THE
BOOK
OF
AMMON

by
Ammon Hennacy

DEDICATION

TO

My Mother
My Wife, Joan

First Printing ..... January, 1965
Second Printing ...... May, 1965
Third Printing .... May, 1966
Fourth Printing .....March, 1968
Fifth Printing .... February, 1970

Introduction

If Jefferson was right that government is best which governs least, it would follow that the perfect government is that which does not govern at all. Some would conclude that the perfect government would be that which did not exist; such is the anarchist view. While I am sensitive to its beauty I cannot accept its logic. I prefer that a policeman be available in my neighborhood, though I am perfectly prepared to concede that ideally he ought to do nothing official whatever.

Such issues having remained unsettled for the hundreds of thousands of years of man's development, will presumably remain so for the predictable future, if not through all eternity. What one can hope is that in the meantime we will keep fresh enough our dedication to freedom — that ideal so elusive because it is a negative — that men will at least be left free to debate it. I am never sure whether our society presently permits Ammon Hennacy to roam the streets because we really want him to be free or merely because the laws prevent our terminating his freedom with our bare hands.

Ammon serves somewhat the same function in the American context that is served by Lenny Bruce, though on another level. Both men outrage us, both see social reality with the fresh eye of the poet or artist, and we make both pay dearly for their presumption.

So long as our Ammon Hennacys merely theorize about a Utopian absence of legal restraint we are disposed to tolerate them. But it is when we are launched upon wars to defend everyman's freedom that we undertake to limit theirs. Of all the unfair charges we bring against them, the most absurd is that of cowardice. It requires enormous courage to live up to the pacifist philosophy. The man who refuses to bear arms is not trying to avoid being killed, he is hoping to avoid killing. It is no sin to be murdered; it is a sin to murder.

The treatment of pacifists in the United States during the First World War was frequently shameful and uncivilized. The nation obviously did not need the handful of individuals involved; their contribution to the war effort would have been negligible. What was at the heart of the vicious harassment meted out to the various anarchists, socialists and Protestants who refused military service was nothing more edifying than the feeling: if *I* have to suffer well, then, by God, you're going to suffer right along with me. Misery not only *loves* company, it is quite prepared to demand it.

Now, of course, there are Catholic pacifists, too. For that matter there always were, here and there. There have even been non-violent saints in the church and certainly there is no question but that in the first years of Christianity the ideal of meekness and submission, of the-turning-of-the-other-cheek, of loving one's enemy, was dominant to a degree that is clearly no longer the case. While all three would protest vigorously at being considered potential saints it is significant nevertheless that when one asks oneself just who, in the United States now might one day achieve beatification, the names most likely to come to mind are those of the dedicated workers for peace Thomas Merton, Dorothy Day, and Ammon Hennacy. It might be argued that the three, though virtuous, are not saintly at all — the embarrassing debate is certainly best put immediately to rest — but all one can say is that if the objection is valid then the Church in the United States today, whatever other virtues it may boast, would not seem to number the development of a calendar of saints among them.

If Ammon has the story-teller's gift it is perhaps chiefly because he has participated in so many stories. How he ever condensed the many and varied events of his life into an account running to just 474 pages I do not know. He has lived in and through so much of our modern history, has suffered so many things and met so many interesting people, that he surely must have acquired more wisdom than most of us, even if his intelligence and sensitivity were no greater than average. His prison adventures alone would have provided some authors with material enough for a dozen books. Those Catholics who suppose that Ammon Hennacy is perhaps the only Catholic who refuses to register for the draft will in the pages of this book encounter men like John Dunn, a conscientious objector who was sentenced to a twenty year term and who, after his release, studied for the priesthood and is now serving the Church in Portsmouth, Ohio.

Our prisons do not, of course, customarily produce priests. They usually teach a man far more about crime and cruelty than he knew when he was arrested and most American penitentiaries stand as tangible proof that we still have much ground to cover in our long march up out of barbarism. The typical American prison — due chiefly to the lust for revenge, insensitivity and ignorance that perpetuates it — is more a zoo for human animals than a place where children of God are rehabilitated. Ammon draws no such sweeping conclusions in his autobiography but by his unruffled, matter-of-fact account of his prison experiences must surely lead all but the most selfish reader to ponder the reality for which our selfishness is responsible.

It is remarkable how many heroes of our cultural and moral tradition were committed to the revolutionary ideal of social development achieved by interior commitment rather than exterior coercion. What an amusing paradox that today's new Conservatives — who spend more time than most in insisting on their own freedom — are more disposed than most to limit the freedom of those who dare to suggest that the status quo cannot be wholly sanctified. Ammon Hennacy acknowledges his debt not only to history's supreme Subversive — and hence most stable Conservative — Christ, but also to Tolstoy, Emerson, Thoreau, Ghandi, Dostoevsky, St. Theresa, St. Francis, Clarence Darrow, Peter Maurin, Dorothy Day and a host of other free and radical souls.

Although it may come as a surprise to him Ammon is a superb historian, if we correctly assume that the historian's function is to interest us in what has gone before. Most of us, even those in public life, tend to find our rut, live out our experiences within its confines, and become aware of the significant events of our time largely by reading or hearing about them. Ammon Hennacy has somehow managed to fall in amongst the marchers on the road of history. He has *experienced* — not just read about — atheism, socialism, anarchism, pacifism, Communism, anti-Communism, violence, poverty, civil disobedience, Christianity, Protestantism, Catholicism, Mormonism, picket lines, freedom-rides, imprisonment, hunger, manual labor, farming, vegetarianism, despair, faith, hope and love. Though the list is incomplete, it testifies to the open zest for bare, natural principled life that seems so characteristic of Ammon and so rare in the rest of us. Even if Ammon were mistaken in every single one of his fundamental beliefs and assumptions — which is true of no man — we could still learn something from him because of his love for the world. Such men cannot be bored. If they could teach us nothing more than how to feel a sense of commitment we should pay them much honor.

Steve Allen

Foreword to the First Edition

Feast of St. Matthew, 1953

Father Vincent McNabb, the great Dominican of England who died a few years ago, said once in an essay which dealt with first principles, that in regard to work, St. Peter could return to his nets and fishing after Good Friday, but St. Matthew, the tax gatherer, could not return to his occupation. It was not an honorable one, this service of Caesar. (St. Hilary said that the less we had of Caesar's the less we would have to render to him.)

It is a good day to write the introduction to this autobiography of Ammon Hennacy, the Catholic anarchist, whose anarchism means that he will also seek to govern himself rather than others, that he "will be subject to every living creature" rather than to the State, that he will so try to abound in goodness and service, love of God and fellows, that for "such there is no law." His is the liberty of the children of God, the brothers of Christ. His love of freedom means that he has put himself in bondage to hard manual labor for a lifetime, not to build up a place for himself in this world where he has no lasting city, but in order to fulfil the law of God, and earn his living by the sweat of his brow rather than the sweat of somebody else's. His love and peace means rejection of the great modern State, and obedience to the needs of his immediate community and to the job. His refusal to pay Federal income tax does not mean disobedience since he is ready and has always proved himself to be ready to go to jail, to accept the alternative for his convictions. He is open and frank in his dealings with all men and far from skulking and hiding in fear, he proclaims his point of view by letter, by article, by picketing, and by public fasting. Many of his "tax statements" appear in this book, and many an account of his picketings. He has done it so often now since the last war, that his fellow workers, Dave Dellinger and I, have begged him to condense, to combine, to shorten, not only to save paper and type, but also to save the reader. He has not done much of it, it is true. The book, from the standpoint of writing, is a sprawling discursive affair, written in spare moments, between hours of hard manual labor, or travelling, or talking to visitors in *The Catholic Worker* office. But he has the genius of the true teacher. If it is necessary to repeat, he repeats, and perhaps when he has repeated his fast in penance for Hiroshima, repeated his picketing, repeated his statement forty times, forty days,—he will have put on Christ to such an extent that people will see more clearly Christ in him, and follow more in his steps. That is our job here, to put on Christ, and to put off the old man, so I am not talking of an excessively religious person, an unbalanced person when I talk of Ammon so living that year by year, he "puts on Christ." We are told by our Lord Jesus, after all, to be perfect as our heavenly Father is perfect, not just as St. Francis, St. Benedict, St. Dominic are perfect.

Ammon has not always been a Catholic, though there is the Catholic strain a few generations back. Surrounded by upright Protestants from his earliest years, he was struck always by the divergence between belief and practice. He distrusted the emotionalism of religious belief too. So it was in his early years that he rejected religious faith. He loved his fellows, he loved this good world which God made, though he was not thinking of it as a created world, then, but as something which had evolved. He loved and longed for the good, and he felt the solidarity of man. He knew that an injury to one is an injury to all, so he early had a sense of the body of Christ, of which we are all a part, potentially, or actually. He served Christ, though he denied him.

This service took him to the Socialist Party, to an opposition to war, which brought him to prison. The story of his prison days will rank, I think, with the great writings of the world about prisons. He had nothing to read there but the Bible, and he turned to that with an anxious, hungry mind, a mind that was tortured by inactivity. Ironically enough, in this so called Christian country, when the guards saw his avid interest in the Bible they replaced the one he had, which had good type, with a small type edition. Prison, after all, is to punish men, not to bring them to penitence.

A penitentiary is a place of darkness, not of light these days of man's cruelty to man. But Ammon saw light, lived in light, those days of his solitary confinement in Atlanta Penitentiary, so great a light, Monsignor Hillenbrand once said to me, that it seemed to blind him. He got no further for the time, than an acceptance of religion and the Sermon on the Mount. He came out of prison a philosophical anarchist like Tolstoi, in rebellion still against Church and State.

I always remember those words of Monsignor Hillenbrand because they were to me encouraging words. Ammon, in his articles, sometimes blasted organized religion, as he called it in such a way as to belabor the Church, Holy Mother Church, and that hurt me as though the blows fell on my own body, as indeed they did. Organized religion was one thing, but the Church was another. I tried to moderate these strong statements of his so that he would be attacking what needed to be attacked, the human element in the Church. But if it had not been for Monsignor Hillenbrand's deep understanding and encouragement at the time (and the Monsignor is not a pacifist nor an anarchist by any matter of means, though a great lover of freedom) I would perhaps have been discouraged from printing so many of Ammon's articles. For by that time, Ammon was a regular contributor to The Catholic Worker, of which I am editor. Every month his article came in, and every month I am sure, each of us members of the staff were shamed by his consistence, his true life of poverty and hard work, his utterly consistent pacifism.

He loved peace, he worked for peace, and he did not do any work which contributed to war. From the time of the second draft, he worked at the back breaking labor of an agricultural migrant. He worked in dairies, and when the withholding tax meant that he would be contributing, though unwillingly to the war budget, he went farther west and south and did day labor, collecting his pay in advance, so that no Treasury agent could catch up with him.

And with the strange inconsistency of us Americans, army men, tax men, were among those who hired him, and with the understanding that they would help him evade paying income tax.

He has led this life of daily labor for many years now. The community around Phoenix, Arizona has come more and more to accept him. Their hostility has grown into love and friendship. Like Gandhi, he calls all men his brothers, wherever they may be, in castles or hovels, in banks or on skid row. He is, what he is attempting to be, a one-man-revolution.

Ammon was baptized on the feast of St. Gregory the Wonder worker, 1952, by Father Marion Casey, of the diocese of St. Paul. He is typically midwestern, tall, lank, long nosed and long faced, thin mouth and warm eyes, enduring rather than strong. He is the average American, and as pioneers have done before him, he stands pretty much alone. Next year, he will transfer his activities to Denver, the capitol of the west, where the president has his summer White House. He will begin again to picket, to fast, to work at hard labor in new surroundings, reaching the man in the street by going to the man in the street. He will still be an editor of *The Catholic Worker,* an editor continually on pilgrimage, a roving editor, doing the work, the speaking and writing that he can do while he earns his living by the sweat of his brow.

And what is he accomplishing, in this one-man-revolution of his? Does he expect to change the world? When asked this last question once he said with characteristic wit, "I may not change the world, but I'll work so the world won't change me."

He told me a story the other day about a Chinese family who were digging a salt mine. The father did not expect to get this done in his life time, the son did not expect to get it done in his, and perhaps the grandson did not expect to get it done in his. But if they kept at it, one day it would be dug.

Ammon is a man of vision, of which there are too few. Sometimes he may seem to be hoping against hope, but I prefer to remember that other quotation of St. Paul's. He has the charity that "rejoiceth in the truth, beareth all things, believeth all things, hopeth all things, endureth all things." Let us pray that he will abound in Charity which "never falleth away, whether prophesies shall be made void, or tongues shall cease, or knowledge shall be destroyed." God bless him.

DOROTHY DAY

The author wishes to express thanks for the use of quotations from Karl Jung, and from the poets Robert Frost, Lillian Spencer and Vachel Lindsay. Thanks also to the following artists for illustrations: Fritz Eichenberg Lowell Naeve— chapter 2 and Ade Bethune

A Final Word from the Author

I had received several notices from the health department to close down the Joe Hill House. An article in the paper said that I was not allowed to sleep more than 10 people on the floor. I asked the inspector what he would do if I had 11. He said he would padlock the door. I told him I would break the padlock and beat him like Brigham Young beat the army, and in mock anger I led him to the door and told him "to get the hell out of here." I spoke to Commissioner Smart and he asked me to present my appeal to the City Commissioners. I did so and Smart said I was saving the city money by putting up tramps. And Mayor Brack Lee said that they would go easy on the regulations for I was doing good work; they didn't want to put me in jail for disobeying their regulations, and he said facetiously that they would have to make an ordinance allowing me to do just what I was doing. A few days later I spoke to a group of social workers meeting at the Salvation Army and I was asked by a minister if I rehabilitated derelicts. In effect I said, "Hell, I haven't rehabilitated myself yet." I did this to scorn their Bible-banging. The next day I received a notice from my landlady to vacate the place. Whether the pious or the law, or between them, had pressured the landlord to chase me I do not know. I tried to rent another place but the inspector told the landlord to give me back my money unless he wanted to spend money fixing the place up. When the inspector found that I was really moving he smilingly said that he would be around to help me when I came back. He could afford to smile for I was on the move. I told him he would try to screw me for I knew his kind. I stored my belongings in three different places and on February 10th went on a speaking trip.

First I went to California, then a week at Cornell University, being invited by a Jew, a Mormon, and a Catholic priest. Then with a friend I made the $99 bus trip from Minneapolis to Seattle, San Diego, El Paso, Washington, D.C., New York City, Buffalo, and back to Minneapolis. Then my friend drove me in half a dozen states in the middle west. As Poulsen was to be executed May 13 I began a 25 day fast in Madison, Wisconsin, cutting my trip short to get in Salt Lake City three days before the execution. Fasting, speaking several times a day, and talking to folks nearly all the time was very difficult, and I will not do it again. I also spoke in Vancouver and Toronto. Poulsen's lawyer got him a reprieve and on November 16th made his oral appeal to the state supreme court. Within 60 days they will make an answer, and within another 60 days the judge in Provo will set another execution date if the appeal has failed. So I will be picketing again for him.

I found that renting a place would only be more trouble so two people sent me money and I paid $900 down on this $9,000 brick house *this side* of the tracks. My payments are $80 a month. I am four blocks from a tavern and few town bums walk the mile or more from down town. It is, as it should be, a place for transients. About 35 is the limit I can handle.

I wish to thank the following who have helped me financially to get this first printing of *The Book of Ammon* off the press: Janet Burwash, Bob Callagy, Dorothy Day, Helen Ford, and Peter Lumsden; to my daughter Carmen who suggested the title, and to Lynn Birkinshaw, my Mormon printer of the Sun Lithographing Company, and to his brother Bill who successfully produced the cuts in the book from old scratched pictures. To my co-workers and fellow Catholic conscientious objectors who are helping me until they are called to prison: Murphy Dowois (the Cajun) and Paul Mann. Also to the merchants, mostly Mormon, who give me food. The paragraph at the end of my citations in the chapter on the Mormons is from my friend William J. Whalen of Purdue University, gathered from his *The Latter Day Saints in the Modern Day World*, John Day Co. 1964.

This book has been written, first in the turmoil of the *Catholic Worker* in New York City, than at the Old Pioneer's farm near Phoenix by oil lamp light, and the last eight chapters at the Joe Hill House here. All this amidst my fasting and picketing so there are typos, and grammatical mistakes that would make a pedant shiver, but I submit that taken as a whole, as our lives will be judged by God finally, the book is authentic.

To the orthodox Catholic who may be scandalized by the tone of the book, and especially by the Epilogue, and to the orthodox radical who looks askance at my religious emphasis, I will say that this terribly acute conscience of mine accepts the basis of what Jesus taught; that I feel at home with the spirit of St. Francis, St. Martin of Tours, and Pope John XXIII and consider myself a good Catholic, although critical of some Church rules, many of which eventually will be changed. To the seeming paradox of being a Catholic Anarchist I will add that my favorite saint is St. Joan of Arc, for she fought the English and the Church and didn't chicken. It is not what you believe but if you are willing to die for your belief. And to live for it. To the radical I will say that Christ, Buddha and Gandhi are essentially more radical than Marx and Bakunin.

To the reader who will see a repetition of thoughts and quotations, I have done this for emphasis. I neglected to say that the picture on page 32 is that of a passport of my wife and myself taken in 1923. And the picture on page 42 is that of Carmen and myself, and our cow, June, at Bisanakee in 1928. To my Mormon friends, regular and polygamous; to the transients with whom I live, I say that I am happy to live in Salt Lake City. At the nominal price of $3 for this book little money will be made, but any profits will go for this lasting memorial to Joe Hill, rebel tramp and poet.

A final word on the recent election. Many radicals voted for Johnson for fear of Goldwater. Hannah Arendt has given them the answer: "He who chooses the lesser of two evils, quickly forgets that he chose evil." Johnson did not need the votes of radicals. They should remember the story of Chicken Little who led herself and small-brained fowl into the den of the fox because she was afraid of something that never happened. Those who voted for Johnson have asked in advance for war in Viet Nam and Cuba, and the protection of capitalism in Brazil, Formosa, and wherever it weakens.

The Vatican Council has adjourned again. It began with glowing hopes under Pope John, and it has now proven, through its by-passing of important subjects, and its emphasis on Mary. that deeds and not words are required. As saints have said: "The Church is Christ in the world and it must needs be crucified as He was." The sad part is that Christ was innocent of evil and was killed because He was a friend of the poor and disposed, while the Church is guilty, being an apologist for the rich and powerful.

Poulsen lost his appeal to the state supreme court.

In Christ the Rebel,
Ammon Hennacy

Mail to Box 2132
Salt Lake City, Utah 84110

December 11. 1964.

*"But Peter and the apostles answered and said,
'We must obey God rather than men.'"*.

(Acts V, 29-30)

"Such problems [our war-torn world] are never solved by legislation or tricks. They are only solved by a general change in attitude. And the change does not begin with propaganda and mass meetings and violence. It begins with a change in individuals. The accumulation of such changes will produce a collective solution."   Carl Jung.

*"You see the beauty of my proposal is
it needn't wait on general revolution.
I bid you to the one man revolution—
The only revolution that is coming."*

Robert Frost in *Build Soil*
A Political Pastoral.

Jonathan and Rebecca Ashford Fitz-Randolph
Author's grandparents on mother's side

Birthplace, Negley, Ohio

Sitting: B. F. Hennacy, Lida, Leah on knee.
Standing: Ammon, Julia, Frank, Lola,
Paul, Lida. 1910. Lorraine born later.

Sharon and Carmen in woods

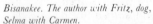

Bisanakee. The author with Fritz, dog,
Selma with Carmen.

Carmen and Sharon making mud pies

Alexander Berkman, Anarchist

The author, fasting in Washington, D. C., 1958

*Francis Gorgen and the author picketing
at Kohler, Wis. 1958*

*The author and U. S. Marshall Raab,
Omaha, Neb., 1959*

*The author greeted by Dorothy Day,
Jan. 1959, Sandstone prison, Minn.*

Carmen and Sharon, 1960

Contents

Note: See middle of page 417 for latest news
of Joe Hill House. See Chapter 22, page
474, entitled, "I Leave the Catholic
Church."
(These additions are not indexed)

Christian Anarchism

Christian Anarchism is based upon the answer of Jesus to the Pharisees when He said that he without sin was to cast the first stone; and upon the Sermon on the Mount which advises the return of good for evil and the turning of the other cheek. Therefore when we take any part in government by voting for legislative, judicial and executive officials we make these men our arm by which we cast a stone and deny the Sermon on the Mount.

The dictionary definition of a Christian is: one who follows Christ; kind, kindly, Christ-like. Anarchism is voluntary cooperation for good, with the right of secession. A Christian Anarchist is therefore one who turns the other cheek; overturns the tables of the money-changers, and who does not need a cop to tell him how to behave. A Christian Anarchist does not depend upon bullets or ballots to achieve his ideal; he achieves that ideal daily by the One Man Revolution with which he faces a decadent, confused and dying world.

(In this book this message is repeated many times. It is worthwhile repeating and studying. At the Catholic Worker in New York City in 1952 I met a Columbia graduate holding prospects of a fine job; and doing post graduate work. He praised my anti-tax articles. In conversation a few minutes later he said, "why everybody pays taxes; they are withheld; you pay taxes; Dorothy pays taxes." He had read my non-taxpaying articles for years and still didn't know what I was doing. Likewise in Phoenix an educated woman had read my leaflets and articles for years and did not know that I really paid no taxes. So, if I repeat myself time after time please remember that I think it is necessary. I have never paid a federal income tax.)

There are indirect taxes that everyone pays. As the saying goes I live in this man's world and if I am going to travel and do propaganda I have to pay tax on the bus. I do not use tobacco or liquor so pay no taxes. I buy Indian articles from the Indians rather than from stores and thus need not pay a tax. To not pay taxes is not my whole message but is is a part of the life of a rebel which I choose to act upon. For despite all talk you either pay taxes or you don't.

Ammon Hennacy

CHAPTER 1.

Childhood - Youth

1893-1916

Ohio - Wisconsin

I am writing these first hundred pages at the Catholic Worker Peter Maurin Farm on Staten Island, N. Y., and will finish the book in my shack on Desert Ranch west of Phoenix, Arizona. Between these farms and Valley Farm, Negley, Ohio, a mile from the Pennsylvania state line and thirteen miles from the Ohio River and the West Virginia state line, where I was born in the midst of the 1893 depression there is a story of a Rebel who travels both in body and spirit as he meets and faces a changing world.

I hardly got born at all, for I was a three and a half pounds, seven months baby, put to bed in a cigar box; and when in a regular bed my mother could hardly find me among the covers. A mud hole just over a bridge on the dirt road was my nesting place when I bounced off of the pillow in my mother's arms, for I was so small I couldn't be held in arms like a regular baby. Anyway that first year I hardly made it, what with pneumonia, colic, and other troubles. After that I was not sick and grew to my five foot nine and a half inches.

My mother came of that Fitz-Randolph family that landed at Barnstable, Mass., in 1720. Ashford and Vail are the Quaker names of my ancestors in this line. My paternal grandfather came from Ireland in 1848 at the time of the potato famine. Whether the name was misspelled in transit I do not know. He fought for the North in the Navy when not fighting booze. He married a Pennsylvania Dutch girl by the name of Calvin. I never saw her. Each of their children were adopted by different Protestant neighbors. Peter Brown, a wealthy farmer, adopted my father. I saw my Irish grandfather when I was a small boy when he came for a visit from California. He gave me a bright penny. Both he and my grandfather Fitz-Randolph were tanners with vats in which to dip the hides.

John Brown and Johnny Appleseed were names familiar in our household and the Coppac brothers who died at Harpers Ferry with John Brown had lived on a farm which was pointed out to me with pride, for here were stations of the Underground by means of which the escaped slaves were helped to Canada and freedom. A bewhiskered picture of John Brown hung in the parlor and I was ten years old before I knew the difference between God, Moses, and John Brown.

1

I was just as ignorant of my own origin as I was of God. Half a mile down the maple-lined road were three stumps. I was told that the doctor had found me in the first stump. My sister Julia was discovered in the second stump, and my brother Frank was hid in the third stump. We would often say, "I'll race you to my stump." As there were no more stumps there, the fiction for the other babies was that the doctor brought them in his satchel.

The house where I was born was a huge brick house built in 1838. Each room had a small grate fireplace, for there was a coal mine on this 333-acre farm. About 100 acres of brush and woods surrounded this mine; blackberry bushes, hazelnut bushes, wild strawberries. Directly back of the house and about a mile up the hill was a lone pine tree which had been planted the day that Lincoln was shot; and thus this hill, down which we went with our sleds in winter, was called Lincoln Hill. Mr. Brown was the first farmer in that community to have purebred Jersey cows; I remember old Cato, a cow with horns like the handle bars of a bicycle. I used to sit on her neck and hold these horns to keep from falling. I never have been afraid of snakes, for in the spring they would emerge by the dozen from the huge icehouse where ice packed in sawdust was kept. Then the hay-tedder would kick up countless copperheads as we were haying. Sloan's Liniment, the Modoc Oil that was sold in the medicine shows down by the river every winter, Peruna and Carter's Liver Pills were always handy, but for regular cuts and bruises a little tobacco juice, my father said, was the best remedy. He ought to know for he had been chewing it since he was eight years of age.

My first memory is that of my Quaker great-grandmother in her bonnet sitting in the east room by her Franklin stove and telling my three-year-old sister Julia and myself of how the peaceful Quakers loved the Indians and were not hurt by them. In this Republican community my father was a Democrat. (I found out years later that when I was a baby he had been a Populist and my mother had baked ginger cookies for Coxey's Army as they encamped on the meadow near us. The reader had better begin to get used to my quick change of gears through these years, from time and place and subject, here and there.) A neighbor girl, Mable Clark, who helped my mother when my brother Frank was born in 1898 taught me on the piano the chorus of the only music which I can play today: "Mid camp fires gleaming; mid shot and shell; I will be dreaming of my own Blue-bell." I shed tears because I had not been born in time to go to war. My first remembrance of money dates from the time in the 1900 campaign when I lost a quarter betting on Bryan. A lot of money for a kid then.

On rainy days we children climbed to the top hay loft and munched apples and salt and bran. A side door showed us Camp Bouquet, a mile away across the lower meadow where it rose several hundred feet high in the V where two creeks met. Indians had camped there for centuries and in the French and Indian War a certain General Bouquet had given his name to the place. Methodists and Baptists had camp meetings there but it was a long way around by road to get there, and I never attended, although we could see the lights and hear the Hallelujahs as they shouted at nights in the late summer. Indians must have stood on this bluff and shot arrows at the game in our meadow years before, for we found many arrowheads there.

As the oldest grandchild I went each summer after the age of ten to help my grandmother in her garden. Her especial pride was ground cherries; a kind of a husk tomato growing on a small bush. These fell off, a few each day, and were taken into a spare bedroom and spread out to dry. Each relative prized the quart of preserves which he was sure to get for Christmas from my grandmother. Here was a huge house of twenty rooms, a red Astrikan apple tree, a spring that never went dry or froze up, out of which water swelled sparkling and cold for the milk and butter in the milk house and for the watering trough for the horses.

As I grew older I cultivated corn the length of a mile-long hillside field, behind Dexter, the old white horse. I shoved back hay in the sheep barn mid wasps and sweat. My uncle Louis would always say, "It'll hold another load." I rode horses bareback after the cows to. the lower farm in the evening. At daylight I walked the mile to the night pasture and warmed my bare feet where the cows had been lying. It seems impossible that a boy could have eaten a dozen or more buckwheat cakes for breakfast—but those were the days!

"Go to sister Randolph's; she's a good woman," was the direction given for miles around to tramps who asked for food. The stories which these "ambassadors" brought of the outside world and the kindness which my grandmother had towards everyone seem to me, now that I think of it, as the first appearance of that "Celestial Bulldozer" which has prepared the way for my unorthodox life. Perhaps I had a good start in being named for my grandmother's favorite brother, Ammon Ashford. (Ammon rhymes with Mammon.) He was the only rebel in the family. He did not belong to church but when he died he left me his Bible with the Sermon on the Mount underlined heavily. He had been a 49-er in California; a sheriff in Missouri who was shot in the leg by Jesse James. He was the local blacksmith when I knew him.

In the summer I met my family Wednesday nights at the local Baptist church, which was only a quarter of a mile from my grandmothers; also on Sundays. I sat through long Baptist theological sermons. Finally, at the age of 12, after cringing at the terrible threats of damnation from the pulpit during a six weeks' revival meeting at our church, I was baptized in the creek and gazed upon by a curious crowd—the only sucker caught in the theological net. This was in the swimming hole which I knew but the preacher did not, so he stumbled on a rock and nearly choked me. During the winter and several summers I did all of the janitor work of the church: filling the huge hanging oil lamps and cleaning the chimneys, carrying coal and emptying ashes from the big round stoves—but then I got to ring the bell and that was something. I did this free of charge and gave $15 a year to the church which was much more in proportion than rich farmers gave. I felt that I should be a missionary.

My father was one of those fine looking, dark Irishmen who made friends in this Republican community so that in time he was elected town-

3

ship clerk, although a Democrat. He was also secretary of the Masonic lodge in a town several miles to the west. One of his best friends was a man by the name of Clark who was a Russelite, or as they called them in those days a "Millenial Dawn." Pastor Russell lived in nearby Pittsburg and said that there was no hell. This was terrible for we all knew that everyone but the Baptists were going there, so to believe there was no hell upset all the countryside theology. This Clark had the local sawmill and cider mill. When he got this new religion he ceased chewing J. T. tobacco, and to help him break this tobacco habit he always had his pockets full of chocolate drops. My interest was not in his losing the tobacco habit but in getting a chocolate drop. These were the forerunners of our modern Jehovah's Witness. (Mr. Clark, unlike modern JW's who seldom have any scruples in doing war work, refused to do any work connected with munitions in World War I, and made a meager living sharpening knives and lawnmowers.)

Now in 1906, which I remembered for two things: the San Francisco earthquake, and the death of Mr. Brown, the farm was sold and we moved about 20 miles northwest to the county seat, Lisbon. This was the birthplace of Mark Hanna, and McKinley had lived there when a boy. Here my father was in the real estate and insurance business, and a lonesome Democrat. There was no Baptist church in this town so I attended the Presbyterian church. I was an usher and helped take up the collection. Two of the Elders who gave out communion were disreputable and unChristian in their daily lives. This caused me to doubt. When I asked the minister about this and about the bloodthirstiness of the Old Testament his only reply was for me to pray. This I did, but the questions kept coming up. Finally he told me to go to Youngstown and hear Billy Sunday, the great revivalist who had thousands pouring down the "sawdust trail" of his tent saying they had been "saved." Then my doubts would all be resolved. I went one rainy night. The blasphemy of this bigot was so powerful that it opened my eyes to the fact that my supposed conversion at a revival meeting was no more real religion than was this wholesale devil worship of Billy Sunday.

I went home and asked more questions. I prayed and read the Bible but the God of Love was never mentioned to me. Around Christmas I got up in the Achor Baptist Church where I had been baptized and said that I was an atheist and did not believe in God or the Bible. My father had wanted me to leave the church quietly as it would hurt his business and political ambitions. I told him that I had splashed in and I was going to splash out.

But I was still a Democrat. I spent the next summer going over the County getting subscriptions for Bryan's paper THE COMMONER. While at my grandmother's the minister who had baptized me, Rev. McKeever, subscribed for THE COMMONER, saying, "Ammon, there is one paper I never want you to read: THE APPEAL TO REASON." I had never heard of it but was in no mood to have anyone tell me what to do. Accordingly when I saw a bricklayer going to work past the house one Monday morning I asked him to take the fifty cents I had made on the

4

COMMONER and subscribe for this new radical paper. I had been told that this bricklayer was a Socialist. My cousin Jessie was there, from her home in Beaver Falls, Pa., at the country each summer. She was a Republican for the same reason that I was a Democrat: her father was a Republican. A man, the age of my father, was there that summer also. He was my second cousin Isaac McCready. He was a radical. His fiery red-headed wife was a beautiful woman. Isaac did not believe in God and all of the relatives who were church goers were anxiously looking for the judgment of God to kill him. He had a "tobacco heart" but outlived most of them. (Here was forming a thread that would weave into my life in a few years. For my cousin, riotously red-headed and beautiful, Georgia, was to marry a man in Georgia who was the son of the chaplain of Atlanta prison.)

I become a Socialist

By the fall of 1910 I had exchanged my lost Baptist heaven for the new Socialist Heaven on Earth. Here in Lisbon the local Socialists were proud to elect the son of the Democratic mayor as secretary of their local. The first Socialist I met was "Curly", a vegetarian. I thought this was a part of the rebellion so the butcher joined the capitalist in the list of my enemies. Then I read Upton Sinclair's Jungle and had more reason both for being a vegetarian and being a Socialist. My father scolded me for my radicalism and especially for spending my Sunday mornings in distributing THE APPEAL TO REASON on doorsteps, rather than ushering, in the Presbyterian church. My father was a good-natured man whose bark was worse than his bite. (In later years he told me he wanted to see if I really was a good rebel and was secretly glad that I kept on with my Socialism.) I introduced Fred Strickland, and Cornelius Lehane—a big Irishman who wore a gold cross on his vest and who was beaten up by the police and died soon afterward in Connecticut during World War I. They stayed at our house and my father talked radicalism intelligently with them. My father allowed me to put up a sign on the public square by the Civil War cannon giving definitions of Socialism. It stood there for years. This was a staid Republican town but it had a little history of rebellion for here during the Civil War lived Clement Vallindgham who favored the South, was put in prison, and ran for Governor of Ohio while in prison. Near here also was captured "Raider Morgan" who got further north than any other Southerner. During a winter vacation I worked in the local pottery and joined the Industrial Workers of the World (I. W. W.) Section 6, Article 2, of the Socialist Party constitution had not yet barred "wobblies," as they were called, from also belonging to the Party.

In August of 1912 my grandfather broke his leg, and this being an easy time to make promises for the winter, I offered to live with him that winter and walk or ride the 5½ miles to the high school in East Palestine, where I would be a junior. Here I met a man about ten years my senior who was a Socialist, Ed Firth. He was also a Sunday School teacher. He was an expert pottery worker. I would have treasured his friendship during all these years, as we had much in common, but he died in prison in World War I. He was indicted with the Communist Labor Party group.

That winter I milked eight cows, morning and night, and worked all day Saturday. I sat behind a huge wood stove nights and studied, taking five subjects. Apples, and cider from the barrel in the dark cellar form the pleasant memory of that winter. Sometimes when the snow was very deep I walked; at other times I went horseback or with horse and buggy. Mother Bloor came to East Palestine and I drove her, with horse and buggy, to organize the first Socialist local among the miners in my home town of Negley. She was a wonderful woman and an inspiration. I was also on the track team and in the mile and half mile run. I was not so fast but I had a lot of endurance. It seemed that the more I had to do the more I did. But this winter was enough of the farm for me. I determined to seek my fortune in the city for the summer.

To Wisconsin

A former Sunday School teacher of mine took crews out each summer to sell cornflakes, house to house. I had never been to a large city or even seen a street car. The first day in Cleveland I made $8, got lost, and ended up knocking at a door across the hall from where I should have knocked, and being abashed by meeting a roomful of girls. By the next summer I had a crew of my own in Wisconsin, Iowa and Minnesota. I sold to retailers and wholesalers.

Meanwhile I had entered Hiram, Ohio, college as a freshman; started a Socialist club there, and had speakers such as J. G. Phelps Stokes and C. E. Ruthenberg, later to be the founder of the Communist Party. Vachel Lindsay had attended this college and here I first became acquainted with his troubadour poetry. Away from home now I thought it was smart to smoke cigarettes, get drunk, play penny ante until daylight, steal canned fruit from the cellar of the Dean's house (for which I was sent home in disgrace for two weeks). This was all of my Baptist "dont's" coming out.

In Portage, Wisconsin, the next summer, I sold a package of cornflakes to a young lady who seemed very nearly to glide down the bannister to answer the door. She appeared holding a copy of Jack London's *Iron Heel* in her hand. I was reading the same book from the town library. This was beautiful Zona Gale, author of *Lulu Bett;* she persuaded me that the University of Wisconsin was better than Dartmouth, so I went to Madison in the fall.

Here I took journalism in the same class attended by Bob LaFollette, Jr. There were a dozen Socialist legislators here, and I earned $17 space rates telling about them for the NEW YORK CALL, and also credit in my course in journalism. I especially liked my class in geology, and if I had not thought a revolution more important I might have been a geologist. I remember seminars of an unofficial sort at the home of the radical Horace M. Kallen. I washed pots and pans at a frat house for my meals, and carried a paper route. At times I would spend a quarter for tickets and popcorn, and take dark, cold, and beautiful Miriam Gaylord, daughter of the Socialist state senator, to a cheap movie. Randolph Bourne lectured here and my roommate, Bill Brockhausen, and I gave up our bed for him. I did not catch much of his message then, but in later years I was to remember his opposition to war and his aphorism: "War is the health of the state." He was the only *New Republic* liberal who did not fall for the war. Emma Goldman, the fiery anarchist who spoke about "free love" and birth control, when these words were only whispered by "decent" people, came to Madison. The one anarchist I knew was working towards a degree, and he asked me to introduce her. I cannot remember what she said, except that she was adept at repartee when people tried to tangle her up in conversation. I had taken public speaking in high school and at Hiram college, but I was the very worst in each class. I did get up at a Socialist meeting and give a talk on the I.W.W. An old time Socialist trade unionist who knew much more than I did criticized me until I was in tears, but I needed it. I asked him how I could be a good speaker. He told me to be sure of my facts and not do as I had just done, talk about something that I didn't know anything about. Then he said to go to some town where I knew no one; get up on a soapbox and commence. After the first speech, if I was any good at all, I would be a speaker.

Here in Madison I took military drill, for I was not a pacifist; I wanted to know how to shoot, come the revolution. I met some young Quaker Socialists and attended their meetings; the only one I remember now is Darlington Hoopes, who ran for Vice President and for President on the Socialist ticket years later. That session of the legislature had a conservative setup, so they increased the tuition for outside of the state students from $24 to $148. I did not have that much money, so when my folks wrote that they had moved to Columbus I decided to go to Ohio State that fall.

I Meet Selma

I spent that summer selling aluminum ware in Wisconsin towns; cooking in churches. The last town I worked in was West Allis. On the day before I planned to go to Ohio, I met a friend from Madison who invited me to a lawn party of young Socialists, the next day. They all knew each other and I was the only stranger. I took a liking to a certain girl and asked for a date but could not get one for four days. Meanwhile I took a friend of hers home. She whispered to this friend, "Better look out for that fellow." Four days later I had a date with my new girl friend, Selma Melms, daughter of the Socialist sheriff of Milwaukee, leader of the Yipsels, as the young Socialists were called, and secretary to the President of the State Federation of Labor. On the excuse that I had to go back to Ohio I had a date every night for ten nights, and we became engaged. Selma was the broadfaced peasant type that always appealed to me. Love is blind, and how much the fact that I was a happy Irishman, much more radical than the staid Germans of Milwaukee, and that Selma was the first radical girl I had ever met (other than Miriam whom we fellows accused of thinking so much of her handsome father that she could never appreciate us) had to do with our engagement is difficult to determine. I went back to Ohio very happy.

That term at Ohio State was one of the best years of my life as a student. I was head of the Intercollegiate Socialist Club and secretary of the Socialist local down town. In my classes in philosophy and sociology there was much room for my radical agitation. I had never been sad about my radicalism, and with this love of Selma in my heart I felt that I could conquer the world. Arthur M. Schlesinger, Sr., was my very good friend at the University. I started the first cooperative second-hand store for resale of books on the campus.

The next summer I sold cornflakes in the New England states and in Ohio. I had been a delegate from Lisbon to the state convention of the party in 1912, and was now a delegate in 1916, so I knew comrades from all over the state. Now during the 1916 presidential campaign I spoke on soapboxes, scores of times, for Allan Benson, the Socialist candidate. We spent several weeks in Dedham, Mass., not knowing then that this town would later be famous at the time of the Sacco-Vanzetti trial. One night when soapboxing in Akron, before about 800 people, my voice gave out. I believed in doctors then, so asked one about it the next day. He asked me what I did for a living, and I told him that I was a salesman. "You talk all day, and you talk all night, and I suppose you smoke cigarettes." "Yes," I answered. "You'll have to stop one of these things," he replied; so I stopped smoking. Later, in Warren, Ohio, I read Alexander Berkman's *Prison Memoirs of an Anarchist*. The next year I was to be in Atlanta prison with him; and the next year in a solitary cell where I could get no cigarettes, so it was a good thing that I stopped smoking. That Celestial Bulldozer again!

That winter it was necessary for me to help at home, as there were five sisters and two brothers younger than myself. I got a job driving a bakery wagon and built up an excellent route by making a special each day of some product which I was sure to have fresh. My smallest sister had been born when I was away at school, so when I arrived with cookies—part of the 10% breakage which I was allowed—Lorraine promptly called me "Ammon-cookie." Meanwhile I had introduced Ben Reitman and Bob Minor and other radicals from the soapbox down town. We had come within a hundred votes of electing a Socialist mayor; had members of the city council, and the president of the school board. It was exciting to be a Socialist and on the winning side for once.

During this winter I studied Yogi, Spiritualsm, and Theosophy. Rosicrucian friends had cast my horoscope: Leo with Saturn in ascendancy, which meant that I would always be in trouble, but never defeated. As if to bear out this prediction of difficulty Selma wrote that she was breaking our engagement, but she would not tell me why. (After we were married I discovered that two Socialists, who claimed to be mutual friends of both of us, had told her long tales about me which had but a faint basis in fact.)

One clear memory I have of Columbus is that of the Rev. Washington Gladden, a Congregational minister of the old liberal style, bewhiskered and benign. So many people came to hear him that he had to have his services in a theatre. He achieved distinction for refusing money from Rockefeller, saying that it was "tainted." These days hardly a voice is raised against the great Foundations who seek to buy respectability by subsidizing individuals and organizations.

CHAPTER 2.

Anti-war Agitation
1917 - 1919

Ohio - Atlanta Prison

About this time we had a huge anti-war meeting addressed by the Rev. Edward Ellis Carr, a portly editor of a magazine along Christian Socialist lines. I introduced him. He told of the hundreds of Socialists in Cleveland who would refuse to register for the draft. He told of his disappointment with European Socialists who had turned pro-war, and that this was all the more reason why we of the U.S. should hold true to our ideals. A local Socialist lawyer, who was of the more conservative group, got up in the audience and opposed Rev. Carr, saying that the prospect of political victory for the party should not be damaged by our traitorous conduct, although he admitted that this war was a fraud the same as all others. Rev. Carr countered this disruption boldly by stating that he would die before

9

he would support war in any way, and ended by calling upon all young men to refuse to register for the draft. As chairman I asked those of draft age to meet with me later, and the group was thus formed which actively put out anti-war and anti-draft propaganda.

I wrote up material for a leaflet and stickers to put on store fronts.

The sticker read:

YOUNG MEN
DON'T REGISTER FOR WAR!

It is better to go to jail than
to rot on a foreign battlefield

The poster said:

YOUNG MEN
are you going to
REFUSE TO REGISTER
for military service in a foreign country
While the rich men
who have brought on this war
Stay at home
and get richer by gambling in food stuffs?

WE WOULD RATHER DIE OR BE IMPRISONED
FOR THE SAKE OF JUSTICE, THAN KILL
OUR FELLOW MEN IN THIS UNJUST WAR.

Signed ....Young Men's Anti-Militarist League

The St. Louis program of the Socialist Party stoutly opposed the war. We had an unlimited supply and distributed them with our poster and sticker. While they did not definitely say that young men should refuse to register, the declaration read: "Support of all mass movements in opposition to conscription." So despite the fact that our presidential candidate, the Revolutionary Rev. Carr, and many other leaders were to turn pro-war, we youngsters knew that we had Debs, Ruthenberg, Wagenknecht and many others upholding us.

Everyone knew that the war was coming on soon. James Cannon, a Socialist speaker from New York City, had been listed to speak at Broad and High on the evening of April 5, 1917. I was to introduce him. By 8.30 there were thousands of people at the meeting and I could not see over their heads. A Jewish comrade came along with his junk wagon and I stepped on top and addressed the crowd. Cannon had not yet arrived; he never did come. The police told me there were too many people around and I would have to come down. I expect there were 10,000 by that time. I argued that I had a permit but they reached for me. I ran across the street to the State House steps and continued for half an hour. Here they had no authority. Finally the state police arrested me and an

10

old man, a dishwasher who was a member of the Socialist Labor Party, who disobeyed his party line and got into trouble. We both spent the night in jail for disturbing the peace and were released on bail with a hearing for May 30.

By this time my father had a good job and my help was not needed. I was routed by the state office of the Party under Alfred Wagenknecht to distribute my own and other leaflets wholesale over the state, and a notice was put in the weekly Socialist paper to that effect. My method was to go to a town and look up a comrade whose name I was given or whom I knew from my previous soapboxing. Often the comrade had already turned pro-war and I had to leave in a hurry before he turned me in. I asked that the leaflets be not wasted and they were not to be distributed until I had been gone for several days. If they could pay for the leaflets that was fine, and if they could not I gave them as many as they wanted. My first town was Cleveland and I was introduced by Comrade Ruthenberg and then sped on my way with enough carfare to keep me going for several weeks. I had to jump across the state line into Pennsylvania to escape turncoat comrades. I took leaflets to my old comrade Ed Frith in Huntington, West Virginia, and also went to the end of the spur railroad in notorious Cabin Creek, but the man whose name I had had moved away and the house was empty. I walked down the tracks carrying two suitcases full of leaflets.

Finally around midnight I noticed a light in a house and knocked at the door. A middle-aged Negro came to the door and I explained the situation asking him if I could sleep there that night and offering to pay him. He said that there were no white folks within six miles and if I did not mind sleeping in the home of a colored person and would say nothing about it to white people the next day I could stay. I was glad to walk into the dimly lighted hall and to hear him say, "Here 'Liza, get out'a that there bed and let this white gentleman sleep." Whereupon a colored girl ran giggling down the hallway and into another room. The bed was warm and I was tired. The next morning I had the regular southern breakfast of grits, biscuits, sowbelly and coffee set before me. My hosts were cordial and found it difficult to understand why I refused their sowbelly. I needed to be strong to carry those heavy grips they said. Somehow they got the idea that it was "my religion" not to eat meat and all was well.

I wore a huge button marked PEACE, yet the dumb troopers, who entered the train the next day and said they were hunting for a score of radicals who were putting out seditious literature, opened my grips and seeing the books on top of the literature muttered something about my being a student returning from college and went on.

Getting back to Columbus the night before I was to have my trial I routed my brothers Frank and Paul and my sisters Lola and Lida and their young friends with leaflets over the university section where we lived and where there were few cops. I took the dangerous downtown section. We would place leaflets and stickers for a few blocks and then skip a few blocks, and backtrack and zig zag. There were no squad cars and radio in those days, so a person did not have to be very smart to outwit a cop. I

11

put stickers on nearly all the downtown store fronts. Finally at 2.30 a.m. I was caught and put in solitary. .

I asked to see a lawyer but was told I could not see one. Detective Wilson said that unless I registered for the draft by June 5th, which was registration day, I was to be shot, on orders from Washington. I was shown a copy of the local paper with headlines "Extreme Penalty for Traitors." I only saw it through the bars and was not allowed to read it. It was not until my release from prison in 1919 that I read this paper and discovered that there was nothing definite in the follow up about the death penalty. This was just a scare headline. However if men take you out to a cliff on a dark night, lower you at the end of a rope and tell you it is a hundred feet and when you get tired to drop—then when you drop it is only two feet; it might as well have been a hundred feet, for you thought it was.

Detective Wilson said that the young Socialists arrested with me for refusing to register had all given in and registered. (Later I found out that he had also told them that I had registered.) I felt that if they gave in some one had to stick, and I was that one. While I was in solitary a statement was given out that the patriotic prisoners had threatened to lynch me and that the sheriff was forced to keep me in solitary. Spike Moore, an I.W.W., sneaked me a note and also a clipping from the paper in which a reporter had asked my mother if she was not frightened because I was to be shot soon. Her reply was that the only thing she was afraid of was that they might scare me to give in. This gave me added courage. My mother never weighed more than 87 pounds and looks like a timid mouse, yet she is one of the few women I have known who have that greatest of virtues: courage.

During this six weeks awaiting trial I was not allowed to be shaved, the excuse being that the barber might cut my throat. I finally paid an outside barber to come in so I was presentable in court. June 5th passed and no move was made to shoot me. But at every step in the corridor I had expected to be called. I was taken out of the dark hole now. Detective Wilson said that the government had postponed my execution thinking that I would give the names of those who had distributed the leaflets. Outside of my folks the only people who came to see me were an old Irish washerwoman, Georgia Crooks, who was a Socialist and a Spiritualist, accompanied by a long-haired American Indian, Karakas Redwood, who was some kind of a Yogi. I had met them often and somehow had come to believe that reincarnation was the only explanation of the injustice in this life. I had a good fighting spirit and did not need religious opium to bolster me. However, if I was executed I had this hope of coming back in another life and raising hell.

None of the Socialist lawyers would defend me and an old Quaker, an ex-judge by the name of Earnhardt, came and defended me free of charge. He was 83 years of age and spoke slowly for it was an effort for him to speak at all. I pled not guilty to the charge of "conspiracy to defraud the government of enforcement of the draft act" because I did not want to get Harry Townsley, the comrade who did the printing, into prison. Technically he was not guilty for he had not printed any of my leaflets *after* the draft law had been passed. I had written asking him to print some and told him to destroy the letter. He got scared and refused to print them but kept the letter and the government raided his place and saw the letter. No one would believe that he did not print the leaflets, as I had asked. I pled guilty for my refusal to register.

The District Attorney, Stuart Bolin, gave the summing up to the jury on July 3, 1917: a regular Fourth of July speech:

"One hundred and forty-one years ago tomorrow the immortal words were written which were to fire our forefathers until they were free from the English tyrant. Today a greater tyrant threatens us. George the III did not cut off the hands of little children and bayonet the enemy alive to barn doors as the Beast of Berlin has done. In 1776 such men as Hennacy would be defending King George and in 1861 it was men like him who would have allowed the slaves to remain slaves. Judge Earnhardt would have you believe that this despicable coward, Hennacy, is a hero. He calls him by the resounding name of 'conscientious objector.' I tell you this man does not have a conscience. The money of our state has been spent to educate him in our university. He would bite the hand that feeds him and would repay the state by knifing her in the back.

"If his ideals which are so glibly spoken of are true why has he not convinced others; why have the responsible Socialists of this city repudiated him and his disloyal actions? Why should he be praised for facing death when millions of men better than he are facing it in the trenches every day for their country? You have the evidence before you where he has ordered his co-defendant to print the treasonable leaflets calling this a Wall Street war and advising young men to refuse to register for the draft. I am only sorry that two years is the limit which can be given; he has said that he would go to jail rather than rot on a foreign battlefield; then give him the jail which he desires.

"As I look over the faces of the jury: faces toilworn with efforts to make this, our great country, the home of freedom, I know that every one of you would not now be here if you were of military age, and you would enlist; you would not need to be drafted." (Several jurors were asleep during this speech.) "You have doubtless celebrated many a Fourth of July with fireworks and oratory. I say to you that you cannot celebrate this national holiday in a manner more patriotic than by giving the limit of the law to this traitor. The blood of those who have died for America rises up in protest and calls upon you to do your patriotic duty: convict this traitor!"

I was sentenced to two years in Atlanta and after this term was served I was to do nine months, for refusing to register, in the county jail at nearby Delaware, as the Columbus jail was always too crowded. I had never occupied a Pullman berth. The two guards who accompanied my partner and me chained us to our berths and gave us sandwiches prepared by their women folks, kidding us that they were marking up good meals on their expense account.

Friday, July 13, 1917 was the date of my arrival in Atlanta. My number was 7438. About fifteen others were in the line when I was admitted, so although my entrance into the Baptist fold was lonely, here I had company into what would prove a greater baptism. I was sent to the top floor of the old cell house, to a certain cell. This was occupied by some one else it seemed, for pictures of chorus girls were on the wall, and magazines and cigarette stubs on the floor. This cell was eight feet long, eight feet high, and four feet wide and was made of steel. In half an hour a large burly but good natured man of about forty-five came in.

"Hello kid; my name's Brockman, Peter Brockman from Buffalo, doin' a six bit for writing my name on little pieces of paper. Got one to go yet. How do you like our little home? What's your name?"

I gave him my name and shyly shook hands with him. Soon we went down the corridors to the mess hall. Several prisoners spoke to Peter and nudged him and winked at me. I was hungry and the beans, coffee, plenty of bread and rice pudding proved a welcome meal. While Peter was reading the evening paper in our cell I picked up a book of prison rules. He saw me reading them and threw the book in the corner, saying, "Don't waste your time on that crap. There's just three rules in this joint: (1) Don't get caught; (2) If you do get caught have a good alibi ready; (3) If this fails, have a guard who will fix it up for you, either because you pay him, or because you have more on him than he has on you." I wondered what the harm could be in reading the rules and Peter said as he sidled over to me and stroked my hair: "You have lots to learn about prison life that's not in the rules, kid!" Just then a gong rang and Peter explained that in ten minutes the lights would be out. He said I was to have the lower bunk which was not so hot and easier to get into. We undressed and Peter came over and sat on the edge of my bunk. I edged away but could not get far. "Don't be afraid. I'm your friend," Peter said, "I've been here four years, kid, and I sure get lonesome. Several skirts write to me off and on but the one I planted my jack with has forgotten me long ago. The hell with women anyway! You can't trust 'em and a fellow is a fool to marry one." "I'm tired, Peter, I want to go to sleep," I said jerkily as he commenced to caress me. "No one goes to sleep so early in this hot jail; the bedbugs are worst this time of year. This is a man's joint and you'll have to learn what that means, kid. Anyway, when I did my first bit in Elmira I had a pal; I was soft and homesick then, and many a night Jimmy consoled me. Jimmy was more beautiful than any girl I ever met. Quiet! I hear the screw!" Peter had finished this last word and climbed into his bunk when a guard stopped before the cell and said: "No more talking there! What's this, your new punk?" he said pointing to me and winking at Brockman. I asked Peter what a punk was and he laughed and said he supposed it wasn't defined in Webster but I would learn soon enough about it.

The next morning after breakfast, Blackie, the runner in the block, brought me a note, saying that he knew the prisoner who had written the note, and had done time with him in Allegheny prison years ago. I read:

> "Blackie, who gave you this note is o.k. See me in the yard this afternoon if it does not rain; otherwise come to Catholic mass tomorrow and I will talk to you there. Your cell mate has paid $5 worth of tobacco to the screw in your cell block to get the first young prisoner coming in to be his cell mate. You are the 'lucky' one. Watch him, for he is one of the worst perverts in the prison. There is no use in making a fuss for you may 'accidentally' fall down four tiers. Get $5 worth of tobacco from the store and give it to Blackie and he will give it to the guard and pull strings to have you transferred out of the cell. This will take weeks; meantime get along the best you can. Good luck.
>
> Yours for the revolution.
>
> A. B."

A note from Alexander Berkman, the great Anarchist! I read it over and over again and then destroyed it, per the first rule in prison: don't keep any unnecessary contraband. For the first time in my life when I had read a book I had sat down at once and written to the author. This was in Warren, Ohio, in 1916, when I had read Berkman's *Memoirs*. I did not get an answer, and now I was to meet him personally. Hundreds of workers had been killed by the Pinkertons at Homestead, Pa. by the order of Frick, manager of Carnegie Steel. Berkman, then a young Anarchist, had stabbed and shot Frick, and had done 14 years and ten months actual time in the terrible Allegheny prison, $3\frac{1}{2}$ years of this in a dark hole. He had been in prison before I was born and here he was again with a fighting spirit that jails could not kill. I had read his paper THE BLAST. The only thing that had saved him from being framed with Mooney and Billings was that he was in New York City when they were accused of dropping the bomb on the Preparedness parade, in San Francisco in 1916.

I had but a faint idea of the word pervert; and I wondered how and why I could talk to Berkman in a Catholic chapel. I remembered in 1915 at Ohio State University when an intelligent sociology professor had assigned me to debate in class *against* Socialism, and asked the daughter of conservative parents to speak *for* Socialism. I surprised myself and the class by giving the argument that the trouble with Socialism was that it was not radical enough, and I gave anarchism as the ideal. As an illustration I gave the story of the wind which sought to compel by force to blow the coat from the back of the traveler. The sun shone gentle rays which made the traveler *voluntarily* doff the garment. Anarchism was thus the gentle way. However, I said that I was not an anarchist because they stood no chance of winning, and it would not be long until the Socialists had gained the Revolution. Now I was to meet the only living anarchist, other than Emma Goldman, Malatesta and Kropotkin, whom I wished to know.

The sun shone brightly that afternoon on the packed ground of the prison yard. In the shadow along one prison wall Blackie had pointed out Berkman to me. I hastened to greet him. His kindly smile made me feel that I had a friend. He told me of a means of getting out letters, *sub rosa,* and explained how to talk in your throat without moving your lips. He said that on rainy Saturdays, when we could not meet, we could see each other at the Catholic chapel, as the chaplain was an ex-prizefighter who was sympathetic to workers and did not mind those who came to visit each other. He gave me four things to remember. (1) Don't tell a lie. (2) Don't tell on another prisoner; it's the job of the screws to find out what is going on, not yours. (3) Draw your line to what you will do and will not do and don't budge, for if you begin to weaken they will beat you. (4) Don't curse the guards. They will try to get you to strike them and then they will have the excuse to beat you up; and if one can't, two can; and if two can't, ten can. They are no good or they wouldn't take such a job. Just smile. Obey them in unimportant details but never budge an inch on principle. Don't be seen talking to me very often, for the guards are watching and will make trouble. Write to me by way of Blackie and I will do the same."

That night Peter again became more aggressive. For about six weeks I slept but a few hours each night until I was transferred to another cell. Meanwhile my goodnatured passive resistance had persuaded Peter that he had better leave me alone. I got him interested in English lessons in the prison school. When I left his cell, he said he would pass the word around that I was nobody's punk, and none of the other wolves would bother me.

I was transferred to the new cell house, with four in a cell. Boston Dave and John were counterfeiters and Johnny Spanish had done ten years in Sing Sing with Gyp the Blood, and was doing five years in Atlanta. He spoke well of Warden Osborne. Later I was to read Frank Tannenbaum's *Osborne of Sing Sing,* and corroborate what Johnny had told me.

A red-headed kid who had a radio without a license was doing time as a spy. He was not a radical or subversive, only interested in radio and did not know he had to get a license. He celled a few cells from me. One noon he slipped me a saw made from a knife, as we were in line going to dinner. It seems that he had cut several bars of a window in the basement which faced outside and was preparing to escape. Some dumb guard had leaned against them and they gave, so the whole cell block was being searched for a saw. The kid had enough sense not to be caught with it. Why he gave it to me I do not know, but now I had it. I stopped and tied my shoe string and secured the saw up my sleeve, and thus got out of my regular place in line and at the table. Here I stuck the saw underneath the table, and it may be there yet for all I know. As we left the mess hall, all of the guards in the prison lined us up and searched for that saw. If they had searched us coming in I would have been found with it, and of course would not have told on the kid.

John, in my cell, was boss of the paint gang and was from Columbus, Ohio. He had not known me, but all prisoners like someone who has put up a good fight and faced death and has not weakened. So he had me transferred to his gang, and when he left in about 6 months I was made the boss of the gang. I had a pass to go anywhere I wanted inside the walls.

The editor of the prison paper, GOOD WORDS, asked me to give him something to print. I told him that was what I got in for, printing things in papers, and that my ideas were too radical for him. He insisted so I gave him this quote which, believe it or not, appeared in a box underneath the editorial caption of the Department of Justice on April 1, 1918:

"A prison is the only house in a slave state where a free man can abide with honor." Thoreau.

This had the o.k. of the warden and was not sneaked in. The ignorant official thought it praised prisons. The CONSERVATOR, edited by the radical Horace Traubel, literary executor of Walt Whitman, was allowed in because they thought it was conservative. The IRISH WORLD which was much against the war came to the Catholic chaplain and he got copies to us radicals through John Dunn, a conscientious objector and Catholic, from Providence, R. I., who was boss of the plumbing gang.

The conscientious objectors were scattered in different gangs and cell houses over the prison. The warden told me that the orders from Washington were to put us all in one place, but he knew better and scattered us out, for if we were in one place we would plot. This reminded me of the farmer who caught the groundmole and said, "Hanging's too good; burning's too good; I'll bury you alive." So we conscientious objectors were scattered around where we could do propaganda instead of being segregated where we would argue among ourselves. John Dunn and I were good friends. His number was 7979 and he got 20 years. When I was sentenced, the Espionage Law had not yet been passed. After his release he studied for the priesthood and is now a priest in Portsmouth, Ohio, and a reader of the CATHOLIC WORKER. Paul was a young, Russian-born Socialist who had quit a good job to come to prison. Morris was a quiet, very short Russian Jewish anarchist, whom I met often at the vegetarian diet table. (You could get all the good toast bread and milk you could devour if you signed up for any certain length of time at the diet table, but you were not allowed to eat anything from the regular table, at the same time.) Louis was just the opposite; an erratic boisterous Nietzschean who felt that everything that you had was his and what he had was his own. Morris was deported at the same time as Emma Goldman and Alexander Berkman, after the war. Louis very recently has come to an appreciation of God, if not of orthodox Christianity. Tony was a Russian who did not speak English, but whose quiet manner marked him as some kind of a religious sectarian. Walter was a college man who came from an old anarchist family who had reviled his father's ideas until the crisis of war brought him to prison. His partner was John, a seaman who belonged to the I.W.W. maritime branch. He had been banished from Australia as a radical, and had refused to register for the draft.

Theodore and Adolph were young Socialists from Rhode Island who were enthusiastic and helpful in any prison rebellion. Gilbert was an Italian I.W.W. who spoke little English. He worked in the stone gang. I never met him personally; we just smiled from a distance. Al and Fred were two older comrades who had unwittingly been sent to prison. They were not left wingers, but were in official position in the Socialist Party, where the extreme conservatism of their communities made them martyrs.

They were not active in any plans that we younger rebels formed. Francisco was the only local comrade from Atlanta in prison against the war; he was a Puerto Rican and had the advantage of his family coming to see him often. The young Hollander from Vermont was not a radical in the accepted sense of the term; he simply refused to fight against relatives who were in the German army. Fritz was a young Russian Socialist who was also quiet, but who went along with us in any of our plans. The Russellites came in later while I was in solitary and I never met any of them. There were about 20 of them including their leader, Judge Rutherford. Nicholas, the Mexican, was dying of tuberculosis. I only saw him from a distance for he lived by himself in a tent the year around. He was a Mexican revolutionist. Two Negro objectors who belonged to some Holiness sect in the Carolinas would not mix with us. I sent candy and other trinkets to them but they did not respond. We were not religious and I supposed we shocked them. My especial friend was William McCoy, of the McCoy-Hatfield feudists in Kentucky. He claimed to have killed six Hatfields. He could not write and I wrote his letters home for him. He had started out with Phillips, a friend, to shoot up the government when he heard that a war was on. The warden was afraid of him, he told me.

Before the transfer had come through for my work on the paint gang I had worked with hundreds of others on the construction gang, wheeling "Georgia buggies," a slang for wheelbarrows, full of concrete mixture and pouring it into the foundation walls for a mill to make duck for mail sacks. There were about 80 of us in a line. The platforms had been built in such a way that we had to make a mighty run to get to the top. So John, the wob from Australia and I took turns slowing up the line; stopping to tie a shoe lace, to look intently at the wheel as if something was wrong with it, etc. About the time one of us would have the whole line waiting he would behave and the other one would take up the sabotage action. One afternoon of this and the boss took the hint and made the runways like they should have been in the first place.

Oklahoma Red had been in Atlanta doing a five year bit and was wanted for a murder rap that he felt he couldn't beat. In a few months now he would be released and turned over to the authorities for trial for murder. One day he saw an old fashioned flat coal car come in full of coal. It was made of wood and in the place where modern cars had a steel brace this wooden car had a nice little hiding place for such a skinny fellow as Oklahoma Red. He was working on the construction gang and said that the next time that car came he was going out with it in this cubby hole at the end where the brakes were. It is an unwritten law in some prisons that if a prisoner can make anything contraband and not get caught making it or taking it to his cell he can have it and no questions asked. Oklahoma Red had outgoing shoes, hat, suit, etc., made in the different prison departments, paying for them in tobacco, and hid this precious bundle of outgoing clothing in the rafters of the cement shed. Several weeks later that car came in. Red found out from the fellows at the power house that it would be switched out at 11.15 that morning. Some of us watched the toilet so no guard or stool pigeon could see Red changing his clothes; others of us kept the guard busy in conversation with head turned the other way. A preacher was watchman at the gate (in for violation of the Mann Act). This preacher trusty was reading his Bible and did not peer closely as the car went out with Red in the hiding place. About a quarter to twelve, guards were scurrying around making another count to see if they had made a mistake, or, if there was a man missing, who he might be. Finally the whistles blew and the guards and the trusties looked in every corner for Red. As far as I know they never got him.

A white man and a Negro had been killed by guards and I was incensed about it. My cell mates laughed and said I should worry about the living, for the dead were dead and no one could do anything about it. That if I wanted anything to do I should raise a fuss about the poor fish served on Fridays by the new mess guard, DeMoss, who had been heard to say that he would make his rakeoff by charging for good food and giving us junk. Accordingly I got cardboard from John Dunn and painted signs which I put up in all of the toilets around the place telling the prisoners to work on Fridays, but to stay in their cells and refuse to go to dinner or to eat the rotten fish. The guards and stoolpigeons tore the signs down, but I made others and put them up. The first Friday 20 of us stayed in our cells. The guards came around and asked us if we were sick. We said we were sick of that damn fish. The next Friday 200 stayed in their cells; and the next Friday 600. That was too many people thinking alike, so on the next Thursday the warden came to the second mess and said that those who did not come to dinner the next day would be put in the hole. Some kid squeaked out in a shrill voice: "You can't do it warden; there's only 40 solitary cells and there's a thousand of us." The next day 900 out of the 1100 who ate at this shift stayed in their cells.

The next Monday I was called to the office and was told that I had been seen plotting to blow up the prison with dynamite, and was promptly sent to the dark hole. This was on June 21, 1918. I was left in my underwear, and lying in the small, three-cornered, very dark hole. I got a slice of cornbread and a cup of water each day. I kept a count of the days, as I heard the men marching to work, and at the end of ten days I was put in the light hole. White bread, which I got then, tasted like cake. This cell was on the ground floor, back of the deputy's office. It was about 18 feet long, 15 feet high, and 6 feet wide. A small dirty window near the top to the east faced a tall building, which kept sunlight from coming in, except on very bright days. A bunk was attached to the wall to the right; a plain chair and a small table, with a spoon, plate, and cup on it. There was a toilet; and a wash basin attached to the wall. A small 20 watt light was screwed in the high ceiling and was turned off and on from the outside. There was a door of bars and an extra wooden door with a funnel shaped peephole through which guards could watch me at any time. I walked around examining my new home. The cell was exactly 8½ steps from corner to corner. The walls were dirty, and initials and home-made calendars with days crossed off had been left by former inmates.

After the dark hole this cell was a relief. A Negro lifer brought in meals, three times a day, and ladled grits, beans, raisins, etc. out of a large bucket onto my plate, while Johnson, the fat guard, stood at the door. The Negro found out that I did not eat meat and he always grabbed my portion. Perhaps this helped him in his favorable attitude toward me, for he gave me notes and candy from Berkman and Dunn, and took my notes in return. The first morning I said "Hello" to the guard, but he did not answer me; after a few days of silence on his part I ceased to bother him with a greeting.

When I had first come to prison I had met the Protestant Chaplain. My red-headed cousin Georgia, who was his daughter-in-law, had told him about me. He wanted to know what church I belonged to, and when I told him I was an atheist he would have nothing to do with me, even when I was in solitary. Catholics were taken care of by the priest and the Protestant had all the rest, so I sent a note to him asking for a Bible to read in solitary, for I was not allowed anything else, or to send or receive mail. After a few weeks a Bible with good print and maps and references in the back was sent to me. After a few days this was taken away, and one with very small print and no maps was given to me in its place. I asked Johnson, the guard, why I was given a Bible with small print, as this was more difficult to read with the small light 15 feet above me, and he simply grunted. The colored trusty later spoke, down in his throat without moving his lips, in the manner we all learn, and told me that anything was done which would make it more difficult for those in solitary. I do not think that the chaplain had anything to do with this; probably the deputy or the guard took this means of teasing one of their caged animals. Outsiders, such as reporters and prison reformers, at times get themselves locked in solitary to get the feeling. But they know they will be out in a day or two. This would then be a vacation, at its best, and a temporary misery, at its worst. When, however, you hear groans of fellow prisoners, when you do not know how many months you may remain in solitary, you have a weight hanging over you that precludes any joyfulness of spirit.

A day in solitary

I hear the six o'clock gong ring for the early mess. I know at 7.20 I will get my mush. I am not sleepy, but I stretch out and relax. In a minute I wash and pull on my few articles of clothing. I pick up my chair and swing it thirty times—up-right-left-down; up-right-left-down. Then I walk 100 steps back and forth in my cell—arms-up-arms-out-arms-clenched-arms-down, as I walk back and forth. This I repeat several times. It is now 7 o'clock. I make my bed and then wash my face and hands again. Then I hear the clanging of the door and I know that breakfast is on the way. I hear the doors open and shut and the jangling of the keys and the rattling of utensils. I sit and watch the door like a cat watching a mouse. The shadows of the guard and the Negro trusty lengthen under my door; the key turns in the lock; the wooden door opens and Johnson, the fat guard, stands back after he has opened the iron barred door. The Negro steps in and ladles out my oatmeal, hands me a couple slices of bread, and pours out a large cup of coffee. Today he has no note for me; tomorrow he may have one. He smiles to me as he turns his back to Johnson and I

20

smile in return. I look up at Johnson but he scowls; no fraternizing it seems. The trusty leaves and the doors are locked. I am not very hungry, and I prolong the breakfast as much as possible to take up my time. At last the food is gone. I leisurely wash the dishes and dry them. Perhaps I spin my plate a dozen times, and see how long I can count before it falls to the floor off the table. I lean back in my chair and think of Selma and of my folks at home. Then I realize that I am within these four walls: a jail in a jail. I walk back and forth for five or ten minutes and then throw myself on my bunk; take off my shoes and hunch up on my bunk.

In a few minutes I am restless and turn on my side. I hear the men marching to work and stand near the outer wall hoping to hear a word or two but I only hear mumbled voices and the shouts of the guards. I hear the whistle of the train in the distance. I kneel by the door and strain my eyes seeking to discern someone in the tailor shop on the second floor next door, but everything is a blur. I walk around the walls reading the poetry I have written and all the inscriptions others have engraved. I am not a poet but my feeling about the Chaplain goes as follows:

THE CHAPLAIN

The Chaplain said that Christ had risen
And that He died to set men free;
But we all knew, who lay in prison,
The lying lips, the mockery;
That He who helped the sore oppressed,
Who scorned the Scribe and Pharisee,
Would never have His children blest
By one who winked at misery.

I try to figure out what the possible history of this or that initial may mean, but soon give it up as waste time. I hear the voice of the deputy in the hall greeting the guard in charge. It is now 9 a.m. and according to my schedule, time to read the Bible. I lie on my bunk for half an hour reading the chapter for that morning. Then I sit on the toilet and take my pencil which I found the first day hidden in a small crack in the plaster, back of the toilet. A pencil is precious. You either have one or you don't. The toilet is near the door and the only place in the cell where a full view of the occupant cannot be gained through the peephole. I do not want to be caught with my precious pencil. I place the toilet paper on which I have written my notes in the Bible and sit on my chair and study what I have written. Then I return to the toilet seat and write some conclusions. Then I lie on my bunk and with my eyes closed think over what I have read.

I then try to sleep for half an hour but become restless and walk back and forth in my cell for a mile and a half and take my exercises. I spin my plate again. I look up to the dirty window many times but can see nothing. For fifteen minutes I look steadily, after I have noticed a bird flying near the window, hoping that it may return. But why should a bird stop by my dusty window? It is now 11.15 and the guards are outside watching the men enter for the first mess. I feel that this is the opportune time to write a few words, which I have not finished, on the wall. I sharpen my spoon on the floor and stealthily carve two letters when I hear a step in the hall and cease my carving.

I walk aimlessly around my cell for fifteen minutes and then sit and wait for the door to open for my dinner. Beans, oleo, bread and coffee. I eat the beans carefully, for often I break my teeth from biting against the stones which are included in the beans. I again wash my dishes leisurely, rest on my bunk for half an hour, then become restless again and walk to and fro for a mile or two. I read for an hour as the afternoon passes slowly. Then make notes and think about the subject matter for a time. I hear the train at 2 p.m. I am tired of thinking and tired of exercising. I again walk aimlessly about my cell, examining the walls. Perhaps I take some toilet paper, wet it, and wash a section of the wall to see if there is a message written underneath the grime; perhaps I figure out a calendar six months ahead to discover on what day of the week Selma's birthday occurs.

I think again of those on the outside and of the radical movement. An hour passess by in this manner and I try to sleep for half an hour but turn from one side to the other. I hear Popoff rattle his chains and groan in the next cell. He is a Bulgarian, a counterfeiter. He invented some kind of a gun and offered the plans to the war department but they never answered him. He does not speak English and did not explain his sickness to the Doctor so it could be understood at once, and was put into solitary for faking. He had sent a poem to the prison paper and this was sent back. He sassed the guards and was beaten up. What with all this he thought if he knocked the deputy warden down, someone would come from Washington and then he could tell them about his invention. He struck harder than he thought and the deputy died. He got life imprisonment, but it was not supposed to be hanging by his wrists from the bars. He was not a pacifist or a radical and when he called the guards names they strung him up.

I take strenuous exercises punching an imaginary punching bag; I try walking on my hands; I sing a song or recite some poetry for another hour. Finally a break in my day comes with the first mess marching by at 4.30. Supper comes and is soon over. I walk aimlessly around my cell. The guards change for the night shift. Now the other fellows in jail, outside of solitary, are getting their evening papers and mail; visiting with each other; playing games on the sly and having a good time. It is dark and the night guard, Dean, turns on the light. Again I read the Bible for an hour and take notes on what I have read. I rest on my bunk; sing some songs; perhaps curse a little if I feel like it; walk back and forth.

Finally it is 8:30 p.m. and my light is turned out. I undress and go to bed. The lonesome whistle of the train howls in the distance. I lie on my back; then on one side; then on the other. Sometimes I cry; sometimes I curse; sometimes I pray to whatever kind of God listens to those in solitary. I think it must be night when the door opens and Dean flashes the light on to see if I am in my cell and shouts to the other guard, "o.k.; all in at 10 p.m." I toss about, am nearly asleep when the bedbugs commence. I finally pass a night of fitful sleeping and dreaming. Again it is 6 a.m. and I cross off another day on my calendar.

A visit from the warden

I had read the Bible once when I belonged to the Baptist church, and now that it was all that I had to read, I commenced with Genesis and read at least twenty chapters a day. I also walked what I figured was four and a half miles a day. Berkman sent me a copy of Edwin Markham's "The Man with the Hoe," and I learned it by heart and recited it aloud several times a day. For the first few weeks the time did not go so slowly, as I was busy planning a routine. I found that on one day, perhaps a Thursday or a Friday, I would suddenly be called by the guard to go across the hall and get a bath. Meanwhile my cell would be searched for contraband. For three minutes at some other odd time in the week I would be taken across the hall to be shaved. It was summer time and I asked to have my hair shaved off to make my head cooler. I could not see myself and whatever the trusty or Johnson thought of my appearance did not make any difference to me.

Once when I was going to get a shave I saw Popoff entering his cell with his head bandaged. This must have been the result of the blows which I had heard faintly the day before. He was mistreated for a year or more until he went insane. Selma and I visited him in 1921 at St. Elizabeth's Hospital in Washington, D. C. He did not recognize me until I said "Johnson, the guard." I sent notes to my sister Lola for the newspapers about the treatment of Popoff. I heard the chains fall which bound him to the bars and then the thump of his body to the floor I would curse the damned capitalist system and the guards and everyone connected with the government and the prison.

Once in a while I would crouch by the door of my cell, on bright sunny mornings, and see the top of Berkman's bald head as he worked at his regular table by the west window of the tailor shop on the second floor of the building next to my solitary. I thought that if he did 3½ years in solitary, in Allegheny prison, in a cell with slimy walls, I could do the balance of my time in this comparatively clean dry cell.

It was now nearly three months that I had been in solitary. Fred Zerbst, the warden, came in and asked me to sign a paper. It was registration for the second war-draft. I told him I had not changed my mind about the war. He said I wouldn't get anything around here acting that way. I told him that I wasn't asking for anything around here: I was just doing time. He said I would get another year back in the hole for this second refusal to register. I told him that was o.k.

It was September 21, 1918. The warden came in again and said this was all the longer they kept prisoners in solitary and that he would let me out the next day; that I would not plot to blow up any more prisons.

"You know I didn't do that," I said.

"I know you didn't," he replied, "but what do you suppose I am warden for? If I had told the prisoners that you were put in solitary for

23

leading in that food sit-down, all of them would be your friends. When you are accused of planning to blow up the prison they are all afraid to know you. Why didn't you come and tell me about the food?

"Why didn't you come into the kitchen and find out; no one but stoolies go to your office," I answered. He left hurriedly.

In about five minutes he returned, saying: "I forgot to ask you something, Hennacy. I'll leave you out tomorrow just the same."

"What is on your mind?" I asked.

"Have you been sneaking any letters out of this prison?" he asked in an angry tone.

"Sure," I replied, smiling.

"Who is doing it for you?" he demanded.

"A friend of mine," I answered.

"What is his name?" was the query.

"That is for you and your guards and stool pigeons to find out. I won't tell you, for I want to get some more letters out concerning the evil things that go on," I replied good naturedly.

He stormed around my cell, somewhat taken back by the fact that I had not lied or given in.

"You'll stay in here all your good time and get another year, you stubborn fool," he said as he left.

It was not for many years that I knew I had used the method of moral jiu jitsu as advised by Ghandi. If you don't give your enemy a hold he can't throw you. Never be on the defensive; always answer quickly and keep the enemy on the run. He is used to trickery and is put off his guard by an honest and courageous opponent whom he cannot scare or bribe.

I picked up the Bible and threw it in a corner, pacing back and forth, thinking and mumbling to myself: the liars, the double-crossers, tempting me with freedom and then telling me the only way to obtain it was by being a rat. This was bad enough, but to talk the Golden Rule and religion, as they did whenever outsiders came around. Love your enemies, turn the other cheek; fine stuff, after they frame you and admit it.

The world needs a Samson to pull down their whole structure of lies. Debs is arrested near my home town in Ohio for defending my comrades Ruthenberg, Wagenknecht and Baker who were doing time in Canton jail and he will come to Atlanta soon. He did time when he was a young man. Now he's not so bitter; but then, he's older, and won't allow the capitalist class to tramp on him either.

Love your enemy?

That night I was nervous and tore off the buttons from my clothing in order to have something to do to sew them on again. I paced my eight and a half steps back and forth for hours and finally flung myself on the bunk. It must have been the middle of the night when I awoke. I had not had a note from anyone for a month. Were my friends forgetting me? I felt weak, lonesome and alone in the world. Here I had been singing defiance at the whole capitalistic world but a few hours before, and had boasted to the warden how I would bravely do my time; now I wondered

24

if anyone really cared. Perhaps by this time Selma might be married to some one else with a real future ahead of him instead of being lost in a jail. The last letter I had received from her was rather formal. Would she understand why I did not write; and could I be sure that some of the letters I had sent her had been received, with the officials opening the mail I had sent to my sister Lola? How could one end it all? The sharp spoon with which I had carved poems and my calendar on the wall could cut my wrist and I could bleed to death before a guard arrived. But then that would be such a messy death. Then the warden would be sorry for the lies he had told me and the tricks he had tried to play. The last thing I could remember before falling asleep was the long wailing whistle of the freight train as it echoed in the woods nearby.

The next day the deputy came in my cell and said that I was looking very pale; that number 7440, a man just two numbers from me who had come in the same day with me, had died of the flu, and that thirty others were buried that week. If I did not get out and breathe the fresh air it was likely that I would die sooner than the others, he said. Why should I not tell what I knew and get out? In reply I asked the deputy to talk about the weather, as I was not interested in achieving the reputation of a rat. He asked me if it was a prisoner or a guard who had sent out my letters. I walked up to him closely and in a confidential tone said, "It was a prisoner or a guard."

I did not know the nature of the flu but thought that this might be a good way to die if I could only get it. Fate seemed to seal me up in a place where I could not get any germs. (Now that I think of it my "Celestial Bulldozer," guardian angel, or whatever the name may be, must have been in charge of events. In those days I believed in germs and doctors and out in the prison I might have absorbed their fears and succumbed. I was saved until I could emancipate my mind from medical as well as all other kinds of slavery.) Late that afternoon I was called across the hall to take a bath. The guard accidentally left my wooden door open when he was called to answer a telephone. I could not see anywhere except across the hall to the solid door of another cell, but I could hear Popoff in the next cell groaning and calling for water. He was still hanging from his hands for the eight hours a day as he had been for months. As the guard came down the hall he opened Popoff's door, dipping his tin cup in the toilet and threw the dirty water in Popoff's face. Then he came and slammed my door shut and locked it. How soon would I be strung to the bars? How long could a fellow stand such treatment?

As soon as it was dark I sharpened my spoon again and tried it gently on my wrist. The skin seemed to be quite tough, but then I could press harder. If I cut my wrist at midnight I could be dead by morning. I thought I ought to write a note to Selma and to my mother and I couldn't see to do it until morning. Well, I had waited that long, I could wait a day longer. That night my dreams were a mixture of Victor Hugo's stories of men hiding in the sewers of Paris; I.W.W. songs; blood flowing from the pigs that had been butchered on the farm when I was a boy; and the groans of Popoff.

The sun shone brightly in my cell the next morning for the first time in weeks. I crouched again by the door and saw Berkman's bald head. Tears came into my eyes and I felt ashamed of myself for my cowardly idea of suicide just because I had a few reverses. Here was Berkman who had passed through much more than I would ever have to endure if I stayed two more years in solitary. How was the world to know more about the continued torture of Popoff and others if I gave up? The last two verses of the I.W.W. Prison Song now had a real meaning to me as I sang them again. I was through with despair. I wanted to live to make the world better. Just because most prisoners, and for all that, most people on the outside, did not understand and know what solitary meant was all the more reason why I should be strong. I sang cheerfully:

> "By all the graves of Labor's dead,
> By Labor's deathless flag of red,
> We make a solemn vow to you,
> We'll keep the faith, we will be true.
> For freedom laughs at prison bars,
> Her voice reechoes from the stars;
> Proclaiming with the tempest's breath
> A Cause beyond the reach of death."

Two months later I heard the whistles blow and shouts resound throughout the prison. The war was over. The Armistice had been signed. It was not until then that I was informed in a note from Berkman that November 11 was also an anarchist anniversary: the date of the hanging of the Chicago anarchists of the Haymarket in 1887. I had ceased by this time my nervous running back and forth like a squirrel in my cell and was now taking steady walks in my cell each day, and also hours of physical exercise. I was going to build myself up and not get sick and die. I would show my persecutors that I would be a credit to my ideals.

I had painted the ceiling of the Catholic chapel in flat work before I got in solitary, and had left no brush marks. The priest appreciated my good work. He knew I was an Irishman who was not a Catholic, but he never tried to convert me. Now, as I studied the Bible, I was not thinking of any church but just wanted to see what might be worthwhile in it. I had now read it through four times and had read the New Testament many times and the Sermon on the Mount scores of times. I had made up games with pages and chapters and names of characters in the Bible to pass away the time. I had memorized certain chapters that I liked. As I read of Isaiah, Ezekiel, Micah and other of the prophets and of Jesus, I could see that they had opposed tyranny. I had also spent many days reviewing all of the historical knowledge that I could remember and in trying to think through a philosophy of life. I had passed through the idea of killing myself. This was an escape, not any solution to life. The remainder of my two years in solitary must result in a clear-cut plan whereby I could go forth and be a force in the world. I could not take any halfway measures.

If assassination, violence and revolution was the better way, then military tactics must be studied and a group of fearless rebels organized. I remembered again what Slim, the sort of Robin Hood Wobblie who was in on some larceny charge had told me once to the effect that one could not be a good rebel unless he became angry and vengeful. Then I heard Popoff curse the guards and I heard them beat him. I remembered the Negro who had sworn at the guard in the tailor shop and was killed. I had read of riots in prison over food and I remembered the peaceful victory which we had in our strike against the spoiled fish. I also remembered what Berkman had said about being firm, but quiet. He had tried violence but did not believe in it as a wholesale method. I read of the wars and hatred in the Old Testament. I also read of the courage of Daniel and the Hebrew children who would not worship the golden image; of Peter who chose to obey God rather than the properly constituted authorities who placed him in jail; and of the victory of these men by courage and peaceful methods. I read of Jesus, who was confronted with a whole world empire of tyranny and chose not to overturn the tyrant and make Himself king, but to change the hatred in the hearts of men to love and understanding—to overcome evil with goodwill.

I had called loudly for the sword and mentally listed those whom I desired to kill when I was free. Was his really the universal method which should be used? I would read the Sermon on the Mount again. When a child I had been frightened by hell fire into proclaiming a change of life. Now I spent months making a decision; there was no sudden change. I had all the time in the world and no one could talk to me or influence me. I was deciding this idea for myself. Gradually I came to gain a glimpse of what Jesus meant when He said, "The Kingdom of God is Within You." In my heart now after six months I could love everybody in the world but the warden, but if I did not love him then the Sermon on the Mount meant nothing at all. I really saw this and felt it in my heart but I was too stubborn to admit it in my mind. One day I was walking back and forth in my cell when, in turning, my head hit the wall. Then the thought came to me: "Here I am locked up in a cell. The warden was never locked up in any cell and he never had a chance to know what Jesus meant. Neither did I until yesterday. So I must not blame him. I must love him." Now the whole thing was clear. This Kingdom of God must be in everyone: in the deputy, the warden, in the rat and the pervert—and now I came to know it—in myself. I read and reread the Sermon on the Mount: the fifth, sixth and seventh chapters of Matthew thus became a living thing to me. I tried to take every sentence and apply it to my present problems. The warden had said that he did not understand political prisoners. He and the deputy, in plain words, did not know any better; they had put on the false face of sternness and tyranny because this was the only method which they knew. It was my job to teach them another method: that of goodwill overcoming their evil intentions, or rather habits. The opposite of the Sermon on the Mount was what the whole world had been practicing, in prison and out of prison; and hate piled on hate had brought hate and revenge. It was plain that this system did not work. I

27

would never have a better opportunity than to try out the Sermon on the Mount right now in my cell. Here was deceit, hatred, lust, murder, and every kind of evil in this prison. I reread slowly and pondered each verse: "Ye have heard that it hath been said an eye for an eye, and a tooth for a tooth . . . whoever shall smite thee on thy right cheek turn to him the other also . . . take therefore no thought for the morrow . . . therefore all things whatsoever ye would that men should do to you, do ye even so to them."

I fancied what my radical friends in and out of prison would say when I spoke of the above teachings of Jesus. I knew that I would have to bear their displeasure, just as I had borne the hysteria of the patriots and the silence of my friends when I was sent to prison. This did not mean that I was going to "squeal" and give in to the officials, but in my heart I would try to see the good in them and not hate them. Jesus did not give in to His persecutors. He used strong words against the evil doers of His time, but He had mercy for the sinner. I now was not alone fighting the world for I had Him as my helper. I saw that if I held this philosophy for myself I could not engage in violence for a revolution—a good war, as some might call it—but would have to renounce violence even in my thought. Would I be ready to go the whole way? At that time I had not heard of Tolstoy and his application of Christ's teachings to society. Berkman had just mentioned his name along with other anarchists and he might have told me more if I had had a lengthy conversation with him; but I never saw him again. I could see the warden's honesty in admitting that he had "framed" me. I could even see that the deputy had only been used to violence in his years of supervising the chain gang. I did not know much about the outside world and it was up to me now day by day to solve this problem of repressed hatred, and when I was finally released to see in what manner I could apply my new ideals to conditions as I found them. The most difficult animosity for me to overcome was a dislike of hypocrites and church people who had so long withheld the real teachings of Jesus. I could see no connection between Jesus and the church.

I continued my study of the Bible. Popoff was still being manhandled. My teeth ached much of the time in solitary and I asked the deputy to allow the prison dentist to fix my teeth. The prison doctor gave one pint of dreadful tasting salts for whatever ailed a prisoner. Very few men would fake a sick call with this dose in view. However, the dentist could not give me a pint of physic for my toothache, and neither could he bring his dental chair to solitary. The deputy replied that I knew how I could get my teeth fixed: that was to tell what I knew; otherwise I could ache for all he cared. So loving my enemies was not altogether a theoretical matter.

It was now early in February of 1919 and I had been in solitary for seven and a half months. Mr. Duehay, Superintendent of Federal Prisons from Washington, and his secretary, and warden Zerbst came to my cell. Duehay wanted to know why I was being held so long here. I told him I was telling the world of evil conditions in the prison and would not divulge the source of my outlet for contraband mail. He felt that I was an intelligent and educated man who was foolish to endanger my health in solitary

28

by trying to better the conditions for a lot of bums in prison who would sell me for a dime. I told him I was learning to take it.

I had read a poem in the APPEAL TO REASON years before and had remembered it and written it on the wall. He and the warden read it and laughed.

SURPLUS VALUE

The Merchant calls it Profit and winks the other eye;
The Banker calls it Interest and heaves a cheerful sigh;
The Landlord calls it Rent as he tucks it in his bag;
But the honest old Burglar he simply calls it Swag.

Duehay changed his tactics and began to swing his arms and berate me as a fool and a coward. The warden had called me names often but he disliked to hear an outsider do so.

"If he's a fool or a coward he must be a different kind, for no one ever stood more than three months in the hole without giving in. He must be a God's fool or a God's coward."

Years later I was to write an account of my prison life and call it "God's Coward." Portions of it were printed in the November and December CATHOLIC WORKER in 1941. It must have seemed especial advice for those about to oppose World War II.

I did not lose my temper or fight back to the warden and Mr. Duehay; just smiled and held my ground. Suddenly Duehay. turned to the warden saying, "Let's make out parole papers for this stubborn fellow. Half of the time I can't trust my own men. This Hennacy is honest and can't be bribed. I will give him a job in the secret service."

The warden nodded and smiled. I shook my head saying I wanted no job hunting down radicals and criminals for I was on their side and not that of the oppressor. . . . The secretary of Duehay was taking this all down in shorthand. Finally in desperation they left.

The next morning a runner came down from the office to measure me for. an outgoing suit, saying:

"The warden told us 'that damn Hennacy wouldn't tell anything in seven and a half months; he won't tell anything in seven and a half years. Get him the hell out of here; give him back his good time and let him go to his other jails. He is too much of a nuisance.' "

The next month went very quickly. It was now March 19, 1919, and I was to be released the next day. That night the deputy came in and said,

"Going out tomorrow, Hennacy?"

"That's what they say; sure a fine feeling," I replied.

"We give; we take. You tell who is getting out your contraband mail or you'll stay here another five and a half months and lose your good time and then another year for refusing to register. You don't think we will allow anyone to get by in bucking us, do you?"

"Tears came to my eyes as I chokingly replied, "I can do it. Go away and don't bother me anymore." After he left I wept, but I was at the stage where I felt strong enough to take it.

The next morning after breakfast I wrote on the wall that I was beginning to do the "good time" that I had lost when the door opened suddenly and old Johnson smiled for once, saying, "Going out of this jail, Hennacy." I did not believe him; and even while the barber was shaving me I thought it was some trick to bedevil me. I was given my outgoing suit and an overcoat. It is customary for the warden to shake hands with those who leave and to admonish them to live a good life out in the world. A guard gave me my $10 outgoing money and a bundle of letters that had come to me while I was in solitary, but the warden never appeared. When I walked out of prison a plain clothes man met me saying that I was being arrested for refusing to register in August, 1918 and would be taken to the County Tower to await trial. We took a street car there, at the end of South Pryor street, and walked a few blocks downtown before we got to the Tower. A second-hand clothing merchant recognized my prison clothes and asked if I wanted to sell my overcoat. I was not handcuffed but I guess my white face from the months of solitary was sign enough to anyone as to my being an ex-convict.

I was ushered into a cell where Joe Webb, a mountain boy, also slept. He had been found guilty of murder, and was to be executed. Through influential friends I was able to get him a new trial, and he got life on the chain gang instead. I was now able to read and write as I pleased. Selma had received some of my contraband letters from my sister. She was cordial and not married to anyone else, so there was still hope. There was not the restriction on correspondents then that there is now, so I had letters from many people over the country. Mary Raoul Millis, a Socialist of an old southern family whom I had met in Cleveland in 1913, lived in Atlanta and visited me in the Federal Prison and also here in the Tower. (She is the mother of Walter Millis, the author of The Martial Spirit, the best book on the Spanish-American War farce.) Peggy Harwell, a pretty young woman who was a Socialist and a Theosophist, also visited me in both jails. They told me that my red-headed cousin Georgia had gone to the warden's office when I was in solitary and raised particular hell because she was not allowed to see me. I asked for radical books to read and among other books Tolstoy's Kingdom of God is Within You was brought. I felt that it must have been written especially for me, for here was the answer already written out to all the questions that I had tried to figure out for myself in solitary. To change the world by bullets or ballots was a useless procedure. If the workers ever did get a majority of either, they would have the envy and greed in their hearts and would be chained by these as much as by the chains of the master class. And the State which they would like to call a Cooperative Commonwealth would be based on power; the state would not wither away but would grow. Therefore the only revolution worthwhile was the one-man revolution within the heart. Each one could make this by himself and not need to wait on a majority. I had already started this revolution in solitary by becoming a Christian. Now I had completed it by becoming an Anarchist. Mrs. Millis was a Christian Scientist and she brought me Science and Health to read. I did so, but it did not appeal to me. Mr. Bazemore, the deputy sheriff, said that "the Fed-

30

erals" wanted him to watch my mail to see if I would divulge the name of the person who had sent my contraband letters out of prison, but he wasn't paid to stool pigeon for them and I could write what I liked for all he cared.

Debs had entered Moundsville, West Virginia prison to start his twenty years. He could not be allowed to receive letters from another convict so I wrote to his brother Theodore in Terre Haute expressing my admiration for one who in his old age was still a rebel. Sam Castleton, who was to be Deb's lawyer in Atlanta, was also my lawyer. My case came up for trial after seven weeks. Castleton told me that if I was not too radical he might get me off with six months.

When I was in court a Holiness preacher was being tried first. He had refused to register, he said, because the Bible said not to kill, and putting your name down on the list of killers was the first thing the government wanted you to do. The first thing for a Christian to do was to write his name in the Book of Life instead of the Book of Death, and refuse to register. He had announced this far and wide but on the night before the draft God came to him in a dream and said that "the powers that be are ordained of God" and he should not disobey them. So he made up his mind to register the next day; but then he took sick and couldn't. It was obvious that he was squeaking, and that if God was talking to him He might as well have kept him well so he could go and register. His wife and children asked the judge for clemency and the judge gave him 24 hours in jail.

My case came next. I was asked if I had really refused to register for the first and second drafts and if I had not changed my mind like the minister and would be ready to register for the third draft if and when it came along. I replied that I had entered prison an atheist and not a pacifist, but that I was locked up with the Bible; that if I had been locked up with the cook book, the phone book, or the Book of Mormon I might have come out an expert on these, but being there with the Bible I became a Christian and a pacifist. Perhaps not a very orthodox Christian, spelling God with a little "g" and two "o's" (good). And that a few weeks ago I had read Tolstoy and had become an anarchist.

"What's an anarchist?" asked the Judge. I could see my lawyer wince and put his finger to his lips.

"An anarchist is someone who doesn't need a cop to make him behave. Anarchism is voluntary cooperation with the right of secession. The individual or the family or the small group as a unit instead of the State. Jefferson said 'that government is best which governs least, as with the Indians.'" I continued for about ten minutes to explain my new radical ideas. The District Attorney, Hooper Alexander, an old fashioned looking Southerner, came up to the judge and whispered and the judge said, "case dismissed." I looked around to see whose case it was and it was mine. My lawyer seemed bewildered and so was I. Mr. Alexander beckoned for me to come to his office and asked me how the hell I got that way. I explained some of my history to him. He had read letters that came to me and said he understood. The reason he had dismissed my case was the contrast between this preacher who was bellyaching out of it and myself who was willing to take more punishment. He liked a good fighter. He was not a pacifist nor in sympathy with anarchism he said, but he realized something was wrong with the world and those who supported the status quo surely did not have the answer. He wanted to know if I had enough money to pay my way to the Delaware, Ohio jail to do my nine months for refusing to register the first time. I told him I had because the Socialists of Columbus had sent me $2 a month to buy candy and I could not use it while in solitary.

CHAPTER 3.

Marriage - Travel in 48
States - Carmen and
Sharon born

1920 - 1930

New York City - Waukesha, Wis.

Ade Bethune

In New York City

I was nervous and in no position to hold down a job. Two scholarships to the Rand School in New York City were open to a boy and a girl from the middle west and they were given to Selma and me. George Herron, a radical professor in the middle west had married a wealthy woman by the name of Rand and they gave money to erect and run this Socialist school. The night of my arrival there was a mass meeting in the auditorium of the Rand School and Mother Bloor was speaking about my case as I entered the back of the hall. Someone told her and she asked me to come forward. I was not ashamed to kiss her in public as she represented to me all that was ideal.

While Selma was not a Christian nor an anarchist, she was radical and understood enough about my feelings to be in accord with my opposition to the church and the state when it came to marriage. Accordingly on December 24, 1919 we kissed each other and made the mutual pledge that "we would live together as long as we loved each other—for the Revolution." (This day was to go down in history for another reason, for it was the day when Vanzetti was accused of the Bridgewater holdup.) So we lived together near Union Square and continued our studies. We lived in Hell's Kitchen and other places. Later I worked with my friend Roger Baldwin of the American Civil Liberties Union as secretary of the League for Mutual Aid. And again as secretary of a building cooperative. Selma worked in the office of the WORLD TOMORROW, a pacifist magazine.

While in New York City I wrote several articles in the I.W.W. paper, THE FELLOW WORKER and spoke at one of their forums. I was giv-

33

ing the pacifist argument when a burly fellow worker said no cop was going to tell him what to do and we had to fight for our rights; being a pacifist was only cowardice. Before I could answer him a small red-headed young man got up and said:

"Yes, you are brave. Last week when the cops raided us on Union Square all you big fellows ran away and left me there alone to fight them all. I'm not a pacifist but I think more of this fellow who does what he says than of you big guys who talk brave and run away."

During my second month in solitary in Atlanta in July, 1918 I had written a poem, Hypocrites, and now in November, 1920 THE ONE BIG UNION MONTHLY of the I.W.W. published it.

HYPOCRITES

I wonder if the devil laughs,
And sings a joyful song,
As to "Onward Christian Soldiers,"
"My Country Right or Wrong."
The Christians each other slaughter,
And lynch and mob and maim,
All those who will not help to kill
In lowly Jesus' name.

I wonder if the devil laughs,
And if his joy's increased,
To see the god of gold worshipped
By preacher and by priest;
Who teach contentment with your lot—
Unless you run the game—
And wink at sin and grab the tin
In lowly Jesus' name.

I wonder if the devil laughs,
And adds oil to his fire,
To make a warm reception for
That saintly son and sire,
Who teach love and the golden rule,
While practicing the same;
By raising rents and burning tents
In lowly Jesus' name.

I wonder if the devil laughs,
Or if he sheds a tear,
As the revolution's growing
Much stronger year by year;
And whether love or dynamite
Our victory shall acclaim,
Our foes will fight with all their might
In lowly Jesus' name.

I also had an article in THE TOILER, the organ of the Communist Labor Party edited by my old friend Alfred Wagenknecht, on the Socialist

Party convention. Around this time about a dozen Socialist Assemblymen in Albany were being expelled because of their radicalism. They were not very radical but the Lusk Committee was out to get even pinks. In their testimony of the trial it was brought up that I had been secretary of the Socialist Party in Columbus, Ohio in 1917, and was routed by the state organization to oppose the war and the draft. Seymour Stedman, once a candidate for Vice President on the Socialist ticket himself, was the defense lawyer and his rebuttal was that I was not a Socialist but a Quaker. Later I wrote to him telling him that he knew the facts and he replied that he had forgotten. The squeaking Assemblymen lost their jobs anyway, and later all of them lived through another war and supported it.

Evan Thomas, Julius Eichel, J. B. C. Woods, and Selma and I met every two weeks, along with other pacifists, and held meetings under the name World War Objectors. We published a large leaflet with a picture of the Perfect Soldier, Bob Minor's huge man with a bayonet but no head, and issued it under the heading Stop the Next War Now. I bought thousands of I.W.W. bronze amnesty buttons and sold them at meetings: a picture of a man behind bars. We went to Margaret Sanger's office and helped distribute her illegal birth control pamphlet and other literature. I remember talking to bewhiskered Edwin Markham, author of that epic that had cheered me in solitary: *The Man with the Hoe.*

Finally in the spring of 1921 Selma and I read Thoreau and Walt Whitman and decided on hiking over the country. I was working as a soda jerk at the Pennsylvania station. We quit our jobs and with $100 set forth. When I looked at the calendar I saw it was on the exact anniversary of my entrance into solitary: June 21. What happened during the next four years I have written in a manuscript entitled *High Roads and Hot Roads.* Suffice it to say that we never thumbed a ride but waited for people to ask us.

We hiked first over Staten Island, viisted Walter Hirshberg in Atlantic City, whom I had known as a CO in Atlanta. His father was an old time anarchist who ran the Boardwalk Bookstore. Got to Norfolk and had a three weeks ride on a leaky coal barge; back up to Boston where we visited with Francis Xavier Hennessey, now a fallen away Catholic, who had been a CO in Leavenworth. Then to see John Dunn in Providence, R. I. We climbed Mt. Washington one night; and found the New England people the kindest folks of the whole country. Visited my folks in Saginaw and Selma's in Milwaukee. Then spent several weeks in Chicago as guest of my old radical friend Ed Smith. Visited Waldheim cemetery where the Haymarket men are buried and placed a rose there. Then down through the snow towards Georgia.

Before we came to Sewanee Mountain in Tennessee, we stopped at a store to buy food and were told that on the other side of the mountain we would see a painted woman on a horse right near the Bottomless Pit. That she would make a sign to a man in the bushes and he would throw us in the Pit. We joked all that afternoon and next day about this prediction. Around 3 p.m. we rounded a corner and sure enough saw a woman about 35, with painted lips, on a horse. She asked who we were and where we were going. We told her and we must have sounded all right for she motioned to a man in the bushes to lower his rifle which had been pointed to us all of the time, saying, "They're o.k." We asked if there was a Bottomless Pit nearby. The woman told us to look around and right behind us was a hole. She told us to throw a stone in it. We did so and could not hear it splash. "How deep is it?" we asked. "No one knows, and if they drop in there they'll never know anything," she replied. We hurried on down the mountain and at dark came to a house. We asked for a drink of water and were in turn asked if we were going over the mountain. "Just came down," we replied. "What, didn't those people on the other side of the mountain rob you?" the lady asked. We told her we had heard a story about the woman on a horse and the man in the bushes with a gun from the other side of the mountain, but no one there had disturbed us. "That's Pop," said a small boy referring to the man on the horse. "You shet up!" said the mother. We camped there that night.

In Rome, Georgia we said hello to the parents of Joe Webb, and they gave us a picture of him on the chain gang. Whether I had done Joe a service to save him from the rope for the ball and chain is a question. In Atlanta we went out to visit the prison. Ex-convicts are not allowed to return and visit. As we came to the outside Tower the guard laughingly said, "Go ahead; I guess you are no ex-cons." We sat on a bench with about twenty other visitors waiting until a guard would show us through the prison. DeMoss, who had framed me into solitary passed several times and looked at me, but I suppose he was not sure about me, As we were going through the yard and got near the house where I was in solitary so long I whispered to Selma and she very sweetly said to the guard who was escorting us:

"Officer, how many people do they have in solitary now?"

"About 30. . . . Oh, we don't have solitary any more," he hemmed and hawed.

As we went through the kitchen the Negro lifer who had given me my food in solitary winked at me, recognizing me.

We worked in Georgia for 18 months. I studied the history of that state for an article for THE NATION in its series on States., but as I recall it was not published. On the streets of Atlanta one day I met a rather seedy man who recognized me. He asked me to come around to his church, but in the midst of his missionary effort he must have remembered that this was the animal he had under his torture for $8\frac{1}{2}$ months while he was deputy warden, for he suddenly stammered and changed the subject before the invitation for salvation had been fully delivered. So even Deputy Girardeau had a conscience. We had a visit for an hour with the DA who had dismissed my case, Hooper Alexander, and he was exceedingly cordial.

Through reading Harry Franck's books on travel we got the idea of going to South America and obtaining a passport. All I had to say was that I had not been convicted of a felony within the past five years. It had been *six* years since I had been sentenced. We left Atlanta in the spring, climbed Mt. Mitchell in the Carolina's, went across Texas and up to Milwaukee in time for the state Socialist picnic in the late summer. We visited our folks leisurely, spent a few days with Haldeman-Julius at Girard, Kansas, where both of them wanted us to link our names as they had. Selma had retained her full maiden name, Selma Melms. Somehow we did not like the idea. Julius insisted that we should visit his friend Charles J. Finger of Fayetteville, Arkansas. When we arrived at his farm he discovered that I was the conscientious objector whom he had planned to see in Delaware, Ohio jail in 1919, but he had to leave the town before doing so. He was a wealthy operator of railroads, junking them or making a success for a syndicate. Somehow he felt that this was a useless life so the whole family sold their houses and cars and bought a farm in Arkansas. Here he wrote books about his early days as a castaway on a cannibal island and other tales of derring do. It was a standing joke in his family that when his sons wanted to roam the world, saying "you did it, Dad, when you were 17," he always advanced the age to 18 or 20. He read chapters from Dickens before the huge fireplace each night. Next we saw "Coin Harvey," who had become wealthy and famous writing about free coinage of silver in 1896 and had started to build a castle at Monte Ne, Arkansas, from which he would direct the World Revolt. A strike of masons interrupted it and it was never finished. Now he was building a pyramid there to contain records of this civilization. He figured Arkansas would be about the last place a conqueror would invade or erosion would destroy.

Very early one morning as we were hiking on a dirt road in Arkansas we chatted for a minute with a farmer going to market with a wagon load of tomatoes. We bought some, Selma liking to eat them like apples, with salt. Haldeman-Julius had given us a score of his Little Blue Books, so, as we finished one we gave them away. Giving one to the tomato merchant-farmer he looked at us closely and said: "Be you all Socialists?"

"Something like that. I was a conscientious objector in jail in Atlanta in 1917-19 and my wife's father used to be Socialist sheriff in Milwaukee," I answered.

"Let me shake your paw," said the farmer, wiping the tears from his eyes, "I haven't seen a Socialist for years. Not since I used to give medicine snake shows over Texas and then end it up with a Socialist speech. You must stop at my house and visit tonight. It's 18 miles down the road; turn off there by the red filling station." We promised to see him that night. His wife was friendly when we arrived, after refusing a ride to Little Rock from a man who had picked us up. We picked blackberries that afternoon and I had my introduction to "chiggers;" that "thang," as they say that gets under your arms and knees and itches and itches and you can't see them at all. After supper our host said we should walk a mile down the draw and say hello to Will who had done time in Leavenworth.

We did so and met a 6 foot 6 jolly native whose voice boomed for a quarter of a mile in regular conversation. I had heard vaguely of such a character but had never met him. He had gone into Texas and worked in the oil fields; then onto farms where with others he joined The Working Class Union, a division of the I.W.W. Along with others he had refused to register and when taken into court and asked by the judge why he didn't go to war he said: "Why don't you go yourself; you old s.o.b.?"

He was threatened with "contempt of court," and told them that is just what he had for the court. Two officers came toward him and he lifted them each by the neck and gently knocked their heads together, as much as saying that if he really wanted to he could do a good job at it. He was absolutely without guile, an "innocent" who didn't know enough to be afraid; and the court had to be adjourned, for no order could be kept with Will around. He got 20 years in Leavenworth and proceeded to act the same way there. An officer drilling the men would slip and fall in the mud. Will would laugh loudly and was put in solitary; here he yelled and made such a noise that they let him out and gave him a job picking up pieces of paper blowing around, with a spiked stick. Some fat guard would order him around and he would run after him saying: "I'll stick this thang in your fat belly," and the guard knew he would. He was called to the "headdoctor," as he called it and asked why he didn't learn how to behave in jail. His reply was that it would "spoil me for the outside." He was finally catalogued as a "natural born anarchist" and discharged, for with Will in jail there could be no semblance of discipline.

We had read of the School of Organic Education at the Single Tax settlement of Fairhope, Alabama, across the bay from Mobile. Passing through there we were persuaded to stay because the history teacher in the high school had suddenly got married and left and they wanted me to teach history. I demurred that I was not a college graduate, was a jailbird and anarchist, and that my wife and I were married common law. They needed a teacher badly, it seemed, so I stayed. Selma had learned how to make baskets from pine needles and was interested in the English folk dances which they had at the school. We lived a mile north of town in a cement block house where huge pine cones and knots of pine made a cheery warmth in the fireplace.

The English teacher told me that Sam said he wouldn't study history and that new history teacher couldn't make him. This was in the Junior class. I told them all the story of the three blind men and the elephant. How one felt the tail and said it was a rope; another felt the trunk and said it was a tree; another touched the body and said it was a house. Of course they were all wrong for it was an elephant. I said it was the same way with history. The history books of one country said that country was right and the others wrong. The history books of a dominant religion or exploiting class said they were right and their opponents were wrong. What was history 10,000 years ago was mostly fable; even at 1,000 years ago we did a lot of guessing about it, and less than 300 years ago we had the fable about George Washington and the cherry tree. What then was the truth? On the Civil War I had learned only the side of the North and the folks here knew only the side of the South. There were three sides to a question: your side, my side, and the right side. Everyone was biased. So was I, but I admitted it; the others generally said they were teaching "the truth." As we did not know for sure about yesterday, let us try and find out about today, for this would be the history of tomorrow soon. Accordingly I told the students I would have the following papers on the rack for them to look at and every Friday we would have an hour discussing current events *with absolute freedom of speech.* They had the regular conservative Mobile daily, the Single Tax COURIER at home, the others I ordered: The CHRISTIAN SCIENCE MONITOR, AMERICA, the catholic weekly, The Milwaukee LEADER, Socialist, The DAILY WORKER, Communist, FREEDOM the London Anarchist paper, FELLOW WORKER of the I.W.W., The NATION, The WORLD TOMORROW, pacifist, the ARMY AND NAVY JOURNAL, and the WALL STREET JOURNAL.

The first day Sam lay down on a bench. Everyone looked to see what the new teacher would do. I had never studied pedagogy but I had had a good course in pacifism these past few years, so I picked up a dictionary and gently placed it under Sam's head and told him to sleep on. He wanted an argument and there was none. The next day he mumbled half audibly to George. I waited a minute and then told him to hurry up and tell George all the good news and when he was finished we could talk about history. He suddenly had nothing to say and from that time on was no bother.

A Disciple Church minister was head of the Boy Scouts and of the KKK in Fairhope. One Sunday he openly said from the pulpit that I should be tarred and feathered and drowned in Mobile Bay, for there was no room in that town for a person who was a traitor, a jailbird, a man who did not attend church, and who was not legally married. They burned a cross by our house. Some folks wanted me to have a guard when I went the lonely mile home from the folk dances at night but I felt my Celestial Bulldozer made way for me. Next week I went to see the minister and invited him to come to my Friday class and give a talk on the KKK. He promised to come and didn't. Three weeks later he was "called" to preach in another town. If I had started to run from such cowards I would be running yet.

Some of the students wanted to skip other classes and attend my history class for they had never had it taught in this interesting manner. I told them they couldn't do that and they had better figure out some other method. Accordingly about half of the high school met in a special history club where all kinds of questions were asked every Wednesday night from 8 to 11; no credit. This was the Organic method with a vengeance.

There was a Shakespearean group and Selma played the part of Autoculous in an outdoor presentation of "The Winter's Tale." During a vacation between semesters I shoveled manure for a Quaker farmer and graded tangerines at a packing shed. I still remember the wonderful lunch at the Quaker farmer's: whole wheat bread, honey and a pitcher of cream. That was all and you could have all you could eat of it.

There was an old fashioned silent Quaker meeting house nearby Fairhope. Selma and I went several Sundays. I found they were of the same Hicksite group as my great-grand-parents, Ashford, in Ohio. Later some of these Quakers went to prison in World War II, and some of them moved to Costa Rica to escape militarism. In late May we went westward across Texas again and climbed Pikes Peak on the night of the 4th of July, 1924. (We learned that next year the history teacher in Fairhope was an ex-army captain, so the pacifist was counter-balanced.) We stopped at Ludlow,

Colorado and took a picture of the cross that marked the burning to death of the strikers and their women and children by the Rockefeller gunmen, years before. (Before this we had stopped at Leavenworth prison and visited Red Doran, Jim Thompson, and other I.W.W.'s still imprisoned. I was surprised to see Zerbst, my old warden from Atlanta. He was now deputy at Leavenworth. He could afford to be cordial now and praised the I.W.W.'s as being skilled workers.)

In Utah toward evening we saw what appeared to be thousands of maggots moving over a distant mountain. Drawing closer we saw they were goats. We watched that evening as the Greeks at the goat corral, backed a goat into a V shaped fence and milked her quickly into a huge washtub. They gave us goat-cheese (something you have to get used to) to carry along. After a few miles we hurried to a cabin off the road and knocked at the door, seeking to escape the rain. The door was slightly ajar and swung open. A sign said: "Cook what you want; clean up, and put out the fire." This was the open hospitality of the west that we had read about. We made coffee and oatmeal and soon it had stopped raining and we left. Later we found we never could buy cherries from the hospitable Mormons, for they always gave us some to eat and carry along.

In Seattle we met Red Doran on the street. He was a barker for a dentist. As we had little money left we hurried down to San Francisco and settled in Berkeley where Selma attended the Arts and Crafts School and I hurried into a job of selling Fuller brushes, taking an extension course in soils, beekeeping, etc. at the University.

Since 1922 I had been a nominal member of the Workers (Communist) Party because of my admiration for Ruthenberg, who had now been released from Sing Sing and was the head of the Party. He understood that I was an anarchist but that I wanted to be doing something and all the anarchists I knew of were a sleepy crowd. Accordingly I taught classes in American History each Sunday morning to the Finnish comrades in Berkeley, down by the waterfront. Each Thursday night I had a class of young Communists in Oakland and each Friday in San Francisco. By the time winter was over I understood that they did not want to learn about American History: all they wanted to hear was the word "revolution" over and over again. I could see no point in continuing my membership. I had never attended a party meeting; paying my dues by mail. I won a turkey as a salesman and Selma and Mother Bloor and a radical newsvendor on the campus ate it for Thanksgiving Day.

One evening in May I came home from a meeting and said to Selma: "Suppose we don't go to South America. Suppose we go to some place in the country near Milwaukee; start farming on a small scale; rest up from traveling, and have some children."

"I was thinking the same thing," she replied.

We bought a sewing machine and shipped it home; a Webster's unabridged with atlas, and a few other things that we knew we would never buy if we did not do it right then. In June we hiked in the breezy weather to the Valley of the Moon and slept near Jack London's place. Hiked over the snow to sleepy Carson City, where we spent a week with Abe Cohen and

40

his hanger-on Dot-so-Lall-ee renowned basket maker. Her husband went fishing daily and brought home 25 fish, selling each one for a quarter, no matter what it's size. We sent home Navajo rugs from here. We rushed throught the Babylon of Reno, through beautiful Truckee (by Lake Tahoe), and crisscrossed California several times, ending up in Whittier, to work a month at an apiary run by a young Quaker woman. Then we had a ride with friends across the worst of the desert. Spent a week at Taos pueblo where we were friends of Juanita, sister of Tony who later married Mabel Dodge.

We zig-zagged here and there to cover some portion of every state. Although we were in many perilous escapades we were never injured in the 22,000 miles we covered; 2,200 of this was on foot. We went by mule to the bottom of the Grand Canyon, and consider this sight by far the best of any in the country.

No matter what church I have attended or what religious teaching I have been studying my conception of God has not been that of a Super-Santa Claus or of a Benevolent Despot, but among other attributes a Force which brings together that of good which every sincere, although misguided, individual, is seeking. At least that much of the good that the person can understand and assimilate at the time. This is not a pantheistic or impersonal approach; it really regards God as dealing more with the person every day than many do who howl about Him on Sunday and especial holy days. So, no matter how many chances we took with people and places unknown we felt that it would all work together for good. (My Celestial Bulldozer again.) We had needed this running around: Selma to counteract the staid, comfortable bourgeois Milwaukee outlook, and I to balance my confinement in solitary. Now we would appreciate settling in one place, while before this any one place would have been a prison in our minds.

On my birthday, July 24, 1925 we arrived in Milwaukee with $105. We bought ten acres of woods with $100 down, built one room in a cozy section of the woods and rested after our long hike. Here, June 17, 1927 I helped the doctor when our daughter Carmen was born, and likewise on Oct. 23, 1929 (the day the Depression started) when Sharon was born. We did not notify a doctor until a few months before that a baby was expected, and had a Christian Science nurse both times. In 1931 I led a strike in a dairy in Waukesha which we won, but I was discharged. We had been happy with our cow and calf, sheep and lamb, police dogs, and life in the woods. We had built with our own hands and with the help of Selma's kid brother, Edmund, four more rooms. I had dug a cellar and carried beautiful rocks of all colors and had a mason build a huge fireplace. Here by the blazing wood, on the Navajo rug near Fritz, our police dog, and mother and child, with the wind whistling outside and June, the Jersey cow securely nestled in the small barn, was a feeling hardly to be improved upon. This house was at the top of a small hill surrounded by woods. I erected a long rope swing for Carmen and Sharon and when I ran under it full speed they would swing over the tree tops below like over the top of the world with screeches of delight. "Daddy, just one more swing," was

41

a never ending request. When Sharon was three she climbed to the top of a ladder to help me fix some telephone wires in the woods. She wanted to be a tree climber. I took her and Carmen to a clearing where there were straight hickory trees and brought a mattress along beneath the tree. Then I boosted them to the first limb and told them to try each branch as they climbed upward to see if it was dead or alive, and to go away to the top. This was repeated many times so that they never had any fear of high places. Later when Sharon was six she climbed to the top of a professional diving platform, held her nose with two fingers, and jumped in. She had just learned to swim and had no fear. When it rained there was a small stream a foot and a half deep and we all had fun wading and playing in the water. Fritz, the dog, would never leave the children and was very careful not to bite them, although he would spring at any stranger. We called our place Bisanakee, from the local Indian "Bisan" meaning "quiet" and "Akee" meaning "place."

After I had led in the strike in the dairy I had no work and could not keep up the payments to the bank. The farmer from whom we had bought the land for $1500 bought the place from the bank for $2,000 and paid off the $700 that we owed. We had $1300 for our six years work and we were allowed to live there in the summer for a few years so the girls had the benefit of country life in their first years.

CHAPTER 4.

Social Work

1930 - 1942

Milwaukee - Denver

Friends had persuaded me to take an examination for social worker in Milwaukee. I told the authorities about my radicalism and that I would refuse to support any war in the future. A headline in the Milwaukee Journal of Dec. 18, 1930 was a surprise to me.

FELONY TERM RULED NO BAR TO CIVIL RIGHTS

The Attorney General sustained the opinion of Mr. O'Boyle that Hennacy did not lose his civil rights because of his convictions. It was pointed out that courts held that the only felonies that can be considered in raising the question of civil rights are those that existed at the time the nation's constitution was adopted and that new enactments, such as the draft act or the dry law, cannot be considered felonies in that sense. Hennacy was convicted while a resident of Columbus, Ohio. He failed to register and also was convicted of conspiring with others to violate the draft act.

In reading Tolstoy I had gained the idea that if a person had the One Man Revolution in his heart and lived it, he would be led by God toward those others who felt likewise. It did not take an organization and signature on the dotted line to accomplish results. This was to be proven in a most dramatic way, and was to usher me into the second great influence of my life: that of the Catholic Worker movement.

In my work as a social worker, it was my business to mark down a grocery order, gas and light bills, clothing, rent, etc. If there was any income it was to be used to purchase groceries. A budget was made out according to the size of the family. A report had been sent in that a certain family whom I visited had an income which was not reported. When I entered this home I told the man that he would not get any groceries this time, because of the income. He wanted to know who had told on him. I replied that I did not know and if I did I was not allowed to tell him. He was a huge man who had worked in a tannery; a member of the Polish National Catholic Church. He locked the door, drew down the blind and took up a butcher knife and made at me. I was sitting at a table and did not get up. He said that he would carve me up if I did not mark down the groceries; that he had locked up two other relief workers in disputes and had always got what he wanted even if he had to do time in the workhouse afterward. He called me all the vile names he could think of. I knew if I answered to this description I should take it and if I did not, then his recital of the vile names would not make it true. He would prance around and swing his fist at me to frighten me and breathe down the back of my neck and tickle me with the point of his knife. I was not frightened for I had learned in solitary not to be afraid of anything. This went on for nearly an hour. I did not answer back a word nor hang my head but looked him in the eye. Finally he came after me more energetically than before and said I had to do something. I got up and said: "I will do something, but not what you think." I reached out my hand in a friendly manner saying, "You are all right but you forget about it. I am not afraid of that false face you have on. I see the good man inside. If you want to knife me or knock me cold, go ahead. I won't hit you back: go ahead, I dare you!" But I didn't double dare him.

For three minutes by the clock which faced us on the wall he shook my hand, and with the other hand was making passes to hit me in the face. I did not say anything more. Slowly his grip loosened and he went to the door and opened it, pulled up the blind and put the knife away.

"What I don't see is why you don't hit back." "That's just what I want you to see," I answered.

"Explain it," he demanded.

"What is your strongest weapon? It is your big fist with a big knife. What is my weakest weapon? It is a little fist without a knife. What is my strongest weapon? It is the fact that I do not get excited: do not boil over; some people call it spiritual power. What is your weakest weapon? It is your getting excited and boiling over and your lack of spiritual power. I would be dumb if I used my weakest weapon, my small fist without a knife, against your strongest weapon, your large fist with a knife. I am smart, so I use my strongest weapon, my quiet spiritual power, against your weakest weapon, your excited manner, and I won, didn't I?"

"Yes, tell me again," was his quiet request. I explained it again and told him how I learned my lesson in solitary.

"Why, you are all right; you did more time in solitary than I did—6 months for beating my wife—last time." I also explained the psychological principle that I had used without premeditation: that of the photographer who when faced with bashful little Mary does not say "Don't be bashful?" but says: "See the birdie." Likewise if I had told him, "Don't hit or knife a good Christian anarchist who returns good for evil. Don't kill this Hennacy; there isn't any more." he would have laughed at me. When I showed no fear and dared him to do me up it woke him up to reality and took his mind off his meanness. The good was in him the same as it was in the warden and the District Attorney but it had to be brought out by the warmth of love which I showed and not by the blustering wind which provoked only more bluster.

"Do you want those groceries?" I asked.

"What do you mean?" he said in astonishment.

"I mean that the door is not locked and the knife is put away. I'll give you the groceries now and skip them next time; all in the same month's bookkeeping." "Well, I'll be damned," was his reply. Adding "And when do I go to court?" "You won't go to court. I don't believe in courts; you have learned your lesson." When I left the house my knees were shaking from the strain although I had not wavered a bit all along. For several years whenever I asked Carmen and Sharon at night if they wanted me to tell them a bear story they would answer, "Daddy, tell me about the man with the knife."

Later at the office, my boss, who was a leader of the American Legion, asked me to testify in court about this man who had locked me up. I refused, saying that he had been imprisoned twice for such tactics and had only learned to do the same thing again. I felt that my way therefore should be used.

"What is your way?" he asked.

For several hours I explained my ideas and experiences.

"You ought to get acquainted with those radical Catholics in New York," he said. He was also a Catholic. I asked Father Kennedy around the corner who was editor of the HERALD CITIZEN the name of such Catholics and he gave me a copy of the current CATHOLIC WORKER. I at once subscribed.

At that time some Fascist-minded American Legion members were putting out a well printed sheet each week calling upon all patriots to run radicals and pacifists out of the city. My boss knew that this was dangerous but he did not know how to combat it. He asked me to speak at a private meeting at his home to several dozen of the more liberal-minded Legionnaires. They had never met a pacifist nor an anarchist before and we had an exciting evening. I asked them to meet my Communist friend, Fred Basset Blair. They went up in the air at the mention of his name but I kidded them about their timidity until they consented to have him meet with them. I was there also. A Socialist and a Technocrat spoke also and by the time winter was over the true Legionaires had argued their vigilantes out of the idea and they disbanded. Meanwhile I spoke on Christian anarchism to the Legion at their Cudworth Post, where Gen. McArthur holds membership. And at their annual banquet I was the only outsider present and was asked to say a few words at the end of the festivities. Later I debated with different commanders of the Legion in two large Protestant churches and at the Jewish Synagogue. I also spoke scores of times to classes at the State Teachers College and at the University Extension classes.

I was given the job of trouble shooter among the social workers for several years and found that evil was always overcome by goodwill. However goodwill did not mean being wishy-washy. The one event of my life which took more courage than anything else was my effort to get an increase in the budget for those on relief. We had a 5% increase in our salaries at the office and I felt that those whom we served needed it much worse than we did. However, I could not get a second of a motion to that effect at the union meeting. I asked my boss about it and he felt that the clients received too much already. I pointed out that grocery budgets were made up by dieticians who fed "the average family" and there was no such thing. Italians would not eat grits and oatmeal. They wanted wine and spaghetti, and so with all kinds of people; they wanted certain kinds of food and would not eat a "statistical menu". I wrote a letter to all of the county officials concerned telling them that I would not accept my $5 a month raise, but would return it to the county treasurer unless the budget of the clients was increased 5%. Twice I went to the office of my boss with this letter and he was not in his office. Twice my knees shook and I was weak at the stomach, for it was more difficult to argue with a boss who was friendly and oppose him on a fundamental issue than it was to call Stalin and the devil names. The third time the boss was in his office. "You can't do that; you put me to shame," he said. "I have already done it, and I mean to put you to shame," I replied. I returned my $2.50 each pay day and it was not long until an announcement was made that the budget of those on relief had been increased 5%. Then those who had not seconded the motion at the union meeting said "fine work, Ammon." I was a delegate to the union of relief clients, The Workers Alliance.

Long before I read of the method of moral jiu jitsu, described by Gandhi, I had used it myself. When a person wishes to engage you in useless vituperation, the clear unexpected answer throws him off his base. One of the best instances occurred when a relief client who had been sentenced to 30 days in the House of Correction for making a relief visitor dance when he pulled out a gun, phoned the office saying: "I have another gun; send your next s.o.b. out and I'll shoot him."

"Hennacy, go make peace!" was the order given to me. This man lived far out in the country. I knocked on his door and being asked who was there I told him who I was. "Hello, you hound." "Hello, hound yourself" was my answer which was not to be found in Mary Richmond's text on social work or in the Sermon on the Mount. But each person has to be spoken to in words which they can understand. I entered the room and the man said gruffly: "I want five mattresses." "Make it six; I am a wholesaler" was my rejoinder. Obviously he did not need that many mattresses but he asked for the impossible in order to be refused and then he would start shooting. "Let's go upstairs and see what size mattresses you need" I suggested. "No body's going up my upstairs," he replied. "O.K. Less work for me," was my answer. "All right come up," he said as he led the way. I found that he only needed one mattress and told him so. He laughed and said, "I won't fight with you." And the whole thing was over. Previous visitors had stood on their dignity and were victims of his spleen.

Another time I had a quick call to visit a family where the last visitor had been thrown downstairs. In this case, as in many others, clients would run up a huge gas or light bill and demand payment. The visitor would refuse and the gas would be turned off and $5 would have to be paid to get it turned on again. A losing game, for the visitor had to order it turned on again. I went up the dark and narrow stairway and entered the room. The man was out. I saw a light and gas bill on the table and marked them "o.k." as they were not too high. Soon the man came in shouting, "I want my gas and light bill paid." I told him quietly that they were already paid. "I don't get enough cornmeal," he said. "What part of the South do you come from?" I asked, knowing that no person in the north asks for cornmeal. "I come from Baldwin County, Alabama," was the answer. "I used to teach history in Fairhope" was my reply. "You know my kind; I won't argue with you," said he smiling. The fact was that the nice clean social workers tried to clean up this old man who was born dirty, born with a tendency to drunkenness, lying and laziness; and they wore themselves out and aggravated him in their efforts. I visited this family every two weeks for four years and concentrated on the teen age children, so that they wanted a better environment and raised the standards of the family. They moved to a better neighborhood and got off relief. About this time the old man asked me for a pair of shoes. I said, "what did you do with the pair you got last month; sell them for booze?" "No, my buddy and I were up north looking for work and got caught in a storm and came to a cabin. Here we rested over night and put our shoes to dry by the stove and when we got up they were all turned up and we couldn't get them on." "And you came home in your bare feet; tell us another one, old man," was my quick reply. He broke out laughing. If I had called him a liar he would have knocked me down. And he didn't get the shoes.

In the early days of the depression the rules were very strict and many who needed help did not get it. Whenever I found it necessary to break a rule I would do so. Once I moved a large family who had been evicted to a place where the rental was above schedule; then I took the rent voucher to my boss and asked him to sign it. "You can't do that," he said. "I already have done it. You do it for your friends; I'm doing it for some one who has no friends." If I did not do this too often I got by with it.

One angry Italian client went to a distribution station and broke a chair over the head of the man in charge. I was sent to his home to make peace. He lived the third flight up and when I knocked on the door it was opened and a chair was raised toward my head. When he saw me he smiled and said "O.k. you're all right Hennacy." Several months before I had visited him and in the course of my conversation had praised Sacco and Vanzetti, not knowing in what good stead it would stand me now.

A group of clients who called themselves the 17th Ward Taxpayers Club wrote to the Governor asking that problems of relief be explained to them. This was a tough neighborhood. My boss called me in and said that he was not going there and lose his temper and get in a fight and lose his job. He asked me to speak for him. I took an Irish friend along, Ray Callahan, the president of the union, in order that anything I might say would not be misquoted. The meeting was in a dance hall in the rear of a saloon. There was standing room only. When I was introduced I said: "You folks did not come here to hear my boss talk; you did not come here to hear me talk; you came here to hear yourselves talk. Go ahead, and if I can answer your questions I will do so, and if I can't I will admit it." "Why didn't the so and so bastard boss come here himself" someone shouted. I knew the details of many rules and regulations and explained them but did not defend them. I gave the anarchist argument of responsibility and of putting up a good fight against exploiters. One man gave a sob story. I told him that if what he said was true to see me after the meeting and I would look into his record and go to bat for him." But on the other hand you may be the biggest liar on the whole south side." Everyone laughed for they knew his number. I left with a vote of thanks.

Life In Milwaukee

Of course an anarchist had no business working for a government, even a county government. I admitted this to all and sundry and I suppose compensated in my mind for this dereliction by speaking in hundreds of Protestant churches on Christian anarchism. My boss, Benjamin Glassberg, had been one of my teachers at the Rand School in N. Y. City in 1921. He had come to Milwaukee and was head of the Jewish Charities, and had visited us at Bisanakee. I had worked for some time for the county before he became my boss. It is not difficult to be brave to someone you do not know but I was reluctant to put him on the spot but I felt I had to do so. Accordingly I went to his office trembling somewhat and said, "I'm going to start a union." He said it would cause a lot of trouble. I replied that there would be a lot more trouble if there was not a union for rumors spread and no one knew for sure what the workers or the employers felt about the issue at hand. I asked him if I could use the big hall downstairs for an organization meeting on a certain night. He o.k.'d it with a smile. By the next noon half a dozen bootlickers in the office had come to him, he told me, saying that I was starting a union. Finally we got an increase in pay from $140 to $175, five days a week, and extra vacation for overtime. I spent Saturday selling the *Catholic Worker* and the *Conscientious Objector* in front of the library, putting even the Jehovah's Witnesses to shame by my fidelity to my post. One of my straw bosses was a Catholic who was sympathetic to the CW. The *Milwaukee Journal* announced that I would have a meeting at his home one evening when I would speak about Conscientious Objectors in World War I who were Catholics. Only a few attended but I was pleased to meet Nina Polcyn and Dave Host, early friends of The Catholic Workers. I also told at that meeting of my friend Ben Salmon, Catholic, Single Taxer, and vegetarian who had done time in Leavenworth and who, still in jail after the war was over, had gone on a hunger strike for over three months and thus obtained the release of the remaining forty-five CO's in Ft. Riley. Ben had been on a hunger strike at Ft. Riley and continued it at St. Elizabeth's Hospital in Washington, D.C. Selma and I had visited him there where he was rooming with the guard who had forcibly fed him at St. Elizabeth's Hospital, and whom he had converted to pacifism. I told of John Dunn and of Francis Xavier Hennessey, a member of the Knights of Columbus, from Boston who was a CO in Leavenworth and whom Selma and I had visited on our hiking trip.

We had several meetings and it was not long until a CW House of Hospitality was started in Milwaukee. Carmen and Sharon sang Christmas carols Christmas afternoon of 1937 while Leonard Doyle played the piano. Muriel Lester of England, gave the House her blessing a few weeks before when she was speaking in Milwaukee. Nov. 11, 1937 was the 50th Anniversary of the hanging of the Haymarket Martyrs. I was able to get Lucy Parsons, the wife of Albert Parsons, one of the martyrs, to speak on Nov. 19th at a Memorial meeting. Fred Basset Blair, Communist leader, also spoke. I told him if he praised Russia I would tell on him, so he kept to the subject. Martin Cyborowski of the CIO also spoke, as did Prof. Philip Persons of the University of Wisconsin Extension. I was Chairman. Sponsors of the meeting, which was well attended, included my good friend Henry L. Nunn of Nunn Bush Shoe Co., a Tolstoian and advocate of 52 pay days a year for his workers, even in the depression. He was much more radical than his employees; a fine man, strict vegetarian and a Christian outside of any church. One of his prized possessions is a picture of Tolstoy carved on a piece of bark by Tolstoy himself and given to a visitor, who upon his death gave it to Mr. Nunn. Socialist and union leaders of Milwaukee and several pacifists among the clergy were also sponsors. The ushers of the meeting were the young Catholic Workers. The diocesian paper did not like this united front of the CW with anarchists and Communists but the CW youngsters stood their ground and distributed a pink leaflet giving the CW position on labor. I had asked old Mr. Bruce of the Catholic Bruce Publishing Company to be a sponsor. He was sympathetic but said he was too old to stand the criticism which would come from conservative Catholics. He wished me well.

* * *

During these years in Milwaukee I never contributed to the Community Fund because many of the contributions came by force from employees in dime stores and other establishments where the pay was low and where there was no union. After a time I was able to get our union to delegate another fellow and myself to protest to the Community Fund on this matter and that year the headline was: "Fund Motto Is: No Compulsion." This was the headline on Oct. 7, 1937. In my speeches in churches and before labor groups I often quoted the following verse from Robert Burns to wake the audience up:

> *"A fig for those by law protected!*
> *Liberty's a glorious feast!*
> *Courts for cowards were erected,*
> *Churches built to please the priest."*

In 1934 my wife and I visited Carleton Washburne at Winnetka, Illinois, asking his opinion about enrolling Carmen and Sharon in the progressive schools there. He felt that the atmosphere was too "goldcoast". Selma and the girls got an apartment there and I went down on week ends to see them. However, by Christmas, we felt that Washburne was right and that it was no place for radicals. We felt that it would be well to allow the girls to see the Jim Crow, deep south, and whatever there was left of progressive education in the school in Fairhope, Alabama, where I had taught history in 1924. Sharon was in kindergarten there. Selma wrote that Sharon was present when her class was marching around in a game with broomsticks. Sharon stood aside and did not play. The teacher came over to her asking, "Are you sick, little girl?" Sharon replied, "I'm Science; I don't get sick." (She had gone to Christian Science Sunday School once, and neither she nor Carmen had ever tasted medicine.) Why don't you play this game then?" the teacher asked. "It's a gun game," was the reply. "But we don't have any guns," the teacher countered. "That's because you can't find them. You would have them if you could get them; so you have broomsticks instead," was Sharon's answer. The teacher grabbed her by the shoulder telling her she must obey. Sharon told her to take her hands off of her; that she obeyed only what was good. Sharon did not pout, but played the next game which was non-military. At this school the old radical spirit was weakening so my wife brought the girls back to Milwaukee at the end of the year.

Selma had the regular atheistic attitude of the old time Socialists among whom she was brought up. When we were hiking we had worked in Atlanta for over a year and had visited Mrs. Millis. Selma had attended the Christian Science church out of courtesy and accepted much of that teaching. I had read the books along with her, feeling that perhaps this approach to religion might be the only one by which she would accept my Tolstoian Sermon on the Mount principles. It was not difficult for both of us to accept the non-medical teaching of Christian Science, whether we accepted their theology in toto or not. Mrs. Millis was the only pacifist among them. The bourgeois atmosphere of their churches did not attract us and their super patriotism made me shudder. We faithfully attended services and studied the daily lessons for years and determined to bring up our children without medicine.

Selma was not a vegetarian and I did not feel like imposing my ideas on this subject on my family. When Carmen was about five years of age she was at the table and asked me why I did not eat meat. I told her that was an idea of mine. "But why?" she insisted. "I don't like to kill animals, and why should some one else kill them for me?" I answered. "But Daddy, maybe, this pig just died; nobody killed it." was her reply.

At times we would go to a movie where there was as much as $1,000 to be won if you took a ticket for their Bank Nite. According to my principles I did not believe in gambling, and would never take a ticket. One night Sharon said, " Daddy, why don't you take a ticket? I never win, and Carmen never wins, and neither does Mother, but you are a good Daddy and you would surely win, but you just deprive your family; you are a meanie!" Now my girls are vegetarians and do not believe in gambling. In those days Carmen would figget in her seat during some exciting scene and Sharon would say, "Relax, sister; heroes never die." Both girls were interested in music, dancing and dramatics. We often took walks up the river both winter and summer on Sunday mornings. They had gone to Christian Science Sunday School twice but it was the same repetition of the Beatitudes, with no sensible explanation, and the girls thought it too dull. One of my best friends was Rev. John W. Cyrus, of the nearby Park and Prospect Christian Church. He was a liberal and asked me to take over a class of teen age boys who had worn out all the teachers. So for three years I only opened a Bible upon request, but answered their questions. I wrote five plays in which I had them take part, and my girls played in them also at times.

Both girls were interested in music, dancing and dramatics.

By 1938 anyone who had studied history could tell that a war was coming on soon. My wife suggested that she take the girls to New York City while I had a good job and before I got into jail. I did not know at the time that she intended to stay there and leave me to my radicalism. We had seen the life in New York City and the girls were old enough to appreciate some of the advantages which they might have there. So in July 1938, we drove there and I came back to Milwaukee alone and sent them four-fifths of what I made. My father had died in June, in Cleveland.

Emma Goldman spoke in Milwaukee in the late thirties. I had not met her for years. Later when I wrote to her in Toronto telling her of the Haymarket meeting and of the Catholic Workers being ushers she wrote to me: I appreciate the good wishes of the young Catholics and I ask you to kindly give them my thanks and my greetings."

In 1937 Dorothy Day spoke at the Social Action Congress in Milwaukee, being invited there by Bishop (later Cardinal) Stritch. She had been upstairs in the office of the LIBERATOR when I had been working in my small office at the foot of the stairs for Roger Baldwin, but I had never met her. Then she was a Communist. Our mutual friends were Hugo and Livia Gellert, Claude McKay, Mike Gold and Maurice Becker. She had left the Communists and joined the Catholic Church in 1928 and in 1933 with Peter Maurin had started the CATHOLIC WORKER. I met her after the meeting and was of course pleased with her words of praise for I.W.W.'s and Communists to the great crowd of Catholics who would not otherwise know much about radicalism. I had but a few words with her on our way to Nina's.

She spoke at Marquette to a room full of nuns, priests and students the next day. I was only able to come late to the meeting and had to sit in the very front row. In answering questions from patriotic questioners she mentioned something of my pacifist record, saying that I was not a Catholic, but an anarchist and that when the next war came she would be with me in opposition to it. Her continued refusal to follow the party line of most churchmen in praising Franco gained my admiration.

One night Peter Maurin spoke at Holy Family House. A Communist friend came to the meeting and when time came for questions commenced to quote Marx. Peter answered, "You did not quote Marx right—here is the correct sentence. Marx got it from the anarchist Proudhon." And then he began to give an Easy Essay on the subject in question. I said, "Peter, you talk like an anarchist." "Sure, I am an anarchist; all thinking people are anarchists. But I prefer the name personalist."

Peter was a wonderful man, the second man of stature whom I had known; Berkman being the first.

Early in 1941 Eric Gill, the English Catholic artist sculptor, died. WAR COMMENTARY, the London anarchist weekly, had a front page article about him by the poet, Herbert Read, which quoted a letter from Gill, "I am really in complete agreement with you about the necessity of anarchism, the ultimate truth of it, and its immediate practibility as syndicalism." Read ended the article with this sentence, speaking of Gill, "He was the most honest man I have even known, or am likely to know."

The opposition of the CATHOLIC WORKER to Franco aroused the ire of patriotic Catholics. During this time I wrote letters to every Protestant church in the city telling them of the coming war and asking for permission to present the Christian anarchist view to their young people. I received but four answers, one of them from a pastor of the Missouri Synod of the Lutherans, which was an accomplishment. On May 20, 1940 I held a memorial meeting for Emma Goldman. Bill Ryan and Ed Lehmann, veterans of the Spanish Civil War, spoke.

I had been selling CW's and CONSCIENTIOUS OBJECTORS every other Monday night at meetings of a lecture forum at the largest Protestant church in the city. On Monday Dec. 8, Jan Valtin was to speak. All of my relatives and comrades advised me not to run the danger of being beaten up by going there. I felt that all of us would be killed for a dime as much as for a dollar, so we might as well sow our seeds and not worry about whether they fell on stony ground or whether we were endangered in the sowing of them. Those who rely on force are reaping the fruits of violence sown for generations. Here is more violence and this is the very time when we must be active. Accordingly I went down to the church with my papers. Half a dozen women spit at me and several men grumbled at me. Suddenly four police grabbed me by the neck and shoulders demanding to know if I was a Communist. "Wake up, fellows. The Party Line has changed. The Commies are on your side." They wanted to know what I was if I was not a Communist. "You wouldn't know if I told you," I replied. "Tell us" they asked, "I am a Christian Anarchist," I answered. "What is that?" was their query. "Someone who doesn't need a cop to make him behave" was my quick reply, as I had told the judge in Atlanta. I asked if either of them were Catholics and each one answered that he was Catholic. I asked if they would like to read what happened to me and the cops during the last war and they replied in the affirmative, so each one departed with a copy of the November CW which had a chapter of my life in Atlanta entitled "God's Coward." I sold papers all evening with no more disturbance. At this time some religious folks around the CW were loath to distribute the paper after Pearl Harbor. I good naturedly kidded them by calling their liturgy an excuse for lethargy.

The radical who is sympathetic to anarchism but who must vote for a "good man" in order to keep the bad men from running the country received an object lesson when Bob LaFollette voted for World War II. He was a "good" man and he knew better but the soft living in Washington must have deprived him of his moral strength. (An aftermath is the fact that LaFollette, who knew enough to see through the alibis of the Communist party line and who asked for free speech for the Trotskyites also, was knifed by the CIO and Communists of Milwaukee for his re-nomination—and that is how Joe McCarthy got upon us.)

One evening there was a meeting of members of the leading peace organization of the country, the Fellowship of Reconciliation, to which I had belonged since World War I. It was held in a local church and the minister who had been Chairman of it for many years was present, along with other pacifist clergy. Somehow a reporter was present, so when the time came for election of Chairman for the ensuing year this cowardly follower of Christ gave a long talk about democracy being needed and moved that for the future we should elect a Chairman for each meeting and not for the year: thus his name could not be given publicity as a pacifist. This man had posed as an American, accepting appointments from the Mayor, when in fact he had been born in Canada and had neglected to apply for citizenship. If he applied now he would have to say he was a pacifist and thus be denied citizenship. So he did nothing.

In contrast to his attitude there was the unsolicited opinion of four leaders of thought in Milwaukee to me as they met me on the street. One of the chief men on a local capitalist paper whom I knew met me and asked if I was going to refuse to register for the draft when my time came. I replied that of course I wouldn't register.

"That is the true American spirit; we need men like you; don't let the government bluff you," he said.

Almost the same words were spoken to me by a leading officer of the armed forces whom I had met once. The first time I met him he said that the way of Jesus, Thoreau, Tolstoy and Gandhi was right, but people would not see it for another 2000 years; and meanwhile we needed an army and he was in the army. A city official who was not a Socialist told me that he agreed with my anti-war attitude and should take the same stand but he was a coward.

Years before I had visited the wealthy head of the Christian Science headquarters in Wisconsin and argued with him that he and his church were wrong in supporting war and capitalism; that among many unimportant utterances Mrs. Eddy had said to "follow me only insofar as I follow Christ and the Sermon on the Mount." And if one had a moral aim and sought to gain it by immoral means, then the moral aim was destroyed by the immoral means. I had not met him for years when he stopped me on the street and greeted me by name saying, "You are right and I am wrong."

I asked what about and he said "War, I cannot forget what you said about ends and means years ago."

"But your church is the only one who will not allow its members to be conscientious objectors," I answered, "and with its supposed emphasis on spirituality it is the most wealthy church in the country."

"I know it sir, I know it sir," was his reply.

I asked him if he cared if I quoted him and he said to quote him if I liked. He left ceremoniously, saying, "I feel better now that I have talked to you, Mr. Hennacy." I wrote to him afterwards but never got a reply. This must have been his weak or his strong moment.

It was not long afterward when the American Legion preferred charges against me for selling CW's and CO's on the street. I had sold them in front of St. Rose's church one Sunday morning, and one of the Legion heads became troubled about it. I went to the corporation council who had charge of such matters. He was a Legion man and an Irish Catholic. A court stenographer took down all the conversation. For an hour I defended my right to be a pacifist and told him that he could discharge me if he liked but I would not quit, and demanded a public hearing. This was on Monday. On Saturday he announced in the paper that the charges had been dropped inasmuch as I was not doing my propaganda on company time.

During this time I went to several Catholic churches each Sunday to sell CW's. About the only other person who helped in this was Jerry, a Coughlinite, who did not agree with the full CW program but who felt he must do something. Now that Father Coughlin had ceased to oppose the war the only thing left for him to do was to sell CW's. For instance on June 14th. I wrote to Dorothy saying, "Made four masses at the ritzy St. Roberts church this morning and sold 33 cents worth. The cop (a Protestant) who had wanted to stop me the first time I sold papers there, was cordial today and wanted to know how I was doing. I had an extra copy of the May (1942) issue with my statement of refusal to register in it and gave it to him and he promised to read it. They sang the Star Spangled Banner after each mass. I did not hear the sermon as the doors were closed, and the ushers were rather dignified—besides I did not have the admission price posted on the door. Tried to sell papers at St. Rose's and Gesu last Sunday, but did not sell one up until 11:30 when it commenced to rain. Sold 28 cents worth at St. Gall's the Sunday before."

My one staunch comrade from 1937 to 1942 in Milwaukee was Bill Ryan. He had been a Communist organizer and with his wife Alba, had gone to Spain and fought with the Loyalists. After seventeen months he discovered that there was not enough difference between the Communists and the Fascists to fight about. He expressed these feelings and was on the way to be executed by the Commies when he escaped. Coming home he was one of the few to tell the truth of how the Commies had sabotaged the Loyalist cause and engineered its defeat through their bureaucratic tactics.

Bill was now an anarchist and also an atheist, although he felt that the ethics of the Sermon on the Mount were a true moral guide. We visited each other nearly every day and on countless evenings met with young Socialists seeking to bolster up their weak-kneed pacifism. Bill, of course, would refuse to register when his time came. When he did refuse I went to local pacifists to get bail for him but they all had some excuse. It was Jerry who went his bail. Four local Communists who had fought in Spain wrote a letter to the Milwaukee JOURNAL in which they said that Bill had never been a Communist, nor had he ever been in Spain. The Party Line had changed and now they were patriotic.

Meanwhile my turn had come. I was supposed to register on April 27th, and prepared a statement of my reasons for refusing. I would also resign my job with the county. On the Friday before, Bill and I rode to Chicago with a Quaker friend and attended a meeting of CO's at a Brethren church. Evan Thomas was there and he was going to refuse also. Of us old timers who were in jail in World War I and who would again endanger our families and jobs and property, there were Harold Gray of Saline, Mich., Max Sandin of Cleveland, Howard Moore of Cherry Valley, N.Y., and Julius Eichel and Evan Thomas of New York City, and myself. Also, of course, the Marquardt family, being the old patriarch and his sons and sons-in-law of Grasston, Minnesota. A. J. Muste, head of the FOR would also refuse. We all felt that we would get five years and were prepared to take it.

I spoke at the meeting, visited with friends, and started hiking home in the late afternoon. I walked about ten miles, and got a ride with an ex-army captain of the last war. He was against this one. Then I walked awhile and got a ride with a young fellow from Zion City. I gave them both CW's containing my statement. I did not have a cent on me and it was dark. I thought of the Chinese who lived on a mouthful of rice a day. Just then I saw an ear of corn on the road. I shelled it and for the next three hours chewed it grain by grain and was not hungry when I finished. Finally after 10 p.m. when it commenced to drizzle a man picked me up and took me to Milwaukee. He admired Lew Ayres who was a CO and was glad to read my statement. Arriving home I received a telegram of congratulation as to my refusal to register from Dorothy who was speaking in Albuquerque. On my last day at the office my Legion friends were very kind to me. The papers had a fair summary and picture on the front page. My argument with the timid souls who felt I would hurt the cause by being radical was that they sneaked off to a CO camp and no one knew they had gone, while if you refused to register it was the man biting the dog and was news. Therefore your ideas went before the world.

The following is my statement of refusal to register as printed in the May, 1942 CW, and addressed to the U. S. District Attorney.

Dear Sir: As a Tolstoian—a Christian Anarchist—I choose to follow the example of the early Christians who refused to place a pinch of incense upon the altar of Caesar. I consider that registration for the purpose of helping this or any other war is the first step towards a defeat of the principles of Jesus as given in His Sermon on the Mount: "Love your enemies . . . turn the other cheek . . ." This does not mean to kill them in war or to commit injustice in time of peace. Personally I wish to frankly admit my inconsistency in having worked for a branch of the government while being an Anarchist; however I did so openly. I refuse to register and will cheerfully accept the sentence of the court, desiring no probation or parole, but willing to sacrifice for what I think is right, as the soldiers and sailors are doing.

In 1917 I refused to register for a somewhat different reason. At that time I was a Socialist who believed in fighting in a revolution, but not in a capitalist war. I had never heard of a God of Love in the churches, and thought I was an atheist. During my two and a half years in Atlanta, I spent eight and a half months in solitary, where my study of the Bible convinced me that the most revolutionary teaching in the world was contained in the Sermon on the Mount. I saw that the Kingdom of God was within every person, but most of us had forgotten it. I felt it was futile to change the *forms* of society—that the biggest job before me was to change myself; this was the revolution most worthwhile. Later, when I read Jefferson, Thoreau, William Lloyd Garrison and Tolstoy I saw that all governments—even the best— were founded upon the policemen's club: upon a return of evil for evil, the very opposite of the teachings of Christ. I saw that all churches supported this essential wickedness of government and were therefore evil institutions—and that in time of war all churches, with isolated exceptions, supported this violation of the teachings of Christ. That is, except the historic peace churches: the Mennonites, Brethren, Quakers, and the Doukhobor, Molokon and Jehovah's sects. Therefore I belonged to no church but spoke in many churches, encouraging them to follow Christ. I became a Christian Anarchist. I saw that the first World War did not make the world safe for democracy, or end war.

In refusing to register, I want to make it clear that the great majority of the people who have supported the economic evils that make for war are acting logically in an all-out effort for war. As an Anarchist, I have taken no part in politics and am not bound to accept the will of a majority whose political battle I did not enter. I honor those who are sincere, sacrificing, war-like patriots. I am a peace patriot. I accept, along with others, whatever punishment is due this generation because of the mistakes of our forefathers. We lied to, and cheated the Indians, and broke nearly every treaty we made with them; we formed our great Southwest by stealing it from Mexico in what Grant and Webster called an unjust war; we fought an unnecessary Civil War to free the Negro and we have refused to give him his real freedom; we grabbed the very islands for which we are now fighting from Spain in an equally imperialistic venture; we started a revolution in Columbia and stole Panama, we invaded Nicaragua and countless other countries to protect foolish foriegn loans and investments; we sold war materials to Japan until recently and helped build up her imperialism in the Far East; we excluded an energetic and noble people from our shores; we refused to support or to build up a decent League of Nations or to live up to our own Kellogg Peace Pact, renouncing war. We do not come before the bar of history with clean hands.

More recently the President, with the aid of his erstwhile opponent, has duped the country inch by inch until we are in this war. Likely, he sincerely believed that "the end justified the meanness" and good would come of it. History has proven him mistaken now, and will increasingly prove that evil defeats itself. His slogans tell this story of trickery: "Fools Gold;" "Cash and Carry;" "The draft is just a census . . . your boys are not going to be sent into any foreign wars;" "all aid short of war;" "lend and lease;" "patrols not convoys."

I predict that we will not conquer Fascism, although we may defeat Hitler; we will have a Fascist dictatorship under the name of Democracy upon us. I predict that Germany and Russia will make a separate peace and that England, as always, will fight only for herself and we will be left to fight the world.

By my action in refusing to register for the draft, I speak and act only for myself. Others have to draw the line where they see fit. I speak, also, for the millions who were fooled by the slogans of the War-Party and who now, but dimly, realize how the President maneuvered them into this war. I speak for the millions of Christians who have been again sold out by their leaders who value church property and power more than they value the example of Christ, and who accept the "lesser evil" rather than the ultimate good and the counsels of perfection. I speak for the millions of union men who have succumbed to the glory of "time and a half," little realizing that they are accessories before the fact of legal murder, in making the weapons of death. I speak for the thousands of radicals whose leaders have forgotten the ideals of Debs, Lansbury, old Bob LaFollette, Berkman, the I.W.W.'s, and Sacco and Vanzetti, and who now support the war. I speak for those individuals and small groups in and out of Protestant and Catholic churches who do not go so far in opposition to war as I do. I speak for my fellow-vegetarians, many of whom have succumbed to this wholesale blood-letting called war. I speak for those in our prisons whose chances for the ideals of Thomas Mott Osborne mitigating their misery are dulled by the fog of hatred which envelops this war torn world. I speak for my own and for millions of children whose hopes of a better world are crushed and who are doomed to the wheel of despotism, fear, greed, and starvation, which will be the outcome of this war.

I speak for a Just Peace and against World War III. I also speak for that better world whose spark has been kept alive by those who are not afraid to face the misunderstanding and scorn of the multitude. I speak with the voice of Thoreau who said: "A minority is powerless while it conforms to the majority . . . one on the side of God is a majority already." I speak with the voice of Peter and Socrates who chose to obey God rather than man. I speak with the voice of St. Francis and of Gandhi who exemplify the life of Christ. I speak with the voice of Jesus who said: "Therefore all things whatsoever ye would that men should do to you, do ye even so to them . . . overcome evil with good." I speak for that time when all shall realize that they are Sons of God and brothers. When all the world is filled with hatred, this is the time when I must not be silent."

Ammon Hennacy

1534 N. 60th St.,
Milwaukee, Wis.
Dec. 19, 1941

While in New York City my wife had joined one of the esoteric cults that spring up in the unhealthy atmosphere of Los Angeles. Their belief in vegetarianism and reincarnation coincided with my own, but their super patriotism and condemnation of radicalism and unions seemed a big jump from that Socialism which my wife had believed in all her life. I went to scores of meetings of this cult trying to see if I could believe in it. I heard the leaders and felt that it was a racket. They spoke words of love and brotherhood but called down fire from heaven to destroy those whom they did not like.

My wife and girls moved to Los Angeles where I visited them in 1940 and 1941 during my vacation. (I had stopped for a day to visit the radical Doukhobors in British Columbia.) This cult did not allow the aura of the husband in the house if he did not belong. When my wife knew I was refusing to register she wrote that when I went to prison my name would be as if I was dead, as far as she and the girls were concerned. I wrote to them cordially all of this time and sent them nearly all I made. The policy of this cult was not to allow correspondence between 100% followers and unbelievers. I had faith in my daughters and knew when they were old enough to understand they would do what was right.

Carmen, then 14, wrote from the Coast: "You may wonder how the Japanese are being treated out here. Well, I don't know about other schools, but as far as I know in our school we treat them better than before, because we think that every other person will treat them bad." My girls bought no war stamps all during the war.

I took my non-registrant statement to the U. S. District Attorney. He had heard Emma Goldman during his college days and thought this war was about fifty-fifty as to guilt. We had a pleasant time and he told me to go on my own recognizance and he would call me when I was to have a trial. The papers wrote about the terrible tongue lashing he had given to a "draft dodger." Bill Ryan was soon sentenced to 2 years in Sandstone, Minnesota prison.

After a few weeks I was called down and put behind the bars. An officer took me to the draft board in my district and the man in charge said "What is your name?" I replied, "You know my name." Again, "Where do you live?" Answer, "You know where I live." Question: "Where do you work?" Answer, "You know where I work." "Here is your draft card," he said. "It is not mine; it is yours. I didn't tell you anything," I replied quickly. And I handed him back the card.

The District Attorney did not tell me definitely what was to be done in my case, but told me to wait and see. It seemed that instructions had been sent from Washington not to imprison those over 45. I was 48. Later my sister-in-law, with whom I was staying, signed a special delivery letter containing my draft card. I returned it personally to the District Attorney, putting it in his waste basket. It was sent to me again. I tore it up and mailed the bits to Washington, telling the authorities I would never carry it. I heard nothing more from them. With all the lies printed by authorities as to the action of radicals I had written to Dorothy Day, at the Catholic Worker saying that if she heard that I had registered not to believe it;

but at least all that any *one* of us could do was to refuse to give in no matter if we were the only ones left.

My wife and girls had left Los Angeles when the cult to which she belonged was denied the use of mails for fraud. Headquarters were established in Santa Fe, N. M. and she followed there. Housing was difficult to find there, so she moved to Denver. Now that I was not tied down to a civil service job I worked at two other jobs and left on the Fourth of July for Denver. After a few days I was working at the huge City Park Dairy where my work consisted in being a social worker to 900 cows. Certain cows that had teats too large for the milking machine; sore teated ones; kicky ones; and those suffering from garget were scattered here and there over the huge barn. The average worker beat the cows and as in the case of human beings they retaliated. I visited my family for a few hours now and then, and on my birthday we all went to the top of the mountain near Golden and visited Buffalo Bill's grave. Here and there along ravines were shanties where squatters eked out a living panning gold.

Sharon was in the eighth grade in Denver. She saw a beautiful white coat in a department store and asked to see the manager.

"My name is Sharon Hennacy. I am a poor girl. I like that white coat in your window. Do you have a larger size also for my sister Carmen?" The manager said that he did.

"Then you have sold two coats if you give me a job wrapping packages after school," she replied with a smile. What could the poor man do? He was propositioned. So I do not need any welfare state or insurance for my daughters, for they can make it.

When Sharon was six and Carmen was eight, Carmen came home from school one day without her gloves and my wife asked her about them and she said she must have lost them. The next day she returned without them saying she had asked the teacher and the lost and found with no success. The following day there came a knock at the door of Carmen's room at school and Sharon stood there asking:

"Are you the teacher of my sister Carmen Hennacy?"

"Yes, little girl."

"Where are her gloves?"

"I don't know."

"Well, it's your business to know. Let's see," and Sharon walked up to the teacher's desk, open the drawer, took out the gloves, thanking the teacher, and walked proudly out of the room. The teacher had been busy; she was not a glove-stealer; she just didn't want to be bothered about such trifles.

I did not know that the dairy where I worked was a closed shop, being organized by the AFL Teamsters Union. Mr. Coffee, the business agent, was soon around to get my $12.50 initiation, explaining that it was being raised to $25 and I was sure lucky to get in now. About 500 attended the first union meeting where I was present. A motion came up to vote $1,000 for Liberty Bonds. I asked to speak against it, but as with about all motions, the idea was to get them passed as soon as possible and start a crap game or adjourn to the nearest saloon. After the motion had passed without any discussion or a dissenting vote, except mine, I asked that my vote be recorded against the purchase of the Bonds. At a later meeting the motion came up not to allow any conscientious objectors to join the union. I was not allowed to speak on this motion either, but had my lone vote recorded against it. I asked Coffee privately why I could not speak on the motion and why such a motion was made. He said that it did not apply to me as I was already a member but that other conscientious objectors in Denver had desired to join and this was to prevent it. I replied that he did not know what he was talking about for I was acquainted with all of the CO's in Denver and none of them wanted to work in dairies. Finally, Coffee admitted that this motion had been made on orders from Czar Dan Tobin in Indianapolis.

Soon after this I was selling CW's and CO's in front of the public library down town one Saturday afternoon. (Our work was from 1 p.m. to 5:30 and from 1 a.m. to 5:30.) A cop came up and asked what I was selling. I handed him copies and said "The best papers in the world. Read them."

He said that I could not sell them without a permit. On the way to the police station he asked for my draft card; I told him that it was a disgrace to carry one; that I had a trial in Milwaukee about it and did not need to carry one. The night captain asked me many questions and said he would keep me in jail all summer until I got a draft card. I advised him to get in contact with my friend Harry O'Connor, head of the FBI in Milwaukee and former member of the union of social workers which I had organized. I was refused permission to phone my employer or to get a lawyer or communicate with anyone.

During the next four days I was shown before the screen in the "Show-up." I must have looked like some one they were after for I had the same questions asked again and again. They must have had some doubts, otherwise they would have beaten me until I confessed or was unable to say anything. This happened to another man in the same cell with me.

After the third day an FBI man came and said there had been a mistake and I was released. I asked the night captain if I could sell papers on the street. He told me to see the Chief of Police. I went up there later and left copies of the papers with his clerk and heard him say in another office that it was all right for me to sell them. I asked for a written permit but was told I did not need one.

The next Saturday afternoon I again sold papers in front of the library. Another cop came up and wanted to know what I was doing. I told him that I had permission to sell papers from the chief. He said "To hell with the Chief. I am a Legionnaire and no one is selling papers like that when I am around." Whereupon he jerked me into the squad car and took me down to the same police station. The same dumb night captain began to ask the same questions again. I told him to look in his record and save time.

He sent me in to the chief of the Military Police. While waiting there I saw several soldiers to whom I had sold papers reading them. This officer was quite gruff, but after questioning me he said it was not in his sphere and took me back to the night captain. I was ushered into a room full of police each of them fatter and more dumb looking than the other. They commenced to swear at me and advance with their fists. I just laughed at them and said I was not foolish enough to give them a chance to beat me up.

At last the night captain told me that if I went out again to sell papers I would be beaten up. "Is that the law talking?" I asked. "That's the law talking," he replied.

My boss did not agree with my ideas, but paid me for those four days I was locked up. In a few days I talked to the Chief of Police who, upon looking at *The Conscientious Objector,* said: "You can't sell that in my town."

"You talk like Hitler!"

"What!"

"You talk like Hitler," I repeated.

He grunted and picked up the CW saying "What is this? You had better see Father Mac at the Cathedral; if he says it is all right it is all right; if he says it isn't; then it isn't." Later I called Father Mac, who had presided at an America First meeting before the war. He said "Why should I put my neck out?"

I corresponded with Roger Baldwin of the American Civil Liberties Union who said they would carry the case to the Supreme Court whenever Carl Whitehead, their lawyer in Denver, wanted to take the case. I talked to Mr. Whitehead whom I had known for years. He did not have time then to attend to the matter but would do so later.

My wife and children visited Ben Salmon's widow and her children with me. Charles was studying for the priesthood and is now a priest in Colorado. My wife did not want to be in the same city where I was being arrested, although the papers had nothing about it, I shed an aura which was too radical it seemed. Accordingly she moved to Santa Fe. I helped them pack.

Two men who operated milking machines in the barn were incensed because of my vote at the union meeting against war bonds and for conscientious objectors. They made slurring remarks against me, trying to provoke a fight for several weeks. They were of mediocre minds and with little intelligence so it was of no use to argue with them. I had to overcome their animosity in some other way. When I walked to the far away milk room with my one bucket of milk I made it my business to walk by their "strings" of cows, which were in the furthermost end of the barn from the milk room, and carry one of their heavy DeLaval buckets of milk along with me. After a few days they cooled down and became friends, although they never did understand the radical and pacifist argument.

MAKE READY THE WAY OF THE LORD —
MAKE STRAIGHT HIS PATHS

Ade Bethune

CHAPTER 5

Life at Hard Labor
Refusal to pay Income Tax
1943 - July, 1947

Albuquerque and Isleta, New Mexico

Christmas of 1942 I went to Santa Fe to see my wife and the girls, and although I was not welcome I did get a couple of hours' enjoyment playing games with the girls. I could not get a job there so went to Albuquerque. Here I obtained work on a dairy farm at $70 a month and keep, 12 hours a day work.

I wanted to get my ideas clear on Christian Anarchism so wrote a book of 150,000 words on the subject much of which was quotations from all of the different brands of anarchists of whom I had read. I sent it to several publishers but did not really care if it was printed or not. It is bound and on file with my other writings in the Labadie Collection at the University Library at Ann Arbor, Mich. After eight months I went to work for Albert Simms who had married Ruth Hanna McCormick. I worked in the cow barn, in the greenhouse and taking care of his valuable calves.

A group in New York City had asked me to write something from Tolstoy against war so I read all of the twenty-two volumes of the Scribner edition and took hundreds of pages of notes, listing them on the subjects of Thou Shalt Not Kill, Christian Anarchism; The Simple Life; and Religion. The first was published in a small green covered booklet and distributed free. The others were much longer booklets and have not been published.

During this time I was aware that a withholding tax would be taken from my pay if I worked on any other place than a farm and that at the end of the year I would have to pay taxes or refuse to pay them. My study of Tolstoy and the emphasis of Dorothy Day in the CW that payment of taxes was unChristian, inasmuch as most of the taxes went for war, helped me to make up my mind openly to refuse to pay taxes. I wrote to the leaders of all of the pacifist groups in the country asking their moral support. All of them but one told me I should write to Congressmen in order that they would act like men; and that one person could not do anything. The one person who approved of my stand was Dorothy Day.

When I refused to pay taxes for 1943 on March 15, 1944, Mr. Simms fired me, saying "You will be arrested tomorrow and I will be disgraced for having harbored you in my employ."

I got a job at a dairy and orchard south of town after working a few weeks for a bee man bottling honey and trapnesting some prize chickens he had. The tax office did nothing about my report.

Meanwhile Sharon had been the guest of honor at a symphony concert in Albuquerque. I met her there and of course was proud of her. Carmen graduated from high school in Santa Fe in 1944. When we had named her Carmen in Wisconsin we had never thought that she would be graduating in a class with many others girls by the name of Carmen as was the case in this old Spanish town. That summer my wife and the girls moved to Evanston, Illinois in order that they might get the best education possible in the piano work which they had chosen. Meanwhile I had visited the Indians in nearby Isleta often and become acquainted with the priest who liked the CW.

THE SUN

The sun, like a blazing ball of gold
Shines from somewhere in infinity
Down upon country and city
To give light, warmth and peace
To the humanity of earth.

One man may think that he rules the world
As he sits upon a golden throne of power
With a sword in his hand and an army by his side,

But yet can he say when the sun shall rise
Or when it shall set in the evening?

No, for the sun is a world of its own,
A part of the infinite space,
A symbol of light and peace,
A blessing to the humanity of earth,
Perhaps our last hope, the sun.

Sharon Hennacy, age 12, in RETORT, 1943

The Simple Life

In June, 1945 the CW printed an article of mine on "The Simple Life" in which I explained the principle of voluntary poverty and non payment of taxes as I had learned them from Tolstoy and the CW. When I was working a man asked me "Why does a fellow like you, with an education, and who has been all over the country, end up in this out-of-the-way place working for very little on a farm?" I explained that all people who had good jobs in factories, etc. had a withholding tax for war taken from their pay, and that people who worked on farms had no tax taken from their pay. I told him that I refused to pay taxes. He was a returned soldier and said that he did not like war either, but what could a fellow do about it? I replied that we each did what we really wanted to.

Here is my story of the simple life: At this dairy I live in an old adobe house. Father Sun, as the Indians speak of the ball of fire, rising over the Sandia (Spanish for watermelon) mountains to the east filters through the mulberry and cottonwood trees to my open door. I turn in bed and relax. A prayer for those near and dear and for those loved ones far away; in and out of prison and CO camp, and in and out of man's holocaust: war. The night before I had cooked unpolished rice sprinkled with raisins. With milk, and the whole wheat bread I have baked, my breakfast is soon finished. It is now 8 o'clock. I go to the dairy to see if any change has been made in plans for work for the day. If my student friend in the milk truck appears, he will take my letters to the mail box; otherwise I will take them myself.

Now the German prisoners have arrived from the nearby prison camp. Paul is to continue his work with me in the orchard pruning dead wood from the trees. Each of us knows a little of the other's language and we each aim unconsciously to please the other by speaking in the language native to the other. "Guten morgen, what speak you?" I say. "Hello Hennacy," he smiles, "nothing much."

In this high altitude it is chilly for perhaps an hour, then we take our shirts off. Perhaps the branches scratch us, but we do not need to worry about tearing our shirts. He wears his North Africa cap and I wear my white Gandhi semi-turban. The orchard has not been pruned thoroughly for some years. We are late with the work, for 5000 trees have accumulated much dead wood.

Mourning doves have commenced to build their make-believe makeshift nests. They will contain two eggs which will hatch out a little brother and a little sister; the former combative and the latter as quiet as the proverbial mouse—that is unless the owl or roadrunner gets the eggs or the young birds. This roadrunner is a carniverous bird, killing snakes and small animals also. It is streamlined, runs swiftly after its prey, and is mostly bill and tail.

As Paul views the countryside from the treetop he says that hardly a house can be seen, and contrasts this with the many houses in sight of his father's farm near the Polish border. A quarter of a mile away we see the morning train coming from Los Angeles. Today we have a row of trees with bits of dead wood scattered near the tops, which takes more time. Yesterday we had old trees, half dead, which required but several large limbs to be severed. Fido and Borso follow us to the orchard and it seems they must lie under the very tree where limbs are falling, gnawing a bone or a bit of frozen and dried apple; but they lead a dog's charmed life and are never hurt. Soon it is noon as Paul goes to the dairy to eat his lunch with Fred, Frank and Karl, and the guard who carries a gun but never uses it. I have cooked a kettle of pinto beans, and not having planted any chili peppers last summer I have added some vegetable shortening and onion for flavor. Orthodox vegetarians do not drink coffee, but not being orthodox in much of anything I have some coffee in cool weather. And of course the balance of the loaf of bread with oleo. For a few minutes I may finish writing a letter which I have begun earlier, or finish an article in a paper. I do not take a daily paper, getting the news from two weeklies. I would not have the noise of a radio around.

Then I usually walk across the road a block to say hello to my Spanish friends; especially my four year old Lipa. She will be kneeling on a bench eating tortillas and beans from the table and will greet me with a mixture of Spanish and English in precise, quick words. The father and older brother are employed on the farm also and I have worked with them at odd times. The older sister passes the orchard on the way to school and likes apples. Now I have to forget my German and see if I can remember a few Spanish words. Lipa will proudly say "apple" and I will say "manzana." She will point to my pocket and say "pocket" and I will reply with "bolsa." Soon it is time to go to work. As I leave, Lipa or some of the family will give the traditional Spanish "come back again." It would be good if I would reply, "Come over to my house," but the accommodations of a bachelor are not conducive to visiting. Brother Joe has been over to practice typing letters, and Lipa has come running several times to "see your girls" (the pictures of my daughters). Seeing the typewriter she took great pride in saying this long word. Another English word which delighted her, in taste and in tongue, was "gingerbread."

The mailman comes in the afternoon. Perhaps today I receive several letters from boys in C.O. camps, discussing Tolstoy and bringing up questions which puzzle them. It is now 6 p.m. and I go to the dairy for my quart of milk, perhaps carry a can of water also, and chop wood for half an hour. Evenings are cool and even in the summer a cover is required.

The apple, cherry and peach wood burns brightly in the fireplace. Even twigs burn well in the range.

It is now early April and asparagus, which has come up for years throughout the orchard, presents a fine supper for the vegetarian. Many times with a half pint of milk, a little pepper and shortening added, it makes a filling and delicious meal. At other times slowly fried and mixed with rice it gives a flavor resembling oysters. (Some meat-eater may correct me, for I have not tasted oysters for thirty years.)

Perhaps a letter or article in the CHRISTIAN CENTURY, which a friend kindly subscribed to for me along with several other papers, suggests an article which I feel impelled to write. Perhaps I am writing another Tolstoy booklet corresponding with my Doukhobor friends in Canada, or writing a digest or review of a book which a friend has loaned to me. My only luxury, a semi-stuffed armchair, is in front of the fireplace; the stove to the right and a table of apple boxes to the left, where my typewriter and current correspondence is scattered. A large table to the back which has been used for apple sorting is used for bread mixing, hectographing, and a general place for material I want within easy reach. I use a board across my lap for a table and have the food handy at the stove.

Before me, above the fireplace, are oil paintings by the former owner of the orchard. This man was a Christian Scientist whose mother knew Mrs. Eddy. Neighbors tell of his reading "The Book" to sick animals and saying that the power of right thought would make grain instead of the weeds grow in the fields. There are undoubtedly metaphysical laws little understood by most of us which show the relationship between the great waves of hatred, fear and war which sweep over and surround the atmosphere of this world and the waves of epidemics, blights, floods and so-called "Acts of God." St. Francis could tame the man-eating wolf of Gubbio at a glance, but he had first tamed the passions, hatreds and materialism which had previously held sway in his own being. Christian Scientists or any of the cults springing from that premise cannot expect to control weeds, insects and wholesale epidemics as long as they bless war and the economic system which feeds on war. When they have the courage and the spirituality of the early Christians then they can surely "take up serpents; and if they drink any deadly thing it shall not hurt them." But warmongers and Mammon worshippers need not expect miracles.

A picture of Jesus at the carpenter's bench finally wore out after I had put it up and taken it down when moving around. My half-pacifist young Lutheran minister friend, Leeland Soker, gave me Sallman's Head of Christ. My unorthodox array of "Saints" on the wall are Tolstoy, Debs, Thoreau, Jefferson, Abdul Baha, St. Francis, Vanzetti and Gandhi. The pictures of my own girls and family and that of an Indian maiden is the only touch of femininity in the house. This room is 14 by 16 feet with two windows and three doors, and the bedroom is 13 by 13. The walls are nearly four feet thick, made of native adobe, and the ceilings are ten feet high.

Tradition tells of treasure hid here in this house at the time of Indian raids. For the house was once an old fort in the times when the whites were encroaching upon the Indian country. The treasure that I have found here was buried, all right—buried deep within my personality, and it took the peace and quiet, the productive labor among kindly, common and everyday sort of people to discover it.

Originally all doors led upon a small patio in the center open to the sky. The east wall is now torn down. Part of the house was used as a Catholic chapel in the early days. Enough cracks here and there allow Brother Mouse to come and go. At a former place where I lived by myself, I was able to stop up all cracks and holes within two months so that mice did not enter. It was their home before it was mine. They have a right to live, to chew and gnaw, but they do not need to do so in my two rooms. There is plenty for them in nearby fields and farm buildings. They do not bother old copies of the CATHOLIC WORKER or other pacifist or radical papers. Their especial taste seems to be for the CHRISTIAN CENTURY—but then they may have developed certain tastes from the former owner of the place.

It is now a bright morning in early May. By this time my skin is nearly as brown as that of Hans. Last year the blisters on my back worried others much and myself but little. This year not a blister came from my exposure to the sun. Two electric pumps bring water from the irrigation ditch and from a well to irrigate the 100 rows of trees. For a short distance the water runs between banks uphill until it reaches the trees. (The saying here is that only a Mormon can make water run up hill. They understand irrigation, are good workers and their system of helping each other could easily be studied and used by all of us. I have some Mormon friends who like to read the CATHOLIC WORKER.) The gopher has made holes in the ditch bank and this is a continual trouble until they have all been stopped up. Hans watches the ditch bank for leaks and I see that the water reaches each tree.

Melons have come up from some left in the field last year. I plant onions, parsnips, rutabagas, tomatoes, carrots, lettuce, blue Indian corn from nearby Isleta pueblo, and the native pinto bean. Later sweet potatoes and peppers will be planted. Last year I planted a small patch of wheat but soon afterward came to work here and did not harvest it. My employer has doubts about my ability as a wheat farmer but I planted about an acre. Much of it is up but some of the ground is black alkili where even weeds will not grow.

Old timers here and there along this Rio Grande have watermills where corn is ground between two stones. They go with exceedingly slow motion but there is no cost, and these stones have been grinding for centuries. If it is possible to get my blue corn and wheat ground at such a mill I will do so; if not, the hammer mill of my employer can grind it. The primitive way of cutting wheat, binding it by hand (for few people raise wheat and use a binder here) and threshing it out by hand on canvas seems queer. By itself it may seem foolish, but taken as part of a pattern of life it has meaning. Orthodox economists tell us that the farmer who uses a horse and a plow and very little machinery cannot afford to compete in the market with the farmer who uses up-to-date machinery.

It happens that I do not care to own property and have it taken away by the government for non-payment of taxes, for most of the taxes in my lifetime will go to pay for World War II and to prepare for World War III. One who eats meat can raise a few hogs and chickens in the country and here turkeys do well. For a vegetarian who simplifies his needs, the cash that is needed for certain purposes can be earned as a farm laborer; and most of the food to be consumed can be raised on an acre or two. To raise food for animals and then eat the animals is expensive. Why not raise the grain and eat it yourself?

I am not competing on the market with others any more than I am losing an election when I do not enter the lists of voting. My ideals are above and beyond that nose counting which takes place at the ballot box, and the economic system which myself and other free spirits follow is above and beyond the market place. The B-29's roar over my head hourly. These planes of death exist, as do the market place and the voting booth, but they do not need to be a part of my life if I do not choose to help pay for them or live in fear because of the warmonger's security in these false gods.

MY BUDGET

I keep ten dollars for expenses and send the remainder to my wife and girls. During the month of May, 1945 my expenses were as follows:

Whole wheat flour, 25 lbs.	$1.25
(could grow own wheat)	
Vegetable shortening, 3 lbs.	.68
Cornmeal, 5 lbs.	.46
(could grow own corn)	
Oleomargarine, 2 lbs.	.38
Rice, 4 lbs.	.58
(price is too high)	
Raisins, 2 lbs.	.23
Syrup, 5 lbs.	.47
Yeast, salt, sugar, etc.	.50
TOTAL	4.55
Electric light bill	1.00
Bundle of CO and CW's	2.40
Postage stamps, haircut, etc.	2.05
TOTAL	$10.00

I bought a quantity of pinto beans (seconds) last year and still have some left. Have a few jars of apple butter which I put up last fall. Get a quart of milk free from the farm daily, and asparagus, wild lettuce, and later fruit and vegetables. Irish potatoes do not grow well here. The ones that you buy at the store now are not worth the money, so I buy rice instead. Another year I should get a few hives of bees.

Reading of the bread-making at Mott St. and of Cobbetts old-fashioned way of bread making, and of Catherine de Heuck's rye bread encouraged me to persevere until I can now say that I make as good bread as I have ever tasted. Here is my method, developed at last after getting the yeast too hot, the oven too hot, and the dough raised too quickly. At noon I put 13 cups of whole wheat flour in a pan. Heat a pint of milk until it commences to bubble, then add water until it is a little more than luke warm. Crumble in 2 cakes of yeast and stir until dissolved. Add 2 tablespoons of salt and 4 of sugar to the liquid and pour liquid in the flour. Mix and add 4 tablespoons of shortening. Knead it a bit and add more water if necessary until it is not too sticky. I then put it in a pan, cover it with a cloth and take it over to Lipa's mother, Reyes, and leave it in her warm kitchen until 6 p.m. (If I left it in my room, Brother Mouse would nose around and perhaps get in the habit of searching for such good food—and my room is too cool for the dough to rise properly.)

At night I knead the dough lightly and make it into four loaves according to the size of pan I happen to have. (The Spanish word for bread is "pan".) I leave these loaves for about an hour and a half by the open oven door where a wood fire is burning. When the loaves have raised sufficiently I put them in the oven; but it must not· be too hot or the outside will burn and the inside be doughy. In about 45 minutes the bread will be done. Shortening applied to the top of the loaf as it is removed from the oven keeps it from cracking. I place the loaves in a roomy and airy oven of another stove which is stored here and not in use, but is mouseproof. In the morning, half of a small loaf goes to Reyes and Lipa and half of a loaf to the growing son of my employer, who prefers it to store bread. A good slice is given as a token to Pat, the bookkeeper on the farm, who kindly brings my groceries from town, as she goes there often in her car.

I have been unable to purchase any buckwheat flour and make my own everlasting dough, added to each day during the winter months. The prepared stuff you buy is a travesty on the name of buckwheat. In winter I make hotcakes from flour, baking powder, salt and sugar and shortening. Have fried mush often for breakfast. When I am out of bread and do not have any yeast I can make fairly good tortillas. One day Lipa said that she had made two for me, but "they are not nice and round like my mother's." (The saying among the Spanish people is that until a girl can make perfectly good, round tortillas, she is not ready to be married.)

A cup of flour, a teaspoon of salt and the same of baking powder and shortening, with enough milk or water added so the dough will not be sticky, will make three tortillas. Roll the dough out rather thin and place on top of the wood stove. Do not have the fire too hot. Keep turning from one side to another until light brown. Then put between the folds of a cloth. Spanish people break the tortilla in bits and dip up beans with it. I have learned to do this fairly well. One night last year when I had taken apples to Lipa I stayed for supper. Lipa jumped up from the table and rolled out a rather lop-sided tortilla and placed it on the stove. Chattering in her snappy English and Spanish, she forgot it and it was badly burned. With a noncholant gesture she said, "That's o.k. Hennacy, take it along and eat it on your way home."

It is Sunday morning. I get up at 5.45, eat a hurried breakfast, take my good clothing in a grip along with about 50 CATHOLIC WORKERS and go to the orchard to look over the situation of the water, which has been running all night. Here the water has gone into another row and missed half a dozen trees; there it is dammed up with weeds and a furrow. I channel the water in the proper places and look over the next row for potential breaks, and turn the water into this new row. I oil the pump, and then a dash of cold water livens me up. Change my clothes, and walk a mile down the road to the seminary chapel, where I give a CW to each person as they enter for 7.30 mass. Then I walk the five miles toward town. Many times a workman picks me up.

If I am early I visit Rev. Soker in his study for half an hour and give him a paper. Then I go in the rear of a large church and say my prayers. The old Irish priest here says what he thinks, his sermons being short and to the point. Some people know me as I stand in front of the church after mass with the CW, but most of them are busy with other affairs. As people go in for the 11 o'clock mass some get a paper from me. Then I hurriedly walk two miles to a church near the University. I have met this younger priest personally; he was a former social worker, so we have something in common. Here the people coming from the 11 o'clock mass and entering and leaving the noon mass can obtain papers from me if they like. Some military men eye my Gandhi cap warily as it bears a neat inscription in red, "Free India Now."

On my way home I leave a copy with my partly pacifist friend of the Christian denomination and chat with him a few minutes. Then I deposit a copy with my Jehovah Witness friends, to whom I have previously explained the mystery of one who is not a Catholic giving time and energy (as they give time and energy for their cause) to distribute a Catholic paper. The fact that I was in prison with Judge Rutherford in Atlanta in 1918 commands their respect. They see the pacifism of the CATHOLIC WORKER but it has the name "Catholic". How could that church be for "the Truth"? There must be something wrong! I have met the Jehovahs in other cities; they have courage, and that pardons much of their intolerance.

Coming home the other Sunday afternoon I stopped in to say hello to Lipa. Seeing me with a shirt and coat she asked, "Hennacy, you been to Ecclesia?" I said that I had. "You say Name of the Father?" "Not very much, but I say benedice for my honey," I replied. Quickly she took me into the bedroom and proudly pointed to two candles burning at either side of an image and said, "See Santo Nino!" (the Holy Child).

One other Sunday I sold papers at the church near the University and the priest said "every soldier who dies fighting for his country goes at once to eternal bliss." An old priest at the big downtown church saw me selling CW's and said "The Catholic church in all of its history has not lived up one jot or one tittle to the Sermon on the Mount. Come in and talk with me sometime." An Indian who was a guard of the German prisoners said to me after reading a CW, "Why does no one tell us about conscientious objectors except after the war is over?" I explained that we were getting them ready for the next war.

The Indian Reservation

One Sunday morning in June I arose early, picked a cup of mulberries from the bush at my door, which with sugar and cream and some bread made a delicious breakfast. I had borrowed a bicycle from Lipa's brother Joe, and after attending to the irrigation of the orchard I started down the road to the Indian reservation in which is located the Pueblo of Isleta, seven miles to the south. The road was uphill and down and quite sandy, so that progress was slow. Here it wound along the edge of the bluff overlooking the two ribbons of the Rio Grande with a wide expanse of sandbars between. Horses grazed on the lush grass along the river in the lowlands near the Santa Fe bridge. Coming into Isleta a rather large adobe house with buildings of the same material occupied the corner between the road and the bridge. An Indian with an exceedingly large brimmed hat was feeding some animals. An auto, partly dismantled stood in the yard. Just south of the bridge is the dam which throws the water through the spillways for the reservation.

It was now 9.30, and upon inquiry of the priest's housekeeper I was told that today's mass had been at 8.00, and the next Sunday it would be at 10.00 o'clock, as the priest had the 10 o'clock mass at a neighboring town this morning. I had taken fifty odd copies of the CW along, and I commenced to knock at each door and give a copy to each family. The houses were on narrow semi-streets winding here and there, as in Santa Fe, and each yard held farm machinery, wood, and the familiar wagon in which I had often seen the Indians from the orchard on their way to town. Nearly every woman who came to the door spoke to me in English and thanked me for the paper. Several extremely wrinkled old men came to the door, and although they may not have understood just what it was they received, thanked me for the paper. Perhaps twenty houses were locked; the people were in the fields or gardens in the outlying parts of the reservation, or visiting. Here I did not leave a paper as I saw I would not have enough. One noticeable thing about the houses is that they are large and roomy, although perhaps a married son or daughter would live in one end of the house.

A man and his wife were on the porch of a nice appearing house, and when I gave them a paper they said that three families lived there. First a pretty dimpled young matron appeared and later another comely young woman, and each got a copy of the paper. While a young sister and brother looked at the paper I stopped a moment to rest. I explained where I worked, and that this was a Catholic paper a little different from the others, in that it did not support war. The young ladies said that about 100 young men from the pueblo had been drafted. Later a mother and daughter invited me in when I gave them a paper. The house was very clean and roomy (more so than my own). A huge coffee pot like we used for threshers in the east stood on the stove. Two stars on the door indicated that men were in the armed forces. I mentioned the story that my Quaker great grandmother had told me of Indians not harming Quakers, who did not lock their doors, fight the Indians, or give them liquor. They recognized the name Quaker, but did not know of any such thing as conscientious objectors, saying that war was bad but boys had to go, and what could you do about it. I replied that many Catholic boys were in concentration camps or in prison in preference to going to war. I told them of the five Hopi Indians who had refused to register and had gone to prison, and of the injustice of Indians being made to fight the white man's wars, after being despoiled of their country and not being allowed citizenship.

A beautiful granddaughter with a clear bright complexion and bright dark eyes, about 8 years old, came in for a few minutes. Her name was Pauline Jiron. Now it was noon and they invited me to eat with them. Peas, with a side dish of chili which made the tears come to my eyes and my mouth burn; bread baked in the oval adobe oven outside the door, and coffee. They brought sugar from the cupboard especially for me, but as I did not use it, nor they either, it remained untouched. I spoke of some old Indian men I had met at the doors that morning and wondered how old they were. "They may look old, but they are not so old" my hostess replied. All families in the pueblo were Catholic except two or three who had a Baptist minister meet with them in their homes.

Nearly every house had several dogs near the door, but not one of them growled, although I was dressed in the white suit I had worn in the dairy, and in my white Gandhi cap, and must have appeared unusual to them. Several notices of silversmiths and their wares were posted at houses. All the Indians had splendid teeth, and not one bald-headed Indian was to be seen. The older men wore hair braided or rolled at the back. The older women wore white leggings wound round and round, and bright shawls. The men wore gaily colored shirts. The children ran to bright colors, as do the Spanish. The generally accepted idea that Indians do not beat their children, that the children are not afraid and seldom cry, was found to be true by my observation, and in answer to questions on that subject. "The Navajo's simply go 'sh-h-h' and the children cease whatever nuisance they are making," one lady told me.

I approached one house where a large wire and wood net or container partly filled with corn hung between four posts. In response to my knock an elderly man asked me to come in. His daughter was there, and later his wife came in. He looked at the paper and saw that it was Catholic, and thanked me for it. He asked me to sit down. I said that this was a Catholic paper that did not believe in war, and taught that all men were brothers and should not kill each other.

"The skin may be different color," he answered, touching his tanned arm," but the Great Spirit is in the heart of everyone. The Sun is the father that gives light and makes the corn grow. If it seems to shine too much for us, we must know that it shines for everybody; for some who need it more than we do. A man who curses the good Mother Earth because the crop does not grow is sinful. We must plant good seed, and God and Mother Earth bring us good food. A good man does not curse God, Father Sun or Mother Earth. Good health comes from the good God."

That man's son is in the occupied German territory now. The father had never heard of conscientious objectors, but felt that war was evil, especially for Indians to fight for the white man when they were not free themselves. He too was interested in the Hopi Indians who had refused to register. I told him about my Quaker great grandmother, the activities of the Quakers in hiding escaped slaves, and of my own opposition to war and refusal to pay taxes.

It was now 1.30, and I went to the house of the priest, which was enclosed to the right of the church behind adobe walls. He was baptizing Indian babies, so I waited on the porch. Corn grew knee high in the patio, and rabbits played in the enclosure bedded with clover. I had brought the housekeeper some asparagus I had gathered in the orchard that morning, and I smelled it cooking. Soon the priest, a big man, appeared. He greeted me cordially. I had mailed him a letter previously explaining that I was coming to his parish to distribute the CW, and had mailed him several copies. He knew the truth about Pearl Harbor and was not in favor of obliteration bombing. He said that, as in the last war, the arms factories of international cartels had not been touched, while hundreds of thousands of civilians had been burned alive. I gave him a copy of the CONSCIENTIOUS OBJECTOR which he had not seen before.

On the bicycle as I was going through the pueblo toward home, several children and older folks recognized my white attire and waved to me. A jeep full of guards from the German prison camp passed me, and one of them who knew me wondered what I was doing down there. They had often met me as I had passed their camp on the way to Albuquerque on Sunday mornings. Nearing home I stopped for a drink of water at the home of cousins of Lipa whom I had met before. As soon as I got home, a look at the well in the orchard proved that the water was running properly. I was very hungry and prepared a good bowl of rice and raisins with a dash of cinnamon and nutmeg, then went to the orchard to turn the water into another row for the night. As Joe was by himself in the dairy I helped him cool the milk.

Having worked during the summer in the orchard seven days a week without extra pay I had earned a vacation in December. My employer had presented me with a fine wool sleeping bag. On Dec. 15th, 1945 I hiked before daylight eastward over the pass toward Amarillo. Walking twenty-three miles and riding 183, I came about an hour after dark to a farmhouse and asked if I could sleep in a shed or barn. It was bitter cold and the man asked me in the house to get warm. Later he insisted that I occupy a spare bed in an enclosed porch, saying that I could sleep in my sleeping bag anytime. His forecast was correct, for of the twenty-two nights that I did not stay with relatives on this hike, this New Mexican was the only farmer who allowed me on his place. I love the land, and it would please me to tell of the hospitality of those who live on the land, but alas, the farmer seems to have the mind of those who live in the city: prosperous and selfish. In Texas a returned soldier in a truck gave me a long ride. Passing a small town, he said, "See that undertaking establishment? Good money in the business. I used to own it, but saw so many dead in Europe that I swore I would never bury one more person. So I sold my business and bought a farm."

On one lonesome stretch of the highway hundreds of cars passed without noticing me. Finally a young couple stopped, told me to put my bundles in the rear, and crowded themselves to allow me to sit with them in the front seat. We struck a snow storm as we arrived in Oklahoma City. I put on my galoshes, which I had carried along with my lunch and other things which might be needed in a hurry, in a flour sack hung in front of me, which balanced the sleeping bag on my back when I hiked. A girth strap of wide leather, wound around the back and buckled in front formed a harness. As on the hike which my wife and I had made years before, I never asked for a ride, but waited for people to ask me: trusting in God instead of my thumb. During two nights in Oklahoma I slept in old vacant houses along the road. Doors and windows were missing, but the floors were dry. Both times I was directed to them by the keepers of small stores who were unwilling to permit me to occupy their nearby sheds. The temperatures these nights were below zero. My sleeping bag was warm enough, but tying it up in the morning was a problem, for my hands became very cold.

In Webb City, Mo., I met several soldiers with bus tickets in their pockets hiking from the west coast, trying to get home by Christmas. No room on bus or train. (My sisters had offered me a round trip ticket, but I felt that I did not wish to be the occasion of the government getting that much war tax. I found that even if I had a ticket I could not have used it. So the absolutist turned out to be practical for once.) In the afternoon a man who had attended Quaker meetings in Philadelphia in his youth, but who was now a Catholic, gave me a ride from near Kansas City to Des Moines. He was an officer in the Kansas Co-op Wholesale and a friend of Monsignor Ligutti. He was much interested in the copies of the CW which I gave him. It was now after dark and bitter cold. I phoned

Msgr. Ligutti and made an appointment for 8:30 the next morning. Salvation Army, hotels and tourist camps were full, so the only recourse for this anarchist was to ask for the hospitality of his enemy, the state. With very little formality I was ushered into a tank cell and was the only occupant of a fifty-bed room. Later in the night some one else came in, whom I found in the morning was a young fellow whose employer had skipped town without paying him. They went around cleaning brass on the front of banks. I staked him to breakfast and a CW and each of us went our way. It was storming. Msgr. Ligutti greeted me cheerfully and I warmed myself before his cheery fireplace in the large house where the offices of the Rural Life Conference are located. He was to leave for Rome the next day. He was interested and sympathetic with my mode of life and enthusiastic about the CW. Presenting me with about ten pounds of literature he wished me well on my trip.

Near Stirling, Illinois, I walked about seven miles and it became dark. Finally I saw the lights of a 24-hour restaurant, had a cup of coffee and went on my way, being told that the next town was about seven miles away. I walked and walked and my fingers were nearly frozen it seemed. I thought I had surely gone the seven miles and stopped in at a farmhouse to get warm and ask directions. The town was still three miles away. Again I walked and walked in the darkness; suddenly I saw another 24-hour restaurant. Looking closer I saw it was the same one, for when I left the farmhouse I had walked four miles back the wrong way. I treated myself to a good omelette, for I was extra hungry and tired. The proprietor had overheard the conversation about my getting lost and suggested that if I did not mind sleeping between bags of onions and potatoes in the basement I could do so.

I was awakened at 5:00 a.m. by a waiter and told that a trucker would take me as far as Joliet. It was now the day before Christmas, and I was 125 miles from my destination, Evanston, Ill. Sleet on the highway and the windshield made this a bitter day—the worst of the trip. The truck broke down and after much walking and a few rides I met my wife and girls. The activities of their sect did not allow my radical aura to befog the atmosphere, so I went to Milwaukee for Christmas.

Later I said hello to my girls for a few minutes and went to Cleveland to visit my mother and sisters and brother. One brother-in-law had been raised a Christian Scientist; he was an ex-soldier, and was interested in the booklet I gave him published by the conscientious objectors who were Christian Scientists. Another brother-in-law lived in a suburb where there was a Catholic church. My sister had tried to give the priest and her Catholic neighbors copies of the CW but without success. I met Max Sandin, CO in World War I. He was also a non-registrant in World War II and one who refused to pay taxes.

Leaving just before dark I took a street car to Berea to visit my hiking pacifist friend, Phil Mayer. He had edited the Walden Round Robin, and although he was a humanist is enthusiastic about St. Francis of Assisi. At breakfast next morning his wife read a few pages from the Little Flowers of St. Francis in lieu of a blessing. It told of the angel in disguise who knocked in such a hurry on the door and of the ill temper of Brother Elias. It seemed to me a good lesson on faith and peace and trust in God. One of Phil's enthusiasms is the reciting of the epic poems of Vachel Lindsay. He showed me a letter from Lindsay's widow, who had been a Communist for years, in which she spoke of her recent conversion to the Catholic faith and her pleasure in knowing that he knew of the Catholic Worker movement.

That evening a lady stopped and gave me a ride for fifteen miles. This was after dark and very unusual. It seemed that a son had been killed by a hit and run driver and she always picked up people, feeling that they would be safer with her than walking on the road. That evening earlier an old couple accompanied by a married daughter and 7 yr. old son in a car picked me up and wondered why I did not ask for rides. I answered, "Oh I am a pioneer and pioneers don't ask for rides." The small boy looked at me with my Gandhi cap and said haltingly: "Oh Mom; a pioneer; a real pioneer; Gee Mom, they had hard times!" After another ride I walked up toward four farm houses but saw folks hiding behind doors rather than run the chance of speaking to a stranger. Down the road I saw the light of a garage; it was one of those 24-hour restaurants and trucker filling stations. While eating I heard conversation that told me that the young proprietor had had a nervous breakdown that morning and had not yet regained consciousness. His wife had worked all day and was weary. One girl had to cook, wash dishes and wait on table. The father-in-law was busy waiting on gas customers. I said that all of my journey had led me to that place that night, and proceeded to wash dishes, peel potatoes, etc. for several hours until the work was caught up. I slept on a bench by the entrance although I did not sleep much because of the noise which lasted that Saturday night until 4:00 a.m. In the morning the wife of the proprietor fixed me an especially fine breakfast and wondered what they would have done if I had not happened to come at just the right time. I told her nothing "happened" in this world, that all things work together for good to those who love the good - God. I had barely stepped out of the place the next morning when a taxi stopped and the driver, who was going to work, took me the twenty-eight miles to Toledo.

This Sunday I walked twenty-two miles. Each place where I hoped to get something to eat was marked "Closed on Sunday." Toward evening I saw a church spire in the distance, and supposing it was a Lutheran church I determined to ask the wife of the pastor for coffee. Coming closer I saw a sign which read "Assumption". Where had I heard that word before? I had only had time to read Dorothy's column in the December CW in Cleveland. Sitting down on my pack in front of the church. I looked it over again and saw that Dorothy had been there a few weeks before. Knocking on the convent door, I asked for Sister Columbiere. I was ushered into the parlor and soon the sister arrived, wondering how I knew her name. I showed her a copy of the December CW in which her name was mentioned, and which she had not yet seen. In a few minutes another sister announced that my venison was ready. I had not said that I had nothing to eat since Monday or that I was a vegetarian but I suppose I looked hungry. Sister Suzanne spoke up quickly, "Oh, I know what he likes, for my father is a vegetarian." So eggs and cheese were substituted. The sisters were interested in my hike and in my anti-war activities. I was unable to see the priest, for he was busy with committee meetings for a credit union and a cooperative freezer locker.

After supper I attended Benediction in the church, hearing with pleasure the clear voice of Sister Columbiere, which matched her radiant countenance. I felt that all things did work together for good, as I had asserted that morning, for if I had received a ride I would have gone through this small settlement and not known I had missed it. The sisters gave me some blankets and I slept on a mattress above the garage. I left early in the morning my pack about five pounds heavier because of the sandwiches, celery, cake, etc. which the sisters had given me.

Arriving in Chicago at noon the next day I had a visit at CYO headquarters with Nina Polcyn, Florence and Margaret, old friends of the Milwaukee Catholic Worker group. I also spent several hours visiting with my old friend, Claude McKay, Negro poet and former Communist, a friend of Dorothy in the twenties, and now a convert to the church. I had a few minutes with Sharon as she practiced music at the University before school, and with Carmen as we walked toward a street car.

As I walked up the long hill on Route 151 to the south of Dubuque, Iowa, it commenced to snow. Cars had slipped off the road all along but the pilgrim on foot made it all right. About nine miles further on I heard the bells of the monastery tolling to the right. A man picked me up and wanted to know where I was going, I told him to the monastery. He wanted to know if I was going to join the monks. I told him that I was not, and that I was a kind of a desert monk myself. Two miles further along a dirt road I came to a parish church surrounded by trees. Going down a deep hollow I saw a fine stone building over the hill. I had lived in desert country but had never seen a mirage. As I walked closer the building disappeared, for it was a mirage.

It was much further on hidden in the blinding snow that I came upon the monastery. Brother Joachim, a native Irishman, red-bearded and smiling, greeted me. Supper was ready, and he personally served me and two other guests. The Trappists do not eat meat or eggs but serve them to guests. Their vegetarianism is practiced as a penance, and not because of any especial regard for animals or health. Several other visitors were at the table, none of whom agreed with the Christian anarchist ideas of the CW. The brothers thought that the lesser of two evils should be taken instead of the ultimate good but they were not unduly insistent on the matter. Soon I met Brother Edmund, a graduate of the agricultural college at Las Cruces, N. M. After supper I attended Benediction. We all retired early, as the brothers get up at 2.00 a.m. and pray until breakfast at 8.00 and then are assigned their labor on the farm. After breakfast I attended high mass in the beautiful chapel. Visitors are partitioned off by locked gates from the brothers. Those in the choir put on white robes instead of the brown habit. They have a vow of silence. They sleep in one room somewhat like voting booths with canvas partitions. They sleep with their robes on. There were 57 monks at the time I was there. In 1849, Bishop Loras of Dubuque offered the brothers 500 acres of land and the monastery was founded that year. The present Abbot is Alfred Beston. I left at 2.00 p.m. the next day. Brother Joachim accompanied me for a few steps outside in the bitter cold and wished me peace and God-speed on my journey. In this world of speed and strife, of atomic bombs and commercial fraud, it was refreshing to rest in the quiet of this peaceful monastery.

That evening it was terribly cold. One man gave me a ride who was a captain in the airforce in World War I. As airplanes went overhead he cursed and said he would never ride in one again; it was all he could do to drive a car; he had a farm and did not want to get far from the land.

I saw the red lights of a radio station ahead and it seemed that I never got any closer as I walked and walked. Finally I came to a filling station and learned that there was but one restaurant in the town half a mile away. I entered, wearily dropped my pack by the stove, and ordered bean soup—double order. A sturdy youth picked up my pack and asked if I carried this on bean soup. "Seems as if I have to, as there is not much left for a vegetarian to eat." Just then the village butcher came in and the youth said: "Mike, if everyone was like this fellow you would have no job." "What you mean, no job?" asked Mike. The youth nodded to me and I explained that I had walked 18 miles and was not extra-tired; that I did not eat meat because I did not like to kill animals and did not want anyone to kill them for me. But I was not in town long enough to hurt his business. Mike was a simple minded fellow from the old country and took all this very seriously, so he answered: "Every day I kill cow and pig; people ask me to kill mad dog and their too many cats, but I never kill one sheep for he look me in the eye and I cannot do it. Someone else has to kill the sheep."

I journeyed through the long dreary stretches of Nebraska and over the exact spot where Crazy Horse had put blankets on the hoofs of horses and escaped the U. S. military patrol, over half a century before. A returned soldier who drove like mad brought me into neon-lit Cheyenne, Wyoming at 9 p.m. The Salvation Army and hotels were full up so I slept in the jail that night. Going south the next morning toward Denver a middle-aged man picked me up. He asked my destination and why I was hiking. He soon said after looking closely at my Gandhi headgear, "I don't like such people as you. You seem to be smart but have no ambition. Going around the country like this and living on charity in a jail. I never took a dime from anybody. I'm going to leave you right here in the desert although I could take you to Denver if I liked." Knowing it was little use to discuss life and its problems with this Babbitt, and wondering how he ever detoured from his bourgeois mentality to pick anyone up, I thanked him for the ride, walked on a mile and a half and got a ride with a jolly U. S. Marshall to Denver by noon.

Here I visited with my old friend Helen Ford, who had a small printing press and who had printed my tax refusal statement. Charles Salmon was studying for the priesthood, but I was unable to locate him. I hiked south and slept one very cold night under a bridge three miles south of Walsenburg, Col. When I awoke two inches of snow covered me. I had not been cold during the night but my fingers were nearly frozen by the time I had tied up my pack. After I had walked a few miles, a man gave me a ride, and I still remember the fine breakfast that I had at the Globe Hotel. Now it warmed up and I was soon over Raton pass and down into New Mexico. Another day, after walking twenty-one miles over dreary roads, I arrived after dark at a small settlement. All of the stores were closed. Going to the house with the brightest lights, I was greeted at the door by a Mexican who worked on the section gang. His wife was away and he invited me in giving me supper and breakfast, refusing any money from "my amigo." I guess he appreciated the fact that I was walking. I gave him my last CW.

An ex-soldier going west to college stopped and asked me to get in. He thought I was an Indian and picked me up because of the pack I was carrying. We arrived in Albuquerque at dark. I phoned my employer to tell him that I had at last come home. A smoldering fire in the fireplace greeted me from my roommate Hovey, the ex-soldier who worked on the farm. I had walked 490 miles and had ridden 3,582, a total mileage of 4,072.

Glad to get back to this land of sunshine I reviewed the results of my trip. I had acquired a sympathetic feeling toward ex-soldiers. It seems that their difficulties had made them kinder than the civilians.

I remembered one evening in Iowa where I had asked half a dozen farmers for permission to lay my sleeping bag in a sheltered end of a building but had been chased away. Later that evening one farmer came to the restaurant where I was eating and slipped a half a dollar in my pocket and said sheepishly, "I am ashamed because I turned you away."

I felt happy with the memory of my family and friends. Carmen and Sharon were continuing their music in Evanston. When a Sophomore in high school Sharon had been chosen to play the piano solo at the Spring Music Festival. She was given Gershwin's Rhapsody in Blue to play and told those in charge that she preferred Mozart. They told her that it was an honor to be chosen and she replied, "It is no honor to play trash; get someone who likes trash." She also refused an invitation to join the music sorority.

I felt renewed faith in that Providence which brought me safely through wind and storm and home again. I brought Lipa some mittens and her small brother Ernesto, a cap. The new irrigation ditch was nearly finished and several months of pruning the trees under the rays of the sun and away from the fog and smoke of the cities awaited me.

This Hovey of whom I speak had been a guard over the German prisoners and had asked me if he could come and room with me when he was mustered out. He had been the errand boy of his father in the moonshine business in the Carolinas for many years and had the easy going ways of his people. Despite this he had a better judgment of character than anyone I have met. Some new worker would come and Hovey would talk to him for half an hour and find out more of his past than a detective. Then he would come to the boss and say: "Charlie, watch that fellow, he's a rogue," or else he would say of another: "Don't fight with that fellow, Charlie; he's the best man you have had outside of Hensley." Hovey called me Hensley because he had once known a man by that name and it was too much bother to learn another name. Once he mailed a letter for me and my wife did not receive it for weeks. I asked him if he had really mailed it and he said that he had. As there was a check for $41.50 in the letter he said that he would pay me this amount if the letter did not reach my wife. But he would not mail any more letters for me. My wife got the letter and Hovey felt better.

Once he asked me to "back a letter for me." I addressed the envelope and then he wanted me to write the letter to his sister, "for you write such interesting letters; write just like you do to your girls." So I told his sister of what we had been doing the past week. "Now sign it," said Hovey. I told him this would be forgery so he signed his name himself. He depended upon me to do the cooking; and if I asked him to chop three sticks of wood he surely would not make a mistake and chop four. His quaint ways and slow motion were a source of joy to me, but one Hovey was enough at a time.

I had been visiting the Indians at Isleta pueblo all along. When the Atom Bomb was exploded at nearby Almagordo in the previous July none of us knew at the time what it was. When we all knew of it I wrote the following expression which I placed in the mouth of a Taos Indian who was visiting. Those to whom I read it felt that it expressed their ideas as well as a white man could.

> *Sun-Father*
> *They mock you.*
> *Fire to glow on the hearth,*
> *Warmth to open the heart of the Holy Corn,*
> *Warmth to melt the snow on White Mountain*
> *Giving water for our crops, our animals.*
> *This, Sun-Father, is good.*
> *Great fire to kill*
> *Is bad.*
> *I kill my enemy with my own two hands*

80

Or he kills me.
That is brave.
To burn and blast every man,
Every woman and child,
All animals and birds,
All corn and grass—
That is cowardly and wicked.
They steal your brightness
For devil-worship;
Sun-Father
They mock you.

In May I received a telegram from Claude McKay in Chicago saying that he was very ill and wanted to come to Albuquerque, thinking the change of climate would help him. Sister Agnes de Sales, head of Catholic Teachers College and a friend of mine and of the CW got a bed on the porch of St. Joseph's Hospital for Claude. He was nearly dead with diabetes, heart trouble and dropsy when he arrived and had to be put under an oxygen tent. I had studied Theosophy, Rosicrucianism, the I AM, Spiritualism, Christian Science, Eschatology, and various other occult cults and at this time was studying Yogi breathing and healing exercises. Their basis was relaxed deep breathing, drawing the strength from God, or as they phrased it: The Great Central Sun. Then this buildup of power was sent with outstretched hands and prayer to that part of the body of the person afflicted. The person to be helped did not need to believe in it; only to acquiesce and not eat meat. I did my best each morning and a friend in Milwaukee who had more experience did the same for him. Whether it was these prayers, those of Sister Agnes and others or not, Claude passed the crisis and in about six weeks was well enough to be released.

The trouble then was to find a place that would accept a Negro. I made a public appeal in a local Protestant negro church but to no avail. Finally Msgr. Garcia made up a bed in his office for Claude. Later we found a small apartment in the Mexican section. I visited him twice a week, took dictation for a book which he was writing, and wrote his letters for him as he was still weak. Bishop Scheil in Chicago was directly concerned about Claude. In speaking of the Bishop, Claude said that he had the same love in his eyes that Emma Goldman had had. Finally the latter part of September Claude was well enough to go by himself on the train to San Diego, where pacifist friends of mine found a good place for him to stay. Later he went back to Chicago and lived several years. It is likely that he did not keep to a strict diet or that he exerted himself too much, for he died about three years after he left Albuquerque.

About the time Claude left I read a short story in COLLIERS and said to myself that if I couldn't write a better one than that I would be ashamed of myself. Accordingly I wrote a story with Indians as characters. After 17,000 words it was not such a short story. The characters seemed real and I could not leave them alone, so continued. After Christmas I had finished a novel of 120,000 words, which I called *Unto the Least of These*. As I visited Isleta pueblo on Sundays I would meet an Indian whom I would develop into a character. In order to develop the characters correctly I read every book that I could find in the University library on the different Indian tribes. The hero was Ramon of Taos pueblo to the north of Santa Fe. My wife and I had visited there in 1925, and she and the girls had gone back there for a visit several years ago. A white girl by the name of Ledra, patterned in courage after Sharon was the heroine. I sought to debunk all of the political and religious philosophies and to develop a spiritual force in opposition to the coming Great War in 1951-52, from these Indians and the Hopi and the Catholic Worker. (Looking back I expect that I only made my characters unreal mouthpieces for my ideas, but at least it clarified my ideas.)

As it was spring now, I heard the lively song of the mocking bird as I irrigated the trees in the orchard. The chirp of the robin and the cooing of the mourning dove were broken by the song of the meadow lark, which my boss says, is translated as "John Greenleaf Whittier." On my way to the pueblo one Sunday I passed the wreck of a B29 that had crashed the day before and all aboard were burned to death but one who was dragged out by nearby German prisoners before the whole plane burst into flames. An army truck came along and a voice cried "Halt." It seemed that a German prisoner had escaped and as no white man walked the roads they thought I was the prisoner. One of the guards knew me and so I was not bothered. I had but fifty papers so went to different homes where I had not given the paper last time.

I was walking this time and I saw a flock of sheep herded by a man on a horse in the lowlands within the river area proper. Indians were watering their stock; some coming in from their fields in their wagons, the men with hair in braids and the women with their bright shawls. Here a colt followed its mother; there a dog barked angrily but jumped up and licked my hand when I entered the yard. I went to different houses this time to give out CW's and as before the Indians thanked me. At one house an Indian dressed in American fashion welcomed me and asked for several papers for in-laws, as he was visiting in this home. He asked what kind of a Catholic paper I had. I told him that it was against the war. He replied, "Yes, this is a capitalist war." Several children were around, among them a small sweet child named Carmelita. I gave them apples which I brought along in a sack with the papers.

I stopped at the house where about fourteen Indians were meeting with a visiting Baptist preacher who gave the same kind of a hell-fire message that I had heard when a child. From this meagre crowd the missionary took up a collection of $21 for, of all things, paying another missionary to go among the Jews and convert them to be Baptists! The absurdity of this cleansing of the outside of the platter was never more evident to me.

I went to visit a young returned soldier who was not religious and who was more attracted to anarchism. His wife was from another pueblo. It was Easter Sunday and I carried the baby for her as she hurried to mass;

her husband following later, and doing as most men did, standing outside. Each of the Indian women had a bright shawl over her head and a small woven rug as a protection from the splintered floor when kneeling.

Coming back home in my white dairy suit I met some Isleta Indian cowboys who good naturedly said "Hello St. John." I was to receive the appelation from another source years later but thought nothing of it then.

In writing my novel I had read much about Indians. I feel that the following poem expresses much of the spirit of the Navajos, whose waste lands stretch from west of town nearly to the Grand Canyon.

OLD SHAMAN

My son was killed in war against the whites
My son's son starved on their way to exile
The son of my son's son is at the white school
I would have taught him Navajo magic
Lightnings and thunders in the medicine-house
While bright noon waits outside;
Wonder of the Holy Corn, grown from kernal to ripe
Ear in a day;
Songs that bring sunrise and sunset to the sacred room.
No other of my blood will swallow great plumed arrows
And bathe in fire without hurt.
I am last to stand the long eagle feather on end,
Making it dance, a living thing.
None will come after me to see in the deeps of the
        hoganda water-bowl
All that was and is and will be.
The son of my son's son reads a book.
He counts one and two.

LILLIAN WHITE SPENCER

At work I was allowed the eggs I would gather from a certain nest and planned for an omelette one noon. As we came in from work we noticed a beautiful bull snake about six feet long stretched out across the road with three lumps rising in his middle. "There is your omelette," said my boss. In my reading of the Hopi I had learned that a snake is not by nature mean if handled carefully. There is a certain grace to its symmetrical winding beauty. I picked the snake up gently, wet my fingers, stroked him, so as not to irritate his scales, and placed him over in the field where he could digest my three eggs in his own good time.

Another time when I entered my adobe house I noticed my coat which was hanging on a chair, moving. There was no wind, and looking closely I saw a large bull snake wound around the inside of my coat collar and in my inside pocket. I stroked him and took him outside. But ever afterward I looked in my sleeping bag when I went to bed.

The night before Christmas there was a celebration in the schoolhouse given by neighboring Mexicans. Some of the young folks who had picked apples with me asked me over. It was called "Santo Nino de Atocha," The Holy Child of Nazareth. Several dozen Mexicans, young and old of both sexes and gaily dressed, sang and danced a short shuffle dance for three hours or more. Special songs were written for this performance whose theme was that the Holy Child had been stolen. It was a song of the Comanche Indians who were hunting for the Child. In the midst of the song someone stole the doll in a crib by the altar. Much of the procession broke up and went from door to door in the village looking for the Holy Child which had disappeared. They know, of course, where it was all along and finally found it and whipped the thief in exaggerated gestures, bringing back the Infant. Then all present went on their knees to the front, placing money in a dish by the Infant. I gave a dime to the smallest girl dancer. One verse told of the time when there was a drought and the Comaches took their children to Santa Fe and sold them as slaves to the white men for sugar and coffee. The old timers here said that this was really true.

One of the Santo nino de atocha verses

> El comanche y le comacha
> Salieron para Santa Fe
> a vender los comanchites
> Por azucar y cafe.

> The Comache men and women
> Went to Santa Fe
> To sell the little Comaches
> For sugar and coffee.

Soon afterwards I asked some young folks where I could get a translation of the verses and they directed me across the road. I knocked at the door and who should greet me but the small girl to whom I had given a dime. She squealed in delight and called her mother. In this manner I found my new friend, 7-year-old Louise Aguilar. In the six months that followed I was a daily visitor and played games with her, or she and her aunts came to my cottage for "huevos"; as they liked the change from beans to eggs. When her young aunt was married I was the only "Anglo" invited to the wedding supper. They knew I did not drink beer or wine but insisted that I have plenty of chili. My throat burned and the tears came at this hot food and they all had much fun at my discomfort. Several years later I visited in Los Angeles and tried to find my small Louise but they had moved again.

One of the last people I met at the pueblo was the elder son of the former chief. He was over thirty-eight when drafted for World War II. In camp he refused to drill, saying he was not going across the water to fight for the white man. His captain asked him if he did not want to fight for his country. He replied that his country was Isleta; that it was nothing the white man had given the Indians, but was only a small bit that they had not stolen. The captain was impressed and asked more questions. He found that this Indian had always fought the Indian Bureau schemes; that he wanted the rich Indian to hire help to clean the irrigation ditches instead of making the poor Indian do it for nothing; and for this reason he was drafted away from the pueblo where he could not bother the exploiters. His father had been fooled or bribed into giving the names of all of the Indian youth eligible for the draft. If he had put up a fight the matter might have been dropped, for the Indians are not citizens.

On trips with my employer I went up the beautiful Jemez River and saw the Jemez Indians. Meanwhile I had corresponded for years with the Hopi conscientious objectors and decided to find work in Arizona in order to be nearer them.

Rose Hennacy, Dan Kutchongva, the author, Thomas Banycya, Joe Craigmyle, my mother.

CHAPTER 6.

Life at Hard Labor
The Hopi

July, 1947 - 1949

Phoenix - San Francisco

I met Chester Mote, my Hopi conscientious objector friend, in Winslow on the third of July of 1947. I had looked for work on farms but could not find any; likewise in Flagstaff. I had just enough money left to get to a suburb of Phoenix, Glendale, with a penny left in my pocket.

Chester told me of an old Catholic priest who had spent many hours talking to his father years ago. He was a good man but Chester cared for no other missionary. The Hopi believe in God just as the white man does, he said, but their God does not tell them to go to war. The Hopi are not sun worshippers. When they look at the sun they think of God, just as the Christians are supposed to look at the Cross and think of God, (but they think of money, Chester thought.)

All tradition is handed down, not written. When Chester was a child he was told that the white man had gone across the water to war twice, and that the next war would be when other white men would come across the water to the white man and give him what he had handed out. When this war was finished there would be but one man and one woman left in the world. This was not meant literally. There would be many, here and there, but each couple would think that they were the only ones left.

Chester had 400 sheep and the government wanted him to reduce the flock to 40. He would not do so and was put in the jail in Keams Canyon for three months. They killed all of his sheep and gave him a check in payment but he refused to accept this blood money. It hurt their book-keeping minds. Later when the Hopi were drafted for war, they were told that if they registered they would be deferred as CO's. The Hopi did not believe the white men but decided to try them out. So all of them who were radicals decided to refuse to register but Chester registered. All of them got the same time in prison.

I walked around that morning asking for work at each farm. Around noon a Japanese farmer gave me as much watermelon as I could eat. Later on I ate some peaches at another farm, and ended up by eating cantaloupe. Just about dark I met a young Molokon who had read my Tolstoy "THOU SHALT NOT KILL" booklet, while in conscientious objector camp. I put my sleeping bag under the trees in his yard. Next day I worked for his uncle in the harvesting of beet seed. It was very hot and I drank plenty of water and had only melon for breakfast. After three days I worked on a farm in the middle of the desert cleaning ditches for ten hours a day, at sixty cents an hour. Then I walked for miles seeking another job. Finally I got a job in a dairy. After I had worked two months, the farmer sold his cows, so I had to look for another job.

I slept at the home of a friend in Phoenix and got up early before daylight, went down to the slave market at Second and Jefferson, and jumped on the first truck going out of town. I did not know if I was going east, west, north, or south. I worked in a field for a big produce company and at night asked where I could find a cabin to stay. Shacks were only for Mexicans and not for white men. I walked down the road and met a Molokon who said he had a shack up the road which I could live in, free of charge. I was soon sleeping on an old spring mattress. I got an old stove and fixed the place up.

I worked day by day for the produce company at sixty cents an hour. I worked at different kinds of weeding in the fields, and one Saturday the man across the road asked me to cut wood at seventy-five cents an hour.

One day I was working with an old man over seventy years of age. He was illiterate and when we signed our names to our checks he made an X mark. When he saw another fellow mark his check with an X he thought his signature was being forged. He asked me, "Have you got the mark of the beast?"

I knew what he meant by this question but asked him. "Has the gov'ment got your number; did you give them your name and get a number on a social security, ration or draft card? For if you did you have the mark of the beast which in these last days seeks to corrupt all of God's children."

I answered that I had used a social security card for three months, but since a tax had been withheld from my pay I had stopped working where it was necessary to have a social security card; that was the reason I was now working on a farm. I had used a ration card for a time, but had refused to register for the draft and did not intend to take any old age pension.

The old man answered; "I have nary a card. Guess they thought I was too old to register for the war and didn't bother me. All of my family made blood money during the war and now my wife and brothers have the mark of the beast again, for they accept old age pension. I will work until I drop before I take money from the beast; from the gov'ment that makes bombs!" And he added "Yes, in these days they number the babies in hospitals when they are born; get boys, and even girls, numbered up for war as they grow up; pester them with numbers when they die. The Mark of the Beast is everywhere. The Bible says that people will be divided, for folks who witness for the Lord can't be a part of numbering and voting and war. If their families prefer blood money then such as I have to go where we are not numbered and do not get The Mark of the Beast. I'm sure glad to find a fellow who only has two marks against him."

"You are a better man than I am," I answered.

Picking Cotton

Having a few free days after the winter lettuce season at the large vegetable ranch where I had worked I went early in the morning to Phoenix where the bonfires were burning, at Second and Madison. Here Mexicans, Indians and Anglos, most of the latter being "winos," were waiting to select the truck in which they would go to work. Just now there were only cotton trucks, there being a lull in citrus picking. Cotton pickers carry their own 8 to 12 ft. sacks, fastened with a strap around the shoulders and dragging behind them like a giant worm. There were eight trucks and several pick-ups. Most of them were shaped like the traditional covered wagon with canvas. There were benches on either side and in the middle. I walked around searching for someone I might know, but my friends of the lettuce fields were wary of cotton picking, considering this the hardest job to be had and one to be taken only as a last resort.

"Last call! Take you there and bring you back. Three dollars a hundred. All aboard gentlemen!" shouted a good-natured Negro in a bright mackinaw. The truck to which he pointed was box shaped, of wood veneer, with a short ladder leaning inside from the rear. I entered and found a seat between a colored woman and a colored man. After a few more calls the doors were shut, and we could see each other only as one would light a cigarette. Later on the truck stopped, and we were joined by a large group of laughing Negroes of all ages. There were three whites besides myself, and one Indian. Our destination was nine miles beyond Buckeye, which is about thirty miles west of Phoenix. After several sharp turns, when all in the truck were thrown this way and that, we came to the field. The Indian and I did not have sacks, so we rented them from the boss for a quarter. This was tall cotton, and harder to pick than the small variety. The field was a quarter of a mile long and a mile wide. A young white man worked in one row, then the Indian, then myself. I had never picked cotton before. The Indian, a Navajo, said this was to be clean picking, he understood. Where the cotton was fluffy it was easy to grab, but where the boll was partly open it was difficult to extract and hurt your fingers.

As we worked along the row from the far end of the field toward the weighing scales and truck, my Navajo friend said that he was learning a lesson which he sadly needed. Now he had just enough money from day to day. Before this he had spent money freely and never had to count his pennies. He paid a dollar a night for a cot in a cheap hotel in Phoenix. He had an older brother who had been quite wealthy before the depression and was a big shot among his people because of his holdings in cattle. Now with the "plowing under" and rationing system of the government he was a poor Indian indeed.

In speaking of the Navajo he said that they had always been poor in these last years, but that the suffering was no greater than last year. If left to themselves, they would be able to get along in sheep and cattle raising and in growing corn. But the government restrictions as to grazing made havoc with the Navajo. These restrictions came about because the best land was owned by the government and let out to wealthy white cattlemen. According to the government treaty, a school was to be provided wherever there were thirty children in a community; but not a fifth of the children were given schools. All this spare time made for shiftless living in the cities. The recent provision of half a million for food from Congress was coupled with three times that amount to "rehabilitate" the Navajo. This was another word for jobs for white bureaucrats to feed on the misery of the Indian with boondoggling experiments.

Navajos do not eat fish, bear, pork; in fact any animal that does not eat grass is not "clean" to them. They will not kill a coyote for the bounty, as do the whites.

After we had worked three hours, we took our cotton in to be weighed. I had thirty pounds and he had forty-two. The white men near us had eighty-five. In talking over this discrepency we found that we had been picking only the clean white cotton, while the more experienced pickers picked the bolls along with the cotton and more than doubled the weight.

As we waited our turn for weighing our cotton, groups were shooting dice in the roadway. A negro woman served coffee, chili, pie, weiners, etc. at reasonable prices. Some of the truck drivers sold food to their passengers.

Returning to the field we picked in more of an orthodox fashion, and in the total five and a half hours the Navajo picked eighty-two pounds and I picked sixty-two. Before we left I gave him the CW to read, with my letter about the Hopi refusing to go to war.

The next morning I met my Navajo friend beside the bonfire at Second and Madison. The truck of Negroes did not go out on Sunday. One truck took only those who had sacks. I got in a small pickup which headed westward about thirty miles to Litchfield Park. Several young girls kept us merry with songs. When we arrived at the field my Navajo friend arrived in another truck. We happened to get sacks at different times, so did not work together.

An old man said that the rule here was "rough picking," which meant everything that had white in it, but no stems or leaves. When I emptied my sack I had fifty-four pounds. The man next to me seemed to work rather expertly, and I asked him what time they quit on Sundays here. He replied that he only came on Sunday's. "Make $1.25 an hour at my job in town, and time and a half for overtime." I commented that unless a person had a large family that was a good wage. "I don't work here for the money," he continued. "I just come out here so I can keep sober. I was drunk from Christmas until yesterday—ten days. I can keep sober if I am working, but I can't stand to be quiet or loaf. And as I have eight kids, I have to keep working."

There was not much cotton left to pick in this field, and the word went around that we would quit about 2 p.m. At that time my sack weighed thirty-one pounds, which, after paying rental on my sack, netted me $2.23. My Navajo friend had not done so well, picking only sixty-eight pounds. He said he had liked my reference to the Hopi in the CW. As we were going into town in the truck the man who picked cotton to keep sober was discussing the merits of different brands of liquor with another picker. This man was telling of going to a town upon receiving a paycheck as a "gandy-dancer" on the railroad, going to the police and asking how much the fine was for being "drunk and disorderly." They said it was $17.50, so he paid it at once, for he intended to get drunk and disorderly.

I did not hear the rest of the story, for the truck soon passed lateral twenty, near where I lived. I proceeded homeward with $3.93 for two part-days spent in the cotton fields. Later in the day, sitting in my doorway resting, I was asked by a man who drove up in a car to work for him for a week, irrigating, at $7.20 per twelve-hour night. Gladly I was willing to let this two part-days of cotton picking suffice. Good pickers can make from $8 to $12 a day, but I was not in that class.

First Picketing

In May of 1948 the Freedom Train came to Phoenix. I felt that as they had invaded "my territory" I ought to say something about the lack of freedom for conscientious objectors, Negroes and Indians. I made some signs and went forth with CW's. About 5000 people were moving inch by inch in five crowded blocks. Shouts of "Communist," "How much does Stalin pay you?" etc. came at me. "Hello, you Communist s.o.b." said one man. My reply was "I'm not that kind of a s.o.b." The crowd laughed and no one was hurt.

Toward the afternoon the American Legion was handing out copies of a forty-eight page comic book put out by Catholic fascists calling names at the Communists. I felt a surge of hatred towards me. One man came up and said "I could knock you down." I answered quickly "You have the right to knock me down and I have the right to picket: that makes us even." Many students asked me questions. An ex-chief of police asked me what I was trying to do and I said that I was trying to prove this was a free country.

About 7 p.m. the police stopped me and said the police captain wanted to see me. After a crowd had gathered and I waited he said that the captain had changed his mind, so I continued my picketing. Later a Franciscan priest told me that the police had phoned him at 7 p.m. that evening asking about my picketing and giving out the CW. He told them that the CATHOLIC WORKER was a good paper and this was a free country so why were they arresting me. The next Sunday he praised my picketing, at mass, in the big St. Mary's church and we became good friends. He had spoken at the Freedom Train but I had not seen him.

When I was sixteen years of age, I had written a page entitled WHAT LIFE MEANS TO ME. I had used this title because my favorite author, Jack London, had written a pamphlet with that title. The substance of my belief in 1916 was: On with the Revolution; there is no God. Churches are opium for the people.

Now on June 1, 1948 I wrote a page listing my attitude on life. Following are the issues that seemed to me most important:

(1) *Courage* is the most important virtue, for, as Johnson said to Boswell, if you do not have it you cannot practice the other virtues.

(2) *Voluntary Poverty,* the fundamental means of the Catholic Worker and Tolstoy, keeps the radical from becoming bourgeois and selling out.

(3) *Pacifism and the Sermon on the Mount* I had learned in solitary and they provided a basis for a worthwhile personal life and for a philosophy upon which to meet all other social problems.

(4) *Anarchism* is the negative side, but necessary to keep one from the treadmill of politics.

(5) *Decentralization* is needed, of course, so that the above principles might work to best advantage.

(6) *Vegetarianism,* which includes no drinking, ·smoking, gambling or medicine, is necessary to live healthily and to be efficient; otherwise with one hand you are pulling one way and with the other hand you are pulling the other way. Keep well.

(7) *Reincarnation* seems a more reasonable theory than the heaven and hell of orthodoxy, although it may be just a deferred heaven that we have to earn.

Tax Trouble

A while before this I had been called to the tax office and told that I should pay something down on my bill. I replied that I did not intend to pay anything, as per my notice to them. The tax man was a Catholic veteran who thought I was a Communist. He said that I would have to go to jail if I did not pay. I told him that I had been there before and was willing to go again.

"Do you think you are right and every one else is wrong?" he asked. "Just about!" was my quick reply. "How could that be?" he queried. "I already have figured it out; it is up to you to figure it out," I replied. "What kind of a country would we have if everyone thought like you?" he asked. "We would have a fine country; no government; no war; no tax man; no police; everyone living according to Christ and the Sermon on the Mount!" was my answer. At this he became angry and said "If you don't like this country why don't you go back to Russia?" "I like this country; it is my country; I want to stay here and fight you fellows who are trying to spoil it," I replied quickly, "and besides I don't speak Russian."

At that time I was working for the big produce company so the tax man said he would garnishee $10 of my wages each week to pay for my taxes due. I told him I had quit my job. He wanted to know when, and I told him "just now" in order that he could not garnishee my wages. He wanted to know where I would work tomorrow and I told him that I did not know yet; that God would see that I got work.

When I first came to Phoenix I received a letter which had been written to me in Albuquerque from an atheist who had bought a CW from me in 1941. He was in Phoenix and I went to see him the next day, and started to work in a date grove where he lived and worked part time. So my propaganda work for the CW lead directly to a job which I needed just then.

About this time, the Bank of Douglas, in Phoenix, had an ad in the paper telling of old times in Arizona and showing a picture of the I.W.W.'s being deported from Bisbee in 1916. I wrote to Frank Brophy, the President of the bank, asking why he, a parasite, had the audacity to slander good I.W.W.'s. I mentioned the CW and my activity with it. He was not sure about his information on the I.W.W. and he already knew of the CW. We met and became good friends.

The Old Pioneer

"Hennacy, fellows like you remind me of Arnold Winkelreid 600 years ago when, 'in arms the Austrian phalanx stood; a living wall, a human wood . . . he ran with arms extended wide as if a dearest friend to embrace' and by his brave death made an opening for his followers to rout the tyrants who sought to enslave the Swiss. The only difference today is that your sacrifice is almost useless for you have no followers and Winkelreid had enough to break the Austrian line."

Thus spoke the Old Pioneer, Lin Orme, one of my employers, as I was on my knees in the hot Arizona sun sawing a tree which had fallen in the driveway. He knew that I had quit a good job for this "Life at Hard Labor" that I had sentenced myself to when I chose to work at day jobs. I replied that my work was not that of an organizer but of a Sower to sow the seeds. If people preferred death and payment of taxes for their own destruction that was their lookout.

Mr. Orme had been head of the Parole Board of the State for 14 years and was now President of the huge Water Users Association which furnished water and power to Central Arizona outside the big cities. In 1916 he was a member of the Rotary Club in Phoenix when the I.W.W.'s were driven out of Bisbee. He resigned from the Club in protest over their approval of this outrage, saying, "If they can drive I.W.W.'s out of Bisbee they can drive Ormes out of Phoenix."

I had worked for him off and on and now he invited me to live in a three room cottage to the left of his house. It was back from the road and quiet. Only an oil lamp, but there was running water. I got the rent free in order that I would give him first chance on my employment, such as mowing his lawn, chopping wood, cutting weeds, etc.

He was not a Catholic, but was a nominal Episcopalean who did not go to church. He was also head of the Old Pioneer Association and appreciated the ideas of Jefferson and his life on the land. His 160 acre farm was rented out to the big company I had first worked for. He knew of my radical ideas and read the CW.

Dates

"The bourgeois get the cream for a thousand years. The time will come when there will be a change," spoke my Yugo-Slav fellow worker, quoting his grandfather in Yugoslavia, as we hewed the jungle of offshoots around the date trees.

"And now Tito has given the peasants the land," he continued. "In my home town when the Nazis came to kill the Partisans the village priest pointed in the opposite direction from which they had gone, but the big priests stood always with the landowners and bourgeois."

"Leo, you talk like a Communist," I remarked.

"Maybe in Yugoslavia I be a Communist," he replied, "but not in this country. I hear Bob Minor speak in Phoenix and he gave good talk and I raise my hand and give a ten dollar bill in the collection, and also a ten dollar bill for my friend who has no money with him. But I find the Communists in this country are chickenhearted. I have a friend who talks communism and one day another friend, a Hindu rancher, heard him and said, 'You been in jail?' The answer was 'no' 'Then you are no Communist; you are a bourgeois,' the Hindu said."

Leo was an expert who knew how to place the huge wedge to dislocate the shoot without spoiling the roots. These date shoots were set out according to variety, and were watered twice a week. There were about 800 in all that we removed from the sides of the big date trees and they would sell from $2 to $6 each.

The man who had left when I commenced to work at the date grove had already tied male pollen in each of the from 8 to 16 bunches of potential dates in the female trees. Three male trees furnished all the male pollen needed and some was sold to other growers who lacked pollen. My job for the next month or more was to saw off limbs that were dead or in the way of picking later on, and to tie each bunch to a limb above, with wire, in order that it would not become too heavy and break. I also clipped out every other string of dates—they were now the size of a pea, thus giving the tree strength to make larger dates of those remaining. Although I cut off thousands of "ice picks" I found later when picking dates that there was always a stray one to pierce my hand or arm at an unexpected time. Some of the trees needed a ladder extended 20 feet and others were younger and smaller. The big ones were 28 years old.

Much of my time in August was spent in putting paraffined cloth bags over the new large bunches of dates. This was so that June bugs and birds would not destroy them, also in case it rained they would not become wet and spoil. The dates ripen a few at a time. Generally the ones most exposed to the sun ripen first, although a few on the hot inside of the huge bunch would also ripen. The bag was slipped over the top and the whole bunch explored from beneath for ripe dates which were put in a small basket and then emptied into wire trays that were carried three at a time to the date room to be sorted and then placed in cold storage until the tourist trade came in November. This date picking began the first day of September. A canvas was placed under the tree to catch.the dates that would fall. All over-ripe or mashed dates were supposed to be placed in one corner of the tray to be used for date-butter. However, most pickers threw these mashed dates out of sight in the grass rather than bother with them. Here I was paid 62½ cents an hour, although in most groves pickers were paid so much per pound.

Christmas morning was cloudy but no rain as yet, so I picked the scattered dates on a few palms. From about Dec. 10 to 20 was a busy time with the dates. My job was to pack the processed dates in containers holding a pound and cover them with cellophane kept in place with a rubber band. If packed too far ahead they would dry out. These were shipped in special containers by customers who bought them for friends in the north and east. The best eating dates were those which could not be shipped. They were brought as needed from the cold storage room. The nice dates you pay a good price for in the stores are generally processed with gas and are therefore not so pure as the ones which may appear wrinkled but have been processed with more natural heat.

"Nonsense, you can't 'catch cold' any more than you can 'catch hot'," said my boss at the date grove when informed that a fellow worker had not come to work because he had "caught cold." This boss is a vegetarian and the fine dinners which are my portion each noon I work there are something to write home about.

Carrots

Early one spring morning, having no work in the date grove or for the Old Pioneer where I live, I walked down the lateral. I went toward the carrot field of the big company for whom I had worked before the tax man caused me to quit in order not to have my wages garnisheed for my share toward the Bomb. This carrot work was piece work and workers were paid as the crates of carrots were filled, so I would have no trouble with Caesar today. Soon my Basque friend picked me up in his truck. Even then I was late, for scores of Mexican families were singing, laughing and working. Around the holidays and later when I worked for this same company cutting lettuce and broccoli at Deer Valley in the sandy ground on the edge of the desert, I had passed the Navajo village and noticed the brightly colored velvet of the Indians as they tied carrots. A friend who had been in the store at noon noticed that the grocer charged a Navajo more for the same article. I had noticed this practice among grocers in the deep south 25 years ago when Negroes purchased anything.

A mechanical digger went ahead and loosened the carrots. The foreman gave me a "claim," a space three rows wide and thirty steps long. I pulled up the carrots and laid them in a row. I was checked out with four bundles of wire covered with tough paper, which cost 4c a bundle and was used to tie 4 to 8 carrots in a bunch, depending upon the size. Larger carrots were put in one crate and medium ones in another. Crooked, broken, small, or deformed carrots were discarded. Farmers came and got them by the truck load for their cattle, free of charge. (Truck loads of culls were also hauled away in the lettuce, celery, cauliflower and broccoli fields where I had worked. Mormon farmers can much of this waste and make juice from grapefruit and orange culls and trade all this for apples and other waste products from Utah, the church in Salt Lake City paying the freight. Other people could do the same thing, but it seems that they would rather hold revival meetings and play bingo. I mentioned this idea of using culls to several priests but they were not interested.)

By noon I had five crates full, which netted me $1.04, after paying for my wire. Then because of the heat (which was around 95 and would wilt the carrots) we had three hours for lunch and came back and worked until dark. Here the carrots were of a good size, but the next day there were too many small ones and it was difficult to make time. The Mexican parents bought soda pop and ice cream at 10c for their children without any coaxing. The children played but when they worked they worked fast and got much done. Several families of Anglos were working in the field and there was a continual harangue on the part of the parents to get their children to work. They made more commotion than the whole field of Mexicans and were the only ones who cursed their children. In three and a half days I made $8.48 and did not go back to get my last 96c, as I had work the next day at the date grove and on my way home saw that the carrot crew had disbanded. Mexican families with a dozen working could make $30 or more in a day, but for a slow, single man like myself the only value in such work was a deflation of the ego.

Every Monday morning I walked four miles down the road to hoe for a farmer. I noticed the same men in the same cars passing me on their way to town, but they never offered to give me a lift. I never met any one else walking. For a few days I hoed maize for a farmer. I worked with a family from Oklahoma. This farmer was away on a vacation for several Sundays so I got up before daylight and milked his five cows before going to Phoenix to sell CW's near Catholic churches. For several Saturdays a young Mexican boy and I dug out and sawed tamerind trees that were interfering with nearby buildings. This was for the Old Pioneer.

Time and piece work

In all of the farm work that I have done this problem comes up. In one lettuce field that I know of the men were paid so much a row to thin the lettuce. The work had to be done over four times as it was not done thoroughly at any time. Most workers if paid by the hour would loaf and soldier on the job. Yet I worked for one farmer who gave me such weedy rows to hoe that I was really paid but 25 cents per hour, although he had promised to pay extra for these bad rows and did not do so. Another time we were paid $1.50 a row, but when more men came the next day for this good wage the boss laughingly said "supply and demand" and cut the rate to a dollar, although the rows were much more difficult. It is necessary to hoe large fields in a short time in order that they can be irrigated again. Thus large crews are necessary to do the work and a foreman cannot watch all of the men all of the time. One employer who paid low wages said it was difficult to get a worker whose mind was concerned with the work all of the time. Did he want both mind and body for $5 a day? Aside from the natural greed of the bourgeois one reason for the importing of Mexican Nationals was the difficulty of getting sober white men by calling for them at daylight at the slave market in Phoenix. With employers passing a "Right to Work" law in Arizona and church authorities refusing to back up labor it would seem that the worker should not worry about the work problems of the boss. I see no solution of this problem under capitalism. At Tempe the other Sunday a very old priest who was visiting asked me to explain this "Right to Work" Bill. I did not know very much about it in detail and as I hesitated the priest said: "Are the bankers for it? If it is good for them then it is no good for me. That's the way to tell about it." We both laughed then for we knew the bankers were for it.

The small farmer seems to have the same vice of greed that the big corporation has as a reason for existence, but without the efficiency of the latter.

In September in the midst of date picking I was called to interview my third revenue officer at the Post Office. This man, unlike the other two, who had been courteous, was a go-getter. He wanted to know if I really meant that I would not pay my income tax; that this was a very serious matter. I agreed with him that it was a serious matter to help pay for the war and the Bomb. He felt that I did not do my share in helping the government; that I got all the gravy. I told him that as a Christian Anarchist I had no share in the government, for I did not vote, accept subsidies, pensions, social security or ration benefits from the government, nor call upon the police, believing rather in turning the other cheek. He asked for the names of my employers saying that as long as I lived in his district he would get the tax money. I suggested that he follow me around in my daily hunt for a job and see just how much "gravy" I was getting. He jumped up and said it made him angry to talk to a fellow like me. Unlike the tax man contacted by my friend Caleb Foote, who felt no personal responsibility of right and wrong and compared himself to his desk, this man gave quite a bit of energy to a defense of the war system. (Caleb was head of the FOR in Berkeley, California; went to prison as a conscientious objector.) The head tax man here is a Quaker. No one *has* to be a hangman; no one *has* to be a taxman. The next day I mailed this tax man a letter explaining in detail my ideas and also marked a copy of the CW. In over two months I have not heard from him but the red tape of bureaucracy moves slowly.

In early November, lettuce harvesting is commencing. I live in the midst of hundreds of acres of lettuce but the big company for whom I previously worked is hiring mostly Mexican Nationals by the week. Until they hire men by the day I can have no work in the lettuce. I took a cotton bus west to the cotton fields on election day. I did not make much: only $1.88, as they quit work to vote at 2 p.m. The next day I missed the cotton bus and walked 11 miles until I found a field in which I could work. I did a little better. Several fellow workers wanted to know how I voted. I told them that I voted every day practicing my ideals against war and the capitalist system which caused war, and did not bother to choose between the rival warmongers who sought to run the country. Each day that week it happened that I got a different cotton truck. The next Monday I disced and harrowed in wheat and alfalfa with a blind mule and a deaf mule for the Old Pioneer. (The mules belonged to a neighbor a mile down the road who loaned them to us). The next day I rode 40 miles west, beyond Buckeye, to a cotton field. I was the only white worker among Negroes. Here the cotton was of fine quality and I earned $4.30.

In a few days I learned to pick cotton with both hands and reasonably fast so that by the end of the week I was picking 200 pounds and making $6.00. I bought a 12-foot canvas sack rather than rent one each day for 25 cents. While a sack will hold 100 pounds I found that to put 65 pounds in it was enough to carry up the ladder and dump in the truck. Time went fast in the open air. I walked the two miles to the highway by 6 a.m. and stood with my cotton sack over my shoulders in the dark so the cotton truck would not miss me. In the truck it was chilly, and each of us was wrapped like a mummy in his sack and wobbled like a pin in the bowling alley when the truck swerved corners or hit bumps. In the center of the truck was a dish pan with sticks of wood burning and smoking. If we ever were upset we would all burn before we could get untangled from our cotton-sack-cocoon. By 10 a.m. I had taken off my shirt and coat and tied them around my waist in the fashion in the fields. One morning I thought I was doing fine as I was keeping up with the man next to me. Looking closer I saw that he was doing two rows to my one and did not seem to work any harder. The man who weighed the cotton and who paid us before we emptied it in the truck was paid by the farmer to supervise the work. He received so much per picker also for bringing us to the field. His mother cooked and sold soda pop. One evening as we were riding home we stopped for groceries in Buckeye. Moving on homeward a young Negro was drinking two cans of beer, being kidded meanwhile by an older Negro who was a teetotaler, and who at the same time was eating a pie and a huge ring of sausage. The young Negro remarked that he had a cold, and never seeming to have heard of starving a cold, he had eaten 7 hamburgers, a bowl of chili, 6 soda pops, a bottle of milk, and now this beer. He did not come to work the next day.

The next day I missed this truck and rode 50 miles near Arlington to a desert cotton ranch which employed none but white people. The man next to me in the truck had recently come from California and said that after a strike last year cotton pickers were now receiving $4 and $4.50 a hundred there. There the union allowed all races to belong. In the packing sheds here I am told that no good paying job is given to a Negro or a Mexican. As we passed a church this man said: "These folks are just playing at church, same as lots of unions just play. They don't mean business or we woudn't be in the fix we all are." Here the cotton was not as easy picking and I only made $4.26. They did not pay by the day but when the truck was full of cotton, so I will have to go that 100 miles again to get my pay. (Later I discovered this is a common trick and that most people never did get their pay.) It is generally 7 p.m. by the time I get home. One effect of this work is the enjoyment of a rest at night.

"There's only one way the poor class of folks can beat this system," said the poor tubercular Oakie as we shivered together on the cotton truck on a dull February morning.

"What is that?" I asked.

":I could take my wife and six kids; rent me a few acres in Arkansas away from the main highway; get me a mule, a cow and an old sow, and no one could boss me and starve me like they do now. I did it once, and I'll do it again one of these days if I ever get away from this damned desert."

"I agree with you. Many professors have written books about just that way of life but few have gone back to the land," I answered.

"Folks hereabouts was talking the other day of breaking in the stores to get something to eat. But I told them they are beat before they start at that game. Got to get back to the land. That's what I told them, but they didn't want to get too far away from the dime stores, shows and taverns," he continued as we came to the cotton field.

This field had been picked over before and now just the bolls here and there that had been missed and the few that had matured late were left. The Oakie went one way and I worked next to two young Negroes. We snapped off the bolls and all the visible cotton, and went half a mile, two rows at a time, before we were back to the truck. I had but thirty-six pounds and when the girl paid me I found that 2¢ a pound was the rate instead of 3¢. I mentioned this to one of the Negroes as we were picking and he said:

"Lucky we gets the 2¢. The other day they gave us slips of paper and told us to come the next day if it didn't rain and they would have the money. I told them to go to hell with such paper; I wanted something that got me my eats and I walked off the field. But most of the others stayed on for they had families."

This reminded me that I still had the slips for $4.18 for cotton I had picked in November at the Jim Crow ranch, fifty miles away, in the desert beyond Arlington. The Negro went to eat some lunch and his row was taken by a husky white man who had lost his job in a laundry when his boss had sold the plant in Phoenix. One of his sisters had married a Church of the Brethren man so he was receptive to my conversation about Conscientious Objectors and nonpayment of taxes for war. Here the cotton was a little thicker and when we came back to the truck I had 72 pounds.

"Got to watch these belly robbers. They'll doctor up the scales and cheat you of half the cotton. The other day I picked around 100 pounds and the weighman said he was only paying for 50 as he was not making much money on this second grade cotton. I wonder what the hell he thought I was making. I didn't like it but I stayed for the day, but did not go back the next day."

"Yes," I replied, "I heard the fellows at the fire by the curb, as we waited for the truck this morning, talking about a cotton contractor who 'short-weighed and ticket-paid' the pickers and made a thousand dollars a month from poor folks as poor as he had been a month before."

He wanted to know if I was a Witness. I told him that I belonged to no church, for each one prayed more and did less than the other. I mentioned about the Oakie who had wanted to go back to the land and he replied that he was sorry he had gone out for day work for he had had more real income and satisfaction on the land. He spoke of several relatives who had made from $50 to $100 a week all during the war in war work. When they had lost their jobs they went to live with his old father who had but $70 cash income a year but always had his cellar full of something to eat from what he had raised on the land.

"You can't farm in this commercial valley though. Takes too much for machinery and if you lose a crop through lack of water, bugs, or poor prices, then the big company grabs your land for what they want to give. Have to get in the sticks," he added with a smile, "away from the places where you think you have to spend money."

We then discussed unions, radical organizations, churches, and the different methods of making a better world. The aim of the Brotherhood of Man and the Fatherhood of God was there but so many things interferred to make us all forget it. All these organizations came first and we forgot our aim.

"And the more noise, the more traffic and the more big whirring machinery, the more we seem to forget that the man next to us is our brother. I know folks back home in the country who never saw a city who feud like all blazes though, so it isn't only *where* you are or *what* you do that counts; it must be what you have inside," my friend said as we quit for the day. He had picked 130 pounds and I had picked 111. It was 4 p.m., and as he lived down my way I pocketed my $2.22 and rode with him eastward. On the way we saw some men forking cauliflower culls into trucks for their cattle, and stopped to get some culls. But they were all gone and only the leaves that were cut from the top of the box as they were packed were left.

One morning I had gone down the highway to wait for the first bus to Coldwater, where I had heard they took on cotton pickers. I had previously asked the colored family on the corner, with whom I had worked, and they said that cotton trucks did not come by on this highway since the holidays. The trucks in town only picked up regular customers and did not bother with the slave market at second and Jefferson in Phoenix. A young driver of a milk truck which bore the sign "no riders" picked me up before daylight and took me toward Coldwater. His first pickup was way beyond Buckeye. After a time we noticed people gathered by the side of the road, and stopping, we saw a motorcycle tangled up against a telephone pole and a young man whose brains were scattered over the ground. Later we found out that he had worked nights irrigating and by some mishap—perhaps being sleepy—had swerved across the road and had been killed as he came home from work. It was not yet daylight. The driver of the milk truck wondered why he stayed here for $75 a week when he had left a $125 a week job in Ohio. And the work of lifting heavy cans of milk on the truck was strenuous. I remembered in 1943 in Albuquerque, when I had swung cans of milk onto a truck for a farmer where I worked. One morning a new truck came for the milk which was an inch higher than the one previously used, and I could not adjust my swing of the can to this higher level for half an hour. It looks easy to swing these cans. One sturdy driver picked up a full can of milk in each hand and held them out at arms length, but he was an exception.

When I got off the truck a mile beyond Coldwater I waited for an hour. A farmer was discing with his tractor. I refused offers of half a dozen lifts as I wanted to be sure to arrive at a cotton field. A young fellow who was walking along told me that a corner, a mile east, was where trucks picked up cotton workers. I had met the Baptist preacher of this small town at a recent Fellowship of Reconciliation meeting. He was a subscriber to the CW and liked Ludlow's articles especially. I had brought several pieces of pacifist literature along. In case there was not work I would visit with this preacher.

Coming to the fire built along the curb for the prospective workers to keep warm while waiting for a truck, which fire consisted of an old tire burning and smoking, I discussed the prospects of work with young and old, male and female, white, colored, and Mexican who were there. One burly, middle-aged man in a bright mackinaw came with his bedroll over his shoulder, a small package of clothing, and a three-cell lantern in his hand.

"Can't leave this stuff laying around. Folks will rob me. Damn working class is their own worst enemy," he muttered as we stood with our backs to the fire.

"You talk like a Wob," I said to him.

"Joined up with them during the free speech fight in Fresno in 1910. But after the war they lost that old fighting spirit. Couldn't beat them when they sang the old 'Pie in the Sky' song, but now nobody sings. Have to keep moving these days to beat all the rules and regulations the master class try to enslave a fellow with," he answered.

Joe Mueller, who had done three years in Sandstone with my friend Bill Ryan, came down from Chicago soon after Christmas and is staying with me. For the first time in eight years there has been a wet season in Arizona. I had but a day now and then chopping wood for the Old Pioneer, so when we saw an ad in the paper asking for cotton pickers we picked out a bright day in between rains and hiked ten miles north on lateral 14. We passed the Navajos in Deer Valley as they squatted in the carrot fields waiting until the carrot digger got out of the mud enough to prepare the way for their work. We saw three crews of cauliflower workers in a field but knew there was no opportunity for a day's work. The view of the mountains to the north and east was magnificient and well worth the hike. As we saw what we thought ought to be the advertised cotton ranch a couple in a very ancient car who were looking for the same work picked us up and we four came to the ranch. We were informed that the cotton was picked several weeks before and they had forgotten to take the ad out of the paper. We rode back with our friends to the bus line and on into Phoenix where we got some groceries, and books at the library.

The night after I had made the $2.22 picking cotton it rained. The field boss had said not to come to work if it rained, for then the cotton would weigh more and he might get cheated instead of cheating us. So the next day I sawed wood into appropriate lengths for our small stove and Joe split it, for although it is mild here in the winter a fire is needed on rainy days. The next day we got up early and walked down the lateral by daylight, getting the bus to Coldwater. No one was here at the corner yet, so we collected some paper and wood. Just then two chunky good-natured Negro women came up with their cotton sacks and we all started the fire. As the flames leaped up a dozen or more potential cotton pickers emerged from the nearby alleys and shacks. Trucks of Mexicans and Negroes whizzed by from Phoenix destined away beyond Buckeye it seemed, but the drivers did not glance toward us. One lanky red-faced, bleary-eyed and slobbery-mouthed individual danced around the fire and in jerky pantomine acted out this story he was telling:

"There is a certain kind of bullet and it only fits into a certain kind of a gun. When a fellow shoots with it just like this then he turns into a dog right away and a big bird comes and picks him up and carries him away and eats him as he carries him. Now if they only made more guns like that . . ."

"Have another drink of muscatel! Get a soapbox! I don't want to listen to such silly stuff. Get a soapbox, I say," spoke up an unshaven man by the fire. He of the imagination saw a truck stop for the two Negro women and ran over and jumped on. We saw him hanging onto it as it disappeared.

"No use of going on that truck. They just pick what cotton lays on the ground—can't make more than 70¢ a day," remarked the man of the unshaven countenance and continued, "Last night the chief of police knocked on my window and wanted to know my name. I told him to get the hell away; that I didn't care for his kind: and did he go!"

A huge fat man with whom I had picked cotton in November winked at me as we listened to this braggadocio. He told of an ad the day before asking for 300 women to sew parachutes in nearby Goodyear. When hundreds of applicants arrived they sorted them out and hired 25, which was all they wanted in the first place. Any who were over 30 or under 20 or weighed more than 120 pounds were not wanted. He added:

"A fat woman I know who is about my size and has had thirty years experience in sewing could not get a look in there. Getting so people's got to be all one size and one age, and I suppose pretty soon they'll want them to all look just alike."

A farmer came along in a car and picked up two women who had worked for him before. This was all he wanted. Joe had been talking to a young man who lived in a shack for which he paid $30 a month. He received a soldier's pension of $90 a month so life was not quite so tough for him as for many others. My Oakie friend told of his wife giving the last of their food the other night to a big man who asked for a handout. After he had eaten he explained that he had been on a drunk and spent his $70 pension and would now have to mooch until his next check came. The Oakie had been in the store the day before and a poor woman with two small children asked for bread, saying she had nothing to eat for today and there was no cotton to pick because of the rain. The storekeeper (who charged from 10% to 30% too much anyway) had answered that he was not running any relief and would not help her.

It was now after 9 a.m. and no trucks came. People drifted away slowly. I asked where the bridge was that went over the Salt River to the Pima Reservation, intending to visit my Pima friend Martin with whom I had worked in the lettuce last year. There was a bridge at lateral 20 I was told, so Joe and I walked down that way. After a few miles one young fellow who had been standing around the fire drove by and stopped, giving us a ride for the remaining four miles to lateral 20. He spoke about not liking to stand around a fire with colored folks and remarked about how he would like to shoot one just as well as to look at one. We did not ask him how many notches he had on his mythical gun but tried to insert a word against such bigotry, but doubt if it did much good. We walked toward the river for a few miles and finally came to a dead end road. It seemed that the bridge was two miles up on lateral 22 and another bridge below at lateral 17 and no one we spoke to knew just where the Reservation was located. So we walked back toward home, stopping to pull a few carrots and sugar beets from the fields for our dinner.

We met some Oakies clustered around a woodpile in their yard enjoying the sun. One boy was wielding an ax and the father rested, snuggled a few inches away against a log, much as cartoons depict certain long whiskered hill billies. The subject of continued rain here and snow further north came up. One young man remarked that it wasn't fair to drop food to the Indians while the white ranchers got nothing. How much he knew of white ranchers was another thing. The inference seemed to be that no airplanes dropped anything near this particular woodpile. All the poor kid knew was depression and war so for him to think of an All Time Santa Claus was understandable.

Nearing home we were picked up by a colored man, partly Indian, whom I had known before when he came to visit me in my cabin last winter when he was irrigating near the Molokon's where I lived. He was, as he described it. "A Witness, for they gives and they don't take, and they are not Jim Crow."

At this time there were articles over the country about migrant workers starving out at Coldwater and nearby Avondale. I had been through these settlements in a truck on my way to the cotton fields and had talked to many who lived there. The starving children spoken of was not an exaggeration. Now that there has been the publicity the Red Cross came; barbers offered free haircuts; and the county hired a doctor by the month to attend to the cotton pickers especially. The little corner stores have slot machines and charge awful prices. The big companies import Mexican labor which is steady and of course much cheaper. All authorities deny this and say that only Mexican Nationals come when no local help can be gotten. But we all know this is a lie. The camp manager should have reported about the starving children but his job was to collect rents. A truck with huge cans of hot soup would help, but there is little chance of getting a CW house started here as long as I cannot get a Catholic to help me sell CW's.

Eloy

"Pick clean, there, men, or else weigh in and go home," said the foreman to a hundred of us who were scratching our hands and faces and tearing our clothing searching out the scarce cotton that the $8,000 mechanical cotton picker had not "picked clean." This machine had bent the tall brittle cotton stalks sideways so it was impossible not to be torn by them. It had also scattered loose cotton on the ground which we were supposed to entangle from twigs and pack in our long twelve foot sack which dragged behind us from the hitch over our shoulder like a giant worm.

Experienced cotton pickers sought out those rows which had the most cotton. The foreman being wise to this had told a few of us to finish some short rows first. When he had gone back to the truck to rest his big body, some of the more decrepit winos had started rows but deserted them and had taken their bottles under a tree. We who had begun our rows to the left of them now found ourselves in the midst of unpicked cotton on both sides. Hence, in part, the rage of the foreman who raced after the winos.

Phoenix prices for picking cotton had been $3.50 a hundred pounds; 50¢ more than before. A good picker in good cotton might make $14 in a day, but "following up the damn machine," as the fellows said, at $2.50 a hundred was the devil's own work — and a better way to deflate one's ego than with liquor I would say. Sure don't feel high and mighty at the end of the day. Regular farm wages had increased from 60¢ an hour to 75c an hour in the last five years here, but cotton picking, despite the subsidies to the growers from the government, remained the same in the cotton center of the state: Eloy.

I came to Eloy to try my hand again at picking cotton. Tradition says that this growing settlement received its name years ago from the Jewish merchant who stopped off the train and whose first words were the Hebrew, "Eloi," meaning "my God," which was ejaculated, not in praise, but in dismay at such a desert waste. This was later Anglicized into "Eloy." If he had viewed this area in the spring or to the immediate north and east had seen the giant suahare cactus and the beautiful desert flowers he would likely have said "eloi" in praise.

Getting in after dark I paid 75¢ to occupy cot number seventeen among the thirty in one of the unventilated cot-houses in the center of town. I did not see any sign limiting inmates to the Jim Crow category as I had noticed in most restaurants, but all whom I saw here were whites. After renting my cot I went to a restaurant and had a small order of friend beans with some kind of Mexican noodles on top, a nice warm tortilla, and pie and coffee. Most of the men were already in bed at 8:00 p.m., perhaps not sleeping, but resting. A few were around telling stories. The red-faced elderly man at my left was asleep. The one to the right tried to sleep but coughed violently and spat on the floor all night. (I don't believe much in germs so I didn't worry.) Across from me was a wino who also wheezed and coughed all night. He was not yet in bed but was spreading his digust with himself and the world to the man next to him who was in bed and to a man sitting nearby.

"I used to drink a quart a day for four years but I quit it. I'm not so damn hot now, for I mess around a little, but I found out one thing in life: that is not to worry about anything; it'll get you down'," said the elderly man in bed next to the wheezing wino.

"Oh, I don't know. That might be true and then again it mightn't; that's just one excuse for not accepting responsibility," said a man up the row, not to he who had spoken, but to the room in general. This wisdom was not taken up, being lost in the void. Meanwhile a man brought the wino a loaf of bread and cheese.

"Ought to have some salt on this cheese; some salt and pepper, mumbled the wino. After he had said this a couple of times the man next to him in bed said he would get him some and got up, and put on his shoes (we all slept with our clothes on in this sheetless and ragged comfort, discomfort. I learned long ago though to always take off socks, for toes must stretch out and rest and kind of breathe). The man walked the length of the room to the office and came back with salt for the wino.

"What, no pepper!" the wino exclaimed.

"Ain't got none," was the answer.

A beefy wino up the way dropped his bottle. After bemoaning his loss for a few minutes he had sense enough to get the broom and sweep up the glass.

"Yes, that Indio is a tough place," a fellow up the line was telling his buddy. "I was shaved, had on clean levies, shoes shined and money in my pocket when I hopped off a freight and started across the tracks to get some breakfast when two bulls pulled their guns and told me not to cross the tracks but to keep on the freight out of town. I told them I had money in my pocket and took it out and showed it to them, and they said Indio didn't want me nor my damn money. And they kept on poking their guns at me so I didn't cross the tracks."

The lights were out at 9:30 and somehow I slept through the night. The manager woke us at 6:00 a.m. as the trucks would be leaving around seven. I got up and went to the nearby restaurant which was crowded with every kind of cotton picker. There was one empty place at the counter which I soon occupied and ordered hot cakes and coffee. To my right was sitting a saintly looking middle aged man who greeted me with a Southern drawl. His kind voice was in keeping with his countenance. Old, decrepit and unshaven men; stocky kids; white and colored women and a few Indians occupied the L shaped counter. I am not especially hardboiled and there have been very few times since I left Atlanta prison that I have shed tears. I know there is suffering and misery, and as Dorothy says, I know that the poor do not have many of the common virtues which the rich applaud. Yet this morning I could hardly eat as the tears came because of this spectacle of those faces around me.

"See that woman who just left," said my friend to the right. "She sure has picked up; last year she was a regular cotton-whore, laying around the trucks all day drunk. Haven't seen her drunk this winter."

I am reminded of the story, think I read it in the Wob paper once, of a man who was leaning unkempt against a store building with a bottle sticking out of his pocket and tobacco juice running out of his mouth. Up comes a well dressed lady who says:

"My good man; why don't you cut out your dirty habits and amount to something. Why, you could work and save your money instead of spending it on liquor and tobacco and someday you might even own this building."

"Madam," the man said, "do you own this building?"

"No," she replied.

"Well, I do," was the answer.

Personally I use neither liquor or tobacco as a discipline, but I dislike to see the Horatio Alger of small virutes handed out to the poor by prissy ones of the upper class whose one vice is that they live off of these dispossessed.

I went outside by the fire along the curb and when the first cotton bus pulled out I was one among thirty in it: Negroes, Indians, young and old whites, and one white woman.

"In-law trouble. I didn't marry the whole damn family," said the young man sitting next to me in the course of conversation. He was from Arkansas and had lived in Louisville for eleven years when he couldn't take it any longer and had left. Had three children and sent his wife money. Came in on a freight and tried to sleep in a box car last night.

We went about twenty-seven miles east and beyond Red Rock until we came to the huge cotton field. I weighed in thirty pounds from my short rows, commencing at 8:00 a.m. Around 1:30 I got hungry and thirsty and took my forty six pounds to the truck. Inquiring if they had beans for lunch I was told they had cow-peas.

"Just what I want; haven't had any since I left Oklahoma," said the man next to me. I took the same and ate happily, along with some crackers, rather than the corrupt white bread. At the bottom of the bowl, a piece of not-quite hairless hog-skin greeted this vegetarian, but it was too late to worry about it.

"Made $9.00 the other day, last week, first picking, but there's always one greedy fellow to spoil it for us. This guy picks bolls and all and when the boss finds it out he brings the price for all of us down to $2.00," said a white man picking next to me. Later I worked next to a young Negro from California who was going back there soon to work in the peas. An Indian from Tucson who knew my Hopi silversmith friend Ralph, worked along by me for a time. He was a slow picker like myself. One Indian woman, a Navajo, was working and they kidded her about putting her baby in the cotton sack and weighing it with the cotton. This didn't happen but she sure earned extra pay by carrying the baby on her back. My last picking was twenty five pounds, making a total of one hundred and one pounds, netting me $2.52. This being Saturday we quit at 4:30. I had worked eight and a quarter hours. At my best I had not learned to pick with both hands efficiently the way I write with two hands — and two fingers — on the typewriter. While we were waiting for the bus to load a dozen men were shaking dice. "A scared man can't gamble and a jealous-hearted man can't work," said one man to a nervous fellow who had lost. Upon the request of several passengers the driver stopped at Red Rock where some men got out and bought a pint of wine. "Marked 45c but they charged us cotton pickers 50¢" they said as they entered the bus. Getting of the bus I was so cramped and sore from the dragging among the cotton sticks that I limped along like the others.

Working for the big company last year I had to work Sundays when there was work. This year I determined not to work on Sunday but to sell CW's at Phoenix churches. Since I have free rent it does not cost much to live. I make enough to send my daughters, in college, a substantial sum each week, and while this day work takes a lot of extra time running around, the work varies and I enjoy it. One Sunday I went to the suburb of Scottsdale. Here I met Father Rook, who is an admirer of the CW. I had heard of him but had never met him; he is assistant pastor in the nearby college town of Tempe. He says mass at Scottsdale and the Yaqui Indian village of Guadalupe in the desert. He took me there that morning. He showed me the addition to the old church that the Indians had built with their own hands in this hot weather. They had not asked for help from the whites but had taken a second collection at mass for the materials. They had never thought of having a bingo party or raffle and in proportion to their income did much more for their church than did their white brethern in Phoenix.

On another Sunday I was standing in front of a large Mexican church when the priest came out and upon seeing the CW smiled and said that he had met Peter Maurin in Chicago years ago. He told me not to be bashful but to shout my wares. This priest is pro-Franco and not a radical but he likes the CW. That very same morning I was chased from a big Catholic church by the priest who disliked anything that was critical of war and capitalism. When waiting for a bus downtown I stand in front of the bus station or Walgreen's store and shout "Catholic Worker." Many Catholics who are not radical greet me kindly as they like to see something other than the Watchtower of the Jehovah's Witnesses sold on the streets. Radicals from over the country also stop and visit with me.

One evening I attended a meeting in town where some visiting Quakers spoke. They knew Dorothy and were glad to know that CATHOLIC WORKERS were being distributed in this far away part of the country. Many years ago I had read and studied all kinds of Yogi and psychic ideas, but for several years I had not had a thought about such subjects. Over thirty-five years ago, in broad daylight, a feeling came to me, on two different occasions, that two certain friends who lived at some distance from me were in trouble; and in my mind I saw that trouble and wrote to them about it. At that very same instant they had felt my thoughts and had written to me about it. At other times I have had friends much closer to me who were in greater trouble and I had no communication or thought about it. While in solitary I had a *gradual* enlightment of mind and spirit but nothing spectacular. In Albuquerque the morning after we knew about the Atom Bomb explosion I was impelled to write a few paragraphs about my conception of what an Isleta Indian would think of it.

Now, shortly before daylight, about four hours after I had been asleep, coming home from that Quaker meeting, I awoke and saw a blue flame burning in the middle of the room. I went to it wondering, for I knew that there had not been a fire in the stove for 12 hours, and this was not near the stove. The fire burned and yet I couldn't see that there was any wood or coal or anything to provide the fuel for the flame. I put my hands in the flame and while it was warm it did not seem to burn or scorch me. I was awed and knelt and prayed silently, shutting my eyes, but keeping my hands in or around this flame. Perhaps this took three minutes and when I opened my eyes the flame was gone. The floor was not a bit scorched although it was warm. I went back to bed and slept for about an hour and then it was daylight. I looked at the spot where I had knelt and there was no mark on the floor where I could tell the exact spot, although I knew about where I had knelt. Before I made any breakfast I sat down and wrote the following blank verse. Bob Ludlow printed it in his CATHOLIC CONSCIENTIOUS OBJECTOR magazine. Here it is:

I have seen the Holy Fire.
I have seen that great Pillar of Flame reaching heavenward;
Burning without fuel, smokeless and brightly blue.
I knelt before it, worshipping.
For the first time in my life I was devoid of all thought of self,
Of worry over causes and events,
Of concern with persons and things.
I approached this Fire humbly, in reverence;
I had not known how or when I had cast my clothing aside,
But unconsciously it seemed I had
Appeared naked before this Divinity.

Today I go about my work;
I write letters to friends and receive letters in return.
I have a tolerable peace of mind.
Yet now after having knelt before this Flame
I know that wars and famines can come and go
And I shall not be moved.
I have seen and felt and been a part of this Holy Fire.
For as I knelt it seemed to envelop me
Without burning my flesh
(Or was I in the flesh or in the spirit?)
Henceforth my faith in the good, the beautiful, the true

Is strengthened.
For I have caught some of that Holy Fire.
That Inner Light has been rekindled.
For I have seen God.

Radical Philosophy

"Is that all your education amounts to?"

"Better lay up some money; who will take care of you in your old age?"

"You with your crazy ideas; how many followers have you got?"

"You write books that no one will print; and articles that no one reads except fools like yourself; you all spend time converting each other."

"Don't be more Catholic than the Church."

Such are the barbs that come from relatives and friends. To have to argue with Christians that God would take care of those who seek first the Kingdom; to have to try to prove to a priest that Jesus really meant the Sermon on the Mount; to have to tell so-called metaphysical leaders that their Mammon worship was not important and that "all things work together for good to those that love God"—all this might seem superfluous, but it is part of being fools for Christ's sake; part of trusting in God rather than in the social security and old age pensions of a war-making state; it is part of that "Life at Hard Labor."

Recently I had letters from two anarchists—one a young man who had been a 4F in World War II (a 4F is one excused from military duty because of ill health or deformity.) He now had intellectually made the jump from this position to that of anarchism. The other is an old man much past the four-score-and-ten, who had given up any hope of educating any portion of the masses against the coming war. Both suggested emigrating to some tropical country away from the materialistic world, where a few of us who knew better could cooperate and survive. These two comrades lacked that which I had lacked before finding the spirit of Christ in solitary. Truth is eternal and as Tolstoy says, no sincere effort made in the behalf of Truth is ever lost.

Wells and Toynbee may write of the significance of history; Churchill may boast of his part in contaminating it; and Hutchins may o.k. the bomb with his right hand (whether he approved of the use of the bomb he stayed there while it was being worked out) and issue the Great Books with his left hand—but all this cannot hide the fact that there once lived a man who faced this issue; who refused to be banished to an island where he could not propagandize the truth, but who instead drank the hemlock. This Socrates tells us:

"Men of Athens, I honor and love you; but I shall obey God rather than you . . . O my friend, why do you, who are a citizen of the great and mighty and wise city of Athens care so much about laying up the greatest amount of money and honor and reputation, and so little about wisdom and truth? O men of Athens, I say to you do as Anytus bids, and either acquit me or not; but whatever you do, know that I shall never alter my ways, not if I have to die many times. I would have you know that if you kill such a one as I am, you will injure yourselves more than you injure me."

I have tramped in all of these United States. As I write I look on the fields of waving grain, the huge cottonwoods that line the *laterals,* and the jutted stretch of seeming cardboard-like mountains at whose feet live the Pima and Maricopa Indians. In and out of prison I have refused to honor the jingoistic Star Spangled Banner. Truly America the Beautiful means much to me. I refuse to desert this country to those who would bring it to atomic ruin. It is my country as much as it is theirs. Despite Bilbo I think of Jefferson; despite Edgar Guest, Bruce Barton and Dale Carnegie, I think of Walt Whitman, Vachel Lindsay and Edwin Markham. Despite the two warmongering Roosevelts and Wilson, I think of Altgeld, old Bob LaFollette and Debs. Despite the Klan and Legion vigilantes I think of the old-time Wobblies, of Sacco and Vanzetti, and of Berkman and Emma Goldman. Despite the warmongering churches I think of the old-time Quakers who paid no taxes for war and who hid escaped slaves; I think of Jim Connolly and Ben Salmon. Despite the warmongering Lowells and Cabots, I think of William Lloyd Garrison and Henry David Thoreau.

It was hard work which built this country. Despite the bourgeois philosophy of the go-getter we worship that machine which now enslaves us. Our military training will not corrupt *every* youth; a few will appreciate the path of manual labor, economic uncertainty, an absolutist stand against war and against the state whose main business is war.

* * *

"You can't cheat an honest man." This saying of the late W. C. Fields was quoted to me by one of my day-to-day employers, in discussing his predicament when he had a building erected by a Phoenix contractor and found that this contractor had not paid $5,000 to sub contractors, so there were liens on his property when he came from the north to live in it. He found some property hidden away by this scoundrel and was able to come out even on the deal. The contractor was a professing Christian. Next time he got a Mormon contractor who was more honest, it happened.

Thinking back over the employers for whom I have worked a sufficient length of time for me to know them: from the Ohio pottery in 1912 where I was told to sort small porcelin fixtures and put the good ones in a barrel for shipping and then was scolded because I didn't shovel them in without looking (this was when I belonged to the I.W.W.), to the orchards where I worked in the southwest, where I was told to place the big apples on top and the inferior ones beneath, each trade has snaky tricks peculiar to itself. Leo, the Yugoslav, whom I meet at the date grove, would say that this was all caused by the capitalist system, and in a measure he is right, although I have a feeling it will take something more positive than the changing of the system to uproot trickery from both worker and employer. I have worked with but very few "white men" who are honest and efficient workers.

One of my employers who had himself played many tricks—and lost his fortune in a bank failure—told me that the dishonest and greedy man was the easiest to cheat, only you had to be one step ahead of him. An honest man was not looking for easy money. I have had one honest employer. He is not an active church member but he believes that it is foolish to build up a reputation of dishonesty. This is the Old Pioneer. He told of the custom in the old days in Arizona, when in order to secure a homestead the rancher had to produce five witnesses who would swear that he had occupied his claim continuously for the required time to prove it. Most ranchers were away working on the railroad and had no immediate neighbors who ever saw them, so a group of men who were loafers and hangers on around the court would swear for all and sundry who approached—for a monetary consideration. These were called "Affidavit men." And in later years to call a man "An Affidavit Man" was the worst insult. One of the most wealthy men of this valley based his fortune on staking any roustabout to a claim and then gathering in the claim for a few more bottles of liquor, when it had been legally acquired by this fraudulent homesteader.

Broccoli

Broccoli here in Arizona comes as near to looking like a tree among vegetables as you will find. Huge green leaves which, even in this dry country, always seem to be wet. Around Thanksgiving work commences on the broccoli. It is four to five feet high and in between the big leaves the succulent broccoli shoots up. Scores of rubber boots and aprons are in the truck. The morning is cold, so I pick out what seems to be boots which are not for the same foot, and an apron, and go over to the fire to try them on. The frost is now off the leaves and two of us get on each side of the cart and two behind. Each armed with a big knife with which we cut the ripe shoots, which are discerned by their purple color. The right way to do is to keep going straight ahead and not turn around for then you will get wet from the leaves. Hands are cold at first and the feet never really do get warm. There is little stooping as in lettuce and the work is not hard, except for the coldness. By the time the field is covered it is ready to be worked over again, for new shoots come up constantly. As long as the price is good cutting continues often until March. I had broccoli for supper while I worked there. The workers are nearly all local Mexicans and a jolly crew to work with.

I Meet Rik

The week before Christmas it rained for the first time in months, so I took several days to make copies of my tax statement and write to friends, for there was no work in any of the fields if it rained. Going home one evening from the date grove I was selling CW's while waiting for the bus. I had gone to a corner where I had never sold before. A young man bought a paper and asked if there was a CW group in Phoenix. I replied that

110

there was not and that I was not a Catholic, but sold the paper because I thought it was the most Christian and the most revolutionary one printed. He was not a Catholic either but had met followers of that paper in Oakland, California. He wanted to know if there were any Tolstoians in this vicinity. I told him that I had not found any. He asked if there was not a Tolstoian, an Irishman who had come from New Mexico and who had not paid taxes—he couldn't remember his name. I wondered if the name was Hennacy. "That's the fellow," he exclaimed. It was thus that I met Rik Anderson who was to be my right hand in getting out leaflets in the next few years. He had read the CW and CATHOLIC CONSCIENTIOUS OBJECTOR in Civilian Public Service Camp, and had formerly been Socialist organizer in Arizona but was not anarchistically inclined. He invited me to his home to meet his wife and children.

I Meet Joe Craigmyle

Several months ago a young man who had been picking fruit all summer in California knocked at my door one evening. He had grown a full beard and I did not know him at first. He had written four letters to President Truman as he had traveled in his work, saying that he was refusing to register and giving his home address as Phoenix. He said that in thinking over the life and death of Gandhi he was ashamed to do anything else than refuse to register, although he had been exempt last time because of heart trouble and would likely be exempted this time if he registered.

The day before, I had visited a young Mexican in the county jail but was not allowed to see him as the only day for friends to call was Wednesday. I sent up a note, candy, and a CW for him. (He had refused to register for the draft.) My bewhiskered friend, Joe Craigmyle, offered to visit him the next Wednesday as I could not leave some special work which I had promised to do on that day for a farmer.

Later in the week I saw that Joe had given himself up and was placed in the county jail in lieu of $10,000 bail. The paper referred to him as a "draft evader". I wrote to the paper giving these definitions:

> "*Evade*—to get away from by artifice; to avoid by dexterity, subterfuge, address or ingenuity."

> "*Resist*—to stand against; to withstand; to stop; to obstruct; to strive against."

I asked them why they did not call things by their right names, but of course they did not print it. I sent a copy to Joe by mail and in due time he received it. I also sent him a blue-covered copy of the Bhagavad Gita, but the ignorant authorities would not allow him to have it as they thought it was Communist propaganda. The next Wednesday I visited both Joe and the Mexican. The latter liked the CW and said that if he had known he was not alone and that there was a group of Catholics opposed to war he would have stuck. He asked for more "good Catholic papers." A patriot from the draft board came up and asked Joe to register rather than go to jail. He asked him how he would like to have the Russians come over and destroy his church. Joe replied that he was an anarchistic vegetarian and did not belong to any church that had a building so the Russians nor any one else could not destroy his church or the truth which he believed.

After much protest by the pacifists in the southwest Joe was released on $500 bail. He at once put signs on his truck reading: "GOD'S PASSIVE RESISTER TO WAR AND THE DRAFT SENT TO JAIL." and toured the town with his truck. A patriot saw him and called a cop, saying, "Arrest that man"! The cop laughed and replied, "This is a free country; have you never heard of the freedom of the press?"

The Monday after Christmas Joe was to have his trial for refusing to register. As the papers tend to hide or distort the witness which he was making against war we thought it would be a good idea if I picketed the Federal Building during his trial. It was drizzling rain that morning and the wind was blowing so that my 2½-ft. by 3-ft. home-made sign took my two hands to keep it steady. It read:
"HONOR TO DRAFT RESISTER BEING SENTENCED TODAY"
"YOUR INCOME TAX FIGHTS THE POOR OF INDONESIA."
Underneath one arm I displayed the current CW. Passersby read the sign to one another and employees in the Federal Building read it from the windows. Half a dozen people stopped and asked questions in a sympathetic manner, some of them youngsters who had never heard of the term Conscientious Objector. To them and to the reporters I gave copies of the CW. The young recruiting officer across the street, out of the rain, came across and read my sign and smiled good naturedly and shook his head, not his fist. What a change from World War I when I was to be shot for refusing to register and for agitating less openly than this! No one openly said a word against my action. One reporter who said he was from an outside-of-the-city paper took my picture. I thought at the time he was from the FBI, and later found this to be true.

The young reporter of the evening paper took half a dozen pictures and questioned me sympathetically about the purpose of my picketing. That night the headline read: "DRAFT RESISTER ADMITS GUILT AS FRIEND PICKETS COURT". Note that Joe was called "resister" instead of "evader." Some of the facts of Joe's history and mine were twisted in the report but the essential quotation as to our purpose was correct. "We are governed by the Sermon on the Mount which tells us to return good for evil. But courts and governments return evil for evil. That's why we would abolish them and let every man be governed by his own conscience."

The reporter must have understood our emphasis for in describing my work in the vegetable fields he coined the phrase "spiritual independence" as the reason for my vocation. The next day the same paper carried a picture of myself and sign.

The Judge postponed the sentence until the following Monday and asked Joe to speak to the probation officer who was in court. This officer asked him if he knew the man who was picketing outside, and tried to argue with him that there was no such thing as a Christian Anarchist. Joe replied: "Well, Tolstoy and the CATHOLIC WORKER and Hennacy says there is, so it must be so." "Do you want probation?" the officer asked. Joe answered: "If I go to jail to witness against war and then accept probation or parole I would then be witnessing only for my own comfort. Tell the judge to do his part; I have done mine."

My anarchist friend Byron Bryant, home from Stanford for vacation in nearby Wickenburg, came down for the trial. He had registered and was granted Conscientious Objector status. (None of the local pacifists showed up although several of them were ministers who had this Monday off.) Bryant came out with Joe at noon and each carried the sign for a few steps as "token pickets." We went to a cafeteria where Bryant stood treat. Then Joe drove us in his truck with his signs on it, to Tempe where we were fortunate to find Father Rook home and had a pleasant visit with him.

On the next Monday I picketed the court again from 10 to 12. Joe's lawyer, furnished free by the Progressive Party, came out and told me that Joe had received a sentence of one year, so my picketing had not hardened the judge. Joe's mother tried to grab my sign for this would aggravate the judge, but luckily no one saw her. The paper again quoted the import of my sign as it reported Joe's sentence. Thomas Acosta, the young Mexican who had refused to register but who had afterward been frightened into registering because he knew no pacifist group, got 6 months. In 1944 the Federal Judge in Santa Fe, N. M., sentenced Jehovah's Witnesses to 5 years and bemoaned the fact that he could not hang a Mexican who had refused to register.

I gave Joe a copy of Dorothy Day's *On Pilgrimage* to read in jail. In discussing non-registration with Bryant before this he felt that if one refused to register nothing would come of it, but the picketing had placed the issue dramatically before the people, where otherwise there would have been but a small item about it.

Walking towards the califlower field on January 30, 1948, I was given a ride by a Basque trucker friend. He had the radio on and as the news came of Gandhi's assassination he said, "Our Gandhi is killed." That seemed to be the feeling of nearly everyone whether they agreed with him or not. He seemed to be the only person in the whole world who exemplified peace and love.

Tax Statement—1949

About this time I sent the Collector of Internal Revenue the following letter, which was later printed in the CW.

I am writing this preliminary statement of my reasons for not paying my income tax ahead of time, as I was recently informed by your office that I would be imprisoned for my constant refusal to pay taxes. Upon my arrest I will give you the correct report of my earnings to date in 1948.

My belief in the iniquity of government, which exists primarily to wage war, has been stated this last six years in my statement to your department when I refused to pay any tax, and also in articles in the CATHOLIC WORKER. To briefly sum them up again for your possible edification:

1. *As a Christian Anarchist I refuse to support any government, for, first, as a Christian, all government denies the Sermon on the Mount by a return of evil for evil in legislatures, courts, prisons and war. As an anarchist I agree with Jefferson that "that government is best which governs least." Government is founded to perpetuate the exploitation of one class by another. In our case it is the exploitation of the poor by a parasitic owning class living on tariffs, subsidies, rent, interest and profit, and held in power by crooked politicians, subservient clergy, blinded educators and scientists, and a prostituted press, movie industry and radio.*

2. *Jesus said "forgive seventy times seven." We make retroactive laws and hang our defeated enemies.*

Jesus told His Disciples not to call down fire from heaven to destroy those who would not listen to His gospel. We have no concern with any gospel but the dollar and with our atom bomb bring fire, not only to supposed enemies, but to whoever is in the way.

Jesus said "Put up thy sword for he that taketh the sword shall perish by the sword." In peace time we draft our boys and prepare for more terrible wars.

3. *World War III, run by the same Big Brass, will destroy rather than save us. Every country which has depended upon conscription has drawn defeat to itself; a country prospers by justice and not by robbery and force.*

4. *Warmongers tell us that Russia will invade us. We invaded the Indians, Mexicans, Central and South America with our dollar diplomacy, Europe with block busters, Japan with the atom bomb. We should talk! Russia wants security. We need not fear Communism for it will fall by its own weight of Bureaucracy and Tyranny of Power.*

5. *In our Civil War no country openly helped either side. In the Spanish Civil War we refused to help the cause of Freedom, but today in China, Greece, and wherever the common people seek freedom we take the side of the Fascists—and do so with hypocritical mutterings of being a "peace-loving nation."*

6. *Capitalism is doomed. It cannot work. With man producing tenfold more at the machine than formerly when free land was available, it is now increasingly impossible for the worker to buy back from what he receives in wages more than a portion of the goods produced. Hence depression or the selling of goods on foreign markets ensues. But there are no markets, so we have a Marshall give-away plan to get rid of the surplus. Capitalism is doomed despite erratic efforts of that demagogic Santa Claus in the White House with his bankers and generals bribing votes with subsidies, pensions and false promises. And, as in the days of Wallace, we destroy crops.*

7. *The Remedy is clear, but the trend today is deeper and deeper in the mire of government paternalism and war, and the distraction of the public by radio give-away programs, bingo, witch hunts, and escapist Youth for Christ, World Government, and such delusions. Decentralization of society with each family unit or cooperative group living simply on the land! Self-government and individual responsibility! Mutual credit and*

free exchange! Freedom instead of government! A realization that you cannot make people good by law and that the Sermon on the Mount surpasses all codes and dogmas!

AMMON A. HENNACY

Cauliflower

"Have a cigarette?" said the young driver of the cauliflower cart, as I was loading the heads chopped off by the men in boots, amid the tall, wet, deep green foliage.

"No thanks, I don't smoke," I replied.

"I noticed you didn't shoot craps with us as we were waiting for the frost to get off this cauliflower. You must be that guy I heard the boss tell about that don't get drunk, eat meat, pay taxes for the war, or even go to church." "Say," said he laughing, "just what the hell do you do to get any fun out of life?"

"I'm that guy alright. What the hell else do you do?" I replied.

"Oh, I like to read stories," he said, as we reached the end of the row.

"Did you ever think that the one who writes get as much fun out of writing as the one does who reads it? I do writing for my enjoyment. Here's a CW with an article of mine."

Coming to the end of the next row I saw a hat propped up, in the damp irrigation ditch and upon looking closer found that it rested on the tousled head of Big Tony. Then I remembered how he came to a group of Anglos that noon and said "Here's a dollar that you "can't throw sixes." After about half an hour with his own loaded dice—he had every cent from his opponents, so he mockingly tipped his hat and said:

"Thank you gentlemen. Now I'll go to Tolleson and get a bottle."

The good natured Mexican foreman had done Tony's work for him that afternoon.

The next day I was told to work in the dry packing stand at the other end of the field. Here the cart loads were dumped and sorters quickly discarded the small, broken, and discolored heads. They threw the good ones on the table where four packers put them in crates and slid them to the cutter—the crates going over rollers —who with an enormous knife, cut off the tops even with the crate. The man at the end of the slide put on the tops, and several fellows loaded the boxes on the truck. An inspector looked at a crate once in a while and if he found culls he would take them back to the sorters and admonish them to be more careful. My job was to fork the culls away so new cart loads could be emptied. Farmers came and got these culls for their cattle. The mystery which I never did get explained, by boss or workman, was why the packers, who had the easiest job of all with no stooping or even skill of sorting out culls, were paid from $18 to $40 a day and the rest of us got 85 cents an hour. It was a custom for the packer to get more was all the answer I could get. I worked here for three weeks, and as the Indian lives off the country wherever he may be, this vegetarian had the one dish of cauliflower every night for supper.

A one-track mind and a one-track stomach. I found a combination of cheese and jelly made good sandwiches for dinner.

Lettuce

Lettuce is the main crop in the part of the valley where I live. The efficient farmer discs, drags, scrapes and floats his land over and over until it is really level. In this southwest everything runs southwest. The field is separated into "lands" about 35 feet wide. Often rye or other green grass is planted and then sheep graze at 4c per head per day. It is irrigated again and again as the sheep graze. Then it is disced and the remaining green and the sheep manure add to the value of the soil. When once water is ordered, it generally takes a day and a night to irrigate a large field. I have irrigated by myself at night in this fresh ground. No matter how careful you may be, the water will tend to furrow in on one side or the other and miss the opposite side. Mormons and Mexicans are the best irrigators. The expert knows just where to put the "checks," extending out like arms from each side to divert the water so that no dry land remains. You may have from two to six lands running at once depending upon the volume of water. First you put a "tarp" of canvas across the ditch, leaning it against sticks and banking it around with dirt making a dam; and generally, further down the ditch, it is well to put a second tarp in case the first one leaks or washes out.

Walking around in this mud to make new checks or to plug up a gopher hole where water is going in the wrong direction, your shins become sore with the rubbing of the boot tops against them. The shift is generally 12 hours at 60 to 70 cents an hour.

After the ground has been soaked, vegetation, which includes the weed seeds, is thus given the chance to grow and then is disced under. When the weather is just right for planting special machines make straight, level beds about 2 feet across, with irrigation runs in between. The lettuce comes up on the very edge of each side of this bed. First come the thinners who generally work by contract and thin out the lettuce to one head every 14 inches. Afterwards it is found that in many places there are two heads, or what is called "doubles." These are then thinned. All this is done with a short hoe; handle about 2 feet long. A worker on the end of a long handle tends to get careless and chop anything in sight if the lettuce is small. Later, when the lettuce is bigger, long hoes are used to cut the weeds and grass. The reason hundreds of people have to work at this job is that the weeds have to be removed before the next irrigation, and then you have to wait a few days until the ground is dry. Meanwhile, at daylight or dusk when there is little wind, an airplane dusts the field to kill bugs and worms. Every season some of these dusters are killed and the planes are wrecked. A liquid fertilizer in tanks is emptied gradually in the irrigation water at the intake. The advantage of having a large farm is that at times the run-off water from one field is used on the next field—or in some cases far out in the desert it is saved in reservoirs. Otherwise the water runs back in the *lateral* and is sold to another farmer.

When a good proportion of the lettuce has solid heads, and especially if the price is high, the long, yellow trailers are at the end of the field. Three men line up on each side of the trailer and two behind it and it is pulled slowly by a small tractor or, if the ground is wet, by a small caterpillar. The tool used to cut the lettuce is about one and one half inches wide, sharp, and curved a bit. The handle is about one and a half feet long. First, you feel the lettuce with your left hand and see if it is hard and, if so, you cut it with the knife in your right hand and throw it with your left hand in the trailer. I generally work on the outside row and, if possible, get the side away from the exhaust, for it would soon give you a headache. This means throwing further but there is less liklihood of there being a collision between human and lettuce heads. At times I have steadily cut lettuce without straightening up for the quarter of a mile row. Generally there are enough immature heads to give you a rest in between. This work pays from 75 cents to a dollar an hour depending upon how many hours you are able to work in the day, for at times there is frost until noon. When there is no frost you can commence at daylight, but when it is hot in the afternoon it is best not to handle the lettuce. If touched when frosty it leaves a black mark on the lettuce. No portal-to-portal pay in this agricultural work as there is, when you enter a mine and pay starts at the time of entrance. You stand around shivering and waiting on the frost to melt and if it is not too hot you work until dark.

The lettuce is hauled to the packing sheds—two trailers at a time — which are in town or in sheds along the tracks. Here the lettuce is wet packed in crushed ice. It is dumped in huge hoppers; one person cuts off the excess leaves or discards unfit heads. Another places paper in the boxes at the head of the belt line. Another keeps him supplied with boxes. One hands the packer the heads and another tops the crate. When the price is high and the crop is coming in heavily, the big money is made in these sheds with overtime. Many make $30 a day. Here the packers get more than the others. The union books are closed and it is difficult for a newcomer to get work in the sheds. If the price remains high the field will be worked over and over again to get all possible good heads of lettuce. We worked half of Christmas. As the saying is here: "When there is work you work night and day, Sunday and Christmas morning."

In the midst of the season crews of Filipinos come from California. There are about 45 in a crew. They man a huge combine. As far as I can make out this is the system they use: a crew goes ahead and cuts lettuce in the rows where the combine travels. This combine looked like an airplane. These heads are placed to one side. A truck with empty boxes keeps pace with it on one side, and one on the other to take care of the full crates. Lettuce heads are tossed on the wings of the combine and worked over just as in a dry packing shed. The girl who lines the boxes with paper, the cutters, the sorters, the packer, and the man who nailed the boxes, all ride on the machine.

They sure ate up the field. They had huge lights and worked most of the night if necessary. The only drawback was rain which would bog down the heavy machine. They worked as a crew and each man received a more or less equal share of the 55c a crate the owner paid. These workers are very quick and sober and dependable. I know of a case where a Filipino leased land and raised lettuce, hiring men of his own race. Some Anglos grumbled about it and so he built a shed and hired Anglos also. This was dry packing of lettuce in the field. He found that the shippers had to repack most of the crates of lettuce which the Anglos had packed. And in the hoeing, the Filipinos could hoe twice as fast as the Anglos and much better. I will admit I would not speed up the average of the Anglos myself.

One morning the boss told us to get in the closed truck and we would all go to the sheds. I had never been there. I found there was broccoli to pack. We finished all there was in a few hours. Meanwhile, I had heard the conversation of the workers and had picked up a bulletin of the union and found that there was a strike of the shed workers. The fields are not organized. I then looked outside and saw the pickets. The foreman told us he would take us home early for dinner and pick us up and pack lettuce until late that day. I told him that I was not working in the shed that afternoon because I did not want to be a strikebreaker. He said "you are already a strikebreaker." I replied that because I was dumb I did not have to stay dumb. Here the pay was about $1.25 an hour but in the fields where I worked from that time on it was 85c and at times 60 cents. Afterwards they never asked me to work in the sheds, and did not discriminate against me because of my refusal to scab, although the foreman would at times, jokingly refer to me as a strikebreaker. Two I.W.W.'s, one of them a Mormon, also refused the next day to scab. The strike finally lost and the head of the union resigned and started a tavern.

One cold morning about fifty of us were cutting weeds out of the beds of small celery. This was done with a paring knife and was tedious work. Next to me was a fellow who had not been there before. He was sympathetic to the I.W.W., and as the work was slow we had an opportunity to talk. I had not found anyone for a long time who knew the meaning of radical phrases and who even quoted Veblen and Plato. He had never heard of the CW and was glad to know of such a paper. I always had an extra one in my pocket. At noon one of the winos who could not help hearing our conversation asked me what I had been drinking. In my younger days I would have uselessly argued with the man but now I only said "I don't drink." In his mind he was right, for what business did educated people have coming to these fields and talking a lingo which the others did not understand. The foreman and a few of the more sober workers knew that I was doing farm work in order not to have a tax for the bomb taken from my pay. I did not have the time nor the inclination to explain this to every newcomer. So, maybe to this man, I did appear "drunk."

All that season a man was in the crew who, upon hearing the person in the next row say anything would immediately begin mumbling a long line of semi-Biblical babble. This was not meant to be a part of the conversation which he was interrupting for he never looked up as he mumbled but this was just an habitual "aside" on his part. I might say to my partner

"I don't eat meat." Immediately this man would mumble: "Meat—now there is all kinds of meat: cow, pig and horse. Then fish is meat and so is chicken. I don't rightly know if an oyster is meat. The Lord said to Peter "Slay and eat; so it must be o.k. Jesus ate fish but what kind of fish did he eat? That is a question. Samson was a strong man and he didn't eat meat. The elephant is the strongest animal and eats grass. Now I eat meat—when I can get it—but I was never really very strong—meat, meat, meat."

If he would hear the word whiskey from Provo that would start a long dissertation on that subject with never a period or a comma between the meat and the whiskey.

Sheep

Now in the fall the 80 acres of lettuce had not matured to full heads because of the unusually hot weather; and the price being low it did not pay to harvest the crop. So the sheep man fenced off any open places along the line with the roll of fine meshed, three feet high wire, rolls of which were a part of his standard equipment. This kept out the dogs and coyotes and kept the sheep inside. Among the several hundred were the two black sheep. (There isn't that proportion of us radicals to the general population of sheep-like followers of authority.) During the day the sheep roamed over the field, always keeping together but running wildly in one direction or another for what would seem like no reason whatever. Toward evening the shepherd brought them towards the windbreak formed by the tall eucalyptus and the spreading chinaberry and pomegranate foliage near the cottage where I live. The Mexican who herded the sheep had a small tent nearby. He did not speak English, the Old Pioneer, who spoke Spanish, told me. So, in my limited manner, I spoke in Spanish to him of the weather, the sheep, the lettuce, and the few words that I knew in addition to the morning and evening greetings. He replied in Spanish, most of which I could understand, but I was at a loss as to proper verbs to use to carry on the conversation.

In the old days if a sheep was missing no attention was paid unless three were gone, for at a dollar a head sheep were plentiful. Now at around $15, each sheep was accounted for. Yesterday as I was gathering some wood for my stove I noticed the Mexican cutting the hide from a sheep that had died. I asked him the reason but he did not know. So the shepherd is always warm in his tent with sheepskins. Herding is a 24 hour per day job, with sleep to be taken when quiet prevails. The pay is around $140 a month with food, stove and cooking utensils furnished. Some ranchers complained that the herder invites countless relatives for meals, but if the shepherd was a good one this overhead was taken—if not with a smile—for a good one is difficult to find. Basques who settled here many years ago make the best herdsmen. When I lived in the shack of the Molokon across the road last winter, the man who herded the sheep was a married Mexican from Glendale. In the summer the sheep are taken to the mountains near Winslow and Flagstaff. A year ago I worked one night irrigating with a young man who had been cook for a sheepherder in Idaho. Each was paid $175 a month and food. He said it was work for an old man and not for a young fellow who wanted to be in town nights.

The lettuce fields to the north of my cottage had been planted earlier and a fair crop was taken from them. One field to the far south was spoiled by the saltmarsh caterpillar. Some say that the DDT used previously had killed the bug that ate the caterpillar eggs, but the DDT did not harm the wooly caterpillar. The big company had imported Mexican Nationals and now did not have work for them every day, but according to contract was obliged to feed them. Of course no local day labor was needed so this meant no lettuce or cauliflower work for me this season.

I like to saw wood. You breath deeply and at times think deeply. During the winter after I had refused to scab I did not have steady work. Ordinarily Mexican men will not chop wood and it is up to the women to do it. The Mexican neighbor women were scabbing at the sheds so had plenty of money and did not feel that they should chop wood, so they asked me to do it. I did it for several days off and on while the men sat by laughing at an Anglo working for them. Some of my pipsqueak friends accuse me of pride but if they could see me chopping this wood they would not see much pride. Although, really I am glad and proud to do useful labor.

It was 24 degrees above at 8 a.m. the other day when I started sawing. Within an hour I had taken off my coat, sweater and shirt, but my feet were cold. This is the work to do in cooler weather. The pungent odor of the wood and the growing pile of cut wood provides a satisfaction of itself. This work is not entirely brawn, for some intelligence is needed to properly judge the grain in splitting chunks of wood. The Old Pioneer has cooked in camps and always provides a wholesome dinner. This wood goes in the kitchen stove of the Old Pioneer. Since I fell and got an ugly gash in my arm last spring I have learned to be careful. A small piece of iron tied to one end of a rope and swung over the outstretched limb, attached to a block and tackle, will pull the limb in the direction desired. Also, learning the proper place to notch a limb is a trick in itself. The Old Pioneer has taught me the value of a bright shovel and a sharp axe.

While doing landscape work for a neighbor the other day I noticed that his small dog was being frightened by nearby children shooting blank cartridges and going through the antics of Wild West thrillers they had seen. My boss of that day had been a salesman most of his life and understood psychology. Instead of telling his boy and girl not to emphasize these shooting escapades he took them downtown and bought them each binoculors in a pretty leather case. It was not long until the other youngsters were waiting in line to look at distant Camelback mountain.

Tax Picketing

It is March of 1949 and I have sent in my tax report. I did not work Sundays this year. I worked for nineteen different farmers and made $1,569. With free rent and often free meals where I work and with simple one dish vegetarian food my actual living cost has been less than $200. I filled out my report accurately, not wishing to have my non-payment of taxes confused by any other issue. In the space listed "AMOUNT OF TAX DUE" I wrote "not interested." The tax man told me six weeks ago he would have me arrested for continual non-payment of taxes, but would wait until the last minute as he disliked to cause trouble. I told him that he should do his duty; that there was no hard feelings on my part, for he had always treated me courteously. Now with Truman calling for universal conscription and the U. S. winking at Dutch imperialism in Indonesia there is less reason than ever for paying an income tax. If I am arrested I am doing time for a good cause, for, paraphrasing Thoreau, a prison is the only house in a war mad world where a Christian pacifist can abide with honor. If I am left free I will continue to be non-tax payer, sell CW's, and aid my daughters. I win either way.

On March 14th, 1949, I carried signs saying that 75% of the income tax goes for war and the bomb and that I have refused to pay taxes for seven years. Right away a squad car came up and I was taken to the police station to see Captain Curry.

"Do you know there is an ordinance saying you can't picket?" he asked.

"Do you know there is a Supreme Court that says in the case of the Jehovah's Witnesses that it is o.k. to picket?" I replied.

"You're a smart guy, eh!"

"Sure, it takes a smart guy to deal with the cops," I answered.

"Smart fellows like you; we take you upstairs in jail and give you 30 days for not registering as an ex-convict," he said.

"O.K. take me up. You got me," was my reply.

Not being used to this moral jiu jitsu he said he would have to go upstairs and see the mayor for further instructions. He came back and in a confidential tone said:

"I fixed it up for you. Just go home and rest and don't picket and we won't give you 30 days."

"I don't feel like resting. I feel like picketing. Go ahead and give me 30 days upstairs or arrest me for picketing; whatever you like," was my reply.

"I have to confer with the authorities some more" he said as he left me. Coming back later he said rather glumly: "Alright; smart guy. You know the law, go ahead and picket, but remember if you get in trouble we will pinch you for disturbing the peace."

"I'm not disturbing the peace. I'm disturbing the war" was my rejoinder.

"You will be on your own" the Captain said.

"I've been on my own all my life; I don't need cops to protect me," I answered.

"If you get knocked down we will pinch you for getting knocked down," was his retort.

"You would!" I said, as I went out to my picketing.

After an hour of picketing the same cop who pinched me before came along and said, "You here again!"

"Captain Curry said I could picket," I replied.

"To hell with Captain Curry" was his answer.

"That's a nice way to talk about your boss" I told him. He advanced to me roughly and said that unless I got a written permit from the City Manager he would put me in solitary. There is a time to talk and there is a time to walk, so this was the time to walk. I went with my signs to the City Hall. The Mormon Mayor, Udall, had offices to the right and he was not on good terms with the City Manager Deppe, with offices to the left. I sat in the waiting room for an hour while their secretaries sent notes or phoned back and forth as to the procedure in my case. Between them, this Pilate and Herod finally came forth with the wisdom that I was to write a letter to the City Manager asking permission to picket and in three days I would get an answer. I wrote the letter and said that in three days all the taxes would be paid and picketing would be of no avail; that I was going out at once and deliberately break the law and they could do as they liked. I did so and was not bothered. Soon the papers had a picture of myself and sign, and were joshing the police for arresting me twice and letting me go. Several months later I had a letter from Manilil Gandhi of Phoenix, South Africa praising my publicizing of my non-payment of taxes in Phoenix, Arizona.

"Hennacy, do you think you can change the world?" said Bert Fireman, a columnist on the Phoenix Gazette.

"No, but I am damn sure it can't change me" was my reply. He put this retort in his column the next day. Since then I have become acquainted with him and although we do not agree on most issues I like him as a man. Since then he has had weekly broadcasts on Arizona history and has not hesitated to give the truth about the despoiling of the Indians by the whites and to praise the peaceful Hopi.

Many people called me "Commie" as I picketed. A man asked me who was paying me. I told him "no one." He asked to what organization I belonged and I replied "None." He next wanted to know how many there were who believed as I did. I told him "Dorothy Day, Bob Ludlow and myself; that makes three and maybe there are more. What the hell difference would it make if there were four?" I gave away CW's to those interested.

American Legion

In Milwaukee I had been on friendly terms with the American Legion leaders. My experience proved that they were men like other men and that it was not impossible for them to understand the radical viewpoint whether they agreed with it or not. Accordingly when the Legion in Phoenix advertised a conference on the problem of Communism I wrote to them saying that I would be outside handing free copies of the CW to those who might be interested. In the letter I reviewed my contact with the Legion in Milwaukee, in public debates with them on the subject of pacifism and anarchism. Drizzling rain all that day did not prevent me from standing with raincoat and umbrella on the sidewalk. The meeting was not open to outsiders. Few men would accept the CW but among those who did were some Negroes and Indians. At the close of the session I went inside and introduced myself to the Commander, an Irish Catholic, and gave him copies of the CW. He was nominally civil but did not discuss the matter.

In Feb. of 1949 the American Legion had the renegade Communists, Ben Gitlow and Elizabeth Bentley speak at a mass meeting in the downtown High School Auditorium. I came early and shouted loudly that I had "The CW, Catholic peace paper; Catholic radical paper" for sale, and I sold fifty. Here I met Frieda Graham, wife of the local Communist leader, Morris Graham. She was handing out leaflets telling of the time two years before when the local police beat up Communists for handing out leaflets at a meeting. I spoke with her at length and found her to be that sincere, intelligent and courageous type which is a credit to any movement. I had met her husband before, when I picketed the Freedom Train. He felt that after we had the Dictatorship of the Proletariat then would be the time for anarchism. He knew my idea that the state would never wither away. This evening I listened to Gitlow bellow forth the terrible danger of The Communist Manifesto (written in 1847 and to be read in any library). Miss Bentley was more demure in her accusations about Communists, but it was plain that neither speaker presented any trace of idealism. The $300 which it is said each received was wasted money on the part of the Legion, for they could not convince any of the danger who did not already believe in the Red Menace, and who were not already entangled in the Red Network.

Not a Success Story

The one event for which I am ashamed and which received its punishment in advance occurred when a chance acquaintance gave me a card inviting me to a secret meeting held in a lodge hall by Gerald L. K. Smith. That night I was at Rik and Ginny's for supper. I was ashamed to admit that I would go to hear such a demagogue, so instead of frankly admitting it I said during the meal that I had to leave early, but hid my reason from my very good friends. My stomach was a better guide than my conscience, for when the meal was nearly finished I excused myself and went to the bathroom and vomited. I was not sick either before or after, and wondered at the time why this had happened. When next I met Rik and Ginny I told them that I had deceived them and how I couldn't "stomach" the rabblerouser. I listened with distaste to Smith's Jew-baiting and hate-mongering, and when the meeting was over I told him that I disagreed with everything that he had said. I asked his opinion on war. He said that he and his office manager both opposed this certain war (World War II) but that he was not a "philosophical pacifist." His mockery of religion by using the word Christian over and over again to bolster his hatred was sickening. No wonder my stomach couldn't take it.

Opportunity Bonds

President Truman announced the sale of Opportunity Bonds on May

16, 1949. Rik made some signs for me and I wrote to the City Manager saying that I was picketing the Post Office that day and asked for a permit to picket; saying if I did not get one I would picket anyway. I was downtown the Saturday night before and strangely did not have a CW to sell, as the papers were late in coming in. I had a few I.W.W. papers, and stood on a street corner trying to sell them when a young policeman came up. He used my pacifist technique against me and won his point. He looked over the wob paper and said with a smile: "I wish you wouldn't sell that paper on *my* corner." I knew that I had a right to sell the paper on any corner but I would be foolish to argue the point and be in jail on Monday morning when I had greater worlds to conquer, in my picketing of the Post Office. Accordingly I replied: "I have a right to sell papers on this corner but as you are so nice about it I will go to another corner."

My signs the next Monday read:

OPPORTUNITY BONDS
BRING:
WAR
DEPRESSION
BONDAGE
BANKRUPTCY
BUREAUCRACY
and
DESPAIR

And on the reverse side:

WHY PAY FOR
YOUR OWN
ENSLAVEMENT?

OPPORTUNITY BONDS
ARE
SLAVE BONDS

On reverse side:

"THAT GOVERNMENT
IS BEST
WHICH GOVERNS
LEAST"

Thomas Jefferson

I gave out CW's and did not have much trouble. The usual calls to go back to Russia and the inquiry of how much the Communists were paying me for my picketing occurred. Many people who had seen me before stopped and asked questions.

During these years several dozen people had refused to pay part or all of their income tax. Ernest Bromley, near Cincinnati, Ohio correlated the publicity on this subject and published the names of those refusing to pay taxes. Most of these were well-meaning Quakers or pacifists who kept their money in banks and had it taken by the tax man. Not being real radicals that was about the best they could do. Others refused once and then decided it was too much trouble to continue the effort. Others earned less than the $600 and so did not have to pay any tax.

Later in the spring Peter Maurin, the founder of the CW, died. I had met him a few times in Milwaukee, but had not seen him since I had been in the southwest. He is the other great man, besides Alexander Berkman, whom I have known personally. He was that rare combination: a hard worker and a brilliant thinker and writer. He was the most "detached" person I have known. He did not at all care for material things but woe to the person who tried to trifle with ideas around him: he would put across his "point" no matter what happened.

The same week my old friend Larry Heaney died. He was at that time on a farm west of St. Louis with Marty Paul. In the old days of the Milwaukee CW there was a drunk by the name of "One Round Baker" who had been a prize fighter of sorts. He delighted in picking out a new cop and spitting on his shoes and before the cop could strike him he would knock the cop down. He always was locked up in jail but he delighted in the sport of knocking down cops. He would come in the CW House and loudly shout that he would knock down any priest. Larry would take him quietly by the arm and walk him around the block and he would be pacified. No one else could tame him.

I had been a vegetarian since 1910. Along with this idea and with my attendance at Christian Science Church from 1922 to 1934 there had been a skepticism about the need for medicine. In fact I took none during that time nor since. The regular vegetarian papers and societies contained such a collection of freaks and frauds that I was repelled from emphasizing this portion of my belief. But to others who saw me refuse meat three times a day it seemed the most important of my ideas. The HYGIENIC REVIEW edited by Dr. Herbert Shelton of San Antonio, Texas—himself a vegetarian of anarchistic inclinations—seemed the best magazine along these lines. Rest and fasting was all that was needed when a person felt ill. Illness such as colds and fevers were nature's way of cleansing the system of impurities. A radical druggist friend told me of the immense profit made from Vitamin pills and of the obvious patent medicine frauds on the market. As we were sitting on the bus one day he pointed to a beautiful girl nearby and said: "See that unnatural look in her eyes. She has been taking that so-and-so medicine for reducing and it is playing hell with her kidneys."

Of all the phony moves the silliest was when Symon Gould, super-professional vegetarian, nominated himself for vice-president and two other men at different presidential elections, for president. He predicted a vote of 3,000,000 for peace, because vegetarians do not kill animals.

The Hopi

In late August Rik and I took a bus to Leupp's Corners, on our way to the Hopi Snake Dance. We had been invited by two Hopi friends. No bus runs to the Hopi so we started hiking the 70 miles to Hopiland. It was a fine clear, morning and although we each carried a medium sized bag, we cheerfully walked northward. After about three miles a woman in a nice car stopped and asked us to get in. She was on vacation too and lived in Baltimore. As Rik and I knew most of what the books said about the Hopi, and as Rik had lived with an aunt for eight years on a reservation where she was a government nurse, our conversation on Indians in general and in particular proved interesting to her. Naturally we told her that our point of contact with the Hopi was the fact that we were conscientious objectors. She was of a liberal mind and seemed to understand what the words meant. Before we reached the Hopi I had given her my current tax statement, a CW and my green card summarizing my tax refusal stand.

Small cornfields appeared bordering in the distant Washes where water sought its level when it did rain. Red buttes glistened in the sun, and finally the brown mesa of thousand year old Oraibi appeared right before us. From our view we could not see the stone houses which formed the most ancient of settlements on this continent. The brown sandstone homes at the bottom of the cliff which formed New Oraibi were scattered here and there. Patches of corn, beans, melons, and trees of peaches and apricots surrounded them. The whole pueblo was an organic part of the desert, with the exception of the white Mennonite church (with white outhouses that could be seen for twenty miles) Rik worked in an architects office and he shivered at this violation of taste, Both Eric Gill and Frank Lloyd Wright would have squirmed also at this monstrosity. If they had to have a church couldn't they have painted it brown?

Chester was working a few miles away in his cornfield, but another Hopi Conscientions Objector friend welcomed us. He had gone to college and on coming home was given the best paid job an Indian could get in the office of the agent, at nearby Keams Canyon. It took him several years to see that the inefficiency, graft, and favoritism to Indians who would blindly follow the whims of the officials was undermining the old Hopi responsibility and character. When the war came he did not register, and was let out of employment. After several visits by the FBI and other officials he finally got a year in Tucson road camp, and later a three year sentence for his second refusal to register. The constitution says that a person cannot be twice put in jeopardy of life and limb for the same offence, but the constitution means nothing to war mongers.

Upon his release he studied the Hopi traditions given by Dan of the Sun Clan of Hotevilla, Advisor and spiritual leader of the real Hopi. Now he is the interpreter of the traditions of the Hopi—of those who do not take old age pensions or assume the rice-Christian status based on gifts from the whites.

Massau'u, the Hopi name for God who rules the Universe, permitted two men to come to this world from the Underground where they had lived previously. Each was given a stone map upon which were inscriptions. This stone is at Hotevilla under the care of the chief of the Spirit Clan. God first made the sun which gives light and warmth to all living things; then the moon which is covered with a deer skin and gives a dimmer light; then the stars; and lastly the great Bird or Eagle which scours the sky awaiting the devouring of the refuse and offal of the earth.

Among the Hopi the wicked or evil one is said to have two-hearts. We might say a split personality. Symbolically speaking the hard hearts of mankind through the ages piled up and piled up until they formed great glaciers. Likewise the white man, hopping around after money, produces the great hordes of grasshoppers which did not exist before the white man came. The Hopi, like Atlas, hold the world upon their shoulders. Every good deed makes for harmony of nature, not only on this earth but in the universe. Every bad deed makes for storms, drought, earthquakes, wars

126

and misery. Prayers accompanied by eagle feathers and proceeding from one who is not a two-heart can overcome evil. As with Gandhi, all true deeds make towards a build-up that is invincible. In fact one good Hopi can save a pueblo from destruction, which the Hopi have predicted from old time will soon some. The prediction reads that the purfication of the world by fire and the destruction of evil-two-hearts will be accomplished by white brothers coming from across the water in what we would call World War III. Somewhere in this turmoil the White Brother who has the replica of the Sacred Stone will appear with it, and when the two are compared and found the same, then peace and brotherhood will begin and a New World with no armies, prisons, government, courts, or Indian Bureaus will cover the earth.

When a bad Hopi dies (and God is judge of what is good or bad—not the Indian Bureau) he still has the feelings of his old time body and its personality, but he cannot be seen by others. From the place where he is buried he can take but four steps a year toward the supiau: the hole in the bottom of the Grand Canyon ninety miles away which is the entrance to the Hopi Underground. Meanwhile he reviews his life of wasted effort, of wickedness, greed or whatever his especial sin may have been. The Good Hopi goes at once to the Underground. When this Third World War has cleaned the world of all two-hearts then the bad Hopi will be judged by "the God of the Hopi" who will push him into a pit of fire if he has not been purified by his four steps a year. Only the feeling body is burned. No soul ever dies. Then all the souls of both good and bad Hopi will be reborn into this new peaceful world. (Babies who die before they are initiatied into the clan when 20 days old are at once reincarnated into the same Hopi family.) This Deferred Reincarnation, with its allied Purgatory of four steps a year, and its life in the Underground of the Grand Canyon is a mixture of the tenets of many otherwise dissimilar religions—all of course unknown to the Hopi.

The real Hopi should not live in town and cater after the fleshpots of the white man. He should not strive for big cars, go in debt or be obligated to any one in a manner which would make it difficult for him to be a true Hopi. He should live from day to day with confidence that God will not let him starve, spiritually or physically. He should not send his children to the devil worship of the public school, accept rations or gifts from the government, register for the draft, vote, or pay taxes to the war-making state. Preferably he should work hard with his hands and be ready to live or die at any time for the True Hopi Way of Life—knowing that perhaps he alone might be left to save the city when destruction comes, and he cannot save it or himself when his mind is chasing after the dollar.

The Hopi are different from any other Indian tribe, inasmuch as they do not have a tribal chief who can sell them out to the whites. Chee Dodge, former head of the Navajos for many years, died worth several hundred thousand dollars. Each of the eleven Hopi pueblos is sufficient unto itself. They practice the anarchistic principle of secession whenever a group disagrees. Over twenty clans have chiefs in various villages with authority only in their own clan and village. Thus it is difficult for the government to bribe so many chiefs.

Some years ago the government placed most of the young educated Indians away from the pueblos in a work project for a few weeks. Then they scurried around and put across the Tribal Council idea among the older folks who did not understand what it was all about. But now that the real pacifist Hopi have explained that the Council is a scheme to put over government policies of exploitation under the false front of democracy, only a few government employees belong to it and it is not recognized by Washington as a factor.

Quakers, pacifists, and other well meaning people do not understand this set-up, and so have been unwitting aids to the war-making government. Thus the Fellowship of Reconciliation and the Quakers called a convention of Indians in Tucson in 1948, led mostly by Quaker Indian Bureau employees of that vicinity, seeking to get cooperation of Indians with the government. With organizations it is easy to bribe the leaders for oil and uranium leases and other million dollar boondoggling dear to the hearts of Bureaucrats. This year the convention was held in Phoenix under the same auspices. Will Rogers Jr., the Governor of Arizona, the head of the Legion, and other politicians were leaders of the Conference. The real Hopi came down and Dan read the now famous letter to President Truman in which cooperation with the government and its war making Atlantic Pact was denounced.

Last year the Quakers established themselves in the comfortable headquarters of the Government school at New Oraibi. They fraternized with the stooge Hopi and never went near the real Hopi who had behaved like Quakers are supposed to behave: They had gone to prison against war. This year they went to work and got as far as the roof of a recreation house. The Hopi have plenty of recreation in their dances and ceremonies; they do not need outsiders to build houses for them. The real Hopi say the government is just as likely to use it for a jail for recalcitrant Hopis as not.

A meeting was called right after the Snake Dance where the young Quakers, Dan and James and other real Hopi, Rik and myself attended.

One of the Hopi explained all this very diplomatically and told how the peaceful Quakers had unwittingly been the means of Hopi who were government stooges putting unethical pressure upon the real Hopi to help in this so-called good work. The Quakers took this criticism gracefully but I doubt if they got its full implication.

One Hopi Conscientious Objector had suggested that I say a few words, so I told them the story of those who asked "Where wert thou when thy Lord was crucified?" and the answer, "I was attending a meeting protesting against crucifixion." This was done instead of carrying the cross. In like manner today those who build schools for the devil worship of a war-mad state, and cooperate with the government, are crucifying the true Hopi. (Later I stopped at the Quaker headquarters in Pasadena. They seemed to be aware of this predicament but did not know what to do about it, still having the illusion of the state and being unaware of the history of the early Quakers who paid no taxes to a war-making state.)

The Hopi Point of View

Hopi Indian Nation,
Shungopovy, Arizona
March 2, 1950

Honorable John R. Nichols,
Commissioner of Indian Affairs,
Washington 25, D. C.

Dear Sir:

We have received your letter dated February 13, relative to the Navajo-Hopi bill. Mr. Viets Lomahaftewa has kindly referred to us for reply. Accordingly we held a meeting in Shungopovy village at which our highest chief, Talaftewa, of the Bear Clan, was present. We have read your letter carefully and thoughtfully.

As village advisors of Hotevilla, Shungopovy we speak for our respective head-men and for these villages that are still following the traditional form (self) government.

You know as well as we do that the whole mankind is faced with the possibility of annihilation as it was done in the lower world because of greed, selfishness, and godlessness. People went after wealth, power and pleasures of life more than the moral and religious principles. Now we have floods, strikes, civil wars, earthquakes, fires and the H Bomb! To the Hopi these are but the smoke signals telling us to set our house in order before our "true white brother" comes. Whom will he punish, a white man or an Indian?

Because we know these terrible truths and facts we the religious leaders of the Hopi people have been continuously opposing the $90,000,000 long-range program. It will not solve these larger issues for us. It will only destroy our moral and spiritual foundation thereby destroying the peace and prosperity of· the whole world. This is the traditional law of this land. It cannot be changed because it was planned by the Great Spirit, Massau'u. He has given us these laws and Sacred Stone Tablets which are still in the hands of the proper leaders of Oraibi and Hotevilla villages. Shungopovy holds all the major altars and fetishes, being the mother village and which represents the true Hopi.

You stated that the $90,000,000 "will be of real assistance to the Hopi people, but it cannot succeed without their understanding and wholehearted cooperation in achieving these desirable goals."

Yet the Land Claims Commission, we understood, will deduct these "helpful assistances" when and if the Indians file their land claims and win their cases against the government. No, we do not want to be indebted to the United States government at the present time.

In a letter to Dan Katchongva of Hotevilla you mentioned the fact that, "you stated that this money is not needed by the Hopi Indians, although you admit that the Hopis have been made poor by the reduction of your land and livestock . . . the reduction of your stock was forced upon you by the severe droughts of the past years."

Suppose you had spent most of your life working hard to accumulate large stock and land only to have someone come to you and force you to reduce your hard-earned stock and land because of "severe droughts". Wouldn't you too say that you have been made poor?

How would you like to have someone make laws and plan your life for you from afar? Pass laws without your knowledge, consent and approval? This Navajo-Hopi bill is being passed by the Senate and House of Representatives without our approval and against our will. Therefore whatever happens in the future the Hopi must not be to blame but the government of the United States.

We are not children but men, able to choose and decide for ourselves what is good and what is bad. We have been able to survive worse droughts and famine in the past. We do not fight droughts and famine with money, but by our humble prayers for more rain and forgiveness for our wrongdoings. Our land will bloom again if our souls are right and clean. No, we are not going to sell our birthright for a few pieces of silver such as the $90,000,000. Our land, our resources and our birthright are worth more than all the money the government of the United States may have. We are still a soverign nation, independent, and possessed of all the powers of self-government of any sovereignty. King of Spain recognized this long ago. Government of Mexico respected it, and it is still recognized by the U. S. Supreme Court. Now why, in the face of all these facts, are we required to file our land claims with the Land Claims Commission in Washington? Why are we required to ask a white man for a land that is already ours? This whole western hemisphere is the homeland of all the Indian. In this fact all Indian people should know.

Now, by what authority does the government of the United States pass such laws without our knowledge, consent nor approval and try to force us to relinquish our ancient rights to our land? Is it only for money? We do not want money for our land. We want a right to live as we please, as human beings. We want to have a right to worship as we please and have our own land. We don't want to have someone plan our lives for us, issue us rations, social security or other dole. Our plan of life have all been laid out for us long ago by our Great Spirit, Massau'u. This is our traditional path we must travel now.

Now if you truly and seriously want to help the Hopi people and honestly want us to understand one another we demand that you come to us who are the religious leaders of the Hopi tribe. This is the only way we can settle any problem. We must come together. The white people seem to be at a loss as to what to do now in the face of the terrible H-Bomb. Why don't you come to the most ancient race who know these things to learn what is to be done? We must meet together so that the common man may have his freedom and security. We want everlasting life; so do you. We are both aware of the fact that we are coming to the same point. To the white man it is a Judgment Day or the Last Days. To the Hopi it is the cleansing of all the wicked forces of the earth so that the common man may have his day.

The Hopi Tribal Council is being reactivated today but to us religious leaders it is not legal; it does not have the sanction of the traditional head-man. And it is composed of mostly young and educated men who know little or nothing about Hopi traditions. Most of the men supporting it are Indian Service employees, men who have abandoned the traditional path and are after only money, position and self-glory. They do not represent the Hopi people.

These major issues must be settled by the highest traditional leaders of the Hopi people and the proper leaders in Washington. It is time we get together peacefully and seriously to settle these matters now. If we fail to do this our lives are in very grave danger of being totally destroyed. Because we do not want this to happen to us or to our people we again demand that you come. Should you fail to come we shall be forced to bring this matter before the United Nations which we understand is for the purpose of settling matters of this nature. Our life is at stake so let us meet together.

Sincerely yours,

Hermequaftewa, Blue Bird Clan, Shungopovy
Dan Katchongva, Sun Clan, Hotevilla
Viets Lomahaftewa, Shungopovy

Chester took me in his car the two miles to the top of Old Oraibi. Here I met his relative Don, author of *Sun Chief,* edited by Simmons of Yale, which I had read several years before in Albuquerque. I had written to Don and he remembered my letter. He spoke English and was an educated, although not an especially pacifist Hopi. He did not need to cooperate with the government, having done well enough by himself by cooperating with Yale. Chester was helping him build a room. Several very beautiful Hopi women graced the doorways as we passed by. The face of the Hopi resembles that of the Hindu rather than the heavier physiognomy of other tribes. Water must be carried to the top of this ancient ruin. I helped Chester attach an oil drum on his car to haul the water to mix the plaster and concrete for his work in helping Don with the room.

Later in the day Dan came over and told me through an interpreter much of the Hopi history. The Hopi do not know the meaning of English radical words yet they have the personal responsibility and the right of secession which are basic principles of anarchism. Thus in 1906 about half of the Hopi in Old Oraibi left to form the pueblo of Hotevilla, seven miles to the northwest. This secession was because they did not wish to cooperate with the government ·as the others in Old Oraibi did. Today Hotevilla is the chief of all the villages in size and in opposition to the whites. As we left Old Oraibi we saw the village chief have his picture taken by white tourists for pay and selling kachina dolls to them. The real Hopi feel that this is making a monkey of Hopi life and traditions. Coming down again we saw small gardens and orchards in the sheltered places.

Some of those who seceded from Old Oraibi in 1906 wished to go back but they were not welcome so they formed the village of Bacobi to the north of Hotevilla. Today they fly the flag of the conqueror and are subservient. At Moencopi, 40 miles northwest of Hotevilla and two miles east of the former Mormon dominated Tuba City, just outside the Hopi reservation, are two villages: upper and lower. The former have cooperated with the government idea of a Tribal Council while those at the bottom have remained true to real Hopi tradition.

As the Hopi were never at war with the whites, as were the Navajo and Apache, they were included by the treaty at the close of the Mexican War in 1845, as given citizen rights, ownership of land, and the right to non-interference in their customs and religion. But the U. S. Government has broken this treaty as it has all other Indian agreements. These villages so far outlined speak one dialect and occupy the Third Mesa and beyond, westward. (This reminds me of Thoreau, who was asked on his death-bed by an orthodox relative if he had made his peace with God. His reply was characteristic of his whole life: "I never quarrelled with Him.")

The Second Mesa is ten or more miles eastward. Here is where we attended the Snake Dance at Mishongnovi, situated on a Mesa towering 400 feet over the valley below. Here the sun is greeted in early morning. Shongopovi and Shipolovi are the other villages here. In each of these villages are many of the true Hopi who have not succumbed to old age pensions and government bribes. They often speak a different dialect derived from the Tewa Indians who came from the southwest after the Great Rebellion of 1680, at the foot of the mesa. According to Hopi custom when any people come and ask to live among them they are asked what especial prayers or abilities they have to give to the Hopi. The Tewa said they would stay there and "protect" the Hopi from invaders. There are no battles on record but the Tewa were good naturedly allowed to remain.

The First Mesa is further east and a little to the north toward the shadow of the Indian Bureau at Keams Canyon. Real Hopi look upon these pueblos as an outpost of Hopiland and hardly a part of it, for they have intermarried with Navajo, Mexicans and whites, have commercialized their Snake Dance, and have taken on the vices of the white man along with his watered-down religion. (The Mormons, Mennonite and Baptist's subvert the Hopi. No Catholic missionaries have been among the Hopi since the Great Rebellion of 1680 when the church was torn down;

a result, many say, of the cruelties of the Spaniards when great beams were carried on the shoulders from the distant San Francisco mountains. I saw one of these beams near Don's home in Old Oraibi.) Hano and Walpi are the villages of the First Mesa. The postoffice is called Polacca. Recently when the Bureaucrats were trying to put over their $90,000,000 budget for the Navajo they got the bright idea of getting the rice-Christian, Hopi Agency interpreter, and some other subservient Mormon Hopi to Washington and have them apply for part of the money for the Hopi. Of course they represented only themselves. The real Hopi will not lease oil or uranium lands to the government or apply for settlement of land claims. They say the land is theirs without any "claims." They say that while they are poor and work hard they do not want any of this 90 million; that maybe the Indian Bureau is poor; for by the time they bookkeep this money it will have been the main source of income for needy Democrats. The Hopi reservation occupies a spot roughly 37 miles by 100.

Our hostess on the road slept in her car under the shade of a tree. About 3 p.m. we went toward the Snake Dance, Chester leading the way in his car. We parked among hundreds of cars at the bottom of the cliff and walked up the cliff this way and that until we reached the narrow areaway between the two-storied houses of the village. Here several thousand people were already assembled waiting for the Dance. I could tell a Navajo man or woman here and there among the Hopi. No cameras were allowed. Our friend from Baltimore feared the snakes so asked us to accompany her to a roof-top right across from the leaf bower which held the snakes. She paid 50 cents for each of us. The sun was in our eyes but we had hats so it could have been worse.

We looked around for the sight of friends: noticed a few of the young Quakers, but could not locate George Reeves and Dave Myers who were supposed to have driven in from San Francisco that day to witness the dance. Likewise we did not see the pretty student nurse from St. Monica's in Phoenix who was returning to her native Hopiland for the dance. We had met her on the bus and gave her a CW and a copy of the letter of the real Hopi to Truman which Rik and I had varityped and mailed for the Hopi.

I will not try to explain all the details of the Snake Dance. If I remember rightly, men and boys of the Antelope Clan danced around the small space in front of us throwing sacred blue cornmeal on a certain spot on the ground and stamping there with one foot. After a few rounds of this dance with a certain chanting, in came the men and boys of the Snake Clan. They were fiercely painted, each symbol meaning some very definite thing to them. Each reached in the brush tent and was handed a snake by the Indian within. This was at once placed lightly in the mouth, about eight inches from its head. With each snake dancer went another dancer with a feathered stick to draw the attention of the snake away from the man who had it in his mouth; although the snake could easily have bitten an ear or cheek. Scientists have examined these snakes after the dance and found them with fangs and with poison; not having been milked out, as some skeptics aver. Several boys roamed around ready to catch the snakes when they were momentarily released, and coiled or glided along the groups to the screams of the audience. Never did a snake get away for these boys grabbed them quickly. I only saw a rattle on one snake, but there may have been rattles on some I did not see. Many were what is called the super-agile and poisonous side-winders— and several were bull snakes. They have to catch whatever snakes they can get in the desert. I expect there were 60 snakes in all, and after each dancer had gone around a certain number of times he would take the snake out of his mouth and put it in his hand and get another one, so that each dancer had six or more snakes by the time he finished. One small boy stood at the end of some dancers and an Indian handed him a huge snake nearly as long as he was tall. The boy held it bravely in front of him, very close to the head of the snake. I fancied I saw a lump in his throat and tears in his eyes, but he held on.

Finally a circle was drawn in the sand and marks were made dividing it to four corners. This was done with sacred cornmeal until the whole circle was covered. Then all dancers threw the snakes in this circle and the small boys threw them back if they tried to get outside. They danced around with a certain chant for a time and then each Indian dancer grabbed a handful of snakes and ran — some to the North, some to the East, some to the South and some to the West. Then these snake-brothers of the Hopi would go in these directions and give notice that the Hopi desired rain for their corn and other crops. And woe to the white man who did not bring an umbrella, for soon the rain came. Once a stranger in a new car was caught in a flood that came thus after a Snake Dance and his new car remains yet in the vast middle of Oraibi Wash.

Don tells in his book about the time when he was young and was lying under a tree. A rattle snake came up and touched his foot and then went away. Came again and crawled up to his knee and went away; then up to his cheek and went away. Don tried not to show fear and he said to the snake, "Dear brother snake; I know I have not been a very good Hopi; but really in my heart I mean well. Please do not hurt me. Look into my heart and see that I am good." The snake came up again and coiled around his neck and kissed his cheek and went away. Don then said a prayer of thanks, for brother snake had looked into his heart and found him good.

Visiting Carmen and Sharon in San Francisco

I had not seen my daughters since that few minutes around Christmas of 1945. They were now mature enough to understand that conversation with their father was not a sin, so they asked me to meet them around the first of September in San Francisco. I left on the bus from the Snake Dance and met them at the home of my friend Vic Hauser with whom I was staying. Vic is a kind-hearted, rattle-brained, half radical who had read the CW and had written to me. Carmen and Sharon were beautiful and somewhat bashful. They had been attending a meeting of their cult at Mt. Shasta and were going back to Northwestern University to continue their musical education. They knew that I considered their cult simply a scheme for its founders to get easy money out of the uneasy consciences of the rich, by their super-denunciation of radicals and labor leaders. This cult, like the Jehovah's Witnesses, claims to use the blazing sword of God to destroy mortal enemies on earth whenever the time comes. My girls appreciated the emphasis on love and the whole Rosicrucian, vegetarian, non-medical discipline which I felt was a cover up for the luxurious life of the avaricious founders of the cult. They figured that my anti-tax and anti-war activity was good enough but hardly in the class of the super-prayers which went forth from the cult. However they were sincere, and the materialism of the cult had not made them mean-minded and hateful. Vic drove us up and down the steep hills and over to Berkeley, and we had a picture taken on Delaware Street, in front of the house where my wife and I had lived in 1924-25.

Vic took me to an I.W.W. outdoor meeting where Tom Masterson, a vituperative atheist held forth. Tom introduced me and I presented the CW ideas for nearly an hour. Tom asked me if I was selling the CW and thus started others buying the paper. I spoke over the pacifistic radio station in Berkeley about my anti-tax ideas and my Christian anarchist ideals. I also attended an anarchist meeting and met readers of the CW. Paul Goodman spoke at this meeting and typified the traditional anarchist excuse for doing nothing in his speech. Some of those present asked my opinion so we had it back and forth most of the evening. To hide away instead of openly opposing the war or the government seemed to be the prevailing anarchist attitude. I pointed out that this was not the program of Alexander Berkman and Emma Goldman. Paul Goodman wrote in an anarchist paper RESISTANCE which I pointed out did everything else but resist. They just talked about it.

Vic knew the Carota's at Aptos and we visited there for a few hours. This exciting young couple had adopted seven babies and had a veritable nursery in their mountain home. I had read about them in the CW, and although they seemed too religious they at least did something more than talk about it.

George Reeves had come to visit me for a few hours in Albuquerque when I worked in the orchard. He was born not far from my home town in Ohio. He shuttled back and forth between gardening and teaching. I had an interesting visit with him and his charming wife. I had corresponded with Max Heinegg, a vegetarian who had quit his job in San Francisco as a commercial photographer at the beginning of the war, as about all the work he did had something to do with war work. He is the first vegetarian per se whom I have known, other than Scott Nearing, who really works. I had heard Nearing speak at Ohio State in 1915; he was my teacher at the Rand School in 1920; and my wife baby-sat his son John, while Nearing debated with Clarence Darrow on the subject Is Life Worth Living? I had met him each year when he came to Milwaukee. He had visited Sharon in Evanston in 1946 and came to see me in Albuquerque later. I do not agree with his emphasis on World Government but admire him as a down-to-earth man.

I Meet James Hussey

During the summer I ran out of work to do, so walked south and east along the highway asking each farmer for a job. Finally about eleven o'clock and four miles away a young farmer, James Hussey, a reserve officer, told me I could cut Johnson grass if I liked. After that I worked for him now and then. On Thanksgiving day I carried but one small sandwich thinking that James would invite me for dinner, but he went to his folks for dinner and I had this small amount of food and cold water. I was digging twelve holes in the middle of a hard driveway for the planting of rosebushes. One of the vegetarian arguments is that people eat too much, and that when the belly is full of food there is not much blood left to work the brains in the head. About 4:30 in the afternoon my brains were going on all eight and I evolved the following philosophy which I wrote down when I got home that night:

"Love without courage and wisdom is sentimentality, as with the ordinary church member. Courage without love and wisdom is foolhardiness, as with the ordinary soldier. Wisdom without love and courage is cowardice, as with the ordinary intellectual. Therefore one who has love, courage and wisdom is one in a. million who moves the world, as with Jesus, Buddha and Gandhi."

My friend Helen Ford printed this on a card for me for Christmas. Later I raised the ante from a million to a billion. Nearly all of my philosophy is a rehash of what I have gained from Jesus, Tolstoy, and Ghandi. But this once it seems that an original thought got through.

Looking back over great radicals I think that Debs showed great love and courage, but all Berger or Hillquit had to do was to say, "Sign here, Gene, it's for the cause," and Debs showed his lack of wisdom by signing. Any amount of radicals, including myself, have great courage and a fair amount of wisdom, but are nearly totally lacking in love. Many pacifist leaders have great love and a fair amount of courage but are so gullible when it comes to being stooges for do-good schemes of no-good politicians that it is pitable. It seems to me that Dorothy Day alone today has the love, courage, and wisdom of which I speak.

* * *

Joe Craigmyle was doing time in the prison at La Tuna, Texas. They told him that the milk from the farm was used for a regular hospital in town. When he accidently saw a voucher showing that the milk went to the Navy he walked away from the farm. The government is notoriously a liar. Countless times have boys in Civilian Public Service been told that certain work was non military, only to discover later that it was military. The FBI came to see me, asking if Joe was hiding around my place. I told them that he was not here and if he was here I would not tell them. I had given the same answer to FBI men who had twice come to me in the orchard in Albuquerque asking about an anarchist who was in hiding. Joe was caught soon afterward and given extra time for escaping. The judge asked him if he believed in "overthrowing the government by force and violence." Joe answered: "I believe in overthrowing the government *without* force and violence."

I told the Old Pioneer that Joe had escaped and that the FBI men were after him. He said if Joe came here to hide him but not to tell him, the Old Pioneer, anything about it.

* * *

Ginny Anderson has a son Keith by her first marriage. While the conversation around the house between Ginny and Rik and myself was pacifistic, Keith read wild west funnies, carried a toy gun (a gift from relatives) and acted like the ordinary product of our breakfast-food box-top culture. The following conversation occurred the other day:

Keith—"Mamma, the radio says they are going to practice throwing bombs again. Who throws those terrible bombs that kill people?"

Ginny—"Governments throw them, my son."

Keith—"Where do they get the money to make them? Must cost an awful lot!"

Ginny—"The government takes the tax out of the pay check and people can't help it."

Keith—"Why do the people allow the government to do this? Why don't they refuse to have money taken from their checks?"

Ginny—"Fathers and mothers must work to get food. They must have a job."

Keith—"Does my Daddy help pay taxes for the bomb?"

Ginny—"No, he doesn't make enough."

Keith—"Does Uncle help pay for the bomb?"

Ginny—"No, he does not have steady work. He does not make enough."

Keith—"Why don't we get in a car and go around and tell people what a bad thing they are doing to pay taxes for the bomb? Maybe they would stop."

Ginny—"We have to work to get food and if we did that we would get in jail."

Keith—"They give you food in jail, don't they?"

CHAPTER 7.

Dorothy visits Phoenix
Washington D.C. Fasting
August Hiroshima Fast

1950

Phoenix - Washington, D.C.
Mott St. - Hopiland

I had not met Dorothy since September 1941 in Milwaukee. I had written letters to her and the CATHOLIC WORKER. She had come to Albuquerque a few months after I left for Phoenix in 1947. Now I was overjoyed to get a card from her saying that she would be here Dec. 29th. I met her at the bus. She had been a smoker until 1940 and now that she had quit as a penance she had a relaxed and peaceful countenance instead of that nervousness that goes with cigarettes. She stayed at Rik's. On New Year's Day we both met Father George Dunne, nephew of Finley Peter Dunne, the humorist, and now at St. Francis Xavier church here. He had been changed from St. Louis to Los Angeles and now to Phoenix because he was ahead of the ecclesiastical authorities on the race issue. He is not a pacifist nor an anarchist, but a fine brave man. We went with Father Rook to the Indian Yaqui mission in the desert southeast of Tempe. Here the Indians who are very poor had built this church or rather had added to the old one —and all without any games of chance or bingo parties.

The leading anarchist of this country happened to be in Phoenix just then, so I asked him if he and his atheistic Italian anarchist friends would like to meet Dorothy. Accordingly we met one evening in an anarchist home. The atheistic anarchists led off by saying that anarchism as defined by Bakunin negates all authority: that of the state and that of God. Therefore for Christian and especially Catholic anarchists to use the name anarchism is unethical. Furthermore it hurts the feelings of Italian anarchists who have felt the lash of the Catholic hierarchy.

Dorothy listened carefully to this reiterated statement and replied that this argument had not been brought to her attention before and deserved careful consideration. She felt that man of his own free will accepted God or rejected God and if a man chose to obey the authority of God and reject the authority of the state it was not unethical to do so. She inferred that we were *born into* a state and could not help it, but accepted God of our own free will. She and Bob Ludlow are converts to the Church.

The atheistic anarchist answer was that it was entirely illogical to use the anarchist conception of freedom to accept the authority of God which denies that freedom. Dorothy felt that the authority of God only made her a better rebel and gave her courage to oppose those who sought to carry over the concept of authority from the supernatural to the natural field where it did not belong. She said that the use of the word anarchism by the CW might shock people; that Peter Maurin, although an anarchist, had generally used the word personalist instead, but she felt that Bob Ludlow and myself used it rightly.

Another anarchist present thought that Ludlow had slipped over the use of the word anarchism on Dorothy. She replied that she stood back of all he said on the subject. This same anarchist repeated the regular argument that religion was opium for the people and that the Catholic Church always stood for the rich against the poor and that The CW was as bad as the history of the church. The anarchist leader felt that if the CW was only called the ANARCHIST WORKER instead of the CW it would be the best anarchist paper going. It was the word Catholic that spoiled it. These atheistic anarchists felt that if I had not hid behind the CW I would have been arrested long ago for my tax refusal. Dorothy answered that I had been a Christian Anarchist long before the CW was ever heard of. The anarchist leader said that Tolstoy in his Appeal to Social Reformers denounced the regular anarchists of his time and therefore should not be considered an anarchist.

I replied that I had read that article of Tolstoy's long ago and that Tolstoy was simply decrying the atheism and violence of various types of anarchists, and saying that without pacifism and the Fatherhood of God there could not be an effective anarchistic brotherhood of man. I also quoted from a book *Tolstoy the Man* by Prof. Stirner issued by Fleming Revel Co. about 1902. Prof. Stirner visited with Tolstoy and quoted him as saying that he was such an anarchist as Jesus and the Sermon on the Mount had made him; not to be afraid of the word anarchism, for the time would come when people would know its true meaning; that one who had accepted and obeyed the laws of God was thereby divorced from obeying the laws of men and did not need them. Stirner was sort of a Fabian Socialist, and he asked Tolstoy if Socialism was not a step on the way to anarchism. Tolstoy answered that it was not, and that it would end in a terrible dictatorship.

Dorothy mentioned the sacrifice of Jesus on the cross, original sin, etc., emphasizing the fact that rebels who sacrifice for a cause need this supernatural help to remain true. The anarchists misunderstood this idea or else were physically unable to accept the importance of sacrifice, saying that what they wanted was better material conditions and not pie in the sky; that religion made people willing slaves. Under pressure from Dorothy and myself they admitted that a good martyr now and then like the Haymarket men and Sacco and Vanzetti, was a good thing; but they did not like the emphasis upon sacrifice.

I felt that this was the trouble with the present atheistic anarchists: that they were not willing to sacrifice enough. I reviewed my prison history to prove that what changed me from being a Socialist and an atheist was the example of that true rebel Jesus. That thus my sanity had been saved and I had emerged from prison an anarchist. That I was associated with the CW because of its brave stand in publicizing my anti-tax campaign when anarchist and pacifist papers said very little about it. That my idea of God was not an authority whom I obeyed like a monarch but a principle of good as laid down by Jesus in the Sermon on the Mount, which I interpreted in day by day decisions as the forces of the state came in conflict with these ideals. And that in the same manner every person had to make a choice between his conception of good and of evil.

The anarchist leader still felt that religious people had no right to use the word anarchist, although we knew that he as an anarchist could not go to law and prevent it. I replied that the atheistic anarchists were more atheistic than they were anarchistic so he should not be adverse to allowing Christians or Catholic Christians to be at least as religious as they were anarchistic, if not more so. That the atheistic anarchist should be glad that the CW had left the state worship of ecclesiastical authorities and were anarchists. I said that the atheistic anarchists did not realize that it was possible for a Catholic to accept spiritual authority and not—like most Catholics, accept the state and temporal authority; that the atheistic anarchist should be glad that someone was fighting authority in one sphere—and the most difficult sphere at that—where the atheistic anarchist stood no chance of being heard. Dorothy told of losing over half of the CW subscribers because the CW opposed Franco and World War II.

The summary of Bob Ludlow on this subject seems conclusive: "There is an incompatability between anarchism and religion only if the Christian insists on transforming the authoritarian set up of the Church to the temporal field or the anarchist insists in rejecting authority in religion. In both cases it comes from a confusion of the supernatural with the natural."

As two of those present were vegetarians, our Italian hosts gave us all that diet. Despite the excitability of the Italian temperament there was good humor and goodwill present at all times. I felt that a fair summary of the question would be that whenever we of the CW became cowardly because of pressure from the Pope, then it would be time for atheistic anarchists to decry our use of the name anarchism. And that as long as they had no Pope to tell them what to do they ought to assert their native anarchism and come out and be as brave fighters against war and capitalism as were Bakunin, Berkman and Goldman, whom they revere.

The I Am Activity

About this time I had a letter from a teacher in Fairhope, Ala. where I had taught in 1924. Her name was Miss DaPonte and she had refused to pay taxes. She told of some boys, Quakers whose parents I had taught when I was there, who had refused to register. The judge in Mobile told the boys: "Well, you pay your taxes, don't you? And a large amount of our taxes goes for war purposes. If you were consistent in carrying out this belief, you would also refuse to pay your taxes."

The main "shrine" of the cult which my wife and daughters follow is at Mt. Shasta in California. I had written every week to my family, and after the girls had been sufficiently indoctrinated in this cult no letters were written by them to me until 1949 when they met me in San Francisco. I did not blame them and even hoped that my wife would get over this infatuation with fake religion, as she had with numerous other cults. She had been raised in the atmosphere of envy of the rich, which is the motivation of too many radicals. Despite my talk of Tolstoy and refusal to cooperate with government, she had never appreciated the real basis of religion as given in the Sermon on the Mount. I was not sure if my girls received the letters and enclosures of articles I had written.

Now, after twelve years of separation I felt that morally my wife and I were divorced although legally we were married by the common law of New York state. I do not believe in either marriage or divorce by the state, so naturally would not seek a divorce. I remembered the good times we had when hiking those four years, and of the early days in the woods where the girls were born in Wisconsin. If she was happy with this patriotic and materialistic religion I had no right and, I felt now, no purpose, in bothering her. So I wrote to the girls each week but not directly to her. With my Life at Hard Labor, vegetarian diet, and mind on The One Man Revolution, I did not have to have physical contact with any woman: I had work to do, and despaired of finding any woman who could stand the pace and who would not seek to tame me.

This did not mean that emotionally and in a platonic manner I had no attachment in my mind toward a certain woman. I had not seen her for nine years and had written often but received a reply only a few times a year. In a few days of conversation we had been able to understand that we had a common devotion to both pacifism and anarchism: and, sad necessity or undue asceticism as it might appear to others, a common practice of a celibate life. She had helped me to formulate my ideas on tax refusal more clearly and, almost alone, had publicized them. She had never once mentioned the subject of joining the Catholic church to me: simply saying that she always prayed for me along with many others. I also included her in my non-church prayers for years. So when Dorothy left, I felt a new reason for continuing my One Man Revolution.

I had become a radical the same year that Tolstoy died. I had a letter and a card from Gandhi in 1934 when he was in prison. I had written to him, "Gandhi. India" and he received it. I had never met these great spiritual leaders yet loved them. How much more then should I appreciate one such leader who was a contemporary and whom I had known for thirteen years. At my age in life the fact that she was a woman did not make as much difference as it would have twenty years before. The men I had known in my radical life had either all turned bourgeois, married women who had tamed them, or had died. So it was natural that I should enjoy the companionship of the one person I knew who lived the ideals which I believed.

In 1941-42 I had walked ten miles each Sunday evening to attend a Quaker meeting. Here in Phoenix the Quaker meeting was held in the morning when I would normally be selling CW's. If there had been one at night I would have attended. As it was I felt the need of spiritual strength in my picketing so attended mass and prayed for grace and wisdom before picketing. In the spring of 1949 the scabbing of seminarians per orders of Cardinal Spellman in the graveyard strike in N. Y. City aroused me. The opposition of the CW to this disobedience of the famous Encyclicals of the Pope, and their picketing of St. Patrick's Cathedral caused me to wish to praise God for such brave action. The best place to praise God was in the Catholic Church so from that time forward I prayed for grace and wisdom at mass, wherever I was selling CW's. But I still had the regular Protestant attitude toward the Catholic church, as being the worst of them all.

* * *

Around this time there was a Brotherhood meeting in the first Methodist Church down town. Levi Udall, Chief Justice of the Arizona Supreme Court was to speak for the Mormons. Frank Toothaker, Supt. of the Methodist Church in this district, and a pacifist of many years, was to speak for the Protestants. A leader of the Jewish charities, Mr. Kaplan, was speaking for the Jews, and Fr. Xavier Harris was speaking for the Catholics. It has always been my custom to read the daily papers carefully to see who is invading my territory, so when these leaders announced that they would speak on Brotherhood I wrote each of them a personal letter telling them that if they talked of Brotherhood and followed their respective churches in supporting war I would get up and say something about it if I had a chance. Also I enclosed my current leaflet and told them that I would be selling CW's outside of the church that night. The Mormon and the Jew came first and greeted me cordially and took a CW. Rev. Toothaker had already read the CW and I found that Fr. Harris had taken it for years.

There are many good things to say about the Mormons: their canning of waste food; their social life around the church; and their tithing. But Judge Udall gave a Fourth of July speech, with little depth of religion or real patriotism. The Jew seemed apologetic and rambled on seeming to want to say something without hurting the feelings of anyone. Rev. Toothaker did not say anything that was especially wrong but sidestepped anything of importance. Fr. Harris gave a real spiritual message but I doubt if many who were there appreciated it, including myself. There was no opportunity for questions. Later I became acquainted with Fr. Harris and found him an understanding radical of the CW type, although not accepting pacifism and anarchism with capital letters.

*   *   *

At this time the priest in charge at the big St Francis Xavier Church here did not allow me to sell CW's there. Friends told me that Fr. George Dunne on Feb. 5th. at mass had told of the visit of Dorothy and myself to him early in Jan. He said that he did not agree with us but he praised the courage and holy life led by Dorothy; gave a summary of my prison experiences, and announced the picketing which I would do on March 14th at the office of the Collector of Internal Revenue. At this time most of the local pacifists seemed afraid to be seen with me in public, and of course none of the ministers who said they believed in peace dared mention that there was a person in town who did not pay taxes openly.

*   *   *

TAX PICKETING

Joe Mueller was a house painter but dabbled in portraits. He made a huge oil painting of an airplane dropping a bomb; and of a battlefield and a graveyard with crosses. I could not get in a bus with such a sign. Having no other means of transportation, I got up early and walked the ten miles into Phoenix with my two signs, papers and leaflets, arriving by 8 a.m. The small yellow leaflet which I handed out was rather saucy and not a masterpiece. Rik varityped it. It read:

WHY AM I PICKETING?

Well, why aren't you? Do the A-Bomb and the H-Bomb make you sleep any better at night? Do you trust our politicians to protect us from destruction in an atomic war? Does it make good sense to foot the bill by paying income taxes?

I am not paying my income tax this year, and I haven't done so for the last seven years. I don't expect to stop World War III by my refusal to pay, but I don't believe in paying for something I don't believe in—do you?

Do you believe that anyone ever "won" a war? Or that any good can come from returning evil for evil? I don't believe it! And I don't believe I need preachers or policemen to make me behave, either.

I do believe in personal responsibility, and that's why I am picketing. Why aren't you?

Ammon A. Hennacy, R. 3, Box 227, March 14, 1950

Many people told me to go back to Russia. The wind blew and I was tired out, holding the big sign. The other sign told of the taxes that went for war and my refusal to pay taxes. The police did not bother me. A few people were sympathetic. One Catholic stopped me and said that Catholics had a bad enough time without my getting them in worse with such radicalism. I told him that I was not a Catholic but if I was I had a right to picket. He wanted to know if any priests supported my activity. I told him that Father Dunne did not agree with my ideas but had announced this very picketing at mass on Feb. 5th. "God bless you, then!" he smiled as he went on his way.

I was very tired by night and was glad when Rik drove me home. Joe had waited until my picketing was over and returned to Chicago the next day with his painting of the airplane that I had carried. The next day the ARIZONA REPUBLIC had a column by Columbus Giragi, old time newspaper man, deriding my picketing and saying that I should be locked up. I wrote to him and told him of two prominent men who disagreed with me but who were my good friends, and advised him to ask them about my sincerity. He did so and asked me to call upon him.

Fasting in Washington, D.C.

Joe Craigmyle felt poor after his release from prison, so he departed from his ordinary life of fruit stand operator to help me rassle 65 pound cement blocks under the beams of the frame house of the Old Pioneer. This was only a job for thin men so Joe and I qualified. We snaked here and there among the gopher holes and skunk apartments for ten days until the job was finished. Meanwhile we had notice from pacifist headquarters in New York that all varieties of pacifists were going to fast during Holy Week and picket the White House in Washington, D. C., against the piling up of atom bombs. If it had been just ordinary picketing I would not have bothered for I could always do that in Phoenix. The CW would be represented which would lend some spirituality to the project; and this would be an opportunity for me to picket the head of the U. S. Revenue office in Washington.

The Hopi had spoken of wishing to protest against the inclusion of their name in the Navajo-Hopi bill, so I wrote to my Hopi friend telling him I would collect money for his expenses from radical Catholics and pacifists here if he would accompany me. I told the Old Pioneer that I would leave on the 26th. of March. Joe is slow to make up his mind on anything and would not say whether he would go or not. When I got word that my Hopi friend was going, Joe decided that we three should go in his Willys pickup.

I already had my summer garden planted, except melons and later crops, and irrigated it on Saturday. That evening Joe came out and got my sleeping bag. Rik made some picketing signs for me and we were there for supper. About 10:45 p.m. we received a phone call that my Hopi friend, and Dan Kuchongva, spiritual leader of the traditional Hopi, were in town and would be over in a few minutes. They brought bed rolls with them and piki bread. Rik's children were wide eyed to see real Indians. We left at 7 a.m. Sunday. I reclined in the back; partly under blankets. We stopped at the Catholic church in Tempe where our good CW priests Bechtel and Rook, held forth, and said a prayer for the success of our journey, Dan sang Hopi prayers and Joe and I thought the best we could do was to say our pacifist-anarchist, non-church prayers. Near Florence we saw beautiful cactus blossoms peeping through to enliven the desert. (Mother Bloor had hiked over the country at the age of 65 and said the most beautiful spot was this very place.) Before we got to Tucson it was snowing and raining and I shivered to think how far we were from our destination.

We went to the home of Ralph, a Hopi silversmith who had done time in chains at Keams Canyon years ago with Dan for non-cooperation with the white conqueror whose policy it was to kidnap the Hopi children and send them to missionary schools. His wife and daughter prepared us an excellent meal and as the rain let up we built the back of the pickup into a secure and nearly rainproof shelter for the one whose turn it would be to sleep there while the other three sat in front.

By 3 p.m. we were headed for El Paso. We had intended to take the middle route through Meredian, Miss., but storms in that vicinity sent us southward. A little later the sun shone through the clouds for the first time that day and Dan stopped and placed eagle feathers along the road side saying the appropriate prayers for our journey. He also scattered sacred corn meal before the car and about ten paces ahead, with prayers. Joe and my Hopi friend took turns driving and we did not stop except for coffee or gas until just before dark when we arrived at Dr. Herbert Shelton's rest home in San Antonio. He had told me to stop and he would give me free copies of his HYGIENIC REVIEW dealing with fasting, which is a basic therapy in his conquering of the disease of people who finally, like the woman in the scripture "suffer from many physicians." He was not in just then but later Joe and I visited him and found him most gracious. He said that at times he felt more anarchistic and at other times more socialistic. He was not religious in the church sense, but strange as it seemed to us opposed birth control because it was un-natural. He felt that the CW program "coddled the unfit," but we did not argue with him for we felt that on the subject of health he was the master, and he did not pretend to be an ethical expert. We found later that a non-radical from Phoenix took a fast of 58 days and was cured of a number of diseases, any one of which could have killed him. Whether he went back to a diet of white bread, white sugar, liquor, cigarettes and canned goods and got sick again we did not know. Rest along with fasting and absolutely no medicine or vaccines is his method.

Here in San Antonio we looked up my roommate of 1915 at the University of Wisconsin, Bill Brockhausen, whom my wife and I had visited in 1923 when we were hiking. He was an advertising executive with a big house and servants headquarters where the Hopi soon were sleeping peacefully. Bill and I sat up until early morning talking over old times. His father had been a Milwaukee Socialist of the old school and Bill had been a natural political compromiser. He greeted me gladly in the midst of that product which has made Milwaukee famous. I had always been an extreme radical in his eyes and I suppose brought back visions of Debs and the old days before he had become so prosperous. In his overflowing good nature he told me to make his home my picketing headquarters if I ever came to Texas to live. Then his old conservatism coming up he said, "You don't do anything constructive, Ammon. Here you are roaming the country with two Indians." I did not argue the point with my extra extrovert friend. We left early without waking him.

We bought some bananas at Houston, massive town of skyscrapers, and left CW's at a Catholic church near where we stopped. All along we gave copies of the Feb. CW, explaining that the Indians mentioned in my article on the Hopi were the ones with us. I had the address of Dorothy DaPonte, a tax refuser in Mobile. She had moved but when we drove into Fairhope across the bay where I had taught history in the high school 26 years before we found that Miss DaPonte was a teacher there. She came of an old Southern family and nearly caused her father to have a nervous breakdown last year when she refused to pay taxes and had bravely escorted a young Negro girl to the front seat with her in a Methodist church. By now her father was getting used to her, only deploring that there were no others in the community who also refused to pay taxes. Two teachers at the school planned to fast with us although they had to stay there and teach. Miss DaPonte would have liked to have come along but had to stay as a witness in some trial about segregation. As many do who are new in a movement she asked why I did not fast-to-the-death on the Whitehouse steps against the H Bomb. I felt that if such an act came as the natural conclusion of a holy life it would be worthwhile if the persecution came from the State as it did in Gandhi's case. It was nothing to be entered into lightly, but required much prayer and fasting.

Several times when we became lost Dan would point a certain way and this would be the right direction. He did not know one state from another and could not read signs but he had a sense of direction. At midnight in Atlanta midst sewer repairs he knew where he was going and we didn't. Toward morning we came to Clarkesville, Ga. and soon to the 800 acres of the Macedonia Cooperative Community. Here my old friend and social worker from Milwaukee, Dave Newton and his brave beautiful wife, Ginny, were members of this adventure in living. Before the first draft in 1940 we had discussed non-registration, but Dave was a liberal, not a radical, so he registered and spent about four years in CPS. About the time the war was over he walked out of CPS and was in Sandstone prison with Bill Ryan and Walter Gormly. He was paroled out to Macedonia. All of the families here were CO's, many of them also vegetarians. Here each family lives in a separate house and breakfast is at home. Coffee at 10 in the common room for those who desire it and a common meal at noon is the rule. Supper is generally at home. There is a common storeroom where such items as have to be purchased are kept. Each one has a key and can take what they like without anyone else knowing about it; only they mark the amount taken on a chart so the stock can be renewed without sudden famine occuring. The main source of income here is children's building blocks and other play apparatus.

146

Expensive machinery helps in this production. Del Franchen, who was already fasting and who would go to Washington for a few days as he made a return trip with furniture, was one of two who attended to a small dairy. They furnished milk for all in Macedonia and living expenses of the two families who attended to the cows. A few garden patches were cleared. One family had lived here for about three years but finally decided that such a life was not for them. It is difficult to find both man and wife who will put up with the deprivations and hard work necessary to make community life a success. For young folks who are raising children it is an ideal place —that is until the arguments commence about private or public school and the desire to raise children for success in a bourgeois world. We left about 9 p.m.

The Hopi wished to visit the remnants of Tsali's tribe who by their rebellion in 1828 had not been deported with the other Cherokee to Indian Territory, so we went the long and mountaneous way to Cherokee. We knocked on all doors about 2:30 a.m. but could arouse no one. Likely the unreconstructed did not live on this sign-decked highway that catered to tourists so perhaps we did not miss anything.

Winding around the beautiful Smokies and asking numerous directions we finally brushed along side a wagon where armed guards were bossing a chain gang in road-mending. Finally we met tall and well built Tilly Brooks, wife of the CO Arle Brooks, of whom Judge Welch spoke in Philadelphia in 1940 that he felt like Pontius Pilate in sentencing Arle to prison for non-registration. I had corresponded with them some years ago. Arle was away in a mountain helping build a house. Each of several families here at Celo, N. C. owned their separate few acres and made their own living as they could.

We drove on steadily, and at 3 a.m. on April first knocked on the door at Inspiration House, 1867 Kalarama Road and under the efficient ministration of Bayard Rustin we were soon sleeping on the floor in the front room. We were among the first to arrive for the fast which had been postponed until midnight. I had many letters from friends feeling that I should not endanger my life by fasting. One of the first people I met was Emily Longstreth, wife of Walter Longstreth, Philadelphia lawyer and Quaker who had also refused to register for the draft in 1942. Both of the Longstreths refused to pay taxes for the war. Also John Baily, a young student feeling his way midst the maze of World Government, back-to-the-land, pacifism, anarchism, etc. Lucile Lord, an FOR member of a month, a pretty young girl, was also a first arrival. We had breakfast of scrambled eggs together in a restaurant. (Before starting a fast you should not eat heavy food.) Soon I met Woodland and Olga Kahler, super-vegetarian Vendantist friends of Scott Nearing. They asked about anarchism and I loaned them my article on Christian Anarchism in THE ARK which had been published a few months before in San Francisco by a group of anarchists who were atheistic but had asked for my explaination of Christian Anarchism. The English pacifist Winifred Rawlins, with whom I had corresponded, was also there. J. B. Fenner, an elderly Unitarian from Pittsburgh, roomed near me. He had quoted my "love, courage and wisdom" in the bulletin of his church. All this anarchism was new to him and for an older man he did pretty well in trying to line it up with his idea of brotherhood in general. He stood up fairly well in picketing. Charles Huleatt of Tracy, Calif. was a young man of much energy whose duty it was to awaken the sleepers in the morning. He had emerged from a religious environment and at this stage called himself an anarchist. Grace Rhoades was an efficient and pleasant lady with whom I had corresponded on the tax refusal question. She spent endless hours typing for the group. Margaret Dungan was an elderly, smiling lady who taught in a high-class girls school. She is also a tax refuser with whom I had corresponded. She was a good sport in picketing and stood up in fasting much better than the super- vegetarians whom I expect watched their loss of weight too morosely.

Toward evening I was pleased to meet Dave Dellinger with whom I had corresponded for years. He is the one man there with whom I feel most in common, anarchistic and not super-religious. He has character and I love him like a brother. His adopted son Howie Douglas slept near me and was the youngest of the group. Janet Lovett, wife of Bill Lovett of the first CO group to go to jail, is a sweet girl always on hand to do her share. She and Bent and Taddy Andresen came from the group at Glen Gardner, N. J. where Dave prints ALTERNATIVE. The Andresen's are critical of religious ideas. Bent was on a long hunger strike in prison. I had known of Francis Hall but had never met him. He and his wife Pearl were religious, and quiet vegetarians, Francis tried to be fair but I felt he stressed religious observances too much.

I had known A. J. Muste, at times called the Number One Pacifist, in 1920 when he was a Trotskyite and again in 1942 in Boone, Iowa at a FOR Conference when he and I each thought we would get five years for refusing to register the next week, I had written to him for five years suggesting that he refuse to pay taxes. He finally came around to that position and does very well. He is edging toward non-cooperation with government. I had only eaten a banana and an apple during the day. Shortly before the fast was to commence Francis and Pearl Hall and Dorothy and I went to a restaurant where we had supper.

Dorothy had said that she would not picket during the week. She came here to pray. There was a long discussion about a 24-hour vigil before a candle—purchased for $3 when one for $1.00 could be had from any Catholic church. It was finally decided that those should pray, who liked, in a separate room. Each evening and each morning sessions were held to decide the action for the day. Leaflets were prepared and much discussion was held upon the exact wording. It was after midnight before the final form was mimeographed—while Bayard Rustin entertained those present with lusty songs of prison, accompanied by his banjo. The good old ladies upstairs could not hear this or they would have gone home at once in dismay it is feared. And all of this activity on an empty stomach.

On Sunday I went to mass with Dorothy, not because I believed in the mass, but because I believed in Dorothy. All these years Dorothy had not spoken to me much on theology. Once in a group she said to me never to join the Church because I loved her and the CW; it was the Church that had to be loved.

She gave out leaflets at Catholic University, and the Kahlers and I went to the Catholic Cathedral with leaflets. Joe did not know whether he wanted to sleep all day or not, but when we got to the Cathedral he was already there. Gordon Zahn, Dick Leonard, and other CO's and Catholics came to see Dorothy evenings. At one open meeting at night the Chairman asked Dorothy to explain about the CW movement. She said that she came here to pray and not to talk; that they should read the CW for information about the movement. Wednesday evening she was called back to New York by the serious illness of Charles O'Rourke, an old timer of the CW staff. Burly Dave Mason came the next day in her place to represent the CW.

Monday we picketed the White House. The group thought my sign saying I had paid no taxes for seven years was too radical, so I carried a sign saying that 75% of the income tax went for war. Others carried signs about The Gandhi Way, not War, being the best, etc. We gave out leaflets and were not bothered. The paper next day had a picture of us. A Committee called on the White House to ask the President (who was in Florida) to rescind his approval of the H Bomb and hinted that he should resign rather than continue his murderous way. Tuesday a committee headed by the Kahler's (Mrs. Kahler is Russian) were greeted warmly at the Russian Embassy and were told that Russia would disarm if we would. A telegram about this was sent to Truman. An Appeal to the Russian People was handed to the Embassy and handed out on the streets.

Wednesday was a day of rest and those who wished to visit did so. Several people felt weak and some had to take orange juice to keep up. I had fasted ten days in jail once and had been in a dark hole on bread and water for ten days in Atlanta, so the fast did not worry me. Voice of America and Tass were appealed to, to give the pacifist message. The Atomic Energy Commission was also visited, as was the National Educational Commission. Dave Dellinger had an Appeal to Workingmen which he wanted to give out at factories but because of the decision to visit Hugh Johnson's Pentagon Building there was a try at an open air meeting instead, and this failing we gave out literature on the street for several hours. Thursday morning, which was stormy, saw Fenner, Lucy Lord, Winifred Rawlins, Ann Rush, a young married woman from Tracy, Cal., Ruth Hartshaugh, wife of a minister who tried to understand all this new anarchism, and myself handing out leaflets at a high school.

I did not want to picket the tax man until I had enough CW's to hand out so I waited until Thursday evening when they came from New York. The group (Dorothy absent in New York) voted not to allow me to jeopardize them by putting out any of their basic leaflets when I picketed the tax man. So on Good Friday morning I went along with Edger Bell, a young Negro tax refuser from Washington, D. C. It was quite windy but not very cold. We did not picket the U. S. Treasury, where they keep the stolen money, but the Department of the Collector of Internal Revenue, where they do the stealing. A cop came out at once and told me I could not picket government property. I told him that I had already picketed the Post Office which was government property, in Phoenix, and had gotten away with it.

"But this is *real* government property," he replied.

"There is a *real* Supreme Court around here someplace that says this is a free country and no permit is needed," I said quickly.

He replied that I would have to go up to 19th. st. and get a permit to picket or he would pinch me. I told him that was a long distance to walk and if I went there and did not get a permit I would picket anyway, and then he could pinch me. I said he ought to call his boss and see what the law was, and then act accordingly. He smiled and said he would check up, and there was no further trouble. We gave out all of our papers and some slips about my non-payment of taxes. Workers came out of the building and asked for copies. Only 15 people who passed refused to take our literature, so we considered our work a success.

While I was picketing the tax man, the group had a discussion about tactics at the Pentagon Building. The nice old ladies would not take any part if there would be any arrests or trouble. And Wally Nelson, a courageous Negro from Cincinnati who picketed Ashland prison when Jim Otsuka was there, would not take part if pipsqueaking tactics were used. I was not present but I understand that A. J. Muste weakened and allowed the old ladies to have their way. They had left for the Pentagon by the time I got back from my picketing. Most of the group stood against the wall in the corridor by Johnson's office. He invited them to hold their prayer meeting in a certain room, out of sight, nearby. They evaded this by going outside of the building and sat on the steps during the Holy Hour of Good Friday, and nearly until dark. Later most of us agreed that the whole thing was a farce, for we should have either disobeyed the cops and had our civil disobedience or never have gone in the first place. Moral: too many old ladies.

There were some late arrivals who fasted for only a day or two or who had fasted in their home towns but were unable to come to Washington the first of the week. One of these was Marshall Bush, a blind man from up-state New York, who had befriended CO's during the war. Ralph Templin of Yellow Springs, Ohio, who had been a missionary in India and knew Gandhi, but who returned to this country rather than swear allegiance to the British Empire was present. He had poise, and was a non-registrant and tax refuser. He and I handed out leaflets one afternoon. Horace Champney and Lloyd Danzeisen of the PEACEMAKER group in Yellow Springs also came. Bill Sutherland and Paula Waxman, and Juanita Nelson, wife of Wally were active in getting our leaflets done on time. Katie Voorhies was an elderly, blind Negro woman from Tracy, Cal. who took money she had saved for burial and came here. Dave Mason was an old time wob. I went to mass with him mornings. Madge Burnham made fine precise posters. Walter Longstreth came down to greet his wife who had weakened somewhat physically while fasting. Elizabeth Haas, a young Quaker librarian from Baltimore who was fired because she refused to sign a loyalty oath, was a part-time faster also. I had met Louise Haliburton in Camp Mack, Indiana when I spoke at a Brethern Conference there in 1938. George Houser, non-registrant and tax refuser whom I had met in Cleveland in 1945 also came late. A young Quaker girl who works as a playground assistant brought her sleeping bag for the last three days.

There was an attempt at the fast to evaluate what we were doing. Some felt that there was too much activity and not enough discussion. Others felt that there should be more prayer. Miss Dungan felt that if a person led a life of voluntary poverty he would miss the aesthetic values: music, beauty, etc. I spoke up and boasted of the scenery and sunsets of desert Arizona which cost nothing and which I liked better than the canned music and organized beauty of the cities. I am reminded here of Dorothy's saying that she liked the chirping of the desert thrush, the cooing of the mourning doves and the varied song of the mocking bird at Desert Ranch just as much as a symphony.

I was asked to give in detail my methods of propaganda. At another meeting on tax refusal Ralph Templin explained to some of the elderly ladies who refused to pay only part of their income taxes that the amount they did pay would be prorated for war, so the only way was to pay nothing at all. Bayard Rustin gave smart answers to questions from outsiders. I felt that this was too much of a varied group to do any one thing very well, although the meeting of so many kinds of people ought to be an education to all.

I did not have a headache during the week and always was nearly last to bed and among the first to get up. I was in good physical condition from my hard work and good care of myself. One night I had supper with my old friend, Francis Gorgen of Baltimore, and it did not bother me a bit to sit by and watch him and his family eat. He drove me over to see my cousin Marie, whom I had not seen since we were youngsters in Ohio. Her father had been a Congressman in the old days of McKinley. I met Fred Libby of the National Council for the Prevention of War, with whom I had corresponded for years but whom I had not met before. The lady from Baltimore who had picked Rik and me up when we were hiking to our first Snake Dance, came over and took the Hopi out to supper. They brought home a pear and an orange for me to eat after my fast was broken.

A few minutes after midnight on Saturday we all had orange juice and/or V8 juice. The Hopi had brought some piki bread which is like cornflakes and I gave some to each person. Bayard and Bill Sutherland and Bent sang some songs. The next morning A. J. Muste read a poem and asked me to read my letter from Gandhi. None of us were the worse for the fast. We kidded Joe about sleeping half of the time, but this is his normal state, and not due to fasting.

The Hopi had met with all of the groups and the interpreter had translated the Chief's message often to those interested. The Hopi fast and pray at home. To picket is not their way, but they were interested in their white brother pacifists. The newspapers took the Chief's picture as a man who did not want help from the government, and it appeared all over the country.

Joe and I went along with the Hopi to the Indian Bureau where we spent five hours interviewing officials. First we met Dearcy McNickel, assistant Indian Commissioner. He is a sophisticated, one twenty-fourth, or some such fraction, Flatfoot or Flathead Indian who had just written a book, *They Came Here First,* lauding all Indians who are government stooges. He studiously insulted the Hopi interpreter by calling him by his English name instead of his Indian name. The Chief spoke of the Hopi way of life; how the government employees of the Hopi spoke only for themselves and had long ago left the true Hopi way. He told of meetings that the Indian Agent had held and what went on at these meetings. While one Hopi was translating the English to Dan, McNickel looked at the recorded minutes of the meeting and whispered to me that the old man was honestly reporting what went on and had a wonderful memory, for he did not make one mistake. McNickel asked Dan why, if he wore a white man's coat and rode in a white man's car he did not support the white man's schools and way of life. Dan drew himself up proudly and replied:

"I have heard these words from traitor Hopi but I never expected to hear them from you." McNickel blushed and hid his face behind his hands in shame.

In the afternoon we met with Commissioner Nicholson who was soon to be replaced by Dillon Myer. He was a pleasant fellow. He asked Dan how he liked the roads and Dan replied that they were good enough for the Hopi but not good enough for the white man to rush around and go nowhere fast and disturb the peaceful Hopi. He asked about the schools and Dan said he did not send his children to government schools for only devil worship was taught there. He asked about water and Dan replied that the government drilled a well right on the edge of the land he used and on the other side were Navajo. He did not use this well for he knew that in time the Navajo would push over and, with the aid of the government, would get the rest of his land. Dan said that there was testing for oil on Hopi land. Nicholson replied that no oil testing could take place without his consent. Dan spoke up:

"You are not there and do not know whether the Indian Agent is in collusion with the oil company or not."

Nicholson asked why the Hopi boys did not register for the draft and get exemption as conscientious objectors. The interpreter replied that the Hopi were traditional pacifists and would have nothing to do with putting down their names for war: that promises made by the government were not kept anyhow. The Christian Hopi and the government-employee Hopi went to war, but not the real Hopi. Dan spoke of the stone tablets which gave the boundary of the Hopi land; that soon the white brother of the Hopi would come with the replica of this stone and the world would be purified by fire in World War III where all who were not true to their ideals would be destroyed. The real Hopi could therefore not make compromise with the oppressor.

While this conversation was being translated the government lawyer, John Jay, who was sitting next to me asked: "Did you read that good article on the Hopi in the CATHOLIC WORKER?" "I wrote it," I answered. Jack Durham, publicity man for the Bureau, was also present and smiled approvingly when the interpreter translated Dan's forthright message. As we got up to leave I gave all those present copies of the CW with my article on the Hopi.

Nicholson put his arm around Dan and said:

"The way of Jesus, Gandhi and the Hopi is right. I think I am an anarchist myself. This whole mixed up world doesn't make sense."

He was on his way out of the Indian Service so I suppose could afford to speak the truth.

Another day we had a meeting for an hour and a half with Judge Witt of the Court of Land Claims, a stern-looking, old man. He explained that the Hopi had one more year to file a claim for the land which they felt the government had taken from them and given to the Navajo. He advised them to get a lawyer. Dan gave the regular Hopi sermon at length, saying that they did not want money for the stolen land; they were here to ask the white man to repent of his evil ways. The judge wiped his eyes again and again and with great feeling said:

"I thank you for the best sermon I have ever heard. I congratulate you on your noble faith and religion. I appreciate your visit and wish you well."

We spent a few minutes with Congressman Toby Morris, typical demagogue and head of the committee on the Navajo-Hopi Bill. He said he did not know how the name of the Hopi got in the bill. While I was picketing the tax man the Hopi interviewed Senator Johnson of Colorado. He had not known about the real Hopi and had the idea that all Indians, like most white men, had their hands out for something from the government.

Tuesday morning after Easter we spent several hours with Mr. Nash, secretary to David Niles of the President's staff. He knew a real Hopi from a government Hopi and tried to say that Truman was a very religious man who would not allow anything to be done to harm the Hopi without first letting them have something to say about it. While the interpreter was translating, I whispered to him that there was a great difference between Dan and the rice-Christian Hopi. He nodded approvingly toward Dan.

Mott Street

After selling CW's at the Cathedral I left around noon with Bill and Paula Sutherland and Bent Andresen, for New York. Bill is dark skinned and the waitress where we stopped for some ice cream said that Negroes were not served here but "Egyptians were o.k.," looking at Bill. He had been called many names but never an Egyptian.

I had visited Mott St., the home of the CW, for a few hours in 1938 and 1939 but did not remember just whom I had met. I had corresponded with Bob Ludlow, one of the editors of the CW, for several years and was anxious to meet him. It was about 9 p.m. when I walked into the kitchen and introduced myself. Several there know of my articles and greeted me kindly. Bob was not in just then. I was soon greeted by Dorothy, and Eleanor and Marge, in the kitchen where the latter lived with her children. Dorothy felt that scrambled eggs and coffee would be just the thing for one who had fasted for a week and I agreed vociferously. O'Rourke, who had been ill, was better, but Tom Sullivan was not to be seen as he was suffering from a breaking-out caused by the backfire of pencillin. I met Bob for a short time around midnight and took to him like a brother, although he was very quiet and difficult to get acquainted with. He is the first anarchist, other than Peter and Dorothy, whom I had known of around the CW and we had much in common.

I went to the top floor and visited with two men who asked questions for a long time. One of them was the head cook downstairs. I did not hear the clock strike 3 and 5 so I must have slept 2 hours.

I was wondering what spiritual result there would be for me in this Fast. I had been busy with propaganda and had met many fine people, but I felt that was not enough. When I awoke I had the feeling that I ought to get a CW house started in Phoenix as soon as possible. I had to find a Catholic to run it and as yet I had not found any to help me sell CW's on the streets. When Dorothy met with the anarchists in Phoenix she had mentioned that "Vanzetti House" would be the name of the house when it was started. I mentioned this to some people later and they thought a CW house should only be named after a regular Church saint. I replied that Vanzetti had been born a Catholic in Italy and had only left the Church because big churchmen had stood with the big landlords against the poor. That his sister who was a practising Catholic, came from Italy to see him before he was executed. That his last words were worthy of a saint: "I want to forgive some of those who are doing this to me." I had never met him but when my wife and I were hiking we met Mrs. Sacco and Dante and the baby several times at Mrs. Jack's. We went with Mrs. Sacco when she saw her husband and we nodded to him and clasped our hands as if shaking his hands, which we were not allowed to touch. I remember how I quit work and my wife and I cried all day on Aug. 23, 1927 when Sacco and Vanzetti were executed. For years I had addressed a memorial meeting on Aug. 23 until in 1942 when I had such a meeting in Denver and but one person attended, I ceased. *Boston* by Upton Sinclair is a novel based on this case and should be a part of the required reading for all young people.

I went down to the kitchen and had a bowl of coffee which was handed to me by a well dressed, smiling, elderly man. Later Dorothy told me he was the Shy Apostle written about in the CW by John McKeon. I accompanied Dorothy to the small Italian church. Only two or three others were there. The walls were covered with life-size murals of my favorite saint, Francis of Assisi, Before this I had always sat still in church but today I felt like kneeling when Dorothy did. The religious meetings at the Fast were boring to me. I felt more uplifted by contact with the Hopi. Ever since I had been released from Atlanta prison in 1919 I had believed in enough orthodox dogma: Father, Son, Holy Ghost, Immaculate Conception, all the miracles, the Resurrection and Ascension, but I did not see any connection between any church and the Sermon on the Mount—and least of all was I attracted to the Catholic church. Mostly because of Franco I suppose. If I had known any Protestant who was an anarchist and a pacifist I would have gone to church with him. Dorothy was the only religious person I knew who had that greatest of virtues: courage. So I was glad to kneel beside her.

Returning to Mott street I saw Bob opening a huge bundle of letters that had accumulated over Sunday. Dorothy asked me to answer a request about anarchism from some Quakers. I was glad to meet Jack English when he came in, and was sorry to miss Irene Naughton who was on a speaking tour to Novia Scotia. Dorothy asked me to entertain seminarians who came in while she was hunting for a new headquarters for the CW, which was being evicted because the house was sold.

I spoke to Fr. Deacy of St. Patrick's on the phone. He had written in the CW. As I knew Roger Baldwin was not in town I told Bob the only two people I wanted to meet just then were Jim Peck and Sandy Katz. I spoke to Jim on the phone but he could not come down. I met Sandy that evening. He was a very intelligent Jewish young man who had done time twice for refusing to register and who also refused to pay taxes. He was an athiest anarchist, much interested in Freud; one of the few regular anarchists friendly to the CW. The columnist Robert Ruark had described Sandy as a Greenwich Village tough who had long hair, dressed sloppily, wore a green turtle neck sweater. Sandy said he had not been in the Village in five years, never wore a turtle neck sweater and above all, any green sweater in his life. For dinner we had good soup and plenty of bread. Baked potato for supper and some chocolate pudding. Nothing fancy. I asked Dorothy who it was that served the food. She said she didn't know; everybody helps; that they come and go and no one asks any questions. This was much different from the Salvation Army places I had stayed when I hiked in 1945 where you had to "sing for your supper." Near the door of the office was a pile of shoes and men came in often to see if they could find any that fit them. One drunk came in singing "Dorothy is a red," but after half an hour when no one disputed his song he left. Another drunk muttered around for hours after we said compline. I left around midnight on the bus for Washington to meet the Hopi and Joe. I had not slept 5 hours straight sleep since I had left Phoenix yet I was not sleepy when I got into Washington.

Homeward

We headed toward Cincinnati where I was to meet my mother at my brother Frank's home. Around midnight we went into a Greek restaurant in Clarksburg, W. Va. Each of the four Greek brothers who ran the place was more decrepit and suave than the other. A person eats thousands of meals yet very few are remembered. This huge Spanish omelette with home-made bread and my favorite pie, raisin, was a treat for $1.05. My mother looked better than when I had seen her in 1945. My niece Patsy I had seen when an infant when I had spoken in churches in Cincinnati. She now attended parochial school, her mother Rose being Catholic. She was excited to meet real Indians and when Dan took a belt from his pocket and gave it to her she was overjoyed. We drove through Indianapolis where Joe had formerly run a fruit stand. It was ten p.m. when we stopped in

Terre Haute. I phoned Theodore Debs, brother of Eugene Debs, but no one answered the phone. My wife and I had visited there twice. He must be a very old man by this time.

In Albuquerque we were welcomed by Msgr. Garcia who had an apartment for just such tramps. By this time our funds were low so I asked my good Lutheran friend, Rev. Soker for $10. After we reached Gallup we went near Window Rock and the Hopi pointed out the original boundary of the Hopi land before the government commenced stealing it. As we came to St. Michael's Mission in the Navajo country we stopped. I knocked on the door and Father Gail answered. I gave him a CW, and his eyes brightened as he spoke of meeting Peter and Dorothy in Detroit years ago. I told him of our trip to Washington. He said that the Indian Bureau was a mess, likely because more recently under Collier they did not favor missionaries. He showed us the beautiful small chapel, whose altar had been hand carved by Indians—and all around were Navajo rugs. Joe and I knelt and said our own kind of prayers of thankfulness for a safe and pleasant journey. Father Gail said they could do nothing with the Hopi. We told him that the Hopi were true pacifists and anarchists like the CW and had nothing to learn from priests who took the part of the government against the Indian and supported war and the capitalist system. He took it in good spirit.

We stopped in New Oraibi, and proceeded on to Hotevilla to take Dan home. He reported to his family in Hopi language about the trip and introduced us. One girl was asleep on the floor and a beautiful girl of 18 was sitting by the stove. I sat beside Dan's brother. The Hopi introduced us to Paul who lived nearby and who, like us, had been in jail as a CO. His wife sat on sheepskins on the floor. She showed us a smiling baby girl born the day before—without government aid. Two small boys played around. I do not feel capable of describing the beauty of Hopiland. My good friend Bert Fireman, columnist on the PHOENIX GAZETTE and commentator on the Ford Hour in his Arizona Crossroads program, has permitted me to quote from a recent broadcast where he tells of Dan's father Yukeoma.

I quote:
"Come, let us visit one of the most inaccessible and colorful of all Arizona Crossroads, the three-fingered mesaland of Northern Arizona, famous as the home of the peaceful Hopi Indians. This is the land of romantic, grotesque Kachina dolls; the home of a people so gentle they sometimes have been called the Quakers of the American Indians; this is a dry land, where nature has provided the people it loves with multi-colored corn that will germinate a foot beneath the dry desert surface; this is a land where the villages are built atop precipitous mesas; where water is scarce and beautiful vistas are abundant; where men are the weavers and dancers and where every community is a separate democracy unto itself; this is the home of our nation's most sensational ceremonial—the Hopi Snake Dance, a nine-day ceremonial for rain that is culminated with the Hopi dancing with live rattlesnakes in their mouths.

"This is Hopiland, beautiful, impoverished, deeply reverent, democratic and pagan—the last outpost resisting Christianity in our country—

yet, strangely, until recently it was absolutely free of the crime and drunkedness and debauchery that the Christian world has had to endure along with the thing we call civilization. This is a land of uninhibited, primitive beauty; of virtue and contentment despite privation and poverty; this is a last frontier of America—this Arizona Crossroads we call Hopiland.

"This was the home of one of the most fascinating men who ever visited the city that is recognized the world over as the capital of progress—Washington, D. C. In 1911, standing before ponderous President William Howard Taft, Yukeoma eloquently recited a philosophy of passive resistance that 30 years later was to make another gnome-like brown man one of the most controversial yet respected men of peace in the modern world.

"They came from opposite ends of the world. One was highly educated, the other was ignorant of his nation's language; one was poor by heritage, the other poor by choice; yet Yukeoma, the Hopi Indian from Arizona, and Mahatma Gandhi, the wizened saint of India's fight for freedom, beneath their brown skins had the same fervent love for the dignity and honor of man as an individual, for the simple old way of doing things, and both had hatred only for compulsion and violence."

My Hopi Friend had told me when we came home that Yukeoma had told Dan many years ago that when he was an old man he would make a trip to Washington by the same route that he had made in 1911 but he would not see the President. We had planned to go by way of Meredian, Miss. but the storms had persuaded us to go by way of Mobile and Atlanta —and this was the route taken by Yukeoma—and we did not see the President, for he was in Florida.

Joe and I came through Flagstaff and left CW's with Father Albey whom I had met before. We came down beautiful Oak Creek Canyon, zig-zagging up the mountain side through Jerome, the mining town built literally on a mountainside. We stopped and said prayers at St. Joseph's Shrine at Yarnell in gratitude for the 6000 mile trip without even a flat-tire. Opening my mail I found two five dollar bills from anarchist friends who liked my anti-war stand; thus my debt to Rev. Soker was paid, and the trip was ended without a deficit. The Old Pioneer had worked an hour a day in the garden. Mulberries were ripe; pomegranate blossoms enlivened the place. The desert flowers of Arizona still seemed to me better than the lush green of the north and east.

My idea of God in May of 1950 is described in a letter to Dorothy: "God is a power-line, and a person can pray and do anything he wishes but unless he connects with this power line he is not connected up. It is all talk. If the average person tries to 'connect up' without using a transformer he is likely to get shocked or killed (maybe that is what happened to me in solitary, as Msgr. Hillebrand so wittily said). Churches should be these transformers to do the 'connecting' but they weaken the current until it hardly means a thing."

Around this time I worked at very hard work for two days with a sledge hammer and came home too tired to eat. I slept for eleven hours and ate three oranges for breakfast, worked hard all day and was still tired and went to bed without supper for 12 hours and woke up feeling fine. When cats and dogs are sick they don't eat, or they nibble at grass to make them vomit.

World Federalists

Two years before, I had been at a World Federalist meeting at the YWCA, sponsored by the pseudo-liberal Unitarian minster. The son of the Mormon Chief Justice in Arizona, Stewart Udall, spoke and the minister sought to convince the audience that unless they converted the city to World Federalism at once there was little use in living. (He soon quit the ministry and has not been heard of since). Now in May of 1950 the new Unitarian minister called for a meeting where the President of the United World Federalists, Allan Cranston, would speak. I was invited to be present.

Cranston said that 75% of our taxes went for war. That without law there could not be justice, and without justice there could be no peace. That we had to have a government to prevent crime. Although he was a newspaper man he talked like a lawyer. He said we had to have a live ideal to defeat the Communist ideal. He was against disarmament.

When the time for questions and remarks came, I said that I was one of those who did not pay that tax for war that he was talking about. That these World Federalists spoke fine words but that their action tomorrow would be just like that of yesterday; that they would all go on paying taxes for the bomb which would kill them one of these days. That they would not gain their World Federalism until they had a majority which was so far away there was no use talking about it. That we Christian Anarchists could practice our ideal right now without waiting on anyone else. That if they were going to overcome the Communists they would have to have an ideal at least as persuasive as the Communists, and not a two-penny second-hand ideal that demands little and gives less.

Cranston replied: "The trouble is that there is too much anarchy now and not enough government. We all know that anarchism is the ideal toward which society reaches, but we have to have World Federalism first."

Tax Garnishee

On June 7th. 1950 I was working for James Hussey, the farmer four miles down the road who is a reserve army captain and for whom I have worked by the day. Mr. Schumacher of the Internal Revenue office asked him how much I had coming and as I had started late that morning I had $5 coming. Mr. Schumacher requested this to be paid on my taxes and wanted to know if I would work for James the next day. James did not know. The tax sleuth wanted him to phone and then he could come out and get my wages. James answered "Uh-huh" and came over later and told me about it, saying that I did not believe in paying taxes and he did, so this was out of his pocket; that in the future he would cooperate with me instead of with the tax man.

The Old Pioneer was in the hospital and the tax man had called on him desiring to know if I had any money coming. I had $12 coming, which had been paid to me by Lin Orme Jr., neither of us knowing that the tax man was headed this way. From that time on I notified my employers that if they paid the tax man any of my wages I would not work for them.

Mr. Schumacher went to each of my employers trying to sell them the idea that if they cooperated with me they were not patriotic and were as bad as I was. But they had been reading the CW long enough to know what it was all about, and besides nobody likes a tax man. So I was either paid in advance, or at night when I finished, or trusted to luck that the tax man did not know where I was working on any certain day. Generally I did not know myself until I phoned to see which farmer wanted me that day. I had told Mr. Schumacher that I would not lie to him but it was his business to find out where I was working. I had given him the names of my employers and my address and I was not hiding. The idea was that I would not pay any income tax.

Irrigating

The water gurgles in the ditch past my cabin all during the night. I hear the soft whistle and song of the Mexican National as he skillfully guides the water evenly, by the quarter-mile-long rows of cantaloupes. Now it is morning and the shift changes. The Big Company has the straightest, cleanest rows, and their ground is well worked. There is a distraint against my wages now so I can't work for the Big Company any more. I do not know much about irrigation, but in the eight years that I have been working in this Southwest I have learned the hard way how not to do certain things. Unless one understands the problem of water in this country, all other information amounts to very little. As I write these pages I am waiting for James to come to get me to irrigate his alfalfa tonight. This type of irrigating is fairly easy. The lands are thirty to forty feet wide and the ports do not have to be dug open and filled in again with the shovel, but are of cement with a tin which is inserted in a groove. We generally run three lands at once. The water comes in supply ditches, called laterals, down the valley north and south on each crossroad, and each road is numbered. I live on lateral 20. As the water comes across the head of the field, the up-to-date farmer has a concrete dam; with a huge tin to open and close it; about four to a quarter mile. Otherwise a canvas tarpaulin (called tarp) is slanted on poles which rest on a beam across the ditch, and this makes the dam. Two skillful irrigators can insert a tarp in running water five feet deep and form a perfect dam.

Two of the farmers for whom I irrigate had a man who slept all night and did not change the lands of water. As the ports are opened and the water rushes into the lands, it goes at a different rate of flow, depending upon the distance from the immediate dam nearby, obstruction of sticks or weeds, or lay of the land. The thing to remember in this Southwest is that the lay of the land is southwest. Walking south to the bus along the lateral, which to the eye would seem to be nearly level, one notices four or more drops, or cascades during the mile. The waste water from the irrigated fields flows into these ditches and is used again and again further down the line.

The chief worry of an irrigator is that rodent vegetarian who fills canal and ditch banks with holes. When you figure on so much water in one place, a great portion of it is apt to be following the serpentine burrowings of Brother Gopher, whose pouches outside his cheeks must literally carry tons of dirt during his lifetime. At least he is "riding high" in the Western country, as did Noah's Ark, built of gopher wood.

Irrigating alfalfa is easy work compared to running the water over bare land, for unless you are used to the field you cannot know just where to put the checks so that all of the land will get wet. I remember irrigating such land for a jack-Mormon (backsliding Mormon) and right even with the flow of water a thousand winged blackbirds would be hopping from dry clod to dry clod, gobbling up the insects which were driven from their sequestered domiciles by the oncoming water.

Walking down the lateral, early one Sunday morning, to get the bus to town to sell CW's in front of churches, I saw a great flock of these same birds roosting and gaily chirping on the backs of the sheep which were grazing on lettuce culls. How they kept from entangling their feet in the wool I do not know, but I never saw one that seemed to have any interference on that account. Maybe this is the way they kept their toes warm early in the frosty morning.

The Old Pioneer

The Old Pioneer is not a radical in the accepted sense. He was on the draft board in World War I and supported this last war. He is an old time Jeffersonian Democrat who wants no subsidies from any government. Like draws like, and God brings together those who sincerely and without counting the cost seek to follow the Truth. If I had asked people where there was a radical farmer for whom I could work I might have been sent to some New Dealer who would certainly not be in sympathy with my anarchism. As it was, I trusted in God and ended up here in the one place in the Valley where there was a farmer of character who chased numerous tax men, the FBI, an Army Intelligence man and a Postal Inspector when they came after me. I offered to leave as Mr. Orme was sick in the hospital with ulcers at time and I felt this nibbling at me by the law would aggravate his illness. "Say here and fight them," he said.

In the old days before dams and water districts, the Indians had irrigation canals. Some of these are modernized and used today by the whites. Land was cheap then but much of it was gobbled up by bankers.

The users of water had banded themselves together in a sort of semi-cooperative Water Users' Association. Soon these bogus farmers and absentee and corporate retainers of wealth had control. The ordinary rancher was at the mercy of non-working theorists, with expensive and impractical plans, who knew little of the procedure of farming and whose chore was to make a living by parasitical living only. At that time the Old Pioneer was in his prime and went from schoolhouse to schoolhouse, evenings, making a fight against these corporate interests. The press jeered at his "one-man revolution." Certain big interests tried to bribe him by giving him a nominal job, but he refused to consider it and cleverly turned their trickery against them. He kept on until he was elected president of the Water Users and fought the good fight there for fourteen years.

In the old days all water gates were locked and the zanjero, or "sankerra" as we Anglos pronounce it, who was the ditch rider, had to carry an enormous bunch of keys. The Old Pioneer ordered the gates to be left unlocked, for only a few would steal water and when they were caught then the gates could be locked. The plan worked. Strange tales are told of supposedly pious men who were water thieves. In those days too a zanjero would often let it be known that the best way to be sure of water when you wanted it was to give him a calf, sheep, or a bag of wheat, etc. The Old Pioneer finally weeded these dishonest fellows out. Feather bedding was not born with the diesel for in the old days here when a crew of Yaqui Indians went out to clean the laterals of weeds and Johnson grass, the custom was to have a foreman, a timekeeper, a truck-driver and a water boy. The Old Pioneer changed all this. One man could drive the truck, keep the time, and be foreman. Ice was furnished and each Yaqui had a rest during the day when he was water boy for his fellows. The Yaqui lived in the desert east of Phoenix. The Old Pioneer built them modern, cement-block houses and a Catholic church. He reopened dozens of cases for Yaqui who had previously been injured and had signed off any demands for a pittance. They received a liberal settlement from him. He also invested a lot of money in a shop where tools were to be sharpened and kept in shape, thus appealing to the peasant-instinct of the Yaqui for pride in their work. At times when I meet strangers in the Valley and they ask me where I live and what I do, I tell them where I am. Sometimes they say "That bald-headed old s.o.b." When I mention this to Mr. Orme he laughs and says "That must have been one of the fellows who were sitting doing nothing with their feet on the desk when I went around the first day; and I made them go to work."

The Old Pioneer instituted another idea based on sound psychology, although he went only to the 5th grade with a little extra study later in mathematics. He had an open office with benches lined up full of people waiting to complain to him. There was no putting people off: he attended to the thing right there. People soon got to know that he was on the square, and in time this cut down complaints. No stuffed-shirt, false dignity with him.

The best stories of his fourteen years as head of the Parole Board in the State of Arizona cannot be told. I am sure I can say without being contradicted by any students of Arizona history that Mr. Orme is one of the very few men, among Governors, Justices of the Supreme Court, Sheriffs, and the Police who could not be bought and who could not be scared. Despite his natural integrity, there is always the chance that he had to learn how and what to do. Thus when he was first head of the Parole Board the Governor asked him to approve the pardon of a certain forger.

The Old Pioneer did so and within a few days this parolee had passed a false check on the Governor himself. From that time on the Old Pioneer listened to no outsiders. He did approve paroles for men who made good. Some of them to this day write to him from distant places. But he had a hard heart toward bankers and felt they had an education and should do their time.

One Mexican who had been fired from the ranch for putting stones in his cotton sack to increase the weight later went to prison for some other theft and came up for parole. He said to Mr. Orme, "You know me." Mr. Orme answered, "I sure do. The answer is 'no.'" When I am writing my articles or my tax statements I give them to him to read, not as a censor, but for correction as to fact or emphasis. Often he says: "Put more Gandhi and Jesus into it."

There was a time, when he was head of the Parole Board, that a man was supposed to be hung for an especially cleverly planned murder. This man belonged to a certain religion, and great pressure came to Mr. Orme from the people of this religion who said: "A . . . has never been hung in Arizona." The Old Pioneer had definite proof, other than court evidence, from one who saw this murder, so his answer was, "A . . . is sure enough going to hang this time." And he did.

At another time several people were caught in a murder, tried, and sentenced. All officials who had anything to do with it except Mr. Orme and the Sheriff had agreed to allow these criminals out on high bail, with the understanding that they would skip bail and the county would be that much richer. This was in the depression when money was hard to get. The bad bargain fell through and the men hung. He was stern, and believed in the rod and in an eye for an eye; but he was just, and never defrauded or underpaid his help, as others did who talked religion. Under another Governor he was offered another job, and was asked to sign his resignation from the Parole Board before accepting the job. "To hell with you and your job" was his answer. He would do what was right and make promises to no one. If he had once accepted the ethics of the Sermon on the Mount he would have had the courage to practice them; there would be no half-way business with him.

Los Angeles Unlimited

With the increasing population in Arizona due to the fine climate and the wiles of real estate men and Chambers of Commerce, there is such a demand for water that the water level is constantly dropping. Last year many in this vicinity had to spend from $1500 to $2500 for drilling new wells, for water for house use, or for deepening old ones. If a farmer cannot afford to drill a new well this is only one more farm to be leased to the Big Company whose giant wells have already in part caused this water shortage. Most of the water used in irrigation here does not come from natural rainfall and snows but from scattered wells owned by the Association. This water has a salty content, and its use for irrigation, along with commercial fertilizers, causes the land to become alkali, so that in the last two years 160,000 acres out of the 720,000 acres under cultivation in the Valley has gone back to desert. New land is being opened up constantly of course. Land has A, B, or C, water rights and the greenhorn had better be sure that his land has schedule A or his dreams of making the desert bloom like the rose will not materialize.

The freehanded Westerner of Arizona was no match for the city slickers in Los Angeles Unlimited, years ago when the Water Compact was made. Arizona is on the high side of the Colorado River and can only gasp for water while the Babylon of Los Angeles and California cheerfully and brazenly siphons and wastes millions of gallons of water away. The Central Arizona Project now up in Congress would give to Arizona what is legally allowed under the Compact, but which was previously prohibited because of the cost of pumping or channelling it. It will finally cost nearly a billion dollars, would have to be paid for by the federal government and would only supplement the water already needed by existing water users. With the trend of corporate farming as it is and the certainty that real estate men would sell more land at inflated price to suckers, the present day evils would only be increased. The rancher whose land is under a lien to a profligate government will soon be a peon as were the helots of Egypt.

This brings to mind the whole question of corporate farming. The Bank of America octopus in California backs the Grapes of Wrath hegemony of that state and the idea has come to this Last Frontier of the country. As I have stated before in these pages it is a vicious circle: people come here for their health and find little work to do. The chief industry is the Reynolds Aluminum Plant employing 1500 men. Reynolds, with his millions, was too poor to build a plant so "went on relief" and got a war plant from the government at a fifth of its cost. Other migrants come from the south and even a few from California. There are the native Spanish and Mexicans who have more recently come over. There is not enough for all at any time, except for a very few rushed months in cotton and cantaloupes. The well paid jobs are in the packing sheds, and the Union books are generally closed. The fields are not organized. Trucks come to the slave market at 2nd and Jefferson Streets around dawn to get workers. At times they pick only those whom they have known previously. Some trucks are run by Big Companies; other by private contractors. Some take only Mexicans, others only Negroes, others take mixed groups. Trucks load up at Tolleson, Glendale and other small towns too.

Field Work

When work is done by contract, that is so much a row for thinning lettuce, chopping cotton, etc., the tendency is for the worker to do a poor job and earn as much as possible. In a big field no boss can see everything. If the pay is sixty or seventy cents an hour or more the tendency is to loaf and kill time. Many Big Companies have solved this by importing Mexican Nationals and having them live, like slaves of old, on the ranch. Indians are also brought from the reservation, paid unbelievably low wages, and cheated in the company stores. The Nationals have general-

163

ly not learned to soldier on the job like the native of the valley, and they are sure to be depended upon until they get "spoiled."

The leveling and working of the land requires expensive machinery which the small rancher cannot always have at hand. Consequently he has to await his turn for custom tillage, work his ground improperly, or get his crop in too late. In marketing produce the Big Companies set the pace and the little fellow is often out in the cold.

As long as so many people live in the cities there will be this unnatural plan, with thousands of migrant workers scurrying here and there to provide the labor needed to harvest the crops of the Big Companies. Too many city workers and farm workers want a pay check, but no responsibility. They have adopted the something-for-nothing philosophy being encouraged by demagogues. They may make good pay but it is soon spent for canned goods. A few hours of work a week in a garden would provide better and cheaper food. Even this is more responsibility than many care to take. The tavern, bingo, radio, movie, dog race, ball game, etc. calls.

*　*　*

"Doing it the hard way, eh?" spoke the Mexican who was driving the huge caterpillar disc in the field next to the 75 by 75 feet garden which the Old Pioneer and I share, and which I was spading.

"Yes, but I eat from this garden every day of the year and don't plow under my crop like you folks do," I replied.

True, the disc was ten thousand times more efficient than my primitive method, but for what? Lettuce and melons are not raised to be eaten but only for the profit to be made. If the price drops the crop is plowed under or sheep are turned in on the field. Three years ago my Molokon neighbor received $5000 for the cabbage on his 20 acres. Next year he put in 40 acres and did not sell a head.

This capitalist system does not make sense. There is no answer to the problem of labor and of agriculture under this set up. Small organic communes, or family homesteads, or groups where a diversity of crops are raised may be established some day, when capitalism dies after World War III. It is more likely—but not necessarily more likeable—that a Communist dictatorship will intensify all the evils of large scale corporate farming, with their forced, so-called communal farms. All the more reason why Catholic Workers and other decentralists of spiritual emphasis should establish themselves on the land now.

My first fast and picketing

Before the Korean War I had told my tax man, a Catholic who thought the CW was a Communist paper, that I was going to picket his office on Aug. 6th.—the anniversary of the bombing of Hiroshima in 1945. When Dave Dellinger and others commenced their two week fast in Glen Gardner, N. J., against the sending of troops to Korea, I wrote to him that although I was unsympathetic with his World Citizen emphasis, I would fast and picket for five days commencing Aug. 7th, from my anti-tax Christian Anarchist point of view. The 6th came on a Sunday so there was no use picketing then.

164

According to the Gandhian technique of goodwill and frankness I wrote to the City Manager and to my tax man, telling them of my extended plans; also to the chief of police asking for a permit and telling him if he did not give me one I would picket anyway. I also wrote 94 individual letters to every priest, preacher, Mormon leader, Jehovah Witness leader, etc. in Phoenix telling them of my fast, quoting "The fervent prayer of a righteous man availeth much." I knew what my CW priest friends thought about it, but from all these letters I received only one answer, from a Methodist minister praising my stand. It happened that his church was not far from St. Matthew's where I was selling CW's the next Sunday, so I went down to his service between masses. In this church there is "open communion" which means that anyone, whether a Methodist or not, could take communion. They have communion about four times a year I think. On an impulse of sympathy with this preacher who had answered my letter I took communion telling him later that the reason I had was because of his sympathy with my pacifism. I had only taken communion before when I was a Baptist—and there a goblet was passed around and everyone took a sip.

About two weeks before my fast I was visiting an enthusiastic young Catholic couple on a Sunday afternoon and discussing the CW movement. A knock came to the door and a young man inquired for me. My host, knowing the ways of the FBI, asked the young man why he wanted to see me. He replied that he had read the CW in Detroit and had come down to visit me. This was the right word to say to get into that house, so in he came. His name was Jack Yaker, a Jewish veteran, who had graduated from Ann Arbor and had somehow skipped the agony of Socialist and Communist activity and had at once become an anarchist. He had read the CW in the Labadie Collection at the U. of Michigan, and the anarchist curator of this excellent library of radical thought had suggested that before he go any further in radical thought or commercial pursuits he should look me up in Arizona. He quit his job and hiked down here in four days. Inquiring as to the location of my postal address he was told that it was west of town. Getting into a bus headed westward he was asked by the driver where he wanted to go. Noticing a CW by the driver's wheel he said that he wanted to get off where that Hennacy was who wrote in the CW, someplace west of town. The driver replied that this bus went north within a few blocks and not west but that I had been on this bus on the last trip and had handed him this CW and he knew where I got off and would let Jack off at the same stop. This was the first time I had ridden on this bus on a Sunday and the first time I had met this driver, so my habit of giving CW's to bus drivers bore fruit.

Jack had the regular anarchist criticism of society, but as with most anarchists he did not have the positive ideas with which to build toward the new society. When we discussed my plans for the fast he offered to be at hand and give me a drink of distilled water every half hour or so. By the time of my fast he had met my Catholic pacifist and anarchist friends here and read old copies of the CW so that he understood the mood in which a fast should be conducted.

165

Rik and Ginny and I had spent hours getting a leaflet out which was headed:

The One Man Revolution

Why do you, a sensible person, now believe that war and the A Bomb are necessary?

Why are poor Oriental peasants who have seldom eaten a square meal in their lives choosing to fight us?

Why does Communism appeal to so many people? Is it because we have failed as Christians?

Why are we in this mess? Because you have sought security outside of yourself instead of accepting responsibility. Because you left matters to the politicians, took their bribes of pensions and subsidies, and their impossible promises of prosperity.

My guilt—For seven years I have refused to pay income taxes for war and bombs. I am fasting for these five days as a penance for not having awakened more people to the fact that the way of Jesus and Gandhi is not the way of the atom bomb. This war, like the last two will not bring peace and freedom.

What can you do now? We made a revolution against England and are not free yet. The Russians made a revolution against the Czar and now have an even stronger dictatorship. It is not too late to make a revolution that will mean something—one that will stick: your own one-man revolution. It is not too late to be a man instead of a pipsqueak, who is blinded by the love of money.

Are you a producer or a parasite? Why not cease voting for all politicians? Why not refuse to make munitions or to go to war? Why pay income taxes for your own destruction?

I had made a hinge in the middle of the handle of the larger sign so I could carry it on a bus. Jack and I had stayed at Rik's the night before. As we left for the bus-stop a carpenter going to work stopped and gave us a ride most of the way downtown. Jack took the signs and waited in the cool of the Greyhound station while I went to St. Mary's to mass. I asked for guidance and light.

I had a small quantity of leaflets, CW's, and folded tax statements in the back pocket of my levis. I had walked the three sides of this block three other times when I picketed against payment of taxes, so the ground was familiar. Shouts of "Go back to Russia, you Commie" were frequent. One Catholic lady who said she had bought CW's from me at St. Mary's cordially took a slip. When I walked on, a man shouted for me to go back to Russia. The lady turned to him and said "Go back to Russia yourself!"

Those who fast do not stop to eat so I kept on during the noon hour. A few now and then greeted me kindly, but most were fearful to be seen speaking to me, and many shouted insults. About 3 p.m. a news reporter and photographer stopped me for an interview. A crowd gathered around. One man was especially noisy, poking his finger in my face and shouting,

"Russia," "the boys in Korea," etc. One big man said that back in his state they took fellows like me and threw them in the river.

"Where do you come from Buddy?" I asked.

"From Ohio, long the Ohio River," he replied.

"So do I, and I was acting like a radical there when I was 16 and no one threw me in" I answered quickly. The crowd laughed. Another big fellow said that if I came back tomorrow with my "damn Communist papers" they would take me out in the desert and throw me up against a cactus and I would stick there. In a very quiet voice, but firmly I said:

"You are not really as mean a man as you make out to be."

At this the crowd melted away, although my two interrogators insulted me as I passed by with my sign again. But they could find no one to back them up. Jack had been on the outside of the crowd and a lady told him, not knowing that he was my friend, that I was not a Commie for I picketed here every year.

After 4 p.m. Mr. Schumacher, my tax man, came up and handed me a card which read:

Seized for the account of the United States on 8-7-50 by virtue of warrant for distraint issued by the collector of internal revenue, district of Arizona. Deputy Collector..........One poster for picket line.

Actually there were three posters but I handed them over saying that I would get some new ones made and picket the next day. I continued handing out leaflets and CW's without my signs until Rik met me at 5:30 p.m.

Rik made new signs that night and marked them "This sign is the personal property of Joseph Craigmyle" *but the tax man did not try to take them.* The ARIZONA REPUBLIC had a good picture of myself and signs on the page opposite the editorial page. The picture showed my large sign which read:

75%
Of Your Income Tax
Goes for War
And the Bomb.

And on the reverse side—

I Have
Refused to Pay
Income Taxes
For the Last
Seven Years

The 7:30 a.m. broadcast gave the above, after describing picketing of a restaurant by the AFL union. One for union recognition. One for peace recognition.

My sandwich sign, in front, as pictured in the paper read: "Reject War. Choose the Gandhi Way." The reverse read: "Your Income Tax Upholds Foreign and American Imperialism." As I picketed I presented first the sign with inch black border which read: "Hiroshima was A-Bombed Five Years Ago. I am Fasting for Five Days in Memoriam."

I was much cheered to receive a telegram at the general delivery window from Dorothy and Bob Ludlow, the spiritual emphasis of which strengthened me as I glanced toward the tax man's window expecting him to come and take my signs away. A Jehovah's Witness was waiting for me in a car and said that he was my friend and had been on the edge of the crowd the day before. I had given him my literature then, he said. He was kindly but advised me to beware of the tricks of the Roman Catholic Church. I showed him Dorothy's telegram and he admitted that he had never heard of such radical Catholics. I also met a young man, a veteran of five years, who said he was atheistic. After reading the CW and other literature, he told me his Irish name and said he was a fallen-away Catholic who had never heard of such a fine radical paper as the CW. Later I received word from him that he would see me at mass at St. Mary's the next Sunday.

Jack kept bringing me water to drink. At 5 p.m. I was so tired I could hardly sit up. I went to Rik's that night and slept 12 hours. I did not have any headache or stomach ache but now realized that I should have stopped for half-an-hour and rested during the day. I felt better the next morning.

I had read in books, and Dorothy and others had told me, that Jesus meant something special. I also knew it from my time in solitary. All this time I could not see any connection between Jesus and the churches which supported capitalism and war. Wednesday morning, before picketing, I went to mass and in the midst of my fasting and prayer and picketing there came to me a feeling that Jesus on the cross here at St. Mary's did mean something especial to me. I have been quite smart in calling non-Christian Anarchists pipsqueaks and in admitting that I had much courage and wisdom. I have known all along that I lacked that love which radiates from Dorothy and true CW's. Now, as I looked over the congregation I did not feel so smart. I felt a desire to be one of them and to help them instead of being so critical. Maybe this is the beginning; but what there is of value that comes to me will have to come from the heart and not from the intellect. This does not mean that I condone church support of war and capitalism. It means that I will not allow it to keep me from God and from Jesus who was a true rebel.

I went with Jack to the Greyhound and rested for half an hour, in the middle of the morning. I also took a salt tablet now and then, as it was 109 degrees in the shade and much hotter on the pavement. (Whether this is a superstition or whether it does me good I am not sure.) My J. W. friend stopped to see me. Two Franciscan priests, whom I did not know personally, took my literature gladly. One priest called my name from his car. I had corresponded with his atheistic uncle and had sent him a CW, so he knew who it ought to be that was picketing the postoffice. The tax man passed and smiled and made no motion to take my signs. There was not quite so much name calling as on Monday. To picket one day is not so bad for you come and go and the super-patriots may not know about it. But to give notice you are picketing for five days gives an opportunity for anyone to beat you up. It only takes one fellow to picket and it only takes one fellow to knock him down. In the afternoon the leader of those who had reviled me stopped with a friendly smile and apologized, saying that he had been drunk; that now he knew what my ideas were. Each day of my fast now he performed kindly acts to help me and argued with others that I was a fine fellow and he was around to keep any others from bothering me, arguing for me the best that he knew how. (Years later I was riding from Los Angeles to San Francisco and a man came down and sat beside me greeting me by name. I did not know him, but it proved to be this very man.) One of my employers came along in a car and took me to a nearby park where I rested on the grass for half an hour. Just at this time some Catholic Anarchist friends came by looking for me, and someone told them that I had been arrested. One of my CW priest friends called Rik and found out that I was still free and picketing. Because of the two intermissions I had, I felt fine that night.

The next morning it was cloudy. The cap that I wore while picketing had a double length green visor and was given to me by a Catholic veteran who had used it in the navy. This morning I forgot it. It seems that God tempers the wind to the shorn lamb for it was not so hot today. I was glad to receive several letters from Dorothy and a card from a Quaker anarchist in Paris who somehow had heard of my picketing. I drank about a gallon of water every day, Jack bringing around the jug about every half hour. I was not very weary and I walked at a slower pace, but I would not have run a mile for a million.

In the afternoon the tax man came along and good naturedly said that he had a bid of $5 for my signs from someone who wanted them as a souvenir. (I did not ask him if he was the bidder) I had given him CW's before and had shown him Dorothy's telegram. Now he was friendly and asked about my life, my daughters, my ideas, and said that he understood my opposition to the status quo. Like the tax man before him he was a Catholic. He felt, as I did, that there was nothing personal. He had his duty to do. He had tried to garnishee my wages, and had taken away my signs so he could report some activity on his part. He said I had a right to peacefully picket and departed in a friendly spirit. We met several times later as I picketed. He did not like my reference to himself as a servant of Caesar in a letter I had written to him. I told him this was perhaps a poetic way of saying it, but I meant it.

The last day of my picketing was the hottest of all. To tell the truth I became a clock-watcher and drank more water than ever. I met a few surly people now and then, but more and more people took my leaflet. One elderly man took my leaflet and remarked that he and his family were friends of mine, for I had given literature to his wife the day before and he had read my tax statement and leaflet to his congregation of fundamentalists at his little mission west of Phoenix. One man whose employment kept him near to my picketing had muttered patriotic obscenities all the times I had picketed here. Today he was pleasant and wondered how I got by without paying taxes. I handed my leaflet to a lady whose face seemed familiar. She refused it, saying, "You gave me one Monday. I took it home and read it and burned it. I wouldn't have such trash in my home." It was my defender of the first day who had told the man to go back to Russia.

During these five days about a sixth of the people called me names. About half of them were fearful, but if one in a row took literature the others followed, and if one refused the others did likewise. The remainder were friendly. Nearly all Negroes and Mexicans took my literature. I began the fast weighing 143 pounds. I ended it weighing 129. Now, a week later I weigh 140. I broke the fast with tomato juice, a peach, pear, plum, orange and grapes, and was digging a ditch at 9 a.m. the next day, and have been hard at work ever since.

One of my good friends in Phoenix is Joe Stocker, New Dealer, and former editor of Anna Roosevelt's daily paper which had a short life here. He is now a free lance writer. He is far from being an anarchist and is not a pacifist. His wife Ida had her first baby while I was picketing and fasting.

Hopi Snake Dance Again

I was rested up from my picketing and went up for the Hopi Snake Dance Aug. 23, starting to walk on the road from Leupp's Corners as Rik and I had done before. After walking 19 miles, the tenth car that came my way picked me up. The air was clear and the sky was bright, and I enjoyed the walk. The snake dance this year was at Dan's home, Hotevilla. A thousand or more people were there. This being the radical village, there was no soda pop for sale or any commercialism as we had witnessed the year before at First Mesa. There were no government or Hopi stooge police, nor any drunks or disturbances. My Hopi friend's small girl, sat astride of my neck during part of the snake dance. A white man came up and asked me how my small daughter liked the dance. I was tanned, but to be mistaken for a Hopi was an honor indeed. The snake dance followed the same pattern as last year and hundreds of years. Knowing hardly anything of Hopi tradition compared to what there was to know, I felt a part of this ceremony without understanding it. I felt at home with the Hopi.

In the morning before we went to the dance I went to my Hopi friend's garden and helped him hoe in the sandy soil. I never saw such a big hoe. I thought I was a good worker but I couldn't keep up with the Hopi. After the snake dance it rained, as it always does. That night I met with about twenty of the radical Hopi at Shungopovy. They asked me questions about my work, my tax refusal, about Dorothy and the CW. As I looked around each Hopi was a distinct personality. They smiled and nodded aproval when my Hopi friend translated my answers to their questions. We left at 2 a.m.

We visited the colorful Butterfly Dance at Hotevilla the next day. This goes on for hours and hours all day, in relays, both men and women dancing. I met a silversmith from Scottsdale, whose English name is Morris Robinson. He had been in jail in Keams Canyon and was a rebel. He had married a Pima Indian. I met the Hopi conscientious objectors. There had been a morning race over desert waste and up the cliff to Hotevilla,

170

and Paul's son won the race, as Paul had when he was younger. The next day I rode with relatives of my Hopi friend to Flagstaff. About half way we heard a noise and there was a hole in the gas tank! The Indian woman quickly grabbed bubble gum from a child and stopped the leak. Ezra, the young C.O. heard us referring to Tucson Road Camp, and in a matter of fact way said "That is where we all will be again soon." The white man would deny the possibility and evade the issue as long as he could. The Hopi face facts. Before I left I spent three hours trying to explain pacifism to Mormon missionaries who were staying in New Oraibi, but I think I wasted my time.

Hopi Message

Around the middle of September I was asked to meet in Flagstaff two young editors of a radical weekly, published in Los Angeles, to go with them to the Hopi, and introduce them to my friends. These young men had been CO's whom I had known by reputation but whom I had never met. The day we arrived was also the day when men from each village were meeting at a Hopi home to prepare a letter to Truman about the draft of Hopi to the war in Korea. While they were busy at this meeting I drove with my friends to Old Oraibi and we met Don; to Hotevilla and Bacobi and over to Shungopovi on Second Mesa. Soon after we returned to the home of a Hopi friend, the government-stooge Hopi, who had been elected by his own kind as Governor of the village, came and gave notice that I and my friends were not welcome here because we were having a secret meeting. We explained that we were here visiting and not taking any part in the meeting, for we could not understand Hopi. I had made the mistake of writing a postal card to my friend saying that we would be here. The postmaster in Oraibi was head of the government Tribal Council so of course the word got around that we were having this secret meeting. My Hopi friends stood up for our rights and their rights to meet as they wished.

The next day, as was our plan, we left for Flagstaff. My friends continued to Los Angeles, and finding that I had to wait for a bus I called up my old friends from Cincinnati and Phoenix, Virgil and Ysobel Maddox. They asked me to skip another bus and come out for the night. Previously they had invited Platt and Barbara Cline over for the evening. Mr. Cline is editor of the Flagstaff daily. He had been reading the CW for a short time and said that he liked my articles about life in Arizona. He had been a member of the legislature at one time and was in the right mood to read about anarchism. He was sympathetic to the Quakers, and his wife was Mormon. From that meeting we became very good friends, and he has given me fine publicity whenever I have picketed. His paper is the only one in this country, other than the CW, which prints the views of the real Hopi as contrasted to the apologies for the government appearing elsewhere.

In the latter part of October TIME magazine had a note that the appeal of the Hopi against the draft was Communist-inspired. It quoted as authority Ramon Hubbell, old time trader among the Indians. I at once sent TIME an air mail telling them that the Hopi were pacifist for centuries long before Karl Marx was heard of. After some more correspondence I received the following note from TIME:

"Referring to your letter of Dec. 7, TIME made no error in its October 23 report on the Hopi Indians. We correctly stated what Mr. Hubbell told us."

My reply was as follows:

"Received your alibi on printing the misinformation of trader Hubbell libeling the peaceful Hopi as Communist-inspired. He has absolutely no authority for this false assertion. In choosing your sources of information you show your plain intent to slander those whom you stand no chance of corrupting. To correctly print a lie is not telling the truth."

For several years I had sent Mr. Hubbell copies of what I had written in the Catholic Worker about the Hopi, but he had not replied. It was not until later that the uneasy conscience of that trader had multiplied the visit of myself and friends into Communists being there to influence the Hopi.

The real nature of the Hopi opposition to the draft may be seen in the following letter which was printed in the December, 1950 CW with the following note: "The above letter was sent out by our friends and brothers . . . The Phoenix papers commented that the signers of the letter represented 50% of the Hopi and were respected leaders."

Hopi Indian Sovereign Nation
Oraibi, Arizona
October 8, 1950

Harry S. Truman,
President of the United States,
Washington, D. C.

Mr. President:

"I also wish to assure the members of both the Hopi and Navajo Tribes that their religion and social customs will be fully respected in accordance with this nation's long-established laws and traditions."

Harry S. Truman.

Today our ancient Hopi religion, culture and traditional way of life are seriously threatened by your nation's war efforts, Navajo-Hopi bill, Indian Land Claims Commission and by the Wheeler Howard bill, the so-called Indian self-government bill. These death dealing policies have been imposed upon us by trickery, fraud, coercion and bribery on the part of the Indian Bureau under the government of the United States, and all these years the Hopi Sovereign Nation has never been consulted. Instead, we have been subjected to countless number of humiliations and inhuman treatments by the Indian Bureau and the government of the United States. We have been dipped in sheep-dipping vats like a herd of sheep. Our young girls and women folks were shamefully disrobed before the people, and they were either pushed or thrown into these vats filled with sulphur water. Our religious headmen were beaten, kicked, clubbed with rifle butts, their hair cut and after being dragged were left bleeding on the grounds in their villages.

These immoral acts were done to us by the government of the United States, all because we want to be peaceful, to live as we please, to worship and make our livelihood the way our Great Spirit Massau'u has taught us.

Hopi Sovereign Nation has been in existence long before any white man set foot upon our soil, and it is still standing. It will continue to hold all land in this western hemisphere in accordance with our Sacred Stone Tablets for all his people who are with him here.

But now you have decided without consulting us; you have turned away from us by leading your people down the new road to war. It is a fearful step that you have taken. Now we must part. We, the Hopi leaders, will not go with you. You must go alone. The Hopi must remain within his own homeland. We have no right to be fighting people in other lands who have caused us no harm. We will continue to keep peace with all men while patiently waiting for our "true brother" whose duty it is to purify this land and to punish all men of evil hearts. Because we have never fought your government, never relinquished our rights and authority to any foreign nation and made no treaty with your government whereby our young Hopi men be subject to conscription laws of the United States. Therefore we demand that you, as President of the United States, now and for all times, stop the drafting of our young Hopi men and women, and release immediately all those who are now in the armed forces of the United States. And we also demand that a full and complete investigation of the Navajo-Hopi bill, so-called Hopi Tribal Council and the Indian Bureau be made by the President of the United States, Congress and the good people of the United States. This is your moral obligation to the Red Man, upon whose land you have been living. Time is short, and it is our sacred duties as leaders of our people to bring these truths and facts before them. We must set our house in order before it is too late. If the government of the United States does not begin now to correct many of these wrongs and injustices done to the Red Man, the Hopi Sovereign Nation shall be forced to go before the United Nations with these truths and facts. We are,

Sincerely yours,

Dan Katchongva, Advisor, Sun Clan, Hotevilla, Arizona.
Andrew Hermequaftewa, Advisor, Blue Bird Clan, Shungopovy, Arizona.

Having nearly fathomed the mysteries of the harness which equipped the blind and deaf mules borrowed from a neighbor (I milked his cow while he caught the wild animals), I hitched them to a disc and prepared the garden, irrigated two weeks before. A clump of Johnson grass here and there defiantly showed remnants of green after the rest of the garden was a pleasant brown. A harrow leveled off the ground nicely. One row of egg plant and peppers remained from the summer garden. The hot August weather had nearly burned them up, but now near the end of September they were blooming again and would produce until heavy frost.

The Old Pioneer brought twine and we measured out straight rows. We hitched the blind mule to the plow and the Old Pioneer led as I made —not the straightest row in Missouri or Arizona—but one good enough for the purpose. We came back over the furrow to make the ground even on both sides of it. By 1 p.m. I had returned the mules and had started to plant. The rows are 81 feet long. I have never worked elsewhere in such fine mellow ground: not a hard lump of dirt to be found. It had rained while I had been up to the Hopi and thus any clods that remained from the plowing around the first of August, when I had driven the mules and Jack Yaker had tried his first stint with the plow, were now dissolved. The furrows were about a foot and a half in depth. I leveled off the ground between them with a rake, then took a hoe and chopped half way down the edge of the furrow to make sure that the ground was fine and crumbly as a bed for seeds. Then I made an inch furrow along this edge where I judged the line of irrigation water would about reach.

First I planted a row of radishes. Then taking a chance that we would have a late frost, I planted 46 hills of Irish potatoes in the next row. Last year I had planted them in August, and it was so hot that they dried up in the hill instead of growing. The trick with potatoes is to have the ground loose and high enough above the furrow so that the top is always dry; the water on either side subbing up and making sufficient moisture. Next I planted two rows of chard, the green leaves of which would mix well with the carrots, to be pulled each day for a salad, from the next two rows. A row of onion seed and onion sets provided a different shade of green in the garden, followed by three rows of beets. We had made four rows for the planting of peas in November; two beds for the tomatoes in the spring and two wide beds for watermelon in the spring. It was after dark before I stopped to eat supper, but all had been planted except two rows of beets.

One Bowl

Long before I had known that Gandhi ate from one bowl—the aluminum one which he brought from prison—I had told the women folks that they cluttered themselves up with too many dishes. Sometimes my sister-in-law at whose home I lived for a year in Milwaukee called me "one-bowl Hennacy" and minimized the quantity of utensils around my place at the table. To my mind the simple life means that one should eat that which is at hand and buy from the store only when it is absolutely necessary. As long as I have Irish potatoes in the garden they form the bulk of my main meal. When they are gone, I do not buy potatoes but eat egg plant, peppers and onions, which are delicious fried. When I worked in a dairy I made my own cottage cheese, but now that is one thing that I buy at the store. Except for the months of August, September and October I have chard and spinach and carrots which make a fine salad, so then I really have two bowls instead of one. When I worked at a chicken ranch in Albuquerque I ate cracked eggs by the dozen. Since then I seldom buy eggs. When I worked in the large apple orchard there and wrote of my visits to the nearby Isleta Indians, I had apples every day of the year—and apple dumplings—and apple cider part of the time, except in April, May and June. Here also I had asparagus seven months in the year. It grew wild in the orchard, and all that was needed was to cut the shoots every few days and not allow them to go to seed. When cold weather came, I never bought this very expensive product of the canning factory having had my share during the remainder of the year.

Apples do not grow in this valley and I seldom buy them. Oranges and grapefruit trees are nearby and pomegranates and figs in season. The Old Pioneer will plant some grapevines this month. We had watermelon each day from June first to August 12th. And of course we had free access to the hundreds of acres of commercial cantaloupes all around us. Our one failure has been tomatoes. While we have had some to eat there has not been enough in proportion to the effort expended. Our rows were too narrow and we gave them too much water and they got too much sun. This spring we will plant them in rows five feet apart and with irrigation only on the outer side. Then the plants can produce leaves and shade as protection from the sun. We have used no commercial fertilizer. I have a small compost pit.

The second Monday after I had planted my garden the Old Pioneer called his brother-in-law, Joe, and he and I hitched ourselves to each end of a broomstick which had a rope in the center, attached to a small cultivator. The Old Pioneer was the driver as we roughed up the ground between the rows. "Damn burros," mumbled Joe.

Broken Arrow

This week I was pleasantly surprised to hear the voice of my Hopi friend on the phone. Catherine Howell, a Quaker woman who had been living for several months in Hopi villages and who had now learned the distinction between the *real* Hopi and the government stooges who accept favors from the whites and thus betray their people, had driven to Phoenix to visit Rik's wife Ginny who was an old time friend. My Hopi friend came along. He wanted to get some information about the letter to be sent to Truman and also to bootleg a job at his trade as a stone mason where there would be no withholding tax for war. He brought a yellow watermelon and some piki. Piki was made a thousand years before Post and Kellogg and consists of rolls of grey or pink toasted corn of the taste

175

and texture of cornflakes. He had never visited my place. I pointed out the middle room which could be his at any time.

I have refused to attend the movies since 1942 as I do not want to pay a war tax. But I hinted to my friends that I was willing to be an accessory-to-the-fact and attend a movie to see the true story of Cochise, the great Apache leader for whom a county is named in the mining region of south eastern Arizona. I had read the book *Blood Brother* by Eliot Arnold and understood that this account of a white man who made friends with Cochise and secured peace between the Apaches and the whites was correct Arizona history—aside from the love story that had to be put in.

So Rik was the host for my Hopi friend, Joe Craigmyle and myself to see *Broken Arrow*. The Hopi said that the Indian customs presented were fairly accurate. The Apache speak somewhat sharply, like the Navajo, while the Hopi are entirely different in expression. The only criticism of the play that I had was the fact that the most stirring and incriminating part of the play was merely referred to, not acted out. This was when the army commander offered a flag of truce and coldly ordered Cochise, his brother, and four others murdered in the tent where the truce was held. The others died right there but Cochise had a knife in his loin cloth, cut a hole in the tent, escaped, and began his famous ten year war against the treacherous whites.

When peace had been made by Tom Jeffords, the hero, the army general made the promise that no soldiers would be stationed on the Apache reservation. Those who have seen this movie and do not know Indian history should be told that Tom Jeffords had to quit as Indian Agent because the government broke its word and sent troops. They should also learn that during the administration of Gov. Safford—one of the many carpet-bag neer-do-wells sent from Washington when Arizona was a territory—a special trip was made by the Governor to Washington where he had the boundaries of the Apache Reservation changed in order that the copper companies could get the land they wanted. Safford is now a copper town. Thus the wealth which enabled the Big Companies to run the I.W.W.'s out of Bisbee in 1916.

Those interested in Indian history should read *Apache* by Will Levington Comfort, the Quaker writer. It is a small book written many years ago and tells of the childhood and life of Magnus Colorado (bloody sleeves), the brother-in-law of Cochise, and of his final death when murdered as a prisoner of war. Now with the whites bribing the Indian leaders for oil and uranium leases, the further robbing of the Indians continues. The message which the radical Hopi bring, along with the CW Christian anarchist emphasis, provide the only hope in this crazy war-mad world.

Truman's Emergency

"How are you going to get people to put up the sword? My son died in Korea. I know you didn't kill him. God bless you!" said an elderly woman as I was picketing the post office in Phoenix, Dec. 18, 1950 in response to Truman's "emergency" declaration. The woman had seen my big sign which read:

"Put up thy Sword
He that taketh
the Sword
Shall Perish
by the Sword."   Jesus' words.

On the reverse of this sign was a picture of a pot, colored green, with a sign on it: *capitalist*. Opposite was a red kettle—*Communist*. Underneath was the caption:

"The Pot Calls the Kettle Black"

My other signs told of my regular refusal to pay taxes and mentioned Gandhi. I attended mass at St. Mary's before picketing and prayed for grace and wisdom. I felt that I would surely get beat up but that the "emergency" had to be met. In another church that morning a CW priest said mass for the success of my witness for peace. I had notified the city manager and the tax man that I would picket against the war emergency. Ginny Anderson stood on one corner to hand me extra literature and be my "lookout," to report trouble if I was beaten. Byron Bryant, Catholic anarchist, home on Christmas vacation from his duties as teacher of English in a Western University, stood on the other corner. There was an unusual number of people coming and going around the holidays. No one advised me to go back to Russia or called me a Communist.

"Extra, extra, all anarchists to be shot at sunrise," shouted the good-natured news man stationed in front of the postoffice as I passed by. When a later edition told of a robbery in Tucson of my friend Brophy's Bank of Douglas, the paper man shouted as I went by: "Extra, extra, Gandhi robs a bank."

A woman looked at my sign and asked if I did not know that Jesus told Peter to sell his clothes and buy a sword. I answered, "Yes, but when Peter showed Him the sword which he had Jesus did not say to cut off the other ear but said, 'put up thy sword. He that taketh the sword shall perish by the sword.'" As the woman walked on she shouted back: "Jesus called for a sword so he could perform a miracle. He never said 'put up thy sword.' You better read your Bible." I told her that I had read it six times in solitary, but there is little use in quoting scripture to these "Bible-bangers."

Somewhat different was a teen-age boy who pointed to an ad of the Marines and said that meant more to him than my sign or my leaflet which he had just read. I told him that if he believed that way—and he was to leave for war next month—that he should do what he thought was right. He refused to take a CW although he was a Catholic and went to St. Mary's. I hoped that he would return safely and could then confer with the priest as to the possibilities of being a pacifist Catholic. It was not his fault that he had never heard the pacifist message before. We parted in a friendly spirit.

177

One gruff fellow asked, "What have you got there?" I answered, "It's either very good or very bad: depends upon how you look at it; better read it and see." He smiled and went his way reading the leaflet.

While Byron and I went for lunch, Frank Brophy, whose bank had been robbed, spoke to Ginny. Although the CW says "Starve the Bankers and Feed the Poor" he reads the CW, and is not ashamed to be seen talking to me on the street, whether I am picketing or just selling CW's at the bus. A Catholic anarchist woman stopped to see us but missed us because of the following incident:

We had only brought along 500 leaflets and now at 3 p.m. they were nearly all distributed. I went to get some more and two friends of Ginny's asked her for my propaganda. So when I returned, I gave her some leaflets and she went in the post office and gave one to each of them as they had requested. A friend of hers in the tax office had asked for one also. I had sense enough to put the leaflet in an envelope for her to give to the tax man but not sense enough to advise her not to give the leaflets to her friends openly in the post office, which was government property.

Later two cops came up and questioned me saying they were having too many complaints about my picketing. They read my signs and leaflet. I told them that what I was doing was clearly subversive and that the FBI and tax man had priority over them in my case and they ought to confer with them. One cop did so while the other asked me questions. Among other things he asked if Ginny had handed out leaflets in the post office. I told him to ask her, which he did, and she explained what she had done. Meanwhile people crowded around and watched my signs. I saw my tax man as he came near; and also an FBI man.

The police wanted to know what had been done when I had been arrested for picketing before. I told them that I had been released and had picketed seven more days without being bothered. They conferred with headquarters and suggested that Ginny and I accompany them to the police station. Here we waited about an hour while detectives and police looked over the signs and leaflet and asked questions. I offered a CW to one police captain but he refused it, saying that no Catholic paper could support such unpatriotic actions as mine. I asked him if he knew Father Dunne and he said he did. I advised him to call up and see what he said about me and the CW. (Later Father Dunne told me that the man had phoned him.)

Byron had phoned a Catholic attorney, friend of the CW, who spoke to Chief O'Clair. The Chief said we could go but I had better not picket or I might get into trouble. I told him that I was used to handling tough individuals and crowds and could take care of myself. He said that any charge such as disorderly conduct, loitering, etc. could be brought against me. I told him that was his business and that I would picket again on March 14th. He grinned and said, "That's another day."

We went back again and gave away our few remaining leaflets. Postal employees looked out of the window and saw that the police had not stopped us. One of the calls against us had come from an ultra-patriotic postal employee who had noticed Ginny handing the two leaflets to her friends, one of the cops told me. The last leaflet I gave out was to a postal employee who had refused it early in the morning and now his curiosity had gotten the better of him. He read it standing where all could see, and praised me for my stand.

Lay Apostolate

During the winter Drew Pearson lectured in Phoenix. I had mailed his manager the current CW, my tax statement and One Man Revolution leaflet. I kidded him about supporting capitalism and war, and like Truman taking the Sermon on the Mount in vain. That inasmuch as he was invading my territory I had to write to him again. I had written to him in Washington, D. C. once before. That I couldn't afford the high price of admission but would sell CW's outside to counterbalance his smoke-screen. A friend gave me a ticket and I went to hear him. He was interesting enough but it wasn't worth even a quarter. I sold plenty of CW's and several thousand people heard, perhaps for the first time, "Catholic Worker, Catholic peace paper, one cent."

* * *

Just before election day of 1950 Rik and Ginny had moved to the suburb, Scottsdale, a small town east of Phoenix that puts on the super-Western dog. Ginny rode around in shorts on a bicycle and Rik, who is by temperment bourgeois, and only anarchist by intellect, chided her about "creating a bad impression in a new community."

Soon afterward we all attended a Democratic election rally in Scottsdale, because Ana Fromiller, the Democratic candidate for Governor, though not an anarchist, was a good friend of ours. Rik thought that the boys would like to sit on the front seat near the band to observe at close hand the machinations of the musical instruments. We all should have known better, but the first thing that happened was the playing of the Star Spangled Banner. Instinctively, and without a look or thought, one to the other, we all remained seated. We could not have put on a "worse show" or "created a worse impression" in this new community than by this action. We heard mumbling, but no action followed. Later Ginny and I kidded Rik about the "good impression" he was so worried about. America, the Beautiful, or even America, are good songs which we could arise to honor, but not the jingoistic "bombs bursting in air." This incident, and one related later in this book, have a direct bearing on one of the momentous decisions of my life, but I did not realize it at that time.

When I was waiting at the bus station one morning to go to Mesa to sell CW's, an elderly woman grabbed a paper from me, saying, "I could cut off the Pope's head and sing to Jesus when I was doing it. I used to be a Catholic; now I am saved and washed in the blood of the lamb. And don't talk back a word or I'll tear you to pieces." I didn't and she went careening up the street.

In contrast, while I was selling papers at the same spot an old man with his few belongings tied up in a sack, hanging from a stick over his shoulder in the traditional manner of hoboes, stopped and looked at my display, saying, "I'll have one." I told him not to bother to unload himself to get the penny and gave him a paper and my tax statement. He had a bright and intelligent eye and replied with a smile: "I'm a good Catholic; on my way to Heaven; name is Collins. God bless you."

Teen-agers, Sharon, Carmen

CHAPTER 8.

Working - Fasting - Picketing

1951

Phoenix - Hopiland

Hopi Initiation

My Hopi friend had invited all of us to the initiation dances in late February. This dance is not public, but, an outsider can come by invitation. It is for children of about six years of age who have received presents on holidays and birthdays from masked kachinas. They are to graduate from this phase of life into the next, or "no Santa Claus" phase: but it is all a ceremonial plan, and not a deceit as it is with us. Even at that early age Hopi children know the how and why of babies.

Rik and family and I left late on a Friday morning by way of Black Canyon Road. Joe Craigmyle had supposedly left the night before with some citrus Ginny had picked for the Hopi and with some of his own from his fruit stand. But you never can tell where Joe is until you actually see him there. He could change his mind or fall asleep on the way. Within 70 miles, Ginny's boys saw the first snow of their lives at Mayer, Ariz.

Getting into Flagstaff we said hello to Virgil and Ysobel Maddox and went to Platt Cline's. Platt had to be out of town at an AP convention. Between the two houses a car skidded into us and we had to stay over a day to get the repairs made. Due to modern technical efficiency the brake man wouldn't touch or give an opinion about the fender; and neither the brake nor the fender man, about the alignment or the motor. But after much red tape we got going shortly before dark for New Oraibi.

We saw in the distance the panorama of the mesas in the setting sun. This alone was worth the trip.

Getting in at ten p.m. we found that our Hopi friend and Joe had waited for us until half an hour before and had gone to Hotevilla where the initiation was taking place. We went there and Ezra, a nephew of Dan, and one of the Hopi CO's, took us to Fred's house where we met our Hopi friend and Joe. We visited until midnight and then went to the snake kiva, which had a side entrance where you did not have to go down the ladder from the top.

The Kiva held several hundred people. A Zuni Indian sat next to me. Kachinas with and without masks danced and then dancers from the other seven Kivas came down the ladder and danced. Children of both sexes sat on benches around the walls, wide-eyed. They had sat there off and on for four days. Women came and gave them a drink of water at times. Rik, Ginny, Ammon, Joe got sleepy in turn and left about 4 a.m. Eight year old Keith stayed until daylight when the kachinas took off their masks. The children were told that they did not live in the San Francisco mountains near Flagstaff but were only aunts and uncles—but not to tell the smaller children. They would learn when it was time. They were then told the duties and admonitions which would make them good Hopi and not KaHopi which means "bad-Hopi."

Mutton and hominy and an especial sweet cornmeal pudding were on hand and everywhere we went we ate some of it. We slept a little and visited with our Hopi friend. We also visited Don, the Sun Chief on top of Old Oraibi; we went to Shungopovy to see Andrew and to ancient Walpi on the huge rock. As we entered Walpi, kachinas were whipping (a form of mock fun) all those who were caught outside of a house, as the procession was coming. We waited with a thousand people for the opening exercises, but as it was getting late we left before we stood the chance of getting lost in the winding unmarked desert roads.

Anarchism

That night Platt and Barbara welcomed us. In true Mormon hospitality Barbara had baked a birthday cake for Ginny. Platt found an autographed copy of Marcus Graham's *Anthology of Revolutionary Poetry* which he had purchased from the author in a hotel in Denver years ago, and gave it to me.

I had written in his atheistic and bombastic monthly paper MAN for about ten years, and when he issued a booklet on Anarchism he did me the honor of giving the definition, although there were many anarchists more capable. I stressed the ethical view. I quote from page 8 on *ANARCHISM, a Solution to World Problems*, issued by MAN, P. O. Box 971, Los Angeles, Cal. 1940.

> Anarchism has been called non-state Socialism. Despite the popular idea of anarchists as violent men, Anarchism is the ONE non-violent social philosophy. It is the very antithesis of Communism and Fascism which places the State as supreme. Anarchists will do away with the State entirely. The function of the Anarchist is two-fold. By daily courage in non-cooperation with the tyrannical forces of the State and the Church, he helps to tear down present society; the Anarchist by daily cooperation with his fellows in overcoming evil with good-will and solidarity builds toward the anarchistic commonwealth which is formed by voluntary action with the right of seccession.
>
> The basis of Anarchism is liberty with individual responsibility; its methods are decentralization of activity and federation of local communes for national and international functions.
>
> Simplicity is emphasized. Courage and freedom are its watchwords. Anarchism, having faith in the innate goodness within everyone, seeks to establish the Golden Rule by working from within the consciousness of the individual while all other systems of society, working from without, depend upon man-made laws and violence of the State to compel men to act justly. Anarchists seek to slowly change the forms of society but do not rely upon that change alone to make people better.

And now a definition from the Encyclopedia Brittannica:

> *"ANARCHISM: the name given to a principle or theory of life and conduct under which society is conceived without government-harmony in such a society being obtained, not by submission to law, or by obedience to any authority, but by free agreements concluded between the various groups territorial or professional, freely constituted for the sake of production and consumption, and also for the satisfaction of the infinite variety of needs and aspirations of a civilized being. In a society developed on these lines, the voluntary associations which now already begin to cover all the field of human activity would take a still greater extension so as to substitute themselves for the state in all the functions."*

March Tax Picketing

About a week before the time for picketing the tax man on March 14, I went over to Rik and Ginny's to make up the leaflet. I had already written what I thought was good, but from previous experience knew that the best things require much effort. That night they were going to see Father Dunne's play *Trial by Fire,* and I was baby-sitting for them. I read the manuscript of my leaflet after supper and Rik asked me if I were going to picket on Sunday. I told him that he knew it was on a Wednesday. He laughed and said that what I had written sounded like a sermon and that it would never do. Ginny agreed

"What are people interested in when they see you picketing? Talk about that," Rik said as he left for the play. After the boys had their numerous drinks of water, etc. etc. and all was quiet, it came to me that most people wanted to know how I got by with it. In a short time I had written another entirely new leaflet.

I never make my signs much ahead of time, for something important may happen that must be used for the substance of a sign. The Saturday evening before March 14th, Rik, Ginny, and I worked until 2:30 Sunday morning getting the exact words for my posters. A hundred suggestions were made but with us no sign is made unless it "clicks" and has the approval of all. The first sign was about my non-payment of taxes, as usual, and needed no discussion. Operation Killer had just been in the news, coming from General Ridgeway and Rik provided the words: *"Operation Killer will bring the peace of the graveyard. Not world peace."*

News had come about the Senate approval of Universal Military Training, and Ginny suggested that something showing our disapproval be given in a sign. It took hours but finally the following emerged: *"The end of the American Dream: Universal Military Training."*

We did not want our posters to be the same as on previous picketings. We hunted through the Scriptures, made scores of suggestions, but the final words seemed to elude us. About 2:30 a.m. the following seemed to ring true: *"God is not mocked."*

So after mass I went forward to picket. A postman with his load on a bicycle saw me as I adjusted my signs and asked for a CW and whatever leaflet I had. Very few people refused the green leaflet. I gave CW's to those who were especially interested.

Two elderly men thought I was advertising some accountant who would help them make out their tax reports. Another man asked me: "How do you get by with it?" I told him that I knew he was going to ask just that question, so I had the answer. He took my green leaflet with that title good-naturedly. One postal employee asked me who paid me for my picketing. I told him that I did it on my own, quitting work on the farm where I would earn $6 and spending as much for my posters and leaflets. "Now that is what I call *believing* in a thing. I'll read what you got there," he said.

I had noticed a sickly looking man with a dog on a chain. I passed him several times. Later he was across the street and called for me to come over, saying that a man in the business establishment wanted to read my signs. I went over, gave them my literature, answered the question again to the effect that no one was paying me; that I was on my own. The man with the dog wanted to read the sign on my back, and asked me to turn around. I did so and he tore it off, saying that I should not use God's name. The proprietor shunted my assailant out of the store saying, "This is a free country. You invited this man in here, and you can't start a rough-house in my place."

I went across the street to continue my picketing, when a woman walking behind me touched me on the shoulder, and taking out a pocket knife, said, "Here, I fix that sign so you can carry it again." It was Tilly Lashoo. A couple of years before when I had been away for a few days I came home and found the screen near my door cut, the door open, and Tilly sleeping in my bed. She had looked up my address, after escaping from "solitary" in a mental institution in Los Angeles. and with much more acumen than most, had found where I lived. She showed me a letter from the CW praising her for work she had done at our Chicago house. She worked in the fields and lived in a sort of shanty-dump away south of the tracks. She claimed that she was very wealthy from properties in Detroit, and that she had been put away in order that others could get her wealth. She said she was part Chinese and part Navajo and had me write letters to her mother who owned a big market in Los Angeles, to her son who was a doctor in New York City, and to her sister who lived there also. Letters to her husband in California, etc., etc., but they all came back. Tilly thought that men, especially Mexicans, were about to rape her, so she kept an ax, a club and butcher knife to properly attend to any males who showed up. She said I was the only man who had not tried to rape her. If I worked nights she would be as quiet as a mouse while I slept or if I was typewriting, and would soak sheets in water and hang them up by the screen and produce a home made air conditioner. But if I was not asleep or writing she would talk my head off. She generally ate by herself. She would stay for several weeks and all at once would be gone, and a shirt or coat of mine would be missing, and in its place would be a lock of hair tied around with a string which would bring me good luck. I had not seen her for a year and now she came along and did me this service and walked on. Months later I received a letter from the court in Los Angeles saying that her husband had died and owned two properties and had money in two banks. I gave Tilly ten dollars fare to go back to California, but she told me a week later she lost it and would hike that way herself. Years later I received a letter from her from the same asylum from which she had escaped. Folks teased me about "my woman," but there was no way of telling her not to come or go, for she did as she pleased.

My first tax man of three years earlier, a Catholic veteran, greeted me kindly. Other tax men asked for my literature and kidded some of their more patriotic co-workers, asking me for literature for them. Cars were parked all along and someone was generally waiting in them. I offered them literature and it was usually accepted.

One man who attends St. Mary's and had openly cursed me and the CW as Communist, tried to pick an argument with me on the idea that the CW was a Communist and not a Catholic paper. I told him that this could not be so for on the night before I had been introduced by Father Bechtel in the basement of Our Lady of Good Counsel Church in the nearby College town of Tempe to the Newman Club, and had openly

185

advocated the Christian Anarchist principle of the CW. This man did not believe it and was going to report me to the FBI. I told him he was wasting his time for they already had a file on me. A priest from St. Mary's came by later and greeted me gladly. Joe Craigmyle, Arizona's only non-registrant, came by and carried my sign for 15 minutes while I rested. A large hotel is across from the post office. I noticed a man whom I thought was a wealthy former employer of mine of Albuquerque. I phoned him and he was surprised to hear me. I did not invite him over but mailed him my literature. Cliff Sherrill, the father of Bob Sherrill, who had given me such good publicity three years ago on Anna Roosevelt's daily, stopped and greeted me kindly. He had been a reporter in Atlanta in 1917 when I was in prison there, had the prison beat, and knew of my story. On my last round a big man struck his fist at my sign. Perhaps I had come too close to him. The newsman was cheerful; one of his helpers had worked with the CW in Boston years ago.

Just as Rik drove up and I had 20 steps to get to his car a young man tapped me on the shoulder and asked me if I had met any veterans that day. I told him I had. He asked me if any of them had tried to knock me down. I replied that they hadn't. His next remark was: "Well, here's one that feels like it." I talked to him for ten minutes before he changed his mind. I can't remember a bit of what I said but it must have been good for I always do better under pressure, like Clarence Darrow.

About fifty people had greeted me kindly and about the same number had grunted disapproval. About 750 had accepted the leaflet and I saw less than a dozen thrown away. I gave out 150 CW's.

It seems that at a certain stage a prophet has little honor in his home town, for the newspapers did not mention my picketing. I had notified the police of my activity, but they did not bother me. That night a radio broadcaster who is the chief red-baiter in this vicinity, quoted from the literature of the Fellowship of Reconciliation, which he called a Commie Front, to the effect that two thirds of income taxes went for war. He had read my leaflet to his audience when I picketed Dec. 18th. and said that I was a Commie and so was the CW Communist. Several people phoned in and defended me. Now I learn that someone brought my leaflet to class at the Phoenix Union High School, and a teacher asked a Catholic girl about it. She had never heard of the CW so she asked a priest about it. He did not know much about it either, so asked a priest at St. Mary's, who explained that the CW was a good paper. So at least one girl and one priest knew more about the CW.

The leaflet I handed out read as follows:

How do I get by with it?

I don't know for sure.

I have picketed thirteen days in the last three years here in Phoenix against war, the draft, and paying taxes for all this. I have been detained by the police and released four times, and been called to the tax office often.

I was a conscientious objector in both World Wars. In 1942 I refused to register for the draft and resigned from a civil service job in Milwaukee where I had been a social worker for eleven years. As I do not believe in shooting I have since then worked on farms where no withholding tax is taken from my pay, so I do not buy a gun for others to shoot. The tax man has tried to garnishee my wages; now I work by the day for different farmers and if necessary am paid in advance in order that no garnishee is effective.

I believe in the idea of voluntary poverty somewhat after the pattern of St. Francis, Thoreau, Tolstoy and Gandhi. I have no car or anything the tax man can get. I make a true report of my income but openly refuse to pay a cent of tax.

I am a non-church Christian. I believe in the Sermon on the Mount, especially because it is more revolutionary than opportunistic Communist tactics. I do not put my trust in money or bombs, but in God.

I am an Anarchist who believes that *all* government exists not to help people but to continue in power exploiters, bureaucrats and politicians who keep us on the run with their continual depressions and wars.

If you believe in capitalism and war and think you get your money's worth in paying taxes that is your business. My message is to those who are beginning to question the idea that preparing for war brings peace. It is also to those who believe somewhat as I do but who are afraid to stand up and say so.

If you begin to see through the assertion of the warmongers that .we are for defense—while we invade foreign countries—then you should read my tax statement in full as printed in the Feb. 1951 CATHOLIC WORKER, 223 Chrystie st., New York City, obtainable from me free of charge on the picket line or by request to my address below.

If you are ready for my message here is a starter:

REFUSE to become a soldier
  REFUSE to make munitions
    REFUSE to buy war bonds
      REFUSE to pay income taxes

      STUDY the Sermon on the Mount
        STUDY Gandhi's non-violent methods
        STUDY Jefferson's idea of life on the land
        "STUDY war no more."

"Better to light a candle than curse the darkness." A Christian Anarchist does both.

March 14, 1951

Ammon A. Hennacy,
R. 3, Box 227,
Phoenix, Arizona.

No State Tax Paid

Aside from paying taxes to the United States I also consider it wrong to pay taxes to the state of Arizona, so on March 15th. I wrote them this letter.

Tax Collector, State of Arizona.

Dear Sir:

I made $1491 in 1950 working as a day laborer for farmers. Whether I owe the state a tax or not does not make any difference to me for I do not intend to pay it. I wrote to your department the last two years to this effect. I am enclosing the statement of reasons why I do not pay my federal income tax and the same holds for the state of Arizona as it is part of the capitalist system and furnished a guard in wars and a militia to put down strikers

I consider that the 2% sales tax which I cannot help but pay is sufficient to pay for walking upon the highways. I do not ask or accept police protection and do not want any pension, subsidy, or help from the state. I do not desire to help pay for the upkeep of prisons, courts and reform schools which deny the Sermon on the Mount. Any services that the state performs could be done much cheaper and better by the people themselves. Neither do I favor handing out millions of dollars in old age pensions to people who do not need it; in many cases to old folks who turn over their property to their children and ask for a pension because everyone else is getting it. This is not the Pioneer Spirit or the true American Way of Life.

P. S. Here is a copy of a leaflet which I handed out when I picketed the federal tax man yesterday.

Sincerely,
Ammon A. Hennacy.

Hopi Protest to Governor Pyle

There was a bill up in the legislature to legalize sale of liquor to the Indians if and when the Federal Government also withdrew restrictions. Four Hopis, the interpreter, Andrew, Dan and Ralph of Tucson stayed over night with me. They dictated the following letter which I wrote for the Hopi to the Governor.

188

Dear Governor Pyle:

In order that it may be fresh in your mind concerning the conversation which you had with us of the Hopi yesterday we are summarizing our thoughts.

It came to our attention this last Saturday that there was to be a meeting of Congressmen here in Phoenix to discuss Indian affairs. One of our leaders, Andrew Heremquaftewa of the mother village of Shungopovy, was busy with religious ceremonials but he felt that this land problem was also important so he left these sacred ceremonials and came to Phoenix.

We are not able to find signs of any meeting and it was suggested that we call at your office. We did so and are pleased to have met you. We find now for the first time that you have signified your intention of signing a bill granting the sale of liquor to Indians. We understand that your desire is not to increase the number of drunken Indians but that you feel the Indians should be citizens and become a part of the white man's civilization and that this approval of the sale of liquor is just the first step in this direction.

Perhaps you have not known of the Hopi traditions. In order that you may understand why we oppose the sale of liquor to Indians we will tell you the way we look at life. The name Hopi means "PEACEFUL." We were the first people to inhabit this land; it was given to us by our God Massau'u. He gave us instructions of how to live pure, clean and spiritual lives. We have held to this tradition even though we have been put in chains, beaten and punished, and our land stolen.

We live where there is no irrigation. We depend upon rain to grow our corn, melons, peaches, etc. The white man has sought to make rain by a machine in the clouds; you have also made huge bombs and have stolen the fire from the Sun for deviltry. Whether liquor is just one part of the white man's way, an essential part perhaps, we do not know, but we do know that we do not want anything to do with the artificial way of life of the white man. *We will get rain if our lives are pure and if we fast and pray and are humble in seeking forgiveness for our sins*

Our God has told us centuries ago of the great wars that would come and of a third great war which will purify by fire this evil generation. He has told us long ago of wagons that run without horses and of men traveling by machines in the sky. All this is not new to us. If we remain true to our traditional teaching of prayer, fasting and true living then we will not be found wanting when that Day comes. If we look around and find our girls and boys drunken we will be judged for having made this possible. You too are a religious man and a leader of your people. You should not take this matter lightly. We tell you that if you wish to solve this question in the truly democratic way you should give the Indians time to have a plebicite in this matter. We are not telling you what to sign or what not to sign. That is up to you as Governor. We are only bringing it to your attention that the white man has always made rules and laws concerning the Indian but never asking the Indian what he thinks about it. You should think this matter over in your own heart and pray to your God for guidance before you do this thing.

There is another matter that we wish to speak to you about. This land that was given to us is held sacred to us as a Peaceful Land. We are told by Massau'u that our oil and minerals must be used for peaceful purposes and not for war. When desolation of war does come there must be some place of refuge; some place where peaceful people are found who remain true to their sacred teachings. We do not wish to be soldiers in foreign countries to kill people. This is also an evil part of the white man's way of life called civilization and progress. We do not want to have anything to do with war. We have made no agreement or treaty with the government regarding our land or regarding our being soldiers; therefore it is a violation of all honor and justice to draft our boys to fight in any war. We will not allow our boys to be soldiers.

A year ago we went to Washington, D. C. and told the authorities that we did not recognize their jurisdiction to decide what land was ours and what belonged to the whites. We are now and have been for centuries a sovereign nation owing fealty only to our God. We have gone to Washington and now to Phoenix but we are not going to have any more meetings in the white man's big cities. We want the next meeting to be held in Hopiland with all of our people and religious leaders. You mentioned that there were different groups of people among the Hopi and you wondered if we represented the majority of the Hopi. We represent the traditional leaders and if you come to Hopiland we will have a meeting of young and old, not in a smoke-filled room in secret, but in the open where the sun can be witness to the truth in our hearts. In the past government men have listened to Hopi who have government jobs and have sought to subvert the Hopi away from their true peaceful life.

> Sincerely yours,
>
> Dan Katchongva, Advisor,
> Sun Clan, Hotevilla.
> Andrew Hermequaftewa, Advisor,
> Blue Bird Clan, Shungopovy.
> Interpreter, Oraibi.

The Governor signed the liquor bill. The night before the Hopi left we had phoned and made an appointment with Congressman Toby Morris at the Hotel Westward Ho. As I went to the desk to inquire for him, I saw him and introduced myself, saying I had Hopi with me who wished to see him. He replied that he already had a meeting with the Hopi. "With the government Hopi," I told him. He looked guilty and said he would be back in a minute, and headed toward the bar. Soon he came around and motioned for the Hopi to come outside in the cold wind where he put his arm around them and told them he was their true friend. We had heard the same words in Washington, D. C. from him.

Around this time Alan Haywood, C.I.O. organizer spoke in the High School Auditorium. I stood outside and sold CW's. And later went inside and listened to second-rate pep talks. After the meeting I spoke to Haywood, gave him a CW, and told him that CW's had picketed St. Patrick's when Cardinal Spellman had his priests scabbing in the cemetery strike. Haywood said he had organized that union, but did not know of the action of the CW. He had bought a copy from me as he went in but I did not recognize him. When he came out of the building he waved to me cheerfully and said "Keep up the good work."

Living Off the Land

"It's good to have you around; you give one confidence in life" said the Old Pioneer when he saw me come home from work and gather my cap full of peas from our garden, and a bowl of mulberries for breakfast from the huge tree by the lateral. "You live off the land like an Indian," he added. I replied that I never bought any canned goods, although at times my fare might seem monotonous to the glutton who thought only of a variety and of out-of-season vegetables. After the peas came fine red tomatoes. Now there is corn, regular sweet corn, Hopi and pop, Okra, a little of which goes a long way, and always onions and carrots. The chard is wilting in this hot weather after being on hand since last November. This year we surrounded some of the tomato vines with stakes and a small mesh wire, and these plants seem to be doing better than before. Bell and chili peppers are on hand now until frost, and egg plant will be my staple in about a month. These are difficult to start but grow like weeds when they have passed a certain stage. We have five rows of watermelons. When I fasted last August and picketed the tax man, I kept thinking of watermelons. Banana and hubbard squash have established ownership of one end of the garden. The oven in my wood stove is no good, so often when I come home from work the Old Pioneer has baked a squash for me. He has an electric stove, but claims that food tastes better with a wood fire fragrant with desert mesquite.

Water

Because of the high price of cotton due to the war every man and his brother are planting cotton. The local papers and then LIFE magazine had articles about a community east of Mesa where a big cotton man from California rented desert land, put down big wells, and drew all the water from a small nearby community, so they had to have water hauled, as they had no money to drill a deeper well. We call this kind of man a suitcase farmer. He leases land, hires custom tillage and custom planting, and often sells his crop before it is matured, so that no matter what happens he cannot lose. He lives in town generally, or perhaps, as in this case, comes carpetbagging from another state. And for us here in Arizona a robber from California is the worst.

Wells that have been here for fifty years are now drying up because of this increased use of water. If a resident farmer has no water or the thousands of dollars it takes to drill or deepen a well, he sells or leases his land to the big company and moves to town, or becomes a farm laborer. This is just what has happened in Arizona, for, according to the census in 1940, there were in round numbers 18,400 farms. In 1950 only 10,300, with more land in cultivation than in 1940.

This last month three resident farmers for whom I work had to drill wells. Adding insult to injury, the big farmers who have already gotten their large wells have now petitioned the courts to halt all well drilling because of the scarcity of water. They have theirs so to hell with the rest. This same Association can unite to hog all the water, but when the CIO wanted to bargain with them in the packing sheds they claimed they were only individual farmers, not an organization.

Few wetbacks work in this section, but the big farmers generally hire Mexican Nationals, for they are steady, sober workers, more so than the average. As I remember my cotton picking days among the poverty stricken and debilitated whites and poor and happy Negroes, I cannot but remember "where wealth accumulates and men decay."

In the latter part of June fires burn in the fields all around: wheat and barley stubble. These shiftless farmers spoil their own land in this alkali country by these fires and deprive the land of humus which results from the plowing under of the stubble. The land also soaks up more water and needs less irrigating where there is this mixture of soil and straw. The big company and the army captain farmer, James Hussey, are about the only ones around here who do not burn their stubble. The Old Pioneer rents his land to the big company and won't allow his stubble to be burned.

"You shovel like a Mexican," said the Old Pioneer as he watched me make a check to dam up the water on the low side of a land in his small wheat field. After eight years in this Southwest I finally have received this compliment. This Irishman generally dug his shovel deep into the ground, put his foot on it and leaned on it, thus making a hole where water could settle and cause a washout—at the worst—and at the best it would make rough ground for machinery that had to go over it. The right way—the Mexican way—is to scoop up dirt in a swinging motion. This is harder, but it leaves no hole for a washout.

CW readers might think that I do nothing but picket. "Hopi," "picket" and "fast" are three different words but to my employers they seem somewhat interchangeable, for when I mention one they ask about the other. They all read the CW and none of them are Catholics. The truth is I have worked every day except the eight days I picketed in 1950 and the time spent for the trip to Washington and the three trips to the Hopi.

There has been very little rain this last year. One cloudy evening James came and got me to come and irrigate his barley field which had recently been planted. Instead of being in lands about thirty feet wide there were about 48 rows irrigated at a time. The water was already set and running in these rows. Bits of straw, sod, or tin kept those rows immediately in front of the entrance of the water from washing out or giving these rows more than their share. Water from a port in the main ditch ran in a small ditch for about 12 feet and then spread out in 12 rows. After a time I walked down the quarter mile length of the field, stopping about every 100 feet to see if Brother Gopher had piled up a mound of fine dirt and had stopped the water in any certain row. Now it commenced to rain. I had brought a raincoat, but with my slushing around in the mud and wielding the shovel and a flashlight I was soon wet around the edges. I had run the pickup nearby so I could get in and out of the rain for a few minutes. When one row would be finished I would remember its number and cut off the water. At the far end water would back up and fill all of the rows. At times I would shut off one port and open a new one. When daylight came I was able to find portions of a few rows that had been missed and to run water down these rows. It had rained most of the night but not enough to provide moisture to germinate the barley.

Now about six weeks later I irrigated this field at night. I crawled into my sleeping bag for a few minutes and soon felt something cold touch my face. It was Cindy James' dog, from half a mile away. She gravely held out her paw to be welcomed. I was only glad she had not brought her eight puppies along. I had made no noise in the field, but she knew I was there, it seemed. Irrigation went without much trouble although I was busy most of the time.

It is evening and I see two Mexicans irrigating perhaps 200 rows of cantaloupes for the big company. They had irrigated last week when the seeds were first planted. Now a small amount of water runs down each row for about 36 hours until it has subbed up and kept the seeds wet in this hot country. (I had not run the water long enough so had to replant my tomato seeds.)

Irrigating

I have been irrigating freshly plowed ground now for three nights for James. He is a reserve officer and is all packed up to go to camp to-morrow. He believed in the previous war, but sees no sense in the farce in Korea. As he is not a convinced pacifist there is little he can do about it. Now the next day when he called for me to irrigate he joyfully informed me that the discharge he had asked for long ago had just arrived and he would not have to go to Korea. He is the most considerate employer I have ever had and has more patience with inefficient help (including myself at times) than I as a pacifist would have had. Instead of driving those who work for him he quietly suggests the tasks that are to be done, and we all go at our own speed. Last week I cut tall Johnson grass along the irrigating ditches for him. Mexicans had taken the two handles off the scythe and thrown them away. I blistered my hands and creaked my back working in the, for me, unnatural posture required to manipulate this scythe. The second day I borrowed one from the Old Pioneer that had handles, and got along nicely. These few days were not as hot as usual, so the work was strenuous but not tiresome.

That kind of labor is a good way of telling whether you are a man or a mouse. Tolstoy at my age, 58, swung the cradle along with his peasants and ate their vegetarian diet. Some of his best works were written while he did this heavy labor.

One thing to remember while irrigating is not to scatter the water. About 50 rows of maize were irrigated at one time. Some rows would be finished ahead of others, so water from one or more rows would be changed over into a dry row and irrigation would proceed twice as fast. I have my same sleeping bag. When water has started down rows or lands it takes a couple of hours to see where it is missing. This is the time to sleep. Dozing with head on knees is not restful. I am a light sleeper and generally take the clock along to gauge the time. In irrigating plowed lands the water has a tendency to flow on one side or the other, and you are never sure just where until it gets going. To wade boot deep in mud which nearly pulls your boots off when you make each step and to make a check that will deflect the water is quite a chore. Always slant the check in the way you want the water to flow—not straight across.

Meet George Yamada

George Yamada, Japanese CO who did time in Civilian Public Service and in Danbury Penitentiary visited me for a week. Aside from Scott Nearing, and my friend Max Heinegg of New Zealand, George is the only vegetarian I have met who is a good worker. Likely this is because he is Japanese and not because he is a vegetarian. George cleaned ditches ten hours a day that week. He kidded and said it was not such hard work for him because he did not have far to stoop as he was built close to the ground.

George had a print shop on the Coast but gave it up rather than pay income taxes for war. He is an expert linotype operator, but will not take the excellent pay this occupation gives, for a withholding tax for war is taken. He has been visiting the Hopi and helping them plant corn. Never a harsh word of Hopi parents to their children he reports. He feels that the Hopi represent a way of life that is an oasis in the world of gadgets. He did not mind my wood stove, oil lamp, and lack of an icebox or air conditioning, for the Hopi cannot afford these things either.

A Legionnaire who is a friend of the Old Pioneer and who says he knows me told him that I was "crazy as hell for there is no such thing as Christian Anarchism." The Old Pioneer told him that he was not of my belief and would not pretend to defend my ideas, but that a thought came to him that might throw some light on the subject. He told the Legionnaire that bluing added to water did not make the clothes blue, but made them white. It could be that anarchism a vague or violent ideal as the case may be, and Christianity, which has not succeeded in following Christ, might be combined and produce something better than either anarchism without Christ or Christianity which follows the war-provoking state.

Babylon

The Valley National Bank, largest bank in the Rocky Mountain states, it boasts, writes of the growth of Phoenix. Along with the Chamber of Commerce and real estate sharks, there is the constant comparison with Los Angeles, and much fuss is made when an industry moves here. The following from the June, 1951, ARIZONA PROGRESS, issued by the Valley Bank, entitled "Comes the Evolution," is worth quoting in full:

"The age of Materialism, spawned by a fertile Individualism and the Industrial Revolution, has lasted a long time. It has produced a multitude of creature comforts. We have invented gadgets to perform almost every physical act, including that of procreation. But all this material progress has not solved the world's social and political problems, nor contributed noticably to human happiness or satisfaction. On the contrary, it seems only to have increased tension, insomnia and ulcers.

"Man, apparently, cannot live by bread alone, or by caviar alone, or even by the escapism of modern transportation and entertainment. He has also had his fill of Supermen and Medicine Men, of puny panaceas and mortal miscalculations. The Pied Pipers of the Proletariat have not delivered a 'more abundant life' but continuous unrest and a long succession of gory wars. When disillusionment sets in, people usually become embittered fatalists or humble supplicants seeking divine guidance.

"Fatalism, of course, is a negative and not wholly reassuring philosophy. Most people must have a spiritual anchor—a basic belief in something. If intangible, so much the better. Said Apostle Paul, 'Faith is the substance of things hoped for, the evidence of things not seen.' Communism is doomed to failure not only because it is bad economics but because it is a godless and soulless doctrine."

Thus speaks Mammon of the Desert, the chief architect which has changed this valley from one of homesteads to commercial farming; which foreclosed on hardworking farmers in the depression, cleverly admits that something might be wrong with affairs. The religious stuffed-shirt who writes this stuff is smart enough to know better, although he may have deluded himself into believing that he is sincere. By hinting that one should pray and that there is really something to religion he seeks to link the predatory traits of his bank with something Holy. "1% is usury Mr. Banker, and time belongs to God, not to bankers."

With further quoting of scripture he tries to put the blame for his own mercenary program's failure to produce an abundant life upon the Communists, accusing them of wars and saying that they are doomed because they are "Godless and soulless." Bankers who are supreme among thieves have the gall which goes with their bloodsucking business in calling others soulless and godless. At least the Communists do not use the name of God to justify their usury. Bankers should not groan about their ulcers and insomnia. They have it coming. They should remember that Jesus who turned the money changers out of the Temple and who said that a rich man could seldom enter the Kingdom of Heaven; that Jesus who told of rich men devouring the portion of widows and orphans. They should think of the time to come when their soulless adherence to money has drained this Valley of water and their warmongering activities has brought destruction to the cities. Then their valued real estate will produce less than the semi-waste lands of the Hopi who lay by two years of corn ahead.

The city parasites are crying to a loan company when they miss two paydays. Until the day they die with their moneybags at hand these bankers will not see the handwriting on the wall which shows that it is they and their lay and clerical apologists who have been weighed in the balance and found wanting. Big Business heads the Freedom Drive for more propaganda against Communism, while they will not allow a radical to speak or write or allow freedom of books in libraries or schools which do not bolster up the status quo. Unlike Babylon and Ninevah Phoenix may then again rise from the ashes of desolation, but if it does it will be without a need of bankers and parasites. It will be at a time when each can have his own vine and fig tree and live simply—without ulcers and insomnia; and without Red Feather charity drives, loyalty oaths and politicians.

In a letter from Lloyd Danziesen, one of those who fasted and picketed with us at Washington, D. C. he says, "You are lucky and of course very wise to be a 'one man revolution,' for you do not have to discuss your action over and over again (with committees) but can swing into action."

Thus I carry papers wherever I go and when I see French soldiers in training at Luke Field on the bus I do not have to belong to a Committee to Propagandize French Soldiers, but I explain that the founder of the CW was a Frenchman and give them CW's.

Tax Fast and Picketing

There was no rush for me to write my leaflet for the picketing and fasting commencing on Aug. 6. However, as with all things of the Spirit, it is best to act when you feel like it and not "quench the spirit" as it says in the Bible. On July 4th. I sat down and in five minutes had finished my leaflet. Later Rik made some fine suggestions as to phraseology and paragraphing but it seemed to "have come out of the blue" for there was no argument between us as to substance, as formerly. It read:

We Have the Kind of World We Deserve
What are We Doing to Deserve a Better One?

We have tried for centuries to make people good by law, by punishment, by war, and by exchanging politicians. We have failed.

We really can't change the world. We really can't change other people! The best we can do is to start a few thinking here and there. The way to do this, if we are sincere, is to *change ourselves!* This is why I am picketing and fasting!

I have been trying to change myself since I studied the Sermon on the Mount while in solitary confinement as a Conscientious Objector in Atlanta prison in 1918.

This is why I quit a civil service job nine years ago and live a life of voluntary poverty.

I work by the day for farmers, because no withholding tax is taken from my pay.

This is why I owe $129 income tax this past year alone, and have openly refused to pay taxes which go for *war and the bomb* for these past eight years.

I am fasting these six days as a penance for being part of the civilization that threw the Atom Bomb at Hiroshima just six years ago, and continues to make bombs . . . and wars.

Our neighbors, the traditional Hopi Indians of Arizona, have not had to change their way of life, for they have had the true way all along!

The white man has stolen their lands, "plowed under" their sheep and cattle, and now this conqueror has told them that the 13th. day of August is the deadline when their time will be up to claim their rights to their tribal lands! The Hopi do not recognize the right of the white man to be both judge and jury, for they are a self-supporting sovereign people who have lived in Arizona for a thousand years without laws, courts, jails or murders. They have never made a treaty with the United States.

The Indian Bureau has bribed some Hopi and has made Tribal Council stooges of them.

Missionaries who have upheld this wicked government have taught them the white man's watered-down religion.

The government has drafted Hopi to fight and die in far-away lands.

All this is wrong and shameful, and we should have no part of it—not even by paying our income taxes to support such fraud.

What Can We Do?

We can rely upon ourselves rather than upon the government . . . We can rely upon God rather than the dizzy plans of dizzy politicians . . . We can work for a living instead of being parasites . . . We can refuse to make munitions, to buy war bonds, to register for the draft, or to pay income taxes . . . Government bribes, medals, and subsidies are trash compared to the peace of mind, love of neighbor, and "Thy Kingdom Come" for which we pray

. . . We sense the illusion of violence, but still cling to the illusion of wealth . . . We need not sow the wind and reap the whirlwind . . . We can begin to be men instead of pipsqueaks . . . The spirit of True Pioneers shall yet defeat the bureaucrats!

Ammon A. Hennacy,
R. 3, Box 227,
Phoenix, Arixona,
August 6 to 11,
1951

I approached this tenth stretch of picketing with absolutely no fear. Heretofore when I even thought through the year of picketing my knees would feel weak, and likewise my stomach. In my mind I was very brave but my body had not caught up with my mind. This year they were both sturdily in unison. I expect that this may be due, not only to experience, but to my deeper study in recent months of the philosophy of Gandhi and of the traditional Hopi both of which emphasized the cumulative buildup of true thought and action into a powerful force, whether outsiders measure things that way or not. Someone has said that no good thought or action is ever lost.

The night before we were to make the signs George Yamada came over and we discussed the content of the signs. When hiking over the country I never did like to go over the same road twice and likewise Rik did not like to make the signs the same as previously. So the rear of the big sign was in a black border, with the first three lines across the sign and the last three given a different kind of emphasis by being in a small box beneath.

I mailed out about 300 leaflets, first class postage, to every minister, priest, rabbi, Mormon, or Jehovah's Witness leader in this community, writing each a personal note asking him to pray for the success of my picketing if he could, in conscience, do so. I knew my CW priest friends would do this without asking and that outside of several Rotary and Legion minded priests they were all sympathetic with my efforts whether they openly said so or not. I knew also that it might take many years for the non-Catholic clergy to get over the fact that I was connected with the CW, although the leading Baptist minister here had mentioned my picketing in a sermon, after having been given a leaflet and CW by me two years ago. I also mailed the leaflet over the country to many friends, and to heads of the Internal Revenue Department in Washington, and to all officials connected there with the Hopi or Indians.

The week before I planned to picket I wrote to the chief of police asking for a permit to picket and saying if I did not get it I would picket anyway. I also suggested that what I was doing was clearly subversive, but not more so than formerly, and he might check up with the FBI and Revenue department and see what the three groups wanted to do about my picketing. I also wrote to the tax office and FBI and told them the same thing. I wrote to my two tax men personally and sent them leaflets.

Orthodox anarchists who like to hide in alleys, whisper in saloons about the great damage they will do to the capitalist, or get social security checks which are not due them and think they have done something, do not like my Gandhian frankness in dealing with officialdom. The idea is I am not "asking" the officials anything. I am "telling" them what I am going to do. I would begin this fast on a Sunday noon and end it on a Saturday noon as the tax office closes at Saturday noon. It is best not to fill up on solid foods the day before beginning a fast but to gradually lessen your intake.

Rik's car was parked five short blocks from the post office, so on Monday morning, after praying for grace and wisdom at St. Mary's and saying hello to my newspaper friends, I loaded my pockets with leaflets, took extra CW's under my arm, and my waterbag with 1½ gallons of distilled water, and walked toward the post office. My old news vendor friend had gone and a new unsympathetic one was at hand. I hung the water bag on a palm tree and walked down the street. My first leaflet was given to a man who stopped and read it and when I passed him again in turn he said:

"I belong to a group that does things like you do: Alcoholics Anonymous. My wife died three years ago and although I had been a churchgoer for twenty years it did not mean anything to me until then, when I prayed. Later I mixed drinks with my prayers, but the AA fixed me up. You are right in not wanting to change the world, by violence; the change has to come with each person first." Thus one Irishman to another.

There were not so many people on the streets in this 105 degree temperature as there were in March, but very few refused to take my leaflet. Only two people mildly asked if I was a Commie. I replied that I was a Christian Anarchist. Whether they knew what this was or not they took a leaflet. Mr. Stuart, the head of the Revenue Department chuckled at my "MENE, MENE, TEKEL, UPHARSIN" sign which Rik had made in semi-Jewish lettering. The headlines on that morning told of the reorganization of the Revenue Department by Truman; the inference being that Mr. Stuart, along with others, had been found wanting and had to go. He was a man of the old school with a sense of humor, and had grinned at my former reference to a tax man being about as bad as a hangman.

In the afternoon a friend gave me a copy of a United Press release of 325 words which had just been sent over the country telling of my picketing and fasting. The account was very fair although it did not mention my emphasis on the Hopi. (I found out later that the next night the London Evening Star had 13 lines about my picketing but the anarchist paper FREEDOM in London to whom I had sent an advance air mail copy of my leaflets never mentioned my activity; neither did the leading pacifist journal, FELLOWSHIP, in this country.) I gave out 400 leaflets and 175 CW's. I only gave the latter when people asked for them or when they seemed especially interested.

"That leaflet of yours is a masterpiece, but there is one thing that spoils

it. It is not dignified to picket like this," said a well-dressed man to me kindly on the second day of my picketing.

"Stop and think a minute," I replied, "How would you ever have read the leaflet if I had not handed it to you on the picket line? And how would the United Press have sent it over the country if I had left it at home in my desk and never picketed?"

The night before Rik sat up very late sewing some striped goods into an apron which had pockets for my folded leaflets and into which I could put 100 CW's. However, I found it impeded my walking so I left it with my waterbag under a tree. (In November of 1952 I was carrying extra luggage in this apron when I got on a bus at Ann Arbor, Mich. Three young men immediately asked me where I got it. I told them in Phoenix, but they would not believe me. It seems that exactly that kind of goods is what their uniforms in prisons nearby had consisted of for some years. They had just been released. They kept looking back at me and laughing. I gave them CW's to read, explaining that I had done a stretch myself.)

Ten CW's and fifteen leaflets is all that I could handle without fumbling them. My fingers would get numb from holding the sign. First thing I met three people who knew me and who wanted to know about my experiences. One was the wife of a CO. She was visiting in Arizona and had been the first of the radical pacifists to visit the radical Hopi. As she was reading the UP release I had given her, a cop called me and asked me why I was stopping people and giving them literature. I told him this was only to friends who were asking for it. He was good natured enough about it but suggested that I go to the police station with him. I told him I had been arrested five times before for the same thing and released without charge but he insisted that I accompany him. So with all my paraphernalia I got into the squad car.

Every time I get a new police captain to educate. This time it was Captain Farley. He seemed good natured enough and wanted to know what I was trying to do. I told him I had advised the chief of police all about it a week ago. I said that there was too much war and materialism in the world and that some spirituality was needed to offset it. Finding that I did not belong to any group he wondered how I thought I could do anything. He thought that anarchists were bomb-throwers and killers. I told him that the biggest bomb-thrower was the government; that a Democrat had killed Lincoln; a Republican had killed Garfield; and an Anarchist had killed McKinley, and he shouldn't have done it, for he let Teddy Roosevelt loose on the world, so the honors were even. He seemed worried how the world would get along without cops when the anarchists overturned the world. I advised him that nothing would happen that suddenly; that today most people behaved and did not need a cop; it was only the weakminded ones they caught.

He asked me what I did with my money if I didn't pay taxes. I told him I gave my money to my daughters for an education rather than to Chiang and Franco. He speculated on what my daughters would think of such an unorthodox fellow as I seemed to be. I replied that they had

200

bought no war stamps during the war and were coming to see me in a few weeks. That when they were asked this question by the War Resister's League when they were quite small they answered:

"We are very proud of our Daddy because he did not go to war and kill people, but we get tired of hearing him brag about it. And besides we did not join the Brownies because they are for war."

The Captain asked me how I got by without paying taxes for war and I explained the matter in him in detail. He wondered what the FBI thought about me. I told him to call up and see. He spoke to Murphy, the head. I offered to leave the room while he talked but he said to remain. He told Murphy he could find no way of stopping this anarchist from parading around the post office and what did the FBI think about it. The FBI didn't give him any satisfaction it seemed. He then called the tax office and asked if there wasn't some rule whereby they could arrest me. He got no satisfaction from them so told me to go ahead and picket. I told him there was no hard feeling on my part and offered to shake hands with him, but he felt insulted, or so he pretended. If he knew what I think of cops he would know that I was really humble for once and tried to be decent to him.

I went back to my picketing. At noon I heard that the UP had inter-viewed the tax office as to my method of working and not paying taxes and had sent an additional release over the wires. Later in the afternoon the Hearst syndicate took my picture for the Los Angeles papers, using a rewrite of the UP article. I met Mrs. Stuart, wife of the tax man, and she deplored my being arrested in a free country. She is Democratic National Committee woman from Arizona. She was always kind and gracious each time she met me while I was picketing. As it happened last year the second night of the fast is always the worst. I took a bath and rested or slept until 6:30 a. m. and felt fine. I had my second wind. My eyes and head were clear. I gave out 300 leaflets and 70 CW's.

The next morning my first customer was the head of the Associated Press Bureau in Phoenix who had been requested by an out-of-town member to report on my activities. This client was told that the policy of the local papers (owned by one man in Indianapolis) was not to "dignify" my activities by mentioning them, although they had given me publicity in the past. Whether now this was because I was emphasizing evil which the white man was doing to the Indian; whether they did not like my poking fun at their stuffed shirt thievery of the bankers; or whether it was the mistaken idea that only wisdom could come from those who wore white collars, and not from one who digs ditches, pickets, and has no desires by which he can be bribed to shut up, I do not know. At least a favorable release was sent AP over the state, featuring my Hopi sign and telling of my non-payment of taxes.

Another cop stopped and questioned me. I told him they had all of my answers at headquarters so he left. One of my employers drove up and asked me to rest in a nearby park for a few minutes. Many of the same people came and went, so I could not expect an increase in the number of leaflets handed out. However dozens who had received the leaflet before stopped and asked for CW's. As before Negroes, Mexicans and Indians nearly always took my leaflets. A leading post office official greeted me cordially and asked for my propaganda, but the two-penny clerks, for the most part had a "loyalty oath" consciousness and were afraid to be seen casting a glance toward me, much less taking a leaflet.

Service Club members marched down four abreast from luncheon in the nearby Westward Ho and glared at me. Invariably the youngest of them would furtively ask for a leaflet. Only the Cadillac-mind seemed impervious to unorthodox ideas. Numerous mechanics in nearby garages with the name "Cadillac" sewed on their coveralls passed by sneeringly. Both of the tax men who had tried to get taxes from me during these years greeted me cordially, not deeming it a disgrace to do so among their fellow workers. Several people reported that my activities had been broadcast by local radios at different times during the day without any bias against me. They quoted my reply to a reporter that while I might not change the world I was sure it wouldn't change me. I gave out 235 leaflets and 100 CW's.

That evening Rik and Ginny had invited Morris, a Hopi silversmith, and family over for supper. (I rode back and forth with Rik and stayed at his house during the week, for the 24 miles a day picketing was enough for me without walking the four miles a day to my place at the Old Pioneer's.) This Hopi had a relative who belonged to the Spirit Clan and who fasted 16 days every year at a certain celebration. About an ounce of soup was all that was allowed each day: no water. On the 15th day this man went to the home of his mother and asked for a drink of water. They refused and scolded him for being a weakling. All this time those who fasted ran over the reservation in a search for spirits or in making prayers at certain places. In fatigue and despair this man entered the hollow where babies had been buried. The spirits of these babies would not let him go. There was a hole which opened out upon a steep cliff. He determined to jump out and commit suicide. Just before he came to the ground, after he had jumped, invisible arms seemed to hold him up so that he landed without a scratch. This taught him a lesson and made him ashamed of himself, so that for the succeeding three years he went through the 16-day fast with honor and without any pipsqueaking.

That night I was not sleepy, so rested on a couch. No matter how the others in the room began a conversation it ended about something to eat. I had to shout and tell them to talk about something else. I received an air mail from Dorothy telling of the picketing of the Atomic Energy Commission in N. Y. by the CW and others on Monday. My wob friend, Askew, in Seattle had heard a report of my picketing on the radio there.

First thing the next morning, as I was picketing, a man stopped and asked me what it was all about. I gave him a leaflet and CW. He asked if I had to pay too much income tax. I told him that I did not pay any tax at all. He asked me to repeat this assertion and said:

"Why you pay no tax at all and I have to pay my tax. That isn't fair!"

"You don't *have* to pay any tax unless you want to," I replied.

He became angry and went away muttering. Several men in uniform took my leaflets. It worried some people to learn that I belonged to no church, was not even a JW, had nothing for them to join that would save them, but advocated that they change themselves. Several fundamentalists exchanged their tracts for my literature, saying that there would be no peace until Christ came, and that I was wasting my time. Rik came to see me at noon as usual and kidded me about my "Indian dinner." The reference being to Indians who when in the desert without food simply drew up their belt a notch and did without, calling this operation an "Indian dinner." Two friendly priests stopped and talked to me. Countless persons in cars stopped and told me to keep up my good spirit. Outside of that first day no one had called me Commie. I gave out 235 leaflets and 159 CW's.

The next day around noon a friend from Tucson who had visited me four years ago when I picketed the Freedom Train came with Ed Morgan, a labor lawyer who was his friend. He had read in a Tucson paper that I had been arrested and so drove up to see if there was anything that could be done. I needed a little rest so we took half an hour off and drove to the ranch where George Yamada was working, and told him of the events of the week. Each time I fasted and picketed because of Hiroshima I had sent my leaflets and an air mail to the Mayor of Hiroshima. This year George mailed the letter for me with his own greeting in Japanese.

When I was picketing a woman shouted from a car:

"Did you just get nuts or have you always been that way?"

"Lady, we all live in a crazy world" I replied.

About 25 cars would always be parked around the sidewalk as I picketed. If any of the people looked interested I offered them a leaflet and later I gave them a paper if they seemed to read the leaflet with interest. Being naturally of a sociable nature if I saw a car from Ohio or Wisconsin I told the occupants that I was from those states, and thus, as Peter Maurin said made my revolution more "personalist." One man in a car to whom I handed a leaflet asked for a CW when I passed again, saying that he was a veteran and an Indian and was sure glad to see my Hopi sign. He was a Cherokee.

Driving homeward with Rik that night I was very thirsty. As we were near the town of Tempe Rik suggested that we stop in a drugstore there and get some icewater. If you drink it slowly when fasting it will not hurt you. As we parked the car we saw next to us the car with Number 1 license plates; that of the Governor, so I left a leaflet and marked copies of the CW in it. Inside the drugstore I introduced myself to Governor Howard Pyle and told him of my activities and of the literature I had left for him to read. He said he felt he would gain some information from what I had left, and although he has the reputation of being all things to all men it could be that some knowledge of the Hopi might counteract his advisors who want the Indians to own land privately and not communally, and to be taxed by the state. I gave out 210 leaflets and 100 CW's that day.

Now it was the last day of my picketing. I felt fine and thought if it was necessary I could fast another week. Working for farmers I seldom take time to look in the small piece of glass I use for a mirror, but this morning while shaving I noticed how bright my eyes were. A woman asked me for extra leaflets and. CW's, saying she would give them out to the women in her church club. I asked her what parish she attended. She said she was not a Catholic. She was a Presbyterian and was going to subscribe to the CW. Two young men who had parked their car came running and asked for literature, saying that they had seen my picture in the Los Angeles paper a few days before. I told them, as I had told others, that my message might seem strange to them but they should take as much of it as they could understand. Saturday noon came and as I prepared to cease my picketing and was on the last round of my course I gave my last leaflet and CW's to an Apache Indian and his wife who just came out of the postoffice.

Weighing myself on the same scales that I had used when I began the fast I found that I had lost 17 pounds. This was much more than last year when I had lost 11. I did not feel weak. I called up the UP Bureau and told them that I had finished my fast. They said that the New York office had requested a feature story about my activity and it would be broadcast soon on a Sunday. I gave out 86 leaflets and 59 CW's. A total of 1320 leaflets and 563 CW's during the week. About 300 people had stopped and greeted me kindly during the week; only three had spoken harsh words.

When you fast your stomach shrinks and you cannot eat as much as you think you can. I drank some orange juice, tomato juice, and ate some grapes and peaches and by 8 p. m. had mashed potatoes, soup, coffee and a small piece of pie. When Ginny was dishing out the soup I asked for three times as much as I could swallow. The next Monday I worked ten hours and in a couple of days had gained back all I had lost in weight. I felt fine.

Hopi Snake Dance

About two weeks after my fasting, Rik and family and I drove up by way of the beautiful Salt River Canyon and Holbrook to the Hopi Snake Dance. This year it was at Second Mesa. We visited the different villages and Ginny was entranced with The Hopi Way of Life. She went to the store to get something and told me that Ramon Hubbell the trader who had blasphemed the Hopi was there. They have stores in many places. So I went over and introduced myself. He was a fat, burly, elderly man who remembered the letters I had written to him and the CW's I had sent him. He patted his belly and shouted that I was a failure like all radicals, that all I wanted was his money. Why didn't I get a job and do some hard work for a change. His wife must have been used to his blustering for she tried to quiet him a little in order that I might have an opportunity to explain myself. He thought some Communists were hiding behind his store in World War I and seemed to think they were there yet. I told him that the two newspaper men and myself were anarchistic, which was the furthest removed from Communism that an idea could be; and that if he had been told we were Communists and were subverting the Hopi he was much mistaken. I tried to tell him Hopi history but he did not want to hear it. I was quiet in tone and we talked for an hour. Then Rik and Ginny came for us to go to the Snake Dance. As I got in one side of the car Hubbell whispered to Ginny at the other side:

"That Hennacy has too kind of a face to be an anarchist." I suppose he was looking for horns.

A group from the American Indian Congress were here talking to the radical Hopi. They wanted to take movies of Dan but he would not allow it for he felt that they would use his picture along with government propaganda. Seems the more educated anthropologists are, the less they know what is going on *today*. They may know all about the bones of the ancients, but they get so tangled up in their details that they miss the real life of the Hopi. Rik and family went back to Phoenix and I went with relatives of the Hopi to Winslow and then to Flagstaff to visit Platt and Barbara Cline.

I Love My Enemies, But Am Hell on My Friends

I receive hundreds of letters from over the world from readers of CW. Most of them praise my stand but a few of them curse me roundly. I answer these letters in as kind a spirit as seems possible at the time. To those who partly agree I tell them more of the same and dare them to live nearer the ideal. If they are too weak to go further then I do not need to be bothered answering them. If they mean business then we have helped each other. I receive a few anonymous letters. One man signed his name, called me a phony, and in every assertion that he made about my activities and character he was as wrong as a person could be. I did not know if he was a Catholic, an I.W.W., a parasite and exploiter, or just a disgruntled chance reader of the CW. I answered each false assertion of his in detail and in good humor; although with some sarcasm. In answer he apologized. Many times we do not know the extent of our efforts, so once in awhile it is good to know that you have overcome evil with goodwill.

I often say that I love my enemies but am hell on my friends. And it has seemed that those with whom I have the most controversy are those who claim to accept the ideals of peace and brotherhood, and even at times, anarchism, yet who follow from such a distance when it comes to practicing these ideals that I feel it is my duty as one who goes a long way to call the bluff of those who say "Lord, Lord" and "peace, peace" in exultant tones which mean very little. To the old man who had "nary a mark of the beast" I am humble, but not to those who boast of being humble. At times those who do not want to have their inconsistencies pointed out say in a super-sweet voice to me "Judge not, lest ye be judged." I reply "O.K., judge me, then."

A woman had written to FELLOWSHIP, the leading pacifist magazine in this country, whining because she might be rated as a "second class pacifist" inasmuch as she still paid taxes. The reply of this pacifist group was that we all had to obey our conscience and that we were all brothers in Peace. To a real pacifist or anarchist who has done time, or who has made a brave stand, but who because of mitigating circumstances could not take an out and out radical stand I would never be critical. But Professional Pacifists who receive salaries as such to water down the ideal to keep an organization going are another thing. Accordingly I wrote the following letter to FELLOWSHIP magazine in August of 1951. Six months later it was published by them without comment.

Editor FELLOWSHIP:

A lady writes to you of worrying because she might be called a "Second Class Pacifist." We are all that kind compared to Gandhi, but that is no reason we should glory in it. We should be ashamed of our timidity in the face of rampant militarism. We are great at calling the Devil names and then we jump to the other extreme and infer that Heaven and World Government or World Citizenship are similar. No wonder we are so weak. We fail to come to grips with reality.

When the organization gets to be more important than the ideal it is supposed to stand for then there is something seriously wrong. That is just what has happened to the churches and the unions and now to the FOR.

In every subject under consideration there is a norm, a standard and a rule by which actions can be measured. But with the FOR there is no norm. You can be an absolutist and refuse to pay taxes, buy bonds, do war work, register for the draft, and if in prison not cry for a parole. The bulk of the FOR membership will blush because of your forthrightness. You can also load a gun but refuse to fire it and remain, not a second class, but a full rate pacifist. Nonsense! The FOR says ten inches is a foot: Father Divine may say fourteen inches; the JW's eight inches. A foot is a foot and a pacifist is a pacifist, and not half a pacifist.

A person can say that there is a certain ideal but they do not have the courage to live up to it, or for the time being it is too inconvenient and that they will follow from afar off. That is too bad but not half as bad as having no ideal at all or alibiing that their temporary convenience is the ideal and that any makeshift is o.k. as long as the dear old FOR has plenty of members. All this is foolishness with God and man.

Sincerely,

Ammon A. Hennacy

I had not attended a Christian Science church for many years. I noticed a lecture advertised on the subject of Peace. I knew that the lecturer would talk the usual jargon about everything being spiritual and that matter was not really existing; only a seeming existence. Nevertheless I stood outside and quietly said "Catholic Worker. Peace paper." Two uniformed ushers came out and asked me to stop selling the paper. I pointed out to them that their church was the only one that did not allow its members to be CO's, but I think I wasted my time talking to them. I only sold one paper to a fallen away Catholic whom I knew; and one of the ushers took a copy to read. I heard the lecture which was as unreal when it came to discussing the subject of Peace as any lecture could be. I told one of the ushers who spoke to me later that in the early thirties when I was in Milwaukee John Randall Dunn, the leading Christian Science lecturer and later editor of two of their metaphysical magazines, had asked me to stop and meet him at the Pfister Hotel when he was there lecturing. He had written an excellent article against war and I wrote and asked him if he meant it. This was his reply.

After some conversation he put his arm around me and said "You are right and the Church is wrong on the subject of war. You did right in going to prison. Keep in touch with me." I wrote to him several times again and did not get an answer, so with so many people who have a momentary flash of truth. The usher felt that people had to make a living even if they worked at war work, and they had to obey the law, even if it was a bad law.

The author speaking at Wall and Broad, New York City, 1956

PRAY and WORK

Ade Bethune

CHAPTER 10.

Work
Fast
Picketing
Maryfarm Retreat

Jan. 1, 1952 - Sept. 21, 1952

Phoenix - New York City

"It'll rain; it always has."

This has been the assertion of the Old Pioneer for half a century when the faint-hearted ones thought Arizona would dry up and blow away. He had studied the data compiled by scientists as to rain and drought, by means of the growth of rings each year as recorded in the tree stump. Our well here had to be deepened twice recently, and all around us farmers were drilling again as the water level lowered. We were 350 miles away from the Hopi who prayed for rain and got it; we believed in machines, not in prayer.

In the last three days of August it commenced to rain and roads were flooded and insufficient water sewers in the cities were overflowing. One man who had memories of the drought of years ago walked in his shirt sleeves on the main street of Phoenix in the rain whistling and saying, "Ain't it wonderful?" When the Old Pioneer went to town the average person scowled at him as if he had brought the rain because he had never been a Jonah of despair. I took these three days when there could be no

208

work in the fields to clean up my cottage and file my correspondence of the previous year, for I had worked every day except when picketing or visiting the Hopi. Of course the water did fill up the dams and it was wonderful for the state as a whole.

Irrigating

By the drilling of the barley crosswise, instead of the length of the quarter mile "lands," I found these last few nights that the water distributed itself with very little trouble, as it did not rush to one side of the land and miss the other side. Several places where the border had been broken between the lands by this cross drilling, the water would escape from one land to another. By going ahead of the water and filling in these low spots the work was made much easier.

"*Don't scatter the water*" is one of the important rules to learn about irrigating. Normally there was enough water—150 inches—to irrigate two lands at once, but due to the dryness of the ground and cross planting of the barley I ran the water on one land at a time. (I only learned this after one night of trying it with two lands at once.) Cindy and her grown daughter came with muddy paws and cold nose to great me as usual.

When the farmer brought me new boots the other night, as three pairs had the left boot snagged, I mentioned the fact to the Old Pioneer. He recalled the old days when the irrigator was supposed to furnish his own boots, and if he had none he was charged a quarter a night rental for the ones used and furnished by the boss. One Mexican would come once a week riding on his burro for 38 miles to irrigate a 48 hour stretch and when he discovered that the Old Pioneer did not charge him the rental for the boots he was overjoyed.

Mexicans

In the old days when there was little electricity in the outlying districts, and before artificial bottled gas was sold, nearly everyone burned mesquite as it grew all over the desert. People cut it as they needed it or Mexicans cut it and sold it. These were the days of carpet-bag Governors and officials sent from Washington, D. C. One such was a very enterprising and ignorant District Attorney who asked the Federal Grand Jury to indict Mexicans for cutting mesquite on government land. The foreman of the jury argued that every one cut mesquite, and to the assertion by the D. A. that the law plainly said that no timber was to be cut from government lands and the Mexicans had been caught in the act of cutting this timber and had thus committed a felony, the jury foreman replied that mesquite was not lumber, it was mesquite, for it was not good for anything else and the work of cutting this thorny tangled mess was a chore which called for calloused hands and not the soft hands of officials. The ignorant D. A. who did not know mesquite from maple was much put out because common men argued with him instead of obeying him. The jury refused to indict the Mexicans.

The other day the headline ran: "Five Arizonians killed in battle in Korea." Four out of these five bore Spanish names. We stole this part of the country from their forefathers (other than the small Gadsen purchase).

We kept them impoverished by our seasonal scheme of work and low wages so that they do not have the education and the knowhow of gaining bullet-proof jobs in the armed forces, as do many of the whites. Hence their high rate of casualties. They are denied admission to clubs and lodges and some unions.

At the State Fair

Other years I had worked one night at the State Fair, taking care of Jersey cows for the Hussey's for whom I irrigate. This year I worked eleven nights straight from 7 to 7 for Hussey and three others, having 72 cattle in my charge. They were there for show and they had to be clean so it was up to me to see that any fresh manure was removed at once. One man wanted to know what we fed cows to produce homogenized milk. I had a notion to answer a fool according to his folly to the effect that homogenized milk came from one teat, regular milk from another, cream from the third, and buttermilk from the fourth, but could not do so with a straight face so I explained to him that homogenizing was done by a machine and that cream was put through this process and thus "stretched" so that a big cream line in a bottle did not necessarily mean anything. These Jerseys tested from 4.8 to 6% butter fat, while the kind of milk you buy at the store is about the legal standard of 3.4%. My daughters were brought up on unpasteurized Jersey milk from our own cow in Wisconsin and had seldom been ill. I had worked in a milk plant in Albuquerque and I knew how skim milk was added to regular milk to increase the profits. There is also a racket in this milk business the same as with white bread. It is not the desire to protect the health of the customer that makes for pasteurizing milk but the desire for profits. To cook the milk to kill all the supposedly bad germs would require from 175 to 200 degrees but this would prevent the cream from rising, so it is processed at 145 degrees which is just sufficient to keep it from spoiling for the several days it may be on the market.

From midnight until 4 a. m. things were quiet, but there would always be a few cows that needed attention. On the second night I heard a disturbance and sure enough a heifer calf had just been born. I felt at once to see if there was any remnant of the skin bag that had held the calf covering its nose to prevent breathing, but all was well and in an hour the calf was walking around. I lengthened the rope of the mother so she could lick the calf. It did not seem to know its own mother and bothered all the other cows, so it was taken away. Besides the milk was too strong and had to be diluted for the calf. A few rows down the barn, twin Holsteins were born another night, and they were a source of delight to the children.

One night I was surprised to receive a 'visit from Oliver Huset and wife. He had read an article of mine on the Doukhobors in RETORT in 1942 and had visited them in Canada. He had been a smokejumper in CPS for four years and had corresponded with me from Montana, but I had lost track of him in recent years. He was anarchistic, and we had much to talk about as he accompanied me on my rounds over the barn. I wondered how he had found me. He said that he heard I was in Phoenix, and, not finding my name in the phone book, had called the Internal Revenue Department and asked them if they knew of a person by the name of Hennacy who did not pay income taxes. My prayers for the taxman must have been of some avail, for they gave him my address obligingly.

My work was at the end of the barn next to the free show given each evening at 8:30. There were Hopi and Apache dancers, hillbilly antics, dancing girls, acrobats and jugglers. The girls came in and practiced their handsprings in the barn, but at the age of 58 my mind was on other matters. The juggler and his wife sat on bales of hay between acts. He juggled six Indian clubs with ease. In conversation with him I learned that he had been all over the world and had given a free exhibition in Atlanta prison, when Debs was there. I gave him a copy of the September CW with my One Man Revolution article and he was pleased to read other copies which I gave to him later. He mentioned that at Le Havre, France, he had put on his act for the soldiers and saw them with trunks full of paper money which was no good outside of France. He inferred that our Truman currency had not reached that level as yet.

The Fair was in the first part of November and the mornings were cool enough, but I never could get used to sleeping more than four hours. It took me two hours to get to work at the Fair, so from Friday morning to Monday morning I only slept two hours on Sunday afternoon after selling CW's at St. Mary's. As long as I was busy working Saturday I was not sleepy. One night I missed the bus and walked seven miles into town to get to work. In the morning I had three quarters of an hour to wait for a Tolleson bus so I sold CW's on the street corner. One man who bought a copy had been head of the Holy Name Society in Los Angeles, but had never heard of the CW. He was much pleased to learn of such a paper. One Sunday morning, waiting at the Fairgrounds for a bus I was talking to a man who was the brother of a Universalist preacher by the name of Kenneth Patton, who had refused to pay taxes for war but had had the tax taken from his bank account. I gave this man extra copies of the CW to send to his brother. Another man asked about work. I pointed out the cotton trucks that were passing by and he answered: "I'll be damned if I'll ever pick cotton. I'd starve first. $1.75 an hour or nothing for me." It seemed that the most recent $1.75 in his possession had gone for liquor so I left him as he muttered about the low wages in Arizona. I work for 75¢ an hour and some Mexican Nationals get 60¢ and 70¢. Some of the men in the barn who worked daytime slept there at night. In the morning about 5 a.m. this vegetarian still liked the smell of the bacon which they prepared for themselves on a hot plate. I waited until I made my own buckwheat cakes at home.

Although the Republican Governor Pyle is a man of kind words to all and of a religious mien, his backers in the state are ultra-conservative cattle, copper, cotton and citrus growers. He appointed a new manager of the State Fair who either from stupidity or from habit as a "free enterprise stooge," awarded the contract for lunches for members of the school bands to a scab restaurant in town where there was a picket line. This was done without bids, and a picket line was thrown at the Fair entrance. Very obligingly the only Republican judge in the county issued an injunction against the picketing.

This disturbance had about died down when a CO friend of the Hopi village of Oraibi communicated to the Governor the displeasure of the Hopi towards the huge 60 foot kachinas erected at the Fair, with bows and arrows in their hand. He explained that the Hopi were never in a war and were peaceful people, and that this special kachina was a particularly peaceful one denoting Life instead of death. The proper emblem should be an evergreen branch symbolizing life. The change was quickly made. In this case I think it was not malice but ignorance on part of the Fair management.

At the same time, an appointment was made for the traditional Hopi to visit the Governor during Fair week, as some of them would be taking part in the weaving and silversmith exhibits. Accordingly, at 2:30 p.m. on a Tuesday I accompanied my friends and a dozen other Hopi to the office of the Governor. Head men spoke of the traditions for peace, non-cooperation with the government, and of their dislike of being forced to take up with the decadent ways of the white man. Dan spoke for the big rebel village of Hotevilla, Andrew spoke for Shongopovi, and Seyestewa spoke for Mishongnovi. David, the weaver at the Fair, heard the Governor say that perhaps in about 25 years the state would take over the Indian lands from the Federal government for a time, and then the Indians could own their own lands individually like white men, although they might not necessarilly have to pay taxes to the state as had been mentioned by the papers before. The Governor also said that many young Indians wanted better clothing and housing and medical care and that he listened to their requests. Now he was hearing from the traditionalists who wanted the old ways. What was he to do? David answered by saying, among other things, "Beware of the Greeks bearing gifts."

The two reporters present gave fair accounts of the conference, although they could not do the subject justice, as they did not understand the Hopi background. The following day another reporter gave an entirely false picture of the traditional Hopi after interviewing the stooge government employee Hopi. They tried to picture these traditionalists as crazy old men and as being subverted by radicals. In fact the Governor must have been advised to this effect by his conservative backers, for after the conference he called the interpreter for a private conversation and asked him if he knew that both the white man who had accompanied them to the conference and the Japanese who had driven them down from Hopiland in his car were anarchists who had done time for refusing to fight for their country. The interpreter said he was of the same belief, so the Governor got little comfort. (The Hopi who had driven them down had a slight Oriental cast of features, so the Governor or his informants thought this was George Yamada.)

About this time, Rik wrote a masterful letter, exposing the thieving plans of the whites and stating that the issue was not whether the Hopi had better clothing but whether their way of life was to be subverted by materialistic conquerors. By some accident this letter was published in the local paper which had editorialized to the effect that this was Only One World and the Hopi had to get along the way the white man wanted.

The Anarchist and the Banker

My friend Frank Brophy, President of the Bank of Douglas, asked me to be on the air with him, as the regular man was away. The program was announced ahead, the announcement stating that a real anarchist and a real banker would be on the air. Accordingly I wrote a five minute talk and gave it in advance to Mr. Brophy. He wrote a reply. Then we went to the station to record these talks and to ad lib for the remainder of the fifteen minute program. It was on Station KOOL, 8:45 p.m. Dec. 3, 1951. The following is substantially what was said on the air.

Mr. Brophy—*I expect Mr. Hennacy, that this is the first time that an anarchist and a banker sit at the same table without the anarchist having a bomb or the banker tearing the shirt off his back. What do you say Mr. Hennacy?*

Mr. Hennacy—*Mr. Brophy, I say that in Russia the enemy of the common man is the Communist and the bureaucrat. In this country the enemy of the common man is the capitalist and the bureaucrat. Just as the pickpocket cries "stop thief," pointing to someone else in the crowd, so do the apologists for the capitalists in this country cry "Communist" to call attention away from their own picking of our pockets. ......
Every step in the boasted high standard of living and "American Way of Life" that has been achieved has been bitterly fought at Homestead, the Haymarket, and by the frame-up of such men as Mooney and Billings, and Sacco and Vanzetti, and is epitomized by the life-long history of Debs, fighting first for the railroad workers and then for all workers. It was radicals such as these and their forerunners, Thoreau and Bronson Alcott, who did the fighting for this American Way of Life.*

This is the way that the radical analyzes the economic situation: the workingman receives a certain wage and can therefore only buy back that much. But machine production constantly increases so that there is a great surplus. When the saturation point is reached production is stopped and we have a depression. Or the goods are sold in foreign countries less developed than we are. The quarrel over these markets brings about the war which seems to be the approved method these days of getting rid of our surplus.

The radical says that no matter what pious wishes and prayers we may indulge in, depressions and wars will continue in greater and greater devastation until we get rid of the capitalist system and put one of cooperation and production for use and not for profit in its place.

There are various ways of accomplishing this aim. The Communist says to organize workers in political parties in order to gain control of the government and have the government run the industries under a Dictatorship of the Proletariat. Then the state will wither away and we will have peace and prosperity for all. At times when the Communists think they can succeed, they do not wait for a legal parlia-

213

mentary change but use violence, as we did in 1776 to get free from England. (As between fellow Irishmen, it is a long time and we are not free yet.) The main thing wrong with the Communist plan as it works out is that the state does not wither away—those who wither away are those who do not buckle to the Dictatorship. And furthermore, there is no peace, but war.

There remains one other method — that of the anarchist. As for this bomb you talk about, Mr. Brophy: today Truman and the government are the biggest bomb throwers. Anarchists quote the Catholic Lord Acton, "Power corrupts and absolute power corrupts absolutely," and therefore no one should have power over others. As the state is founded on the power of the police and the soldier they would do away with the state by refusing to obey it. Many anarchists talk loudly of the violence they will commit, but it is mostly talk. Anarchists like the Russian Tolstoy, the Italian Malatesta, the Englishman William Morris, and the American William Lloyd Garrison were also believers in the ethics of the Sermon on the Mount and against the use of violence and war.

I am myself in this category and call myself a Christian Anarchist. The Christians do not like it because I belong to no church and decry their approval of capitalism and war. The anarchists do not like it because I quote Jesus, St. Francis, and Gandhi, and write in the Christian Anarchist paper, THE CATHOLIC WORKER. We would, by our daily action of non-cooperation with government and war, and by our cooperation in useful production, create, as the I.W.W. preamble says, "a new society within the shell of the old." This is a slow process but built upon the rock of brotherhood of man and the Fatherhood of God and not on the shifting sands of politics and nationalism.

Mr. Brophy, if all the Communists would die we would still have this problem of capitalist non-producing parasites living off the rest of us.

Mr. Brophy—*Mr. Hennacy, it appears to me that you may be beating a dead horse. Many people will be shocked at the idea that capitalism is dead—or at least moribund shall I say, but that is the way I feel about it. England was the leading capitalist nation of the world at the beginning of this century. Now what is England? She has become an out-and-out Socialist state, with a powerful but little known Communist group working within which hopes eventually to push England into outright Communism. For many years Norway and Sweden have been semi-Socialist states. Germany and Italy were National Socialist states before the last war and today both are undoubtedly closer to Communism than to Capitalism. And how about our own country? The Democratic party which was supposed to be the guardian of the magnificent Jeffersonian dream of the American Democracy, has now become the captive of the Socialist, Collectivist, and Communist groups in this country. Of course, rank and file of the party do not realize* *this yet, but that does not alter the fact of the matter. The American Labor Party in New York with strong, Communist connections for example, is occasionally in the position of being able to decide elections there, and I think the record will indicate that it has always been in favor of the Democratic ticket. Former Vice President Wallace, Senators Pepper, Benton, Humphries, Lehmann, Murray and Representative Marcantonio are listed as Democrats. However, if you were to check their voting records I think you will find that what they favor is some sort of collectivized or Socialist state. Certainly it is not capitalism as you understand it.*

Anyway, you and I come closer to some agreement when you speak of war. You believe that wars are fought over markets, and that is one of the abuses of the Capitalistic system. To that I would first say that such wars are the product of Imperialism rather than of Capitalism —but since the Imperialists were mostly Capitalists I suppose you might say I am quibbling. However, the point I wish to make is this: Call them the wars of Imperialism or Capitalism if you like, but for the most part they were 19th Century struggles or early 20th Century. Today wars are fought to retain power in the hands of bureaucrats and dictators. That is a curious change which has come about in the past twenty years, and I doubt if the dumb Republicans have discovered it yet. That's why I can't be too hard on a mere Christian Anarchist.

Let me just quote a few lines from a Washington financial service that came to my desk this week. It was speaking of the Administration's approach to various difficult economic and employment problems that it will have to face before the next election. I quote: "This is the basis for many rumors in Washington (and some originating in surprising places) that the Administration does not now want a truce in Korea." If there is any truth in such speculation that does not sound much like a Capitalistic war to me.

Mr. Hennacy—Capitalism already dead. You mean it wants to make us all dead. Capitalists are the pawns of the bureaucrats. Nonsense! Does anyone seriously affirm that the President today bosses Standard Oil, Du Pont, Ford, General Motors? He may worry them somewhat and make them do some extra bookkeeping. His friends get mink coats and deep freezes, but nothing like Reynolds Aluminum's getting a 32 million dollar plant for six million. Call it Capitalism or not, it is an evil thing. It surely does not make for peace and prosperity.

Wars are caused, of course, by the selfishness and greed of men but unless these are organized in a state they would never result in more than a McCoy—Hatfield feud. It takes a state with taxes from Christians to make A Bombs. It takes a state with politicians seeking power to make wars. It takes a state giving fat contracts and a guarantee of increased wages as a bribe to workers to make the munitions of war.

(Just then when we were off the air, "that man's getting the best of you

215

Brophy, you'd better wake up," said the owner of the station who was listening to us. Mr. Brophy asked me, "What's the best objection to your idea?" "Ask me how the hell I am going to get my ideas in effect," I replied.)

Mr. Brophy—*Well, Mr. Hennacy, it looks as though you and I both agree that "our common enemy is the state," as Albert Jay Nock has written. As you say, the state does not just wither away. It grows, while the helpless citizen watches it grow, and as it grows in importance the individual citizen diminishes. I suppose you and I are what our Socialistic and New Deal friends would call rugged individualists. You, a Christian Anarchist, and I, a Christian Banker, if there is such a thing. After all, Mr. Hennacy, as an anarchist it is up to you to get rid of the state. What I want to know is how you are going to do it.*

Mr. Hennacy—*That's easy. If you want to change things you have to get 51% of the ballots or the bullets. If I want to change things I just have to keep on doing what I am doing; that is every day the government says "pay taxes for war." Every day I do not pay taxes for war. So I win and they lose. The One Man Revolution —you can't beat it. The only revolution that is ever coming, as the poet Robert Frost says.*

Mr. Brophy—*I'm inclined to agree with you again, but when I think of the One Man Revolution I think of it in terms of individual revolution rather than in terms of political action. If, for instance, every one in the country had a one man revolution himself and gave up greed, chiseling, and the other vices that all lead to war, then perhaps the good world that you and I both dream about might come to be.*

Mr. Hennacy—*Anarchists do not believe in political action. Anarchists do not need a cop to make them behave. Amen, brother.*

Mr. Brophy—*Mr. Hennacy, I cannot allow an anarchist to have the last word, so I will say, Amen.*

During the summer I received a letter from Carl Owen, a young man who came from a KKK atmosphere in South Carolina. He had openly refused to register but no one in his vicinity had paid any attention to it. His state has a heritage of revolt, so perhaps one who did not jump when Washington called was not to be handed over at once. He had hiked to a Quaker seminar at Sedona, Ariz. and had been arrested and held for not carrying a draft card at the same spot where my friend Jack Hewelcke had been arrested for the same reason in 1946. This was on the mesa, just west of Albuquerque. Carl had read Emerson in high school and somehow got away from his provincial surroundings. He had played around with the Progressive Party, being on their national platform committee in 1948. A Quaker lady had sent him a clipping of my One Man Revolution article in the Sept. 1951 CW. Now in Feb. of 1952 he came to visit me for a few weeks before he was to report in Albuquerque for trial. We dug ditch and trimmed trees together.

Carl was not a "sleeper" in the sense that the Old Pioneer meant when some one had called me on the phone and I had asked who it was and he replied "One of your sleepers I suppose." But after a day's work I never knew a fellow so hard to awaken as Carl; you literally had to pull him out of bed to get him awake.

Another time the Old Pioneer answered when I asked him if I had any mail. "Only some of your outlaw papers."

Carl was not at all religious or anarchistic minded. He had plenty of courage and did not need any shot in the arm from me. He was of course interested in my prison history. We had a pleasant time together. He then left for Albuquerque and on Feb. 19th Judge Hatch offered to let him go free, saying that the only proof of his non-registration was his own testimony. This is perhaps the only case on record where a prisoner refused freedom, for Carl said if he was for the war his place was in the army and if he was against it his place was in jail. He acted as his own lawyer and produced his own testimony that he had violated the law by refusing to register. Papers all over the country reported his sentence of 3 years in El Reno, Okla. prison, but Phoenix papers, true to form, never mentioned it. Carl does not want a parole and has the makings of a true rebel. At the same time another young man got 3 years for refusing to go to war.

Picketing

Now picketing time in March approaches. As usual, I had sent letters to the chief of police, the tax man, and the FBI, telling them that I was going to picket; that what I was doing was clearly subversive, but not more so than usual; that they should make up their minds what they were going to do about my activities and not make themselves look silly by pinching me and then letting me go to picket again as they had done previously. I sent copies of these letters to the local press, and, inasmuch as they refused to mention my name last year, I was surprised to see in the morning paper two days before my picketing (March 12), the headline on the front page of the second section:

"ONE MAN REVOLT ENTERS ITS NINTH YEAR
One Against 150,000,000."

After giving the facts about my letter to the authorities, the article added:

"The U. S. attorney's office says there's no jail penalty for refusing to pay taxes. But a fraudulent return can be punished by a prison term. The city police say there's no law against picketing. The FBI says Hennacy's acts are not within its jurisdiction. And the revenue collector says his office can't prove Hennacy earned $1,701.91, or owes $192 in taxes. But that's not all, unless Hennacy has attachable property, the only thing that could be done would be to assign a tax agent to trail him and levy on a day's pay, or change from currency tendered in any purchase, 'and that,' opines Stuart, 'would cost thousands of dollars.' So, it's still one against 150,000,000."

217

A few days later a radio demagogue who specialized in calling all people Communist who were a little left of center, received a phone call on his "We the People" program. This person asked if it would not be a good thing to tar and feather radicals so people would know who they were. The commentator said this was rather drastic, but on the other hand it might be worth considering.

I had written the basis for a leaflet, entitled *Why Do You Pay Your Income Tax?* Rik, Ginny and I had spent two nights writing and rephrasing it. Our Hopi silversmith friend and his wife were over, as usual when we develop our picketing propaganda. It is good to have friends who will unmercifully criticize my brainchild. Ginny made the suggestions which made the leaflet a direct instead of a preachy emphasis. But on her own she would never do for she gets too sentimental. I pay no attention to rules of grammar but go by the sound and feeling of what I write. Rik puts out neat and tidy mimeograph work and posters and so has a tendency to want to make my wise cracks grammatical. I tell him that the whole point is lost unless it rings true—grammar or no grammar.

As a hangover from his days as a Socialist organizer Rik tends to appeal to the masses, but, after a little argument, agrees with Ginny and me that the true Christian Anarchist must appeal to those about ready to make the next step and must know that these are very few indeed. Thus to appeal to the masses the idea would be to appeal to present day grievances such as too much regulation, taxes being too high, and not enough pension from the state. And also not to knock anything which has the approval of the masses such as churches and the Boy Scouts. The rabblerouser will always be able to get the masses on immediate issues. The Christian revolutionist therefore gives the basic idea of reliance upon self and God and not upon politicians and the state. We can live and die and never change political trends but if we take a notion, we can change our own lives in many basic respects and thus do that much to change society.

A generation ago any minister who talked pacifism would never think of having the militaristic Boy Scouts in his church; now they all have this group and as a result it is difficult for them to question the ethics of their action. Another reason for writing and speaking on basic issues is that the very elect would lead people astray with such fakes as World Government. I have recently read Lewis Mumford's *The Conduct of Life* in which he feels the only hope is to have millions support World Government. Aside from the fact that he writes wonderful peace propaganda in between his support of wars, this refusal to accept the reality of "the density of the population" precludes any serious attention being paid to his well written optimism.

My Picketing Leaflet read as follows:

WHY DID YOU PAY YOUR INCOME TAX?

Is it because you think that taxes, like death, are inevitable?
I know the decision to pay taxes is a voluntary one, because I have

218

openly refused to pay my tax for the past nine years. This year alone I owe $192.

Is it because you feel that you are protecting yourself against war with Russia? Certainly there is a definite connection between war and taxes, for from 80% to 90% of your income tax goes to pay for war, past, present and future. As a conscientious objector in both World Wars I believe that war is destroying us, and has actually created the Russian Communist threat. The poverty and misery of the Czarist Empire culminated in the First World War (with Russia on the side of the Allies), and brought the Communist state into being. The world wide destruction, poverty and totalitarianism of the Second World War (with Russia on the side of the Allies) made the Soviet Union a world power and a real threat to our military machine and our capitalist aspirations.

The Marshall Plan and our attempt to arm the non-Communist world has directed the hate and distrust of our allies towards us. By trusting in our own armed power instead of trusting in God we have created the very conditions which are helping promote Communist Russia: the conditions of insecurity, fear and hate. The poor of Europe are tired of fighting. The wealthy classes there have used our money to retain their Asiatic possessions and to fill their own pockets. The "Voice of America" tells those behind the Iron Curtain to revolt, and boasts of the freedom in capitalist America. But with our loyalty oaths and with the building of new concentration camps (two of them in Arizona), we are rapidly becoming a Police State like Russia. Here in Arizona even druggists must now sign loyalty oaths . . . next it'll be undertakers and corpses!

This nation was settled by many folks from Europe who sacrificed everything to escape religious despotism and the tyranny of military conscription. While we have achieved separation of church and state, we are more in danger of a military despotism than ever. The early Christians refused to be soldiers, and some of them are official saints of the Catholic church for this reason. When they were thrown to the lions in the Roman arena they died singing. Truly "the blood of the martyrs was the seed of the church." Today most Christians join the Lions Club, or Rotary, sing "for he's a jolly good fellow," and die respectably of ulcers. They bless war, and their churches are built out of the profits of an unjust economic system. If we continue in this manner, war and income taxes will be the death of us yet.

Do you pay your income tax because you are afraid of the sacrifice that trust in God and opposition to the state may involve? I decided long ago that, while all of us must die, I could choose something worthwhile to live for and die for. You might as well die for what you do believe as for what you don't believe. Remember that Johnson said to Boswell, "Courage is the greatest virtue, for without it you cannot practice the other virtues."

If you want a better world you will not get it by trying to make men out of Congressmen through writing them letters, by voting for any politician since they all believe in war, or by expecting very much of a World Government composed of these same ignoble politicians. Neither will the mocking of God by saying prayers for peace while making munitions and paying taxes for war be of much avail. That kind of prayer bounces back!

If you want to think a little further about this, here are the first steps (you will know in your heart what is right for you); Study the Sermon on the Mount, and the lives of such dedicated men as St. Francis, George Fox, Tolstoy and Gandhi. Try to make whatever you do coincide with Christ's teachings. Ask yourself whether returning evil for evil in courts, legislatures, prisons and war is not denying Christ. If your answer is yes, then stop doing it. But be honest with yourself. Don't alibi by saying you have to do this evil for your family's sake, or, blasphemously, for Christ's sake. Ask yourself whether you are a producer or a parasite. A third of us lead parasitical lives as salesmen, lawyers, bankers, politicians, policemen or soldiers, or else make a living out of the weaknesses and vices of our fellows. Most of the clergy give a very counterfeit return for their money. In a society based on a return of evil for evil, these jobs may be necessary, but they wouldn't exist in the society envisioned by Jesus where evil is repaid with good.

Do you give your children an example of honesty and Christian conduct? Aren't you really coercing your children into un-Christian practices when you boast of your "within the law" business deals, and when you indoctrinate them into giving their first allegiance to the state in such militaristically motivated organizations as the Boy Scouts, and by banning any textbook that doesn't praise capitalism and war? If you teach your children to conform at any price, how can you ever expect them to stand upright and self-reliant before men or God?

To sum up: REFUSE to register for the draft or military training!
REFUSE to buy war bonds!
REFUSE to make munitions for war!
And when you get around to it,
REFUSE to pay taxes for war!

(my name and address)

If you want a free copy of my letter to the tax collector as reprinted in the Feb. 1952 CATHOLIC WORKER, ask me for a copy or write me.

Before starting to picket on March 14th. I said prayers and asked for grace and wisdom at St. Mary's, and stopped as usual at the newspaper office to see a reporter friend. It had rained every day all week, and the

Old Pioneer wondered if the Lord and the weatherman would favor me, on this, The Ides of March. The day was sunny and not windy. The first person to greet me as I picketed was my banker friend, Frank Brophy. It seems that in this society today the only free men are ones like myself who practice voluntary poverty and do not care for money, and the banker who has too much money. Of course, Brophy is an exception, for he speaks out, while most bankers are stupid in everything but collecting money and do not have the intelligence to express themselves or the courage to do so. The newly rich are the ones who are scared the worst and cannot stand any sign of unorthodoxy. I had only brought 377 leaflets and 200 CW's containing my tax statement, thinking this would be more than enough. The first hour I gave away 100 leaflets and 30 CW's, and saw that I would run short.

This was the day that Senator Taft had announced he would come to town. Around noon big-shot Republicans commenced to gather at the Westward Ho Hotel, right across the street from my picketing. Soon Mr. Republican himself, looking out of place in a cowboy hat, appeared. Whether he saw my signs or not I did not know. As a fellow Ohioan I had written to him telling him that I would be picketing, and enclosing a copy of the CW with my tax statement. He may not have received the letter. I had told him that I considered himself and Supreme Court Justice Douglas as men who were fairly honest and not quite so corrupt as their associates, but that this was very faint praise, indeed, and that he was wrong in wanting war in China.

Mr. Stuart, the head tax man, whom the headlines this morning said would soon lose his job in the reorganization of the Revenue Bureau, greeted me kindly, as did his wife. They had read Dorothy's book and enjoyed it. One out-of-state tourist good naturedly wanted to know what my racket was. "The government that it getting the taxes has the racket," I replied. Several people shouted from cars that I should go back to Russia if I didn't like this country. My answer that I like this country silenced them. The same employer who always comes in his car and gives me a little rest by driving around the block came again today. A reporter from the AP interviewed me and said a photographer would be around later, and the story would be sent over the country. Ted Lewis, of the N. Y. DAILY NEWS introduced himself to me. He was with the Taft entourage and knew of me through his friend Ed Lahey, Washington correspondent of the Chicago DAILY NEWS, Detroit FREE PRESS and other Knight papers, who had interviewed the Revenue Department in Washington about my activities and who had written clever articles about my fight with the government. A reporter on the local paper, who had reviewed Dorothy's book recently, also introduced himself to me.

A local writer and radio broadcaster, who along with the demagogue I mentioned before, makes a living as a red-baiter, spoke to me for about fifteen minutes. I had met him at the Gerald L. K. Smith secret meeting. His group had announced over the radio that Dorothy, the CW, and myself were Communists, and when Dorothy cancelled her engagement here in

January, took credit for having frightened her away. Although this red-baiting outfit claims to have the backing of the American Legion and the Catholic church, I know from friends in the Legion and the many friendly priests here in Phoenix, that these claims are exaggerated. I wrote a letter giving the facts of the matter, and so did Frank Brophy. To our surprise both letters were read on this red-baiting program, with the remark, "No comment." However I dislike the ideas of a person, I am unable to dislike people, so this man and myself had a pleasant and not too controversial conversation. (Later this red-baiter left town).

"*I'm a Russian and I think I'm free,*" said a beautiful peasant type woman to me. She referred to my large sign: "THE RUSSIANS THINK THEY ARE FREE. SO DO WE." I asked her if she was a Molokon, and she said she was, mentioning her name which proved to be also that of my nearest neighbors who are Molokons. She lived near Glendale, on lateral 20.

Rik and Ginny attend Quaker meeting here and brought home a booklet describing the visit of Cadbury and others of the English Quakers to Moscow. I was surprised to learn that the Russians they spoke to thought they were free and we were behind a dollar or "velvet" curtain. Of course the ones who had opposed Stalin were already dead or in far away prison camps, and those remaining did not want any more than they had, so in that respect they were free. It is all a matter of perspective. The pygmies thought they were the biggest people on earth never having seen anyoue else. And the old saying goes: "In the kingdom of the blind the one-eyed man is king."

This booklet gave me the idea for my poster. Here we are free to vote for one or the other of politicians whose nomination is cooked up beforehand. I am free to picket, and although I am happy that an increasing number of people respond to my propaganda, I know that they are bound by their bourgeois lives to keep on supporting the system, albeit griping now and then.

The reverse of this big poster read: THE POWER TO TAX IS THE POWER TO ENSLAVE. The sandwich sign in front read: I CHOOSE NOT TO PAY INCOME TAX FOR WAR AND OWE $192 for 1951. The sandwich sign from rear view quoted my friend of pre-war days at the U. of Wisconsin, Randolph Bourne: "WAR IS THE HEALTH OF THE STATE."

During the day about 50 people stopped and warmly congratulated me on my picketing. Later I learned that a friendly priest had brought another priest from his town to meet me but had somehow missed me. From the point of view of acceptance of my message, this, the 21st day of my picketing in four years, was the best so far. Rik and Ginny drove along at 5:45, and I took this opportunity to take 50 CW's of the March issue which had just arrived, to St. Francis Xavier Church, and to kneel there and give thanks for my successful day. The two Phoenix dailies did not mention my picketing. The Flagstaff daily had an AP story with my picture on the front page. The tax man and his wife own the Prescott COURIER and they carried a four-column head on the front page about my picketing. The reports were factual and not a bit slurring. The radio here also had decent comment.

The Vigilantes

Soon after my picketing and after the tar-and-feather propaganda on the radio, three young men, two of them Mexicans, knocked at the Old Pioneer's door and asked for "Yancy." I happened to be there talking on the phone to the Hopi who had arrived in town, so I told them that I did not know of any one by the name of "Yancy" but my name was Hennacy.

"You are the guy then. You put those leaflets about not paying taxes in our car." Meanwhile I had invited them in and asked them to be seated, but they stood around nervously. I told them that I never left leaflets in any car; that I gave them to people who took them.

"Who told you such stories as that? I've been selling the paper here for five years in front of Catholic churches and I never would have lasted that long if I was Commie," I replied, and added "Who sent you here and what are your names?"

"We won't tell you. We go around all over after such fellows as you." Come outside there on the concrete and we'll rub your head in the cement."

"What's the rush? What's the rush?" I said good naturedly.

"You are a Communist and this Catholic Worker is a Communist paper and we don't like it," said the leader. "You don't have to like it. Lots of people don't like it."

"If you would beat me to pieces and if what is in my leaflet is true and if what is in the CATHOLIC WORKER is true, then it would still be true if I was dead. And if it isn't true why bother about it?" I asked them. They muttered about my being a Commie and to come out and take my beating.

"You can beat me up right here and it doesn't take three of you; let the smallest one start right now. I won't hit you back. Go ahead." I said smilingly. They looked at each other and didn't make a move, muttering something about me stabbing the boys in Korea in the back by not paying taxes for their guns. I told them of Saul persecuting the Christians and seeing Stephen stoned to death, and the Lord spoke to him later and he became the Apostle Paul. But my words were wasted for these Catholic boys did not seem to know Paul from Moses. I told them that they oughtn't to get excited about dying in Korea, for the Americans had taken all of this country except the Gasden purchase from their forefathers in the Mexican War.

"Well if we hadn't taken it from them they would have taken it from us" was the not too intelligent reply. They listened to some of my pacifist explanations for an hour and did not attack me. They asked where I would be selling CW's next Sunday and I told them at St. Mary's and the leader marked it down on an envelope. As I shook hands with the leader and they were leaving, Rik and Ginny came in to take me to see the Hopi who were at their home. I did not know that they were coming so soon. They told me that they saw a gunny sack tied over the license plates of the Vigilante car. These men did not need to fear for I would not report them.

The next Sunday three very husky young men came up to me and in a surly manner each bought a CW. One was Mexican and the other two were Anglos. They pointed to me and at the paper and discussed the matter between themselves but took no action as there were too many people coming or going at St. Mary's. I told those who had been to beat me up that if they could find me on the highway or in the fields working they could beat me up if they thought they could solve anything by doing it.

Several times down town I met two different fellows who looked enough like the leader of the group to have been his brother. Whenever I hear of a person swearing in court that a certain person committed a crime I am very doubtful. I looked at this man for an hour and we were nor more than two feet apart, yet I could not be sure of this identity. It is now nearly a year since this happened that I am writing and I have heard nothing more from the vigilantes. They were not especially vicious but had been told lies about my being a Communist, so they were not to blame for their action.

Work

It is a good thing that I like to do manual labor on a farm. A life of not paying taxes and of voluntary poverty, such as I have set for myself, requires work as a basis. To talk about the dignity of labor, of life on the land, of a vegetarian in his own garden, of refusing to pay taxes, and then to mooch for a living gives the lie to all conversation. The best feeling that I have had during the past year was to look at the two rows of potatoes which I had laboriously hilled just right and planted before a storm broke over the mountains and the driving rain made me seek the refuge of my cabin. It happens that I also like to write articles describing my life and my ideas. (I think better as I type). But the pleasure in writing an article or a book is outdistanced by my work in the garden and the fields. Working for a wage without enjoying the work that you do puts you in the class of the rich man whom some one has said is just a poor man who has money; you are a poor man who makes money.

During the past ten years I have had nothing to do with those props of capitalism: Rent, Interest and Profit.

Today I spent spent nine hours pulling weeds in our garden and just before dark I planted two dozen each of eggplant and peppers. I work, but I eat freely from this garden every day of the year.

For the past six months I have irrigated barley often at nights for Hussey's. This is really not difficult for the water runs slowly. The only experience new to me in this work is that the sugar and malt in the barley mix with the dew, as I walk through it checking the flow of the water, forming a paste which when dry make my overalls a veritable coat of armor. As usual Cindy and several other dogs came up with cold noses and muddy paws, but after I had greeted them they went on their way exploring gopher and skunk.

Coming to the farmhouse at 7:30 a.m. after my night of irrigating recently, I saw the big bull loose in the open driveway, pawing the earth and snorting. Just then James Hussey, my boss, came up and walking gently toward the bull he finally grabbed him by the ring in the nose and led him captive to the pen. This was the real pacifist way of handling the problem, performed by a reserve army captain. As my grandfather told me: "Don't run from a bull or a billy goat; they have four legs and you have two, and you can't make it."

On the way home that morning (April 8th.) I saw pickers in the strawberry fields. I had always wanted to do this work but have been too busy. They pay 70¢ an hour now, rather than by the basket as very few are ripe. I remember eating berries at 10¢ a quart in 1942 in Milwaukee. I tried raising them one year here but was not successful. They have to be irrigated every four days in the season and weeds pulled from them the year around when irrigating. If there is a big head of water on, or if the crop is high enough to impede the water, the regular cement port will not allow enough water to go through so a low place is left in the bank where extra water is let through. As with country people the name given tells just what happens for this is a "helper."

Personal Responsibility

Digging ditch for a neighbor recently I heard bottles smash on the highway. Two teen-agers had found them along the side of the road and were smashing them in the middle of the highway.

"That's not a damn bit smart," I shouted at them. They could not see me, and I suppose thinking this was their conscience or something uncanny, hastened onward. This lack of responsibility belongs not only to youth, for while irrigating one night I saw a big car stop on the highway and a man take out sacks of bottles and junk and throw them along the side of the road. This was not a slum dweller who had no place to put his garbage, but a big city bourgeois who seemed to want to save the expense of paying a garbage man to haul his refuse away. A lady wrote a letter to the local paper about a dead cat on the street and bemoaned the fact that no one came to remove it. The city replied that this street was just over the city limits, and that it was up to the county. The county said their contract was lapsed with the S.P.C.A. and action would depend upon a future board meeting. In an anarchist society each one would be responsible and would not have to write letters to papers or to call the cops to have something done. They would do it themselves. Coming home from helping my friend Joe Craigmyle pick oranges and grapefruit the other night I mentioned this lady and the cat, and said that the Sunday before I had seen a dead cat on the lateral on my way to the bus, but being late I did not stop to remove it. On my way back in the afternoon, after hundreds of cars had passed and numerous Mexicans going to the bus, I noticed that the cat was still there and stopped to throw it off of the road. As we were talking we noticed a two-by-four with four spikes sticking up on the highway. We swerved around it and were a quarter of a mile past when Joe said, as an afterthought to my remark that this would cause somebody some trouble: "I'll back up and you can throw it in the ditch." In my mind, then, Joe, who has not been much of a man of action rose from a one-cylinder to a two cylinder anarchist.

In early summer when the new crop of citrus is on the trees the old crop is still there too, and is extra sweet and juicy. The only thing to be careful of is not to knock the blossoms off when picking the old crop. As with apples, there is a "June drop" of small citrus, and this is all nature's way of providing larger fruit, for if none fell off at all, none of the fruit would be of much size. If a person has time it is well to thin out fruit, as I did with the dates. When picking grapefruit or oranges you can tell when they are light. Then they are pithy, and no matter how good they may look on the outside, they are no good inside and are thrown on the ground while picking. When we return to the fruit stand the load is graded as to size.

Putting the Worst Foot Forward

When traveling around and broke, when my wife and I were hiking, I worked for several years, off and on, selling Fuller brushes in Georgia, California and Wisconsin. Although I spent a lot of time in radical propaganda, I was always near the head amongst the salesmen in my district. As I did in social work, I broke all of the rules, and yet succeeded. The company wanted salesmen to sell not individual articles but whole sets. All sorts of tricks were used to get the sale. Individual salesmen were given quotas and prizes, and burdened with pep talks. I would never set a quota. If I thought a woman could not afford a flashy article I took more pride in selling her something really better and not so flashy. And I never pressured potential customers. If there was any weakness in the article as to color, size, weight, etc. for that individual, I admitted it at once and then spoke glowingly of the good points. For if I did not admit any weakness, the customer would not listen to my good points but would be thinking of this glaring weakness.

Likewise with ideas I admit at the start that myself and those like me are not going to win, for the whole trend is toward the welfare state and bigger and better churches. The trend is not toward individual responsibility and the voluntary poverty and simple life of the early

226

Christians—all the more reason we should keep on trying, though. When I first meet a priest, I tell him I am not a Catholic and how terrible his church is; that the other churches would be just as bad if they knew how. Then I stress the CW, the Sermon on the Mount, and Gandhi. I can't say anything worse, so from then on I am saying something better. If I should hem-haw and dissemble, and say maybe I'm right and maybe I'm wrong, I would not get the attention of the person to whom I am talking. Why waste time talking to sleepy people? I aim to wake them up at the start. If they get scared away by my frankness they are a weak porridge anyway, who would not stand much of the truth. Of course a person has to be goodnatured about it and quick on the trigger when it comes to answering objections. As when a priest was trying to argue against pacifism by saying that according to natural law a person had to defend himself against a robber, or defend innocent children and the grandmother about to be raped.

"Do you have a gun, Father?" I asked.

"Why, no!" he answered.

"Then you are in an awful fix: you have nothing to depend upon except God!" That ended the conversation and he got the point.

When someone on the street asks me if the CW is a Communist paper I answer: "Worse than that; it is Christian Anarchist, best paper in the world. Better read it." This is Gandhi's moral jiu jitsu again. The idea is that no matter how strong a man is, he cannot throw you if he cannot get a hold. Likewise when opponents call you names or go after you violently, the successful method is to never crawl or excuse yourself but always advance in counterattack that throws your opponent off his mental balance. By answering an objection before it is voiced you have already made the ammunition of your opponent useless. Do not let your opponent set the norm. Generally a minority is jeered at because they are so small. It is *quality* and not *quantity* that is the measure. "One on the side of God is a majority" is the perfect answer which I have given dozens of times with success.

Selling CW's

"Is that the Communist paper that uses the name Catholic, that they tell of on the radio?" four people asked me one Sunday morning after the local-red-baiter had denounced the CW. I told them that it was not Communist, but had been blessed by the Pope, and was the best Catholic paper in the world; to ask the priest about it. They all bought a copy without further argument. "Is that the good Catholic paper that is sold on the streets?" asked a lady as I was selling CW's in front of the bus station. I replied that it must be for it was the only one sold on the streets. "I'm not a Catholic," the lady said. "I belong to the Grey Ladies and we visit hospitals. I have heard patients ask for it. I want ten copies." One professional man invariably hands me a nickel or dime for a copy but won't take it: "Makes me mad to read it. It is all true but what can I do about it?" For a year or more a certain elderly lady has pointed to me and told all who would listen that I was a Communist and the CW was a Communist paper. I paid no attention to her. One day when I was speaking to a Catholic friend who, for some esoteric reason, won't touch a copy of the CW because it opposes Franco but who stops and talks to me cordially—this woman came up and said that I am a Communist and the CW is a Communist paper. The friend answered; "I have my own bone to pick with the CW, but I read it, formerly, for years and I know Hennacy from his articles for ten years. I am telling you that neither he nor the paper is Communist. Ask the priest and he will tell you that I am right." The red-baiter went away grumbling, "Communist, Communist!"

Another time a member of the air force was going to Korea in a few days. He was visiting here, coming from New York City. He asked what kind of paper I had, and said that he had never heard of it. I told him that it had been published in his own town for 18 years. The name Worker sounded to him like Communist he said, and he wanted to know if he could ask the priest who was standing nearby about it. He did so, and the priest who is neither pacifist nor anarchist, answered, "If it's good enough for me it's good enough for you," showing him the CW in his hand. I spoke to the man for half an hour and gave him several old copies.

On a downtown street corner, a soldier with half-a-dozen service bars on his uniform smiled and said that was the kind of paper that was needed: a peace paper, and bought one. Another time a sewer worker from Seattle, a Mormon and a .Wobblie, who said he had read the CW in the library greeted me by name as he knew I would be the one selling papers on the street in Phoenix. A lady said "Hello Mr. Hennacy, don't you remember me?" This was in front of St. Mary's. I told her I met many people and did not remember her. She replied "Why I bought a paper from you last year when I came here for two weeks vacation."

The Hopi

When my Hopi friends visited and were able to pick real oranges and grapefruit from trees, to ride up the escalator at Porter's store, and to see an Indian with feathers sitting there, they were delighted.

We discussed Governor Pyle's schemes for getting the Indians to be like white men. In conversation with newspaper and radio men who had known him for years, I got the impression that he is primarily an actor who.sincerely believes that there is no conflict between his religious phrases and attitude and his support of capitalism and war. His talents are a grade above the banjo-playing vote-chaser. He has a pleasing voice and gracious personality. This could all be true and yet he could never have an original thought or never once take a courageous stand against a system of society that degrades whites and Indians alike.

Did not McKinley make the best stooge Mark Hanna could desire? McKinley prayed to God and God told him to bring the Bible to the poor Cubans, so we had a war. He did not know there was a sugar trust ready to impoverish the natives and grab the land. He did not know there was a venal Hearst and Pulitzer cooking up a war. Such "innocents" make the best stooges.

My Hopi friends brought along a copy of Jan. 1952 CRISIS which had an article on the Hopi by our mutual friend George Yamada. Here the land question is discussed. Governor Pyle deplores the fact that 83% of the land in Arizona is owned by the federal government. What he does not deplore is that too much of this land is rented out for practically nothing to his wealthy cattlemen backers. (They bellyache always about government restrictions but they still lease the land from the government.) The Hopi have only a fourth of the land that they had before the Indian Bureau moved the Navajo in on them. The Navajo were moved in because the cattlemen needed more land. There is plenty of land, but the wrong people have it. The Navajo could easily be given some of this government land and the Hopi could be given back the land stolen from them. But this will not be done by politicians from Washington.

For all good causes

"I don't wear a label; I'm for all good causes," replied a young conscientious objector, who, passing through Phoenix, had called the local paper to find my address, and found me one evening when I was caretaker of Jersey cows at the sale of purebreds at the State Fair grounds. Many people write to me, or come to visit me, who are drawn by different phases of my philosophy. So as to save time, I try to find out if their emphasis is I.W.W., Catholic Worker, pacifist, anarchist, vegetarian, life on the land, or tax refusal. This slogan of not wearing a label is fine for kids, I told my new friend, but at his age of 31 he ought to begin to have ideas that lead to some definite belief or action. I admitted that it was a sign of progress for the average person of bourgeois tendencies to look at the Republican and Democratic parties and to realize that wearing their labels was meaningless. Like the housewife, in the days when women did the baking at home, who put the initials "T. M." on the top crust of one pie meaning " 'Tis Mince;" and the initials "T. M." on the top crust of another pie, meaning, " 'Taint Mince," such labels surely did not have any meaning.

The thought behind my friend's no-label attitude seemed to be a desire to approach as many people as possible, on the street, in buses, at dances, etc. and to "make friends and influence people" by not scaring them with such words as pacifist or anarchist. He wanted to rattle half-truths and half-criticisms as a build up "for all good causes," and as a monkey wrench thrown into the status quo. This is a mass approach. Mine has been to get the individual in this mass, if possible, to think. People can be jolted into thinking but I have yet to see any who have been "maneuvered" into doing anything more than maneuvering.

I remember 40 years ago when well-meaning friends had told me that to use the word "Socialist" was defeating my purpose, and that some word such as "Progressive" that did not have such a bad meaning should be used. My reply then was that whatever word was used to designate a radical belief, that word would have a bad meaning to those who were being denounced. Today the word Socialist only means collaborationist with war and capitalism and it has lost all its old radical meaning. Even many timid anarchists prefer the word "Libertarian" for fear they will be called bomb-throwers. I explain "an-archy" means "without-rule;" nothing to do with bombs.

I told my young friend that he could always get a crowd to applaud mild criticism of war and for the lowering of taxes and raising of wages, but that this same crowd would really follow the blazing torch of super demagogues who spoke, as did Coolidge, of "the great native intelligence of the common man." Yes, men by themselves are not so bad, but in a crowd or in a political campaign where they wear "labels" they are only suckers. I pointed out that spiritual power was the greatest force in the world, and that beside it all the two-penny political victories did not mean a thing. Too many of us dissipate our energy by being "for all good causes," attending meetings and passing resolutions, organizing and presenting petitions—all this effort to change *others,* when if we really got down to it we could use this energy to change *ourselves.* This can be done by spiritual means and it does not wear one out but is invigorating. We become tired radicals because we use our weakest weapon: the ballot box, where we are always outnumbered, and refuse to use our strongest weapon: spiritual power.

Culls

As I was helping a farmer polish the horns of his cows for the sale the next day, he said he had heard that I was an educated man and wondered as to my being a day laborer. I explained my method of working at day work on farms in order that no withholding tax for war should be taken from my pay. He wanted to know more about these ideas and for the next hour he heard the words anarchism and pacifism undiluted by "all good causes," and departed with the current CW and my promise to mail him future copies. In contrast, another farmer whose cows I was attending wanted me to go back to Russia if I did not like this country.

The cows for sale were listed in a catalogue, with pedigrees and a record of their production of butter fat. The manager of the sale was discussing with one farmer about certain unregistered and non-pedigreed cows which are called "grades," and many times these cows give more and richer milk than the purebred stock. But there is no guarantee that a heifer from such a cow will be a good producer; more than likely she would be a throwback from scrub stock.

In Albuquerque I worked for two men who specialized in extra fancy chickens. At one place I gathered eggs each hour from a trap nest, and marked the number of the chicken, taken from a leg band, on the egg she had just laid, and also in a record book. Those who did not produce a great number of eggs were thus culled out. "Why feed the culls?" my boss said. Each day a dozen or more hens would die of "blow-outs;" which meant that the very efficient egg-producing machine had overstepped itself. The mediocre hens lived longer and did not blow out.

At a dairy in Albuquerque where I worked, my job was to go to any of the eight corrals and in the mud and manure drive the next string of cows to the barn to be milked. Nearly every night a calf would be born in this wet and cold discomfort and my job was to carry it in the morning to a warm stall. (Josephine, a heifer, had her first calf, which being a bull I carried away and she never saw it again. For months she followed me and "moo-ed" whenever she heard my voice.) Very few of these calves coming from cows that were "grades," died. Later I worked for a multi-millionaire who had highly priced purebreds. My job was to keep a fire in a stove in the barn at night and to feed these calves egg, with specially prepared milk. Yet the death rate among these purebreds made my boss groan. Tuberculosis and Bangs disease (premature birth of calves) seems also to be more prevalent among the inbred purebreds.

Super-efficient bankers jump out of windows when red instead of black ink records their business schemes. Efficient assembly line workers go berserk, and we read of an especially good bus driver driving right on to Florida to escape his treadmill of efficiency. At its best, our system is efficient only in turning out quantity, and at its worst it is trying to bomb us to death. And really it is not so efficient either, for very expensive garden tools these days are held together only by the paint on the handle and are of very inferior design, workmanship and material.

When I was a social worker in Milwaukee in the thirties we were often derided by well-to-do Republicans for "coddling the culls" when we helped the poor. From time to time I have heard radicals who were especially scientific and eugenic-minded look upon the ideals of Jesus and Gandhi as perpetuating the life of the unfit and the misfit. When I helped in the formation of the CW House of Hospitality in Milwaukee in 1937, I will admit that my interest was limited to its pacifist and anarchist slant and that I felt this coddling of the bums was not so important. After my study of Tolstoy, my acquaintance with Peter Maurin and Dorothy Day, and my ten years as an actual laborer—rather than a radical theorist with a good job.—I have come to view this whole matter in a different light. The conversation about grades and purebreds that night, and my meeting with the young rattle-brain who was "for all good causes" helped me to clarify my ideas along this line.

In this age of the assembly line, of super-markets and super-advertising schemes, of radio get-rich-quick guessing games, and of Service Clubs to put a little holy oil of goodness on this theft, the illusion persists that this is a scientific and efficient age. Yes, we produce, but for what? If somehow we do have bums, poor housing, ill-health, new diseases, and poverty, these can only be attended to by Community Funds, Heart, Cancer and Give-a-Dime campaigns, pensions and social security payments by the state. Charity Incorporated has no room for Houses of Hospitality where there is no record of aid given or even the name of the recipients, no "singing for your supper." "They won't work if you keep on feeding them!" "They sell the clothing you give them around the corner for booze," say the well fed parasites who also refuse to work and do not help the poor except to give away a suit that is too small for their fat bellies, or to give a very dim and distant contribution to a fund, much of which goes for overhead. The idea of these professional do-gooders is to give "coals and treacle" to the poor, as Shaw said, and to keep them out of sight in order that the rich may not be reminded of the filth and degradation which is the foundation of their wealth. And on this matter of clothing being sold for booze, the clothing given to St. Vincent de Paul, Goodwill Industries, and Salvation Army is many times purchased by stooges of the second hand stores. All that is left for the really poor is the sorriest stuff. In my work as a social worker, I discovered that no matter how many rules you had to keep from giving relief to frauds, that it did not take a very smart person to scurry in between our red-tape and beat us at our own game. Good social workers are told not to "become emotionally involved" with their clients. Again, the mechanistic approach.

The CW breaks through all this sham. Instead of living in fine apartments to which we can repair after witnessing the other side of the tracks, we who accept Lady Poverty have given up worldly goods, insurance, and much of our privacy. This cull in the breadline; this drunk or prostitute; this maladjusted and perhaps lazy man—all of these may not be improved a bit by our help—and yet one may be helped now and then. Ours is not a Success Story; the Way of the Cross was also a failure. He at least might have led a rebellion against the Roman State instead of dying on the Cross and forgiving His enemies.

Where are we to look for those who are going to bear the Cross today? It is true that St. Francis, Tolstoy, Malatesta, Kropotkin and Gandhi left their inheritance and, choosing voluntary poverty, were able to accomplish much. We also print the word and deliver the lecture to purebreds as well as to the culls. We make no mistake in thinking that because a man is ragged he is holy, for if he is avaricious he is as much a slave to money as is the rich man. (My banker friend Brophy jokingly told me that he would have to write a defense of the rich for the CW. I told him that he would end contradicting himself, and that the best defense for the rich could be obtained by the oratory resulting from a few drinks given to a poor man on the street.) The Old Pioneer tells of stopping at a stand in the desert recently and being charged 15¢ for a soft drink. "This is 500% profit for you" he told the proprietor. "I'm not in business for my health" said this greedy and seedy defender of the capitalist system. And might have added "For anybody else's health either." The Old Pioneer also tells of being charged 25¢ for one common needle in the old days when everything coming into Phoenix had to be hauled from Maricopa Wells station beyond South Mountain. "The freight is what costs" was the alibi of the greedy merchant. How much freight on a needle?

Neither do we count the purebreds, Tommy Manville, the dear old DAR ladies, the useless royalty of Europe and the Maharajah's of India, our own inbred Du Ponts and intellectuals who have nearly without exception prostituted their talents toward the making of bombs. There is some hope that among the bums we may find a John the Baptist to carry on the work when we have gone. There is little hope from politicians whose integrity has already been purchased, or from the super-educated to whom a doctor's degree, a deep freeze and a television set mean more than fighting for a lost cause.

How will we then come to a sensible way of life? Without war work we would have a terrible depression. Hardly a person but will gladly earn this blood money! Hardly a person but will pay taxes for more bombs! The rich will not give up their riches and the poor will not give up their pensions (for the young will not help the aged; preferring to "keep up with the Jones's"). The froth at the top has little right to scorn the scum at the bottom; meanwhile we who do the work of the world try to understand them both.

The Old Pioneer remarked recently that Jefferson's plan of not having great wealth inherited was the right idea. This reminds me of the old Russian proverb one of my Molokon friends told me: "Do not lay up money for your son, for if he is any good he can make his own money; and if he is not any good he will lose it." So in our writing, our picketing, our speaking, our help to the poor in Houses of Hospitality, we must needs show our sincerity by our own voluntary poverty. No one would think of bribing us, for by our lives we have established the fact that we need nothing. We need not fritter away our time by building up "all good causes," which are not so good for they accept the tyranny of the state and operate without questioning its framework. When they are ready for it, the rich, the bourgeois intellectual, the bum, and even the politician and the clergy may have an awakening of conscience because of the uncompromising seeds of Christian Anarchism which we are sowing. To all of these we make our appeal and from all it is not impossible to gain a few adherents for that time "when each shall give according to his ability and receive according to his need." For what does all of our bookkeeping mean but a denial of this ideal?

Johnny Olson came back from a sojourn in Texas. In a splurge of affluence he bought five mouse traps and set them around our house. He caught the whole population which consisted of three mice. While I, as a pacifist vegetarian, would not cause the death of Brother Mouse yet as an anarchist I have no right to deny Johnny the right to catch them . . . The old mules, belonging to a neighbor, which I have used for plowing the garden these five years, are now muleburger. They did not enter this incarnation legally, for they were not killed in time for the new government regulation which allows equine meat in weiners.

Irrigating

Today, May 15th I received a notice that I owe $2.15 interest and penalty on my $192 tax bill for 1951 and unless paid within ten days my property and wages will be attached. This is an old run-around and I am not worrying. Today I ate the first Irish potatoes this year from our garden, which is more important in the life of man than paying taxes. The persimmon tree which the Old Pioneer's daughter-in-law gave me last winter now bears premature fruit. Watermelon, eggplant, tomatoes, squash, peppers and onions are doing fine. I am irrigating tonight and soon I will be irrigating maize for James. Now in June I have been irrigating about three nights a week. Because of the heavy rains there is plenty of water this year and it is not rationed. If a farmer does not use up all the water he has ordered or is allowed in one year, he is not permitted to carry it over to the next year, for no one can tell if the next year will be one of drought or not. Various crops need various amounts of water. In this two crops a year valley, melons, lettuce, wheat and barley require 2 acre-feet. Cotton takes 3 to 4 acre-feet, and the ground has to be really soaked before the cotton seed is planted or it won't grow. Alfalfa 7 to 8 acre-feet, and celery the most of all: 9 acre-feet. The average amount used by a farmer is 4 acre-feet. Melons are irrigated with a small flow of water down each row for as long as 24 hours, the idea being that the moisture will gradually sub up to the roots. Thus not so much water is used as when a whole field of alfalfa is flooded. In this hot country, when most seed is planted and irrigated another irrigation must soon follow so that the seed will be sure to start growing. To explain an acre-foot is a very technical matter, but for the layman it is sufficient to know that it is the amount of water that would cover one acre a foot deep. The zanjero has a measuring device whereby he can tell how much water goes over a board. Thus 20 inches flowing over a board 6 feet long for 24 hours is a acre foot.

Generally, James uses 150 inches for three days and nights, switching the water from alfalfa to newly plowed ground or wherever it is needed most. If the ground is very dry the water may shoot over it in a hurry and not penetrate to much depth. Then the next irrigation will use up much more water. The other night three lands ran smoothly in newly plowed land and required no attention from me. Two other lands were not level and I had to make checks all along, as the water went to one side of the land entirely. Last night I did not cut off the water soon enough from the end of the quarter-mile run and too much of it flowed into the highway. In this field there was no ditch to catch the overflow; the ditch being across the highway, so I hot-footed it to make openings for the water to escape. There is a fine for flooding the highway. I always jeer, in a high-minded way, toward those who let water run into the road, and now I, myself, am the guilty one. James said he would get the blame for being a poor farmer, for of 50 people who might pass, only one would know that I was the hired man who was the culprit, but all knew him.

Field after field is flooded with lights at night these past few weeks for the Navajos and Mexicans who tie carrots all night. Some camp in the bushes along the lateral; others come in trucks from town. Little money in this work. As I was walking to a neighboring farm the other morning, some young Mexicans who knew me pointed and motioned for me to come to the field where they were turning melon vines out of the ditches where they were irrigated. I shook my head and said, "le otra," pointing to another job toward which I was headed.

The out of state person who comes here and wants to raise even a small garden has much to learn. The seed catalogues are not written for this dry climate. And even the good articles that appear in the papers do not sink in. One has to learn by bitter experience. These newcomers say it is a dry country so everything must have plenty of water and they proceed to pour it on. The sun bakes the gound and cracks it open and the air gets in to the roots and the plant dies. *Do not pour water on top of the ground.* The right way is to make a trench and run the water in this trench beside the plant until it subs up and moistens the roots, the top soil remaining dry. When tomato plants are blooming, lay off the water for they will not set and form tomatoes but will grow into tall green bushes with few tomatoes. And after the tomatoes are green if you water them too much they will not ripen. Same with watermelon; when the blooms appear, go slow on the water; then when the melons form give them the water which makes watermelon. Irish potatoes seldom bloom in this climate. We have been eating them for about a month, but we will have to consume them quickly or give them to friends, for in this dry climate the potatoes will soon wither away. The Old Pioneer and I agree that it is unethical to sell anything from our garden. The work is a labor of love and not commercial so the product should not be commercialized either; so we give away our surplus.

Whittaker Chambers

The Old Pioneer and I had read the summary of WITNESS by Whittaker Chambers in the Saturday Evening Post. Any Irishman detests an informer. I had never heard of Chambers in my radical days, except that my wife and I knew Esther Shemitz at the Rand School in 1920 and later on we heard she had married, but didn't know it was Chambers. As I read his articles, I recognize the type of sentimental radical who had just enough conscience to not enter fully into Communist trickery for a long stretch of time; and who had just enough knowledge and feeling of religion to use it as a cover for his weakness of character. I have met many tired radicals and those who have frankly decided that their radicalism was youthful folly, so for the remainder of their lives they would eat, drink and be merry. I have also met former radicals who have become holy jumpers, Jehovah Witnesses' and even Christian Scientists, but in each case they carried their radical sincerity and self sacrifice into their new belief. I have also met radicals who have gone away over to the other side.

As I read of the life of the early Quakers I could not place Chambers into any sincere relationship with them. He did quit the party. That was good. He could still have been a radical after studying Kropotkin and Tolstoy, for a man of his learning could not be ignorant of the anarchist philosophy. If he liked life on the land he could have made a living on the land instead of accepting the 30,000 pieces of silver a year from that super apologist of capitalism and war, TIME Magazine. Whether all that he said about Hiss is true or not is not important. The problem is not, "How bad is Hiss?" but "How good is this Chambers who talks about God and Freedom, and who after the travail of body and spirit must return to his capitalist vomit?" There is no sackcloth and ashes worn by this capitalist farmer and successful writer who has chosen to prostitute his clever mind to capitalism instead of to Stalin. This baby business about "being on the losing side" does not come well from one who seems to be winning plenty of applause and cash, in his new venture as the poor bashful boy from the wrong side of the tracks who fought the well-dressed and high-and-mighty money changers in the State Department. In this election year, when the slimy policies of our statesmen may be due for a change in direction, but not in sliminess, Chambers may well be on the winning side.

The comment of the Old Pioneer on Chambers was that he was reminded of an old-time owner of a saloon and dance hall here in Phoenix who was quite a drunkard. One night he was drunk and went outside and slept off his spree on the pile of horse manure which was there, in the days before automobiles. He was awakened by the scream of a woman, and staggering into the dance hall with the horse manure sprinkled all over him, he shouted: "I come to defend the honor of woman."

The Real Issue of 1952

This being election year I thought it well to summarize the anarchist argument against voting, in my leaflet given out during my seven days fast and picketing, Aug. 6 to 12.

> You, as a citizen of the United States and a registered voter, are asked to vote for politicians representing certain political parties. Have you ever stopped to think what this voting really means?
>
> You are told that if you do not vote you are irresponsible. If you do vote, then you are indeed irresponsible, for the very act of voting is dodging your responsibility by passing the buck to others. You have no kickback if your elected representative does not live up to his promises. You are told that unless you vote, you have no right to beef about the way things turn out. The answer to that one is very simple: when you vote you have no way of knowing that your candidate will win. If he loses, the issues he has endorsed will have failed. If he wins, there is nothing to prevent him from turning his back on these same policies or conveniently forgetting about them. In either case, win or lose, you will have consented, by having voted, to accept the winning candidate's judgement as superior to your own. You know, of course, that politics abound with examples of these situations. If you have any lingering doubt of the validity of this, just ask yourself who it is that actually selects your candidates for you?
>
> Now you might agree with me so far but be tempted to say: "But if the good people don't vote for good candidates, the bad

men will run the country." A really good candidate makes an ineffective official because he won't stoop to the low methods that are essential to the efficient operation of government. Nowhere is this conclusion more eloquently demonstrated than in the autobiography of that famous muckraking journalist of 40 years ago, Lincoln Steffens, whose experience in "cleaning up" many American cities made him an authority.

If voting is not all that it is cracked up to be, how did we get into this state of affairs? Have things always been this way? You are far too young to remember the days when there were no nation-states as we know them today. Of course you recall from reading the Old Testament that there was a time when there were no rulers in Israel and "each did what was right in his own heart." The people grumbled and asked for a king. The Prophet told them that a king would take their sons for war and their daughters for concubines and servants, and would pick the choice of flock and field for himself and make slaves of them, but still they wanted a king. They got a king, and from that time on went down hill, ending in the Babylonian captivity.

Throughout several centuries before the advent of nation-states, various kinds of city-states developed in many regions and endured for long periods of time. The democracy we associate with the Greek city-states rested upon a slave economy and extended the blessings of democracy to the slave-owners only. In the city-states that flourished during the Middle Ages, people had never had it so good. They knew no wars as we know them. Professional "soldiers of fortune" fought, except on Sundays and the numerous holidays, on rather well defined battlefields. Civilian lives and private property were fairly well respected, and conscription and rationing were unheard of. While they did not have our gadgets, they had perhaps a larger degree of security than any people have had before or since except in jails or under slavery. When the guilds had pride in their work, artisans produced fine goods with skill and loving care, and the same spirit made the functioning of these medieval city-states one of the most outstanding examples of decentralized government ever to have existed. The guilds and the city-states fell, finally, for the same reason that modern craft unionism has become an "old man of the sea" on the back of the labor movement—they refused to help and protect the unskilled worker. That "Cradle of Democracy," the New England town meeting, is democratic only during that one day of the year that it meets, for the rest of the year delegated authority usurps the real democratic idea. But it tends to work better than any other democratic form.

The advent of capitalism in England with the invention of the steam engine divorced the worker from the ownership of the tools of production. The Enclosure Acts, which aimed to produce wool for this new system of factory production, resulted in the farmers losing their lands and becoming the pitiful wage slaves described in the novels of Charles Dickens. Capitalism paved the way for the modern nation-state. The nation-state did not acquire its ultimate power until Napoleon introduced military conscription, centralizing and consolidating power in the all-too-familiar pattern of today. This myth that teaches the right of an omnipotent state to lay claim to the allegiance of the bodies and minds of its citizens and today masquerades under the high-sounding phrase of "Selective Service" is the backbone of strength of the nation-states of today. Destroy this myth, and a tremendous stride will have been taken toward the day when nations will live at peace with each other.

Prior to capitalism the feudal worker was exploited by his guild-master during the years of his apprenticeship, but was given food, clothing and lodging. When his term was up, his guild-master gave him a purse of money, the tools of his craft, and a certificate attesting to his merit. As a journeyman he was free to travel anywhere he wished without being subjected to immigration restrictions or jurisdictional disputes.

Today most workers do not own the tools of their trade. Yet where these tools consist of industrial processes or the factory system, today's productivity is many times that of the feudal worker. Today's worker is paid not in the terms of the worth of his labor or skill but is paid a portion of it, called a wage, and the difference which he does not get is called a profit and is taken from him by the owner of the productive process as tribute. Since the worker cannot buy back more than a portion of what he has produced with the wage he is paid, the owner is always in danger of stock-piling an unsalable "surplus" (as happened in 1929). This condition holds true even when the nation-state owns or controls the productive processes as in Fascist Italy, Nazi Germany, or the Soviet Union, not just in countries where capitalism is still more or less privately owned. All modern economies answer this problem of the "unprofitable surplus" by directing this portion of their economy's output into the production of goods earmarked for destruction—tanks, guns, uniforms, battleships, bombers, and the like. Before these implements of warfare became entirely obsolete, "practice" wars are waged, as in Spain and now in Korea, and the hoary alibi of "national defense" perpetually justifies the continued production of these expendible materials—at the expense of the peace of the world. This is done by tacit mutual consent between the various nation-states. And this, briefly, is why neither the United Nations nor any other combination of nation-states can possibly end the threat of war. So wars are not accidental—if we didn't have this war in Korea we would have to have one somewhere else, or face the alternative of another depression. Do you remember the sharp stock-market slump during the short Korean cease-fire late last year? President Truman was forced to interrupt his Florida vacation and vigorously deny any cease-fire agreement before the stock market recuperated. And as for the truce talks which have lasted for more than a year, do you really believe a truce will result until agreement is reached upon a new battle zone?

Have you ever considered what kind of a world we would have if men and women of all nations were suddenly to come to their senses and agree upon a scheme of life which left no room for exploitation and war? Our technology today is sufficiently advanced that our forests, mines, mills and factories can produce commodities far more rapidly than the world can wisely use or consume them. Agriculture, transportation and communication have also kept pace.

This is the only valid issue of 1952. And you will pardon me for saying that while the issue is hardly a new one, the solution is respectably ancient also. Jesus knew it, and summed it up masterfully in the Sermon on the Mount. Tolstoy, Thoreau and Gandhi re-stated it, and practiced it successfully. In 1952 it can still be stated that evil begats evil, and that only good can overcome evil. And while it is essential that we begin practicing that as a personal code, it is equally essential that we apply it as a people in our corporate acts. An objective analysis of the motivation and actions of the governments of any of the nation states will reveal to what an enormous extent they return evil for evil. In our own country our national governments represents the largest single example of the organized return of evil for evil, both in foreign relations and domestic affairs. Since our national government has truly been created in our own image, it is obvious that the place to begin any reform of government is not by "voting for the good candidates" but by changing our own motivations and actions. As an instance of the satanic ingenouity of this organized evil, our government, in cahoots with the real owners of our economy has assumed the major share of paying for the "unprofitable surplus" produced by our economy and earmarked for destruction, and has reached into the worker's wages through the device of the withholding income tax to compel the workers to pay the brunt of this "profit insurance."

The withholding tax was scarcely two years old when President Truman secretly ordered the atomic bombing of Hiroshima on Aug. 6, 1945, just seven years ago this week. Six months previously the Japanese had sued for peace through the offices of General MacArthur. The terms upon which they were prepared to surrender were identical with those we later accepted on V-J Day. The history of the war reveals that during the months following this bid for peace we engaged in the bloodiest battles of the Pacific island fighting, climaxed by the most dastardly action of any war in history—that atomic bombing of Hiroshima and Nagasaki. This act, which earned us the label of being the bloodiest killers of all time, was done in OUR name, yet we were never consulted on this policy of atomic bombing or even informed of our adoption of it.

I feel impelled to commemorate this infamous anniversary by picketing the local office of the Bureau of Internal Revenue during these seven days from Aug. 6 to Aug. 12. I might add that I have absolutely no stomach for food when I contemplate this monstrous act, so I am abstaining from eating for these days also. Were I only concerned for myself, I would not have prepared this explanation of my picketing. If you are still at a loss to know how best to challenge our government's iniquity, you might do worse than follow my example of refusing to pay income taxes. I have not permitted the government to collect the tax it says I owe for the past nine years.

I am fully aware that my message may seem too far-fetched to have any place in the world of today and, that in self-defense, you will wish to dismiss it and write me off as a crackpot. I would almost be inclined to agree with you if it weren't for the fact that we have, right here in Arizona, a thousand-year-old example of a people already living this good life, having had no need for government, election campaigns, courts, prisons, murder or warfare. I speak of the traditional Hopi Indians who have found the key to living harmoniously together. The major sin they recognize is to try to get even with the neighbor who may have wronged them. Their wholesome culture rests upon each individual's complete acceptance of responsibility for the consequences of his motivations as well as his actions, and their keen awareness of the spiritual significance of life. In our culture the name given to this way of life consistent with the above mentioned requirements of the better world is Christian Anarchy. You can approximate it today, here and now, without passing the buck (through voting) or waiting for the rest of the world to achieve it. While it rejects voting for politicians or going to war, directly or through subsidizing its cost, it embraces that radical practice known as returning good for evil. Should you wish a free copy of my letter to the Collector of Internal Revenue as reprinted in the Feb. 1952 issue of the CATHOLIC WORKER, ask me for it, or send your request to my mail address.

Ammon A. Hennacy,

Rt. 3, Box 22, Phoenix, Arizona

Picketing and fasting Aug. 6 to 12, 1952

Rik's varityper had broken down, so we had to work all night to get even 80 leaflets for distribution on the first day of my picketing. Byron

Bryant, radical friend and recent convert to the Church, was with us that night and he and I attended mass at St. Mary's where I prayed for grace and wisdom to guide me in my seven days fast and picketing. Then I visited my newspaper friends, giving them my leaflet. The AP man was very cordial and sent out a good story over the state the day before, telling of my activity, stressing the fact that I, who was not a church member, went to mass each day to attain that frame of mind necessary for the kind of Gandhian picketing which I engaged in each year, and that upon the completion of my fast I would enter a five day silent retreat at Maryfarm, near Newburg, N. Y. He stressed also, "the 59-year-old Christian anarchist picketing in accordance with the Gandhian principle of open opposition to the state and its war-making functions." Two local radio stations gave good factual reports of my opposition to taxes and war. As usual, the local press, per instructions from on high, would not "dignify" themselves by mentioning my name or that of the CW.

Fasting

The subject of fasting is difficult for many Americans to understand. I claim to be a One Man Revolution, yet I get ideas from others. I began my fasting in 1950 without reading in detail of Gandhi's opinion on this subject. My experiences in solitary in Atlanta in 1918-19 had taught me to really love my enemies. Therefore when I had fasted I had the most kindly feeling toward tax men and officials. My fasting and picketing was not to discomfort them or trip them up, but to wake up and encourage the timid pacifists and anarchists who did not dare oppose the powers that be. Later I read that Gandhi had nearly died on his first fast of seven days, because he had some mixed feelings of hatred toward the oppressor. On his other fast of twenty-one days his mind was clear and he got along fine.

On Monday night, Rik and I had some chop suey at a restaurant. I was to begin my fast at 4 p.m., the next day. Accordingly I had in mind eating a few extras that I could not get out in the country: a malt, grapes and pie. But in my mind I had ·already commenced to fast and these specials did not taste good and I did not finish them. I got weighed at 4 p.m. and weighed 140. I lost about two pounds a day. I went home with Rik every night and drank distilled water. After the first day I was too weak to reach across the table for anything if I had wanted to. I was strong enough when I got in my "picketing harness." I did not picket on Saturday or Sunday as the tax office was closed; but I did not rest, as new CW's had arrived and I was distributing and selling them. Some friends felt I could eat a bite or two for strength on these two days, but I told them that I wouldn't "cheat" and that if I did take a bite my stomach would growl for more and I would be worse off than before. Also that my strength came from prayer and ideals and not from food. I got a letter from Dorothy each day holding up my hands—and feet—as it were. On the morning of the sixth day I got my second wind and felt like a new man. I was clear-headed and light-headed, and walked as if in the air, with no fatigue. Each day the AP wanted some news, so I told them of the weight

I had lost. During the last 5½ hours of my fast, I lost 4 pounds; 17 pounds in all. I broke my fast with a special mixture of vegetable juices, with Rik, at a juice bar. As Rik and I touched glasses in a toast to The Green Revolution, the waitress said: "What good nerves you have; your hand is so steady." I explained that I was breaking a seven day fast, and she couldn't believe it.

The meaning of fasting, although explained by me personally to many people, could not penetrate to the general public. One woman who spoke to me about twice a day when she came by, and who argued with me good-naturedly but not too intelligently, told me on the last day of my fast that I could get a good lunch for 35¢ at the YMCA. "But I am fasting these seven days," I replied. I had given her my leaflet, in which I mentioned my fast, but she had either not read it or did not comprehend it. She backed away from me quietly and whispered, "You are a saint." Of course I am not a saint, and I was the same right then as I was before when she thought I was eating meals regularly.

On Sunday, I stopped to rest on a chair in front of the church where I was selling CW's. A lady who had likely noticed me there for years wanted to know if I was sick. I told her that I had been fasting for the past five days and was tired.

"What are you fasting for?" she asked.

"Seven years ago they threw the Bomb and that was a terrible thing to do wasn't it?" I asked.

"Yes," she replied.

"And they are still making materials for them out at Reynolds Aluminum and other places," I added.

"Are they?" she queried.

"Yes. And you don't suppose that God would pay much attention to prayers for peace from Christians who are making bombs, or throwing them, or helping in the armed services, or paying taxes for all this, do you?"

"I don't suppose so, but I never thought of that." was her reply.

"Well, I am fasting as a penance for those who are doing all this ignorantly, or who are weak and do it knowingly. I don't make bombs, or go to war, or pay taxes for war."

"Oh, one just man saves the city," she said reverently.

"What do you have there?" said a well-dressed man to me, when I was picketing again.

"Oh, some good anarchist literature," I answered rather smartly, for as I have said many times I do not believe in minimizing my wares.

"That's just what I want. I heard Emma Goldman and Alexander Berkman when I went to Yale, and I haven't met a real anarchist since. Tell me, what are you doing?"

I explained my anti-tax program in detail. He was a mining engineer from New York City who had properties in Arizona and in leaving he gave me a dollar "for the cause."

I had no trouble at all with the general public or the police. I had, as usual, notified the police, the FBI, and the tax man that what I was doing was clearly subversive, but not more so than usual. I gave out around 150 leaflets and 50 CW's a day. Many people who had heard reports on the radio and who happened to have seen an out-of-town paper stopped and asked for literature. Ed Lahey, of the Chicago DAILY NEWS, came to see me, but I had left for the day. He left a note. He had written about me previously.

When I finished my fast and picketing I started East.

I drank some more juices on the bus and ate fruit. The AP had told what I planned to eat on my first meal at my friend, Platt Cline's home. Barbara had mashed potatoes, apple sauce, custard pie and coffee and toast. Also some peas. This was at 11 p.m. But at 4 a.m. I was hungry and got up and ate some grapes and a peach. On the bus to New York there was little sleep and not much variety of food for a vegetarian. I had some watermelon with Sharon at midnight in Chicago, and my mother and younger sister gave me some lunch in a box at Cleveland, as they met me at the station. Sunday morning in New York City, after going to Mass with Dorothy, I got weighed and it was exactly where it was when I started: 140 pounds.

Maryfarm

As we drove past West Point to Newburgh we shivered and took new strength in our opposition to this ancient nest of legalized murder. (Selma and I had passed it on the boat in 1921 when we had gone to visit Ruthenberg in Sing Sing.) The bombers were to disturb us all week, at Maryfarm, as they buzzed and dived. While fasting I had been looking forward to the good whole wheat bread which Dorothy promised me she would bake at the retreat. She taught the girls there to bake also. There were about forty of us there. Father Casey, who gave the retreat accepted the Christian Anarchist position of the CW. We were not supposed to talk to anyone but him, so I got acquainted, and was charmed with his honesty, humor, clear thinking, and courage. One evening we talked about the evils of capitalism and I had said that time belonged to God and not to bankers and that even 1% interest was wrong. He felt that I might explain some of this to the others, but I told him I had better be quiet for there was so much that I did not know spiritually. I said I would needle him from the sidelines if he got too far astray from the radical left. The next session he was quoting from the parable of the talents and of the man with one talent hiding it instead of putting it out to interest. With a smile he said, "Beg your pardon, Ammon." I took notes on his lectures, asked questions as to church history and dogma, went through all of the masses, compline, rosary, benediction and singing in Latin without knowing too much about what it all meant. In fact, I got blue marks on my knees from kneeling so much on the hard floor. Toward the last I had a faint glimpse that there was a green pasture beyond the high, jagged and thorny theological fence. Whether I would nibble at it or not I did not know, but I continued to pray for grace and wisdom. I had brought along some notes from Tolstoy, Gandhi, etc. and among them saw this poem by the Protestant Vachel Lindsey, which I had somehow copied with the special one of his I liked, "The Leaden-Eyed." In this atmosphere of radical religion the one radical and the one religious poem fitted. Here they are:

The Leaden-Eyed

Let not young souls be smothered out before
They do quaint deeds and fully flaunt their pride.
It is the world's one crime its babes grow dull,
It's poor are ox-like, limp and leaden-eyed.
Not that they starve, but starve so dreamlessly.
Not that they sow, but that they seldom reap.
Not that they serve, but have no gods to serve.
Not that they die, but that they die like sheep.

At Mass

No doubt tomorrow I will hide
My face from you, my King.
Let me rejoice this Sunday noon
And kneel while grey priests sing.
It is not wisdom to forget
But since it is my fate,
Fill thou my soul with hidden wine
To make this white hour great.
My God, my God, this marvelous hour
I am thy son, I know.
Once in a thousand days your voice
Has laid temptation low.

It seems that no one had pulled the weeds from the flower beds for a long time, so I took a busman's holiday by mowing the lawn and pulling weeds, for half a day, in between conferences.

Sacco and Vanzetti

I had not known that the Vigil of St. Bartholomew, Martyr, was on the 23rd of August, the day on which Nicolo Sacco and Bartholomew Vanzetti had been done to death by the frightened bourgeois just 25 years before. I mentioned it to Dorothy and Father Casey, and we three together with Joe Monroe and Kenneth Little got up at midnight and went to the chapel, where by candle light we said some of the Matins with special prayers for the souls of these martyrs in praise for their noble lives and courageous death. We remembered the last words of Vanzetti who forgave those who were killing him. The retreat was over at noon. Dorothy had phoned to New York City to see where there was a memorial meeting for Sacco and Vanzetti, but in all that city not an anarchist, I.W.W., Socialist or Communist had a public word to say. They were either gone bourgeois or busy building their respective—and now respectable—organizations. Dorothy said we would have to have our own meeting then on Union Square. She had to meet some people at the bus and Father Casey detoured to say hello to Ed Willock, so Jim, a seminarian and Roger O'Neil, kid anarchist who gave out men's clothing at the CW, accompanied me to Union Square.

244

Some Christian Front Catholic had the crowd and was going strong against "atheistic Communism." I tried twice and spoke for about ten minutes each time but had no soapbox and a very small crowd. We walked back to the CW. Father Casey had just arrived and wanted to know about the meeting. Late as it was he said we would go up and have a good one and he would help me by standing and asking me questions. Sure enough the presence of a priest drew the crowd away from the fascist and we had a meeting for several hours until 1:30 in the morning.

Whittaker Chambers Again

Several letters came in protesting my denunciation of Whittaker Chambers in the July-Aug. CW. I answered them. Dorothy gave me the penance of reading his book, saying that I was about the one person who was of the age and time of Chambers who had not turned bourgeois, who was still an uncompromising radical, and who had no ulterior motive in asking Chambers to join any group for his salvation. I read the thing and wrote him the following letter.

New York City, 223 Chrystie St.
Sept. 9, 1952

Dear Mr. Chambers:

I mailed you a leaflet some months ago from Phoenix, Arizona which I distributed on the 300th anniversary of George Fox becoming a Quaker. Later I had an article in the CATHOLIC WORKER for July-August in which I made some cutting remarks about your activity as an informer, ending with an illustration uncomplimentary to your character, as spoken by the Old Pioneer with whom I live.

I had read your articles as given in the POST. Several readers wrote saying that I had been uncharitable and unfair to you. I have read your book and find it much worse than I ever expected it could be. Your talk about God and your being a sacrificial lamb to save this atheistic capitalism from Communist atheism is blasphemy.

I am happy that you find some peace of mind on the land and that you plan to stay there. I also appreciate that you did hard labor on the streets in Washington, D. C., and that you give theoretical justification to the answer of Johnson to Boswell that courage is the greatest virtue, for without it you cannot practice the other virtues.

I am coming to Washington within the next month and if it is convenient for you to meet me there or at your farm I would be glad to get acquainted with you on the chance that there "is that of God in you" which may make you evolve from the damning position of choosing the lesser of two evils rather than the ultimate good, which you claim is the true Quaker message and which you refuse to accept.

Regular bought and paid-for informers, like Budenz, do not deserve the attention of real Christians, Catholic or otherwise. Their mouthing of slogans indicates no prayer or thought. Your case is different for you have not exulted in your informing. It is difficult for any of us to understand ourselves, much less other people. However, as you have handed it out by the hundred pages you ought to be able to take it, so here goes.

First, to introduce myself I will say that my wife, Selma Melms, and I knew your wife at the Rand School in 1920 . . .(*Then I gave my personal radical history, with which the reader is familiar.*)

My attitude toward Communists may be explained by saying that if any of them were arrested in Phoenix where I live I would picket the court at the time of their trial with signs saying:

"In Russia the enemy of the Worker is the Communist and the Bureaucrat.

"In this country the enemy of the Worker is the Capitalist and the Bureaucrat.

"This trial is Stalin's way; not Jefferson's."

In a frank and sincere spirit I would like you to consider the following questions:

1. How can you boast of a Messianic role of martyr, identifying yourself with the early Christians who refused to put even a pinch of incense on the altar to Caesar, or seek to expiate your crime for the sin of being a Communist, when with both of your hands you offer your clever mind and the body of your son to Caesar?

2. How can you expect the American public to leave their materialism when you offer them only a defense of that materialism against a rival materialism?

3. It is true that St. Francis and Gandhi inched around and retreated before they found the path to sainthood, but once they found it they did not blaspheme by calling evil good. You may be weak, and may have sinned, and may not aspire to sainthood, but to hide your weakness and cowardice behind the facade of God and Freedom is sainthood in reverse.

4. The Good Thief on the Cross admitted his thievery and asked to meet Christ in Paradise. You continue your wickedness and are unrepentent.

5. You do not need to choose the lesser of two evils and uphold war and capitalism. You do not need to forget the plight of those workers whom you claim to have "humanized my soul for the rest of my life." You can still choose voluntary poverty, life on the land, and dissociate yourself from both capitalism and communism by accepting Christian Anarchism. Does not the example of Jesus, St. Francis, George Fox, Tolstoy and Gandhi mean more to you than the acclaim of the makers of the Atom Bomb?

Sincerely,

Ammon A. Hennacy

246

I did not receive an answer. When I was in Philadelphia some Quakers said that Chambers was taking instructions with a priest and likely would join the Catholic Church and that then all of the stoolies would have joined and the Quakers would not have to be ashamed of his blasphemy.

The Catholic Worker

I had visited on Mott street for a few minutes in 1938 and 1939 and had spent the day after Easter of 1950 there. Now I was glad to visit the two Catholic Worker farms, stay for two months, and get a knowledge of what the whole thing meant. I was not yet sold on the advisibility of majoring in "feeding bums." I was for more and more propaganda. Dorothy had asked me in the spring to write my Autobiography, so I looked through the files for the last fifteen years and picked out copies of my letters to her and the CW. Many events had happened the memory of which was hazy, and some I had entirely forgotten. I took quiet hours in the library at Peter Maurin Farm in outlining this book and in writing the first portion of it. At other times I explained the CW ideas to visitors, spoke to different radical groups in and around New York, went up to Maryfarm again to speak to a meeting. I met the Shy Apostle of whom John McKeon had written and many others who came and went. I had thought that Tom Sullivan would be a grouch who would dislike my radicalism, as he is neither pacifist nor anarchist. I was delighted to find him a fellow Irishman whom I loved. I found myself going easy on Mike Harrington who was a luke-warm Socialist, he got so much razzing from everyone else. I was there for two mailings of the paper and sat around at different tables getting acquainted. I kidded Betty Lou and Pat, as I had Jane and Helen at Maryfarm for being too pious. The bedbugs bothered Joe Monroe and Mike, but I was next bed to them and they did not touch me. Maybe a vegetarian's blood is too weak for them—or too strong. I spoke three times at the Friday night meetings; the last time about the Hopi. Tom said this was my best meeting. I told him that was because there was more Hopi and less Hennacy in the conversation. Bill Ryan was in the city for a few months, having relinquished his job as editor of the I.W.W. paper because of their timidity. I had not seen him since 1942 when he went to prison, so we had many hours of good companionship. Julius Eichel, old time CO of both wars, came over with his family to one meeting. I visited twice with Roger Baldwin. We did not argue about our differences and each respected the other. I was glad to meet the other non-Catholic contributor to the CW, Fritz Eichenberg, who came to two of my meetings.

Not enough physical work and too much starch in the diet I thought, although the fellows in the kitchen always gave me something extra when I took no meat. I had thought I would help Father Duffy in some hard work at Peter Maurin Farm but with a few rainy days and my writing and meetings I didn't get much done. Quiet Hans and efficient Ed kept things going there. Tamar Hennessy is one of the matter of fact, practical women of whom there were very few in this upset world. I played with her children and off-and-on had a little conversation with Dave Hennessy. His radicalism stops on "back to the land" while mine begins there.

A letter came from Archbishop Francis of the Old Catholic Church inviting me to see him in Woodstock, N. Y., beyond Maryfarm fifty miles. I had planned to visit Holley Cantine and Dachine Rainer in nearby Bearsville, so made the two visits at one time. I had corresponded with them for years and was glad to spend the evening and night there in their log house and beautiful wooded hills. They are pacifist anarchists, so we had much in common. After getting lost up a mountain, Holley brought me to see Archbishop Francis whom he knew. This kindly, thin and agile old man was my match in conversation. Bob had told me I would only be able to get a word in edgewise. But he was not really that bad. He knew many old time radicals whom I had known. I had only vaguely heard of the Old Catholic Church. It started around 1871 when groups, in Poland, Holland and England mostly, refused to go along with the infallibility of the Pope. Other leaders had died until now Archbishop Francis was the head of the group in the world. There are about 70,000 members in this country. As I understood it these people were not radical, but had meekly followed their leaders just as many others do. Father Francis was also a vegetarian. His big church in Woodstock was burned during the war, whether by Vigilantes or "act of God" no one knows. He had moved to the edge of town on top of a mountain and built this beautiful small church decorated with wooden screens like the Middle Ages and other wood carvings. He also worked quite a garden. He had signs and pictures of St. Francis warning hunters not to kill anything on his premises which extended way back. He would ring a bell when hunters approached and this scared the game away. I attended mass that Sunday morning. It was in English. At the close he introduced me to his congregation along with praise for the CW. I talked informally to some of them. He had a friend drive us to Maryfarm where he thought he would meet Dorothy but she had just left for New York City. As we entered the yard Father Faley approached to kiss the Bishop's ring, but he jerked his hand away, saying, "I'm schismatic."

I was not attracted to this small denomination because it did not seem to have any life, but I was attracted to the good Archbishop with his simplicity, kindness and spirit of love. Coming back to town I visited for half a day with Hugo and Livia Gellert, old time radical friends. They were non-religious and radicals, but not anarchists. Hugo's brother had been a CO in World War I. They knew of my association with the CW and were pleased with my anti-tax campaign. It is good to meet friends after thirty years and to feel perfectly at home.

It was about this time that the "grace and wisdom" for which I had prayed for the past four years, and the prayers of my good Catholic friends coupled with that Celestial Bulldozer of which I have spoken made it imperative in my heart that I should become a Catholic. I had written nearly 100 pages of this book before I surprised myself and friends by changing the title of the book to Catholic instead of Christian Anarchist. In the next chapter I tell of this in detail.

CHAPTER 11.

Traveling

September 21
to December 16, 1952

In the East
and Middle West; to Phoenix

Ade Bethune

LORD·HELP·US·TO·BE·CHRIST+BEARERS

"I didn't know the Catholic Worker had a right wing," said a young Quaker social worker to me as we met in the office of the National Council for the Prevention of War in Washington, D. C. I had just mentioned in conversation that Tom Sullivan and Mike Harrington chose the lesser of the Second and Third evils in the current campaign. Tom had put in his column in the CW that he was for Stevenson. We were reading proof at the printers and Dorothy said to him, "Tom, this is an anarchist paper. I crossed off your reference to Stevenson." She told me, "Tom won't speak to me for a few days but he will get over it." Which was true. We had a Pacifist Conference at Peter Maurin Farm, early in September, and Mike had spoken for Socialists. He was practically alone among us anarchists. In defense he said that if Socialists were in power then he would be an anarchist. We told him to wake up and join the procession. Dorothy and I and others had gone through that parliamentary stage long ago. This Quaker in Washington had heard me give a Four Minute Man speech at the end of the staff meeting of the American Friends Service Committee in Philadelphia, a few days before.

Arlo Tatum, alumnus of Sandstone prison, with whom I was staying, had introduced me to the Service Committee as "A Christian Anarchist who lives like the early Christians," so I commenced by telling hem that as they expected the worst I had better put my worst foot forward and give it to them strong in the few minutes I had. I said that my Quaker ancestors had hidden escaped slaves before the Civil War and had thus met the challenge of that day. Today, since Aug. 6, 1945, when the Atom Bomb was dropped at Hiroshima the challenge was whether we approved of that devilish action. Dorothy and I refused to pay income taxes but all those present had taxes taken from their pay to support war and in doing so they were committing a terrible sin. I mentioned that I had been a social worker myself for eleven years, and now had been doing menial manual labor in the fields for ten years, so that no withholding tax could be taken from my pay. I knew what endless work it was to pick up the pieces of human wreckage at the bottom of the cliff, but that we of the CW did this now, and we did more than this, for we had the one sure radical method of seeing that people did not fall over the cliff in the first place. This method was that of the One Man Revolution within the heart of man, without depending upon political revolutions which only changed masters. I repeated my anarchist argument, as given in the Frontispiece of this book. I ended up by telling of Dorothy's kneeling while they sang the Star Spangled Banner in Church. Afterwards some well known Quakers congratulated me on my strong message, while others walked out in a somewhat dazed condition, asking Arlo how they ever allowed such a fellow inside the premises.

I had spoken also to an adult group at a Quaker church in Philadelphia where 98% of the members were pacifists, and had sat on the fronting bench during the silent meeting. My good tax refuser friends, the Longstreth's had invited me there. I also spoke to the War Resister's League and met Ned Richards and family, CO's and tax refusers from away back. I met a fine group of young pacifists in Philadelphia.

Washington, D. C.

Here I arrived at the very minute that my friend Ed Lahey of the Knight Newspapers was leaving by plane for New Orleans, so I missed him again. I spent the night and spoke at St. Martin de Porres House where Llewellyn Scott has held forth almost alone for years. He works to pay the upkeep and does well to give out clothing the year around and to have something hot in the winter months for those who need it early in the morning. The young folks at Friendship House were an earnest group, with a fine spirit. I had more time and tried not to be so blunt as I had been with the sophisticated Quakers, but in the end I said about the same. Father Owen beamed his approval throughout my talk and Mary Huston, the leader, thanked me.

I had written to Fred Libby of the National Council for the Prevention of War in 1917 when he headed a peace organization. His secretary sent me money for help in my anti-draft campaign, saying that this was from her personally, as the organization was more conservative. Libby is an agile and friendly man of 77, from generations of farmers up in Maine, Henry Beston told me. He works with politicians and has hopes of disarmament, but I was glad to meet him again. He appreciated very much the extreme left position of the CW and introduced me to Jim Finucane and his office staff. I spent the night with him and his charming wife. His "thee and thou" reminded me of my Quaker great-grandmother. The weather was rainy and cold.

I met one friend at the Indian Bureau who had met the Hopi that Easter week of 1950 and who appreciated the true Hopi. He did not begin to be as radical as many with whom I associate, but he knew what the words meant, read the CW, and enjoyed the Hopi songs which I played on his player that night at his home.

Boston

In Boston I was happy to meet John and Helen Cort and their five bouncing children. They had recently moved to a big house on a hill in Brighton overlooking Cambridge. The view out of the kitchen window was enough to make any woman forget the worries of housework. John is organizer for the Newspaper Guild, spent years around the CW, and knew Peter well. Dark and handsome Irish, Joe Dever came over one evening, and he and John received an antidote to their enthusiastic support of "the people's choice." They had heard the anarchist message before, but they could not yet be so radical. I told them that they were young and there was no hurry. After mass John went upstairs and later came down with an article "The Charms of Anarchism," for the COMMON-WEAL, which he read to me. Joe laughed and said "First he praises you and then he sticks in the knife." I told them I was used to that and could take it.

John drove me over to meet Pirim Sorokin at Emerson Hall and came for me after I had visited for several hours with my old friend from Ohio State University in 1915, Arthur M. Schlesinger, Sr. Sorokin had been imprisoned both by the Czar and the Communists, under sentence of death for six weeks by the latter. He accepted the Christian Anarchist position, but in small letters instead of in capital ones. His approach was that of getting the same result, if possible, by having educators giving their fine minds to this problem. He had figured out something similar to my Love, Courage and Wisdom thought. Bob Ludlow had said that I would meet my equal as a conversationalist when I met Sorokin, so when either one of us would stop for a breath, or out of good manners, the other would get in a word. The remark by Bob was proven justified. I had admired Prof. Schlesinger because he was chairman of a committee that had asked the Governor of Massachusetts to allow a statue of Sacco and Vanzetti to be placed on Boston Common. Too many liberals and radicals forget their ideals as they become older.

Schlesinger and John Cort had wanted me to meet Comrade Felicani, anarchist printer and old time friend of Sacco and Vanzetti. I was glad to meet with him for half a day. Some one had sent him a clipping of Father Casey and me holding the only 25th anniversary meeting for Sacco and Vanzetti, on August 23rd, and he was pleased, although puzzled at the connection between priests and anarchists. I told him of Peter Maurin, founder of the CW, who in June 1934 had answered a certain John Cummings who had wanted a Catholic Political Party by saying:

"A Catholic political party cannot stop Communism or Fascism, whether Catholic or Protestant. Fascism is only a stopgap between the rugged individualism of bourgeois capitalism and the rugged collectivism of Bolshevik Communism. The Catholic Workers Movement fosters Catholic action and not Catholic political action."

I told him in detail of the five priests in Phoenix who support my anti-tax efforts, and of the work of Dorothy and the CW. He said he would be pleased to read her book and receive the CW. I was glad to meet this old-time anarchist.

Henry Beston

Henry Beston, who ranks in my mind as a writer with Albert Jay Nock, had written to me in 1945 praising my rendition of what an Isleta, N. M. Indian thought about the Bomb: "Stealing the brightness of Father Sun for devil worship." He had sent me maple syrup at Christmas and letters written in his superb handwriting. I came to his country home after dark, near Nobleboro, Maine. A more gracious man, with both hands extended in greeting, I have never met. Henry is not a political or economic radical but opposes modern materialism because of his love of nature.

The Bestons have a great collection of cow bells of all weights, tones and shapes. Every time you open a door a bell jingles, and when I left, Elizabeth waved her hand and rang the big dinner bell outside as a farewell greeting. This is also the House of Books and of Baskets. The only place I remember where I could not reach out and touch a book was on the middle of the stairway. Baskets of every shape, age, and color were in the places unoccupied by books and bells.

One of the tests of a man is whether he knows how to prepare his own food, says Henry. Fire in the fireplace early in the morning, coffee boiled the old New England way on the stove, and a dash of Saturday baked beans greeted me the first morning. I played the Zuni Sunrise Song before Elizabeth was out of bed and together with the other nine records they were a source of happiness to the Bestons.

I had not known that Elizabeth Beston was Elizabeth Coatsworth the poet. I read a book of her poems while there and liked especially the "Song of the Rabbits Outside the Tavern," and the poems about nature. I copied seven of them to read to friends as I travel back to Phoenix, and I know the Old Pioneer will like the "Green Fields." I was also entranced by the book of Fairy Stories written by Henry thirty years ago. The Beston's, like all farmers, go to bed early, so for once in this last two months I did get the right amount of sleep.

Yoné

Yone Stafford had come to the Pacifist Conference at Peter Maurin Farm in September, and asked me to stop at her home in Springfield. She has been a friend of the CW for years although not a Catholic. Here I met with a small group of pacifists, four of whom were Catholics. One of them, Mary Moore, has read the CW from the first issue, and formerly taught school near Mott street. Yone's house is one of the very few where I have been that seems really built to live in. An iron frame with outlets for the hot air forms a fireplace. The bricks are built around it. Unlike most fireplaces it does not smoke. The whole force of an architects office was upset by the idea that a room could be built with a 12 foot wall at a slant instead of square. This forms a bookshelf and gives a sense of area to the room instead of having the walls crowd in on you. The bed here is the best in which I have slept. Yone opposed the war all during the war and wrote countless letters to the local press under both her own name and the name "America," as the characters in Japanese for "Yone" and for "America" are the same.

Traveling Westward

I helped distribute leaflets, with Bob and Mike and other CW and War Resister friends, at Times Square, the night of a blackout and display of supposed patriotic efficiency, in case of an air raid. Each of us had a different corner. Cops told us to move on and so we went to another corner. I had about 2000 leaflets which I gave out. One fellow argued with the cops and then got arrested for "beating up the cops." It is not wise to picket or hand out literature if you are going to get hysterical. You have to practice pacifism right then and there.

Arriving in Rochester, N. Y. after dark I was met at the bus by Francis Anzilone, and was shown the very clean and orderly CW house. I knew that their works of mercy had more of the social worker approach, which I had discarded ten years before, and that most of them did not appreciate the pacifist, anarchist message of the CW. However, I was pleased to meet the small group who were interested in my more radical interpretation. Next day, after some stray bus riding and phoning, I met the Thorntons, Vincents, Dvoraks and Betty Clendenning, at Edinboro, Pa. Here different stages of progress in thought and agricultural effort were being worked out. Zigzagging again on buses I looked in on Mike Strasser's philosophy class at Duquesne University in Pittsburgh, and spent the night with his charming family. Erica thought of me as a desert father I guess, and gave me *Desert Calling* about Charles de Foucauld. I had known Mike in the old Milwaukee CW days. Despite our respective turns to the right and left, this old CW bond held us in a brotherly feeling. A conversation on the phone with Fr. Hugo and Fr. Meehan was the best that I could do in the rush of this Smoky City.

The next day I phoned the authorities at Chillicothe Prison and asked permission to visit my CO friend, Carl Owen. I was no relative and I was a jailbird, and thus by the rules should ordinarily be refused admission. We visited far enough away from an official who was busy reading incoming mail so that we could say anything we pleased. Carl was thinner, but clear-eyed. As with all of us in jail the first few months are the worst, but when we begin to do time we can take it. Carl liked his bacteriological work in the hospital. He did a lot of reading, a chapter from the Bible each day along with the rest. After nearly two hours he introduced me to Fr. Soltis, the Catholic chaplain, who asked about the ideas and activities of the CW. I had to wait an hour by the gate before the officials of the prison made sure that I was properly identified, but finally the electric gate, which decorated the super-electric barbed wire enclosure, opened and I was on my way. In other years I had meetings at the home of the young Murrays who had other Catholics present.

That evening I had supper with Father John Dunn at the Mercy Hospital in Portsmouth, Ohio, where he is chaplain. We had been pals in Atlanta, as CO's in 1918, before he had studied for the priesthood. He had always been baldheaded, so now he looked just a little older, and with that merry twinkle as of old. I explained the peaceful life of the Hopi to the nuns and played Hopi records before the evening Benediction. John is the one priest I have heard who said the Rosary and other prayers as if they were a fresh, newly discovered thought. Each of us remembered names and incidents from Atlanta that the other had forgotten. John had two copies of Douglas Hyde's *I Believe* and gave me one to read on the way. I found it very interesting and a relief from the stool pigeon mentality of the Budenz-Bentley-Chambers type. Hyde put his finger on no one and named no names for Scotland Yard to pounce upon.

My brother Frank has always made money with little effort. He played a violin in the orchestra of the Socialist local in 1917 but since then has always followed the capitalist way of life, though with tongue in cheek, for he believes neither in capitalism or radicalism or in any religion. He has never voted, not because of anarchist ideas but because he didn't think it worthwhile. He had a Stanley Steamer in the old days, and has played around with airplanes for a score of years. He took me up 5000 feet in the air and we hovered over Loveland and tried to guess where grailed the Grail. Then he drove me in his car to see John and Mildred Loomis who edit the INTERPRETER, the decentralist organ which has at times mentioned my anti-tax effort. We ended up at Ernest and Marion Bromley's in Sharonville. He is leader of the tax-refusers and Marion quit a good job as secretary to A. J. Muste of the FOR rather than have taxes taken out of her pay for war. They still deduct war taxes in that organization which is dedicated to peace with a capital P. Frank's wife, Rose, was cordial to me, although not interested in radical ideas.

At the Grail I met Helen Adler and Mary Buckley who greeted me warmly, and I spoke and played Indian records to a small select group, until evening, when we had supper with Jim and Grace Rogan whom I knew from old CW days. They were leaving for Africa soon. The founder of the Grail here had asked me years ago for carbon copies of all of my notes on Tolstoy. She was now in Africa and those in charge were fearful of the implications of Tolstoy and Jesus in this mad world. But all of us must go step by step on our own road at our own speed, and we all do what we want to.

I visited in Columbus for a few hours with a nephew whom I had not seen for years. He is manager of a big store but is interested in this uncle from far away, who brought another world through the CW's which I left with him. I spent a week in Cleveland with my mother who is now 81. I went to the Greek rite church mornings in the next block, and with her to her small Baptist church. I read my favorite hymn, "Faith of our Fathers." I visited with my nieces and nephews and five sisters and brother. "Mamma, you are a pipsqueak," said six year old Gail to my sister Lorraine one morning. Seems she had not been quite asleep the night before when I was telling my adventures downstairs and she heard this new word spoken. Dorothy tries to ration me to say "pipsqueak" once a day only, but at times I am sure I exceed my quota. My sister Lola had old letters of mine from prison days packed away, including letters to her from Emma Goldman and Alexander Berkman, about me. A pleasant visit with Bill and Dorothy Gauchat of the Cleveland CW, with Max Sandin, CO and tax refuser, and strange as it may seem, a pleasant visit with the Catholic columnist of the Universe Bulletin who disagrees mightily with Dorothy and myself.

The kindly atmosphere of the CW house in Detroit and the cheerfulness of Lou and Justine Murphy and their happy children is outstanding. These folks are not very radical and they listened to my extreme message with goodwill. I had breakfast with my old friend of CO days, Carl Haessler, and spent the night with Harold Gray on his big farm near Saline. Harold was one of the six of us who had been in jail in World War I and who refused to register in 1942. The cooperative feature of their farm, which appealed in the lean days of the depression, was now dead, having succumbed to the big wages of the city. But Harold and his wife held forth with their life on the land. This was election night, and we were talking of the Green Revolution and never tuned in for a minute or thought of the battle between Tweedle Dum and Tweedle Dee. Harold drove me to the CW farm at Lyons, where I said hello for a few minutes to the couples living and building there. Then to Ann Arbor where I looked in the files of the Labadie Collection at the University Library, where all of my writings are filed, each article from the CW being cut out and listed under the heading "Christian Anarchist." Mr. Harris is the custodian since the death of Agnes Inglis.

I had lost track of beautiful Virginia Beck, after knowing her with the CW in Milwaukee and visiting her ten years ago in Denver. On a chance I wrote to her through her husband Vincent Smith, who teaches philosophy at Notre Dame. He met me at the bus, and I had a good visit with Fr. Leo Ward, Fr. Putz, Julian Pleasants and others that evening, and a super breakfast-dinner at The House of Bread with Ruth Farney who had set up the ovens at Peter Maurin Farm. The good spirit of all these folks who listened to my extreme views of the left spoke well of the depth of their understanding.

For the second time in seven years I phoned the Nuttings and promised for sure to see them next year. Later Father Casey loaned me Nutting's *Reclamation of Independence* which I read on the train and enjoyed. Here are a few gems of his:

"A believer in the Green Revolution is simply an anarchist who happens to like farming."

255

"If we are to exalt the common man, the common man who stays common must be the hero—the man who makes his way without unmaking the way of others, who earns his living and that of his family without working for someone else or having someone else work for him; the man who makes use of material things but not of men."

"If a man raises wheat to sell, success depends not only or chiefly on the amount of wheat produced, but on the market quotations for wheat. If he raises wheat to feed his family and animals, the market price makes no difference whatever. If he has grain he has succeeded."

The next night, in Wilmette, I met Dorothy, Monsignor Hillenbrand and Monsignor Newman, at John Mella's and at Dorothy's meeting at the school. I had not seen Sharon for over three years. She teaches music at a private school in Winnetka. The cult she belongs to does not damn the Catholic Church and she told me she was glad I planned to join the Church. She told Dorothy that her cult believed in the Ascension of Mary before the Pope proclaimed it. She is sweetly serene, dedicated and pure, tolerant and beautiful. Her cult does not believe in medicine or vaccination and her boy friend has withstood the army for a year and a half, despite court-martial threats for his refusal to take the shots. I met with several groups in Chicago, and enjoyed the hospitality of Peter Maurin House, which is practically an adjunct of the Alcoholics Anonymous and not at all radical, although you get a CW there if you ask for it. They have a hard enough time saving themselves from booze without saving the world. With John Mella and FOR friends I met Elly Mayr of Vienna, Catholic pacifist daughter of Casper Mayr, leader of Catholic pacifists in Europe. Also a short visit with Father Teresivich, a gentle and also a radical priest.

In Milwaukee, I spoke in the Summerfield Methodist Church, where I had given a pacifist sermon from the pulpit at regular services fourteen years before. Al Cortez, an I.W.W., was the secretary of the FOR, the first active Spanish rebel I have known. I visited with Henry L. Nunn who read to me some pages from his forthcoming *The Whole Man at Work* concerning my activity. Several friends on the Milwaukee JOURNAL greeted me kindly, as did dozens of my co-workers of the Department of Public Welfare whom I had not seen for ten years.

I stayed over night with my friend Ray Callahan, first president of the union which I had organized, in the office in 1935. He now works at the zoo, and says that he is succeeding with social work among the animals. "I am trying to get the elephant to eat meat and the tiger to eat grass; and I'll succeed; that is I'll succeed as quickly as those in the world who try to maneuver folks around in social work," he said. A meeting with Betty Van Ells, Florence and Jerry of the old CW group, and kind words from the Cardyn Center and I was on my way.

In Minneapolis, on a Sunday morning waiting for a bus to get to Fr. Casey in Hutchinson, I introduced myself at Quaker meeting and a CO who was present and who had heard me speak at the University in 1938 came forth. He planned a small meeting for that night and I met many friends, among them Prof. Mulford Sibley who had read my book on

Christian Anarchism in manuscript seven years before. Someday I may rewrite it from the Catholic Anarchist view.

In the next chapter, on my conversion to the Catholic faith, I tell of meeting Dorothy at Father Casey's and of our visit to old man Marquardt's at Grasston. "Weep and howl, ye drunkards" the old man had said to the court, explaining his refusal to register in both wars. He "judged no man" but stood adamant against the forces of church and state that made war. He made this braggart feel humble in his presence. In 1942 when those of us who were over 45 had to disrupt our lives (and our wives) by refusing to register, the eight Marquardt boys and near relatives who refused to register and did time in Sandstone cheered me. The old man had five farms to tend to, with only his wife and daughter to help. He lost two of the farms.

I had corresponded with David and Beverly White who teach at Macalester College in St. Paul, but had never met them. They had some Yogi meeting on that night, so had planned for me to speak at McCosh's Campus Bookstore, near the U. of Minnesota campus in Minneapolis. Beverley drove me there. Two of the Marquardt boys greeted me happily, and the older one stayed until 1:30 a.m. when the meeting broke up. Here in this radical and non-religious bookstore I was pleased to find CW's on display, with a tin can to put the pennies in as they were purchased. Every variety of radical was present, and there must have been some one with a knowledge of Catholic history, for the St. Paul daily paper, under the caption THEY SAY, had a picture of Pope Pius XII and myself (to the left).

It quoted the Pope: "The church is realistic. It believes in peace. It reminds statesmen that the most complicated political situations can be solved on a friendly basis." Then they quoted my Love, Courage and Wisdom phrase—see page 136. At the end, it said "Ammon Hennacy, Roman Catholic 'Anarchist.' "

In Madison I had the best meeting of my trip, at St. John's church, near the campus of the University of Wisconsin. Father Kutchera had prepared the way at mass that morning by announcing the meeting and saying that Catholics were directed from the Pope on faith and morals, and on charity above all, but otherwise they could be as radical or conservative as they chose. Fourteen years before I had spent the night with Father Kutchera and we had discussed Tolstoy until early morning. I had been advertised then to debate with the head of the ROTC at the Student Union. At the last minute the military authorities had forbidden an officer to debate with a pacifist so I had the meeting to myself.

I had many questions from the floor this night, and many of us adjourned to Father Kutchera's study until midnight. My old time Quaker friend, Francis Hole, was out of town so I enjoyed the hospitality of John McGrath, circulation manager of THE PROGRESSIVE, and long time admirer of the CW. The following night some Quakers and pacifists and Father Kutchera met with me at John's. I also spoke to a group of students at the University Baptist center where my old friend Shorty Collins held forth. I had him speak in Waukesha in 1929 on "Stop the Next War

Now." I was glad to meet Ivan Bean, who with Bill Ryan and myself, were the three non-registrants in Wisconsin in 1942.

My old-time friend, Francis Gorgen, now lived in his home town of Mineral Point, Wisconsin. He came to get me, to spend Thanksgiving.

Real tax refusers are difficult to find so I couldn't miss Walter Gormly whose car had been taken by the tax man a year ago. He met me at Cedar Rapids in a car not registered in his name and we had a pleasant evening, along with a professor at nearby Cornell College who was interested in my anarchist ideas especially. I promised to speak to his class next year. Walter is a technician and an expert on efficiency for small business. He had done time in Sandstone, after quitting a good job because of the war work in the plant where he was employed.

Dave Dunn and Mignon McMenany met me at the bus in St. Louis and I spent several days in and around the Pio Decimo press. I especially enjoyed the sung mass at Monsignor Hellriegel's Holy Cross Church, and his robust faith and energy. We drove out to see Cy Echele and family and met with Quakers and young Catholics interested in the more radical CW program. Father Joseph Becker, at St. Louis University, introduced me to his class which was studying unemployment. I stressed the fact that there was no unemployment on the land. He read some of Peter's Essays and we all discussed the anarchistic implications of the Green Revolution. A very fine man indeed was Father Becker. Before I had joined the Church I had often used the word Jesuit in the Protestant connotation, which meant double talk, but now Father Becker and my memories of Father George Dunne in Phoenix gave the word Jesuit a new meaning.

Larry Heaney had been my especial good friend in the Milwaukee CW, so I was pleased to meet Ruth Ann Heaney and her children. Two of them resembled Larry. Marty Paul had met me at the train. We went over rough roads until we reached the farm. Here I felt at home among the oil lamps and wood stoves and cold bedroom upstairs. Marty had worked hard with very little result, until now he begins to see growth. Their four children danced around, bashful and happy. Jack and Frances Woltjen came over the next morning, and after a pleasant visit by Ruth Ann's fireplace they drove me to the bus. We all talked theories but we also knew something of hard work—and the loneliness that goes with detachment on the land.

It was nearly a twenty-four hour ride on the bus to Denver. I sat next to a boy who was going to work at the atom bomb plant in Washington. He had graduated from high school and looked hopelessly upon a possible army life. He offered no patriotic comments as I gave my conscientious objector history, read a CW that I gave him, but was bound to follow the line of least resistance. In Denver I was glad to stay at the home of a lady who puts CW's in the book rack at her church: Mrs. Kennebeck is a CW fan and the mother-in-law of my old friend Elliot Wager who says that my debunking of everything in the world, except the CW, at an anti-war meeting of Wheeler in Milwaukee in 1941 gave him the push which ended up in his joining the Church. I had not met him since then. Two Jesuit priests and other young Catholics came one evening to the most enthusiastic of small meetings of my trip. I had spent four days in jail in Denver in 1942 for selling the CW on the streets, but despite the super-patriotic atmosphere of secular and ecclesiastical Denver I feel that there is a real basis for a CW house there. Helen Ford and Mildred Mowe of the FOR left welcomed me; I had never met Paul Kermeit, who had done time as a CO, and was happy to meet him here at their evening meeting.

In Albuquerque my friend Monsignor Garcia welcomed me although he disagrees entirely with my ideas and with CW radicalism. An evening with Al Reser and Bob and Betty Reagan was the extent of the CW interest in this community. Al and Catherine had bought a house west of town. I had hoped that they would get as far as Phoenix. My good friend Rev. Soker of St. Paul's Lutheran Church was called out of town, the night before I arrived. I was pleased to see a sign "open for prayer" on his church door. I visited employers with whom I had worked during my five years here, and walking the six miles out in the country after mass early one morning, I did not at first recognize Lipa and Ernesto about whom I had written in the CW in 1945. Pickets walked in front of the chain stores, as they did in Denver. I had only a few CW's left but encouraged the pickets and gave them CW's. I spoke to Brother Mathias at his clean and orderly House of Hospitality where the atmosphere is that of social work and not radical like the CW. Father Schall was not home when I went to Isleta Pueblo. I visited old friends among the Indians there. They liked my report of the Hopi. I spoke with a leader of the Jemez Indians who came to see Monsignor Garcia. He was Catholic and appreciated the CW which I gave him.

I met my daughter Carmen in Santa Fe. She met me at the bus as did also some friends with whom I had corresponded for years but had not met: Peter and Florence van Dresser. Carmen teaches music here at the home of that cult to which she and Sharon and Selma belong. I had an extra fine vegetarian supper with her and the cult friends where she rooms. She is of a more demure type than her individualistic sister, but despite the years of separation she was kind and sweet to me, and she lives the same dedicated life as does Sharon, and is gracious and beautiful. A boy in this home had refused to do any work for his employer on a job at Los Alamos so had lost his job. Carmen looked through my missal and knew the Kyrie, Gloria, etc. from her musical studies. She also was sympathetic to my becoming a Catholic, as there was no chance of my belonging to her cult.

I spoke to a group of Quakers, FOR members and Catholics in the home of the grey uniformed nuns, medical missionaries next door to the house where Carmen rooms. This order has hospitals in India and here in Santa Fe and Augusta, Ga. They perform maternity services on call, as these two areas have the greatest infant mortality in the country. Dorothy had spoken here six years ago, and I was welcomed by the intelligent nuns who did not let their interest in their immediate problem keep them from seeking to understand the wider Christian Anarchist view of the CW, which I presented.

"Scabbing on the system," said my friend Peter van Dresser, as he pointed to the stone battlements built to hold his windpower generator. We had driven up from Santa Fe the sixty miles north to this beautiful 50 acres, stretching in narrow strips at the base of orange cliffs, through which ran a small mountain stream. Half of this acreage had been cultivated for many years. A road wound up from the village three miles away and on toward the nearest neighbor twelve miles distant. Peter and Florence had sought for months for just such a place and in despair had driven west toward California. On the way they had come across this Shangri La and had bought it from Mexicans living there. The adobe house was falling apart and now this new one was being built. Peter is one of the expert decentralists of this country: a house builder, and one of the few people I have met whose radicalism extends over into definite action. In this Land of the Sun the house will be heated by solar heat. Peter is a designer and builder of machines also. The workshop, which will come next along with the food grown in this sheltered mountain retreat, will prove that no one has to live in a town and be a slave to a boss but that every one can be self-sufficient. Sun, shade, water, earth, mighty cliffs, and not far away the magnificent Sangre de Christo (Blood of Christ) Mountains. Eleven-year-old Steve had helped his parents make a relief map of the immediate country and recently before the first deep snow had come he hiked one afternoon by himself over a rough, snaky mountain with pack, lunch and compass.

On the way from Santa Fe, we had stopped a few hours for a visit with Father Cassady, at Espanola. He is one of the few priests in this state who appreciates the CW. Peter and Florence are not members of any church and were enthused to find a man of the cloth who had been raised in this vicinity, knew its problems, and understood Eric Gill and the decentralist problem.

It was after dark as we came back through Espanola, and thus we were able to see the cold and formal lines of the lights, at the atom bomb plant at Los Alamos. This was a great contrast to the varied sprinkle of lights, here and there in the valley, coming from the homes of humble people. The story goes around here that an old man had a school where he sought to develop the mind and spirit of students, and that when the government confiscated it and built the greatest force of destruction known to man on his beloved mesa, he died within a few months. (I was to meet the daughter of the founder of this school, Peggy Pond Church, in a few months in Phoenix. The old man from whom the government took the school had owned it since the death of Peggy's father some years ago. Mr. Pond had established a school in the lowlands to the east and had been flooded out so thought this mesa would never be flooded. A flood of hate however reached up and now envelopes the mesa). Mammon is not satisfied with sending the murderous product of Los Alamos abroad, but in order to make the slaves employed in this devil's work contented the manure from countless small farms has been bought up to make the grass grow an unnatural green on

260

this murderous mesa. A social worker told me that an excessive number of maladjusted children live in Los Alamos.

In Flagstaff my good friend Platt Cline met me at the bus. He had just returned from Hotevilla where he had learned of the death of Fred, one of the Hopi conscientious objectors who spent four years in prison. Fred had been injured when a bus overturned. Platt has a tape recorder and I was pleased to listen to the words of Andrew, as interpreted, telling of the Hopi traditions. Platt caught me unawares and recorded my picketing experiences as I was talking. He was interested in my reasons for becoming a Catholic and just why I joined the Church, so this was also recorded.

The papers recently carried a story about the Civil Air Patrol, seeking to build up an excuse for their existence by planning to drop Christmas presents to the Navajo and Hopi Indians. The true Hopi announced that they did not want presents through this anti-social channel. The Hopi work hard and they are poor, but they want little to do with the white man and his Coca-cola culture . . . A visit to the American Friends Service Committee local office with their hazy goodwill activities, the other extreme from the air-plane Santa Claus, completed my visit in Flagstaff.

Arriving in Phoenix after four months and four days abroad, I found it raining, and within a few days was irrigating and working as usual.

Fr. Marion Casey and the author

MAKE STRAIGHT the WAY of the LORD

Ade Bethune

CHAPTER 12.

I Become a Catholic
September 21
to November 17, 1952

Maryfarm
Chrystie Street
Peter Maurin Farm
Hutchinson, Minnesota

"When will Ammon join the Church?" asked a friend, of Father George Dunne.

"When it get's underground, I suppose", he answered.

I felt that in ten years or more the capitalist or the Communist dictatorship might have all of us radicals in jail, and then would be time enough for joining a church. I had always said that a priest or preacher who blest war could not bless me.

When picketing that Wednesday in August of 1950, I had momentarily felt drawn to the Church. Also for a moment at Fr. Casey's retreat at Maryfarm in August of 1952 I felt that there might be something inside the Church that I ought to have, but that was only for a second and I thought of it no more. I attended mass daily after that retreat because I was at the CW and loved them all. So when Bob Ludlow went to Uniate mass at the Ukranian church, each morning I got up early and went with him. If I was at Peter Maurin Farm I went to mass there. I did not understand much of it and it did not mean much to me. I was busy writing on this book, speaking to all kinds of radicals, and answering letters that came to the CW. Father Casey had left for Minnesota and I was glad to have met him. I told him that if I ever joined the Church he would be the one to baptize me, but I felt no reason to even think of joining it now. Dorothy had said not to join the Church because I loved her and the CW, so if, in addition, I loved Fr. Casey, the first anarchist priest I had met, this only meant that I had fine radical friends who were Catholic. The Church which upheld the rich landlords in every country when it was in the majority and who still blessed Franco and Peron, and still blest war—that was the Church that people thought of when the name Catholic was mentioned, and not the Catholic Worker.

It was Saturday the 20th of September when Dorothy mentioned that she had to talk to a Communion Breakfast at the Hotel Biltmore the next morning to 600 employees of Gimbels. I knew what these confabs consisted of: they all got together and said: "God, Jesus, Gimbels! God, Jesus, Gimbels!" Pretty soon they were saying "Gimbels, Jesus, God", and finally ending up with only the word, "Gimbels". It was the old Pie in the Sky racket. As the old I.W.W. song went:

> "Long haired preachers come out every night;
> Try to tell you what's wrong and what's right
> But when asked how 'bout something to eat,
> They will answer in voices so sweet:
>> You will eat
>> Bye and Bye
>> In that beautiful land
>> Above the Sky.
>> Work and Pray;
>> Live on hay;
>> You'll get pie in the sky
>>> When you die."

Around 9 p.m. I was typing in the office when Dorothy stopped on her way to the church. She said she did not know what to say to such a crowd so she would have to pray about it and ask for guidance. She came back in a couple of hours.

We all wished her good luck as she went, as the saying was, into the jaws of the lion next morning. In the afternoon Tom was called to the phone and received the message that I was to accompany Florence Quinn, who did secretarial work for Dorothy at times, and who had questioned me about "Rendering unto Caesar" at my first talk at the CW, to some free opera down in the village. Dorothy had mentioned about going there and I told her I didn't care about such things. Florence had tried to get reserved seats but only got a number to call to wait in line. I thought that as long as I was there I might as well stay for we could just as easily get 3 seats as 2. While we were talking about it Dorothy came up. She had been to see her sister Della after the talk at the Hotel Biltmore. She described how the big shots from the store and the chancery office breathed hard when she commenced her voluntary poverty, reliance upon God rather than insurance companies and capitalist effort, non-payment of taxes for war and Atom Bombs, etc. She described going to mass in the big Church nearby, and that right after Communion without any reason or warning the big organ burst forth with the blasphemy of the Star Spangled Banner. This was a most holy moment after partaking of the body of Christ and it was broken up by this war-mongering. Everyone stood up in honor of this God of Battles. Dorothy did that thing which only St.Francis or Gandhi would have had the spiritual insight to do: *she knelt and prayed.*

Hearing her tell of this gave me the one positive jolt of my life since I knew in solitary in Atlanta that I loved my enemy the warden. Here was I, brave and boastful about my great One Man Revolution. I had faced the taunts of crowds and of the police, had felt nearly alone in opposing the draft in two wars. I was making a good fight. I remembered right then of my debate with the head of the American Legion in Milwaukee, Sam Corr, at the Grand Avenue Congregational Church in 1941, before Pearl Harbor. The flustered assistant minister stood between Sam and me on the platform before the crowd, saying "Now what song will we sing? Oh, Onward Christian Soldiers, with your permission Mr. Hennacy." "You fellows can sing it. I won't", I replied. Accordingly I sat stubbornly in front of them all while they stood and sang. I felt mean and I expect I looked mean. And they glowered at me. I was the first to speak. I said, "I suppose you folks will wonder why I did not have the courtesy to arise and sing with you. I wouldn't sing such a song in prison and stood the chance of going to solitary many times. One young fellow walked out of prison chapel when they sang it and did a month in solitary. So I'll be damned if I'll stand up for such a war mongering song on the outside." The next day the Milwaukee JOURNAL commented on my stubbornness.

Now all this came back to me. I called myself a non-church Christian. I was just a stubborn smart-alec—perhaps with more knowledge than many others I met, but still moving along with a handicap of lack of spirituality. Now I knew my lack of it. How was I going to get it and where? I did not dare admit to myself outloud that I was slipping, but I did say then with tears in my eyes to Dorothy, "You have shown me a great light; you have made me ashamed of myself. This is the biggest jolt that I have received in my life. Where it will lead I don't know, but from now on life is going to be different for me."

That next week was full of meetings. One night Dorothy and I had planned to visit a certain Communist whom I had known 30 years before, but it rained very hard and we did not go. Saturday we called up and invited this Communist and family over to Peter Maurin Farm for the Sunday afternoon. That morning we went down to the old church near Tamar Hennessy's where they go to mass. The old priest had set aside a plot where Peter Maurin's body could be moved from far away Brooklyn to be near the farm named in his honor. I had promised to clean weeds off the plot, but this had already been done by a caretaker. So Dorothy and Tamar and I carried rocks and made the boundaries of the plot.

Around 1 p.m. the Communist and his wife and teen-agers came. We

264

all went upstairs, above the chapel, to the library where there is a loom and spinning wheel. We all teased and carded and spun and rewound wool. The oldest teen-ager asked me to explain anarchism. I did so. For several hours we all discussed Communism, anarchism, pacifism, war, capitalism, etc. We were just as far apart as people could be: Communist-atheist and Catholic-pacifist-anarchist. Yet all that time there was not one harsh word or loud voice or intemperate bit of speech. We did not agree, but there was that spirit of brotherhood which ought to be over the whole world. There was that thing that the Catholics call Grace. There was that thing which we of the CW called The Green Revolution.

For supper we had home-made baked beans and all the home-made whole wheat bread we could eat—with a few loaves wrapped up for the Communists to take home. The Communists had recorders with them, and they played all kinds of folk and popular songs. Without anyone requesting or suggesting it they commenced to play Christmas carols. None of us remembered to play The Red Flag. As they left the teen-ager said, "Ammon, I want to thank you for explaining anarchism to me." Now I'll swear that among all the radicals and pacifists and even Catholic Workers, I never met up with such good manners as this.

Dorothy took them down to the bus. I looked around for something to read and saw a book on the table, *An Anthology of Russian Short Stories,* and of course looked up the one by Tolstoy. It was one I had never read: "The Diary of an Insane Man". I have not seen it since and my memory of it might not be accurate, but the impression I received was that this man said that when he was a boy he had not hit back when another boy had hit him, and people had called him foolish or crazy. Then again, when he had grown up and the peasants had stolen wood from his forest, he had not done like others and taken them to court, but had said nothing about it. This was also foolish and crazy. And now, yesterday, he had sold all he had and given to the poor and had been committed to the insane asylum. How Tolstoian!

Dorothy went upstairs at once to read and write and I went towards the barn, where I slept upstairs, above Fr. Duffy's room. It was quite dark. Without any conscious intention it seemed I walked into the chapel instead of going upstairs. There was a candle burning by the Little Flower. (I didn't know what the Little Flower was. I had always bought Carmen and Sharon a red rose every day or two and had brought one for Dorothy when I could get one. I did not know how I was "working against my stubborn self", for Dorothy had put a rose by the Little Flower and it was there while I prayed and meditated for an hour or more.) I had always prayed for grace and wisdom when in a Catholic Church, and I did so now. Much of the time I was just quiet and did not say any prayers. I did not hear any "voices" but there came to me a clear assurance that the Catholic Church was the true Church, that whatever I did not understand would be explained to me, that I was not hurting the Church by remaining outside: I was only hurting myself. For I needed this spiritual insight that Dorothy had when she knelt and the main thing now in my life was to work toward getting it.

I did not think anything about theology. I had the confidence in my heart that this was the road upon which I was now entering. How fast I would travel depended upon myself, and upon more of this Grace from God that I had prayed for since 1950, and that had been present all that day. It was as if the Communist family represented my first Marxian Socialism by which I had gotten away from a bourgeois surrounding. God had brought them there to bless me by their kindness, tolerance and courage. It was as if Tolstoy himself was there, as represented in his short story, sent by God to bless me in my life of voluntary poverty and hard labor, in my tax refusal and anarchist emphasis. It was as if Dorothy had brought us all together by her great life of love and sacrifice, sent by God to bless me in deeper spirituality. I was very happy. I said to Dorothy in the morning, "I'm a Catholic! What am I supposed to believe?" I would have believed that Jonah had swallowed the whale if I was supposed to! She said not to be in a hurry but to study and pray and get the cobwebs out of my brain. She gave me Karl Adam's *Spirit of Catholicism*. A few days later, I had come upstairs from supper and was typing in the office. Dorothy was leaving soon on a speaking trip to the West. She called from the corner of the stairway. I looked up and here she was holding a whiskey bottle, half full, which she had just retrieved from an "ambassador" who had thought himself hidden in the dim hallway. I poured it in the nearby toilet.

In the morning, several of us got up early to go to the bus with her. We could not get out of the premises, for several men were sleeping against the iron gate at the bottom of the front stairway. They finally awakened and made room for us to get through to the street. We all went to mass at the ornate St. Francis church near the bus station, and as we left Dorothy placed the current red rose I had given her, with a prayer, at the statue of St. Francis to the left of the entrance. We went to the small lunch room down the street as it was not yet time for the bus to leave. In the midst of our meal a big taxi man came in and quarreled with a smaller one about some parking arrangement; finally swinging at him and bloodying his nose. The smaller man quickly picked up a sugar bowl and threw it mightily in the face of his opponent. The latter went outside screaming and seeking to rub the broken glass, sugar, and blood from his eyes and face. The owner of the restaurant was wringing his hands about who would pay for his damn sugar bowl. Dorothy asked me to open her grip which was near me. She took out a towel, got some cold water and went outside and bathed the face of the "aggressor". Thus her exit from New York was to be typical of the problems of New York and of the world.

Saying goodbye at the bus Dorothy remembered that I had not digested all of the events of the past ten days clearly in my mind. While I knew the direction in which I was headed I did not know how fast I would go in my search for spiritual truth. I had thought that I would read Karl Adam's book and the one *Lessons on Love* by Goodier published by the St. Meinard Press, the Catechism and other material, talk to Father Dunne in Phoenix and be baptized by Father Casey in the fall of 1953, when I again went to his Maryfarm retreat. I would meet Dorothy in Phoenix around Christmas and tell her of my spiritual progress. All that I remembered was that she whispered for me not to forget about "that other", meaning my spiritual growth. She says that she quoted from the Psalms "My heart is ready, O Lord", but I do not remember it.

Two nights later I talked on Christian Anarchism at the S.I.A. (anarchist) hall at 813 Broadway. I did not enter into Catholic dogma for I did not yet know much about it, but did as I had done for years, praised the CW. Most of those present liked my militant opposition to war and the payment of taxes for war. Several did not like my reference to the CW and one comrade waxed especially strong in his denunciation of the Church and the hierarchy. Before I could answer, up jumps Bill Ryan with a defense of the CW and the Sermon on the Mount, although he was atheistic. Bill had admired and known Peter in the old days.

With my heritage of disgust at Billy Sunday's hell fire and the "once saved always saved" Calvinist doctrine, which also linked capitalism and Protestantism as of God, I had always thought that the Catholic church must be just a little worse in every way than the Protestants. It seemed to be so dogmatic and did not admit of any of the whittling away of doctrine like the Unitarians, where a good book review takes the place of religion; or like the Quakers where their witness against war simmers down to admitting such a renegade and open advocate of war as Whittaker Chambers.

With all of my wrong ideas about the Catholic Church, I was now committed in my heart to become a Catholic, so it was up to me to see what all their theology meant. I had always said that if the Catholic Church was from God then it deserved all the more condemnation because it had departed so far from the Sermon on the Mount as to support war and capitalism.

Now as I read Karl Adam's small book I began to get a clearer idea of what the Church meant. I will go into detail on this subject because until this was made plain to me I could not really call myself a Catholic. The reader who knows all this can bear with my insufficient knowledge and understanding, and the non-Catholic who reads can go along with me in my search for truth. I do not want to become a theologian but I will at least have to know what certain terms mean to me.

Original Sin. I had for the most of my adult life followed the philosophy of Rousseau to the effect that we were born perfect but were corrupted by society—that is by government mostly—and by organized religion which commercialized the teachings of Christ and other great teachers and had blasphemously called evil good. Naturally I had not known the Catholic doctrine and had been antagonized by the extreme hell-and-damnation Protestant teaching. I knew that an anarchist society could not exist until people chose to do good of themselves, and as I looked around among anarchists and almost everyone else, it seemed that there was an awful lot of meanness in the world. How come? Even if the Roussean idea was correct, what could be done about it? So when I understood the Catholic teaching of original sin and how it was to be overcome by the Grace of God, then this was the main theological obstacle overcome.

267

In his book Karl Adam said:

"Though original sin brought a weakening of nature, it did not bring as well a physical deterioration or corruption of our bodily and mental powers."

This was an entirely different thing from being "conceived in sin and born in iniquity." The Grace of God brings man away from his blemish and the sacraments keep him away. If this has not worked out correctly for many Catholics, that is not my business. I had better attend to Hennacy first.

St Thomas in the Summa puts it this way:

"In relation to Adam we are to some extent like the children of a millionaire who has lost all his money. We cannot begin life with as much power as our father once had. But we have, through our own free will and the grace of Christ, the power to build up our fortune in good works. If we sin instead, it will be our own fault."

What had seemed to me a mumble jumble of holy water and criss-crossing, I now saw was the LITURGY, as the daily redeeming grace of Christ present. I blushed at the wisecrack I had often made when a Catholic mentioned Grace and I said, "or Ethel." I had quoted Giovannitti, the I.W.W. poet, to the effect that "The holy wafer is but kneaded dough . . . spit on their God." As a non-Catholic I had thought that the Holy Eucharist had a magic which dumb Catholics used as an excuse to keep on sinning, with the o.k. of the priest and the Church. I now saw that the priest might be fooled and a person taking communion might possibly fool themselves and those present, but God was not fooled. The sacraments *were* the actual body and blood of Christ. Whether Giovannitti, who was a fallen away Protestant ministerial student now turned against religion, wanted to scorn both the communion of sincere and hypocritical Catholics, and what proportion there were of hypocrites who attended mass was not my problem. I repeat that I had better attend to Hennacy and his growth in understanding things of the spirit, first.

As Karl Adam says,

"The sacramental grace flows directly from Jesus into the soul of the believer. The sacrament is no more than an appointed sign of Christ, an objectivisation of the gracious will of Jesus, a visible and perceptible 'I will, be thou made clean.'"

Now as I went to mass daily I saw that if a person was spiritually alive and wished to keep that way the perfect thing to do was to go to mass and take communion daily. This was not being priest-ridden. It was a means of spiritual growth. I was to join the church to praise God for the spirituality of the CW and for the Communion of Saints. The Catholic Church was open day or night and one could go in there and pray; it was not just a matter of listening to dreary theology on a Sunday.

I had looked upon the HIERARCHY as a lot of despots ruling the dumb masses who went to mass. To my astonishment the anarchist idea of no majority rule worked right along with this idea of the hierarchy and against the majority rule whereby Protestants elected bishops, and factions fought one against another. Not that there was no "politics" in selection of Catholic bishops, Monsignors, Knights of Malta, etc. But historically a guiding hand always seemed to produce saints among these materialists. Closely connected with this new discovery was the idea that there was more freedom *within* the Catholic church than there was on the outside where radicals would quote Bakunin or Marx and would no more think of being a heretic to them than a Catholic would be to the Pope. Yet here was a queer thing: all through the history of the Church there were bad Popes and scheming Cardinals and corrupt alliances with corrupt kings; yet somehow, there always arose a St. Francis, a Hildebrand, a Catherine of Sienna, and now the CW, to bring such a great light that there was a step forward despite the mistakes made. I was wrong to look at the corruption in the Church as being the whole Church and forget that within this great body there was a spirit which also produced great saints. This was not too obvious, and if a person wanted freedom in the Church he had to fight for it. But it has always been the case anywhere that the best things in the world have to be earned the hard way. Easy things come easy.

We are urged to speak the truth. Adam says:

"When He (Jesus) called the Pharisees whited sepulchres and a breed of vipers, and Herod a fox He was not inspired by any sort of hatred against individuals, but by the tremendous earnestness of truth."

In the small book *Lessons on Love* Goodier says:

"Our Lord was troubled in the Garden, but we are not told that He was troubled at the sight of the Cross."

Also *"Faith teaches us to believe in everybody, not as satisfied optimists, but as men among our fellow-men. Hope gives us the confidence that nothing we do is wasted. Charity goes further; it bids us not easily to miss a chance of doing good, not to act on the defensive, never to use the argument that we are not obliged as a reason for standing aloof."* Here is enough idealism for a radical.

THE POPE, I was to find out, is not a despot. He had to go to confession to any common priest. If ignorant Catholics followed him or ignoble members of the hierarchy when they spoke as very fallible human beings, and refused to listen to him or them when they spoke with theological authority, that was their discrepancy. As a good Christian and as a good Catholic I would do the opposite. Adam spoke of Pope Innocent III's being wrong when he inveighed against witches and of the Church's being wrong in opposing Galileo. These were matters of opinion, not of Christ and God and faith and morals. There was this thing also, that the value of the sacraments did not depend upon how good an orator a priest was. In themselves they brought grace. So with the Pope, he could be good or bad, but the truth of the Church was there all the time and even a dozen bad Popes could not kill the real Church. Adam says that no one can be sure, even the Pope, that he is in a state of grace and really saved Only God knows. I had often said and have heard others say that they needed no priest to come between them and God for they could deal with God directly. Generally this was an alibi, for while they *could*, they practically never *did* get a direct contact with God. And by taking communion from the poorest excuse for a priest there surely was no attachment to a great orator or divine by which notice of God would be deflected.

THE IDEAL. Adam says:

"Wherever a purely human ideal seeks to assert itself and men are taken captive by values less than the ultimate value, then the Church proves herself an irreconcilable opponent." And when the Church fails to do this it is also living up to its tradition for *"it is a field of wheat in which there is much cockle, a net that contains both good and bad fish."*

As Cardinal Newman says, *"The Church is ever ailing, and lingers on in weakness, always bearing about in the body the dying of the Lord Jesus, that the life also of Jesus might be manifest in her body."*

FREEDOM . . . CONSCIENCE ABOVE ALL—Karl Adam says that a man is bound to that which appears to his conscience to be God's will, although the judgement of his conscience be objectively false. No less an authority than St. Thomas stresses this obligation of the erroneous conscience. Even in so vital a matter as a belief in Christ, a man would act wrongly who should profess this faith against the judgement of his (erroneous) conscience. He also says that the Vatican Council condemns blind faith. *"He is bound to follow his conscience and conscience alone."*

Concerning pastoral authority, Adam says *"There is no absolute certainty that all the particular measures of the pastoral authority are according to the mind and spirit of Christ."*

Therefore if I, as an anarchist and pacifist, do not agree with the prevailing support of capitalism and war by the clergy that is perfectly o.k. I do not have to agree with them. I have freedom. There is also this dogma, that it is Grace from God and not the great brains of theologians and the hierarchy that have produced real Christianity.

LOVE. Adam points out that the supreme test was *"See how these Christians love one another."* So this is the best of arguments why those of us of the CW who stress returning good for evil and are pacifists and anarchists are really working with the spirit of the Church. How can those who bless the killing of Catholics by Catholics in wars love one another?

Adam says that many theologians become so narrow that they do not see the luminous truth that,

"The Kingdom of God is not a kingdom of the sword, that a man should forgive his offending brother seventy times seven times, and that fire should not be invoked from heaven upon unbelieving cities."

Father Goodier says,

"Love does not always calculate, does not always consider pros and cons, is not always prudent, as some philosophers understand that virtue, does not always look for success, but once aroused shuts its eyes, 'gives and does not count the cost, fights and does not heed the wounds, toils and does not seek for rest, labors and looks for no reward.' lays down its life and does not think about it. Such a nature is dangerous? Yes . . . it is

270

the essence of all greatness to face what is dangerous . . . The man who would truly love, and know to the full what it means, will beware of that timid, limping thing which sometimes parades, and hides its littleness, under the name of prudence."

And Goodier again,

"A stoic, ancient or modern, who boasts of being above emotion, who acts by his reason and that only, who prides himself on doing his duty, has triumphed over love, scotched it if he has not killed it; it is a gruesome triumph, the triumph of the polar ice over the underlying land. Beauty there may be of a kind, beauty, and strength, and stillness; but life, and warmth, and growth, and fruitfulness there can be none . . . Love is a restless thing. Idleness and love are incompatible; love cannot go asleep . . . The wastrel who meets you may not deserve your penny; if he receives it he may even chuckle at his fortune, and your weakness; nevertheless, as often as not, he goes away with something more than a penny in his hand, something in his heart of which he is not aware, but which someday will bear fruit; the memory of one who has treated him above that which he has deserved, the memory of a kind deed done."

FOR ALL PEOPLE—Adam points out that for those who can understand but little the very minimum is required and for those who can understand and practice more, then more is required and expected, up to the criterion of St. Augustine who says, *"Love and do what you will."* What could be more anarchistic? And the final criterion, *"If thou wilt be perfect, go sell that thou hast and give to the poor; and come; follow me."*

"In the Catholic Church alone may we discern an organic growth in the consciousness of the faith. There is no petrifaction here. . . . thus the church has a message for men of every age . . . She does not hesitate even to take over pagan ritual and pagan symbols, whenever such things can be Christianized and reformed. This is not weakness, or unprincipled accommodation, but practical Catholicism. It is a direct consequence of that fundamental Catholic conviction that every genuine value, everything that comes from pure and uncorrupted nature, belongs to God and has citizen rights to His Kingdom."

"Other sheep have I which are not of this fold." Adam says, *"Wherever the Gospel of Jesus is faithfully preached, and wherever baptism is conferred with faith in His Holy Name, there His grace can operate. When the disciples would have forbidden a man who had not attached himself to Jesus from casting out devils in His name, Our Lord declared: 'Forbid him not.'"*

And again.

"In those non-Catholic bodies in which the apostolic succession has been maintained by means of valid Episcopal ordinations, as in the schismatic churches of the East, and in the Jansenist and Old-Catholic churches, she still recognizes the validity of all these sacraments."

Adam also says that among Protestants, and Jews, Turks and Japanese, Grace can abound and saints occur; especially among the Russians. It was

Pope Clement XI in 1713 who especially rejected the proposition that "outside the Church there is no grace." The praise of Gandhi by the CW has aroused the ire of the near followers of the excommunicated Father Feeney who feels that no one but Catholics can go to heaven.

HERESY—When I was speaking in Minneapolis someone asked me if I was a convert of Bishop Fulton Sheen. I replied that he converted the big convertibles and that I came in the Left door. The same person wondered if I was trying to "bore from within" the Church. I answered that my purpose was to gain spiritual growth and everything I did would be in the open and in the tradition of the best of Catholic saints I hoped. He wondered what I would do if the Pope ordered me to pay taxes. I told him that I was willing to take the risk that this would never occur. A friendly priest gave me a good answer to this by saying "The Pope tells me to walk on my hands. So what?"

No use in speaking of such foolish things. However the priest said that in Catholic teaching a person was bound to live true to his conscience or there was no basis for morality at all. So I was glad to read what Karl Adam had to say about heresy.

"Catholicism has sometimes repelled and rejected outright an heretical position with all its implications, reasons and consequences in order to prevent any contamination of revealed truth, and then, when the danger of such contamination was past, has taken over these elements of truth which heresy had grasped but wrongly emphasized, and moulding them into harmony with the whole of revelation, has consciously built them into her teaching and maintained them."

I can now see that it could be that the emphasis on Christian Anarchism by the CW might cause the hierarchy to ban the CW. Karl Adam says that Aristotelianism is used by church authorities today, but was forbidden as "the source of all heresies" and not allowed to be taught at the University of Paris in the 13th century.

In the first edition of this book when I had been a Catholic less than a year I said that if I were the editor and were ordered by the Pope or the Cardinal to cease publication, I would do so for the ultimate good of the Church. But after mature deliberation I decided that I would not do this. In February of 1960 for instance, while I was speaking in Chicago at the Catholic Worker house at 164 Oak Street, a phone call came from the Chancery office and a loud voice could be heard roaring that unless we took the name Catholic off our headquarters they would send the police and have the place closed up. It was a Monsignor who had evidently been angered at the complaints of Catholics who objected to our distributing anti-tax leaflets in front of the Federal Building and protesting the arrest of Rose Robinson for non-payment of income tax. I told Dorothy about it later that day and she said, "His bark is probably worse than his bite. We have had this kind of trouble before."

And she mentioned how she had had to go to the Chancery office to hear complaints about some of Robert Ludlow's articles in the past.

272

But Karl Meyer, who is a fine young man, but only 22, did not question the order and changed the name of the house to St. Stephen's, after the first martyr who had been a server of tables, and whose feast is celebrated the day after Christmas.

I do not blame Karl for who at the age of 22 fights the Chancery office. But I felt to rationalize this and say that the name Catholic Worker means nothing and that we could act just the same under any other name is cowarly. Dorothy disagrees with me on this and does not think Karl cowardly. I feel that Dorothy because she is kindly and motherly naturally upheld Karl in his stand. Under such circumstances I would not obey, but I would go and try to talk to the Cardinal or Chancellor first and explain my right as a Catholic to act according to my conscience. I do not think that I will be excommunicated for disobeying Caesar and being a radical anarchist, for I do not deny Church dogma, but only the support of Churchmen for exploitation and war but if it ever did come to that I would consider myself excommunicated like St. Joan of Arc. Those folk excommunicated themselves, not her. I would still be in the *real* church, the church of the saints.

SAINTS were fellow-workers of Christ. Much of my attraction to the Church was for this Communion of the Saints. While some Catholics might seem superstitious and foolish in their veneration for certain saints, yet this has to be allowed, for with it can come great spiritual growth at times.

INDULGENCES. I had often asked about them, but never did get a clear explanation. Adam made it appear logical, although in the past they were a source of great scandal. And today they are not the most important feature of the Church but are a means of helping weaker Catholics—out of the great reservoir of sanctity of the Saints. Adam says that *an indulgence is not a remission of sin but only of the temperal penalties attached to sin.*

CHURCH AND STATE—Adam says that the Church has not for long been the handmaiden of any state, although this has happened at times. I feel that it has happened nearly all of the time, but if the name Catholic means universal then it really means it was not Italian, Spanish, American or any other church, but a Church Universal.

SEX. I had often said that Catholics did not believe in birth control because they wanted more children born so there would be more Catholics and more money for the Church. It really isn't that bad. A woman wrote a letter once to a vegetarian paper saying that there were two main sins: White bread and birth control. There is no doubt that they are both unnatural and detrimental. Catholic teaching on sex (outside of the native Irish who get so puritanical they put the Puritans to shame) is much more natural and wholesome than the terrible Protestant "garment of shame." It is not my fault that the Church makes itself look foolish by insisting on the wickedness of birth control because it is mechanical when she takes all the rest of the mechanical civilization that goes with it: Atom Bombs and all. It is a sin not to have a child conceived but when he grows up it is o.k. to kill him and have him kill others in war.

I over-simplify this for emphasis, but if the reader gets the point I will add that the Church condemns birth control because it frustrates the end of action. Like eating for pleasure and vomiting after, like the Romans did. It is contrary to natural law and therefore immoral. But so is killing!

Now after ten years I tend to agree with Dr. Frank Lorimer, Professor of Sociology at the American University, Washington, D.C. and honorary president of the International Union for the Scientific Study of Population, who in the Winter 1963 issue of CROSS CURRENTS, reviews a book, *Family Planning and Modern Problems*, by Fr. Stanislas de Lestapis, S.J. I quote "Nevertheless the statements of some priests imply a tolerance of irresponsible reproduction as the natural consequence of the unregulated satisfaction of sexual impulse. High fertility, as such, and large families in particular have been honored without respect to conditions, motives, or consequences. Fr. de Lestapis repudiates this point of view. A true interpretation of Catholic doctrine supports the ideal of responsible parenthood . . ."

The accusation has been made that the use of contraceptives leads to sexual abnormality and perversion. Dr. Lorimer answers this objection, "This thesis lacks substantial basis and is an unwarranted slander on the private lives of many non-Catholic couples and of some high-minded Catholics who do not adhere to the teachings of their church in this respect." And he adds, "Are not desertion, illegitimacy, and irresponsible procreation greater evils than contraception?"

I have heard whisky faced, obese priests, who would seem never to have controlled their gluttony to tell young couples to sleep together but to have "self-control."

I Am Baptized

Dorothy had not planned to be in Chicago but suddenly a meeting was arranged and she wrote to me in Cleveland that she would be there November 7th. I had planned to be there about that time also, and was glad to meet her and tell her of the progress of my reading and thinking and praying. I had planned to be in Hutchinson, Minnesota to see Father Casey around the middle of the month but was two days late getting there. Dorothy had not known just when she would speak there but she arrived a few minutes after I came, not knowing I was there.

In conversation I asked Father Casey what was the first thing to do when you joined the Church. He said it was to be baptized. I asked him how much you had to know to be baptized. He replied that no Catholic really ever understood everything as he should, and had to accept much on faith. There would always be some ideas for each of us that would remain a holy "mystery." He and Dorothy spoke of the Ethiopian who wanted to be baptized right away, while there was the opportunity. I read the Catechism and the Creed and said I believed it all, although there were some points that needed to be cleared up. Father Casey felt that I had a better understanding than many who were born Catholic or who were converts. In studying the Catechism I asked him about the question of obeying parents and from this it flows that we should obey civil laws. We agreed that if a Catholic in conscience felt that it was a sin to register

274

for the draft, pay taxes for war, and otherwise be a denial of the Sermon on the Mount, then that person was bound to disobey man and, as St. Peter did when arrested twice for breaking the law and speaking the name of Jesus on the street, answer, *"We should obey God rather than man."* It would not seem logical that by saying "Render unto Caesar" which meant giving taxes to kill in war; to spread hatred and lies about the enemy; to return evil for evil; that Jesus would nullify all of His Sermon on the Mount.

When the Catechism came to the commandment "Thou shalt not kill," it was asked when was it permitted to kill? The answer was, "in a just war, in capital punishment and in self defense." While this might be the rule for those who follow the old eye-for-an-eye teaching of Moses, we felt that a Christian who was led by the Sermon on the Mount could do none of these things. Today there is no "just war," for civilians are being bombed, and even by the regular rules of a just war the idea of war is out. Many states and countries do not have capital punishment and murder is not more prevalent there. Despite that fact I live in a state and a country where it is the law, I am not called upon to be an executioner or a prison guard. If I pay taxes to support such a government I am denying Christ, and am a part of returning evil for evil instead of returning good for evil. And of course when it comes to defending oneself by violence, I have already defended myself in a better way when the man locked me up with a knife—and a person should not go backwards and take up the sword. So to one who tries to practice the Counsels of Perfection, to do less is to follow Christ that much less. Therefore to be a better Christian Anarchist and a better Catholic is perfectly logical and within the theological setup of the Church.

Dorothy had said that she would be my Godmother when I was baptized, and Bob Ludlow would be Godfather by proxy as he was in New York. That evening Dorothy spoke in the church basement to Father Casey's people and I was asked to say a few words. When a man asked me about "Rendering unto Caesar," Dorothy spoke up before I got my breath, saying, "The less of Caesar's you have, the less you have to render." After the meeting was over Dorothy, Father Casey and I meditated and prayed for a time in the church, and then, after further explanation as to the meaning of baptism I was baptized. It was all very sacred and solemn. I saw that water, salt, oil—necessary parts of nature—were linked with my entry into the Church, and as Dorothy had told me once, sensing my objection to holy water, "All water is holy; it makes the corn grow for the Hopi."

Later that night I made my first confession to Father Casey. He encouraged me in my faith, abjured me to keep up my radicalism, and told me that he had baptized me "Ammon St. John the Baptist Hennacy." I did not know that a new name was given for the New Life in Christ. Later I asked him if that meant I was to have my head cut off like John the Baptist. He inferred that this might take place and be performed by a Cardinal, as such was the history of many true rebels.

In traveling around I had lost track of the day of the month. I found that I had been baptized on Nov. 17, my mother's birthday, and the Feast of St. Gregory the Wonderworker. Both Dorothy and Father Casey said I would have to do more than move mountains.

The next morning we all went to mass and I took my First Communion. I was very happy.

After mass we drove 110 miles, picking up Don Humphrey, and went to Grasston, Minnesota to see old man Paul Marquardt. He and I were the only ones who refused to register in both wars. He had read the CW for years and was overjoyed to see Dorothy. He was "A little shaky from the last round with the officials" but his eyes were bright and he was tolerant and friendly, although he belonged to no church, reading the Bible here on his farm. We all felt truly humble in his presence, knowing that he was one of those "not of the fold" of whom Jesus spoke.

In the beautiful mass at Monsignor Hellriegel's in St. Louis, meeting with Fr. Kutchera in Madison, Wisconsin and with Father Becker at St. Louis University, as well as with many friendly Jesuits on my trip, I was welcomed and asked to speak on my radical Christian Anarchist ideas. Here in Phoenix, Father Dunne, Father Xavier Harris and fellow priests at St. Mary's, and my old friend Father Lawrence in the parish where I am a member, all explained very kindly matters of doctrine which puzzled me or which were new to me. Father Bechtel asked me to speak again to his Newman Club, in the nearby college town of Tempe. When Dorothy came to Phoenix for a week in January, I took the time off and was able to go to mass and communion daily. I have much to learn and much humility and love yet to learn, but I feel I am on the right road.

Before and after Conversion

Reading over my ideas on religion, as written on August 31, 1951, in the light of being a Catholic, naturally I found that I would place a much different emphasis, now. But all of the criticism which I have made of pious frauds in the churches still stands. Likewise all of the really religious and ethical ideas still seem to me worthy.

I will review my ideas paragraph by paragraph, placing first what I thought in 1951 and right afterwards what I believe now.

"All things work together for good to those who love God."

Naturally if I believed in this truth then, I doubly believe in it now. GOD, or Good, as I prefer to spell it, is the only *real* force that exists. That only is real which is eternal, and evil is temporal and defeats itself. Despite all the churches and prayers, very few people really believe in God; for if you *believe* in a thing then you must *act* as if you believed it. Otherwise you are just talking about it. Most people believe more in the power of evil for they do not trust in God, but put their trust in government, insurance, politicians, medicine, war, and anything but God. (1951)

God, of course is supreme, although it may look as if the devil is running the world, including most churches. It is foolish to take a Pollyanna attitude that evil does not exist. To work with it against good is even worse. *I feel that positive action in "living the life" is more important than calling names. I feel that the system of violence is falling to pieces and those of us who believe otherwise need to "keep the torch burning," as the saying is, so that there will be some hope. When evil piled on evil destroys itself, there will be those of us who will help with that* real *force, God, and be His instruments.* (1953).

THE BIBLE in places reads like the word of God, especially when speaking through brave prophets like Daniel, but mostly the Old Testament is an alibi for tricks which the Jews worked upon their neighbors to get their land and women, and then put the blame for these tricks upon Jehovah. Practically every sin is condoned for the benefit of the Jews. (1951).

The Bible still needs to be interpreted by Grace from God and not by every little, loudmouthed Bible-banger who starts a holy-jumper church. My criticism came from my Protestant training of believing every word as literally coming from God and not as the growth of spiritual understanding during those centuries. To be sure I had never been as ignorant as it is said Governor Ross Sterling of Texas was, in the thirties, when he was quoted: "What good will Greek and Latin ever do for our children? If the English language was good enough for Jesus Christ, it's good enough for Texas."

I remember just now that the Communist whose gracious spirit helped me that Sunday at Peter Maurin Farm to come to prayer and meditation when I decided to become a Catholic, was Jewish. So despite my former anti-Semitic attitude I find that a true Christian should have no animosity toward any race. I shall seek to remember this. (1953).

JESUS taught something entirely different from the Old Testament. I believe that Jesus was born of a virgin, but this is not the important thing; the important question is—do we follow Him? His message of returning good for evil, of loving your enemy, of turning the other cheek, had been said by the Rabbi Hillel and others, but it was mostly conversation, for no one had been noted for living up to these ideals, much less dying for them. This of itself would have made Him a spiritual leader. But others have spoken holy words and lived in caves and done miracles. Jesus chose his disciples not from these hermits but from live men in the world, and He met the issues of the day instead of talking "pie in the sky." He said that a rich man could not enter the kingdom of heaven; He spoke of the wrong which lawyers, church officials, and landlords did to the poor—and He drove the moneychangers out of the Temple. The lesson to us today from the life and methods of Jesus consists in the fact that:

He had an ideal.
He recognized the evil which the rich did to the poor.
He wrote in the hearts of men a Way of Life which they themselves must use to save them from sin.

When He had to "put up or shut up" He bravely died and did not pipsqueak.

If we claim to be His followers we should likewise be brave. (1951)
All that I thought on this matter I still believe and with the added idea that He brings Grace to help us live according to His ideal through the sacraments, daily mass, and communion. (1953).

THE EARLY CHRISTIANS lived as brothers, holding property in common. They were also pacifists, for they "could do violence to no man," and many were martyred because they would not be soldiers. They were also anarchists inasmuch as they took no part in government, were denied communion if they went to court on anything, and no one was exploited. All this was changed when Constantine the Great was blest and took over the Church. It has since then always been an organ of reaction. (1951).

The Early Christians. I agree with all that I wrote on this subject. The only difference now is that although the Catholic Church and other churches have been organs of reaction I feel that the Catholic Church does not necessarily have to keep on in this role. What the other churches do is not my problem. It is not impossible for the spirit of the early Christians to be prominent again in the Catholic Church. (1953).

PAUL AND THE CHURCHES—have turned this message of Jesus around to mean nearly the exact opposite of what Jesus intended. His Mercy and Love they have turned into a bargain counter whereby to "sin and be sorry" is all that is needed to join a church, get "pie in the sky" and pay little attention to life on the earth. The fundamentalist Protestant churches are the worst in this respect. Witness the following from a leaflet handed to me while I was picketing and put out by the Palmcroft Baptist church here in Phoenix: "I offer full pardon; YOU'VE nothing to do; just TRUST ME; I'll keep you and take you above; and make you forever 'a son of My Love.'" (1951).

Anyone has a preference as to apostles and saints. I admire St. Paul's courage and his 13th chapter of First Corinthians, but generally speaking I believe that his influence was to dissemble rather than to clarify the ethics of Jesus. So with St. Peter, I choose to emphasize his "obey God rather than man" and not to follow him when he praises those in government authority. I think that he denied Christ the fourth time when he spoke contrary to the Sermon on the Mount in upholding the return of evil for evil. Neither he nor St. Paul can be blamed for the mechanization of religion, done since, in their names, so I would not now phrase my opinion of them in the same harsh terms. (1953).

PRAYER—"The fervent prayer of a righteous man availeth much." By the same token insincere prayers are just so many wasted words. My prayer said often while working is: "Great God of Truth and Love, bring peace, protection, enlightenment, and encouragement to," then listing my friends and especial enemies. On Sunday's, while fasting, or when passing a Catholic Church I enter and kneel and ask for Grace and Wisdom for me, a sinner, directing my appeal to Jesus on the Cross. I use no holy water and do not cross myself. (1951).

I agree with all that I have written above on this subject except now I do use holy water and do genuflect and cross myself with meaning, as a help toward spiritual growth. There is spiritual power when spiritual people recite the Rosary. (1953).

THE CATHOLIC CHURCH has produced saints like Francis of Assisi. Personally I do not believe in the fall of man, Heaven and Hell in the accepted sense, or in bargains in sins according to rules set up, not by Jesus, but by warmongering theologians. The Catholic Church seeks members, quantity, not quality. Those who get promotions are not holy men, but business men. They all support war and capitalism. (1951).

Of course my expression on the subject of the Catholic Church has changed very nearly entirely. As explained elsewhere I could find no better explanation of evil than that given by the Catholic Church. The priests to whom I have spoken tell me that "it doth not yet appear what man shall be," so no one knows exactly of what heaven consists, and as to hell, it is best described as absence from God, or darkness, perhaps a burning or yearning of conscience, but not necessarily the fiery hell where one would have to be composed of asbestos to function in this place where fundamentalist Protestants and some Catholics would send the unsaved. I know personally of Cardinals, Archbishops and Bishops who have praised the radicalism of the Catholic Worker. A few super-patriots among the hierarchy stand out as companions of Joe McCarthy but many of the others blush to think of his tactics. As a whole the hierarchy is more radical than the laity. So while the CATHOLIC WORKER is the leaven it is not the only leaven for there are radical Catholics in France and other countries too. (1953).

REINCARNATION—the belief of Gandhi seems to me to be more logical than one chance for heaven or hell in this one life. Belief in it is not very important. It is "living the life" that counts. (1951).

Reincarnation does not now seem to me to be important. The important thing is spiritual growth. I accept the Apostles' Creed as to life after death. As much as I or anyone else can improve spiritually here and now is all to the good, no matter what the exact measurement of the future life may be. (1953).

"Do you really believe it?" said the Old Pioneer to me when I returned from my trip last December and told him that I had been baptized a Catholic. "I sure do," I replied. "I had a kid brother who 'got religion' at a revival meeting when he was 16 and it lasted all of his life. He was a good man," said the Old Pioneer, and added, "Do you feel certain now and not afraid?" I told him that I was never uncertain nor afraid since my time in solitary in Atlanta, and the reason I had joined the Church now was to praise God and for the Communion of the Saints. He had been reading the Bible all winter. He had several versions including the new Catholic New Testament (Young Orme gave that to me to remember the old man by). Most old timers around here already know the Mormon Bible and they either believe it or they don't.

One Saturday afternoon while I was cleaning the Old Pioneer's house for an hour, I noticed some teen-agers on bicycles pass by my shack, to the left of the garage. I thought nothing about it, as people often come in here, thinking this road goes some place, only to find it a dead end. When I went over to my shack a little later, I found all of my papers, books, etc., piled in the middle of the floor and some articles of value missing. I had heard of other places being messed up by youngsters. When I told the Old Pioneer about it he was very angry and said I should call the sheriff; that the kids should be "whupped"; they didn't do enough "whupping" these days.

After I had told him I would say nothing of it to the authorities and would pray for the kids, as I had for vigilantes who had come after me here, in order that they would not get into more mischief, he calmed down. Later he was reading the CW and said to me, "Every time I read Dorothy's column I get ashamed of myself in such a big house; why, do you know 100 families could each have a house and more than an acre on this land—but then I'm too old to think of such new things." Then, as if he had admitted too much, he added with a wry smile, "I can't see Dorothy feeding all these bums who never work and wouldn't work. They do nothing but drink. But who am I, a sinner, to tell Dorothy anything?"

One evening he told me "If I ever joined any church it would be the Catholic. You believe it, Dorothy believes it. It is the only church that doesn't whittle things away into nothing." I told him that I was not the one to tell him to hurry for I had been nearly 60 years about it myself. When Dorothy was here he told her that he had advised me to join the church. Perhaps he had this in his mind to tell me, but he never really told me. He was only glad that I did. He had always admired Ghandi.

280

Although he had never been in any war, he was a great student of history, and knew the details of battle formation from almost any battle you could mention. He knew Arizona history, too, and admired the Hopi. He had met my Hopi friends when they came.

Three times in the five years that I had been here, he had been taken to the hospital for several weeks because of his stomach ulcers. Several times I noticed a light in his house around 2 a.m. and came over and asked if he was sick. He had spells of vomiting. I wanted to sleep on the couch here so I could be near if he wanted me, but he felt this would be giving in, and he wouldn't have it. I had wanted to feed the chickens, or gather and pack the eggs, but he felt this was his job and no one could do it just right. I had taken the morning off twice a week through February in order to accompany him to town when he took the eggs to the store on Tuesdays and Fridays and carry them in for him. He had stopped to have an examination by the doctor and took different kinds of medicine. I had planned to go to the Hopi with Joe Craigmyle on Feb. 28th, and when I came back he was going to the hospital, but that day he felt worse and his son took him in. Right before I left he did show me the details of the care of the chickens.

I called him on the phone several times when I returned and the day before I picketed, March 13th, I visited him. I had sent in the *Arizona Sketchbook* by my banker friend Frank Brophy for him to read and it was the last thing he read. (Brophy had good naturedly inscribed it to "The One-Man-Revolution from a Pipsqueak.") The Old Pioneer's ulcers had healed and formed scar tissue which closed the duodenum so that he would starve to death if not operated upon, and there was only a chance that at his age of 80 he might stand the operation. He wanted to know about the chickens, and told me to eat all the cracked eggs I liked "and even some good ones." He was operated on the 14th and came out of the ether alright. Several days later when I had worked all day and all night and was very tired and was sleeping soundly, I awoke feeling that something was wrong with him. I prayed for him. The next day his son said they had been called and he had nearly died at just that time. He held on and did not get worse for a few days.

I phoned Father George Dunne whose name the Old Pioneer knew from my mention of him before, and asked him to call at the hospital. Father Dunne called that evening and said something about his being an "old timer" who had many things to do yet. Mr. Orme corrected him sharply, saying, "Old Pioneer sounds better." He then asked to be baptized. A doctor, a Catholic nurse, and a Catholic woman who happened to be visiting just then, were witnesses. When Father Dunne left, the Old Pioneer said "God bless you, Father Dunne." Two days later, on March 26, the old Pioneer died in his sleep.

Both of the Phoenix papers and the ARIZONA FARMER had editorials about his death. While I was waiting in the funeral parlor, I became acquainted with the Secretary and Vice-President of the Old Pioneer organization, recognizing them from conversation I had about them previously with Mr. Orme. As his wife and son and daughter-in-law were Episcopalians, it was thought best to have the funeral under that auspices; they were glad that Father Dunne had been there to give him the peace of mind which he desired.

The papers spoke of him as being an Empire Builder and of his fine services to the Valley. But up to the very last he was just as much an enemy of the bankers and industrialists who sought to commercialize the Valley as he had been 20 years before, when these local papers had made fun of his "one-man-revolution" saying he could not overturn the bankers who had control of the Water Users Association. The old man had denounced this control which they had gained by subdividing big holdings into names of dummies who thus gave them more votes. He got the rules changed and was president of the Association for 14 years.

They forgot to mention that in 1916, when the I.W.W.'s were driven out of Bisbee by the copper owners, Mr. Orme resigned in protest from the local Rotary Club which approved this action, saying, "If they can drive I.W.W.'s out of Bisbee they can drive Orme's out of Phoenix. To hell with you."

He it was who also told me when I offered to leave his place, rather than to have him bothered with tax men nibbling at me for my anti-tax attitude, "stay here and fight them." He knelt to no man. Now, belatedly, he knelt to God.

One night recently after irrigating for a long stretch and when I was thus sleeping very soundly, the Old Pioneer appeared to me in a dream. He looked very tired and not at all belligerent. With a soft smile he said, "I wouldn't 'whup' them. I wouldn't 'whup' them, now." I then awoke. This was not a vision like that of the Blue Flame; it was just a dream, but it was real and full of meaning to me.

The Old Pioneer

282

CHAPTER 13

Jails and Picketing

1961 to 1964

*New York City; Las Vegas,
Nev.; Cape Canaveral, Fla.;
Washington, D.C.; Omaha;
Sandstone Prison;
Polaris in Conn.*

*Eileen Egan, Jewish student, the
author, Walter Kerell, CW assoc.
editor. Picketing at the last air raid
drill held in New York City: 1961,
at City Hall Park.*

The only place I was bothered was at 43 and Lexington where I was told I had to have a license. I explained to the cop that the Jehovah Witnesses had settled this in the Supreme Court years ago, but he didn't believe me and took me to the police station and then to the magistrate's court on 2nd Ave. near the CW where the judge released me on my own name for a few weeks. (The night before Dorothy and I had been walking along that street and she said, "there's the jail." I said I didn't care, but the next day I was in it.) Patricia Rusk, an ex-airplane hostess, who then lived with us came along to help me sell CW's daily, and the next Friday at 43 and Lexington another policeman tried to stop me but I talked him out of it. The next Friday Bertha Tisius and Eileen Fantino stood on the east side of the street and I took my accustomed place at the pillar at the entrance of the Peerless stores. Dorothy was to come also, but she was late. I told the girls jokingly that if they got pinched first I would call the office and if I got pinched first they should call the office. They were talking and faced away from me while the cop of the first encounter grabbed me and took me to the police station. When Dorothy came and wanted to know where I was they waited and looked around and finally called the police station, whereupon Dorothy stood at my usual place and sold the CW the rest of the afternoon, saying, "Ammon Hennacy, one of our editors, was just jailed for selling the CW; buy the Catholic Worker." And along comes the atheist anarchist Jackson MacLow and helps with the sales.

The American Civil Liberties Union wanted me to be the guinea pig to prove free speech for the Democrats, Republicans, Socialists and Communists who moved on when a cop told them to. So I deferred my anarchistic principles for them and allowed Emanuel Redfield, a friendly Wall Street lawyer, to appear in court with me and plead not guilty for me. The judge would not listen to any argument for free speech and told my lawyer to appeal the case if he wanted to, giving me a $10 fine or 5 days in jail. Patricia was in court and visited me in my cell with Mr. Redfield wondering why I did not pay the fine for I could get it back again but could not get the 5 days back. I explained that I would never voluntarily give the government any money.

We jostled in the prison wagon up to the Tombs which is near the City Hall. After a time I was lodged in Lower D12 with Dan, in for drunkeness, who had bought a bottle of liquor when he cashed his $55 Lackawanna check and had been rolled. Now he was picking up butts. I offered to buy him a package of cigarettes from the trusty but he said they charged 50¢ after lock up and it was better to buy Bull Durham when the regular commissary wagon came around the next day, so I gave him a quarter. One aged Jew got ten days for selling pretzels on Wall Street without a license (and the city won't give you a license). He had not learned yet to pay off the cops. We were fed on trays which were pushed into our cells. There was a runway where in the daytime we could walk back and forth. In the morning my name was called "for Rikers," which meant for Rikers Island, part of the men's prison. As we lined up in the outside corridor a screw with a cigar in his mouth yelled out our names, but his articulation was thus impeded; few could understand what he was saying. It seems he was an educated man for he used seven lettered words instead of four lettered ones as he shouted, "Get in the . . . . line you . . . . bums."

Again we were packed in the wagon and jostled to 134th street where we were not permitted to leave our smoke filled vehicle for the breezes on the ferry. About 150 of us sat on benches in the big receiving room at Rikers Island and were counted and recounted and finger printed. We all stood naked and all body openings were examined supposedly for dope which we might smuggle in. The wine sores on the old men, the stooped and broken bodies of many, presented a sorry specacle compared to the beautiful shiny black bodies of the Negroes among us, for there was no segregation here. We all took chances that the clothing handed us would fit. Most of us were short timers who went to Dorm 8 in the workhouse division.

My number was 419327 and Emil had the number next to mine. He had done 30 days for drinking and had only been out a few days and by some miracle of police inefficiency only drew 5 days this time for being caught in a doorway drinking from a bottle. Emil is a counterman and swears that in the future he will stick to beer, for this he can take, but not whisky. After he had done his thirty days he went to the blood bank but his blood was too thin to be taken. In this dormitory there were upper and lower bunks. I had a top one, and as is the custom in these modern jails there were no mattresses, only springs and several blankets and sheets. The man on the bottom bunk told of bits he had done and of the corruption of the police and of the regular payoff to them.

Marching from Dorm 8 at the far side of the workhouse with about 150 inmates we came at 5:30 a.m. to the main building where there are eight or more three-story cell blocks where those live who are doing from one to three years in maximum custody. We marched two by two and when I saw through the glass door the dining room full of convicts hunched over their aluminum plates eating their meagre fare in assembly line speed, tears of rage and pity choked me. This was the first time I had been in jail for 35 years. Was this all that our boasted civilization meant? I remembered what Tolstoy had said when he had first gone to Paris and saw an execution by guillotine and he had then started on the thought which led him to be a "Tolstoyan": "There is no such thing as progress in the world," he felt if this was all that man could do to man. And again these immortal lines from Edwin Markham's, *Man With The Hoe*, that I had recited hundreds of times in solitary in Atlanta years ago, came back to me:

> "Down all the caverns of hell to their last gulf
> There is no shape more terrible than this;
> More tongued with censure of the world's blind greed;
> More filled with signs and portents for the soul;
> More packed with danger to the universe . . .
> Through this dread shape humanity betrayed,
> Plundered, profaned and disinherited
> Cries protest to the Powers that made the world;
> A protest that is a prophecy . . .
> O master, lords and rules of all lands
> Is this the handiwork you give to God . . .
> How will the future reckon with this man
> How answer his brute question in that hour
> When whirlwinds of rebellion shake all shores
> How will it be with kingdoms and with kings
> With those who shape him to the thing he is
> When this dumb terror shall arise to judge the world
> After the silence of the centuries?

"Don't go away mad. Just go away." This is the sign as you enter and leave this House of Correction. By the most visionary use of the word no one would suggest that anyone is ever "corrected" there. For from the time you are told not to smoke by a guard who takes a cigarette out of his mouth to tell you to get in the . . . . line until your fingerprint is taken the second time as you leave there, there is nothing but the assembly line of the "count" and changing of the guards. It took us from 8 to 10 to get checked and rechecked and about 75 of us left on the ferry Tuesday morning with the usual seven lettered word thrown at us by the screw. Emil accompanied me to the CW where we were welcomed by Murray Kempton of the *New York Post* who wrote in his column the next day on the contrast of McCarthyite Catholics and us at the CW. A Monsignor Martin had complained at a Communion breakfast here in New York City that $5,000,000 had been raised to fight

McCarthy "solely because of his Catholic ideal." Kempton said that "The forces against Ammon Hennacy have far more than $5,000,000; they are all arms of all states from the traffic cop up to Georgei Malenkov. It is, he remembers, better to light a candle than curse the darkness . . . We have no more radical instrument in our society than the Catholic Worker group. Its members are pacifists, reconcilers, and anarchists, and they believe that the service of Christ involves secession from the state." He ended by saying that upon my return from jail I "seemed altogether the least lonely man on earth."

Patricia had shivered in the cold selling CW's on the corner where I had been pinched while I was in jail and on the next Friday we went up there again to disobey the law, "for a bad law is no better than any other bad thing." The same cop was there and he told us to go ahead and sell CW's for all he cared for he would not be the servant of the priest who had complained against me. Patricia and I went to the Church down the block and wanted to see the Msgr., but he would not see us. We came back again in an hour and we heard his voice saying he would not see us, whereupon I asked his housekeeper for stationery upon which I wrote: Dear Msgr.: I would like to know if you or any one in authority complained about my selling the CW at the corner of 43 and Lexington. If you did, out of courtesy to the Church I will go across the street, and if you didn't I'll stay here for I have earned the right to do so." I never heard from him afterwards. The appeal of the ACLU to the next court was lost but the appeal to the higher court in Albany was won unanimously. I had the right to sell the CW and my book as I was not engaged in a commercial venture. It was six months before this decision was reached.

On a Sunday morning I was selling CW's across the street from St. Patrick's Cathedral as usual when a cop came along and said that his brother was a priest and I had no right to sell my Communist paper here. I told him it was not a Communist paper and if it was that this was a free country and I had a right to sell it here, showing him a newspaper clipping of the court decision.

"I don't care anything about the law. If I don't want you here I'll arrest you and you won't be here. You will be in jail. And if the judge lets you out and you come back I'll pinch you again; and if he lets you out and you come back I'll pinch you again; I'll wear you out."

"What if I wear you out?" I asked.

He laughed and went away. If you are not ready to die you are not ready to live.

JUNE 15, 1955   *Air Raid Drills*

In the spring of 1955 I saw in the paper that there would be an air raid drill on June 15 and all were supposed to take part or suffer a penalty up to a year in jail and $500 fine, this being a state law. I told Dorothy and said we must get ready to disobey this foolish law. I contacted Ralph DeGia of the War Resisters League and he got in touch with others, F.O.R., American F.S.C. & W.I.L. and so accordingly when the time came we had a whole group in City Hall Park ready to disobey when the whistles blew. The television men were there and asked Dorothy to tell why we were acting as we did, but she asked me to speak as my voice would be louder so I told them

286

that if a bomb dropped there would be no police left to arrest us and that the whole thing was a farce. Robert Fisher, a young man uptown who was working as a social worker in lieu of going to the army heard me on television and took a taxi and came down and went to jail with us. He is a Unitarian. Just before the whistles blew we gathered at the War Resisters Office at 5 Beekman Street where Bayard Rustin advised all of us not to refuse shelter unless we were ready to take the consequences of perhaps a year in jail and $500 fine. There were some who handed out leaflets until the last minute and then took shelter. Dorothy and I had signed a leaflet which was well printed by Dave Dellinger which we distributed. It began "In the name of Jesus who is God, who is Love, we will not obey this order to pretend, to evacuate, to hide . . . we will not be drilled into fear . . . We do not have faith in God if we depend upon the Atom Bomb" . . . ending up with our pacifist anarchist idea of refusal in every way to support war and governments.

We were ordered to take shelter and refused to do so. We were packed into vans and when we were waiting to be booked at Elizabeth Street station we noticed an elderly man with a badge on his cap whom we thought might be an attendant. I gave him one of our leaflets and it was not until later when our indictment was read in court that we discovered that he was Rocco Parelli, a bootblack, who had been sitting in the park knowing nothing about the air raid drill, who happened to be the first one arrested. Our indictment thus read: "Rocco Parelli and 28 others wilfully refused to take shelter." It was entirely fitting that this common man, not a scholar, intellectual or radical, should symbolically head the list, representative of the workers of the world we were trying to awaken. There were ten of us from the CW: Dorothy and I; Carol Perry, a tax refuser from San Francisco; Patricia Rusk; Mary Ann McCoy; Eileen Fantino and Helen Russell of the group who work with Puerto Rico children in Harlem. Mary Roberts, an artist, Stanley Borowski who has helped in selling CW's and picketing, and Michael Kovalak, who with others had picketed the Chancery office at the time of the graveyard strike in 1949. A. J. Muste, Ralph DeGia, and Bayard Rustin were old time War Resisters. Jackson MacLow, our atheist anarchist friend; Bob Berk, a young radical I had known in Tucson, and Dale Brotherington, a Quaker who had corresponded with me from Florida. Andy Osgood, a War Resister who had visited me in Phoenix and Hugh Corbin of the same group who had picketed with us in Washington, D.C. Also Edith Horwitz whose husband had been a CO, and Jim Peck, an old time CO. I had not met Henry Babcock, an elderly Quaker, or Henry Maiden, a Quaker with whom I celled. Kent Larrabee, head of the New York City Fellowship of Reconciliation. Orie Pell of the Women's International League for Peace and Freedom, but the Queen of us all was Judith Beck, the actress who was supposed to be playing Phaedra in The Living Theatre that night but who went to jail with us. Dick Kern had promised us at the War Resister's office not to "go limp" but to put on his show by himself elsewhere, but true to form he became enthusiastic and so the papers had a picture of him being carried by the police into the van. And Joan Hamilton had walked into the group and did not seem to be able to make up her mind whether she wanted to go through with it or not; as she was pregnant and she was later released.

By chance we fellows had sandwiches but the women did not have anything to eat all day. Around 11 p.m. we appeared before Judge Louis Kaplan. As our names were read off the Irish clerk it seemed did not wish to admit that an Irishman by the name of Hennacy could possibly be among these radicals so he persisted in pronouncing my name as "Hennacky." Some of the girls laughed lightly at this and the judge pounded his gavel and wanted to know what was the matter. Judith answered pertly that she had had nothing to eat and was giddy. The judge asked her to step up and she did quickly, and not demurely. He told her to stand back and shouted angrily, asking her name, where she had been born, and who paid her rent. She answered without the customary "your honor" with which these dignitaries inflate their ego. This enraged him all the more and he wanted to know if she had ever been in a mental institution. "*No, have you?*" was her classic answer which will reverberate through these musty halls until the time when courts and prisons will cease to exist. The audience laughed and the judge shouted "Take her for observation to Bellevue psychiatric ward." Judith screamed dramatically and her husband who was one of the audience in the courtroom, a Yale graduate, stood up and shouted "You can't do this." The place was in an uproar. The judge ordered the courtroom cleared by the riot squad and we were all put back in our cells. Later he had us brought in and read off a written statement saying, "*Theoretically three million people have been killed in this air raid and you are the murderers.*" He placed our bail at the unheard of sum of $1500 each.

At that time we of the CW had not discussed the matter of bail so we accepted it after being held for 24 hours. I had thought to plead not guilty with the others to show our solidarity with them, but Dorothy being a better basic radical than I am persuaded me to plead guilty on the anarchist principle of "we did it once and we will do it again; and no legal quibbling." So Dorothy and I, Carol, Mary, Stanley, Dick Kern and Judith pled guilty, but Judge Bushel deferred our sentence until those pleading not guilty should have their trial.

After our arrest the diocesian paper, The *Catholic News*, N. Y. City, felt that we were presumptuous in our "private interpretation" when the Church always upheld obedience to duly constituted authority. On the other hand the *Commonweal* in a long editorial praised our stand: "The saint and the radical (and they are often the one and the same) share a common, ironic destiny, honored by posterity, they are usually persecuted during their life times . . . We honor the saint and the radical — dead; alive we find them too uncomfortable for our tribute . . . A society without its radical is a dead society, just as a Church without its saints is a blighted Church . . . we need them to remind us of uncomfortable truths, to rebuke our slothfulness and ease." The Ave Maria magazine although not agreeing with our ideas felt that we had the right to disobey the law. The *Nation* and the *Progressive*, the *Pittsburg Post Gazette*, and of course Murray Kempton in the *N.Y. Post* praised us. The *Chicago Tribune* also praised our stand, and *Harpers* magaine for October ended a long semi-editorial under "Personal" with this sentence: "Two of the group — Dorothy Day and Ammon Hennacy, of the Catholic Workers movement — have a long and honorable history of getting arrested for doing what ought to be done but no one else cares to do. In meekly running to cover, the rest of us have only compounded the dishonesty of a Civil Defense program that is neither serious nor safe." However the *St. Louis Catholic Register* devoted pages to prove from a legal and theological view that we should have obeyed the law. *The Boston Pilot*, oldest diocesion paper in the U.S., did not refer editorially to our case but had an editorial written in their August 13, 1955 issue headed *Need for Confession* by the editor Monseignor Lalley, our good friend, saying: "*The greatest single act of human destruction in the history of the world must be placed on our doorstep — and we did it the second time at Nagasaki the next day as if to show that it was no accident . . . . The supreme tragedy of this moment — a decade later — is that we still refuse to strike our breast and acknowledge our sin . . . American aid around the globe . . . We cannot buy back our innocence with all the gold in Fort Knox; guilt must be washed away in penitence . . . The nation would be appalled even today if an international tribunal should suggest that those who decided to drop the bomb should be called to some new Nuremberg to answer for it. But God is not mocked! We must wonder, however, how long He will wait for our repentance.*"

Fritz Eichenberg, who had been in court, provided us with a sketch for the front page of the July-August CW. The case dragged on and on and finally on Dec. 22 we were all found guilty and sentence suspended. We had all expected to get time and when I came home Tom Caine had prepared a card wreathed in black on my desk, "To express our sincerest condolence on this sad occasion." Opening it I saw in big letters: "So Sorry! NO JAIL!"

JULY 20, 1956

This year the night before the air raid drill Dorothy spoke with others at the Quaker Meeting House on East 20th Street and we distributed our leaflet headed BAN THE BOMB, BY PERSONAL PROTEST and signed by Dorothy and me. This time we chose Washington Square and there were more reporters and television men than there were of us, and also the police. We gave our message to all of New York City. There was a fellow sitting near me whom I did not know and he happened to be the first put into the police van and I was the second. I asked him what kind of a radical he was: "I'm no radical; I am an instructor of Physics at Purdue University and I was visiting in town and reading a book and you folks surrounded me and now I am pinched with you." Later in court he told this to the Judge saying that he knew by his study of the effect of explosions and bombs that if all the City of New York offered a visitor was to stand in a doorway to be safe, he knew it was foolish for he would have to be 500 feet underground to be safe. The figures were that 4,372,939 would have died in the city in our mythical warfare. So David Caplan was fined $25 and set free. Reporters who were present offered to pay his fine but he had the money and paid it himself. From the CW Dorothy and I, Stanley Borowski and Deane Mowrer went to jail. Jim Peck and Ralph DeGia who were arrested the first time, were with us again. They and Tom Rick, Al Uhrie of Ossining, and Marcus Cohen were of the War Resistors League, as was Patricia Daw a young pregnant woman. Of the Quakers Bob Gilmore, Sec. of the American Friends Service Committee in N.Y. City, George Willoughby of Philadelphia, sec. of the Central Committee for Conscientious Objectors, Dale Brotherington, who was with us last year, Mrs. Elizabeth Quigley of

Agawam, Mass. and Dan O'Hagen of Pa. Others were Nathaniel Cooper, a Zionist, Hollis Wyman who had been in the air force at Hiroshima but was now a pacifist, and Michael Graine, a young atheistic anarchist friend of mine. Our case was postponed from time to time until October 31 when we appeared before Judge Kaplan who told us we were no different from other criminals and he would give us the works. He told us to come back on Jan. 15 and he would sentence us. Dorothy and I, Deane, Stanley, Dan O'Hagen and Michael Graine pled guilty and the others stood trial.

We were all prepared to get 6 months but the night before Little Tommy in the office showed me an item in a late paper that Judge Kaplan had been promoted to be a judge in the Court of Special Sessions at $3500 a year increase in salary. We wondered if he would hold our case over or if we would get a worse judge. We were relieved when a kindly Irishman Judge Comerford appeared and listened patiently to us about our ideas — even a lengthy poem by Mike Graine. He gave us $25 fine or 5 days in jail although the D.A. wanted to hold me on a charge of conspiracy. This judge was sympathetic to the I.R.A. in the old days we heard, and was marshall of the St. Patrick's Day Parade. We all did the 5 days and many people picketed the Women's House of Detention where the women were jailed. I took half a dozen books with me thinking I would have plenty of time to read them but I was not allowed to take them inside with me. As we were being processed a guard at Hart's Island asked me "Where's Dorothy?" I said she was in the woman's jail. "Where's Hennacy?" he asked. I told him who I was and he said he had read the CW for years. One of my fellow prisoners was arrested for sleeping down by the river; he had on an overcoat but no shirt. Another was arrested for panhandling and had $43 on him when arrested. His defense was that he "didn't ever want to be broke." We each had a separate cell with a mattress but the radio blasted until 9:30 p.m. Later Mike and Stanley went to Dorm 4 and Dan and I went to Dorm 16. There were about 80 prisoners in a dorm, two-thirds of them Negroes and very few grey headed men. The light went out at 9:30 and we were up at 5:30. For the first time in two years I had a good rest. We were not hurried at meals as we had been on Rikers Island and the guards were not so ill tempered and profane.

JULY 12, 1957

This time the protest was practically a CW one and it was made in the small park opposite the CW on Chrystie Street. Television and newspaper men gave us good coverage. Those arrested were Dorothy and I, Deane, Kerran Dugan who at that time lived with us and was an Associate Editor and young Karl Meyer, a convert whom I had met at St. Peter Claver House in Washington, D.C. several years before. Michael Graine and Dan O'Hagen again, and Judith and her husband Julian Beck. Sandy Darlington came from Seattle to take part with us. He did not know exactly what he believed but he wished to be counted with us. Later at Times Square a young Methodist couple, Richard and Joan Moses, had parked their car and all alone disobeyed the air raid warning. We met them in jail later. The judge this time was a tough Catholic by the name of Walter Bayer. He told us to read the Bible and said that we were a "heartless bunch of individuals who breathe contempt" of the law. He did not give us a chance to explain that most of us were anarchists who took no part in making laws so we did not consider any judge as our servant to enforce them. He gave us 30 days.

"*Unfit.Committment No.483325.Ammon Hennacy,Hart Island,Department of Correction.30 days. Admitted July 13,1957.*" So read my yellow card.

It was not until then that I remembered that it was July 13, 1917, just 40 years before that I had entered Atlanta Prison in World War I. I was called "unfit" for labor because I was over 60 and was put with the old men in Dorm 12. I helped as houseman a little and spent the rest of my time pulling weeds from my favorite vegetables (egg plant and peppers) in a small garden nearby. The Warden called me in and wanted me to rewrite something he had composed about traffic safety. I made it alive in a few minutes. Just then the prison doctor came in and the warden addressing me said that he had a plan to lower taxes which was to make bingo legal something like the pari mutual in horse racing. He asked what I thought about it and I told him it was crazy as hell for the charge which a third of the people came to prison for was gambling — the numbers racket — and it did not need to be sanctified by the state, as it had already been by the Church. He said he had a job for me in the Commissary department. I worked there for the rest of my time, getting $2 worth of goods a week for my work which was doing a little cleaning and checking of stock. Karl was under 20 and was sent to Rikers Island. Julian, Mike, Kerran, Bob, Sandy and I met in the yard at times, as we worked in different places, and sat in the sun with our shirts off, as did other prisoners. The glum guard imprisoned on the other side of the 12 foot fence had an unhappy time marching back and forth "guarding" us and took out his discomfort by telling us to put our shirts back on. The bread here was white but fairly good. Two thirds of the inmates were Negroes and were in mostly for selling dope. The fellow in the next bed to me had started at Elmira as a juvenile, had been transferred to Dannemora, and had been out only two years since then. I met Fr. Higgins the Chaplain and in his dealings with prisoners he appreciated my quote from John Dewey: "*A good man is one who, no matter how bad he has been, is getting better; and a bad man is one, who, no matter how good he has been, is getting worse.*" I had met him at Fordham before as he teaches there.

Meanwhile there was continual picketing of the women's jail where Dorothy, Deane, Judith and Joan were incarcerated. We picketed 24 hours a day. From 10 a.m. until 6 p.m. young women with their babies in carriages, and scores of students enlivened the atmosphere. We sang radical songs and had a good time. The cops, and the matrons at the jail were generally friendly after they got used to us. The *Commonweal* said that few Catholics protested when Dorothy was in jail because she protested against the destruction of mankind. "Those who protest against risque movies are given Catholic Action medals." And the *Boston Pilot* said, "The conscience of Dorothy Day is clear — can we say the same of our own?"

MAY 6, 1958

We had been picketing the Atomic Energy Commission at 70 Columbus Ave. for several years and there was a week of picketing going on when we heard that the air raid drill would be on May 6th. Bob Gilmore was told by the Quakers that he should not take the chance of getting three or more months in jail by disobeying the law with us, but he and I said that to cease our picketing for 10 minutes because of an order by another arm of the war making state would be indefensible on our part. So both Bob and Stewart Meecham of the Quakers joined Dorothy and me and Deane, Kerran and Karl Meyer. Al Uhrie came along for the second time and Art Harvey, a vegetarian anarchist whom I had known in Detroit and at Cape Canaveral disobeyed also. We made clear radical statements in court and were surprised when Judge Kenneth Phipps, a Negro, gave us 30 days and suspended the sentence.

APRIL 17, 1959

The night before the air raid drill some Socialists led by Dave McReynolds in the Village met with us and said they would also disobey the air raid drill, and Dave had an article in the *Village Voice* saying he would be with us. We issued a leaflet stating our position which was distributed in City Hall Park. Besides Dorothy and I and Deane and Karl and Arthur Harvey fourteen others disobeyed and we were all arrested. We five refused bail and the others were releasd on bail which I suppose I upped to $1000 for when he asked me if I did not believe in law and order I said "no" and was cut off before I could explain that I believed in God's law. The others were Dave McReynolds, Al Scott, a former CO, Scott Herrick FOR member and real estate man, Sheldon Weeks, Quaker, Thomas Grabell, Martin Smolin, Joe Caldwell a Catholic, Gil Turner, Joe Fraser, Walter Crutchfield, Bob Schoenhold, Joe Schulman, Milton Chee, and Bob Peck. Deane & Dorothy knew but not the rest of us until we met in jail that brave Janice Smith had come with her two children to the park and had been arrested also, but they released her. She reads the CW and says that her husband bought it from me at 14th and Broadway. After four days we five were released on our own name and had a day of freedom before we all appeared before kindly looking Judge Roe. Dorothy was at one end of the line, I was in the middle, and the judge commenced at the other end asking each one how many times he had been arrested on this charge and why he disobeyed the law. Attorney Glass spoke for the others saying that if the object of the law was to deter Dorothy it had not done so and would not do so, that he was not empowered to speak for her but had, as a man to express his thought. Dave McReynolds spoke clearly about Germans being asked to disobey Hitler and be true to their consciences so we also should be free to obey our consciences. Gil Turner, a folk singer gave logical reasons for his action. I said that I followed St. Peter as a Catholic and Thoreau as an anarchist, that I had no personal animosity toward judges, police, tax men, and civil defense men, but that they were all in a bad business. The judge asked me about rendering unto Caesar and I told him Caesar was getting too much around here and some one had to stand up for God. The *Village Voice* for 4-29-60 in a front page headline said *"TOO MUCH TO CAESAR, TOO LITTLE TO GOD. A judge and an anarchist traded Biblical quotations last Friday morning."* We five got 10 days in jail or $25 fine, and the others had sentence suspended as this was their first offense. I was in the Tombs on Sunday and went to Confession. The young Chaplain said "Hennacy, what about obeying the civil authorities?" I didn't know he knew my name but replied that the way I understood it we were supposed to obey God rather than man. He replied that the Catholic Church was not in favor of pacifism and the breaking of laws, but after a time he gave me absolution. Just before Mass he stood before us saying "This is the second Sunday after Easter. In the Epistle today it says to obey the civil authorities." It said a lot of other things but it seems he had to get off his commercial. The sermon was no worse or better than the average on the outside. Two guards at Hart Island wanted our literature, remembering me from the other times and also on television they said, when I was on Nightbeat. My number this time was 516337. I had a good rest and read historical novels, as there was not much work to do. I met several prisoners who were in for "jostling" which is an ineffectual attempt to pick pockets in a crowd.

There was mass picketing of the women's jail in the Village. *Commonweal* drew an analogy between Dorothy whose conscience opposed atom bombs now, and Major Eatherly, a Catholic, who had dropped the bomb at Hiroshima. For years he has been in and out of mental institutions as his guilt has deranged him. The *N.Y. Post* said editorially: "We feel a certain kinship with those behind the bars. For the notion that modern man can snugly protect himself against the hydrogen bomb by conducting such fire drills is a form of self delusion almost indistinguishable from madness."

MAY 3, 1960

I came home by plane from Spokane in the midst of a speaking tour in the west to be here for the air raid refusal. I had thought if we would have 50 it would be a great victory. When then sirens blew, there were 500 in the City Hall Park and another 500 on the sidewalks who laughed when ordered by the police to take shelter. *Janice Smith* had collected about 80 women with their children and there were hundreds of students playing hookey from school. *Kay Boyle*, the author, was right behind me singing *"Civil Defense Is No Defense; We Shall Not Be Moved. "Norman Mailer* and *Dwight MacDonald* were there also but the police were frustrated when they called upon us to move and no one moved. They wanted to know if we were not Americans and most people laughed. They arrested a few here and there, 25 in all, being careful not to get any leaders it seemed. Later in court I asked Officer O'Hearn who arrests us every year why he had not arrested Dorothy and me. "Why didn't you ask me?" he said, but we were in plain sight with our signs. I told him that next year there would be a thousand of us and he had better get more police. When the sirens had stopped blowing Dave McReynolds got up on a bench and shouted "This law is dead," and we all cheered. Television men asked me to lead a song celebrating our Victory so I sang John Brown's Body and said that we would all be back to break the law next year. Zita Ferron, Diana Lewis and Thomas Franz, a student, were Catholics among the 26 arrested. Judge Calazzo gave a patriotic lecture and sentenced them to 5 days in jail. I picketed the Tombs that night for 14 hours and Bob Steed picketed the women's the next night. On Sunday there was mass picketing at the women's jail, and I picketed for two nights.

The *Village Voice* had pictures of the demonstration and the *Nation, Commonweal* had editorials favoring us. The *N.Y. World Telegram* had an editorial entitled *Exercise in Futility*, saying "Yesterday's test can be called meaningful and successful only if a potential enemy's plan is to drop marshmallow puffs on N.Y. City — and to advertise in advance what time they are coming." Murray Kempton in the *N.Y. Post* had a typical article on *Laughter in the Park* which put the Civil Defense authorities in their proper place. On a Saturday night we had a party for the jailbirds and friends in Debs Hall where A. J. Muste and Paul Goodman spoke and Muste gave diplomas to the jail graduates. And later at the Community Church James Weschler, editor of the *N.Y. Post*, Kay Boyle, Norman Thomas and others spoke. Bob Steed and I picketed Brooklyn College in the rain supporting the hundreds of students who refused to take part in the drill there. 59 were suspended for four days, but as in our case, the leaders were not touched. Finally the college authorities gave in and rescinded some of the heat; a Fellowship of Reconciliation Dean being the one who suspended them. It was his job I suppose but he put his job above his pacifist ideals.

AIR RAID DRILL PICKETING

On October 3, 1960 Mary Lathrop, Jack Baker and I from the CW, and Ralph DeGia and others from the War Resisters and others from peace groups commenced to picket the Civil Defense Office at 46th and Lexington. We had told them in advance of our plans. We picketed 5 days a week from noon until 2 p.m. My sign read:

CIVIL DISOBEDIENCE

We

Call for 5,000

To Refuse to take part

In the compulsory

Air Raid Drill at

City Hall Park in 1961

Ammon Hennacy, Catholic Worker, 39 Spring St.

At times twenty people would picket with us and at times there were only the three of us. The employees at the Civil Defense were friendly. Linus Pauling stopped and greeted us kindly. I did not know him but Mary had heard him speak and introduced me to him. One fellow came with an umbrella and signs said that this was the perfect shelter. The police did not bother us. Many stopped to take our pictures. As usual students came and picketed for a few hours with us. Jim Peck came often and walked along with his premeditated stride. After 2 p.m. we went to a restaurant nearby and had coffee and warmed up. Carrying our signs there and to and fro in the subway we were often praised by people who saw us nearly every day. The Canadian Broadcasting Company asked me questions and while they played only a small part of the conversation they sent me a check for $100 for my trouble.

Once when there was a heavy snow we shoveled a walk for us to picket in. The lazy attendants at the Civil Defense did not clear the sidewalk, although all along the street the snow had been removed. Finally we shoveled the entire walk for them. If they are so worried about clearing people from the streets in an air raid and cannot even get the energy to clean their own sidewalk it is time they folded up. We continued our picketing until Jan. 1, when Mary went south with Dorothy on a speaking tour, and I went north and west. Jack picketed intermittingly during the spring.

APRIL 28, 1961

I had come home from Salt Lake City to be in time for the air raid refusal and held a sign saying that for the 7th time I had openly refused to take part in the air raid drill. I saw Col. O'Hearn and he saw my sign, but as the year before Dorothy and I were not arrested. A powerful leaflet was distributed, headed *"Brave Men Do Not Hide."* There were about 2,000 people refusing this time. I was asked to say something, and others spoke. About 40 were arrested and got varying sentences. I picketed for the women at their jail, and all night for the men in the Tombs, leaving in a few days to start the Joe Hill House in Salt Lake City.

After the demonstration Murray Kempton asked me to autograph my sign for his teenage college daughter whom I had not met when I visited him in Princeton several years ago.

VICTORY

In 1962 the farce of the air raid was so obvious that there was no compulsory drill.

TAX PICKETING

After the Old Pioneer had died in 1952 I stayed on at the farm at the request of his son until the estate had been settled. Meanwhile I had written a Declaration of Conscience giving my history, which was printed in the July-August 1953 CW. In it I quoted Thoreau: *"How does it become a man to behave toward this American government today? I answer, that he cannot without disgrace be associated with it. If 1,000, if 100, if 10 men whom I could name – if ten honest men only, if one honest man, in this state of Massachusetts, ceasing to hold slaves, were actually to withdraw from this co-partnership, and be locked up in the county jail therefore, it would be the abolition of slavery in America."*

During my first day of picketing a woman told me that she had a letter from her son in Korea, and that her three other boys would go to jail before they would go to war. "God bless you," she said. Now for the first time in my fasting I was a Catholic and I went to Mass and Communion each morning. I always notify the FBI, the tax men, the police, etc. of my picketing ahead of time, and this year I sent a typed letter to the 165 clergy in Phoenix asking them to pray for the success of my picketing if they could in conscience do so. I started the fast weighing 142 pounds. The scales which told fortunes on slips of paper came out with the dubious advice that read: "Don't always follow the line of least resistance."

Near quitting time on the next to last day a young fellow whose appearance marked him as of the nervous intellectual type, and not that of a rowdy, stopped and asked me if this was my sign that I was carrying. I told him that it was. He said that I had better call the police for he was going to take the sign and tear it up and dance on it, for no Communist could carry such a sign in his town. I told him that I was no Communist; that I was a Catholic and an anarchist. He replied that he was a Catholic. I asked him what parish he belonged to and it was St. Matthew's, the same as mine. I inquired if he had been at Mass the last Sunday and if he had noticed me selling CW's in front of the church. He had been to last Mass and had not noticed me. I told him that if he had looked closer he would have noticed a candle burning before the Blessed Mother for the success of my intention in this picketing and fasting. He didn't believe it. I asked his name and he told me but would not give me his address. I said that I did not believe in the police and if he got any pleasure out of tearing up my signs he could do so. He took them and tore them off the standard and danced on them there on the sidewalk. He refused to take a copy of my leaflet or the CW, muttering "Communist, Communist." I advised him to see our parish priest and get straight on the matter of the CW and he promised to do so. I then called the priest and told him what had happened. He did not remember the name of my patriotic friend.

I wanted to see the AP man on another matter so I went to the newspaper office. Here I saw my friend with the signs telling a reporter about the Communist he had found. I recognized the reporter from pictures I had seen of him although I had never met him. The reporter said that I was not a Communist for they all knew of my picketing activities for years. The patriotic Catholic said that he was a veteran from Korea and repeated that no one could carry such a sign in his town. The reporter said that he was a veteran of two wars and he had fought for just such things as freedom for Hennacy to carry signs and picket; that if the young man did not like my signs he could do as the pickets in front of the Whitehouse in the Rosenberg case did: get other signs and picket the pickets. The reporter also said that I was standing up for the freedom which was true Americanism, and although he disagreed with my ideas, that the patriotic young man was acting like a Fascist or a Communist in denying me freedom. The young man said he would come down the next day and take any other signs I would have. The reporter told him he was lucky he was opposing such a person as Hennacy when he broke the law for I would not take him to court. The AP carried the story of my torn signs and some reporters wanted me to prefer charges so as to make the story more exciting, but I explained my anarchist ideas which did not allow retaliation. No one bothered me the next day. Ginny and her boys came up at 3:30 and broke my fast with me and I left for New York on the 4 p.m. bus stopping at Platt Cline's in Flagstaff and to see the Van Dresser's in Santa Fe. Here the local paper which goes to the atomic workers in nearby Los Alamos printed the next day a factual account of my opposition in paying taxes for their bomb.

My first picketing in New York City was at the Custom House down near South Ferry where the wind blew the signs mightily at times. The CW printed a special leaflet about Hiroshima Day Aug. 6 also being Transfiguration Day. John Stanley, Stanley Borowski and Roger O'Neil helped me picket and Dorothy came around at noon for a couple of hours. Catholics said they had phoned to the Chancery office and that they were going to stop me. A cop said I was not allowed to picket and I told him I would call the Civil Liberties Union as to my exact rights and would be back in half an hour. I called and they said to go ahead. The cop never came back and a few days later he walked by and smiled. A cop argued with me about paying taxes and conferred with the tax man inside and I was not bothered. Several men stopped and said they would report me to the FBI. On the last half hour of our pickting some Catholic teenagers had Dorothy and me backed up against a car calling us Communists. Just then the lady who had called the Chancery office and found that they were "not for us and not against us" stopped in wonder, for she had not seen Dorothy picketing before. We were very tired from buffeting the wind and wear and tear of answering questions and we left inviting the youngsters to the CW. Now eight years later a boy is working in our office for the summer who spoke to me that day and got a leaflet and a CW. His father is a detective but he and his brother are Catholic conscientious objectors.

In August of 1955 Carol Perry who had quit her job with the telephone company in San Francisco and had done housework in order that no withholding tax would be taken from her pay, signed a statement with me and we picketed the tax office, Dorothy coming along at times also. One of my signs read *"The individul conscience Versus the atom-bomb? Yes, there is no other way." (Life magazine editorial Aug. 20, 1954)* Bob Steed had just come up from Memphis and he helped me picket, as did others, among them Judith Beck who had a dainty sign reading, *"Love and Life, not Death and Taxes."* A passer by demanded that the cop on duty "Arrest that man!" The cop did not know if he had the right to arrest me so he went to headquarters to find out and came back smiling, telling me to go ahead and picket. The employees in the building greeted me more kindly and there was no red ink spattered on us from the windows above as had happened last time. We gave out as many as a thousand CW's in a day.

About an hour before we had intended to go home on the last day a nervous ex-marine walking along with his girl friend worked himself up into excitement and a small crowd finally collected around Jackson MacLow, Bob and Dorothy. Carol and I were handing out papers at the other end of the street just then and we had gone to make a phone call. As we returned my heart jumped to notice a larger crowd and much loud talk, expecting to see Jackson, Bob and Dorothy in their midst, but happily they were picketing from the far end of the block up to the crowd. Later I heard what had happened. A sort of well dressed man said that all this picketing was a disgrace to his Church and wanted the crowd to beat up the Commies who pretended to be Catholics. He wanted Bob's name and called a cop who took Bob's name and address and went away. Dorothy had the good sense to refuse to argue with such excited people, so she and Jackson and Bob left the crowd to argue among themselves and went on picketing. Then an important and portly well dressed man came up and dispersed the crowd saying that he had heard Dorothy speak years ago and that the CW was a fine group of people, and that he was not going to allow any harm to come to these good Catholics. He showed the crowd his Knights of Columbus membership card and in a few minutes the side walk was clear. Coming over he addressed me by name and I recognized that I had sold him a CW at Pine and Nassau. We continued to picket for an hour with no more bother from anyone.

August 1956 I was picketing again at the Custom House and this was the first time since 1949 that I did not have the police or mobs bothering me. The Friday before my fast a new Irish tax man had come to the CW office to collect my taxes. He called me in his office on the seventh floor on the first day I picketed asking about my "hidden assets." After a time he seemed persuaded that he was not going to get any money from me and said he would pass my case up to his superiors. Later a tax man from last year met me on the picket line and in a friendly manner inquired about my fasting. Last year two T men came from Washington and questioned Dorothy, Carol and me several times at the CW and at 90 Church Street, saying that they would report their findings to Washington and would see what was to be done about our open refusal to pay income taxes. Each day Bob Steed helped me picket. A Catholic whose folks knew Sacco in an anarchist club in the old days came during his noon hour and helped hand out papers. One man seriously thought that I was advertising a service whereby people could learn how to get out of paying taxes. While resting for five minutes in the park each hour I noticed great shoots of Johnson grass disfiguring the scenery as they appeared between the neat evergreen border. Ordinarily I would exercise my anarchist prerogative and uproot them but I was too tired to lift a hand. On the last day as I was again resting, along comes the park attendant and asked the occupants of each bench to move in order that he might sweep a few dead leaves from behind the benches. Then he proceeded to sweep this refuse along the hedge, pushing it along with his broom indifferently so that some remained along the hedge to blow around again. It was not his job to beautify the park by getting rid of the unsightly Johnson grass. It was nobody's job it seemed, so my last act in the park was to pull it up.

In 1957 the tax office had moved to Varick and West Houston Streets which was nearer home, and as it happened this side of the building was almost entirely in the shade. Here I picketed from 6th to the 17th. Frances Rogosz from Minersville, Pa. helped me during the rush hour at noon and Bob Steed and Janet Burwash helped at times. As I had just come back from my strenuous Las Vegas picketing in the heat I was persuaded to drink buttermilk and orange juice at times during this fast. I had many expressions of sympathy from passersby and hardly any criticism.

In 1958 Zita Fearon of St. Cloud, a small blonde, helped me picket often, and Bob, Deane, Anne Marie Stokes and others cheered me from time to time. The peacemakers had invited me to address their conference but I could not do so as I was picketing, so they came for a day and visited and helped me picket: Ralph Templin who had known Gandhi in India, Bob Luitweiler who had been with me at Cape Canaveral, and Ernie Bromley active on many pacifist fronts. During all these years many of us had picketed uptown near the Japanese Embassy telling them that we were sorry our government had been guilty at Hiroshima and Nagasaki.

In 1959 my tax statement quoted William Lloyd Garrison, the first Christian anarchist in this country that he would not equivocate and he would not be silent and he would be heard. One of my signs read *"It is a high crime to break the laws of Jesus Christ in order to yield obedience to earthly rulers.*

Pope Leo XIII." Jack Baker, pretty Ellen Hollinde in her bare feet, and Hugh Madden, "my shadow," helped me picket. Hugh has whiskers like Uncle Sam, and is an ex-farmer, ex-Trappist novice, with a scratchy twisted rope around his neck. He fasted also and knelt at prayer every so often. A huge bale of paper fell from a truck in the middle of the street and no one paid any attention to it. Finally I left my picketing and edged it over to the curb. No trouble from anyone this year.

Picketing Tax Office, N.Y. City 1960

I commenced this picketing Aug. 6th as usual at the branch tax office at Varick and W. Houston Streets, but after a week found that the main office was at 484 Lexington Avenue, at 46th Street, so I picketed there for a week also. Tax men would come out of the office and greet me kindly, take a CW and argue with their fellow workers about how I got by with it. I was on NBC for a few minutes with a factual interpretation of my ideas. Mary Lathrop helped me picket daily and other friends came around at times, among them Diana Lewis who had been in jail on the air raid refusal.

One day a small jerky young man bumped into me as I was picketing. Each of us said "excuse me" to the other. As I turned around and came back he danced in front of me like a gorilla, saying "You might get in trouble carrying that sign."

"Oh, I'm always fixed for trouble," I said confidently, as if I had a dozen guardian angels at my side.

"You like the Japs?" he asked, seeing my Hiroshima sign.

"Sure I like the Japs. I like everybody. I like myself. I like you. I am a peaceful man."

"I bumped into you on purpose; I wanted to see if you would fight. You are a peaceful man; I am too," and he walked away.

A reporter from Phoenix who knew me but whom I had never met was visiting in N.Y. City and was happy to write me up for his paper. The Belgian priest who had been in house arrest by the Communists in China for 6 years, who had spoken at the CW, and who felt that the enemy of the Chinese people was not the Communists but Chaing in Formosa, stopped and blessed me as I picketed. The uptown cops came around and asked questions but no one bothered me.

Atom Bomb and Missile Picketing

I belonged to a committee of pacifists who had planned to enter the atomic test grounds and if necessary be atomized as a protest against the biggest bomb which would be dropped in August of 1957. As I had been picketing the tax office during that time for many years I did not want to leave this front for another front, so I wrote to the authorities in Las Vegas, to the Bishop in Reno and priests in Las Vegas that from June 17 through the 28th I would fast and picket the Atomic Energy Commission to waken up pacifists, as it was 12 years since we dropped the bomb at Hiroshima. In New York City when we had picketed the Atomic Energy Commission I had become acquainted with the Publicity Director, Mrs. Grace Urros. When she learned that I was going to picket in Las Vegas she said that she would write and tell them to be nice to me, and she was coming out there a few days later and would see me. When I began to picket Lt. Col. Hunter greeted me kindly and said he would do anything to help me except to cease dropping bombs. And he had Don the guard bring out a chair each morning in order that I might rest in the shade at times. And also I was invited in the air conditioned office to cool off and for a drink of spring water. All of the folks there were cordial except two Irish Catholics; the Spanish Catholics being especially friendly.

I did not know until I came back to N.Y. City that on the day before I started picketing the *Las Vegas Review Journal* had an article, *"Bishop Dwyer in Warning Against A-Test Attitude.* Bishop Dwyer referred to the recent appeal of His Holiness, Pope Pius XII, for a cessation of tests of atomic weapons. He explained, however, that the appeal was directed to the whole world, and not limited to the Nevada proving grounds . . . Regarding the proposed plan of Ammon Hennacy, staff member of the *Catholic Worker*, to picket the Las Vegas AEC office, Bishop Dwyer said in a private interview, 'this man does not have episcopal approval for his effort.' Questioned about the status of the *Catholic Worker* as representing the mind of the Church in organized labor, Bishop Dwyer explained that it has no official status. Again, in a democracy, he said, 'we subscribed to principles of free speech and a free press, and certain forms of extreme liberalism can under certain circumstances be as dangerous as some of the other "isms" circulated throughout the world today.' Bishop Dwyer re-affirmed that basically the Church is concerned with the eternal salvation of the souls of men. At the same time Catholics in every part of the world are bound in conscience to respect and support lawful authority of civil governments."

In a book just published by the AEC they say that the winds carry this atomic dust eastward in an east and west, but not much of a north and south direction, taking from four to seven weeks to encircle the globe. "About 10% of the debris stored in the stratosphere descends to the earth annually. Strontium -90 produces anemia, bone necrosis, cancer, and possibly Leukemia . . . Most of the strontium-90 in the present world-wide fallout, however, is in a water-soluable form . . . there is evidence that in the local fallout the strontium-90 constitutes a smaller percentage of the total fission products than it does farther away . . . the lymphoid tissue — tonsils, adenoids, spleen and certain areas of the intestinal lining — is one of the most radio-sensitive of all tissues . . . In Japan . . . there was an increased incidence of miscarriages and premature births, and a greater death rate mong expectant mothers."

Here it was from 100 to 120 degress and I faced the sunny side of the building all day. I was able to get a reasonable hotel a block away. My signs quoted the Popes against atomic war and for the arousing of the Christian conscience. I went to Mass downtown at the St. Joan of Arc Church and the Msgr. was cordial when I told him of my plans. The next day I went another mile and a half the other side of town to St. Anne's where the priest was much opposed to my ideas, but as I went there every day he soon became friendly. The first day Don Ashworth of the *Review Journal* and a photographer interviewed me and that night a good front page picture and article told of my ideas and mission in Las Vegas. Reporters from Hearst, AP, UP, N.Y. Times, the Japanese press and television from Albuquerque also took pictures of Col. Hunter and me. The correspondent of the ABC papers from Barcelona with headquarters in Washington, D.C. was happy to see a radical anarchist.

I knew that the Irish Catholic Chief of Police had once studied to be a priest; when he stopped on the second day and asked me if I had ever been convicted of a felony I told him that I had. He asked me if I had registered myself at police headquarters as an ex-convict. I told him that I did not believe in obeying such laws and he replied that I could get 30 days for it. He already understood that he could not imprison me for something that had happened so long ago, and besides Roosevelt had given all CO's a pardon in 1933. He really wanted to discuss pacifism and anarchism with me and we visited cordially for a time. That night I was on television (Stetson hats; I told them I would not appear with any cigarette or fake medicine ads). My sign and book were shown and I gave my message. The folks at the AEC said it was good. Later I discovered that the head of the television company had phoned a priest to find out if the CW was on the subversive list and was told that we were very radical but were good Catholics. The priest they phoned was my friend at St. Anne's.

In the morning at daylight I got up to watch the atomic test 75 miles to the west. First a flash like lightning, then the thunder, then the mushroom cloud rising and remaining stationary in the air until it would be blown toward Salt Lake City and points east. On another morning I waited to see another bomb go off and nothing happened. It seems that fifteen minutes before the button was to be pushed that the wind turned toward Las Vegas. They abandoned the experiment for that day for they were not going to have the poison hitting their city; it could go elsewhere.

One Jehovah Witness tried to tell me that it was wrong to oppose the bombs for they were being built up for Armegaddon. No one called me Commie during the whole 12 days. On the next to last day of my picketing I got up early to see the test where a bomb twice as big as any was to be dropped. 2,000 Marines were waiting on tip toe to enter the fatal area and many animals were half dressed with clothing to see the effect on their bodies of the radiation. We all waited and waited and the explosion did not occur. About 10 a.m. Col Hunter came back from the field saying "Hennacy, you stopped this one, you had better get back to N.Y. and let us get to work." They had pressed the button and the bomb didn't go off. My son-in-law later showed me the Pasadena Sunday paper with the headline "Atomic Test Foe Scores 'Victory'" saying that I had an accidental moral victory inasmuch as this bomb was a dud. After I left the AEC folks sent me an article by Mr. Ashworth in the *Review Journal* headed "AEC Picket Gives Up 22 Pounds to the Cause." I drank sauer kraut juice to break my fast, wanting something sour, and next day my daughter Sharon in Pasadena had an avacado salad for me.

I had planned this Las Vegas picketing in time to get home for the air raid drill in which this time, as told before I got 30 days; and I got out of jail in time to begin my tax picketing. During this time a group led by Larry Scott went to the actual atom grounds prepared "to be atomized for Christ and humanity." They had dressed prepared to sleep out in the area and to offer civil disobedience to the death and several of them "went over the fence" and were arrested. A pacifist lawyer made the agreement with the authorities that if they went home and didn't go over the fence again as planned, there would be no charge; if they went over the fence again they would get 60 days. They prayed and held a vigil all night and God told them to go home. This is terrible: to go to thousands of dollars worth of expense and then to chicken out is a poor way of advancing a cause.

Picketing Missiles in Florida

Half a dozen Peacemakers met by plan at Cocoa Beach, Fla. on Saturday April 12, 1958 to protest the missiles at Cape Canaveral. Most of us had other plans, Art Harvey and I to refuse to take part in the air raid drill May 6 in N.Y. City, so we did not plan to offer any civil disobedience in Florida. That night we spent at the home of a CW reader by the name of C. D. Preston in Orlando, who is the head of Christian Science pacifists, this being the only church that does not allow its members to be conscientious objectors. Here we made our signs and each of us chose a church where we would distribute leaflets in the morning. I also carried a sign which I wanted to use later and put it by the fence near the Catholic Church in the suburb of Rockledge. I had phoned the priest twice to say that I would distribute the leaflets but his housekeeper did not get the message to him.

"Take the word Catholic off that sign and leaflet. You don't have permission from the Bishop or from me to use it. You give Catholics a bad name," said Father Le-May at St. Mary's Church in Rockledge.

"We are laymen and we do not need permission from the Bishop or from you to oppose missiles for murder," I answered, and continued, "The Church has had a bad name long enough in supporting wars. I like the name Catholic and I am trying to make it mean something like the early Christians meant it to be when Christians couldn't go to court or kill in war. I venture that in the years to come the Church will be proud that we Catholic Workers opposed missiles and war and that we gave the church a good name."

My sign read *"We Protest Missiles for Murder, Catholic Worker, New York City. Peacemakers."* and *"Missiles Attack; They Don't Defend."* The priest said that he had heard of the CW and that we could picket any place we liked but not to use the name Catholic. We discussed the whole matter of pacifism for about ten minutes. I said I had as much right to us the name Catholic for peace as Catholic war veterans had to use it for war. The priest was not angry but we could not agree that I couldn't use the name Catholic in pacifist literature. As I was talking to Father LeMay the ushers had torn up my sign and broken the stick in pieces. (Before we left Marge Swann took a snapshot of me standing by the Church with this broken sign in the shape of a cross.) As it was an hour until the next Mass I took a walk around town looking for a store where I could buy a paper. I saw a Presbyterian Church and gave the minister copies of our leaflet. Just then I saw my four Catholic usher friends talking to the Chief of Police, a young man by the name of Hubert Aslup. He took me by the arm and escorted me into his office, locked the door and motioned for the ushers to go away. Pointing to our leaflet he said, "You know about everybody makes a living on these missiles around here. These fellows outside are Georgia Crackers, and I brought you in here to warn you that they are going to lynch you, or tar and feather you, or throw you in the river. And I won't defend you either. If I didn't have my uniform on I would beat the hell out of you myself. You better start walking out of town."

I explained that I had had the KKK after me near Mobile, Ala. before he was born, that I didn't run then and wasn't going to run now. The Chief did not believe that I was a Catholic and called me a Communist. I replied that I was an anarchist. He wanted to know if that meant "no cops," "Yes, and no government and war" I answered. As I walked the two blocks away from the station I toyed with the idea if it was worthwhile to be beaten up by these ignorant men, but found my feet walking naturally toward the Church. As I reached St. Mary's the police chief eased up behind me and said "Better get your ass out of town or these guys will get you. Go to the Presbyterians, don't bother these Catholics, I'm warning you!"

I listened to the sermon sitting out on the Church steps and could see the four men waiting across the street for me. I had about ten pounds of literature in my pockets and this would help me sink in the water if they threw me in. Drowning was a quick death and just a choking. And hanging was also a quick death. Folks don't die of tar and feathers and I didn't see any pot of tar handy. If they took me away ten miles from town and took my clothes off and beat me up I suppose I could find the other picketers in time. I said a prayer for protection and walked to the sidewalk and commenced to give out leaflets as people left the Church. About five people had received them when the reddest-faced Irish looking usher grabbed me and rushed me over to the other side of the street. Then ensued the old name calling of "Communist;" that I had no right to hand out leaflets with the name Catholic; and if the Bishop knew of it he would have prevented me. I asked the name of the Bishop but they didn't know. Finally I remembered it was Bishop Hurley of St. Augustine. They told me that Father LeMay and Chief Alsup had told them "to take me over the hill" and prevent me from handling out leaflets. I said I didn't believe this. By this time all had come out from the 11 o'clock Mass.

As the four ushers were calling me insulting names one man said, "I wouldn't beat up that old man. You should have respect for age; that will make him a martyr and that is just what the Commies want." He was the only one of them who took a CW to read. They said that it seemed that the Church and the police couldn't stop me but they sure could, and the red-faced man said "We'll take you over the hill and throw you in the ocean just as soon as you make a step to the curb to hand out another leaflet." I told him I would sit down by the tree and rest a bit until the people came out from noon Mass and then I would give out at least one leaflet.

"You'll go over the hill. We don't fool around here with such as you!"

Just then Chief Alsup and another cop drove up and motioned for me to get into their car. They were taking me to the Mayor's house and I waited while they conferred with him for a time. When they returned they said they could arrest me for loitering and for disturbing religious services. I replied that I did not disturb any religious service; and that I only disturbed the already disturbed Catholic Vigilantes. They could arrest me for whatever their law said; that I wouldn't sue them for false arrest for I didn't believe in courts.

"We got to be careful; that's just what you Commies would do," the chief replied.

By this time we had come to the town of Cocoa and to the Police Station. As I was ushered in a khaki-clad officer in charge said, "If I didn't have my uniform on I'd beat the hell out of you; you New York Communist." He repeated this twice again within a few minutes. The officers conferred again in another room for about ten minutes and I could hear them arguing about false arrest, etc. Finally they told me to take the leaflets out of my pocket and they piled about 100 of them on the desk saying they would distribute them for me. Then they told me to go. Everyone won this game, for I did not chicken and kept my integrity; the Catholic Vigilantes won for I gave out no more leaflets at their Church; the Police won for I could not sue them for false arrest, they didn't arrest me; they just detained me.

The next day the local paper, the *Tribune*, gave a good summary of our ideas, saying also, "The pacifists met with a chilly reception. At St. Mary's Catholic Church in Rockledge, police were summoned to prevent at least one of the group from disturbing services. He was escorted in Cocoa by Police Chief Hubert Alsup and warned to leave town." Sunday night I spoke at a Negro Baptist Church and Marge Swann spoke in several churches. Bob Lutweiler spoke to the Episcopalians and Methodists and on the whole we had a fine reception instead of the "chilly" one referred to above. The next day Marge and Bob had a conference with the Police Chief of Cocoa. The leaflets were still on that desk and he said there were a couple of things he didn't agree with in the leaflet: breaking laws and anarchism. He said the Mayor didn't quite agree with the leaflet either and wanted to see us. We had wanted to have a street meeting but the Mayor offered us the free use the next night of the Municipal Auditorium if we would debate with the Air Force people, but they were not allowed to debate the issue they said, so we had no meeting. Marge and Dick Fichter spoke on the radio the next day. Dick is a charming wild man (without his beard and beret). Harry Scheirer, a Quaker from Philadelphia, dragged his slight body manfully with us. Patricia Parkman, with Fellowship House in Washington, D.C. lent her charm to the scene. The Orlando and Miama papers gave us good coverage when we marched in the rain the next day picketing through the air base on the public highway.

Dave Dellinger and some others had entered the AEC office in the Washington suburbs, and sitting down refused to move or to eat until Admiral Straus would speak to them. They went for 7 days and had a few minutes talk with him at last. This is not good manners and is a negative fasting with which I would not take part. I explained in my picketing leaflet which had the cut of John the Baptist saying "Make Straight the Way of the Lord," *"I am fasting, not to coerce or embarass the A.E.C. but as a penance for our sinfulness in bombing Hiroshima and Nagasaki and for our continued testing of hydrogen and atomic weapons in our mad race for a supremacy that means only death. I am fasting to awaken the consciences of those who are a part of the war machine, those who are half-hearted pacifists and those Christians who see no contradiction in following Christ and Caesar."*

Previous to my fast I had hiked a day from Frederick, Md. with others on a Peace Walk to Washington, D.C. and took part with their picketing on a Sunday. The AEC office was at 1717 H St. I roomed near the Cathedral, went to Mass each morning, then down to buy a N.Y. Times, read it and rest, and then picket from 9 to 10; resting on the grass in the park by the Roger Smith Hotel half a block away. Then I picketed 20 minutes and rested 40, then to picket during the noon rush until 1:05. Then to rest for the remainder of the afternoon except for the 20 minutes around each hour when the A.E.C. shuttle bus from Germantown would arrive. Thus I picketed four hours and rested four hours. I only missed one rainy day and one day I attended the Hopi hearings with Viets of Hopiland.

"You couldn't be more right than you are. I know as much about the effects of atomic radiation as any one in this country. Keep up your picketing. Good luck to you," said an Atomic Energy employee to me on the 28th day of my fast. Three days later Admiral Strauss, who had seen me there daily as he came from their main headquarters remarked, "You look wonderful." We would mock salute each other in the morning.

To those who have never fasted and who are so fearful or so medically minded that the loss of a pound or of a meal is a major disaster, the announcement that I would fast for 40 days as a penance for our atomic sins brought letters of protest that I was committing suicide. On the 17th day of my fast a man who works at the AEC building quietly told me that he had fasted 62 days with McSwiney, Lord Mayor of Cork, who had fasted 78 days for the freedom of Ireland and died in 1920. He greeted me kindly several times later. Nine others of McSwiney's followers had fasted 94 days in prison and had lived. Many of the early Christians fasted 60 days in the hot desert. Pythagoras fasted 40 days before he took his exams and he would take no one as a student at the University of Alexandria who had not fasted for 40 days. Mrs. A. G. Walker, a noted Rhodesian singer, in Capetown, Africa, in 1931 fasted for 101 days to lose 63 pounds, as she was much overweight. In a supervised fast a man by the name of Succi ran up the steps of the Eiffel Tower on the 40th day of his fast. Harry Wills, the Negro prizefighter, fasted 30 days each year when he commenced training for a fight. Freddy Welsh, onetime lightweight champion of the world, always started his training for important fights with a week's fast. The most spectacular achievement was that of Gilman Low, artist and athlete, who in December 1903, at Madison Square Garden before 16,000 people, at the end of an 8 day supervised fast broke nine world records in weight lifting, such as raising 950 pounds three times in four seconds, and raising 2,200 pounds 29 times in 20 seconds. Bob Hoyt of the Knight newspapers who wrote three articles about my fast had asked a leading nutritionist at the University here if I could fast for 40 days without injury. He replied that if I had a strong will it would not hurt me.

A young Mormon soldier in uniform asked me questions for half an hour. Art Harvey picketed with me for 5 days and fasted 10 days. Bob Steed fasted in N. Y. City with me for 8 days. Terry McKiernon of Notre Dame, good Catholic anarchist, fasted with me the last 9 days. Others in this country and in England wrote about their fasting with me. Mayanna Manion of Mt. Angel, Oregon, fasted 13 days. Bob Grant of Santa Fe drove by and took me to visit the Little Sisters of Charles de Foucauld who are charwomen at the Catholic University of America. The priests at the Cathedral were very unsympathetic to my fast but Father Coen at the Catholic Information Center downtown had my book and Dorothy's and prayed for me daily. Virginia Glenn brought my mail to the park at times and planned a talk for me at the Bagdad Restaurant to the Washington Pacifist Fellowship near the end of my fast. And she introduced me to The Venerable Narada, a Buddhist priest whom I came to know fairly well. I listened to their lectures at the Burma and Ceylon Embassies.

I lost 31 pounds in my fast although for 11 days I did not lose a pound. Noticing strawberries gave me a hankering for them and I mixed some in a juicer with buttermilk at Dick and Byrd Sweitzers where I stayed for a few days. Dick is secretary to Mormon Congressman Udall from Tucson who is my friend. His wife Lee drove me to Mormon Church and helped me drink the strawberry buttermilk as I broke my fast. I read the lives of Jack London, Ibsen, and the Quaker John Woolman during my fast.

Sandstone Prison 8-26-59 to 1-24-60

"Over the Fence" at Omaha Missile Base

AUGUST 24, 1959

Omaha is the brains of the Missiles, where you touch a button and they go off all over the world. Pacifists whom I know had a project there for several months, most of them going to jail for 6 months for "going over the fence" in civil disobedience at the air base. Karl Meyer was the Catholic among them and I felt I should offer him my company, so the day after my tax picketing was over I left for Omaha, first stopping in Chicago where Dorothy and I spoke at a meeting of the Quakers. Francis Gorgen, my old time friend from Wisconsin, drove me from Chicago, picking up Janet Burwash who was going to visit her folks in Peoria. Catholics had phoned from Omaha that we should stay with them. The judge had told Arthur Harvey when he asked him if he had anything to say in court that he didn't want to hear it, so I wrote to the judge giving my reasons for being the last of the group to "go over the fence."

Francis drove me out to the Mead Air Base in the morning. Our friends told us that for several days the radio had announced that I was coming from N. Y. City for civil disobedience. We waited awhile at the Mead Base in a line of vehicles until the guard said, "You're the pacifist; the picketing place is two miles down the road." We asked a trucker and went down a dirt road to a dead end and across a ditch, noticing tar-paper covered buildings dotted here and there. We asked where the headquarters was and offered a CW to workers but they seemed afraid to take them. Finally a clerical worker took us ceremoniously to the brass at the front gate. They were waiting for us and we had somehow got in the back way. The U. S. Marshal handed me a typed notice from the head of the Air Base ordering me off the premises, and they opened the locked gate for me to get out. I went out and immediately stepped over the small fence and was officially arrested by Marshall Raab, but no handcuffs or chains were put on me as had been the case with Karl Meyer. The publicity given him had made them more careful. Marshall Raab asked me if I was an anarchist-vegetarian like Arthur Harvey and I replied that I was and in addition I was a Catholic. He said that he had heard an anarchist speak at Hyde Park in London that summer but had not paid much attention and wanted to know if I was a real anarchist. I told him I was, and that I had written a book about it. He wanted to know if he could read it. I told him I had brought it along for the judge and would autograph it for him and the judge and he could have it first. When we came to his office a newspaper man was there and told me that he was tired of writing up about us and would not give me much publicity. Before I could say a word the Marshall said, "He is not in it for publicity; he has reasons; he's different." The office secretary spoke well of Marge Swann whom she had taken to Alderson, W. Va. prison recently. Francis was allowed to come in to visit me and to be in court at 3 p.m. The D.A. wanted to make sure that I knew enough to plead guilty and he finally understood that I did not want a lawyer, so my plea of guilty was accepted. Judge Robinson wanted to know if I had anything to say before sentence was pronounced. I asked him if he had read my letter and he said that he had. I told him that I had nothing more to add. He gave me 6 months with $500 fine and costs, but as I found out later this fine was not "committed," which meant that I would always owe it but did not have to sign a pauper's oath in lieu of payment. Marshall Raab said that he had taken Arthur Harvey to the newly re-opened Sandstone, Minn. prison between Minneapolis and Duluth, and I supposed I would be going there instead of with Karl to Springfield, Missouri.

Twenty six prisoners were sleeping on and under bunks and on the floor in a space in a cell tank supposed to be for 12. It was hot but there was a fan and it could have been worse. The food is miserable as in most county jails. A friend of Mike Gold's sent word to me from the floor below. After a night and day I was moved to another cell with another prisoner and at 5 a.m. the next morning he and I and a Negro prisoner were chained and handcuffed and went in a car with a Deputy Marshall and a decrepit, foul-mouthed ancient who got a per diem for helping escort us. We had to drink coffee and eat sandwiches handcuffed in the car, but Marshall Raab had been more considerate with Arthur, taking him unbound into restaurants. In the afternoon we arrived in Sandstone.

Sandstone Prison

Sandstone is a town of about 1500, entirely destroyed by fire in the forest fire of the 90's but now rebuilt. The reservation is several miles out of town and was used mostly for conscientious objectors in the 40's, and later as a state mental hospital, but this year it was reopened as a medium security Federal Prison, with about 50 transfers from Leavenworth, and more coming in from Terra Haute and Milan prisons, with a few like us from the courts. At the time of my entry there were 70 and at the time of my release there were 354. The prison consists of two story buildings erected around a compound of about two acres in the midst of 3,000 acres of swamp and farm, the latter not being run just now. Mostly we lived in dormitory custody with about forty five in each dorm. E building contains cells where those who have a detainer against them are housed; and then there are 13 solitary cells, painted yellow, upstairs, with a mattress on the floor. Mostly you get regular eats and you can get books from the library to read while in solitary. Newcomers are put in A and O (Admission and Orientation) for three weeks or a month. Here we were two to a cell. I met one fellow who had done time in Parchman, Miss. where the wife has overnight visits with the husband prisoner each week. (There have been prisons too where the officers bring prostitutes for certain prisoners and make money for themselves.) A couple of farmers were in for feeding corn which the government had bought for surplus, to their hogs, or for figuring out their income tax differently from the way the government accountants figured. A bookie from the big city became my friend and threatened to reform. Most of the men were in for stealing cars over the state line, many others for peddling dope, quite a number for variations of mail fraud. My one especial friend was an Indian who had stolen a horse. He knew that the horse belonged to a neighbor but being drunk he didn't care. There were about 100 Negroes, 30 Indians and half a dozen Mexicans. There was no segregation in the dorms or in the dining hall.

One morning we were marched to the front office and given shots at the medical office. I told them that I did not believe in shots but they said they would strap me down and make me take them anyway, and that Arthur had taken them after an argument. So I took them. About a week later we were called up to take more shots. I told the officer that I was not going up to take them and asked to see the Captain. He said to see him at the medical office so I went along. The medical officer kept me until last and grabbing my arm told me to hurry up and take my shots and to argue afterwards. I said that was just the idea and I wanted to see the Captain. Finally he got him on the phone and I said, "Captain Driscoll, there are three things you can do: (1) Give me the shots, (2) Allow me to be a conscientious objector to shots, (3) Place me in solitary for the duration of my time," the medical myth being that I would carry disease to the others. The Captain had sense enough not to make a martyr out of me so I took the shots after which the medical officer said, "I'll make you come back and take all the possible damn shots."

But in a few days when I went before the Classification Board the medical officer was all smiles (he had given me the shots and could afford to smile). Warden Meier who is a pleasant quiet man entangled in government red tape said that he understood my radical ideas and asked about the CW. I gave him our ideas and history. He wanted to know if there was anything I wouldn't do around the prison. I told him I wouldn't kill chickens and he had better not put me to teaching history or I would teach it radical as hell. I said that just as Kruschchev and Eisenhower could disagree yet coexist, so could I do my time graciously if that was the way they wanted to run things. I was told to go to the Educational Department and be ready to help set up the school when the educational director arrived. Meanwhile I helped Arthur set up the library as he set it up with some peculiar classifications of his own. Later with the approval of the director we ordered several hundred liberal books including all of Jack London, Erich Fromm and Aldous Huxley.

The warden read my book and liked it and I allowed him to have it for the guards' library, as it was not allowed in our library, at least while I was there. We have two copies of Dorothy's book in the library. Mr. Durham, an active Southern Baptist from the El Reno Reformatory, was my boss as educational director for a month. He was liberal and had never met a radical who was a Christian. He took pains to understand my pacifism and wanted to read my book so I had my mother send him one. (I have half a dozen of my books in her attic for Judges, Wardens, etc. Or if a Pope or a Cardinal wants one I ought to have one handy.) The present educational director, Mr. Earhart of McNeils Island Reformatory, is a quiet liberal who understands our ideas, and he was friendly to Arthur and me. One day the Warden brought Rev. Bolton from Sandstone to see me. I had just discussed with Mr. Peterson, the genial guard at the library, about gallows not hanging, or prison doors not locking themselves, and that when people refused to be judges, hangmen, guards, wardens, or madames of houses of prostitution, then these things would cease to exist. I had said that all Judges, D.A.'s, Wardens, etc. ought to do thirty days in a regular jail. And he said that if we prisoners were Warden for a day we would see what a Warden had to do put up with. I told this to the Warden and said I supposed he had a time with the old time sadistic guards.

Prison Routine

Lights on at 6:30 a.m. and breakfast from 7 to 7:30 in the cafeteria-like dining room with four to a small table. You can choose with whom you eat. I was generally with my Indian friends. Always hot and dry cereal, coffee, toast, oleo, and some kind of stewed fruit. At times pancakes, french toast or scrambled eggs. On a Sunday or a holiday we have just coffee at 8 and "Brunch" which is lunch and breakfast at 10. Generally two strips of bacon then. To work at 8 and lunch at 11:30 which consisted of potatoes, meat, several vegetables, and jello, cake, pie, pudding and tea or in the summer, Kool-aid. To work at 12:30 and to count in your dorm at 4:30 when the whistle blows on work days. Supper at 5 to 5:30 which is plentiful. Corn on the cob in season, and generally too much starch. Cornbread at times which was good, but the whitebread was not as good as in the New York prisons, it being more like storebread. I ate very little starch and Arthur and I gave our meat and fish to those who asked for it. I fasted from Thursday night to Saturday noon or until after Mass on Saturday morning. Count again at 9:30 and lights out at 10:30, but at times those who wanted television could listen until later in another room.

After supper on week nights prisoners can go to the library or to classes until around 9 p.m. I worked extra at nights and on Saturdays, Sundays and holidays in the library, and while I know just about the exact location on the shelf of each book I never got to read much as I was busy shuffling Zane Grey and other rubbish for the prisoners as they returned and took out books. We are not allowed to visit a prisoner in another dorm. Some guards are more fussy about this than others. We had a skating rink and hockey games, and in good weather baseball, volleyball, football and tossing horseshoes. At this latter Arthur and I played and ran about even, but the Indian could make a ringer nearly every time. We played 107 games of scrabble and I only won 10, so there is no doubt that Arthur is smarter than I. You can buy a certain amount of candy, cigarettes, etc. at commissary and afterwards there is a scramble to pay gambling debts. Some of the most religious were the worst gamblers.

Religion

Father Smith told us that he did not want us to consider him as a Chaplain, but as members of his parish, which we were geographically. He has two parishes and does not have much time to confer with us but he is kindly. I attended Protestant services with a Lutheran friend, not taking part except to sing "Faith of Our Fathers, in dungeons dim," twice. A choir leader sang a song, "When God Forsakes You Turn To Your Friend." He likely meant when your friend forsakes you to turn to God, but it rhymed better I suppose. And he also sang about "when the waters cover the sea." I always thought that they covered the land, but this was another rhyme. For a minister to be a Chaplain in the armed forces or in prison and accept the pay, and in some cases wear the uniform of the officers, is in my mind as bad as to have a Prohibitionist wear the bartender's apron behind the bar and hand out temperance leaflets. Churches ought to pay the salaries of their Chaplins and then they could be independent. For if they don't know what goes on they cannot be of much use, and if they do know and do nothing about it, that is worse yet. I know of cases (not in Sandstone) where Catholics did not go to confession because they felt that the Chaplain was too friendly with the Warden. They may have been wrong but this feeling kept them away from confession.

Later in Milwaukee the chief probation officer who is a friend of mine told me of social workers and others collecting money under the name of some club and paying the salary of the court Chaplain. In this manner prisoners would not feel that he was biased for any especial church and certainly he was then not an arm of the State. Here the Huber Plan whereby certain prisoners work at their regular jobs and live at night in the jail and turn all of their salary in to feed their families or to pay fines, and also their keep at the jail is a system. This is a terrible strain on a prisoner and under creditable officials it can be a help, but a jail is always a jail.

Many of the guards in Sandstone are recruited from the farming community. Most of them seem to be afraid of their jobs, of us, and of themselves. Some are naturally kindly and others find ways to needle us with regulations as to know we fold a blanket, happen to look in at another dorm, or not follow some silly regulation to the letter of the law. Guards are like pacifists, anarchists, vegetarians, Catholics and others; they can be kind, generous, intelligent, and courageous, but they can also be arrogant, perverse, selfish, greedy and tricky.

"There are two kinds of people in the world; those who have done time and those who haven't," said a lifer to me in Atlanta prison in 1917. In prison and out of prison about a third of the people are stool-pigeons who are ready to name names for a profit to themsevles. In a recent issue of the prison paper in Leavenworth there was a reprint of an article by Judge Lebowitz in New York City praising the Russian prisons that he had visited. Here families could visit and prisoners were paid the going rate for their work. Nothing

was said about political prisoners. Like Martin who wrote, *Break Down the Walls*, that Carol Gorgen reviewed in the CW once, I am not interested in making bigger and better prisons. The current issue of the Atlanta prison paper says in an editorial that 95% of the men there are recidivists, that is they come back again to prison. It would be around 85% in Sandstone. I know men there who have been in jail for many years and have not learned a thing. I know others who have been caught in a mail fraud which is no worse than regular business who will now be more careful and who will not knowingly break the law again. I know kids from Milan who will likely go in and out of jails for years to come. None of the officials ever used the word "rehabilitate" without excusing themselves, for they know it is a farce. Attitudes towards prisoners range from the sentimentalist who says that "there are no bad boys," and that most prisoners are incarcerated unjustly, to sadists like J. Edgar Hoover who wants more jails and more punishment. There are bad boys and bad people who knowingly choose to do evil. Jesus gave us the method of overcoming evil when he said to the woman caught in sin, "He without sin among you first cast a stone at her." If the early Christians went to court they were not allowed to go to Communion for 6 months, and if they were in the army and killed a man they had to do penance for ten years. Since the time of Constantine the Church has tried to cooperate with the State and capital punishment, prisons and war. All this is done in the name of Christ while Christ is denied.. The darkest place in the world is a prison and this is where light is needed. When I left Sandstone I told the Warden and Mr. Earhart, who had already met Dorothy who had come to meet me, that the prison had not hurt me any, and perhaps I had helped in my attitude of being the kind of radical who does not believe in prisons at all but who while there tries to give his fellow prisoners the idea that there is a different way of looking at life, on the inside and on the outside. My time in prison was not wasted and if in the future I do up to five years for civil disobedience I think it would be time well spent on my part. I often say that a fellow who is any good on the outside does much better on the inside, for as Debs said, "While there is a lower class I am in it; while there is a soul in prison I am not free."

Father Casey, Janet Burwash and Bill Henry visited me. I was restricted to write to 7 approved correspondents. Upon my release I had 640 Christmas cards from over the world.

There would not be one chance in a million of arriving at the number 7438 if you chose four digits from 4 to 84,000, but the current issue of the Atlanta prison paper had an interesting writeup about how a prisoner enters prison and what is done from time to time. They might have taken any number as a sample but they chose this one — 7438, which was my prison number in 1917 there. The Milwaukee papers tell of the acting Postmaster who "mishandled" $17,000 and was fined $1,000 and placed on 5 years probation. I slept near a Negro from Milwaukee who got 5 years for a minor theft. The *New York Times* of 6-22-60 tells of Judge Lester D. Salter of Chicago giving two ex-policemen three years probation for stealing $1,800 worth of appliances, saying that their take home pay of $350 a month was not enough to live on, and that when off duty and stealing they "were engaged in free enterprise."

JUNE 6 TO 19, 1960

Brad Lyttle had organized this Action to protest the atomic subs which with 16 H bombs can kill fifty million people. The leader of the march was Adrian Maas, a young Hollander, now living in New Jersey. He has lived a bit in South Africa and is the second Christian Scientist pacifist whom I have met. He graduated from their college, Principia, near St. Louis and argued with them for years, and with his draft board. He is a fine young man and deserves much credit for fighting the patriots in his church nearly alone.

The march had started June 10th from the Battery in New York and Hugh Madden of our group had started with it then. Charlie Butterworth and I caught up with it at Columbia University the next day, Saturday, he coming back after a few hours and I continuing with the others to New Rochelle. Each night we were provided shelter with friends. I was fasting but the walk of around 20 miles a day was no more than I did regularly when picketing the tax man. My sign said, *"Yes, for Life and the Green Revolution; No for Death and the Polaris bomb."* Groups of students joined us in the towns and the police often escorted us cordially through the towns, but the nearer we got to New London the more hostile the police and the people were. In one town two beautiful 16 year old Quaker twins, Merry and Mercy, walked with us and Hugh and I were fortunate to stay at their house that night. We were called Communists in many towns, but in three instances I gave the CW to Catholics who were questioning us and made friends of them.

Half a dozen atheistic anarchistic students, two Quakers, and a schismatic Western Orthodox young priest by the name of Itkin were the walkers that went most of the way. Hugh did not like to walk with "unbelievers" so soloed on the side or forward or backward. Scott Herrick and Joel Greenberg had sailed in a sloop from Cape May, and Harry Purvis, John Davenport and Bill Henry had rowed from Manhattan. And Arthur Harvey had met us on the way. In New London on the next Saturday dozens of folks came from New York and Boston to help us: Janice Smith and her children, Pat McMahon, Dave Dellinger and Ralph DeGia, and Bob Gussner.

About thirty of us marched over a long bridge and got wet in a soaking rain on the way to Groton and the Electric Boat works. Here hundreds of workers were gathered in a narrow street by the factory entrance with angry looks toward us. We made the mistake of twice huddling in a meeting before continuing our march. When we got to the worst of the crowd a 14 year youth by the name of Timothy Hutchinson from Cambridge, Massachusetts was at the head of the line and I was second. A saloon keeper tore Timothy's sign and tramped on it, and tore mine and a CW I gave him, and so on with the others. Three of the kid anarchists hurried back to give out more leaflets and when Brad went to tell them we were going home someone from behind hit him on the jaw. We gave out thousands of leaflets in the park when the Harvard Yale boat races were going on, and later that night we had a meeting in our office at night where some workers attended and gave patriotic arguments. The action went on until the first of September but I had tax picketing in August, and this was enough on the Polaris front.

There has been a strike on at *Kohler Co.* in Wisconsin for five years. They are a paternalistic concern paying good wages but not believing in unions. Both sides had committed violence. Bob Steed, Deane and I picketed the sales room on Park Ave. once a month for years and when I was speaking in Wisconsin I picketed the Kohler plant with my friend Francis Gorgen and two former employees, Bohemian Catholics.

We have picketed the Spanish Embassy, the Spanish Travel Bureau, and ships in port, protesting against the Franco regime where Catholic as well as anarchist students are tortured. At the Travel Bureau I told them that we were anarchists similar to Francisco Ferrer the educator whom the Church and the State did to death in 1909. They remembered that.

With Ann Marie Stokes we have picketed the South African representatives here. Every Saturday in the summer of 1960 we help CORE (Committee On Racial Equality) picket Woolworth's. Bob Steed fasted for 46 days and picketed the courts here a couple of hours each day on the Chessman case, and he and I and others picket Sing Sing from noon until 10 p.m. when there was an execution there. Someone has to offset the old eye for an eye mentality of the traditional Catholic clergy who seem to be the only ones to advocate the death penalty or to call for more punishment when the question is up in the legislature. Some non-Catholic friends of ours were lobbying at Trenton against capital punishment and when they saw two priests there they innocently thought they were there on the same mission, but the priests knew nothing of such a bill; they were there to lobby for bingo. Each December for years I have picketed the Whitehouse in Washington, D.C. about political prisoners.

December 2, 1960 Mary Lathrop and I picketed Sing Sing from 4:30 until 10 p.m. A young man had hit an older man in a fight on the Bowery and the old man died. The young man was persuaded to plead guilty and told he would get clemency. As it was he did not have a good lawyer and was to be executed that night. Hundreds of people came up from town and read our signs. One guard said that there was hardly any capital punishment now, only four or five a year. Some guards coming to work took our leaflets and were cordial. We had walked the 72 steps up the wooden stairway which is a shortcut to the prison from the streets below. At ten minutes to ten we said the Rosary and at ten when the lights went dim we were praying for the soul of the young man. We did not know for sure whether he had been executed until we read it in the paper next day. I cry very seldom, but all the next day I was in tears.

Other New York Meetings

Ordinarily a prophet does not speak much in his own town but New York City is so big that I speak often in churches, schools, and special groups. The Quakers have groups of students whom they take to the UN, different embassies, and as a final treatment to the CW, or at times I have spoken to their groups in an all day seminar with others such as Erich Fromm. All of these speakers believed in patching up the system so it was well that someone was there to give them hope when their patchwork failed.

I had a three cornered discussion between Sid Stein of the Communist Party and Sam Karp of the Socialist Labor Party at a forum. Also a discussion at Hofstra College in Long Island between Arnold Johnson of the Communist Party, Lynne Trugeon defending capitalism, and myself with the anarchist position. And twice at Hunter College Hyde Park Day where speakers from all parties, except the Liberal who would not associate with Communists, spoke and later had a soapbox under a tree for hours. This later meeting was on May 4th. Cardinal Spellman's birthday; Karl Marx's being the 5th. The present line of the Communists is to be reasonable and historical and not especially radical. The Socialist Labor Party is of course the oldest Socialist Party, more like a fundamentalist church in its dogmatism, purity and absolutely no sense of humor. In an editorial they called me a "Parlor Radical." They are always well financed from the capitalist system which they disavow and never risk going to jail which might disrupt their organizing. In all of these meetings none of the radicals mentioned the basic Marxian principles-, so I gave them: *The Economic Interpretation of History*. If a Catholic sheepherder in the west clips wool and a Catholic stockbroker in Wall Street clips coupons, they may both pray alike, but their outlook on life is different because they make their living in a different way. This does not hold good for every human being but in general it is true. *Surplus Value*. If a man makes $40 a day for his employer and gets back in return but $10, then he can only buy back that much and the surplus piles up and we have depressions and wars. The capitalist system commenced to fall apart in 1914. I doubt if it lasts until 2014. and maybe not until 1984. I would not push it for it is already falling: billions spent to pay farmers for not growing wheat, corn, etc. and to store this surplus — with half the world underfed. We don't deserve to survive. *The Class Struggle*. Between those who work for a living and those who own for a living, as Scott Nearing says, there is a struggle. All this the Catholic anarchist believes with other radicals. But Communists believe that the way to solve this problem is to have a Dictatorship of the Proletariat, and afterwards the state will wither away and we will have a stateless society which would be anarchism. Anarchists do not believe that any state will wither away and they agree with Lord Acton, the Catholic who fought the declaration of infallibility by Pius IX, that "Power corrupts and absolute power tends to corrupt absolutely."

I spoke to several meetings of Communists to greet my old friend *Elizabeth Gurley Flynn* when she was released from Alderson prison for violation of the Smith Act. The Communists are realistic in most of the world but somehow here their wires are twisted for they think that by opening their meetings with The Star Spangled Banner they are proving their patriotism. Neither Dorothy nor I would stand up when on the stage when this was sung. I always told them that they couldn't sing it, and did not believe it, and were not fooling anyone; that next time they invited me I hoped they would all sing the Red Flag like we used to in the old days. The youngsters applauded me but the old folks were puzzled; they couldn't leave their party line. Howard Fast had asked me to speak at their May Day meeting on Union Square but I told him I might front for them but I would do it in my own way. So in 1960 when some Hunter College students asked me to speak at a 4th of July Anti-Japanese Treaty rally I did so. I kidded them about the Star Spangled Banner and then I said: "When anyone is for peace, justice, freedom, or higher wages he is called "Communist." That is an honor and I am glad to be with you today. When people are for good things they are never called "Christian" or "Catholic" for we have not earned the right to be so called. But there was a time when being a Christian and a Catholic meant something: that was when if you went court you were not allowed to take Communion for six months and if a soldier who was a Christian killed any one he was not allowed to go to Communion for ten years. All over the world where we find a tyranny we find the Catholics supporting this tyranny; they have forgotten the message of the early Christians. We are trying to make our Church have the old time message of the early Christians. And last year the hierarchy put thumbs down on the efforts of the poorly paid Catholic Puerto Rican hospital workers here to have a union. Although if I was in Russia I wouldn't last long being an anarchist, but here today I am happy to be with comrades who are not only against this Japanese Treaty, which is the subject of the day, but for other items of justice."

Another time I met with the Trotskyite leader, Myra Tanner Weiss at a forum. Her grandfather Tanner was an old time Mormon. I spoke at the College of Complexes which was a meeting place where liquor was served. An anarchist, Slim Brundege, has a place like this in Chicago also where radicals and others can speak. When I had finished, a drunken Irishman got up saying that he was an athiest and worked on the *New York Times*, and he wanted to know what kind of a so-and-so God I believed in: the Catholic God, the Mohammedan God, the Buddhist God, The Mormon God, the Jewish God, etc. I told him, "Folks, this man is all mixed up; he doesn't know God is an Irishman."

The latest instance of pacifist action is that of the young Christian Science leader of the Polaris march to New London, Connecticut, Adrian Maas, who in August of 1960 was approached at the pacifist headquarters by three sailors who said: "You are a pacifist?"

"Yes."

"That means that if I hit you in the face you would not hit back."

"Yes." So Adrian was hit three times in the face by the sailor. Meanwhile, Julius Jacobs, a pacifist, stood by. To defend Adrian with fists was wrong, and he did not have the words to say or the right action to prevent this assault. He did, however, have the pacifist principle to not use violence.

"Now you would shake hands with me after all this?" asked the sailor. "Surely," said Adrian, whereupon the sailor hit him in the face again. Adrian and Julian have been strengthened by knowing that they were true to their principles. Whether I would have said anything or done anything in a pacifist manner to stop this violence I do not know. The pacifist technique is not a recipe to live forever, but it is a way of life, that if lived, goes from victory to victory rather than from defeat to defeat.

As I have said before, he who gets there fustest with the mostest will win, so if your loved one is attacked you should have a weapon to defend her. To be without a weapon is not to be a pacifist; it is to be an inefficient militarist. To pick up an ink bottle or use your fists to defend someone may prove that you are brave, but if you desire to defend someone, all you do is to aggravate the attacker and provoke added violence. Pacifism is to be used only by pacifists. As a last resort one could place his body between that of the weapon and the attacker and deflect the blow if there was an opportunity to do so.

Theologically speaking, if one is in a state of grace he is ready to die, while the attacker is obviously not ready to die. It could be, if you die as a pacifist, as Stephen did without throwing back any stones, by this very action you might be able to awaken your attacker, as Saul was awakened. God knows, you do not.

The author, Mary Lathrop,
Picketing at Air Raid Office
46th and Lexington: Oct. thru Dec. 1960.

CHAPTER 14

CATHOLIC WORKER

New York City

1953 to 1963

Holy Family Picture

*6 by 9, on wall of First Joe Hill
House, 72 Post Office Place
Salt Lake City, Utah.
Painted by
Mary Lathrop, September, 1961*

We are a paper and a movement and a house of hospitality. As I said before, we are station where folks who have lost their way stop for a time until they can decide where they want to buy a ticket to — a monastery, the Ford Foundation, a union job, the Carmelites, marriage, or lower down on skid row. While there are perhaps only fifteen of us who will admit that we are anarchists, there are thousands who call themselves pacifists — that is between wars, and likely there are a hundred thousand who praise us for our works of hospitality and our emphasis on voluntary poverty.

As a House of Hospitality the CW is unique in that we who are "front office" live here and work for our keep. In organization we are truly anarchistic, for even in the smallest debating club or PTA much time is spent in making up rules and by-laws and writing a constitution. There are just about two unwritten rules here: (1) don't bring liquor in a bottle in the house. We don't search the "ambassadors" but we pour out the liquor if we see them drinking. (2) We never call a cop, although twice when Dorothy did not know it someone called the police.

The following describes our place at 39 Spring St. Now we are at 175 Chrystie, feeding folks on the first floor.

Dorothy designates someone to run the House and as long as they can do it without wearing themselves out they are the boss of how many people can be "paid out" for a flop when we do not have the room. Now we have eight apartments and pay for everyone else in a hotel or rooming house, but in the old days up to sixty slept in the house. The cook has charge generally of what he wants to order from De Falco, our old grocer friend from Mott St., only we cancel lemon extract generally, for the tendency would be to use it for drinking instead of cooking. Roger O'Neill at Chrystie Street, who cooked when the cooks were drunk, used to have two kinds of meat and two kinds of omelette, rice, sweet and Irish potatoes, with no warning. As a vegetarian I would ask if there was any meat in the soup, and receiving a negative answer I ate it and found a bone, or as I would say "a feather" in the bottom of the bowl. In the old days we had a coffee line in the morning, and a soup line at noon, and supper for those living in the house. Now we are forty-two steps up on the third floor and it is not worthwhile for a man to come up for such a small bit, so we have a meal at 11:30 with sandwiches to carry out for later if they want them. The men come early and sit around, as first come first served, and we have to have a man at the bottom of the stairs to ward off the drunks who might fall backwards before they reach the top, and to tell the late comers that there is saturation point in the feeding.

In my early days at 223 Chrystie Street when just then most of the kitchen crew were drunk I got up at 5:00 a.m. and helped pour coffee for the line and scrubbed the slime from the hall and kitchen floor. Some men would come back as much as three times in the line. Often one drunk would preach to the line telling them that they were all no-good bums.

What kind of people come to us? All sorts of tortured souls who have no other place to go. Peter said that we had to put up with one another the way God puts up with us, and Dorothy said we loved God as much as we loved the person we loved the least. By this measure I am a failure and so are most of us. The only thing is that we have different points of touchiness and tension, and a different breaking point as to how much of any certain kind of misery that we can take. And I suppose we get a "tolerance" toward certain irritations and an added intolerance toward others. One kind that is especially difficult for me to take is the scrupulous, over-pious person always wanting to put a scapular on me and hovering near the holy water. They are sure to burst out in vituperation a little later. We have had some of the quiet, withdrawn scrupulous type who have generally been good workers in detailed filing, etc. But once they are presented with an emergency their frustration and hatred of life has resulted in their violently attacking whoever is in their way. Then we have the loud-mouth braggart who when drunk by his very noise would upset everything. One such who has been here for twenty years exasperated me by his noise when I was trying to phone and I said to him, "How long do I have to put up with you?"

"How long do I have to put up with you, you damn intellectual?" he replied. This is wonderful, for the Catholic Worker is a place for derelicts, and we intellectuals talk pacifism, anarchism, and go to Mass. All some of these folks want is one more drink and in between they have to listen to us.

Then there are the hysterical women who quarrel, accusing each other of selling clothing we give them for drink, and who fight as to where they are to sit at the table, etc.

The first day I came to the CW in 1953 Dorothy said, "Here is Susie; she wants to meet you," and she left me for hours with a woman who chattered and chattered. She was a chronic pest whose noise would send the average man to a monastery or the asylum. I got used to her in years, but she is still hard to take. Later that afternoon there was a scuffle and noise in a room across the hall. Dorothy asked me to see what it was. There was Albert, a stocky part-Negro who had a huge cane as he was crippled. He did not allow "niggers" to come here and was trying to evict a huge Negro much bigger than himself. Foolishly I jumped between them saying quietly to the huge Negro, "You oughtn't to pick on a cripple, don't you think?"; and to Albert, "You are not the boss around here. This man has as much right as you have here; now lay off." They each one went to another corner of the room. I wouldn't advise this as a tactic for I might have been clubbed by both of them.

Bob Steed came up from Memphis, having asked permission of the Bishop there to sell the CW, and later having this permission withdrawn when there was a strike and it was noticed how radical we were. One summer afternoon, right outside my office window, two drunken men, one Negro and one southern white, each had a knife and was daring the other in the foulest of language to knife him.

"Oh, we must do something; we can't see these men kill each other," said Bob.

"You are not God and you are not a cop; just hold yourself," I said.

"But we are our brother's keeper; we are pacifists and we can't let this violence continue," said Bob.

"You are young and you are going to see a lot of violence; you are in the midst of evil here on the Bowery, and you will see more of it."

"But it's our duty, it's our duty." Bob said as he went towards the door.

"Duty, my eye," was my reply. After half an hour the two men got tired of shouting and each walked in a different direction. If we had interfered we would have provoked these two men to make good their boasts and threats and all four of us might have been knifed. We are going to have to put up with a lot of trouble or we shouldn't be here.

All those who come to the CW for any length of time come through mixed motives. I had a crush on Dorothy but got over it in a few years. She is the best ever and has more integrity about what is worthwhile than any two radicals or Christians I have ever known. Everyone is enamored of her and calls her a saint. One woman wanted to know if she saw visions and she replied, "Hell no." She is wonderful, but is not a saint, and what she says goes. This is no democracy and if it was I wouldn't stay a month. For the weaklings would always outvote the few courageous ones. Everyone is not meant to be a Trappist and when Bob Steed was at the Trappists for two years it upset him so much that he left to get refuge here. He varied between scrupulous sanctity and anti-clericalism. Seeing Kerran Dugan and me reading the *Daily Worker* he was bothered and went to the local priest asking for written permission for the editors of the CW to read the *Daily*

Worker. The priest said that Dorothy and I could read anything, it wouldn't hurt us, but Steed, he would have to see the Chancery Office about that. Of course nothing was ever done about it and in a few days Bob was off his scrupulous emphasis. Another time when I was fasting and picketing the tax man and was going to leave for my daughter Carmen's wedding in California Bob had just taken over the running of the office. In a rare spurt of efficiency he wrote out checks and paid all bills, but forgot to check up and see if all checks from the month before had been cashed yet. Now, being overdrawn, he said he thought it was God's will that I should stay home and not attend the wedding. "Don't blame God for your stupidity," I told him. I like Bob and when he learns how to work and discipline himself he may develop.

Stanley Vishnewski, my co-editor friend on the CW, says: "Hurry up and die, Ammon, and I'll make a fortune out of you selling *Special Hennacy Hamburger;* Ammon always liked them."

One rainy day I went downstairs to lunch and came back and found that some "ambassador" had lifted my coat and raincoat; the latter for comfort, the former to sell for liquor, I suppose. I was to go to court the next morning and did not have a coat. In the mail the next day came a coat which Tom Sullivan brought to me, and it just fit. Tom was here for about eight years after some time at the Chicago CW with John Cogley. He was not a pacifist nor an anarchist but, I think, the best fellow we have had around here to run the house. He was kind to drunks and homos, and not so understanding with the half insane. Charlie Butterworth has taken special interest in the balmy folks and does the best he can with the drunks. I appreciate those who have done time no matter who they are, and the young folks seem to like to tell me their troubles and to listen to my tales of radical achievement. Most of the folks around here visit those who are sick in hospitals but as I don't believe in medicines I am not especially interested in this activity. When Judith Gregory was here she was interested in farming communes and co-op housing. So through it all we have a variety of interests and everyone gets taken care of by someone. I meet with all kinds of radicals of the left, and with leftist union leaders, and the Association of Catholic Trade Unionists. I also am the Catholic who meets every other month with The Central Committee for Conscientious Objectors of Philadelphia, which is the group doing the most for those in trouble with the draft.

Certain women come daily with handbags to haul out clothing which they sell, and often the woman who had been in charge of the clothing room got extra money for liquor or cigarettes by the sale of such clothing. We have an honest one now. At Chrystie Street we always had a night watchman who was always very very surly with any he did not know. One night John Cort from Boston who was with us for years, came to say hello and told who he was, but this stupid watchman would not allow him inside. The old adage of Lord Acton that "power corrupts and absolute power tends to corrupt absolutely," which I quote often in this book, holds true in the lower echelons also. Most of the men here who are sober for a day or two, if given power to allocate others to the table to eat often abuse this power by telling someone that he is too drunk to be with us, when they themselves were that way yesterday and will likely be that way again tomorrow.

A book called *Subways Are for Sleeping* came out a few years ago which described some characters around the Bowery that would seem incredible. And a documentary *On the Bowery* was filmed in which "Doc," the second most important character, was formerly of our house. Some film was taken of us, but was not shown in the final picture. The main character was offered $40,000 a year in Hollywood but all he wanted was one day's work now and then to earn enough money for a few days' rent where he could lie with a supply of wine and drink himself into oblivion. He said to give the $40,000 to someone who would appreciate it. We have some such men here.

Readers of the CW in the thirties will remember the wonderful articles by John McKeon about the people he met around the CW and the Bowery. The one on *The Shy Apostle* who got tea and Chinese food after midnight in the cold nights and stood up those liable to freeze to death and fed them is one of his best. Raymond is still with us, a sober, good-natured, industrious, kind-hearted pack rat. On Chrystie Street we worked together pouring coffee in the morning. He would bring bags of chicken bones to be used for soup, and leave them in every corner until the place was full of rats. Old clothes, junky furniture, anything that wasn't tacked down he would pile to high heaven, on the roof or in hallways.

I have taken men to one of the cheap hotels to pay them in and later that night would see them drunk in the gutter. They had planned with the night clerk at the hotel to return the money so they could get drunk.

When Charlie Butterworth was new at running the house a man came in with an ancient phony slip for an appointment to a hospital, wanting thirty-five cents carfare. He was obviously a fraud. Just now he was sober. Charlie was in a quandary for if he refused him money he was "denying Christ," and if he gave him money he might be contributing to his forthcoming drunkenness. The man argued for twenty minutes and outfoxed Charlie who was a Harvard law graduate, so that Charlie asked me what to do. "For Christ's sake give him the thirty-five cents; he has earned it," I replied. The thing to have done was to chase the man out at once rather than to have argued with him. Young pacifists and Christians make this mistake of preaching and arguing with drunks or those who are not a bit interested in ideas. Your time is entirely wasted. I remember when I was new here and a very Irish man appealed to me as a fellow Irish radical for carfare to see his dying mother. (He might have done it on a wager to see how gullible I was, for this was such an obvious fraud that I aught to have known better). I gave him the $1.25 necessary and of course he and his buddies got a bottle.

Before Charlie Butterworth had charge of the house two FBI men came in and showed their credentials, asking for a certain fellow who helped in our kitchen who had been AWOL from the Army for over a year. Charlie used delaying tactics and said that he was not the boss and that he would have to see Bob Steed who was in charge of the house. He knew Steed was not around, but he couldn't tell a lie, or the truth, so he told the man in the kitchen that the "law" was after him. He then came back and said he couldn't find Steed. Of course we helped the man get out of town. He was not a radical, just a fellow who had too much of the Army and got down and out on the Bowery.

The FBI came around and charged Charlie with "harboring" a deserter which could have a penalty of five years; and for helping him to escape another five years. Coming in from selling CW's on Wall Street one Tuesday the FBI men were here and when I entered they wanted to know who I was and what I though about Charlie's action. I told them I hoped the whole army deserted and they never found any of them. They asked Steed what he thought about it, and he said the same as I did. Then they teased him about not notifying the draft board of his moving from Memphis. As he was twenty-seven this was only academic interest. They asked Charlie if he had his draft card. He answered, "I am a weak brother; I haven't torn mine up yet." (Since then he has done so.) He is thirty-two.

When Charlie came to court he acted as his own lawyer and gave a good presentation of his reasons for not turning anyone in to the police. For in the middle ages all lawbreakers could seek "sanctuary" in a church or monastery. The judge had given five years to a Communist, but said that his son was of the age of Charlie and took the CW and he looked upon Charlie as his own son, and gave him six months, sentence suspended. When I went to get the $1500 bail money back several of the clerks said they had read my book while at college. Now Charlie runs the house, continuing to be kind and courteous, but making decisions more quickly.

Bob and I happened to be standing in the front window and saw a young man take off his overcoat and give it to a friend and come to us and ask for one. We told him he had better get it back from his friend. A drunk can be rolled and come to us barefoot without a shirt. No matter if he had $1000 sailor's pay the night before he really has nothing now. We outfit him and if he is not over his drunk he can mooch money until he gets drunk again and come again barefoot the next day. We don't ask any questions as to names and reasons or keep any books about what we do. One fellow we called "Dear Soul" had charge of the clothing for a day or two and wouldn't give some one clothing because "you are a drunk." He was lucky he didn't get beaten up in some alley for it is not those who have plenty of clothing who need it, it is those who are poorly clad. In a great number of cases people who get clothing from us or from any charity sell the clothes around the corner at a second hand store for very little. One of the common methods is to take a coat and ask for $5 and a "retainer." This means that the merchant gives you $5 for your good coat that he may sell for $15 and gives you in return some old rag of a coat worth $3 that can keep you warm. Likewise with shoes, you get a dollar and an old, old pair for a fairly good pair. If you ask a man if he is going to sell clothing for booze of course he will tell you that *he* would never do such a thing. If you have spies to watch the man then you will have to have spies to watch the spies, and besides we don't believe in any spy system.

This "Dear Soul" was a twisted unfortunate orphan who had made the rounds of about all the Trappist and many other monasteries. He feigned an ungodly limey accent. Coming in he would greet you:

"Good morning, dear soul! You are looking fine. And what is your problem?" By the time you had heard this said to a dozen people and twice to yourself each day it got to be monotonous. So after about two weeks of this I told him:

"I am no damned dear soul; and I always feel fine, I never feel any other way; so cut out this pious phony crap." He didn't bother me any more. He outshone nearly every one in his energy. He always wanted to work and though he would just as likely put something in the wrong place and undo what others had done, at least he was moving. He liked to attend fires, hospitals, and funerals.

At one a.m. I was walking with a beautiful young woman who lived near us, coming home from the Village, when we saw a huge man sprawled across the sidewalk in a drunken stupor. It was in the early fall and not really cold, but she thought we should do something about it. I asked three drunks leaning against a pole to help me lift the man to a large doorway nearby, but they laughed, saying that all they were interested in was another drink. So I started over to the CW to get Bob to help me. On the way I saw a drunken Negro blabbering at a fire alarm box thinking it was a police call: "Come and get Mable; she is a bad whore; she is an awful whore." Bob and I came back with an overcoat (better than I ever wore) to place over the drunken man. Two fire engines, a dozen cops and a hundred people were gathered around, and a cop was questioning the drunken Negro who had some how turned in a false alarm in his effort to get the police to corral his Mable. Bob and I partly lifted the drunken man while the girl lifted his feet and we dragged him to the doorway and placed the coat over him. We might have killed the man and could have robbed him and were now dragging the body and not a cop or anyone noticed us. In the morning going to Mass I stopped but the man and the overcoat had long since gone. Drunk people lay all over the Bowery and few people pay any attention to them. I deserve no merit for this good deed for I only did it because of the admonitions of a pretty woman.

One night about 9:30 p.m. Dorothy and I were walking a few blocks from the CW when we heard a screaming and saw one gang of teen agers chasing another gang with steel pipe, clubs and what ever they could get. No police were in sight on this main thoroughfare. A block away from our place here on Spring Street a dozen Italians beat up a bewhiskered young man and broke the jaw of a long haired friend who was visiting us. These youth were not real "beats" but they were outsiders to these several blocks. Father Natallichio of old St. Patrick's spoke to us one night and told of two of the youth of the parish beating up an old drunk who was sitting in a doorway: and this happened with a priest not far away. The priest called the cops but the boys went away. Another time a man was murdered two blocks from the Church. And this is not a really tough section like parts of Harlem and Brooklyn.

Several times when I have done time on Hart's Island I have met a short fellow with a limey accent who is quite learned. I see him looking through garbage cans nearly every day some place. I think his specialty is rags. Others collect bottles, others food. People leave an awful lot of fairly good stuff in garbage cans, which if retrieved soon enough is usable.

Anna is a sweet old Jewish woman who drags a couple of paperboard boxes with twine strings attached containing whatever junk she has picked up from garbage cans and doorways. She had been a seamstress in her

youth. No one knows much definitely about her. She had long hairs strag-
gling out from her chin and pretty blue eyes. She was forever asking for a
smoke, thinking that she was too unworthy to have a tailor-made cigarette,
but wanting a bag of Bugler to roll her own, and picking up butts. She
would not sleep in a room or on a bed, but would lie on the floor in a doorway or hall. She did not seem to realize that cigarette butts thrown away
when she emptied ashtrays into full wastepaper baskets caused fire and so
she was an unconscious firebug. Her mind was hazy about people and places
and if she did not see a person for a day or two she would ask if he or she
had gone on a long trip or if they hat gotten married. Once we had a call
that she had been hit by a truck and both legs broken. We went to see her
in a hospital and she has not been to see us for several years, as the Jewish
charities now take care of her.

One highly placed mechanic liked our works of mercy and was our friend
for twenty years but when we commenced to get arrested on the air raid
drill he ceased to come around. Dozens of seminarians come and work for a
few days, weeks or months, and after they become priests they come back
and say hello when they can.

Another fellow had worked for the State Department in the Near East
and was getting a divorce from his wife there, or rather she was getting the
divorce from him. He came to us perhaps a little high on dope or perhaps
this was his rather insane manner. He brought an assorted group of homos
and drunks with him. He was always dressed as a gentleman and had an
Oxford accent. I expect because I listened to him he thought I was a fine
fellow. He would come in and "write his book." When anyone crossed him
in the slightest detail he would take a pencil and mark off a page in his book
saying, "I have crossed your name out of my book." One day he came in
from the television room saying to me, "That was sure fine the way you told
off Bishop Sheen." His mind went this way: (1) I like Hennacy. (2) I don't
like Bishop Sheen. (3) If Hennacy told off Sheen on television that would
be wonderful. (4) Therefore it happened.

Paul was a quiet middle-aged man, perhaps a little queer, but never to
be noticed one way nor the other. He lived wtih us and cheerfully ran certain errands. One day he was missing and word came from an insane asylum that he had ben picked up for some irrational activity and was being
kept there. A bank book had been found on him with a credit of $2,000.
All this time he was with us he had not slept in his bed but had been a night
clerk at a flop house and had banked his money. The State took all his
money for his keep and then paroled him back to us. He does not get drunk
very often and is quiet and of little trouble, but has given up doing much
work.

Lena is a not unattractive Italian woman who propositioned several old
Italian men to go into business with her, and after she got their money she
vanished. They came around here and wanted their money. She ate here
off and on. She was forever running to Church and one day came with the
news that a certain Puerto Rican glutton who ate as much as three at our
table, was dead from an operation on his extensive stomach. She had the
priest say Mass for him and we put up a notice in the office for prayers for
Pedro. Soon afterward we saw Pedro at Mass. It seems that he had been

sick and was taken into the ambulance with his eyes closed and she thought he was dead. We all teased her at the "resurrection of Pedro" because of her prayers.

A very dapper young man worked in our office and wrote an excellent article for our paper. Whether it was dope or booze or both we do not know, but after a time he was gone. Two phonies that I remember: one was grooming himself to run for President of the United States, dressed well, and inveigled us into making long phone calls for some mythical mooch. Another had a scheme for world peace and was disappointed because we would no turn our mailing list over to him. He did get hold of lists and had suckers paying the postage and addressing envelopes to any list he could get with all kinds of crazy schemes. We kept him for a few weeks but did not let him get near the files.

Selling CW's at St. Patrick's one Sunday morning a social worker in the midwest whom I had not seen for twenty years introduced a young man to me whom we thought we could help. He came to us and slept on a cot among several others. Near morning we heard a hissing like a snake and then he had a terrible screaming fit running madly around. He did not froth at the mouth. He finally told us that he had escaped from an asylum and had not been taking his medicine. He banged himself around us for months until he finally went back to the hospital. We have had several others who were escapees but we did not know it, who were not violent, but depressed.

We had news from a nun that a certain Negro girl had her face burned and needed skin grafting. We published an appeal for funds which were sent to the nun. After a time the nun wrote to send no more money for this family used the girl as a come on. They would not give her up to the doctors for an operation unless the nun bought them a house, a car, and gave them a certain sum of money. They had been subsidized these few months and now they moved on to some other town for their game of fleecing the gullible.

A good looking young Negro couple with half a dozen children gave some story about being out of work and we fed them several times and gave them food to take home. Accidently we saw them get into a nice big car a few blocks away. One Sunday morning they came very late to eat and the man made up story about working overtime. His wife spoke up and said he was dancing with bad women all night and never went to bed at all. Scores of men and women who come here will get a job working in hotels in the mountains, or other short time jobs, but the trouble is that they ask for money ahead of time and get fired, or if they last a time they will come home and drink it up. They cannot handle money and at this age they will never learn. Many of them really think that this time they will keep sober. We have men who work in the kitchen who will get drunk perhaps only twice a year and who are fine workers. Others are hiding away from their families, or have prison parole. Many are too shaky to hold a job if they had one.

One fellow who has been here for many years hates anything religious. He does a little work but not much. He does not smoke or drink and is very surly. He has grown up children somewhere. He asked us for $7 a month because we spend that much on others for tobacco and he does not smoke. We told him we would charge him $21 a month to live with us and knock off $7 and he owed us only $14 then. He may be a miser who has money saved in a bank.

One night just before a Friday night meeting a young man who is not a Catholic but who knew us brought a red-faced half drunk Irishman out of the gutter to me saying, "Hennacy, here is Christ. Take him and clean him up." I told him to bring him in and he could clean him up; we don't have to go out asking for customers. The man wanted another drink and in our warm room he felt uncomfortable. Another visitor would bring men in to us with wine sores on their legs and want us to clean them up. Days would be spent trying to get them into hospitals. As long as they drank they would have these wine sores and little could be done about it. Priests would see a drunk uptown and phone us saying they were sending a man down for us to kept over night. It was generally the old story; the man took the carfare and went into the nearest saloon and never reached us. But one night around 11 p.m. the Traveler's Aid phoned saying there were two Scottish Catholic girls at the Union station stranded and all welfare agencies were closed. What could I do? I had never heard of a Scottish Catholic girl, so I told them to visit until I did some phoning. I met them and carried their suitcases, one to Eileen Egan's and one to Janet Burwash's apartment.

A certain middle aged woman of vituperative voice that would frighten a regiment has a stodgy son who is deaf and dumb, a victim of meningitis. She came to us with a story of being defrauded by landlords, neighbors, etc. and having no place to live. We publicized her plight and tried to get her a place. Finally someone sent us $50 a month rent for her. In our innocence we gave it to her for the rent. After five months she was thrown out for the non-payment of rent. She had never paid a cent of it. She would not ask for relief for if she did her son would be sent to an institution and she would lose her son as a "come-on." We felt that she pinched her son and made him yell so she could get sympathy. She would have half a dozen coats for him and take him out coatless in the cold saying, "My poor boy needs a coat." She would take him into saloons and in front of churches to get donations from folks who would pity her or who would give her money to get rid of her. Finally no one would put up with her and we took her in and gave her a large room downstairs next to the kitchen. The $50 a month still came for her and she gave out to everyone that we were getting rich from her money. When she saw anyone ask for a second helping or get an extra cup of coffee she would yell, "You can't have it; my money pays for it." To have her around was worth $500 a month wear and tear on all of us. She would steal anything she could get her hands on and sell it. I had a call from the Quakers and one from the St. Vincent de Paul chiding us for being too hard on this poor woman and robbing her of her money. I told them they could have her if they wished. When we put in the sprinkler system we had to tear up her room and this was an excuse to get her right off our hands. We found stores of sheets, clothing, etc. that she had hidden away and not sold yet. One day a woman lawyer from the west who had written that she had wanted to learn how we did things in our "social work" came with a friend to look us over. I had told her not to expect much, and that we could do very little; we had to put up with a lot of misery. She and her friend were inspecting our kitchen. Two stairways led up from it to our office. She came up one stairway and her friend the other and they met on either side of this woman and her dumb son who was shouting and roaring. This was enough; they ran out quickly. We could not have staged it better if we had tried. Stories come to us now and then of people and agencies who have been taken in for months by this woman, but we are the ones who bear the brunt now. We pay this rent — $50 a month and feed them.

I have three people in mind who were terrible pests, and although I have a lot of patience, I could hardly take them, but finally each of them have gone out in the world and achieved integrity and greet me now casually as an old time friend.

There is my friend Larry the cook who sweats daily and puts up with intellectuals who gabble at the table or come late and prolong his working hours. He has more patience than I.

"Saviour of the World, save Russia," is said at the end of each Mass at St. Michael's Church. The Communists are supposed to be our idealogical enemies. We feel that it is hypocrisy for us to pray for our enemies and at the same time want to drop bombs on them. Father Connell the theologian advocates a *limited* germ and atomic war against the Communists, and Msgr. Conway although expressing sympathy with the "sentimental pacifism" of the CW, also believes in a limited atomic war. Whatever that will turn out to be! So we really feel kindly toward the Communists here and in the world.

When the 65,000 papers come to our office each month I go uptown around noon, first to the Communist Party and the Worker headquarters on West 26 Street, give them a dollar as a good will offering for their expenses (for they have families to keep and do not get any Moscow gold or any donations from Corliss Lamont, skip day days, and are poorer than we are). I know all of them and gven them a CW and talk for a few minutes about anything of interest. Then I go to the Catholic Charities where Janet Burwash and other friends work and give them some papers. Then to the American Friends Service Committe (Quakers) where my good friend, Bob Gilmore holds forth, and present them with the latest news from the left. The remainder I take to the Jefferson Bookstore (Communist) on East 16 street near Klein's Annex, where they are given out free and put in good display.

"Where did you come from and where are you going?" asked my priest friend at the Catholic Charities, good naturedly.

"I'm coming from the Communists and I'm going to the Quakers."

"Which one do you like the best?"

"Why, the Communists, of course; all you others are pie-cards living off the miseries of others at a good salary," I replied.

When I was on Nightbeat once I was asked, "What did you do today?" I told them of getting the mail after going to 7 o'clock Mass, answering the mail, selling papers on Wall Street, and then I got a red nose and took it to my old time radical friend, the Communist Elizabeth Gurley Flynn, as I was visiting her. By this time my interviewer got nervous and asked me other questions.

In 1956 the U.S. Revenue Department illegally padlocked the premises of the Communist Daily Worker for taxes for which they did not receive the bill of until the next week. They did not owe these taxes but it was at the height of the McCarthy hysteria. I remember Dorothy sitting at her desk to the right in the front office at Chrystie Street and boiling over and writing the following which I took to the protest meeting at Carnegie Hall where it was read. And later we printed it editorially in the CW.

"We at the CW express our sympathy to the Daily Worker in the eviction they have suffered even though their beliefs are contrary to our own. Freedom of the press is a concept fundamental to Jeffersonians and libertarians and freedom in general is essentially a religious concept. The Smith Act itself shows that our country is so superficially religious that it is not willing to take the risk and consequences of a faith in freedom and man's use of it. If we only had the space and could be truly charitable and hospitable we would offer the use of our offices and even of our mailing list, since the bureaucrats have confiscated yours, and we are sure that we would risk nothing in such a gesture but achieve a healthful clarification of thought. Yours for a green and peaceful revolution. The editors of the CW."

Later we withdrew the offer of the mailing list which was made under emotional stress and in a facetious manner. In February of 1957, Dorothy was invited as one of half a dozen non-Communist radicals and liberals to be "observers" at the Communist 16th Annual Convention where 350 delegates debated the issues of Poland and Hungary and what the Communist' Party should do about it. Various McCarthyite papers called Dorothy an "Enemy of the Cross of Christ" for associating wth the Communist enemy. In an article in the March issue she quotes Wm. Z. Foster as saying in his opening speech, Who Is The Enemy, certainly not those gathered together there at Chateau Gardens (a few doors from our Chrystie Street House of Hospitality), but the men of Wall Street. And furthermore, a greater enemy to the worker than the government has been the corrupting influence of our prosperity, our soft living, Foster said. "Foster himself has never hesitated to embrace the Cross though he would not call his sufferings such. Father Kaszinsky on the outskirts of Pittsburgh helped him in the great steel strike of 1919, and called him friend. It was a strike which most of the American labor movement disowned as a 'Hunky' strike, engineered by 'foreign propagandists.' But Foster is an American . . . not enemies of the Cross, I thought, as I reviewed in my mind the case of Dorothy Blumberg, whom I had met the day before and brought home to supper at St. Joseph's House. She had spent two years in Alderson Federal Penitentiary . . . convicted as one of the 'top' Communists . . . in the struggle ahead is it the capitalist or the Communist who will be easier to convert?" Then Dorothy told of my five Communist delegate friends from Wisconsin who came to our place for supper and said it was the best meal they had in New York City. And Gurley Flynn's sister was there too. I also met Alfred Wagenknecht whom I had not seen since 1917 when I was secretary of the Socialist Party in Columbus, and he was state secretary of the party in Ohio.

The CW opposed the execution of the Rosenbergs and we have had several articles against the continued imprisonment of Morton Sobell, and we have had Mrs. Sobell speak to us. I tried to visit Morton in Atlanta but was not allowed inside. About this time Mike Gold in his column in the Daily Worker mentioned Dorothy and me whom he had known all these years, and our voluntary poverty, pointing out that, "Money has become the opium of the American people. Not religion, or art, or science, but the fast buck is the topic of most conversation here."

Whenever I have had a Saturday night free I have gone to the Libertarian League on Broadway where they had their dinners once a month, with Spanish and Italian cooking. Later this group split up and the younger folks are on St. Mark's Place and the older ones on John Street. I have spoken on how an anarchist could be a Catholic several times before them, and Dorothy has also spoken to them. Most of these good comrades are of Italian and Spanish Catholic upbringing but do not feel at home in the Church because of the support by the Church in Spain and Italy of the exploiter.

The anarchist paper, Iindividual Action, which had a short life of three years and in which I wrote a column, had discussion by readers about my being a Catholic. In the English anarchist weekly *Freedom* there was also a discussion about my being a Catholic. One of their main contributors said in speaking of different kinds of anarchists: "B is an out-and-outer of a different sort, rather like our friend, Ammon Hennacy in America. He pays no taxes and arranges his life to avoid any compromises with the state. He is a tireless propagandist who 'lives out' his anarchism."

Milton Mayer in the *Progressive* has often mentioned my absolutist position and of the CW he says, "The CW is the best anything in America." Once Eileen Egan invited me to speak to a small group of students from Viet Nam. I was introduced and later a girl said, "Glad to meet you Mr. Heresy." So at the office I am called "Father Heresy" at times. Donald McDonald of the *Davenport Messenger* had written an article saying that the works of mercy of the CW and the life of Dorothy was fine but to pay no attention to Hennacy and pacifism and anarchism. I wrote a reply but it was not printed. Later I met him in Milwaukee and he said in his column, in part: "As often happens people are never quite what we imagine them to be when we judge them only on what they have written, and on what others have written or said about them. I half guessed that Ammon Hennacy who is now 66, would be a gaunt, thin, emaciated man in beggars rags. Instead he is well-built, healthy looking, and has a quickness of movement and an alert responsiveness that one usually finds in men half his age . . . I had also though that Ammon might be dogmatically insistent on non-essentials and relativistic about the basic principles of Christian life. He did mention his vegetarianism, his non-smoking and non-drinking, but not in the manner of an aggressive zealot. And with respect to the irreducibles of Faith and morals, he gave no indication of any compromise or easy tolerance. . . . It seemed clear to me that this man, who has suffered a great deal (inside and outside of jails) for his convictions, does not hate any man. I am sure I could not say the same, with any confidence, about certain other Catholics whose "orthodoxy" is beyond reproach . . . Is Ammon Hennacy sure in his own mind that his anarchism and pacifism are the answers to universal war and hate? I do not know. But of one thing he is sure and that is that he must bear constant and personal witness to what he thinks is right. Perhaps few of us are called to bear the same kind of witness as Ammon Hennacy's. But I would think that all of us are obliged to achieve the indomitable quality of Ammon's perseverance and the generosity of his charity."

While I was in Sandstone prison, Murray Kempton of the *N. Y. Post*, had a column about me entitled, "Ammon and the Wolf," quoting from my column in the CW about conditions there and giving my history. He said that "I hadn't realized how much touch I've lost with the consequential lately until I found out that Ammon Hennacy had been in and out of prison for five months with me none the wiser . . . I cannot believe that Sandstone will ever be the same. It is obviously a sound policy for our society to keep Ammon Hennacy moving along."

In 1956, *Time* magazine interviewed Dorothy and asked her when she as representing the furthest left a Catholic could be, would ever get together with the right wing *Brooklyn Tablet*. She said "at the Communion rail." *Time*, on July 22, 1957, had this item: "Led by Roman Catholic Pacifist-Anarchist Dorothy Day, ten members of the Catholic Worker movement (*Time*, March 12, 1956) were arrested for failure to take shelter during Manhattan's civil-defense drill. After registering their disobedience as "a matter of conscience and a refusal to take part in what amounts to a deliberate campaign of psychological preparation for war, they were each sentenced in Manhattan arrest court to 30 days in jail."

Another time a few years ago according to the *N. Y. Times*, report of a Communion Breakfast following Mass at St. Patrick's Cathedral "Father Kelleher, pro-synodal judge of the ecclesiastic tribunal of the Archdiocese of New York . . . praised Dorothy Day at a saint."

Various right wing Catholic papers call Dorothy and me Communists, and some priests and laymen have said that they have definite information that Dorothy was at present a card carrying member of the Communist Party. Many of the clergy have praised us for our ideals and have told us to never give up our struggle for real Christianity. Prof. John A. Abbo of the Catholic University of America is the author of *Political Thought: Men and Ideas,* published by the Newman Press, with the Imprimatur of the Archbishop of Baltimore. He has some pages on Anarchism, and after discussing Bakunin and Kropotkin, and Tolstoy, he says: "A similar theory, although highly personalized and interpreted with a touch of Thoreau's and Gandhi's ideas and ideals, is preached by the American Ammon Hennacy, a Catholic pacifist, and some of his associates in 'The Catholic Worker' movement. Hennacy's principles and beliefs are interestingly told in his *Autobiography of a Catholic Anarchist*. The following is a recent statement of Hennacy on his group's doctrine and policy:

> 'We are motivated by Christ and St. Francis to a life of voluntary pover-
> ty with no reliance upon bullets or ballots or formal organization to
> achieve our ideals. . . . We feel that we have creatively used Gandhian
> dialectic in taking the thesis of the Counsels of Perfection of the early
> Christians as contrasted to the antithesis of the acceptance of the indus-
> trial-capialist system by most of the clergy today; and we have emerged
> with the synthesis of living poor, in the vanguard of civil disobedience to
> air-raid drills, payment of income taxes for war, and in the absolutist
> stand of refusal to register for the draft, creating . . . the new society
> 'within the shell of the old.' "

Steve Allen in his Autobiography, *Mark It and Strike It*, Holt, Rinehart and Winston, N. Y. 1960, says on page 167: "Man has always done rather well when it comes to the formalities of religion; he will willingly burn incense, sacrifice lambs, make pilgrimages, bow toMecca, light candles, sing hymns, march in processions, mutter prayers often without thought to their meaning, flagellate himself, make certain signs and gestures, tithe his salary, and all the rest of it, but he will usually be God-damned (if you will pardon a play on words in this paradox) if he will love his neighbor. . . . Because of this I admire tremendously a Christian like Ammon Hennacy, the penniless Catholic pacifist, more than I admire, say, two high churchmen who stand on opposite sides of a boundary of war and bless the killers (more reluctant, some not) who advance toward each other's throats. I sympathize with such prelates, however. It must be very difficult, if one is trapped by office and circumstance, not to commit the absurdity of blessing Mussolini's bombers."

Just now we are mailing out an appeal for money and the outer office is filled with men and women of the Bowery who are stamping envelopes, and in a few days they will be putting stamps and stenciled addresses on them and inserting our appeal. The custom is to buy cigarettes, candy, ice cream, etc. as a sort of thank you each afternoon when this extra work, and the mailing of the paper is done. Most of these folks do not believe our radical ideas, and some are very opposed to them, but they feel that the CW is "our paper." Last week we had published the fact that we returned $3500 interest to the city on the money paid to us for our Chrystie Street house which was torn down for the subway. Some in the office said, "They send back this money to the city and now they beg; I don't understand it."

One of the last to leave at night is a middle aged woman from the middle west who sweeps out the place; and one of the first to come in the morning is an aged Irishman who sweeps out the inner office and empties waste paper baskets. Italian Mike is big and heavy but he walks to the Ninth Street bakery every day for bread and to the Fulton market for fish on Fridays. And George has enough energy to run a whole restaurant, but considers that being "head waiter" here is satisfactory.

Before I went to prison in Sandstone, a reporter came in and asked questions about the CW. He said he was writing a book. I have had many like this and never heard from them again. What was my surprise to find upon my release, a chapter devoted to this interview entitled, "Give Us, Miss Day, Our Daily Bread," being in a book, *The Bowery Man*, by Elmer Bendiner, Thomas Nelson & Sons, N.Y. 1961. He was former managing editor of *The Nation*. This book presents an interesting history of The Bowery from pre-revolutionary days, with a score of illustrations. He interviewed "Mission-stiffs" and contrasts the CW treatment of the Bowery man with the Bible-banging of the missions. I told him about the Shy Apostle, and of some of the frauds we have to contend with.

He quotes me as saying that a man asked me if I didn't know that he was a fraud. I can't remember the answer I gave but I suppose I did say, "That's one problem you can't bring to us, Mac. If you're a fraud, that's between you and God." I go around at a merrygait and I never thought of myself having time to relax, but Bendiner says I "have the relaxed self-confidence of a man who knows he is right." He says that I seldom give money to panhandlers for "they drink just to keep on dying." He says that "until Babylon is broken up into idyllic communes under the banners of The Green Revolution, this little band will go on operating its charity and its paper with the blithe confidence that comes from knowing that nothing can be done about anything in this worst of all possible systems."

Salt Lake City readers can get this book at the University library, for I gave them a copy when I first came here, along with the first edition of my Autobiography.

REWARD

FOR INFORMATION LEADING TO THE APPREHENSION OF —

JESUS CHRIST

WANTED — FOR SEDITION, CRIMINAL ANARCHY-VAGRANCY, AND CONSPIRING TO OVERTHROW THE ESTABLISHED GOVERNMENT

DRESSES POORLY, SAID TO BE A CARPENTER BY TRADE, ILL—NOURISHED, HAS VISIONARY IDEAS, ASSOCIATES WITH COMMON WORKING PEOPLE THE UNEMPLOYED AND BUMS. ALIEN—BELEIVED TO BE A JEW   ALIAS: 'PRINCE OF PEACE, SON OF MAN'-'LIGHT OF THE WORLD' &c &c   PROFESSIONAL AGITATOR RED BEARD, MARKS ON HANDS AND FEET THE RESULT OF INJURIES INFLICTED BY AN ANGRY MOB LED BY RESPECTABLE CITIZENS AND LEGAL AUTHORITIES.

Art Young

CHAPTER 15

SPEAKING
1953 to 1961

Wall Street; Fordham; Other New York Meetings; New England States; South; Mid-West; Mountain States; West Coast; Canada.

Joan of Arc

Painted by Mary Lathrop, 1963.
Hanging at new Joe Hill House
1131 S. 1st W. Salt Lake City, Utah

Wall Street

Here is the center of exploitation of the world. Actually Wall Street begins at Trinity Church and ends at the American Sugar Refining Company at 120 Wall where it runs into Front Street. As Eric Gill would say metaphysically and commercially Wall Street extends to Times Square, St. Patrick's, Fordham, Columbia, and to all the places where the Sermon on the Mount is ignored or watered down, and where the devil is worshipped.

Here in New York City I spoke for the season in 1954 at Broad and Wall Streets. The law in this state is to have a fairly large American flag. I also had a standard with a cut of St. Francis as drawn by Eichenberg with the current CW attached to it, and I stood on a small aluminum step ladder. I kept this parapanalia at the I.W.W. hall lower down on Broad Street. Once I had the flag upside down and a woman made a complaint to a cop and once an inch of it touched the ground and I was ordered to lift it higher. But one cold day my nose dripped and I could not get at my handkerchief without getting someone to hold my flag and sign, so unknowingly I used the flag for a handkerchief. My audience must have been entranced for no one noticed it. A CW girl standing by told me afterwards about it. Some-

333

times I would have the competition of "The Bishop," a husky Southerner in a homberg who arrived in a limousine and denounced "The Whore of Babylon," meaning the Catholic Church. Sometimes I got his crowd away and sometimes he diminished mine. After years when I was not speaking but was selling CW's nearby and would walk by he would take a paper from me and tell his crowd, "You know what I think of the so and so Pope, but this CW is a good paper, and my friend Hennacy is what I call a good Catholic who goes to jail for his ideas."

Patricia Rusk and I had visited John Moody, of The Moody Investment Service and Moody Manual of Business. He had known Peter in the early days, was a convert, and had been a Single Taxer, which was quite radical then. I had told him that time belonged to God and not to bankers, not even 1%. He bought my book and later wrote to me saying:

"I pray for your success every Tuesday when you are speaking on Wall Street. You are getting under the sculls of people. I hear about it. God bless you."

Another time a man said to me, "For 41 years I was a Catholic and now I left the damn church." "That's fine. It wasn't for you. For 51 years I was not a Catholic and now I joined the Church, and we are both happy."

Once a man said to me, "What are you first, a Catholic or an anarchist?" Some months before a Protestant had asked how I evaluated my ideas and I had put being a Catholic fourth. In October of 1954 I was confirmed at Newburgh by Bishop Flannery (Administrator) of St. Patrick's Cathedral, along with many others. I had given his secretary a copy of my book and four years later I discovered it was on his desk. Whether he had waited four years to read it, or read it again after four years I do not know. I never spoke to him personally." I had not noticed anything special at this confirmation. But now I guess my confirmation caught up with me for I answered:

(1) I am Catholic and go to Mass and Communion daily, worthily I hope.
(2) To live poor, for the world's baggage bogs you down.
(3) To love your enemy, not everyone but your enemy.
(4) To bring this out in small groups of like minded people.
(5) To be a worker and not a parasite and this cuts out all Wall Street.
(6) To be an anarchist, for if you live a dedicated life and vote for this and that politician to return evil for evil in courts, prisons and war, you deny Christ.
(7) I do not smoke, drink, eat meat, or take medicine for if tomorrow "come the revolution" I can't revolut if I am tied to an aspirin or a cigarette.

At Fordham

I spoke there seven times but not until I had stood outside the gates for some years selling CW's and getting acquainted. I was finally invited to speak to The Economics Club, the Suarez Society, and Fordham Political Union on "The Position of a Political Anarchist in the Catholic Church." I had to tell them that the term "political" was a misnomer. I told them, "that when I spoke to Protestants they asked why I had joined the worst church and when I spoke to Catholics they asked how they let a guy like me in. I replied to the Protestants that of course the Catholic Church was the worst church; that they would be just as bad if they knew how; they were jealous. And to the Catholics I said that I was baptized by an anarchist priest, Father Casey near Minneapolis, the only one in this country (there was one in Yucatan and one in Canada but they were too far away) and that you did't have to be a Democrat or a Republican to be a priest. And when I was baptized I had to had to read the Catechism. The *Fourth Commandment* said to honor and obey your parents and from this it followed to obey the civil authorities.

"What kind of a Church am I getting into; have I got to mind the cops?"

"No," said Father Casey, "That's just for people who don't know any better. We know better, we have to do better. There's likely a little corner in Heaven for Catholic hangmen. They don't know any better. No one told them; right next to the bingo players. But there is another place where Saint Francis, Saint Martin of Tours and others are. If we want to see them we have to try to be like them. *This is what this commandment means today: when Jesus was asked what to do with the woman caught in sin He said: "he that is without sin among you first cast a stone at her." And His teaching was to love the enemy; forgive seventy times seven; turn the other cheek. So today if you vote for any one who makes a law saying 5 days, 5 years, life or death if you do something; or if you don't do something; or if you vote for the judge who pronounces the sentence; or if you vote for the governor or president who appoints the hangman or the jailors — then these men are your servants; they are your arm to throw the stone and you deny Christ."* Now you folks don't have to be in a hurry to be an anarchist for I was 59 years getting to be a Catholic, But I am sent here to waken you up and you can't say you never heard it; you will have to sweat a little from now on; you will have to approximate the anarchist way if you want to be a real Catholic or a real Christian.

"And the *Fifth Commanment* says Thou Shalt Not Kill, but the Catechism says it is permitted to kill in a just war, capital punishment, and self defense. Father Casey said that of course there was no just war; that capital punishment denied the Sermon on the Mount, and that I had defended myself much better when I shook hands with the man with the knife, than if I had used a knife; that I couldn't use knives and guns like other Catholics, for I knew better so I had to do better. Now, of course, on the subject of war the Holy Father has said that a Catholic cannot be a conscientious objector in a just war. And there are no unjust wars for the Catholics in any certain country. They are supposed to obey their rulers. It is the other country that has the "unjust" war. So in Italy Catholics killed for God and Mussolini, and in Ethiopia they killed for God and Haile Selaissie. And in Germany for God and Hitler; and in this country for God and the man who said "I tell you again, again and again that no boys will be sent across to war." The fact is that the true meaning of the word "Catholic" is universal and God does not have any country, for we are all brothers. Once a Sunday School teacher was reading from the Bible and she read the passage where "God spoke unto Joshua saying kill all the Ammonites, Jebusites, Moabites and suffer not a one to live." A little girl raised her hand and said:

"Teacher, that must have been before God got to be a Christian." "*Life* magazine a few years ago had an old English woodcut showing the hanging of pickpockets. This public spectacle was supposed to deter pickpockets, but at this public hanging the pickpockets worked the crowd. When I was in prison in Atlanta I met many counterfeiters; they were not the best ones; they were

the second best, for the best ones were out making money — I mean making money." Then I told of my life in prison, of my anti-tax activity. I spoke later half a dozen times to classes and as I travel over the country I find former Fordham students who greet me.

A priest from a ritzy Bronx church asked me to speak at a Communion breakfast just before St. Patrick's Day. I suggested that Dorothy speak as I would be too radical. He replied that he wanted me to jolt the "lace-curtain" complacent Irish in his parish. It was a very ritzy breakfast in a hotel with an Irish audience of police, FBI, etc. character. Naturally few agreed with me. When the meeting was over the priest said "Mr. Hennacy is an anarchist and he is a Catholic, and maybe a better Catholic than I am. It is good for you to hear him and that is why I brought him here to waken you to the possibilities of what our Gospel might mean to us." I spoke in classes in Catholic high schools and to the Information Center on Staten Island, and to the Newman Clubs at Brooklyn and Brooklyn Technical. Here the priests made it plain that they did not agree with me but wanted the students to hear what I had to say. A meeting at the Walter Farrell Guild where liberal Catholics hold forth was very interesting. The liberals who are for good capitalism, good wars, and the impossible task of trying to make sense out of "workers councils and employers councils" and no class struggle between the two, per the Pope's encyclicals no doubt find the forth-right radicalism of the CW aggravating and seemingly unreasonable.

May the first in 1958 was a busy day for me as I spoke, wearing a red ribbon, to the Bronx Science High School which is one of the two best schools in this country according to TIME magazine of that week. Here the students were enthusiastic and I was to meet some of them later in picket lines. Then a bus load of students came up from Drew University, for the third time in as many years, and I spoke to them, and at midnight I attended a committee meeting against atomic tests.

Nightbeat is a program on television where John Wingate interviewed two people for half an hour each. This was not previewed. His secretary read my book and interviewed me. I never saw Wingate until the minute I entered the television room when he said to me, "My last question will be about Cardinal Spellman. Will you answer it?" I replied that I would. Mr. Wingate picked out of half a dozen definitions in the dictionary on anarchism the one which mentioned "chaos" and gave a statement from any anonymous theologian that a Catholic could not be an anarchist. I gave my definitions of anarchism and explained my application of it, and of course there are all kinds of theologians and none of them bind me to disobey my conscience, and besides I was baptized by an anarchist priest. Mr. Wingate goodnaturedly chided me on my vegetarianism, pacifism, and refusal to take medicine. He asked me if I believed in the infallibility of the Pope. I said I did when he was infallible, and when he wasn't, he was talking through the Pope's hat. I explained that we respected Spellman as a Cardinal, but were not bound to agree with any of his patriotic and anti-union ideas; that he had a lot of patience with us and had never picketed us. And that I was bound to obey my conscience above any Church authority. Stuart Cloete, the novelist from Africa followed me on the program. As we were waiting I traded books with him. He had whiskers and most of his time was

336

spent in a defense of wearing them. The night before Christmas Mr. Wingate's secretary phoned and asked if I would be on their Christmas program. A Baptist minister from New Jersey who had a Christmas party in July to get clothing for an Indian mission in the west explained his novel scheme. Some Salvation Army lassies explained their procedure. A chorus of Negroes from a Harlem Church sang. I suppose I was to represent the Catholics. Mr. Wingate went over all of my wild ideas and goodnaturedly kidded me about them. I replied in like manner. Christ and the Sermon on the Mount is my guide to determine truth. For years I have met people on the street who saw me on these programs and stop and ask me questions.

For several times in the fall I spoke at a Socialist picnic at Massepaqua Long Island, along with Earl Browder and Norman Thomas. I knew Earl in the old days when he was released from Leavenworth as a CO in World War I. He gets further and further away from radicalism. Norman is always a good speaker and fighter for what he believes, but he gets less and less radical as he grows older. It was up to me to speak of the old days of Debs and Mother Bloor and to dare them to come alive.

Father Meyer at the Episcopalian Henry Street Settlement on the lower east side is a friend of ours. He gets his money from the corrupt Trinity Church but he puts it to good use. If any of the kids in the gangs are fighting and one of them touches his hands on Fr. Meyer's Church that is sanctuary. His work with the gangs is the best that has been done by anyone. He has spoken here at the CW twice and Dorothy and I have been down to his Church speaking to his young folks twice.

In the New England States

Holy Cross Seminary at Worcester, Mass. is a conservative Jesuit college. A student from there had bought a CW and my book from me at 43rd and Lexington and wrote for me to come there. I got there at 5 p.m. and he said, "You very nearly didn't have a meeting." "How come," I asked.

"At 1 p.m. the Dean called me in and said, 'I find that the Catholic Worker is subversive, and Hennacy is the worst one. The meeting is cancelled. I'll put a guard at the gate and not allow him on the campus."

At 2 p.m. the student received a letter from Bishop Wright saying,

"I hear our mutual friend Ammon is speaking tonight. I would like to attend his meeting but cannot do so for I have a meeting of my own. Have him call this phone number at 9:30 and I'll see him in the morning. God bless Ammon and the Catholic Worker."

The student showed this letter to the Dean and he said "Have your meeting." The room was crowded and I was answering questions in the students' rooms until 1:30 in the morning.

About the same time a Methodist and a Lutheran student who had heard me in the mid West and who were now studying to be missionaries in foreign countries asked me to speak at the *Hartford Theological Seminary.* When I got there the students told me I very nearly didn't have a meeting. It seemed that the Professor in charge of meetings in the building where I was supposd to speak was afraid of the word "anarchist" and asked my friends if they could get me to speak without using this dreadful word. They said that was one of my especial words. This professor conferred with the president and he did not wish to take the responsibility so the board of trustees decided that if I said I was a "Catholic anarchist" and not a Protestant one I could have a meeting. So for once I hid behind the Church.

At *Dartmouth* the Christian Union turned out to hear me with much interest but the Catholic youth who had suggested my coming got frightened, and when he heard that I was speaking to the class of a Catholic prof. in the morning he notified the young conservative Catholic Chaplain who tried to stop my talk to the class. I spoke. But later the Bishop of New Hampshire would not allow me to speak in that state. He died and I have no contract with that state since and it is just as well as it has a bad reputation in jailing Rev. Uphaus.

Prof. Bourcier of *Middlebury College in Vermont* had invited me to come there and speak but the authorities thought I would be "too controversial." He ordered four of my books and gave them to these men to read and I was invited to speak, having fine meetings with hours of questioning at the College and a large meeting at St. Mary's parochial school. I had stayed at the home of the priest that night and in the morning he looked up the definition of anarchism which meant "chaos", but after my explanation of it he phoned to the grade school and had me speak to classes there. I had also spoken to Trinity College in Burlington and to nearby St. Michaels, as well as meetings at Brattleboro and Putney College.

I spent a night at the home of a Quaker, Herbert Leader, in Burlington Vt. and he told me I was to speak to some classes at the U. of Vt. the next day. The first one was on labor history. I sang I.W.W. songs, told them of Mother Jones, Debs, and Joe Hill and answered questions for a long time. the next class was in Sociology where a student gave a review of an article by Protestant ministers who had visited Moscow. I had heard these ministers here at the CW and gave further information, and also the report of a Catholic priest·who had been imprisoned by the Communists in China for six years and who emerged more friendly to the Communists than to the usurper Chaing. Too many priests there are agents of "American imperialism" and it cannot be expected that the Chinese would like them. The next class was a two hour seminar on social work, so I was at home describing my life as a social worker and life now on the Bowery. That night I spoke to a large meeting of students on CW ideas. I was interested in St. Albans, as this was the town where Morgans Raiders held up and robbed the local bank after their escape from Plattsburg prison in the Civil War time. Raider Morgan had been captured near my home town of Lisbon, Ohio. Later Joanna Sturm and I saw a movie based on this St. Albans robbery.

New England Town Meeting

With my farmer vegetarian friends Bob and Ann Stowell I visited the Town Meeting to which they belong at Cabot, Vt. A preliminary meeting had been held where anyone who desired questions to be discussed could present them so that each voter now had a printed booklet on the 28 motions to be voted on that day. There was much discussion of an increase in tax for roads. About two-thirds of the town population were there and there were more women than men present. Only those who paid a $10 poll tax could vote at the meeting, although this did not prevent them from voting in state or national elections, if they did not pay their town poll tax. The Moderator is only paid for one day of the year at this meeting. He had been elected for years and was an employee of the local cheese co-op. He was voted out because he took the unpopular side of desiring a centralized school for three towns which would cost $10,000 interest. It was defeated by 168 to 7. And a prosperous farmer became Moderator. The five Catholics present voted for free taxes for 5 years for the local Masonic Hall; they might as well be good humored about it. Men are elected to run the town not according to political party, banjo playing or baby kissing, but because all these folks know each other and there is no passing the buck if you are found inefficient. As an anarchist I could stand for this decentralized *administration of things, not the legislation of morals.*

A man by the name of Francis had a meeting for me at his house for *Amherst* students and friends. A neighbor whose first name was Francis received the CW and by mistake it was delivered to my non-Catholic friend Mr. Francis who liked it, and invited his neighbor. At Harvard, Yale, Boston U., Springfield College I had interesting meetings. I spoke to classes at the U. of Connecticut at Storrs, having come there on the invitation of the Newman Club, but the priest got scared and cancelled the meeting a few hours before it was scheduled. In Provincetown I went to visit my friends Lee and Vicki Pagano and my two god-children Pier and Jackie, and spoke to resident artists and friends, among them the old time radical Harry Kemp; who became a Catholic before his death. Somehow I spoke to a business man's club at the Agawan Catholic Church and after a couple of hours most of those present understood me even if they did not agree with me. I also spoke at Brandeis College on that trip.

In February of 1957 I accepted the generous invitation of Dr. Paquette of Waterville, Maine to extract 19 roots and make an upper plate. I had gone around for years with one tooth in front, figuring that the education of my daughters and the printing of my Autobiography was more important than my looks. Seems that most of my teeth were chalky and broke off all of these years. After X-rays I had these roots extracted in four sessions, at my insistence, without the aid of any drugs. It did hurt a little and I could not help a tear now and then, but I had inadverdantly chosen a skillful dentist who did a minimum of goughing and who had a sure grip on the forceps. I found I could say "Mississippi" without any lisping. In fact I spoke to two meetings the first night and meetings every other night while this dental work was going on. I spoke to my first *Lions Club* telling them what I have mentioned before, that "the early Christians were thrown to the lions rather than put a pinch of incense on the altar to Caesar, while the modern ones join the Lions Club." I spoke to some students at Colby College. Father Gower of the local Catholic Church had me speak to some laymen and a tape recording was taken of my talk. My message was so radical and so new to these good men that I had to spend two other nights explaining and answering questions, with the help of Father Gower and a retreat priest from Augusta, until they were convinced and in all good humor felt that a Catholic could also be a radical. This layman came down to the CW for a week later to get better acquainted with us. I also spoke to a social worker group at Gould Farm, Gt. Barrington, Mass.

The Canterbury Boys School is a ritzy place founded by Havemeyer Sugar at New Milford, Conn. There is a priest there but the teachers are lay people. I have seldom been so enthusiastically received by an audience, although nearly all that I said was new to the boys. They crowded around and bought twenty of my books, wanted to know "if I believed in unions," etc. Later they sent a large donation to the CW. In later years I have met them as I was talking in other colleges or was selling CW's on the streets.

An anarchist instructor invited me to speak at Brown University and a Monseignor came to the meetings.

Speaking in the South

There are very few Catholics in the South outside of Louisiana and the tendency is to try to appear patriotic and regular for they are in a disliked minority. For years I had written answers to the capitalistic letters that Bill Stevens, a convert, had written to us from Charlottesville, Va. Finally he met me at the bus when I was on my way to Florida and we became acquainted. He had a page introduction to my book inserted in it when he gave it to the public library in his home town. It read in part:

"Hennacy's mother is a Fitz-Randolph. He loves Thomas Jefferson, Francis of Assisi, Tolstoy and Gandhi. His 'bomb' is the Sermon on the Mount; his 'persuader' instead of the hydrogen bomb, which he abhors with a passion, is the Palm Branch, a durable weapon . . . Hennacy puts the phony gliberal in his place and gives a clear perspective to true Convervatism (of the individual)." Numerous friends had me speak at Norfolk.

Bill and Gay Houston had me speak to student friends at Morehouse University where he was then teaching, in Atlanta. Francis Coyle had me speak to classes at the University of Georgia, but the meeting at the Newman Club was cancelled as being "too controversial." This was at Athens. At Chapel Hill, N. C. Ronald Gosslein had me speak at the home of a radical professor, and I met the Catholic Chaplain who was liberal. Dick Bayer of the *Charlotte N. C. News* had me speak at the Unitarian Church in nearby Monroe. Mrs. Williams, a Catholic, had asked her priest if she could come to the Unitarian Church to hear me. Her husband, head of the NAACP, and later publicized as one Negro who would use a gun instead of the pacifist method against white aggression, accompanied her. I saw the bullet holes in their car where the White Citizens Council had shot at them. I had written to all six of our subscribers in Nashville, Tennessee telling them that I would be through their town on a certain day and I would like to meet them. A professor at Vanderbuilt University who was not a pacifist but who liked the CW for years, phoned me at Tell City, Indiana and planned a meeting for me, where I spoke to his class in theology. Some subscribers from the Methodist magazine *Motive* in that city who liked us came to this class. No Catholic took the paper in Nashville and the Catholic Chaplain was aggrieved because someone of the CW had spoken in classes instead of a patriotic Catholic.

Mr. and Mrs. Doering teach at a plush boys school north of Birmingham and had written to me to come and visit them. A fellow teacher asked me to speak to these white, Protestant boys and I spent all of my two days answering questions. Later I discovered that on the last afternoon a police van from

Birmingham was outside and they were getting ready to defend me. I had been talking about jails all along so it seemed natural for the police to be after me again. But nothing happened. I stayed two days at the Divine Word Seminary at Bay St. Louis, Mississippi, an integrated school where a Negro, Father Perry is the head, and where white and colored students live together. The only manner in which the state punished them was not to allow them any surplus commodities. Father Perry is one of the finest priests whom I have met. In New Orleans I spoke at Tulane, Notre Dame, Xavier, Sisters of the Blessed Sacrament and the Caritas group. I met a seminarian who said that I had argued with him for years on Wall Street until he had quit his "unholy" job and come here to study to be a priest. At Dean Stephen Ryan's I had the pleasure of meeting Father Fichter, known all over the country as a courageous priest. At Lafayette Fr. Sigur and Dr. Ward made me welcome and I met many interested students and faculty members at this large Southwestern University. The diocesian paper here and the local paper and also the New Orleans paper gave me a fair story. In New Orleans I spoke to Protestants who had read the CW for years. The wife of one of these ministers asked me, "What can I do with those War Bonds my folks gave for my children? I can throw away the guns and turn off the gangster shows on television, but I can't throw the money away." I remembered a friend of mine who at Christmastime had a date with a Southern divorcee. Just before coming to her home he had received a telegram from his friend Joe that he was sick and had lost his job. He mentioned this to the woman and she said, "Mr. Pat, your friend will have a miserable Christmas. This will never do. Here, send this to him." And she went to the large family Bible and gingerly took out a $50 bill and gave it to my friend. "I keep this money in the Bible to perhaps purify it, for it has the picture of that Yankee Grant on each bill."

My answer to this woman was to cash the War Bonds, thus not being guilty of receiving any more bloody interest, and place the money in not too large or too small bills in the Bible, and as occasion offered for any especial personal need of others to give it out, but not to organizations. If any remained when the children grew up it would be for them, and if it was all gone then it had already served a good purpose.

In Oklahoma City I stayed at the home of Byerly's, Quakers, and had a fine meeting at the Catholic Secular Institute where priests, nuns and visiting students from Norman attended. The diocesian paper, The Courier, gave me a fine write up saying that I had "a firm theology all his own." A fine picture on the front page with the inscription "A visit with an anarchist," and one on the inside with two nuns. Here a Carmelite brother wanted me to answer the article in the October 1959 *Homiletic and Pastoral Review* by Father Leslie Rumble entitled "Catholic Pacifism Repudiated," supposed to be an answer to the *Morals and Missiles* by English pacifists. Father Rumble said that Christ never implied anything against war in His teachings in the Sermon on the Mount or elsewhere. Denying Christ he quotes the theologian to the Cardinal of England as saying, "if asked, the confessor must declare conscientious objection to be wrong and sinful." For Father Rumble to declare Catholic pacifism "abnormal" and his declaration in favor of war normal is to forget Benedict XV who in his *Peace of God*, 1920 said, "The Gospel command of love applies between states just as it does between individual men." Father Rumble commits the same mistake in 1960 as happened at the time of Joan of Arc when those in the employ of the English exploiters and rulers, and who spoke for the Church, burned her. To follow Father Rumble is to place the Church where Communists today say it is: on the side of oppression, exploitation and war.

I was welcomed by radicals and Catholics at Las Vegas, N. M. and spoke to classes at Highland University there, first going to early Mass at Montezuma Seminary where hundreds of Mexican seminarians are studying. I had been in Santa Fe many times visiting my daughters, and after I was a Catholic I became acquainted with the Medical Missionaries, the good nuns who delivered babies within a radius of forty miles, for free for the poor Mexicans and Indians. Dorothy had spoken there and I spoke to them at a meeting where Quakers, anarchists and pacifists came. Carmen lived next door to them for some years. Someone got to the Bishop with the word that the CW was Communist and he sent word that I was not allowed to speak to the nuns, so twice I have visited with them, but have had meetings at private homes of interested Catholics. This is the Bishop who became so excited about a girl appearing in a beauty contest but who says nothing about the atom bombs being made for years in nearby Los Alamos. I have reviewed several books in the CW dealing with the history of Santa Fe and the Indians and am glad that my daughter is married and living in this beautiful city 8000 feet high, with the clear air and the Indian traditions.

When living in Albuquerque from 1942 to 1947 I had met with Protestant pacifists but had not known any Catholic pacifists. The Newman Club at the University of New Mexico run by the Dominicans is a beautiful place. Just as I was announced the bells tolled reporting the death of Pius XII. I had to tell over and over again my realistic approach to pacifism and war which is that, as Gandhi said, "it is better to kill a tyrant than it is to knuckle and obey him, but it is much better to make him your friend." And quoting Forrest the Southerner, "he who gets there fustest with the mostest wins." If we are not pacifists then to talk of us disarming is foolish. As long as we are exploiters we must guard our loot; only when we give up our capitalism and imperialism and our loot can we talk of acting like Christians. Ed Abbey, author of *The Brave Cowboy*, about two anarchists in an Albuquerque jail, drove me to Carmen's in Santa Fe that night after the meeting.

It is very seldom that a prophet has honor in his home town, and I consider Phoenix one of my home towns. When I was a pacifist and not a Catholic there for 6 years I was a scandal to the bourgeois minded pacifists and Quakers, although they liked me in private conversation, but I was always getting arrested it seemed. And when I came back as a Catholic of 6 months my Catholic friends and priests liked me but it was too sudden for them to sponsor me at public meetings. So it was not until 1960 when I was back after my release from Sandstone prison that Bea Trudelle had a meeting in a northern suburb for me at a dancing studio. And through a labor minded lawyer I was asked to speak a few words at the Catholic Labor group at the ritzy St. Francis Xavier Church. But no one knew I was coming so it did not excite anyone. My very dearest friends are in Phoenix but that does not mean public meetings. There is no rational way of explaining why the Mayor of Phoenix, Jack Williams, should have me speak on his radio station and give my radical ideas without censorship. And later when he refused to run for mayor he still had me on the air. He does not agree with any of my ideas, but he liked the Old Pioneer and stood up for me even when I was going to jail and he was only a commentator, and did not own the station and was not Mayor. Likewise Don Dedera has given me a good hand in his column quoting me as saying, "A man has two means of protection — the Bible or the gun. No man or country can hold a Bible in one hand and a gun in the other . . . He is a Christian Anarchist. Through penance and exposition, he is trying to do away with the atom bombs." The Allen Family in Tucson with their ten fine children always had meetings for me when I came that way. Friends at the Arizona Ranch School had me talk to their boys. Father Fowler had me speak at St. Joseph's Academy. Dick and Byrd Sweitzer, Tom Bahti and Elizabeth Baskette are fellow "Indian lover" friends of mine there, while Phil Burnham and Mike Cudihay always make me feel at home.

The West Coast

Over the country it is tit, tat, toe as to where the CW is welcome and where it isn't. In San Diego there is lots of Navy and Bishop Buddy likes the Navy so we can only speak in a home now and then, although I did speak at San Diego University to the class of a Prof. who had been fired from a Catholic College because he had as reference some book in his English class that no one but a Jansenist would disapprove. Although when I visited Frank Scully, the man "who has one lung, one leg, and one idea: Frank Scully" an old time friend of Dorothy, he wrote a column about me in the San Diego diocesian paper. In Los Angeles it was Cardinal McIntyre who told Dorothy that she was doing God's work and never to give it up. I spoke to a crowd there at the Little Theatre on June 9, 1954 (the saints day of two fine martyrs, Primus and Felician, who wouldn't give in although told by the soldiers that each one had weakened.) Father Bruscher introduced me here at Loyola, and I have spoken to Quakers and to small groups many times when I go to Pasadena to visit my daughter Sharon. At Stanford and Santa Clara the Steinke's always arrange meetings for me, and many students are interested, despite the conservatism of the authorities.

In San Francisco years ago Archbishop Mitty said that a Catholic can't be a conscientious objector so I visited Arthur Duffy and George Lillis doing a 6 months sentence because of the letter sent to court from the Chancery Office. Individual priests are friendly here and there and I have spoken in meetings at Catholic bookstores and in private homes. And at St. Albert's, the Dominician seminary in Oakland. In Berkeley at the Newman Club and at Wheeler Hall at the University, and before Quaker and pacifist groups many times. I have spoken on KFPA many times, and for a time I prepared a tape every two weeks here in N.Y. City of what I thought about the world and sent it to them and they broadcast it. A most interesting meeting was at the Cloven Hoof in the "beat" section. When I have finished getting acquainted with the Mormons around Salt Lake City, I plan to go to San Francisco for good, so I will be glad to see Vic and Emma Hauser, George

Reeves, Warren K. Billings, Gordon Koller, Byron Bryant, Bob Pickus and my other friends there again.

I had some fine meetings in the old gold rush country at Marysville and a good write up in the Yuba College paper there. Likewise in Corvallis and Eugene in Oregon.

Portland is the one town in the west where we are welcomed by Catholics, Quakers and liberals. The Blanchet House where 1800 people a day are fed was started by young college students awakened by the CW. I spoke there in 1954 but in my two later visits the leader was not interested in our radical philosophy for the men, but was cordial to me personally. At Catholic Portland University, three classes at Lewis and Clark, and two exciting meetings at Reed, and several Quaker meetings. I ran the whole gamut of possible questions. One cordial Jesuit priest heard me give the very radical CW position as I spoke to Quakers at the YWCA. Wanting to pour oil on the troubled waters he said:

"On the subject of pacifism, anarchism and war, it could be that you are right and it could be that you are wrong; and it could be on these subjects that the Church is right, and it could be that the Church is wrong; isn't that the way, Mr. Hennacy"?

"No, I am right and the Church is wrong," and I added, "Father Feeny in Boston said that no one but a Catholic could go to Heaven. That is the line in Spain, but not in Boston, so he was excommunicated. On points of faith like Heaven, Hell, Purgatory I will not argue; I accept what the Church teaches on Faith, but on being true to that radical Christ whom I found in solitary I will obey Him rather than any Church authority."

Out at Mt. Angel Mayanna Manion and her large family have always been our friends and they plan meetings for us, and the good nuns there are our especial friends always, having us speak to their classes. Reuel Amder, young non-church anarchist and John Little, school principal in the country are our good friends for a long time.

Seattle has an old I.W.W. tradition so I spoke one night for the "wobs" at Washington and Occidental where men had been killed years ago to prove the right of free speach. I came as near being beaten by a drunk that night as I ever did. He was just drunk enough to be nasty. The Salvation Army was playing on an opposite corner and this was old time "interference" as the wobs would say. I spoke at a liberal Church of the People and at the Unitarian Church, and to small groups of pacifists in their homes. Velde (of the Un-American Activities Committee: a good name for them) was coming there soon so a meeting at the University was cancelled. The hierarchy there seem to be afraid of us, although numerous priests are friendly. Our old friend Isobel MacRae always had a meeting for me, and Jean David the French Professor who knew Peter always greeted me gladly. Bob Casey, a union seaman who does not follow us all the way, but who takes my books in ports over the world, planned several meetings at forums there in 1960. And the Diocesan paper gave a fair write-up of what I believed in. My old friend Ed Lehmann who fought in Spain lives here, and June and Farrar Burn live away out in the Sound on their island. Last time I stayed with Sue and Mike Miyake, Dorothy's niece and her husband.

I had spoken to a Catholic group and a young priest got up and unmercifully denounced me as being devoid of any understanding of Christ's teaching. I am not mad at any human being so far and I am not going to start now being angry at a priest. I answered him firmly but kindly. The next day he wrote the following letter to me, which was later printed in the CW: "I realize that after all you have been through you must be inured to most kinds of insults and misunderstandings of your character and aims. But I am afraid that what I said last night, that you don't seem to go all out in accepting your Catholicism, might have cut into the sensitivity of even a man of such high ideals and contempt of human opinion as you are, since it was an accusation I don't suppose you hear too often, and since it denies what you really are doing to your fullest capacity. If this was the case I hope you will accept my apology.

"I also hope that you will accept my congratulations. It takes more courage than most of us can muster to accept, with no compromise, what we know is the complete spirit of Christ's teaching. Christ didn't think too much of those who insisted on the letter of the law but didn't live the spirit. As you said last night, there must always be at least one to tell the emperor that he's naked. Maybe others will try to shut him up or embarrassedly ignore him, but they are still glad that he did say it, and do not realize that there is still some hope for the survival of truth if there is at least one man living it.
"I will pray that God will continue to give you the grace to fulfill your mission of shocking men from their immersion in the letter of the law to a realization of the full spirit of Christ's law, even if they can only live up to that spirit in a mediocre way. Since we are men, and not apples, one good man can make a whole barrel, the whole world better.
Sincerely in Christ,

Mountain States

In Spokane Sister Bernice had me speak twice to teachers and students at her Maryclif High School. And at Gonzaga College seminarians met me at the bus and had me speaking about very waking minute at their college. Just one student who has nerve enough to speak up is enough to get a speaker to come to give the message and answer questions. I will not go to any group unless it is known ahead of time that I am an anarchist and a pacifist. If they are afraid of these words they are not ready to think or to learn. I wouldn't waste time on them.

Brother Martin Gaines has a House of Charity where he feeds many people and houses them. He is the "Lord's beggar" getting practically everything by asking for it from all kinds of people. He is a pacifist, a convert, who heard me in 1954 at St. John's in Minnesota. We had a meeting also at a home of Catholic friends of his, and I spoke to the people at his house. I'll be nearer him when I am in Salt Lake City and count him as my good friend.

A lone printer from Brooklyn takes the CW in Boise, Idaho, and he asked me to speak to a few friends at his home. This town hid away in the mountains reminds me of Santa Fe. I will have much more to write if there is a second edition of my Autobiography about Salt Lake City, but I will begin now to tell you of my interest in the Mormons.

345

In Phoenix I noticed 3000 Mormons going out on a Saturday to pick cotton for the Church. I had read the book of Mormon and saw more blood in it to a page than is in our Old Testament. I had written to the heads of the Mormon Church in the Second World War and asked them if a Mormon could be a conscientious objector. The answer was "they could be, they wouldn't get the idea around us." There was a fellow by the name of Bryan in Springfield, Mo. prison as a conscientious objector who it is said was some kind of a Mormon. The Mormon Church has always been bloodthirsty and conservative, but in their early history as told in books by Vardis Fisher and others they had a "United Order" and today they help each other rather than have the welfare state do it. They also tithe and do not take collections in their churches. And their meetings are very interesting. I have good Mormon friends in Flagstaff and Tucson. When I was selling CW's at 43 and Lexington a woman told me of a Sister Mary Catherine, a Carmelite nun, whose folks were polygamists and whose relatives are the Romney's, Apostles in the Church. I corresponded with her and she read my book and she reads the CW, and I visited her in Salt Lake City. A Jewish man by the name of Herbert Rona became a convert to the Mormons. An atheist gave him a CW and he wrote to us saying that he was a pacifist. He had me speak at his home and ex-Gov. Bracken Lee, LeGrande Richards (one of the 12 Apostles), Professor Bennion and Judge Anderson, all Mormons, came to a meeting at Rona's house where I explained my radical ideas. I also met a leader of the polygamous Mormons who are out of the Church and found that he was a pacifist, did not vote, and was a vegetarian. He had done time for having half a dozen wives and still has them.

I also know radical priests in Salt Lake City. I like to work in orchards so by the time you are reading this I will be out there in farm and orchard work. How much of regular Mormon or polygamous Mormon is worthy and how much is phony you will hear about as I live among these good people. The Catholic Bishop here has been very conservative, for the right-to-work law, and out-doing the Mormons in being conservative, at the same time subverting them by bingo, which Mormons are not allowed to indulge in. I do not know the attitude of the new Catholic Bishop.

While I am living among the Mormons I will do them the courtesy to abstain from tea or coffee, meanwhile fasting my regular day a week as penance.

Ed Heustis is a union sympathizer in Anaconda and a CW reader for years. He had me come there and after some questioning by the local priest I spoke at the Catholic Central High School. I would like to visit and speak in Butte, Helena, Billings, Deer Lodge, etc. later,

Once I had thought of living in Denver for a time, but the conservatism of Catholics there does not appeal to me and there is no especial attraction to that city. I have spoken to pacifists half a dozen times in their homes and have gone to nearby Boulder to speak to Quakers. Cheyenne is the home of a wonderful woman with a wonderful family: Mrs. Robert Leybourne. I had sold her sister a CW in Phoenix ten years ago and she had bought one for Mrs. Leybourne and she had become one of the six subscribers in Wyoming. When I was fasting for 40 days in Washington D.C. and picketing, Mrs. Leybourne thought that if I had been in Cheyenne I would have been picketing the dedication of the missile base there the next day, but I couldn't do it for I was busy in Washington. Some one ought to do it maybe she ought to do it. So the next day she takes her 6 children and four months pregnant with another, and shivering they ride in their station wagon, saying "Hail Mary's" the 30 miles to the missile base where she parades with a sign saying, "Missiles are for Murder." The cops came, but she didn't budge. She did not know that some Quakers and pacifists had planned to come there from other parts of the country and picket and go to jail, so when they came her home was the headquarters for activities. I visited her and the children — one girl is named Dimity and another Felicity — and I had a meeting of pacifists at her house. She introduced me to the Bishop who knew of her activities and did not scold her. Her father had been an old time I.W.W. and she is Irish and I suppose that helps, but she *did* the thing while others talked or wrote letters to Washington, D. C.

In Kansas City Bob Hoyt of the ill-fated Catholic daily had me meet friends in a huge antiquated stone house. These were all liberals but they were cordial to the CW. In St. Louis I have spoken several times as I crossed the country at the Catholic Center near the University and always have had spirited meetings. The German influence of state worship is prevalent here and our anarchist approach is not liked. Minneapolis and St. Paul have long been a center where the CW is popular among priests and students. Radical students at the University always plan a meeting for me, and at the home of Orin Doty who was in jail as a CO, at Maryhouse where women live together and do charity work. A Baptist College greeted me gladly but at the same time the Sisters at a Catholic high school who had invited me, even when I had been in Sandstone prison, reluctantly had to cancel the meeting because the priest in control disliked us. The present Bishop in St. Paul denounced the coming of Kruschev to this country and does not seem to be as tolerant as his predecessor. *The Wanderer* is a right wing Catholic weekly that carried articles denouncing the CW and Dorothy, saying that she had gone to prison in Nevada against the atom bomb. None of us went to prison there, and she had no part in that demonstration. I visited with the editor for half an hour and convinced him that when his paper said "it is rumored that Dorothy Day is a communicant" that he was doing an injustice to a great and noble Catholic. (Later they had a long editorial against Dorothy and I and our support of the Cuban revolution.) I have spoken three times at St. John's Seminary near St. Cloud and have always had a good response from the students. The reporter in the St. Cloud paper printed an interview with me that showed a great understanding upon such a short acquaintance. J. F. Powers, the short story writer lives in St. Cloud and I value visits with him. He and George Collins, are the only two Catholics whom I know of that refused to register for the draft in World War II. They did time in Sandstone prison. I spoke at Father Casey's in Hutcheson, and later at Belle Plaine, and to the parishes of several radical priests in small Minnesota towns. I answered questions to a large group of seminarians at St. Mary's in Winona. In Duluth I met with the Finnish I.W.W. folks who publish a daily paper. Across into Wisconsin at Ashland I was welcomed by a Jewish professor at Northland College where I spoke to classes, and by John Chapple, a right-wing extremist long before the days of McCarthy, who is a Catholic convert and friendly to the CW for what might seem odd reasons. We disagreed on Russia, but it seems had the same enemy: the welfare state.

"Mamma, can that man who was in prison because he didn't want the world blown up, sleep in my bed?" asked 5 year old Jeffry Lippink in Two Harbors, Minnesota where I was speaking in their home the second night after my release from Sandstone prison.

"Yes, Mr. Hennacy can sleep in your bed," mother replied.

"Then I'll help 'gainst the war, won't I?" Jeffry answered.

In LaCrosse I had spoken at Viterbo College in 1954 and at the Methodist Church where my friend Winslow Wilson was pastor. He was the first one I heard of who refused to register for the draft in 1940. Although he was already exempt as a minister, and his wife was 7 months pregnant, he refused to register and got 2 years in Sandstone prison. I collected small sums and sent to his wife. Later he became a subscriber to the CW and I have spoken to his folks several times. He is now superintendent of the district in Madison. I treasure knowing him and his fine family. In Milwaukee I have spoken in journalism classes of Dean O'Sullivan's, in their library, and across the street at Cardyn Center. Also at the Newman Club at what was formerly State Teacher's College but is now University of Wisconsin, Milwaukee. Also to small groups in houses, and always to my Communist friends under the auspicies of their leader Fred Basset Blair. There is not much of a pacifist grouping now among Protestants there, but I spoke to them once since becoming a Catholic.

Friends in the Ford Foundation wanted us to apply for a grant, saying that we could receive money each year for five years with no strings. Dorothy wrote refusing any of their money as it was "blood money", being taken from the workers. She remembered the first president of the Ford local who was beaten by Ford thugs. Now of course, Ford, and even Rockefeller are respectable. But the point is they are not *sorry* they are a part of the war system and capitalist exploitation. About the same time a man from Massachusetts wrote that he wanted to send the CW some money but he was a tax man and perhaps Hennacy wouldn't like it. I wrote to him saying that if St. Peter and St. Andrew had a day off from preaching they could go back to their old job which was fishing, but St. Matthew couldn't go back to his old job — that of being a tax man, for it was wicked. Now, if this man could continue being a tax man, unlike St. Matthew, then he should give his money to the Bishops and St. Vincent de Paul, they were not particular, but we were. If he was sorry he was a tax man and as a penance wanted to give us something, we would take it. We didn't get it. I told this to Father George Dunne, a Jesuit, and he said I would make a good Jesuit. And I mentioned it at Marquette and Dean O'Sullivan said that the Jesuits would have gotten the money.

When Bishop Meyer was in Milwaukee I was not allowed to speak openly in churches or in societies having a Chaplain, but in 1960 when Bishop Cousins came from Peoria and was Bishop in Milwaukee I was allowed to speak both at the Cardyn Center when I had a meeting for many hours, and at St. Francis Seminary where I met the President and answered questions from the students for hours.

Of course in Chicago, Nina Polcyn of St. Benet's book store always welcomes us. I spoke at the University of Chicago and to Quakers and small radical groups but not to any churches, or to Catholic colleges. The CW here works closely with other pacifists. The new Bishop in Peoria cancelled my meeting as being "too controversial." I spoke at the Universalist Church. At Notre Dame I had spoken at the home of Prof. Willis Nutting, and to a small meeting at the University Library sponsored by Father Leo Ward. In 1960 he had me speak at a larger meeting there, and the next day to his classes and those of another professor. One student quoted Christ chasing the money changers out of the temple and wondered what I thought about it. I said that if He came back here He sure would upset some of the plush around here. I was pleased to meet Prof. O'Brien, head of the teaching of courses in Criminology. He had formerly been head of all the prisons in Indiana. We did not disagree as much as one might think. In Bloomington some students had me speak at a luncheon informally. Someone at the next table heard part of my conversation and gave a garbled account of it next day in the college paper.

I had been through Indianapolis many times but did not know anyone there, until a young priest from Purdue had me speak at Marian College to several classes of students. All of the priests I met were cordial except one who said he would not have allowed me in his diocese if he were Bishop. He said that a true Catholic should obey his Bishop, who was "Christ on earth" regarding a "just" war, and even if the Bishop was wrong, the sin would be upon the Bishop and not upon the one who took error as being truth. I had not heard this echo from the Middle Ages for some time.

At Joe Zarella's in Tell City, Ind. I met cordial priests from St. Meinrad's. At Purdue University I had as fine a welcome as I have received from a Newman Club. Here three young priests work with the students. At a Communion breakfast and later with a tape recording for the local radio I was able to help there fine young folks realize something about "Christ the revolutionist."

In my home state of Ohio I am always busy speaking to colleges. Antioch College is radical, and at my first visit the Catholic priest in the town was very cordial. My meeting with the students here is always interesting for they are intelligent and full of questions. The Catholic students have had the idea of fighting Communists without knowing what it is all about. I met with them alone. The College *Record* said, "Whether his doctrines are right is largely immaterial. But the man is right, and therefore dangerous, because of the way he treats his opinions. He makes issues out of them. He heckles bureaucrats. . . . For all I know, Hennacy may have found a teammate or two this weekend. At any rate, if President Gould meant what he said last fall — 'let me say as strongly as I know how that there are no subversive activities at Antioch,' then somebody outfoxed the President. Tartly candid, unreconstructed Ammon Hennacy is a subversive activity. And his subversiveness is both impossible and disreputable for a court or prison to combat, let alone a college . . . "

I spoke at Oberlin College to a large meeting. Forty years before I had put out anti-draft literature on their campus. I have always been welcome at the Grail where these fine girls learn the homemaking arts. In Columbus my especial friend is Dr. Wm. Mitchell, who founded a home for spastics, later turning it over to an Order. He had me speak to them and introduced me around the Chancery office. The Bishop was away that day. The good Doctor had written and published booklets at his own expense favoring McCarthy, and had come to the CW giving us money for helping the poor "but not for that radical Hennacy." I became acquainted with him and although we disagree on some things we each appreciate the integrity of the other. On the 5th of April, 1947 I spoke to the Newman Club at Ohio State University there. This was exactly 40 years from the night I had been arrested for opposing World War I. In Cleveland I spoke at the Unitarian Church one night while a meeting of Gov. de Salle's Democrats was supposed to be going on, but they were late so the Democrats came in and wanted to know what this "anarchist-no-voting" meant.

I have spoken to Father Hugo in Pittsburgh several times on the phone but have never met him. Now that my friend Bishop Wright is in Pittsburgh I hope to visit that city more and more. In Philadelphia I have spoken several times to the Quaker colleges and at Pendle Hill. Also to a coffee house of my friend Bill Basnight. At the Christian Brothers La Salle College I was introduced to a huge meeting of students by the Brother who said, "This man has been cleared; this man has been cleared." The students had signs like at a political convention saying "Welcome Ammon Hennacy." They asked stimulating questions for hours afterwards. That night I met with professors and friends until 2 a.m., among them John Stokes, former conscientious objector, and now a wealthy manufacturer, and Catholic convert. Later I spoke to his conservative Catholic friends at his home. He has developed *Mary's Gardens*, offering seeds and flowers named for Our Lady.

In Washington D.C. I spoke to St. Peter Claver House, and to small groups of students attending Catholic University, friends of Peggy Reeves. In Lancaster, Pa. I spoke twice being invited by Kitty Shenk, a former Catholic, but now a Unitarian, who had me speak at her church and to Catholic groups, and also to the Evangelical and Reformed Seminary. The college paper said the next day, "Anarchist fascinates, bewilders." I also played Hopi records and spoke to the children of the "hook and eye" Amish in their school. They looked at me puzzled for their founder was Jacob Ammon, Friends in the local York paper had me speak to Catholics and others there. One stormy night I spoke to students at the Lutheran Muehlenberg College at Allentown, Pa. And another time at Drew University in New Jersey. I spoke to the Newman Club and to an economics seminar at Rutgers before being invited to speak at an assembly dressed in a gown. I spoke at Cornell but the Catholics were abashed at my radicalism, the other students being more cordial. In Rochester at the CW house I spoke to small groups several times.

In Cànada I visited for a few days with Tony Walsh at his Labre House in Montreal and was introduced by Murray Ballantine when I spoke. I become acquainted with Karl Stern, the psychiatrist, whose book *Pillar of Fire* I had read years before I became a Catholic. In it he said that when he joined the Church he brought with him "all that was good from Gandhi and Tolstoy." I also visited the Little Sisters of Charles de Foucauld, who work in factories and live among the poor. Later I met women of their group in

Chicago and Washington, D.C. They are not as radical as we are but they understand and are sympathetic. I spoke to a small meeting of the Newman Club at McGill University, staying at the home of a Quaker, David Kirk, whose wife had the same great-great-grandfather as I on my mother's side. They have adopted several children of varying nationalities. Going on to Combermere I visited a day at Catherine De Heuck's headquarters and spoke to those living there. A young Belgian seminarian invited me to speak to the White Fathers in Ottawa. They are missionaries who work in North Africa. I was surprised to receive a letter from the Father in charge later appreciating my visit, for I had not thought that my extreme radicalism would go over there. Later the young Belgian, now a priest, stopped at the CW on the way to his field. The next day I spoke to students at the University Seminary in Ottawa, and this being the Pope's birthday they had the day off, so I was busy answering questions every minute.

In Sudbury, Ontario I was guest of Vicky Smits, a young housewife who emigrated with her husband Joe Holland nine years ago. Joe works at the Frood-Stoble unit where he blasts 700 tons every 8 hours. The shoemaker says there is nothing like leather. Here, the nickel center of the world, there is nothing like nickel. The big name there is INCO (International Nickel Company of Canada.) Another name that also looms big on the horizon of Sudbury Basin of the 130,000 acres where John Foster Dulles was once Chairman of the Board of INCO, is Local 598 of the Mine, Mill and Smelter Workers, established in 1943 after a score of years of lockouts and violence, and now numbering 14,000 workers. There are at least thirty nationalities in this growing town which is not far from the uranium mines at Blind River and the gold mines at Virginia. In this latter town untl recently native born Canadians received the highest wage, then immigrants, then Indians, all doing the same work. When the union convention was held in Sudbury recently the Chamber of Commerce aroused dissident racial minorities against "the Commie union" and picketed the union hall. My hostess Vicki, picketed the pickets with a sign "Our Leaders are Tops."

My visit was complicated somewhat by the situation of 70% of the members of this left wing union being Catholic, and of the opposition to the union of all the clergy, both Catholic and Protestant. Vicki had planned my schedule as she had lived in different parishes and knew several priests. First I spoke to a group of men employed by INCO who were anti-Communist, at St. Anne's Church. Father Regimbault there disliked both capitalism and communism, and like Father Murphy and Father Kaptean with whom I spoke later, believed in unions. That night and at a Communion breakfast on St. Patrick's Day at the same Church where I answered questions for hours it was difficult for them to gain an understanding of the pacifist anarchist ideal, as they had the idea that anarchists and radicals acted like a goon-squad from Mine Mill that had beaten up a Steelworker organizer brought in to rival Mine Mill. I tried to bring the message that as the Quakers reply to the assertion that you can't trust Communists. "No one said we should trust Communists, for we should trust God and love the Communists." I tried to arrange a meeting between priests and the heads of the Mine, Mill. The union men were willing but the priests would not talk to non-believers. The clergy had tried to prevent the showing of *Salt of the Earth*, the story of a strike at Silver City, N. M., and had told Catholics that they could not receive Communion if they sent their children to the summer camp of the union. The Church did not provide any summer camp for the children in this desolate area where the copper fumes kill nearly all vegetation. I visited the camp with Weir Reed the camp director.

On a tour of the smelter at Copper Cliff I saw as much as a visitor is permitted to see; the mixing ore and its roasting in the gas oven. The fumes did not allow us to go very near the room where the refuse was being skimmed off or near the kilns where men entered to clean out the accumulated sooty refuse. The guide said that his brother had refused to go in a kiln when it was too hot for he had already had an ear burned, but the foreman went in, and to escape the heat had madly rushed out and fallen several stories and was killed. Helmets, boots with steel over the toes, and aprons and gloves, and gas masks cannot always prevent a splash of metal from injuring workers. Some mining is a mile underground.

I was in Arizona when *Salt of the Earth* was being filmed at Silver City, N. M. and I sent money to help the women pickets. The injunction was against the men so the women picketed and finally won the strike. The film was not allowed a public showing in most of the U. S. so I despaired of seeing it. Reid ran the picture with me as an audience of one. Jencks who played an important part in the film is currently being hounded by the authorities, not because he may have signed a non-Communist affidavit falsely, but because he put up such a great fight against those who make wars and profit out of wars. The picture showed that it was radicals who were brave enough to be beaten up and to organize unions when the going was hard. I spoke to a meeting of the union where I met old time I.W.W.'s. To both Communist and Catholic audiences I say, "In Russia and the Iron Curtain countries the enemy of the free worker is the bureaucrat and the Communist; in this country the enemy of the worker is the bureaucrat and the capitalist." I spoke also to a group of women, the auxiliary of the local Lions Club, and to enthusiastic students at Sacred Heart College.

SPEAKING TOUR 1961

Leaving New York City January 2nd I spoke to a group at the Catholic University of America gathered together by Father Robert Hovda, I visited with my friend Bob Hoyt, of the Knight newspapers. He attended the new Catholic Church at McLean, Va. built like that in Holyoke, Mass. in a circular manner, with built in plate glass sound proof rooms for women with crying babies . . . the priest here, along with most I met in or near Washington, was not a bit interested in social problems, least of all my radical approach to them. Bob's young boy had been told about my being a vegetarian and working a garden the year around in Arizona, and proudly showed me some plants he had set out in their small garden.

Several times when I had been fasting in and around Washington, D.C. I had my last meal with Bob and his boss, Ed Leahy. This consisted of onion soup in the National Press Club restaurant. Ed had written up episodes of my argument with the tax man in the string of Knight newspapers over the country, stressing in a humorous way that I was still fighting windmills, and the tax man did not seem to know what to do about it! "The Bureal of Internal Revenue in Washington doesn't like to be asked about Hennacy. A spokesman declares that the case of the Phoenix non-taxpayer has not come to their attention at the main office. But if Hennacy's writing arm holds out, they're going to have to put him on the docket eventually."

I had a standing room only session at the big Unitarian Church across from the Mormon Church, and met with a small group of pacifists also. I also met with some AFL-CIO officials and was glad to meet I. F. Stone, whose dynamic weekly debunks much that goes on in this city of politicians. I always visit Stewart Udall and some of his liberal Democratic Congressman friends, Senator Gene McCarthy, and Ed Leahy and Bob Hoyt of the Knight Newspapers.

A lively group connected with Rev. Ballard's Naturalist Vegetarian Church in Baltimore was something new for me. Then I went to Philadelphia and addressed a Quaker Day School, after which Patricia Rusk drove me back to Baltimore for a small meeting at Goucher College. An exceedingly interesting meeting at St. Johns University at Annapolis showed me that I should have planned a stay of two days there in order to answer all of the questions propounded by those freewheeling minds. A teacher drove me hurriedly to Woodstock Seminary where the seminarian Czyparek, our friend from New York City, tramped with me to a cabin in the woods where before a huge fire of logs we discussed radical ideas for hours. It had taken several years of speaking a few words as I was selling CW's at 14th Street before this seminarian finally became an enthusiastic CW fan.

Mike Strasser obligingly met me at 4 a.m. at the bus in Pittsburgh and I spoke to a group where Eddie Egan teaches philosophy in a Catholic school. Father Rice, who picketed with us in the depression spoke to me on the phone, and the priests at St. Vincents at Latrobe came and got me for a large meeting. One student had made a bet that he could get me angry, so when the time for questions came he insulted me and dared me to hit him. I told him to come up and strike the first blow and then I would turn my cheek for the second blow. Later we were good friends when he told me of the wager. Their school paper had a good writeup of the meeting.

Russ Gibbons, secretary of a national group of Catholics interested in civil liberties, had planned meetings for me at Rosary Hill College, to a Newman Club at another college and to the Knights of Columbus in the suburb of Hamburg. I was challenged by questions from many who had never heard the radical message before. Nicole d Entremont gave a very good account of my ideas in their paper Ascent. And at the K of C meeting the head of the Democratic party in Buffalo, an Irishman by the name of Crotty, exchanged witticisms with me, in all good humor.

I had been invited by a student to speak at one of the two seminaries in the world established by the Popes, the one in Worthington, Ohio, outside of Columbus, but some minor official there became frightened and cancelled it. The student appealed to the head priest and he knew of the CW and said it would be good to liven them up with a few unorthodox ideas. I never saw so many red sashes outside of a May Day parade. I told them that there was little opportunity in their closed world for them to know what was going on. That I was part of a revolutionary movement like that of the early Christians and that God had sent me to make sure that they didn't go asleep on their job. That what I said was going to get worse so they had better play sick and leave if they couldn't take it. Although the questions are nearly always the same, as given in my chapter on questions and answers, they came fast and furious at this meeting. Dr. Bill Mitchell, my McCarthyite friend from Columbus, took me to his home after the meeting.

In Chillicothe I visited my old time friends where they now lived on a farm. Two priests of the Glenmary Order of Home missioners who had corresponded with me came over for the evening and invited me to speak to their Order near Cincinnati, where also some nuns came to the meeting. Then I had a day in Portsmouth with my old pal of Atlanta prison days, Fr. John Dunn, and went on to Cincinnati where I visited by brother Frank and spoke to a meeting of Quakers and Peacemakers. I was glad to see my friend Maurice McCracken again who had been deposed from his Presbyterian ministry for not paying taxes for war. And of course Ernie Bromley and family, leading Peacemakers. A new group of girls were at the Grail where I spoke to them at length.

I have always found a welcome at Antioch College, and visited at the home of a pacifist who refused to pay his income tax so his $9000 home was sold by the tax man for the around $500 tax that he owed. No one else bid on his house so he bought it back, and of course paid the taxes. Earlham College at Richmond, Ind. had invited me to speak, but cancelled the meeting. This is a Quaker College that has R.O.T.C. so I did not expect much from them. I arrived at Purdue in the midst of exams so only met a few students and had a meeting at the home of a Catholic family. Fr Frazee at Marian College in Indianapolis greeted me gladly and I answered questions practically all day as the students crowded around. One student had heard me answer the same question three times, so the fourth time it came up, he answered it boldly before I could get a word in. The Athletic coach wanted me to tell the teachers at the table at lunch about my fasting and being a vegetarian. He said he had a difficult time getting them to walk short distancse rather than riding in cars. Again in Milwaukee I spoke at Marquette University and to the Cardyn Center nearby, and visited many old time friends. And of course at the Catholic Center at the University in Madison I am always welcome. Likewise at the University of Minnesota and at the homes of pacifists I had interesting meetings.

I arrived at midnight in Winnipeg and was met by a young Catholic who put me up at a downtown hotel. This is the only city in North America where the Communists have members of the City Council and the school board. In these Provinces the government furnishes the buildings near the regular University for the Catholics and for the Church of England, and they pay a small token rent, and teach their religion, philosophy, etc. They make no effort to compete with the regular College in the physical sciences. I was busy all day with meetings. Father Forsythe drove me downtown to the Communist Party headquarters where I introduced myself. A young Communist vegetarian was eating his lunch and invited me to eat with him. Later I met the Communist officials and told them of the CW.

Parochial Schools

This reminds me of the whole idea of aid to parochial schools here in the United States where there is supposed to be a separation of Church and

354

State. When Al Smith ran for President he said, but to little avail, that he believed in the Catholics running their own schools without the help of the state. President Kennedy ran on the same platform. Until his election the National Catholic Welfare Conference, the spokesman for the Church, did not have the nerve to come out and ask for money from the state. It is well known that outside of Cardinal Cushing, most of the hierarchy are so conservative that they would rather have a wishy-washy man like Nixon as President than a liberal. And it was this kind of Catholic in Congress who killed the President's effort to help the public schools. Catholics say that it is unfair for them to pay taxes for public schools, and then for their own parochial schools. This is no more unfair than to make a bachelor to support big families of children. Nor here in Utah where no Mormon in good standing is on relief, for the Mormon Church takes care of their own. Mormons pay a tithe for this and also taxes to feed the Gentiles. If Catholics would lay off their gambling, drinking and smoking they could have enough to run their schools. The following is from TIME magazine of August 25, 1961:

"Msgr. George W. Casey, 65, is a Boston Irish Catholic who looks on the folklore of Boston Irish Catholics just about the way that a small boy with a pin looks on a cluster of balloons. In his lively column for the *Pilot*, weekly newspaper of the Boston archdiocese, Father Casey has lampooned South Boston's 'convivial, congenital, incurable' Irish for boozing it up on St. Patrick's Day, critized parish priests for being 'tyrants,' and even suggested that nuns wear modern clothes — all to howls of Hibernian protest.

Last week Columnist Casey's latest shock was front-page news in Boston. He blandly urged U. S. Catholics to abandon parochial grade schools and concentrate instead on high schools and colleges. 'Since it is quite clear by now that Catholic schools are not going to get any financial aid from the federal government.' Father Casey argued, 'We should move our resources to the front of greatest challenge.'

Casey challenged the assumption that primary grades are the best time and place to carry out the chief mission of Catholic schools, 'preservation of the faith.' While 'neatness, sanitation, table manners and so on can be ingrained in these early years, it is not evident that doctrine and abstract ideas can be.' More important are the crucial years of high school: 'Let us have priests and the Sisters around in the grades where boy meets girl, and where both meet the Reformation, the Inquisition, Communism, Darwinism, Freudianism, and all the other religions and philosophies. They are much more needed there than where the boys and girls meet spelling, times tables and long division.'

Sending Catholic children to public schools, argued Casey, will help 'avoid most of the less pleasant by-products of separation and inbreeding.' Moreover, 'we will all be relieved of the financial strain that so distorts our devotions and parish programs. The parishes will not have to erect the enormous bingo signs that disfigure all the church lawns in certain areas, or run a lot of novenas for palpably profit motives. Sunday Mass will not take on the quality of a fly trap designed to hold the people until three collections are taken up.' "

In Saskatoon the Catholic lady with whom I had corresponded for years had to be out of town for some weeks so my contract was with the Doukhobors. Koozma Tarasoff had visited Russia and asked a Greek Orthodox priest about conscientious objectors and received the reply that he didn't know anything about them, and besides all Christians should fight for their country. He had met some Doukhobors who had picketed against militarism and had been sent to Siberia for a year. When they returned they lived in a colony with other Doukhobors. The understanding being with the government that if they kept by themselves they would not be bothered for military service. They told Koozma that they would like some of the "wild" Doukhobors of Canada to come and picket and go to jail and liven them up. My friend A. J. Muste met Baptist pacifists who had done alternative service in Moscow. How many were killed during the Stalin regime there is no means of knowing.

Here in the vicinity of Saskatoon thousands of Doukhobors lived in the early 1900's. They were persecuted and many fled to British Columbia. Now thousands of them live in a prosperous manner, own individual farms, sing their songs, and practice their religion which might be described as similar to pacifist Unitarians, but with the Russian tradition. I spoke at an annual dinner they had and happened to sit next to a young couple who lived up to the non-smoking, vegetarian ideal of the early Doukhobors. Outside of my talk, which was revolutionary, the tone seemed to be to be a part of the Canadian culture. I also spoke at a meeting in one of the Doukhobor meeting houses where the older folks came on a Sunday afternoon. I addressed a meeting of liberals on pacifism and anarchism, and had a small meeting with students at the University. Koozma is now married and lives in Vancouver and has written a 1000 page book on the history of the Doukhobors. He is getting his M.A. degree there.

In Edmonton Prof. Rose of the English Department welcomed me and he had planned with the Christian Student Council to sponsor meetings which were well attended, and good reports in the *Gateway*, the student paper, followed, especially one by Bentley LeBaron who analyzed my ideas as (1) individualism, (2) intelligence, (3) spiritual power, (4) pacifism, describing my ideas more coherently than I did, I expect. I also spoke at the Unitarian Church. Looking at the map it is not so far to Fairbanks, Alaska, and some time I hope to be invited to speak there. I had corresponded with Jim Milord, who teaches at Hobbema, on a Indian Reservation fifty miles south of Edmonton, so I was glad to spend a couple of days with him and his charming family. These Indians have oil royalties which have demoralized them. I listened to a speech contest and made friends with a young health minded Indian boy.

I spent a week with Helen Demoskoff, Pete Maloff, and other Doukhobor friends. I visited Doukhobors in Grand Forks where a Russian paper is printed and was greeted kindly by the editor who reads the CW.

In Spokane my friend Brother Martin at his House of Charity took me 35 miles to the top of a mountain which a Catholic Msgr. had bought for him, this being a 500 acre tract, where alcoholics from the city could build shacks, raise their food, and be so far away from a saloon that they stood a chance of reforming. We tramped for half a day midst magnificent pines, over streams, and to the high plateau where there is room for 100 cabins or more. In this society that is the only way to help the alcoholic, for if he is in the midst of temptation he will generally succumb, and drag down with him his weak friends. I spoke to a whole gymnasium full of boys who were anxious to get out and play. I only had fifteen minutes but I made one of the best speeches of my life. I suppose it was the challenge of these kids and the short time at hand that made me do my best. Due to a misunderstanding I was not able to make the meeting at Carroll College at Helena.

Salt Lake City

Arriving here on April 6th. I thought I would look around and see what the prospects might be for work when I came back in May. I went on the bus a few miles north to the town of Bountiful but found very few people at home. Then I realized that this was the 131st anniversary of the founding of the Mormon Church and that most people were at the semi-annual conference in Salt Lake City. I got a few leads for work later and after three hours of knocking on doors I came to the Stake Farm where Mormons in that vicinity produced milk for the needy. I asked if there was any work I could do and I was put to work digging post holes and setting posts for the next seven hours. Men were coming and going putting in as much time as they had in repairing chicken a house. A young married woman lived in a cottage. Her husband had lost his job because of illness and so he was employed at a nominal wage on the farm and the rent was charged up to them to be paid when he got regular work. I spoke later to the wife of the farm manager and she was very critical of high up Mormons. She told me of a "good Mormon" up the road whom I contacted when my work was done. He had a chicken ranch and cherry orchard and told me if I was back here in cherry picking time he would have work for me. He had gone away from Mormon country when he was young for 15 years but now was back for good. He had seen the world and did not think much of it. In May, Mary and I were taken by a contractor to pick cherries at his place and I was glad to meet him again. Prof. Wormuth of the Political Science Department at the University, whom I had met while selling CW's at the New School in New York City a few years before, invited me to speak to his class. He told me that of the 50 students all were Mormons but three. I told them of being bothered by the KKK when teaching in Alabama, that there were three sides to a question, your side, my side, and the right side, and kidded them about the Mormons giving up polygamy in 1890 when it cost them money. I had a barrage of questions, and to my surprise half a dozen young men came up and thanked me for opening up new ideas to them. The next day, Bishop Neal Maxwell, of the Mormon Church, who had been in the room and heard me, asked me to tape a record for his television program of all of my radical ideas. I said that surely he did not want all this radicalism, and he replied that Mormons were supposed to search for the truth and if I had more or less of it it would be good for the students. The tape was played later twice when I was in New York City. I bought a typewriter and work clothes and stored them with a pacifist friend and hurried back to New York City to perhaps be arrested for refusing for the 7th time to take part in the air raid drill, but as related elsewhere I was not arrested.

357

CHAPTER 16

IN THE MARKET PLACE

New York City

1953 to 1961

3 Hebrew Children

Painted by Mary Lathrop, 1963.
Hanging in new Joe Hill House.

Tom Sullivan, associate editor of the CW, gave the above title to my activities on the streets of New York City. As a salesman I understand the value of being at the same place at the same time with the same article for sale, and not to jump around, or have a perpetual "gone to lunch sign" in your window. There is another thing that I have learned which is that the wider the sidewalk where you are standing the less likely it is that anyone will break through the line of moving people and buy from you. Also if people are burdened with shopping packages they are not likely to put them down and buy a paper. Also if people are rushing to make a subway to get home they would not take five dollar bills if someone was handing them out. If there are four people selling one block apart they will sell more than if scattered.

During the Fall· and Spring season there are free lectures on *Monday night at Cooper Union*, and from 9:45 to 10:45 as many as 2,000 people may emerge. It is true that many just go in there to get warm. In 1920 Mrs. J. Sargent Cram of Peace House, a wealthy pacifist, and a descendent of Peter Cooper, had planned a meeting where Senator Borah would speak. He was three quarters of an hour late and she asked me to get up and talk until he came. I can't remember what I said but I held the crowd. Students and "Bowery philosophers" often interrogate me as I am selling CW's there and we go to the all night restaurant across the Bowery and discuss radicalism. One person cannot take care of such a crowd, so Patricia Rusk helped me for a time and others around the CW came along. Once we met a seminarian who had formerly been in the army and who said that he could love the enemy and kill him at the same time. Theological discussion had gone on for a long time when Pat looked up at the seminarian and innocently said, "You say this to me now, and you tell this to God when you die." That was the end of the conversation.

Tuesday from noon until 2 p.m. I hold forth at Pine and Nassau, a block north of Wall and Broad where I formerly soapboxed. This is a narrow corner and Catholics coming to and from Our Lady of Victory Church two blocks to the east on Pine have an opportunity to know about the CW. A well dressed man said hello to me mentioning my name and I said that I couldn't remember him.

"Oh you wouldn't know me. I slept on the floor at your place all one winter and saw you come and go. Booze had dragged me down in the gutter of the Bowery. I had lost my job and family. But with you folks I sobered up, then went to the AA, and now everything is fine."

I meet people who have heard me speak on the street years ago. Several guards from the banks have bought from me. At times I have had young folks, seminarians, and visitors come down and each one take a corner so that the name "Catholic Worker" resounded. On snowy days I did not sell so many papers. I always have a place handy where I can get warm. The Watchman in one bank chased us, but the others were more cordial. I took friends to see the stock exchange. I suppose it is some old Fenian blood, but I felt an urge when looking over the balcony at the thieves quarreling over their loot, to have a bag of feathers and throw them all over the place, as one pacifist from Kansas did twice among the Congressmen in Washington, D.C. "First time I ever bought a paper from the editor of a paper," said a customer to me.

9:45 to 10:30 p.m. Tuesday's at New School, 12th St. near 6th Ave. Very few Catholics attend this liberal school of adult education but I have many friends there who tell others about the CW. They accepted my book in their library. One night a cab driver waiting for his "fare" who was at the school said, "There's a guy in there talking against you folks, name of Blanshard." I didn't believe him, but in a few minutes a man whom I knew by his moustache was Paul Blanshard, the professional anti-Catholic, came out.

"Have a Catholic Worker, Mr. Blanshard," I said handing him one.

"How much?" he asked.

"Nothing, you need it bad," was my reply. He gave me a nickel.

A man who had known Vachel Lindsay in the old days talked with me for a few minutes, and when he heard that I had attended Hiram College he was glad to know that I quoted my favorite poem of his to the students often: The Leaden-Eyed. *The Village Voice* had a picure of me selling CW's there, and later when I was in Sandstone prison they said I was not able to sell CW's for a time and folks had better subscribe for the CW as they were missing something good.

Wednesday from noon to 4:30 *at Fordham University Uptown* 190*th St.* This is about the noisiest place in New York City, what with the elevated, the Boston Post Road whizzing by with trucks, and students running like mad to make a train. In many other campuses there are a dozen places where students come and go, but here you can get them all at once as they come out. One student liked Eichenberg's drawing of the six workers and bought 300 CW's in order to send them as Christmas Greetings to his friends. I have met hundreds of nuns and priests from over the country who are visiting or going to school at Fordham. And every day many students ask me questions about CW ideas. And in traveling over the country speaking, priests who have met me when they were seminarians at Fordham will tell of the cold days when we both shivered in the wind, they as they came down the quarter of mile walk to the street, and I as I buffeted the wind on the street. One priest was talking to me and later that day he told me that his superior had noticed us together and had said, "Don't encourage that Hennacy, for after a student hears him it takes five years to get him back in the groove."

14th Street and Broadway, Thursday, 6 *to* 8 *p.m. (and for years noon to* 2 *p.m. but in* 1960 *picketing Woolworth's at that time.)* This is a cosmopolitan place where you meet every kind of person. It is also a very noisy place, and very windy. Competition here is great, for two or three street merchants will be shouting their wares and looking for a cop, for they are not allowed to do business without a license, and the city will not give them a license. I have witnessed one fellow selling toys get pinched four times in two hours, but he kept right on selling. I have made many valuable contacts here.

"Give me a dime. The fellow down the street says for you to give me a dime," said a short fellow with a string tie. I gave him one.

"Make it a quarter," he said cheerfully, and like a rabbit before a snake I was charmed and handed it over. A few weeks later he came into our office and said to Dorothy, "Here is $2. Ammon loaned me 35c recently."

Drunks who hate Catholics, and sober people who despise us call me "Communist" and say they are going to call the FBI. Spanish Priests who are Fascists hurry by not looking my way. One pious woman had just come from Mass and wanted to know if the CW had an imprimatur. I told her that only diocesion or Order papers had an imprimatur, and that there were many papers printed by lay people. "Ask a priest about us; here comes one," and I turned to see our own Father McCoy whom I had never met down this way before. He of course told her we were the best.

43rd and Broadway, Friday noon until 2 *p.m.* enormous crowds pass by here. I am really part of the pillar by the Peerless store, so am not pushed around by the crowd. A young man told me that I had a kind face and that I must be a very good man. I told him that I was not a "goody-goody" but I aim to do the best I could, and not the second best.

I'm in such a fix that any way I turn I am in a fix. I know if you would say a prayer for me it would help."

"What's your name?" I asked.

"Jimmy," he answered.

"Alright, I'll pray for you at Mass each morning," was my reply.

Going home I stopped at a market to get some yogurt for a friend and the manager came running out shouting, "What did you steal. Let me search you. You look like a crook. My man saw you stealing something."

I told him to search me and he did so but found nothing. How am I going to please the public? One man wants me to pray for him, and another thinks I am a crook. A year later Jimmy greeted me, "Better keep on praying Hennacy, I'm just making it by the ragged edge."

I am always telling success stories but there is once that I had to admit defeat. A tall Irish drunk came up and asked me if the CW had an imprimatur. I told him it didn't need to have one. Somehow in his befuddled mind he though I must not be a good Catholic if I sold a paper not formally approved by the Church. So he said give me some, and took a dozen and commenced to shout:

"*Catholic Worker, free copy. No imprimatur.*" And pointing to me he added, "Don't buy from this jerk." I couldn't argue with a drunk man and I do not believe in calling a cop. I thought he would tame down, but he kept on for about ten minutes and no one took a free copy from him, those who knew me took papers and paid me for them. I got tired of this and thought if I walked quickly around the block I might lose him. Half way down the block as I neared St. Agnes he caught up with me and whispered in my ear:

"I am your persecutor! I am your persecutor!"

I walked faster around the block and looking back did not see him. I stopped in a restaurant for a cup of coffe, but before it was served he was beside me saying again, 'I am you persecutor!" and he handed a copy of the CW to the waitress saying, "Free copy; no imprimatur." I walked out and back to 43rd and he followed me. I had 15 minutes yet before quitting time, but I was defeated, and I went home. I never saw him again.

A lady coming from Church wanted to know if the Church supported the CW and I told her it was not for us or against us, and to ask some priest about it. Just then I saw a priest walking our way and I said, "Ask him." And again it was our friend Father McCoy who was on hand to reassure the good woman that the CW was good for her soul.

At times I wear sandals that friends give me. A kind old man saw me thus attired and said that he would come back and bring me a pair of shoes that he thought would fit me. I thanked him and said that I had shoes at home. Several times innocent Catholics who hear the name Catholic as I shout will stop and buy a paper and say "God bless you. I am glad to see someone besides a Jehovah's Witness on the streets selling papers." Yet at other times Catholics will say it gives the Church a bad name to be out on the street. At times Protestant ministers, seminarians, and even high school students such as 16 year old Judy Shafer, who played hookey from school for the aid raid demonstration, will stop and help me sell CW's.

A Jewish man who often buys a paper from me here told me of his 8 year old boy who was showing a neighboring Irish boy how to hold a bat. This boy did not want to be shown and said, "You can't show me anything, you dirty Jew!" In a sober and innocent manner the Jewish boy replied, "You have committed a mortal sin."

"Why don't you get a job?" asked a kindly elderly man.

"I don't need any," I replied, "for I work for my keep at the CW."

"I'm a retired policeman with a pension, and I make $65 a week on an easy job.

"We believe in living poor near the Bowery," I told him.

"I am happy and I want you to be happy and have a job too," was his rejoinder.

I told him to read the CW and see how we could be happy without bosses. He wanted to know how much the paper cost. I advised it was a penny and he replied that he didn't have any money on him, so I said to read it and pay me next time. I never saw him again. An Irish woman bought four of my books and offered me an Irish sweepstakes ticket for free. I told her that I did not believe in gambling, bingo, chances on Pontiacs, etc. for this was the something for nothing idea that was the basis of exploitation and slavery. An atheist stopped and said that the Catholic Church was the source of more evil in the world than any other institution. He did not call the Church the Whore of Babylon as fundamentalist Protestants call Catholics. I believe in putting my worst foot forward, and after that my best foot, so I replied: "Sure, compared to the good it is supposed to do, the Catholic Church is the cause of much evil, by watering down the Sermon on the Mount, by justifying wars and exploitation, by ransoming slaves but seldom opposing slavery; by insisting on married people living together midst fighting, malice and hatred, and the Jansenist idea on sex: expecting men and women to live together in "self-control" when this advice often comes from the mouths of clergy who never could be accused of any self-control in eating and drinking. I suppose if all this accumulated misery was on one scale it might seem to out balance the good that the lives of saintly nuns and priests do in consoling the wife of a drunkard, the mother of wayward children, the man yoked for life with a termigant, the nursing of the sick, and all the works of mercy. The Church as a whole as Monsignor Guardini has said is the Cross on which Christ is crucified, for in His name they deny Him, but yet through the Church comes a St. Joan and a St. Francis of Assisi and all the saints down through the ages. So while only God knows how the scales balance, I would venture that there is more good than evil."

St Patrick's Cathedral, 8 to 10 a.m. Sunday's. I am across the street, for the people seem to come out in a flutter or in a daze. Many pass me by but I do meet folks from all over the world who know of the CW, and others who are surprised to learn about us. The priests never bothered me here but I have had to educate a few cops as to this being a free country. On very cold days I have a few friends who invite me for a cup of tea after 10 a.m. The parades, swinging of flags, playing of Star Spangled Banner and Onward Christian Soldiers and the visiting dignitaries, and the whole spirit of obeisance to Mammon makes this an odd place for a radical. I did go to Mass there at 8 a.m. for years, generally being one of the first to take Communion in order to get out and sell CW's. Once the priest handed me the paten and I officiated as his server for twenty minutes before Cardinal Spellman and the Cardinal from Australia who was visiting. (This ought to get me inside the pearly gates.)

St. Francis of Assisi, near Penn Station, 11 a.m. to 1:30 p.m. Sunday. From 1954 through 1958 I sold CW's here. One priest who acted more like a cop than a priest shouted at me and Pat or whoever was helping me sell CW's to get away. I was to the side of the entrance and would have moved down aways if asked to do so in a civil manner. The priest said he would call a cop and I told him to do so. I showed the cop the Supreme Court decision as to my right and he said I had the right to sell the CW any place, but suggested that as we were all Catholics and for the sake of peace would I move down a bit. I told him that out of courtesy to the Church I would move down, and I did. Again a visiting missionary priest said I was not allowed to sell the CW in N. Y. City, and that he would call a cop if I didn't go. I told him this had been tried before, and if he didn't believe it to ask inside. He didn't bother me again. For the past two years I have been attending the 10:30 Uniate Byzantine Rite at St. Michaels Mass back of old St. Patricks, near us on Mulberry Street. I like the singing, which is done more by Irish than Russians. The Czar could be blessed for all I understand it but the sermons are honestly religious and no political propaganda against the Communists and for capitalism.

Julie Lien, a girl from Ohio, was with us for a time and helped me give out CW's once a month at the National Maritime Union. Finally their goon squad came and chased us. One of them grabbed her papers and she took them back and sweetly said, "One at a time, Mister," as she gave him a CW. We had fed these men in 1936 at the time of the waterfront strike and had been thanked by their leader, but now the line is to make a bargain with capitalism. I have enough to do fighting ordinary cops and the State, so I left this labor front.

From May 8, 1942, Milwaukee Journal. The Paul Marquardt family on trial for refusing to register. in Duluth, Minn. Paul had not registered in 1917.

CHAPTER 17

*COMMUNITIES
1921 to 1963*

*ALL OVER THE
U. S. AND CANADA*

Flight into Egypt
*Painted by Mary Lathrop, 1963
Hanging in new Joe Hill House.*

The Amish are an off-shoot of the Mennonites from the 18th century in the Palatinate in Europe, led by Jacob Ammon. For over 150 years they have developed the farm land in Pennsylvania until it is the most valuable in the country. My friend Vincent Tortora, a Catholic who has written about the Amish, drove me through the Amish country here around Lancaster, Pa. where over the rolling fields I saw the Amish farmers plowing and harrowing with horses and mules. You knew the "House" Amish because they had windmills and no wires or telephones or electricity, and no tractors in the yard. They are so-called because they have prayer meetings and services in their homes instead of in churches. The "Church" Amish have churches and use tractors and automobiles and perhaps have a telephone and electricity. Another name for the "House" Amish is "hook and eye" Amish because they use no buttons and are very strict. Tradition says that in Germany in the old days the most conspicuous point of attire of a soldier was his brass buttons, so they used no buttons in protest. All these Amish vote and pay taxes and mostly are allowed by the government to stay and work on their farms instead of going to war. To them the outside world is called "gay," as the Gypsies call the outside world, much as the Mormons call all others "Gentiles." Their children are taught in parochial schools or in public one room schools where the teacher is sympathetic and all the children are Amish. Vincent took me to one such school where he knew the teacher and children. When I was introduced, the children looked at me attentively. I did not realize then until I saw signs on bill boards advertising companies with the name "Ammon," so my first name stood me in good stead. I played some Hopi records and told them Indian stories. The girls in their blue dresses on one side of the room and the boys in their broad hats and long-cut hair on the other side listened with bright faces to my talk. Lunch time came and the older girls crowded around Vincent asking him to bat on their side in the ball game outside. He knocked a homer.

There are 10,000 Amish in and around Lancaster; none of them need sign a note for they are absolutely honest in business; some put money in banks, but most of them do not. The Amish have very little heart trouble or tuberculosis. They do not carry insurance, and if a building burns all the Amish get together and have a "bee" and the new building is up in a few days. We passed "black-bumpers," which are cars with the chrome painted over by the Amish for otherwise they would be thought "gay." The Amish do not live in town or carry on any business. Dairying and chicken-raising occupy them for long hours each day. Their land grows in value for they use only natural manure from cattle and horses, and no commercial fertilizers, hence their land is never worn out, but grows deeper top soil as generation after generation of these old country Christians continue their culture in our atomic age. The Amish do not go to court in any circumstance. If any one steals from them they do not report it to the police. Vincent told me of cases where outsiders had reported someone stealing from the Amish and the judge had given them the limit "for stealing from these good people."

The Hutterites

Professor Joseph Eaton was co-author in the December 1953 *Scientific American* of an article about the Hutterites in South Dakota, Montana, and Canada. These descendants of the Anabaptists in Transylvania had been tortured, robbed and exiled by Catholic civil authorities and the clergy. (Their founder, Jacob Hutter was burned at the stake in 1536). Driven from town to forest and given sanctuary now and then by some noble, they were driven out again and again. Many recanted but in 1874, 102 families came to the Dakotas. They were persecuted because of their pacifism in World War I, and the Hofer brothers died in solitary in Alcatraz. I have corresponded with their family in Canada. These brothers were buried in the army uniforms which in life they had refused to wear.

I had corresponded with Professor Eaton and visited with him for an hour at Western Reserve University in Cleveland. He suggested that I visit the King Colony Ranch near Lewistown, Montana. I wrote to Rev. Joseph Stahl there, and his bearded son Joseph met me at the bus in the midst of an unusual snow storm on April 30, 1954. He is the manager of this 7,000 acre ranch where 61 Hutterites live, all of them being related, so that, the young folks told me later, when they wanted to marry they visited other Hutterite colonies where they had no relatives, and in a couple of weeks in August there was some quick courting going on. There are three other ranches within thirty miles. Rev. Stahl greeted me kindly. He is an old man who after illness two years ago relinquished his position as minister of this community to a younger man who was just recently ordained by the religious head of the Hutterites who lives in Canada. He knew of my pacifist history, but in a forthright manner was disconcerted about three things: (1) Why I had waited until 59 years of age to be baptized a Catholic. (2) How I could be a Catholic as well as a pacifist, for the Church upheld war. (3) Why I did not live with my wife. I had given him a copy of my book, and showed him one about the Hopi, and also Dorothy's book, and he remarked, "Did Jesus have any books?" And looking at the medal of St. Francis which I wore, he said, "And would Jesus wear a medal?" Nevertheless he gave me a doctrinal book on Hutterite history and theology. His daughter, Mary, asked questions about the CW, and other teen-agers and men and women of the community came back and forth. The women dressed plainly with polka dot kerchiefs over their heads. The family of this house of children and grandchildren ate in the dining room, but I ate with Rev. Stahl in my alcove near his room, his wife having passed on five years ago. He folded his hands in a German blessing and thanked God after the meal, Services are held each day about 5 p.m., but there were none that day as the Chapel was being painted. The meeting lasts for two hours on Sunday morning.

During the evening I was asked questions about Catholic faith and customs, and later when the older folks had gone to bed the teenagers showed me their hope chests, where all that they were allowed to own was placed. Once in a while one would place a picture of a movie star on the inside of the lid, but this was very daring indeed. They freely discussed the outer world and their happy life within this community. They had met some sweet nuns at a hospital but had read Maria Monk stories and had much to learn. Statistics show that there is less mental disturbance and a higher birth rate among these folks than any other of record. They do not send mentally ill people to hospitals but take care of them at home, which is the CW and anarchist ideal. I asked them about discipline in the community. They said that a certain boy had stolen a bicycle from a neighbor in the "outer-world" (my daughters of the I AM religion speak of the outside in this exact term also). He broke it trying to ride it and he was paddled and had to stand ashamed before all in Church. The community repaid the value of the stolen article in wheat. Later this boy enlisted in the army and now writes back that he has learned to obey and when he comes back he will consider himself lucky and will behave. If a person of adult age did evil he confessed his sin before all in church and if it was possible to undo the injury he did so, A more serious crime where there was no repentance resulted in the person leaving the community. No cases were ever taken to an outside court. Seven boys from this community were in Civilian Public Service in World War II, and none having been sent to date to alternative service in the draft which continues today. Some rabble-rousers led by a military man from the city tried to use KKK tactics at the time of Pearl Harbor, but as the Hutterites have the respect of the community this soon died down. There are 98 communities of the Hutterites, divided as follows in the 1954 Almanac shown to me: 7,264 in Alberta and Manitoba, having 88 ministers; 372 in South Dakota with 24 ministers, this number being included in the Montana groups who have 12 ministers. There are 472 in Paraguay with 7 ministers and 124 in England with 2 ministers. Each colony is on its own, although they may trade produce if they desire. This colony has 200 cows, 700 sheep, 2,000 chickens, and 20 hives of bees. No tobacco is used but beer and wine is made and is consumed by these German folks without drunkenness. No ornaments, musical instruments, radio, television, dancing or going to movies are permitted. No photographs are ever taken.

These folks do not like being called Mennonites, for they are Hutterites. Rev. Stahl read to me from Acts telling about obedience to authorities, the payment of taxes to Caesar. Here they pay $5,000 local taxes for roads and schools, and some federal income tax. They liked my idea of simple life on the land and did not mind my vegetarianism, admitting that they ate too much meat. They are not out to disturb and convert the world as are the Doukhobors, and told me that I would make a good Hutterite, but I felt that while it was wonderful to visit these good folks their atmosphere was too puritanical for me.

When a young man is married he then grows a beard, and he gets a bed, 25 pounds of feathers to make quilts, a bureau, a spinning wheel and a sewing machine. With more children they get more rooms. There is no honeymoon. Each farmer is allowed a dollar a month to spend if he has to go to town for anything. As they buy wholesale many of the local merchants do not get Hutterite trade and so restrictive laws as to their expansion have been passed in South Dakota and Manitoba.

The Doukhobors

I have visited these anarchistic pacifists four times in the past 19 years. They broke off from the Greek Orthodox Church in Russia about 300 years ago.

"Each priest argued that the Holy Spirit was in favor of his own way of making the sign of the Cross," Peter, their leader, continued. "I rose from behind the trees where I had been sitting. 'You are both wrong,' I told them. The Holy Spirit is not concerned whether you make the sign of the Cross with two fingers, three fingers, or with all fingers of both hands. And if you priests had enough of the Holy Spirit within, you would not be squabbling over such foolish things."

" 'Oh,' said the Governor, bearing his teeth at me like an angry dog, 'You are wrestling with the Holy Spirit, eh?' *You are a spirit wrestler; a Doukhobor;* tie him to the post and whip him across his back."

This quotation is from J. F. C. Wright's *Slava Bohu* (Praise God), a story of the Doukhobors published in 1941 by Farrar, Rinehart. I have corresponded with him in Vancouver where he is a newspaper man.

As a Tolstoian, I had read of these 7,000 Christian Anarchists coming from concentration camps and the wilderness of Russia to Saskatchewan in 1889. Tolstoy's royalties from *Resurrection*, with money from the English Quakers, provided their transportation. After seven years of homesteading, they were asked to swear allegiance to the king, but as they did not believe in king or czar they refused and gave up their land and moved to British Columbia, 150 miles north of Spokane, where they bought land. *Alexis Carrel* in his *Man, the Unknown*, says of them: "The Doukhobors of Canada have demonstrated that those whose will is strong can secure complete independence, even in the midst of modern civilization. I know with them that: 'Christ said turn the other cheek. Some among humanity must begin, must set an example. Our ancestors did not give way to the Cossacks. We will lead the way, will suffer for our principles come what may.'"

Tradition says that the Doukhobors come from the Three Hebrew Children of the fiery furnace. In 1893 at the village of Kars in Russia, they had received word from their leader who was in prison in Siberia, that they should reform their lives and burn all guns, knives, ikons, tobacco pouches, vodka containers, and that there should be no more division of rich and poor among them. When they built this fire, Cossacks beat them with knouts and trod them with their horses.

In 1954 in upper California, I met aged Fred Sorokoff, who at the age of 12 had witnessed this terrible scene. His son had been in prison as a conscientious objector in World War II.

They burned schoolhouses rather than send their children there to be taught militarism. They took off their clothes in court as much as to say, "You have taken our land, our children because we would not send them to your schools, now take our clothes, take everything." St. Francis divested himself of his clothing in the public square at Assisi rather than be a part of the commercialism of his wealthy father. George Fox went naked in the streets of London, so it is an old tradition. In 1941 I met Peter and Lucy Maloff, and later Helen Demoskoff who was my interpreter as I spoke at Krestova where a score of men and women stood naked after a vegetarian meal, singing their religious songs. Helen had been in jail for 11 years off and on for going naked in court, refusing to send her children to school, and for burning down community property which the government had confiscated and turned over to other Doukhobors whom they could train more or less in Canadian ways. Helen also burned her own house for good measure. Dorothy has also visited Helen and looks upon her as a sister. After thirteen years I visited the Doukhobors again and was pleased to see the calmness of her grey eyes, the lucidity and spirituality of her conversation, and the warmth of her love which the hounds of the government could not lessen. The governmenet had taken hundreds of Doukhobor children and kept them for five years in the New Denver Sanitorium to brainwash them into patriotic ideas. The Quakers had sent a certain Emmet Gulley from Portland to help the Doukhobors and he gradually turned into a persecutor of them and worked hand in hand with the government. I reported this to the Quakers in Philadelphia and Pasadena several times until they finally removed him. In fact, the *Vancouver Sun* had a cartoon of a Quaker kidnapping a Doukhobor child and turning it over to the Mounties. Bloodhounds were used in some cases. Now after my fourth visit in 1960 I find that a compromise has been reached and all children are returned to their homes, no patriotic history is taught in the schools, there is no homework, and girls are allowed to wear the traditional Russian blouses and skirts. But recently a teacher asked children who had been brainwashed for five years what they wanted to be when they grew up and two boys answered that they wanted to be policemen. So it was about time that they came home where the parents could counteract some of the devilishness taught in the schools.

The Doukhobors are divided in five factions. The great majority live in *Saskatchewan* and are on big farms and have for the most part succumbed to Canadian ways, voting, eating meat, no communal life, smoking, drinking, but they are legally recognized as pacifists and do not have to go to war. They support the Red Cross instead.

The *Orthodox* led by Johnny Verigin, nephew of Peter the Lordly Verigin who sent the message from Siberia in 1895, lives in Brilliant and there are a great number of others around Grand Forks to the west who are still pacifists and live fairly simply, but who are tired out and have finished with community living and with any opposition to the government. They meet in prayer and singing and keep up many traditions and for the most part accept old age pensions. *The prophet Sorokin* came here but some years ago migrated to South America and did not come back. He has some followers of varying adherence to Doukhobor ideals who await his leadership. *The Reformed Spiritual Community of Christ,* some of whose members may also follow Sorokin, and who in the past burned down schoolhouses, went naked in court, and refused to send their children to school. Some of them live in a sort of communal group in Krestova. They have not promised to cease their violent tactics, and as I drove toward Nelson recently at night, police were stopping all cars to see if any Doukhobor was up to mischief; and a guard is at certain bridges and schoolhouses all night. *The Lebedoff Faction* is a smaller group to which Helen belongs. They have formerly burnt houses and gone naked in court, and they feel that they have already established this witness, and the time is now ripe to emphasize more positive aspects of Doukhobor tradition, such as in the old time, and a refusal to accept pensions from the government. There was also a very small group under the leadership of Michael Verigin, now deceased, where communal living and communal marriage was practiced at Hillyers, B.C., near Vancouver. One child was born there and was given the name of the mother as it was impossible to tell who was the father. Helen's brother, Joe Podvinikoff, was one of the leaders. This group has now disbanded. There is much animosity between all of these groups, much high-sounding intellectual hair-splitting, each accusing the other of not being a good Doukhobor, when in fact there are some in each group who do smoke, drink, eat meat or vote, and there are some in each group who fall away from one or more of these Doukhobor ideals.

In my 1960 visit I got acquainted with Helen's husband Pete, and her brother Pete who had both done time in prison. Her brother Philip nearby has a small flour mill where wheat is stoneground. Unlike the Hutterites and some other communities, the Doukhobors have not succumbed to white bread. Helen made some wonderful pancakes, and her husband warmed up a steambath where you sit on a table with feet on a bench midst steam made from dashing hot water on hot stones, and wash yourself with hot and cold water and finish off with a switch of tree branches.

The Canadian government negotiated with the Russian government to move the Doukhobors back to Russia and Helen's brother Joe was on a committee that went to Russia to see about it. They signed away their Canadian citizenship to take effect when they were on a boat going to Russia. Helen and about 50 others do not consider themselves the citizens of any government, so they are now free it would seem. But negotiations have bogged down and nothing has come of this removal.

I went with Helen to Nelson, B.C. and we visited the newspaper office and in a few days a picture of us appeared saying "Anarchist Visitor . . . with Helen Demoskoff, member of the Sons of Freedom . . . an admirer of the Doukhobors 'because they have been in jail so often in defense of their beliefs.' " My last evening this time with the Doukhobors was spent in hearing about thirty of their youth practice songs at Pete Maloff Jr's. house. I was asked to speak to them and I only wished that they lived in the United States, for then I could teach in their home schools, and rest up between jails with these wonderful comrades, but I could only stay in Canada a short time without being deported as a subversive. I plan to visit the Doukhobors soon in Saskatoon.

The Molokans

Molokan means "Milk Drinker." This name was given to them in Russia by the Orthodox because they were dissidents from the regular church, led communal lives, and were pacifists.

Thousands of them came to Arizona and central California at the turn of the century. Each family had a quarter of an acre strip of land for their home and cow, chickens, etc. and all farmed in common. Any extra money earned outside was turned over to the local Molokon preacher. In 1917 in Phoenix about fifteen Molokons went to federal court for refusal to register for the draft. One of them was David, who worked for the Old Pioneer with whom I lived in the late forties. In court the Molokons wanted to sing and pray, but the Old Pioneer told them this was not allowed, but spoke to the Judge about it, and of course the Judge had to uphold the dignity of the court. The Old Pioneer told the Judge, "you had better let them sing for they will do it anyway." So they sang and prayed. They all got time for opposing the war.

Later David's wife Stella said that it was not fair for her and her husband who worked hard, and had no children, to turn their money over to the Molokon preacher. "The serpent has entered the garden," the Old Pioneer said. And sure enough in a few years all this communal life was abandoned and now Molokons have big cars, get drunk, and in 1952 I was asked by two young Molokons down the lateral to go to court with them as their brother was up for being against the war. He had registered but the authorities did not want to defer him. Now there was no singing and praying. About the same time David and Stella revisited the Old Pioneer. Now he is a wealthy Molokon preacher and there is no radical talk. One Sunday I went down the road several miles to the Molokon Church. Not many young folks were there. The men sat around a table on benches, and the women sat in the back of the room on benches. They have no musical instruments, but do a lot of singing in Russian. As each one enters the church all present get up and bow. There is a short sermon and all kneel on the floor and pray. When this is finished, each man kisses all the other men and each woman bows before each man and he in a stately manner puts his arm around her and kisses her. Then each woman kisses all of the other women. The preacher here is a farmer who gets no salary. He hears confession, but it is not obligatory. There is no collection, but anyone can place money on the table for the poor if he likes, but I never saw any poor Doukhobors around Phoenix. They keep the Jewish holydays too, and do not eat pork or lard, and at certain times the the preacher blesses the crops in the fields. Dorothy and I have visited some of the old timers who were in jail in 1917 and whenever I go to Phoenix I always visit them. In August many Molokons visit in California who are equally prosperous. Many of them are friends of some of the Doukhobors in Canada.

Single Tax

Arden, Delaware and Fairhope, Alabama were started in the 1890's as Single Tax colonies. At the former Upton Sinclair lived. An obnoxious anarchist shoemaker had him arrested under the old blue laws for playing tennis on Sunday and he left. My wife and I spent a week there in 1920, visiting its founder Frank Stephens, and Don Stephens, who was a conscientious objector in World War I. Those who lived there were artists, or retired people, or bourgeois radicals who made a living in town. The intellectual atmosphere was better than most places. It was not intended to be the center of any revolution, only in the matter of land there was not any exploitation. Profit and banking were not disturbed. As related in the first part of this book my wife and I lived for six months in 1924 in Fairhope where I taught in the progressive school there. I have made two visits since that time to Fairhope. It is growing in population and is surrounded by real estate speculative land, but the Single Tax idea is practiced as of old. I stayed at the home of the secretary of the Single Tax Corporation, Cornie Gaston, and he explained the idea to me. Tolstoy and other anarchists were friendly to the arguments of Single Tax, but as in practice a government is sanctioned I am not interested in it. Fels of Fels-Napha and Lincoln of Lincoln Electric Co. have left millions for Single Tax propaganda but it seems that no one is enthusiastic enough to work overtime or to sweat, let alone die for the cause, so it progresses not even as much as we poor anarchists. I quote from the Single Tax leaflet: "Under the Single Tax the government, not the land holder, is entitled to that portion that is now paid to the so-called 'owners' of land, as rent. Ownership is a term that can be properly applied only to those things that come into existence as a result of man's labor applied to land. Land, by its nature, and by reason of man's necessity to use it must be treated as common property so far as rent is concerned, if justice is to prevail. . . Since much of that which results from man's labor on the land cannot be separated from the land upon which it is produced, it follows, that to have for himself the full ownership, of that which he has produced he must have exclusive title to the land involved in the production. To prevent such exclusive title from constituting a denial of the equal rights of all others, the single tax requires the holder of such title to pay into a common fund, for the equal benefit of all, an annual rent (single tax) equal to the value of the special privilege of exclusive title to the land. This value . . . is measured by the market value set by those who want land to use at its fullest productive capacity. This makes it unprofitable to hold land out of use or for inferior uses."

Llano Colony

This was started near *Leesville, La.* around 1912 by Job Harriman, Socialist leader who was defeated for mayor of Los Angeles because of the McNamara Brothers confession of dynamiting the *Times* building. My wife and I spent a couple of weeks in the colony in 1922. They wanted us to stop and teach in their school, but we still wanted to hike over the U. S., and we did not like the dictatorship of Pickett, who was the manager. We met Kate Richards O'Hare and her family there, and Bill Zeuch. The plan was for radicals to gather in this utopia where they would cooperate and not be exploited. The price of admission was $2,000. Old cut over land had been bought cheaply and somehow instead of cultivating and building homes on the land they had, they bought more and more land, and also some on the Isle of Pines to grow tropical fruit. They had a good bakery and dairy with milk and bread routes toward Leesville. *The Llano Colonist* was a well written paper with a growing circulation. When we were there they were filling the silo. Last year there were dozens of trucks with silage and only a couple of people to tramp it in the silo. This year there were half a dozen to do the tramping but only a truck coming in now and then. The manager did not want to thin carrots for that would be wasteful, so we had thin, spindly and crooked carrots. Now anyone could come if they only had two mules and 10 children. The old timers were leaving and the newcomers were loafing. In religion no one agreed on anything. The only thing all agreed on was that they did not like capitalism. My brother .Paul roasted the peanuts, ground them into peanut butter, and packed it in cans or glass for sale. He was there for ten months and got tired of the continual quarrelling among the leaders. New folks came and the older ones left until around 1936 it was dissolved. Pickett hung on until around 1957 on an acre or two. There is some committee in Los Angeles that claims some of the assets. Llano was bound to fail for the same reason that others failed such as the New Harmony colony of Robert Owen, the Phalanges in Wisconsin of the Fourierites, etc., etc., because these colonies were made up of people who came to escape life, with very little ability to work, and very little desire. What they wanted was a hand out. They could have been held together by some religion perhaps, but they had different religions or none.

The Bruderhof

They began in Germany after World War I, had to go to England when Hitler came into power and then migrated to the wilds of Paraguay. With their German efficiency they cleared the wilderness, built a hospital, and provided for themselves, however they hired natives to do unskilled work. They were pacifist, but decidedly not anarchist or vegetarian. Later they established a group at Rifton, N. Y. where they manufactured wooden toys. Anyone can join, but they are looked over by The Servants of the Word, a self-perpetuating group who pray and are led by God to do the right thing. Everyone has to think alike and there is no deviation from the norm. You cannot wear whiskers if that is the line, you cannot travel unless you get permission, you cannot write anything for publication unless it is o.k. A young fellow could not court a girl unless the Servants of the Word felt it was best. When Vivian Cherry took pictures of our Newburgh farm for *Jubilee* in 1955 we stopped at the Bruderhof at noon. I knew some folks there who were vegetarians and suggested that I eat at the vegetarian table with them. "Oh, we are not vegetarians any more: we have achieved unity." This is another name for brainwashing. There are folks who have been pushed around in life and they turn over their worldly goods to the Bruderhof and have security. If they like it, then it is the place for them. If they can change their ideas and habits to suit the Servants of the Word and think they are doing God's will then they are happy. I do not know what the rate of turnover is here. A few years later I was visiting the Macedonia Colony for the second time. The Bruderhof was just in the process of liquidating it and selling out, moving the members either to another colony in Pennsylvania or the one in Connecticut. I asked the son of the founder, Mr. Arnold, if a Catholic could be a Bruderhof. He said: "You could come here and live and we would search for the truth. There is just one truth, not two." And of course that would be the Bruderhof. It is therefore no place for an anarchist, but for those who do not mind being regulated and ordered around it is fine. It is also a haven for tired radicals or those who do not wish to oppose the system. To say that they are demonstrating anything about a future society is foolish: what they are doing is to provide a haven for those who are tired of fighting and who want to feel secure. (Dorothy Day does not agree with my ideas. She likes both the society of Brothers and Hutterites and points out that their rule is voluntarily accepted.) I have friends in the Bruderhof in Paraguay and in England, as well as in this country, but they as a whole are too organized and medical minded to suit me. But they don't have to please me: there are plenty of people who will appreciate them.

The Koinonia Community

This group is not far from the site of the old Andersonville Prison of Civil War time. It is near *Americus, Ga.* and is comprised of 1100 acres of fairly good farm land where cotton, peanuts, pecans, etc. are grown. Two Baptist ministers started it around twenty years ago with the understanding that colored and white folks could live together. The ministers were put out of the Baptist Church, and they continued to be a source of cheer to the poor Negroes around there. After the Supreme Court decision, the White Citizen's Councils got excited and bombed the road stand where the colony sold hams and other produce. They also shot at random with rifles at night through the windows of the houses, cut down thousands of young trees, and raised a lot of terror until finally no Negro would live on the premises. Any neighbor who would deal with the colony or any store or even a bank who would deal with them was also bombed. They had to go 50 miles to buy feed or gasoline, and of course they could not sell any produce. Even the insurance company cancelled their insurance. So they bought pecan shelling machinery and made a living shipping the non-perishable nuts. Friends took up the slack of the insurance so that in effect they are insured. Members were beaten up in Americus and brought to court on false charges and fined. An effort was made in the legislature to make them illegal. But Clarence Jordon, their leader, remained adamant; he would not run away. Three of us from the CW have been down there on night watch and Dorothy had bullets sprayed around her but no one was hurt. The few days I was there, there was no shooting. I worked in the shed packing pecans. While these folks are Baptists, they do not shove their religion at you the way some colonies do. Of course people come and go for various reasons. They are pacifists, but not anarchists or vegetarians. I have no criticism of Koinonia and would enjoy another visit.

St. Francis Acres, Glen Gardner, N. J.

This 17 acre wooded community was founded around 15 years ago by the man whom I consider the best fellow I know, David Dellinger. He had been in prison as a conscientious objector and bought this land and established a printing press, bringing young pacifists and their wives to establish the new life. But the women wanted the pretty things in town and both men and women wanted other spouses and soon they all left, but others came and left. and now others came and stayed. As it happens all but one, beside Dave and his sons are now Catholics. They have a common purse and democratic meetings as to how to run the colony, but the trouble is that very few people there are responsible workers, except Dave. I lived there for five months while the first edition of my book was being printed. If people are all of one religion it is possible for them to live together in harmony, but this is not the case at Glen Gardner. If after living in a community for many years the common pocketbook idea is found among people who know each other that it fine, but to begin with that impediment among people who come there because they can't make it on the outside, does not make for a growing successful community.

The Amana Society

These pacifist Germans lived in community in *Iowa* much like the Hutterites, having a blacksmith shop, some small industries, a brewery, and farms. Around 1942 they ceased their community living and divided the industries into shares like capitalistic organizations, and each now owned their farms. I stopped there when hiking in 1946 but could not get any interest in pacifist ideas from anyone I spoke to. The older ones did not understand English and the younger ones I suppose were now sold on The American Way of Life. Now the Amana Refrigerator is widely advertised.

Celo Community

I visited this beautiful valley among the North Carolina mountains in 1950 when the Hopi and Joe Craigmyle and I were on our way to Washington, D.C. Each one has five or ten acres and owns it outright, but there is a provision that he cannot sell it to anyone who is not approved by the community as a whole. There is a Quaker hospital nearby where some of the colonists work. I had corresponded with one of the first conscientious objectors. Arle Brooks, and wanted to see him here, but he was miles away chopping wood, so I visited his wife Tillie as related previously. Some old folks have come here to retire, and while the tone of the community is pacifist, it seems to be a resting place rather than one which is alive. As I understand it, no Negroes live here; whether this is planned that way I do not know, but they do not have any racial trouble. It would be too quiet and too medical for me, but for some it would be, and is, the good life.

374

As mentioned before, this group was liquidated by the Bruderhof. I had visited it in 1950 and knew most of its members. They had a notation of the amount (not their name) on the score board, so that it would be known when the barrel was empty. They had a fine dairy and a milk route in town. They also made wooden toys and raised vegetables and had a small school. There was a great variety of religious beliefs here, and continual turnover, as some were very pious and others atheistic. They were all pacifists. The community was bound to fail because of this controversy on religion. The Bruderhof was the answer, for now they could all believe the same, with exception of a few who did not go with the Bruderhof.

Meadowlark, Newton, Kansas

When I spoke to the college of the Brethren in Newton I went out to Selma Platt's place called Meadowlark. Here she took care of mentally ill people, for free and also for pay. She had enough land surrounding the main house for cottages for others, and some came from the defunct Macedonia Community. The spirit was cordial, well organized, and more of a venture than a real community. There was no religious basis upon which it could be founded. It could function as a helping hand. The people there tended to be liberal rather than radical.

Gould Farm

This large farm began half a century ago as a rest home in the Berkshires near *Great Barrington, Massachusetts* where mentally disturbed people came for rest and received treatment from specialists in the nearby town. Some of them could pay and others couldn't. There is a Protestant religious atmosphere with chapel and evening meetings but it is not forced upon the members of the community. There are a dozen small cottages where those who need privacy can have it. I attended a convention of social workers there and gave the CW radical philosophy. Later I was invited again and spoke to a smaller audience. Pacifists and anarchists have at time been part of the staff, although the foundation that runs the community pays salaries and is liberal rather than radical. With these limitations I feel that they are performing a good service.

Harold Gray, Saline, Michigan

Harold had been in jail in World War I and had inherited a large farm near Saline, Michigan. Here he gathered pacifist friends and had a large dairy, and raised pigs, chickens, and fruits and berries. They had milk, and other routes whereby they sold their products. Harold was Episcopalian and the others were of varying beliefs or none. All were pacifists. However when big wages in the city beckoned they all left for the fleshpots. I visited there twice when Harold was in the process of selling his herd of cows as he could not hire men to tend them. He often went to the CW farm at South Lyons to get their whole wheat bread, and in fact drove me there once. Now he is building houses for city folks on his place and is a landlord with no idea of the community with which he started. He just couldn't buck the whole Ford way of life.

In 1907 in my home town Jacob Beilhart bought an old farmhouse on the edge of town and started a religion by this name. A relative of the man who brought up my father joined it and was known as "Ma Young." The local newspaper wrote terrible stories about them worshipping the devil, and when finally a girl there from Chicago had a baby, they were driven out of town and went to Kansas, where after a few years Jacob died of appendicitus. As I remember it, he dealt with spiritualistic mediums, was against all exploitation of capitalism, and there seemed to be some kind of communal marriage. Everything of course was held in common and those who came gave all they had. There seemed also to be an idea that money would come in abundance if prayers were directed toward the cash. Jacob's brother in nearby Columbiana was a Socialist. He kept a harness shop and distributed some of my anti draft literature in 1917.

The Shakers

This was an old time group of craftsmen and farmers of the early 1800's. They did communal farming like the Hutterites, but the men lived in one huge stone house and the women lived in another huge stone house. When my wife and I visited what had been such a community in Kentucky in 1923 the very old lady told us that there were times when the supposed celibacy was overcome. They were prosperous but after the Civil War they seemed to get no more recruits, what with the expansion of agriculture to the west and the conscription which had disturbed the even keel of Shaker farming.

Paul Williams, Nyack, N. Y.

This pacifist inherited money from his father and bought the side of a mountain and began to exercise his unorthodox architectural ideas in housing. He called this a certain cooperative name, built homes for artist friends, charged them a nominal rent, and presently they live in a congenial community. Each one makes his living as it happens. I visited there one afternoon and found each home " a castle" as it is supposed to be, with privacy, and yet with the understanding that each neighbor was sympathetic.

The Lemurians

This group started in *Wauwatosa, Wisconsin* in 1940. They were young folks who were pacifists and vegetarians but particularly not anarchists, for they envision a perfect society with a constitution somewhat like that of the United States, but without war. This was all to happen in 1953 when a new continent called Lemuria was to rise from the Pacific, and meanwhile we here would sink. They moved to California near Los Angeles and bought a farm and prepared to perfect themselves for the great event of 1953. They printed all of their literature in green ink. But time went by and nothing happened in the Pacific. I do not know if they advanced the date or not but they are still on the farm in California. I was not able to visit them last time but will do so on my next trip west as I knew them as personable young folks who printed my statement of refusal to register for free in 1942. Two of them going as conscientious objectors to the CW camp in New Hampshire. In their community in California they lived in common, each giving all they had when they joined. I have no idea of what the turnover has been with them.

Individuals on Farms who Like the CW Idea

A CW farm was started in the depression, bought for $1,000, and now *Carl Paulson, Ridgeroad, Upton, Massachusetts* with his wife Mary and nine children live there. He makes a living in stained glass window work. I have visited there half a dozen times. Bill Roach and his wife and nine children also live there. He works in a church furniture factory nearby. The O'Donnells formerly lived in another house but they have scattered. Carl's father and mother have built a home nearby also. Each family has a garden and there are some fruit 'trees. I have visited thousands of families over the United States and I would not hope to find a finer one than that of the Paulson's. Carl went to Danbury prison as a conscientious objector. He had married a young artist friend of Ade Bethune who was a trustee of the farm when it was a communal farm. If I was a young man with a pregnant wife I would build a house there and make a living selling milk and honey to the others and to neighbors.

R. 1, Springboro, Pennsylvania

Jack and Mary Thornton, a farm and a lot of children. Jack worked until recently in a foundry in Erie and does a lot of farm work. I have visited there several times and have made calls for friends to come and help Jack. There is room for a dozen families to live on the farm, but they would have to get work in town to supplement their income. *Bill and Dorothy Gauchaut, Avon, Ohio* (near Cleveland) formerly had a small acreage and ran a home of hospitality on Franklin Street in Cleveland for years. They sold their acreage and bought at a bargain a large well-built house. Here Dorothy take cares of spastic and other crippled babies and gives hospiltality. Bill works for a utility company. I have visited them several times.

At *South Lyons, Michigan* between Ann Arbor and Detroit, Father Hessler, the pacifist anarchist Maryknoll priest in Yucatan, gave a small farm to the CW in Detroit. Part of it was deeded to Lou Murphy who runs the Detroit CW, and the rest of it to several families. They built their homes and have their gardens and some animals. They make their main living working in hospitals or at other work. There has been a spirit of friction here for years, and although each family may be very good, they do not seem meant to live so close together. *Glen Johnson* is the one whom I know on the farm now.

Jack Woltjen, Bluffton, Missouri read the CW after he got out of the army, and used the GI Bill to borrow money to buy a large farm. I have helped him build fences and feed hogs the times I have visited there. He works in a hospital part-time and hopes to be out of the red soon. Here is room for many families to live and the place is big enough so that they do not need to be too near each other. They are a fine young couple well worth knowing. Nearby *Ruth Ann Heany,* widow of Larry Heany, my good friend in the CW in Milwaukee, lives. She has five children and a small place. Marty Paul tried to farm with the Heanys but gave it up and moved to the city. Her black-Irish children are beautiful.

Bob and Ann Stowell of Cabot, Vermont head workcamps in the U. S. They are pacifists, anarchists and vegetarians, but not Catholics. I have visited them several times. He has been a teacher at the University of Vermont and does small job printing too. They work at a southern community in winter. *Eric Freedman* and wife, a young Jewish couple decided to go to Alaska and came over to the CW to give help and get ideas. They landed in northern British Columbia and live off the land.

Communities that I have not Visited

The Huntington Library, Stanford, California, have a book on twenty efforts at communities in the history of California. I visited Kawea up in the sequoia region where there was once a Socialist community. They have only a very small post office by a rushing mountain stream now. The big tree that you drive through there is called General Sherman was first named Karl Marx, but that was in the old days of the community. There was the Home Community of anarchists on Puget Sound but it did not last very long. There was the Theosophical community of Madame Tingley, and many others. I have been not far away from The House of David at Benton Harbor, Michigan, but I never visited it. Their lawyer was a federal judge in Los Angeles in World War I and resigned and joined this pacifist group, which is really better known as bewhiskered ball players. The son of this lawyer was a conscientious objector with my friend Rik Anderson in a camp in California in World War II.

Ottawa Housing

In 1957 when I was speaking in Ottawa, *Paul Harris* invited me to his home which was one of 80 built cooperatively. *Father Morosco,* now Bishop in Toronto, had about 80 families meet weekly and study cooperative housing for a year and a half until they were ready to pool about $300 each to form a cooperative for a house for each one. They had met weekly in small groups and all together once a month, mostly Catholics with a few Protestant friends. Reasonable loans were made and each did as much work on his own house as possible with the help of friends. The houses are with four bedrooms so that Catholics can have large families. They have a common skating rink and a park.

In Notre Dame

About ten years ago, *Julian Pleasants* and friends who were teachers at Notre Dame, bought a farm on the outskirts and measured it out in five acre lots with unpaved roads running through. No one made any profit out of it and each had a place with congenial neighbors where living was cheap. I visited them twice in the winter so do not know just what they could raise in the summer. The houses were not zoned to be expensive. I don't think they have much of a community life, but at least they have the basis of cheap housing.

I visited their printing plant and the huge hotel in which they house their four hundred workers who print millions of copies of books and work for their keep. They have fine meals and luxurious quarters, and it is considered an honor to come from all over the world and work there for free. Like the CW, workers do not earn a wage so do not pay an income tax for war. All of the pacifist societies take a war tax from the pay of their employees. It was formerly the rule that those living here could not be married, but this was recently changed, some say, so that some of the big shots could be married. All the JW's live under a discipline that would make any anarchist shiver, and having little sense of humor, I suppose they take it and never know what happens. They formerly had a farm near our farm on Staten Island and I visited that twice. They knew who we were and had brought us some vegetables when we first came there. They now have a much larger farm and a school in up state New York.

Short Creek, Arizona Mormons

On the Sunday morning in 1953 when the Korean War was ended over 100 state police and deputies came to this peaceful community to arrest 26 men, 38 women, and 154 children because polygamy was practiced. Short Creek is in "The Strip" which is an area as large as New Hampshire, Delaware and Rhode Island combined, and with a population of 700. It is north of the Grand Canyon and logically would belong to Utah but it is in Arizona. To get from the county seat, Holbrook, south of the Canyon, is 430 miles around through Nevada and Utah. This great rebellion against the "decency" of metropolitan Phoenix was engineerd by Republican Governor Howard Pyle in a theatrical attempt to gain votes, but it was one of the reasons for his defeat in the next election. The real issue of course in Arizona is that the copper companies never have paid their share of taxes, and the big land companies have prevented any law regulating the ground water that they pump out and thus impoverish ordinary ranchers. All this dust storm about the immorality of the Short Creek Mormons was used to keep the minds of the people from the real issues. When the state police, camera men, reporters, etc. arrived to conquer this great rebellion against the soverign state of Arizona, the children were neatly dressed and stood in the early dawn singing *God Bless America*. The men were taken to Holbrook and then to Prescott to prison and the women and children to Phoenix where the Welfare Department portioned them out in rest homes. After some months in prison, the men were released with the half-promise that if they were quiet they could see their children. However, the women were not allowed to see their husbands and the children are not permitted to see their fathers. An article in *Colliers* for Nov. 11, 1953, describes the situation. Ray Williams is one of three school teachers in Short Creek. He is a Mormon who has one wife and three children. He has never practiced polygamy but unless he promises that he will never practice it in the future he will not be allowed to teach. Furthermore, he is not allowed to see his children or his wife unless he gives up his religious belief of polygamy. Another man of Short Creek is married but has no children, yet he is not allowed to see his wife unless he promises to give up his ideas of polygamy. Meanwhile the parasite Tommy Manville is free to have a dozen wives and the courts over the country grind out fake divorces for him and for others. There are many cases of Navajo men having several wives for the women here own the sheep and the more sheep he has, the more wealth he has. The government winks at this and calls the extra wives "boarders." Maybe it is because the Navajos are so scattered and it is difficult to tell them apart. Before I came east, the last money I made as a migrant worker was given to the Catholic lawyer who was defending the Short Creek folks. Perhaps by this time promises have been made by the Mormons which they never intend to keep and the families are together again in Mexico or some place else. I plan to visit Short Creek sometime and see how these folks live in community.

The Order of Aaron

Maryellen Fullem drove me the 230 miles southwest of Salt Lake City, through the town of Delta to within six miles to Eskdale on the Nevada line where this group has 3000 acres in the desert, a school of 50 children, and 17 adults who raise food for the colony and alfalfa for their stock. At Partoun, 50 miles north, they have 5000 acres where Mr. Card, an early convert to the group, lives and helps take care of their land. They also have a sawmill at the top of a mountain near Price. I had met Mr. Conrad, a cheery outgoing man, who with his wife are teachers here, two years ago when Mary and I were picketing the tax office. We visited some classes and later heard the string orchestra play classical music. I spoke of the Indians and made friends with 10 year old Mary who was especially interested. Mr. and Mrs. Conrad receive a salary from the state for teaching these children and this money is a help to the colony. They have 8 of their own and a divorcee is there with 5 children. The others are boarded at $30 a month from families of the Order who cannot live here at present. Members also tithe to Bishop Glendenning and he has a Council of Twelve, and a Patriarch, as in the Mormon Church, and a successor determined in case of his death. He is 72 years of age.

The custom here at meals is to eat silently. The girls wear blue corduroy dresses, but the boys wear whatever they happen to have. Fields of alfalfa dot the desert. The Snake Mountains are about ten miles to the west and the colony is six miles off the highway leading from Delta to Ely, Nevada. The nearest town is Garrison, Utah. They have their own power for lights and for pumping water from a diesel outfit. Their small houses are of wood and unpainted. Water is pumped into a wooden tank so they have water pressure. Small trees stick up hopefully around the place.

We spoke for a time with Mrs. LaRue Snow Young (a good Mormon name) whose husband until his death two years ago had been one of their leaders. These folks are ex-Mormons who believe in living co-operatively with all in common, like the Hutterites, whose King Colony in Montana, where Dorothy and I have visited, they have also contacted. This cooperative effort they call *The United Order*, this being the Mormon term used by Joseph Smith and Brigham Young. They also live *The Word of Wisdom*, which means that they do not smoke or drink, like good Mormons are supposed to do. Those who use tea or coffee do so as long as they feel they have to but this is frowned upon. They are pacifists and teach that the Lord will soon come, so they have unsheathed their sword and taken up the Bible, and all their young men go to alternative service rather than go in the armed services. They are not polygamists, although many people around here think there would be no other reason for so many women and children to be hidden away in the desert.

While we were picketing the tax man here in 1961, Mary and I were invited to a singing fest of this Order at a private home, and I was asked to say a few words. A chiropractor by the name of Dr. M. L. Glendenning, had started this group 30 years ago, but it was not legally chartered until 20 years ago. I subscribed to the CW for he and Mr. Conrad in 1961. I looked up their address but Dr. Glendenning and his wife were in Arizona. I spoke to a middle aged woman in charge and she explained the principles of the Order and I bought a book, *Now My Servant, by Blanche W. Beeston, Caxton Press, Caldwell, Idaho, 1957,* which tells of the life of Dr. Glendenning. According to this book he is said to have heard a voice supposed to be Elias speak to him since the age of 14. These messages are collected in *The Book of Elias.* He has been directed, he states, to documents left by his ancestors, in this country and Scotland, proving that he is a lineal descendant of *The Order of Aaron,* and that he was directed to continue this Order. Converts have been made in Provo and Salt Lake City. At the semi-annual Mormon Conference April 6, 1931, because of the activity of Dr. Glendenning, Joseph Fielding Smith declared that no messages or revelations were bonafide unless they came to the President of the Mormon Church. An attempt is made to prove from *The Book of Mormon* and their *Doctrine and Covenants* that this *Order of Aaron* is not spurious. I have spoken to men outside this group who know Dr. Glendenning and they say he is sincere and acts fair with those who join the *Order,* and that it is not a fraudulent group. I have met leaders of other religions who have claimed to have received Divine intsructions and I have found that their main emphasis was upon collecting money from the gullible. and that their private lives were materialistic and gluttonous, and far removed from the ideal which they preached.

At Eskdale they keep Saturday as the Sabbath, but in Salt Lake City they keep Sunday. I have attended their Sunday meetings and find them a cheerful and sincere group. If I meet Dr. Glendenning later and more of this group I will be able to form an opinion about them. Right now I am favorably impressed. Those who join the Order are on probation for a year, and after the first noviceship anything that they turn over cannot be refunded if they leave the Order. The writer of this book says that Dr. Glendenning will allow a person whom he has chosen to do any certain work the freedom to make mistakes, for by this method he will learn the hard way and the lesson will stick. This is the only pacifist group that I have met that have come out of the Mormon lineage. It is easier for those raised for generations in an "out-of-this-world" religion to remain "unspotted from the world." But for the Bruderhof, Koinian in Georgia, and this group to take people out of the commercial life of the cities and expect their children to grow up and not to go back to the fleshpots is surely a problem. The personality of a leader may hold them together as long as he lives, but generally there is a fight over who is to succeed in authority. This has happened among the Doukhobors, Molokons and Bruderhof. If the organization squelches all discord affairs may run smoothly, but it is likely that the spirit may be lost, as has happened to all orthodox religions. If these new groups cannot prove by their lives, as the Hutterites have done, that they do lead the *true* Christian life, then they have no excuse for existing.

Always there have been remnants of the early Mormons who felt that their freedom of religion allowed them to have more than one wife, despite what they called the "sell-out" of the Salt Lake Mormons. They felt also that the centralized authority of the banking and other industrial interests of the rich Mormons in the big cities of Utah was not the real spirit of those. early Mormons who trekked the desert and worked and suffered in common. Somehow, also, these Mormons got away from the bloodthirtiness of their Book of Mormon and took the pacifist attitude of The Sermon on the Mount. Without using the words, these folks were primitive pacifists and anarchists, for they had seceded from the state and were breaking the laws of the state. They lived with everything common except wives, just as the early Christians had lived.

There was the New Home colony on Long Island founded by Josiah Warren of Bunker Hill lineage. It lasted until that generation had died away and the young folks became city and capitalist minded. There was the Socialist Colony in Ruskin, Tennessee founded by J. A. Wayland of the *Appeal to Reason*. Debs went there once. It lasted only a short time. And of course there was the classic *Oneida Community* founded by John H. Noyes, which lasted only part of a generation and ended up as a financial success in the famous Oneida Community Silver. Books have been written about the community of wives here and of the discipline whereby the sexual act was prolonged. There was a lot of opposition to this community but Noyes, who was a brave and forceful man, fought for his rights. Whether his leadership kept anyone else from developing sufficient strength to carry on when he gave up or not, at least the community did not last for long.

The Catholic Worker

"People shipwrecked on an island — that's not a community: that's a disaster — that's the Catholic Worker!" All of the things that made for the failure of other communities that have failed or that are now on the skids: we have all that and yet survive somehow. We take in those that no one else will have, and for many there is no other place to go, and some of them stay with us until they die. Our New York group had its first farm at Easton which was taken over by some families.

We did some good for many, and how much we will never know. There were many retreats there, vacations for children, but as a farming commune we were a failure.

Our next, Maryfarm at Newburgh was again the occasion of many retreats where spiritual seed was sown, and we raised plenty of food, but civilization in the form of jet planes that worried cows and chickens, and liquor too close by, coupled with the fact that it was really too far from New York City, caused us to sell the farm. Our Peter Maurin Farm on Staten Island grows plenty of vegetables, and we have retreats and meetings there, but it is in no manner self sustaining. It is really just another House of Hospitality such as we have in New York City. It serves a purpose and it is a community, somewhat as a jail is a community — not that you can't leave the farm, but it is a place that never can be considered a community in the sense of any of the others which we have discussed: it is like our place in town — a station where people come and wait until they can make up their minds where to buy a ticket to, and if they can't make up their minds, they stay.

Conclusion

It would seem that the only communities that carry on successfully are those of a small religious sect who feel that they have *the truth*, and they also have a discipline that keeps them away from the outside world. The test comes when it is seen if the second generation carries on the idea. The most successful would seem to be the Hutterites. I have read of communities in England such as the Taena, which is Catholic and nearly a part of monastic life, and of Lanzo De Vasta's L'Arche in France and numerous ones in India. I do not have enough first hand information about them to form an opinion. For myself I would rather live out in the world and propagandize "the heathen" and fight the devil there. Within the next few years readers of the CW will see from my writings what I think is valuable about the polygamus Mormons in Utah, Idaho and Arizona. I intend to visit the Argenta Community near Nelson, B. C., Canada.

Seated: Dorothy Day, Helen Demoskoff
Standing: Helen's husband and
brother Joe.

CHAPTER 18

*Book Reviews
1950 to 1960*

*Carol Gorgen and the author
Picketing at Las Vegas, Nev. AEC
Easter week 1962*

Inasmuch as I have gained insight from others, a short summary of the most improtant book reviews I have written for the CW and in the I.W.W. paper *Industrial Worker* is given.

The Hopi Way by Laura Thompson, and *Culture in Crisis*, former U. of Chicago Press, and latter by Harpers. The thesis of *Culture in Crisis* is that the influence of the missionaries, especially Mennonite, has broken down traditional religious beliefs of the Hopi in the villages of New Oraibi, Upper Moencopi and Bacobi. And also that the coercive measures of the government have produced "rigidity and ultra-conservatism" in the outstanding rebel village of Hotevilla and in a lesser degree in Shongopovi. As the white man's world crumbles the Hopi are shown to have a world outlook, a faith, a Way of Life more satisfying and wholesome than that of the ancient Greek city-states or of any modern Utopia. Will the Indian Bureau succeed in demoralizing the Hopi? Will the missionaries, the army, and the cattle and oil men succeed in getting the souls and bodies of the Hopi? The author says that "The Navajo-Hopi land dispute was not legally settled until 1943, when the Navajo were confirmed in the use of three-quarters of the original Hopi reservation which they had usurped and were occupying, leaving the Hopi the use of only 986 square miles of desert land."

The Bending Cross, a biography of Eugene Victor Debs, by Ray Ginger, Rutgers Univ. Press., New Brunswick, N. J., 1949. Born in a Catholic family, he was not baptized and seldom entered a church, but he was a better follower of Christ as far as I knew than any so-called Christian leader of his time. Even in the 90's he refused to speak before a segregated audience. He was not a pacifist, nor an anarchist, but when Emma Goldman, the anarchist said, "Mr. Debs, you're an anarchist." Debs clasped her hand and said, "Not Mister, but Comrade, won't you call me that?" He said that "The capitalist politician tells you how intelligent you are, to keep you ignorant. I tell you how ignorant you are to make you desire to be intelligent." His speech to the court in 1918 in Cleveland is a classic. He boldly gave the revolutionary position and got his ten years in Atlanta. Here he was beloved by all prisoners, and refusing to go to compulsory chapel, the warden abolished compulsion for all. In his early days when he was ordered by a group of thugs out of Colorado, he said, "This will either be the beginning of organized labor in Colorado or the end of me."

The Autobiography of Mother Jones, Mary Field Parton, Charles H. Kerr Co., Chicago, 1925. Reviewed in Dec. 21, 1951 *Industrial Worker.*

"There's only one thing to be afraid of . . . not being a man." This was the characteristic brave answer of Mother Jones in 1919, at the age of 89, during the steel strike when a union official felt it might compromise their fight to allow a Communist to put out leaflets in the union hall, lauding the Russian revolt. She was born in County Cork of a family of fighters against British terrorism, she taught in a parochial school in Monroe, Mich., had a dressmaking shop for the rich until burned out by the Chicago Fire of 1871. She then became an organizer for the United Mine Workers until her death at the age of 100. She led hundreds of the wives of miners, armed with mops and brooms and banging on dishpans, to the mine pits, straight up to the machines guns of the Colorado thugs. On elections she said, "You don't need to vote to raise hell . . . you need convictions and a voice."

The Life of Mahatma Gandhi by Louis Fischer, Harpers, N. Y., 1950

In dealing with the enemy it was Good will to the enemy that Gandhi always had. Fischer said that "Victory came (in South Africa) to Gandhi not when Smuts had no more strength to fight him but when he had no more heart to fight him." Gandhi's idea of fasting is little understood in the West. Fischer quotes him as saying: "One may fast against those who love you, not against a tyrant." Gandhi said, "We must widen the prison gates . . . Freedom is to be wooed only inside prison walls and sometimes on gallows, never in the council chambers, courts, or in the schoolroom." Fischer contrasts Churchill and Gandhi: "Churchill is the Byronic Napoleon. Political power is poetry to him. Gandhi was the sober saint to whom such power was anathema. The British aristocrat and the brown plebian were both conservative, but Gandhi was a nonconformist conservative. As he grew older Churchill became more Tory, Gandhi more revolutionary. Churchill loved social traditions. Gandhi smashed social barriers. Churchill mixed with every class but lived in his own. Gandhi lived with everybody. To Gandhi the lowest Indian was a child of God. To Churchill all Indians were the pedestal for a throne. He would have died to keep England free, but tried to destroy those who wanted India free."

The Pictorial History of the American Indian, by Oliver LaFarge, Crown Publication, N.Y., 1957.

This book accomplishes the difficult feat of interspersing 350 illustrations of American Indians with their historical perspectve and debunkng much of the fiction in our history books, so that it ought to be required reading in every high school in the country. The map giving the ancient location of over 200 tribes ought to help put the white man in his place geographically, while the details of the government's deceit ought to put us in our place ethically. Indians lived in New Mexico 20,000 years ago and for 3,000 years grew corn. The way the white man got the land of the Indian was, "get him drunk, talk him into signing a mortgage he cannot pay off, does not understand that he must pay off, and in due course foreclosure . . . that is the system." "Many missionaries think that a man cannot become a good Christian unless he dresses as the missionary does, lives in the same kind of a house, eats the same food — despite the fact that, as Indians sometimes point out, Our Lord wore His hair long and wrapped Himself in something very like a blanket. The same line of thinking led well meaning schoolteachers on the Navajo reservation to propagandize their pupils urgently against eating the 'disgusting' parts of a sheep, until a study by the Association on American Indian Affairs showed that only by eating the whole animal could the Indians achieve a balanced diet, and that those who followed the teachers advice were more susceptible to tuberculosis than those who did not."

Cherokee, by Don Tracy, Dial, N.Y., 1957.

True to the history of Tsali, who by his bravery in refusing with his band of mountain Cherokees to accept the white man's false promise of freedom in Indian Territory and by his voluntary death at the hand of the U. S. Army, was able to purchase the freedom of the remnant of his people, this thrilling story gives the customs and traits of this noblest of eastern Indians. The love story of Suti, the boy who killed two panthers with his blowgun and darts, and of Meg, the daughter of freedom-loving pioneers, is more gripping than most of the romances of modern whites.

The Royal City, by Les Savage, Jr., Hanover House, N. Y., 1956.

This book tells vividly of the rebellion of 1680 led by Po-pe, esthetic cacique whom power led into a gluttonous life and deserved death when he visited Acoma. In a natural consequence of character and historical events the author gives a thrilling story of Luis, the young American born Spaniard, who tried to get justice for the Indians whom the greedy zealots of the Inquisition robbed for their own profit and that of wealthy Spanish nobles. He tells of the relation of Luis and his relation with three women: Condesa, the courtesan, Kashana, the Acoma maiden, and Barbara, the Spanish aristocrat whose love for the wholesome desert country around Santa Fe ennobled her life more and more as she saw through the wickedness of her aristocratic surroundings. The contrast of the corruption and intrigue of Mexico City with the simplicity and integrity of the Acoma cacique who fasted in nakedness for the sins of the whole tribe; the sunrise and sunset of the Sangre de Christo (Blood of Christ) Mountains near Santa Fe; the smell of the mesquite burning from countless fireplaces in the morning air — all this to those of us who have lived with and known the Pueblo Indians and have loved their "way of life," makes this book one to be enjoyed and remembered.

The Hopi Indian, by Harry C. James, Caxton Press, Caldwell, Idaho, 1956.

Mr. James knows much about the Hopi from scores of years spent near them. He tells of the beating to death of the Hopi Juan Cuno, of Oraibi in 1655 by Friar de Guerra. He says that "the best of the Hopi have no desire to lead the easy, parasitical life of the rationed, clothed, housed, and protected 'ward'."

America's Concentration Camps, by Carlos B. Embry, David McKay Co., N. Y., 1956.

The author is a liberal southern editor who sympathizes with the Indians but would solve their problems by assimilating them into white society. Until 1834 an American citizen had to have a passport to enter Indian territory. And the Red-Cloud Treaty was the only one ever made by the U. S. where the enemy received all its demands.

Conquest of Violence, The Gandhian Philosophy of Conflict, by Prof. Joan V. Boudurant, Princeton University Press, 1958.

"Oppression Ceases," Gandhi taught his followers, "when people cease to fear the bayonet." Unlike regular anarchists Gandhi sought by negotiation with politicians to achieve the stateless anarchist ideal, and also unlike most anarchists he was able to develop both personal and mass resistance to the state and to exploitation and to overcome the government. The author quotes Bob Ludlow in an article in the CW as saying, "It is the political element that will destroy Gandhi's teachings in India for he did not realize that Satyagrah must be united with an anti-state philosophy." The author replies, "nevertheless with Satyagrah as the functioning socio-political technique of action, anarchism could conceivably result." Gandhi said, quoting from the Gita that "when there is no desire for fruit, there is no temptation for untruth." Gandhi says, "Do not resist arrest; if taken prisoner, behave in an exemplary manner ... do not expect guarantees for maintenance of dependents." Courtesy to the opponent was shown in India when "Satyagrahas ceased their civil disobedience at midday because of 'the hardship this would work on European opponents who were less accustomed to extreme heat ... and postponing an action to spare the Englishman for his Easter Sunday services and celebration.' The author quotes Gandhi as saying, "I do believe that when there is only a choice between cowardice and violence, I would advise violence ... Non-violent conduct is never demoralizing whereas cowardice always is." Fasting is primarily a penance and according to Gandhi "there can be no penance where the accused person is not conscious of having committed a wrong ... Fasting ... no one who has not earned the right to do so should use this weapon." The author shows an understanding of anarchism when she says, "Anarchists urge freedom from politics rather than political freedom."

The True Believer, by Eric Hoffer, Harper, N. Y., 1951.

"Who is the true-believer? . . . He's a guilt-ridden hitchhiker who thumbs a ride on every cause from Christianity to Communism . . . When we renounce self and become part of a compact whole, we not only renounce personal advantage but are also rid of our personal responsibility." I read and reread this thought provoking and cynical book. Most of what he says is true for nearly every "true believer" you meet, but it is not necessarily true of all, and these few like Debs, Tolstoy, Gandhi, etc. who acted and whose truth somehow diffused itself in the hearts of people rather than to be organized into corruption. To cast his incomplete self on the bandwagon after the pioneers have blazed the trail; to take benefits of the union scale of wages after having scabbed in thought or deed for years; by the impact of his numbers to water down the purity of any cause. "The mass leader: this strength lies in his blind spots and in plugging all outlets but one."

The Autobiography of Big Bill Haywood (reprint from 1929) *International Publishers 381 Fourth Avenue, New York City, 1958.*

In the face of a 20 year prison sentence, Haywood was asked in court if he was conspiring to interfere with the profits of the munition makers. He answered, "We are conspiring to prevent the making of profits on labor in any industry. We are conspiring against the dividend makers. We are conspiring against rent and interest. We want to establish a new society where people can live without profit, without dividends, without rent and without interest if it is possible; and it is possble, if people will live normally, live like human beings should live. I would say that if that is a conspiracy we are conspiring." Wonderful words! An old "Molly Maguire" taught him unionism when he was working in the mines in Nevada as a boy. He helped found the I.W.W. whose slogan was, "overtime is scab time, any time there are some working no time." He was born in Salt Lake City. He married Nevada Jane Minor and delivered the baby himself on a lonesome ranch. He attended two terms or a parochial school in Salt Lake City and knew Father Hagerty, who it is said wrote the I.W.W. preamble. Through the famous Moyer, Haywood and Pettibone trial when the stool pigeon Harry Orchard perjured himself and Darrow finally won the case, and through the days of 1917 when hundreds of I.W.W.'s were in jail against the war Haywood stood firm. The I.W.W. was the only union that had the rule that "any one who joined the army, the militia, or the police was forever denied membership." Haywood was a lover of centralized power in administering the I.W.W. Many of this union became Communists and went to Russia. I disagree emphatically with his skipping bail and going to Russia, but I tend to remember his good fiight up to that time rather than to castigate him. His wife died in 1917 and his two daughters also passed away before Haywood died of diabetes in Moscow, May 18, 1928.

Attorney For The Damned, by Clarence Darrow, Edited by Arthur Weinberg.

Simon and Shuster, N. Y., 1957.

This is a lengthy book which gives excerpts from some of the greatest summations which Darrow gave over the years, but one would have to feel the tone, see the light in his eyes, and observe the swing from nonchalant humor to heart rending emotion to know how he swayed juries and never lost a case. His summations lasted at times for three days with never the use of a note. In 1894, when he was general attorney for the Chicago and Northwestern Railroad, and Debs with his American Railway Union had a strike on the line, Darrow resigned his good job and represented Debs. He is known for his speech to the prisoners of Cook County jail:

"Preachers will tell you that you should be good then you will get rich and be happy. Of course we know that people do not get rich by being good, and that is the reason why so many of you people try to get rich some other way, only you do not understand how to do it quite as well as the fellow outside."

And again Darrow said, "If a doctor were called upon to treat typhoid fever he would probably try to find out what kind of milk or water the patient drank, and perhaps clean out the well so that no one else could get typhoid from the same source. But if a lawyer was called upon, he would give him thirty days in jail, and then he would think that nobody else would ever dare to take it (that is the typhoid fever). If the patient got well in 15 days, he would be kept until his time was up; if the disease was worse at the end of 30 days, the patient would be released because his time was out."

Anarchism by Paul Eltzbacher, Libertarian Book Club, GPO Box 842, N. Y. 1.

This book is mentioned by Kropotkin in the Encyclopedia Brittanica as the best book on anarchism, and Alexander Berkman told me in Atlanta prison that this was the one book I should read. The author analyzes Godwin, Proudhon, Stirner, Bakunin, Kropotkin, Tucker and Tolstoy as to law, the state and property and as to means of achieving the revolution. I agree with Tolstoy in critical idealistic anarchism, no law in the future, no legal relation, and pacifism. I agree with Godwin in no law in the future and no legal relation. I agree with Tucker in pacifism. I agree with Bakunin in having both individual and collective property. I agree with Proudhon in critical idealistic anarchism. There is also an article by Rudolph Rocker on anarchist communes in Spain and other of his ideas. This book as a guide to the anarchist writings is invaluable, for anarchism remains, if taken with the pacifist approach, as the only hope, for all other roads lead to tyranny and death.

Anarchism, by George Woodcock, World Co., 2231 W. 110 St., Cleveland, Ohio, 1962. $1.95 paperback.

"Anarchism has thriven best in the lands of the sun, where it is easy to dream of golden ages of ease and simplicity, yet where the clear light also brightens the shadows of existing misery."

"Two recent historians of anarchism, Alain Heslier and Claude Harmel, have discovered *the first anarchist in Jean Meslier, the 18th century cure of Etrepigny,* whose resentment against the ecclesiastical and civil authorities of his time festered into a great Testament which he left to his rural parishioners (it was intercepted after his death by the Church authorities and never reached the farmers for whom it was meant) and in which he denounced authority of every kind and advocated a bucolic society based on friendship among peasant communities." And *Jacques Roux, a country priest, in 1790 led a group called the Enrages,* said that land belonged to all equally, and burned chateaux. He was sentenced to death by a revolutionary tribunal, but he cheated the guillotine by killing himself, saying, "to die placing liberty above law is the death of an anarchist." *"In Italy on Aug. 1, 1877, Father Fortini, the priest of Letino,* welcomed the anarchists as 'true apostles sent by the Lord to preach His divine law' . . . Guided by Father Fortini, the anarchist band set off for the next village of Gallo, where *Father Tamburini* came out to welcome them, and went from house to house, shouting to the people, 'fear nothing. They are honest folk'."

Tolstoy said that *"the man who wishes to abolish the state must cease to co-operate with it, refuse military service, police service, jury service, the payment of taxes."* "Perhaps the most impressive example of Tolstoyan influence in the contemporary Western world is—ironically in view of Tolstoy's distrust of organized churches—the Roman Catholic group associated in the United States with the *Catholic Worker* and particularly with that saintly representative of Christian Anarchism, *Dorothy Day."*

In Spain Pi Y Margall, a Catalonian bank clerk, was the first active anarchist. Pio Baroja, the author of *Red Dawn,* was a great anarchist writer. "The Inquisition effectively stifled any tendency toward religious dissent during the 16th century, anarchism has in fact taken on the character of a delayed Reformation movement. . . . All anarchism, has of course, a moral-religious element which distinguishes it from ordinary political movements, but this element is far more developed in Spain than elsewhere . . . for in the eyes of the Spanish libertarians the Catholic Church occupies the position of anti-Christ in the Christian world . . . *the anger of an intensely religious people who feel they have been deserted and deceived"*

The conclusion of the author is well stated: "The great anarchists call on us to stand on our own moral feet like a generation of princes, to become aware of justice as an inner fire, and to learn that the still, small voices of our own hearts speak more truly than the choruses of propaganda that daily assault our outer ears. 'Look into the depths of your own beings.' In this insistence that freedom and moral self-realization are interdependent, and one cannot live without the other, lies the ultimate lesson of true anarchism."

The author picketing at Dugway, Utah
Military Base, Easter Week 1962

CHAPTER 19

QUESTIONS AND ANSWERS

1950 to 1964
Over the U. S.

Joe Hill House of Hospitality and
St. Joseph's Refuge, 1131 S. 1st W.
Salt Lake City, Utah

QUESTIONS AND ANSWERS

1. Why do you deny the authority of the state and accept the authority of the Catholic Church?
2. Why do you refuse to pay taxes when Christ said to render unto Caesar?
3. What about Christ chasing the money changers out of the temple? Does this not justify war?
4. What would you do if Russia attacked us?
5. You are not Catholics, you are Communists?
6. You are not practical.
7. You Catholic Workers knock the bourgeois society yet you depend upon donations from the bourgeois to feed you.
8. How are you going to run things without cops and soldiers if we abolished them all tomorrow?
9. Why are you so critical of other people? Is it kind?
10. Why do you fast in public when Christ said to do this in secret in your closet?

11. Why don't you work like other men do?

12. Christ ate meat. Do you think you are better than Christ by not eating meat?

13. Why don't you vote for the good man for office? You just help the bad man by your negative attitude.

14. Would you defend some one dear to you who is being attacked?

QUESTIONS AND ANSWERS

"Why do you deny the authority of the state and accept the authority of the Catholic Church?"

Because I consider the function of the state as essentially exploitative and immoral with its denial of the Sermon on the Mount in the return of evil for evil in courts, prisons and war. While the Church in practice approves of exploitation and war this is not an essential doctrine of the Church but a perversion of what Christ taught and the early Christians lived.

Around 1845 Thoreau was asked to pay taxes to the Church and he refused, saying that he was not a member, and asked for a piece of paper on which he wrote, "I am signing off something I never joined." He then asked for another piece of paper on which he "signed off" from the state into which he was born but never joined. Likewise I have seceded from the state and give it very little. To churches where no bingo or gambling prevails I will give generously, but to commercialized churches I give a nickel.

When I became a Christian I did so because I felt Christ was a rebel against the same old eye for an eye policy which has made the world a shambles. When I became a Catholic later I did so because I was first drawn to the pacifist-anarchist policy of the Catholic Worker, and came to see like Karl Stern, that I brought with me into the Church all that was good from Tolstoy and Gandhi. So the Church that I joined was the real one founded by that St. Peter who said to obey God rather than man. I accept the authority of the Pope on the essential matters of faith when he speaks ex Cathedra, but on matters like anarchism and pacifism where he differs I am free to follow my understanding of the Sermon on the Mount. In Boston Father Feeney said that no one but a Catholic could go to Heaven. That is the line in Spain but not in Boston, so he was excommunicated. On television here I was asked if I believed in the infallibility of the Pope and I answered that I did when he was infallible. When he talked through his hat his opinion could be no better than that of anyone else. So his views on Franco, Communism, war, etc. are worth as much as they are worth in fact, and no sanctity need be given to them.

If I go to the wall and push a button which says light, another which says heat, and another which says refrigeration and I get the results expected I do not tear down the wall to see how the wires are put together, for, not being an electrician, I could not put them back together again. I accept the word of the electrician and leave the wiring as it is. But I do not take the word of the electrician about Franco, war, capitalism, etc. Likewise I accept what the Holy Father says about the Faith but not on matters of Franco, war, capitalism, etc.

The Church allows me more freedom than the state. The state has arrested me thirty times, and the Church through police only twice. Out of courtesy I will address the authorities of the state in good humor and announce my proposed acts of disobedience, but I have no hope nor intention of reforming the state. I try to live as a good Catholic and I have some hope that this leaven may help to bring to light the teachings of Christ and the early Christians and be a leaven in the commercialized mass of the Church.

There is no contradiction in my denial of the authority of the state and accepting that of the Church unless the Church makes me be a servant of the state in issues which I consider immoral, which please God, I hope I will never do.

"Why do you refuse to pay taxes when Christ said to render unto Caesar"?

Dorothy Day gave the best short answer quoting St. Hilary, "The less you have of Caesar's the less you have to give to Caesar." Those who believe in rendering unto Caesar will still do so no matter what I may say. To those who may have a doubt I will give several thoughts to build up their "render-unto God" instead of to Caesar. When Jesus was asked what was the greatest commandment He told them that the first one was to love the Lord with all your heart and the second one was like unto it, to love your neighbor as yourself. "Who is my neighbor?" asked those who wished to argue. Then Jesus told the story of the Good Samaritan.

Again Jesus was taken up into a high mountain by the devil who told Him if He fell down and worshipped him He could have the whole world and in fact would not have to pay any taxes at all. Jesus told the devil to go back where he came from.

Then again He was asked if He believed in paying taxes to Caesar. In those days different districts had different money and the Jews had to change their money into that of Rome, so Jesus asked, not for a Jewish coin, but for a coin with which tribute was paid, saying "Why tempt me?" Looking at the coin He asked whose image and superscription was there inscribed and was told that it was Caesar's. Those who tried to trick Him knew that if He said that taxes were to be paid to Caesar He would be attacked by the mobs who hated Caesar, and if He refused to pay taxes there would always be some traitor to turn Him in. His mission was not to fight Caesar as Barabbas had done, but it was to chase the moneychangers out of the Temple and to establish His own Church. Whether He winked as much as to say that any good Jew knew that Caesar did not deserve a thing as He said, "Render unto Caesar what is Caesar's and unto God what is God's," or not, no one knows.

The U. S. government considers that I owe over a thousand dollars in income taxes and if I offered them a penny they would consider it an insult. Christ insulted Caesar when He offered Caesar a penny.

Once in Phoenix I had announced that on Monday I would picket the tax man for a week. On a Saturday night a policeman told me that I could not sell papers on a certain corner. I could have stood on my rights and insisted and spent the night and Sunday and Monday in jail and not been able to be on hand for my main battle. Jesus had to choose His battleground.

Now it was also said to Pilate by Christ that he would have no power over Him unless it came from God. Despite what anyone says each of us has to decide forhimself whether to put the emphasis upon pleasing Caesar or pleasing God. We may vary in our reasons for drawing the line here or there as to how much we render unto Caesar. I make my decision when I remember that Christ said to the woman caught in sin, "Let him without sin first cast a stone at her." I remember His "Forgive seventy times seven," which means no Caesar at all with his courts, prisons and war.

"What about Christ chasing the money changers out of the Temple? Does this not justify war?"

Christ was "true God and true man." He was hungry and thirsty and He hungered and suffered and bled on the Cross. In this He was the man. He saw the Jewish Temple made a den of thieves and evil being done by hypocrites who kept the letter of the law — taking legal advantage of the rate of exchange and of technicalities that the poor and untaught knew little about. As He suffered when scourged so did he suffer at this blasphemy and He chased the cattle that would not move without the lash. Whether He actually lashed the money changers or whether their guilt made them flee we do not know. But we do know that He did not try to exterminate their families or to imprison and kill them. He used no man-made law against them. "Let him who is without sin first cast a stone." So Jesus was without sin and was the only one who had the right to chase the evil men out of the Temple. And for this among other things they killed Him.

Likewise during the agony in the garden when He knew that Peter, despite his protestation of great faith would soon betray Him those three times, His flesh was tired and He told Peter to sell his clothes and buy a sword. Peter said there were two swords. Jesus replied. "That is enough." Then when Malchus was arresting Jesus, Peter took one of the swords and cut off the ear of Malchus. Jesus was God and He did not tell Peter to cut off the other ear, but performed His last miracle by healing the ear. He then disarmed Peter and all of us by saying, "Put up again thy sword into its place; for all that take the sword shall perish by the sword."

The whole essence of the Sermon on the Mount is to love the enemy, to turn the other cheek, and to return good for evil. The enemies of the Jews were the Romans. Jesus did not join with the Macabees and Barabbas in violent insurrection against the government. He did not show any hatred toward them and even said that if a Jew was asked according to Roman law to carry the pack of a soldier one mile, he should cheerfully carry it two miles instead of grouching about the one mile. What aroused His anger was hypocracy in the Synagogue. Jesus knew that to exchange a Roman despot for a Jewish despot was not worth dying for. He had a better way which was to overcome the enemy permanently by love. Today we find those who trust in violence, both in the courts and in war, who justify this violence by quoting this passage about the chasing of the money changers out of the Temple. If they would take it in its context they would look at the Churches today with their bingo and selling of chances and charge of admission at the door, all to keep up a big show, and know that He would overturn these tables also.

"What would do if Russia attacked us?"

Kneel and pray for our sins that have brought the attack upon us; and pray for the Russians.

We have scattered obliteration bombing in Bremen, Hamburg, Tokyo, and atomic death in Hiroshima and Nagasaki, and we continue our atomic testing which spreads Strontium 90 over the world. We have spread death over Europe in two wars; now we will learn what it all means here at home. We have taken the sword and now we are dying by the sword. In Dugway, Utah at the U. S. Proving Ground in 1960 "a healthy rabbit died in seventy seconds after a military scientist had placed a droplet of an unnamed nerve agent in the animal's eye. Sparky, a black mongrel in a glass-enclosed cage, was instantly paralyzed — and rendered painless — when an aerosol was 'vented' into the air he breathed," this being all a part of our chemical, bacteriological and radiological warfare.

"He wins who gets there fustest with the mostest," said a Southern leader in the Civil War. If we believe in the military way of life we ought to be armed with the most terrible weapons and have the facility of using them quicker than the enemy. To be inefficiently armed is not to be a pacifist. To disarm without ceasing our exploitation would be foolish for we are told in scripture that he who hath great possessions keepeth them by being well armed until he who is stronger taketh them from him, but to trust in the Lord and spiritual values rather than in much possessions. A clean about face toward the principles of love and brotherhood of the early Christians is needed. And we are the nation least probable to acknowledge our sins and repent. The whole history of our country has been militaristic from the time we tried to exterminate the Indians to our Mexican and Spanish American wars. And our dollar diplomacy in the banana republics and our stranglehold through loans to most of the South American countries is a scandal, let alone our support of Franco, Salazar, Chiang, and until their overthrow seemed at hand, of Batista and Trujillo. We have spoken for years of the natural result of capitalist imperialism and of the need to expand. As Randolph Bourne said, "war is the health of the state." Even if now war has become suicidal our exploiters must needs live up to the tradition of all exploiters.

So if Russia attacked us with missiles or atom bombs all that we would do, if by some miracle we would be alive, is to help those nearest to us in whatever way we could. We would obey any necessary routing or traffic regulations but it is likely that we would find it necessary to circumvent the red tape of the bureaucrats and help people on our own as we did during the depression and as we do now. By our contact with the enemy we would not show fear or hatred and by our actions we would try to make them ashamed of their oppressive tactics, but we wouldn't "preach" to them. With Wall Street destroyed maybe some of us could get together in small communes and live like we ought to without exploitation or government, but by mutual consent.

"You are not Catholics, you are Communists" —

Call up the Chancery office in New York City and they will tell you that we are Catholics and that they are not for or against us. We are members of the Catholic Press Association for twenty-seven years and this would not continue if we were Communists.

Now as to being Communists it is true that we accept the Marxian analysis of what is the matter with capitalist society, but as to what is to be done about it we differ. Communists want the state to do everything, and after the dictatorship of the proletariat the state will wither away and we will have the stateless society, which is anarchism. The anarchists don't believe in any state at all and they agree with Lord Acton that "power corrupts and absolute power tends to corrupt absolutely."

With the Communists we believe in (1) *The Economic Interpretation of History,* which means that for the most part the way people make their living determines how they think. As the western Catholic sheepherder who clips wool and the Wall Street Catholic broker who clips coupons: they pray the same but they think differently about life. (2) *Surplus Value.* If I earn $40 a day for my boss and get $10 in wages I can only buy back $10 worth and the balance piles up and we have depressions and wars. (3) *The Class Struggle.* Between those who work for a living and those who own for a living there is a struggle and we are on the side of the have-nots; and we choose to live poor among them and help them fight in a non-violent way and a non-political way against exploiters. And where those who run the Church side with the exploiters we oppose them and side with the exploited even if they are Communists, being critical of them as anarchists and pacifists should be, but with sympathy.

"You are not practical"

I am the most practical fellow you can find. The dictionary says being practical is "pertaining or relating to practice or action." You might say that we anarchists are the original "do-it-yourself" folks, for we do not depend upon politicians and bureaucrats to do things for us.

Being an anarchist means being responsible for the needs of yourself and others without being told or ordered by authorities. While walking to the Post Office one morning for the mail I saw a block ahead of me a two by four full of spikes fall from a truck into the middle of the street right at a cross walk. Dozens of cars whizzed by and scores of pedestrians edged around it but no one picked it up, for they didn't put it there, and neither did I. But I picked it up and put it in the container for waste by the curb. Another time when I had been fasting for ten days and picketing the tax man here in New York City I noticed a huge bale of paper junk fall from the rear of a truck into the very middle of the intersection at Varick and West Houston Streets. No one did anything about it until I laid aside my sign and pushing with my shoulder with all my might I finally edged it over to the curb. Likewise when walking the roads in the country I always removed nails, glass, dead cats, limbs of trees, etc., which would impede traffic, so that I think the government owes me money for my scavenger work. I do not feel a bit guilty in using the roads for which I pay no income tax to build.

If being practical means piling up money and worrying yourself sick saving for a sick day, or to retire with your ulcer then I am not practical. If organizing thousands of people into a group promising to do good, or pledging themselves to revolutionary action is practical, then I am not practical. When I have been picketing the tax office I did not need a committee to coordinate or regulate me, for I can organize myself. This is what the one-man revolution is supposed to do.

"You Catholic Workers knock the bourgeois society yet you depend upon donations from the bourgeois to feed you."

Who else lives among the poor twenty-four hours a day? Sure, "we comfort the afflicted and afflict the comfortable" until the latter shell out voluntarily to help us do the things that need to be done, that the state neglects to do. We do get money in small bits from many people who are poor; very little of our money comes in large amounts. We refused to apply to a large foundation that offered us money, and we returned $3,500 interest to the City of New York because we did not believe in interest. One millionaire gave us a thousand dollars for Christmas for helping someone he had known on the Bowery. The next year he wanted to give us more and wondered if it was deductible from his income tax. We told him that we were not an "accredited" charity organization, and that he would have to give from his heart and not from his deductible surplus. We didn't get it.

We couldn't live in this society and get our money from anyone else; and whatever money we as writers or speakers get we turn in to feed the poor.

"How are you going to run things without cops and soldiers if we abolished them tomorrow?"

We are not going to do anything tomorrow or the next day except perhaps die from the atom bomb. The welfare state is here to feed us with bread and circuses into complete senility. Even then no one is ever going to get all people to think alike — the Catholic Church has been trying it for two thousand years and they have millions saying the same words but their quality is nothing to boast about. For as the Indians said, "If everyone thought the same every one would want my wife."

This wholesale mass idea of doing things is what is the matter with this world. There will be cops and soldiers for a long time yet. I have already resigned from the need of cops or soldiers to protect me for I rely on a greater power. Obviously if I do not believe in voting or shooting, I or a million like myself, could not begin to think of overturning society. What I have done is to remove the need of my dependence upon these instruments of violence

Democrats and Republicans do not make good anarchists. When we have enough pacifist anarchists in any geographical area who resign from the state and its coercive measures then we will begin to have a small anarchist society. The radical Hopi Indians have had it for centuries without being anarchists in the true sense of the word for their action comes more from a communal tradition.

There is no reason why people interested in the transportation industry could not meet in local, regional, national and international conventions, much as chess players, scientists and others do, and discuss how best to solve the problems of transportation in any given area or weather condition. A railroader, a truck driver, an airplane pilot, and a steamboat man all are prejudiced as to the efficiency of their own way of travel. But when profits are not the measure, but service, then the true solution can be arrived at. Not by baby kissers or banjo players or lame ducks appointed to commissions to regulate commerce, but by the very men who do the work. A decoration of, say, The Order of Frank Lloyd Wright, would be a greater incentive than political glory. Anything that the government does, except make war, all of us could do if we got the idea of doing it, and we could do it better.

"Why are you so critical of other people? Is this kind?"

There is a great difference between kindness and weakness. To give a derelict a "dime for coffee" because you are too weak to say no, knowing that it is for liquor, or to give money for carfare when a walk of a mile for an able bodied young man would help to waken him up a little, is also weakness. Sometimes we act through stupidity. In Salt Lake City at our Joe Hill mission a red faced town bum and an anemic whitefaced old man asked me for 80 cents for carfare to go to the bloodbank to sell their blood. They promised faithfully to pay me back that afternoon. I have no regular donors who give me money to pay the rent and utilities and could really not spare even that amount, but I gave it to them. They would not take blood from the old man for he had hardly a pint in him to work on, let alone any to sell, and, of course, the town bum never showed up again. How stupid can a fellow get? With all of my experience I should have known better. To make a decision is a sign of growth, but any of us postpone decisions for we cannot accept the idea that we might be wrong. No matter how humble we may appear, our basic motivation here is pride, and not the humility and kindness that we front to the public.

"I was just going to ask you for a dime," said a well-heeled non-Catholic acquaintance of mine to a young man on the Bowery who had just asked him for a dime for a cup of coffee. The young man looked dazed, stammered a bit, and reaching in his pocket took out a dime and a nickel and handed my friend a dime. This was too much for my friend whose conscience hurt him. He ran after the derelict saying, "Here I'll trade you the dime for this quarter," which he did.

The moral, as I told my friend, is not to be sentimental and weakminded. My friend robbed the derelict on the Bowery of whatever faith in human nature he might have had. To do one good deed that day would have perhaps built him up, but now he would think, "I have met another phony."

There are people who have been babied by their relatives and as they whine their way through life most people are too "kind" to jerk them to their feet. One such person stumbled up to me, tramping on my toes and excusing himself by saying that he hoped he was not in the way. I told him he sure as hell was. And what could he do to help. I told him he could keep out of my way and sit in a corner. I said this in an alert manner and not with venom, and finally after some years there is no animosity between us. It was not unkind of me to educate this young man to be less rather than more of a nuisance. To encourage nit wits is not to help them. Useless conversation just to be saying something is the worst waste of time. The congenital blabber-mouth, even of pious words, needs conversation like I need a third eyebrow. In our office and in every city where I have lived, there is one or more such meddlesome pious souls sputtering superlatives to cover up their ignorance. They cannot be squelched, but it is weakness and not kindness to encourage them.

There are too many "Uncle Tom's" who by their sycophantic attitude mess up values. I have met such ones who praise me and agree with me when I know that they have just the faintest idea of what it is all about. These phonies do not need encouragement.

There are able men who are basically sentimentalists. They enthuse about "the revolution" or they are trigger happy about "dying for Christ" in some protest, but when it rains they run for cover, "to live again to run away another day." These folks are not insincere, but they clutter up any movement with their bubbling froth which soon settles down.

Then there is the clever manipulator who is sincere, but who is determined never to sweat overmuch or to neglect being paid for overtime if by chance he is found on the job after the whistle blows. To contrast these pie-cards of today with Debs, Mother Bloor, Mother Jones and Bill Haywood, is to know the difference between the real McCoy and the counterfeit.

I have worked with radicals in and out of jails for half a century. There is not one of them whom I have met that I would not gladly meet and work with again, but there are several who are hard for me to take, and a little bit of them goes a long way.

Walking through our office just now I notice a score of derelicts, each one of whom if you take them by themselves with even the doctored history which they have seen fit to tell us, cannot be blamed overly much. They are weak and they have been buffeted by "the system." To these folks I am not critical, but neither do I fall for their alibis, but good naturedly refuse them.

In a mushy atmosphere of pollyana optimism anyone who clears the air by calling things by their right names and facing facts runs the chance of being called arrogant and egotistic. This could be, but I submit that if taken as a part of my whole life and philosophy I have, by placing myself in a limited pacifist-anarchist-Catholic sphere, put myself in a glass house. If so I must needs take whatever stones come my way. I have the right by my life of integrity to criticize, but I must also take whatever criticism comes my way in all good humor. If I hand it out I have to take it.

When speaking at a Catholic girl's high school in Tucson I had occasion to deflate an arrogant young priest who was misquoting Christ. A girl brought up on respect for the Cloth was amazed and innocently asked me, "Mr. Hennacy, do you think that you are better than other people?" "Sure, but I have too good manners to say so," I replied.

Another time a spoiled and arrogant priest wanted to know if I was "holier than thou." I told him that I hoped by Christ I was, for if I wasn't I would be in a hell of a fix. I used this blunt method to deflate his spurious piety.

Those who criticize me me for criticizing others, are themselves criticizing, and by what right are they above criticism themselves. I do not claim to be above criticism; I am not going to allow such accusations to keep me from exposing fraud.

"Why do you fast in public when Christ said to do this in secret in your closet?"
If I was doing this for any vainglory it would be terrible, but it is, like

the small top of the iceberg appearing above water, only an indication of the huge mass beneath. It is only the result of a dedicated life which appears because of an emergency in the war mad world, meant to say "Danger" to those about to be wrecked. You can't obey all scripture at once. You have to choose. Christ also said to "shout from the housetops," and "not to hide your light under a bushel." If I did not speak and fast the very stones would cry out.

I also fasted before I was a Catholic. I do this as a penance for all of our sins. I do not do it to coerce or embarass my enemy the government, and the tax and war officials. I do it to waken up the timid pacifists who know better and don't do better. Someone has to raise the ante of what should be expected of a Christian and a Catholic. Talk is cheap and in this gluttonous world fasting can be a means of waking up some people.

If anyone thinks the mainspring of my action is egotism I would ask by what measure they value their own actions. I am willing to be judged as a man, not a mouse, by my fruits, both now and hereafter. My message is not meant for those unable to receive it.

"Why don't you work like other men do?"

I could answer this in these days of automation with the old wobblie refrain, "How in the hell can I work when there is no work to do?" for they work for companies where a withholding tax is taken from their pay for war. I have to bootleg my work and work by the day where there is no tax taken out, such as migrant work or in self made jobs such as speaking in colleges and schools.

I work for my keep just now here at the CW, getting up early for the mail, recording the income, answering letters, selling CW's each day on the streets, which is much harder than walking around; speaking upon call at the office to visitors, and when called upon to do so travelling over the country. Now, since November of 1961, I am in Salt Lake City directing the Joe Hill House of Hospitality and St. Joseph's Refuge, collecting food daily to feed thousands who come here from the freights. I will describe this elsewhere in more detail in this book. If anyone thinks that sleeping on the floor by the door with from thirty to fifty people snoring, coughing, mumbling in the after affects of liquor, answering the door a dozen times a night as drunks pound for entrance is fun, let them try it.

I am sixty nine and I do not ask the state for any social security or old age pension. I have worked up to the age of nineteen on a farm, and eleven years not long ago at stoop labor on the ranches of the southwest. I have worked eleven years in Milwaukee as a social worker, and six years on a farm near there.

I fast and picket the tax office each year and several times have fasted for over forty days and picketed. If you think this is easy work, try it.

"Christ ate meat. Do you think you are better than Christ by not eating meat?"

If He hadn't eaten fish He would have had a hard time; that's what His disciples were for the most part; fishermen. I am a vegetarian for sentimental reasons: I don't like to kill animals and I don't want someone else to do it for me. And for pacifistic reasons I won't kill capitalists.

400

John the Baptist, Buddha, Gandhi, and the Trappists, Camaldolese and other Orders are vegetarians. It is a matter of where a person draws the line. The Essenes of Christ's time were vegetarians and He did not reprimand them. He was asked why He and His disciples did not fast as John's disciples did. He reached a different class of people: wine-bibbers and gluttons for whom the Gospel was also meant.

In old English law a butcher is not allowed on a murder jury for fear that his occupation as a killer would make him too hard hearted towards the prisoner before the court. Primitive man had to kill and eat or starve to death. He had no supermarkets where he could buy vegetables. Outside of the Eskimos who have little vegetation there is no excuse for modern man consuming so much meat. And doctored up before they are killed to produce more fat, and preserved by questionable chemicals. The eating of these fowl and animals is not conducive to spiritual or bodily health.

Those who wish to kill their own animals for food are welcome to do so, and for those who wish to be kind to animals the best advice is the vegetarian slogan: "Be kind to animals by not eating them."

There is the cartoon of the Father Bear with a gun pointed at the hunter who is asking for mercy because "of my wife and children at home." The bear replied that the hunter had killed his wife and children, not for food, but only to show off to his friends. "I won't do it again," promised the man. "You won't have a chance to do it again," said the bear as he aimed his gun.

"Why don't you vote for the good man for office? You just help the bad man by your negative attitude."

A good man is worse than a bad man for he finds a good reason for doing a bad thing that a bad man couldn't figure out, so he lends his goodness to evil. The devil doesn't have horns, he has a halo as big as a hoop. We elected Wilson to keep us out of war, and Roosevelt when he said, "I tell you again, and again, and again, that no boys will be sent across to foreign soil."

A good man cannot get any legislation passed or enforced unless he plays ball with the bad men who have a head start on him and surround him. He has to vote for their postoffice, harbor graft, or other larceny minded bills to even get his bill out of committee.

I only voted once in my life and that was in 1916 when I voted for Allan Benson, the Socialist candidate for President, who was against the war. And before I was out of Atlanta Prison, Benson was for the war. I might as well have stayed at home. My capitalistic brother is not a pacifist nor an anarchist, but he had sense enough never to vote in his life, as he does not trust politicians.

In 1960, I was asked to run for Vice President on the Vegetarian ticket, but of course I refused to do so. Both major party candidates believe in the return of evil for evil in courts, prisons and war. The Socialist parties believe in violence and Socalism, so as a pacifist and an anarchist I could not vote for them.

I have already seceded from the idea of government. If I voted for a pacifist and he was not elected, I would be honor bound to obey the winner, who of course, this time (1960) would either be Kennedy or Nixon, both of whom believe in greater armaments and in war as a means of defeating Communism, although, of course, they say they believe in peace. I vote every day by my anarchistic actions.

"Would you defend someone dear to you who is being attacked?"

Christ was defended by Peter who cut off the ear of the attacker. Christ gave the answer when He said, "Put up thy sword; he that taketh the sword shall perish by the sword."

Pacifism does not mean to stand by and do nothing. It means to do something: to use the strongest weapon, spiritual force, rather than the weaker weapon, violence. But you can't use it if you don't have it. First, you must not be afraid, for even animals can smell fear. Second, you must feel that there is good in your attacker. Third, you must have the agility of mind to speak sincerely without preaching in *"very few words"* that will deflect the violence. This can't be learned in a book. It has to flow from a life of integrity, with the minimum of show-off. If you invade an army camp you must not expect them to act like pacifists toward you; you are asking for trouble.

I hope I would defend those dear to me as I have defended myself many times, by spiritual understanding rather than by violence. But none of us can be sure until the last chapter how we will actually act in a given circumstance. My friend Bayard Rustin was asked this question, and he said that once he acted in one way and once he acted in another way. He was in a barricaded cabin in the deep South with other Negroes where the surrounding KKK were masked ready to lynch them. Bayard opened the door and stood with folded arms, saying, "You came here to lynch us; start with me." They went home in shame. If he had spoken in anger and called them bastards he would not have won. Another time he was in a taxi on the Bowery and he saw a Negro being beaten by two white men. He jumped out and kicked and hit the white men in the appropriate places and drew the Negro in the taxi away to safety. My friend Ned Richards was in the Near East at the time of World War I. He was a young man doing missionary work and was the oldest male among women and children at the time when a crazy Armenian was standing on a hill nearby and shooting at each one as they came out of the house. After a time Ned walked with hand outstretched, a perfect target, up the hill to the Armenian whose gun was pointed at him. The Armenian handed him the gun and commenced to weep.

An AP dispatch tells in Bloomington, Illinois in 1936 of two bandits who held up a small restaurant where a girl and her father were the owners. The girl asked them why they held the place up. They said they were hungry. "Sit down and eat," she said. "You will call the cops," the replied. "You are between me and the phone and the cop went by half an hour ago," was her answer. They ate and whispered and returned the money. If she had screamed when they came in she would likely have been shot as well as robbed. Another time two robbers held up a filling station run by Father Divine's followers in Philadelphia. "Peace, Brother," said the attendants when told by the robbers, "Your money or your life." However, the guns were brandished or whatever the admonition was to hand over the money, all that the men said was "Peace, Brother." It was impossible to rob such people, so the robbers went away.

CHAPTER 20

Mural, 12 by 15, of the execution of Joe Hill.
Painted by Mary Lathrop, on the wall of first Joe Hill House, 1961.

JOE HILL HOUSE
Salt Lake City, Utah
1961 to present

Time: May 1961 to Present
Place: Salt Lake City, and West to the Coast

After speaking here in April of 1961 at the University I hurried home to New York City to take part in the air raid refusal. 2000 protested and some were arrested but few leaders, so I came toward Salt Lake City. Arriving in Cleveland, Ohio to visit my mother and brother and sisters I had a phone call from Mary Lathrop in New York City, saying that she had quit her job and wanted to come with me to Salt Lake City to help start the Joe Hill House. Mary's father had been a Communist organizer so she knew the radical part of the CW message. She had been a Catholic only a short time. She had met my mother while traveling with Dorothy before. We left for Notre Dame where I had several meetings; staying at the home of Terry McKiernan, who has the House of Bread; then to Nauvoo where we saw the grave of Joseph Smith, and I spoke to the Catholic nuns at their school. Mary had been here with Dorothy previously. Then to visit my daughter Carmen in Santa Fe, a week with Phil Burnham in Tucson where I had a meeting at the Allen's; and a week in Phoenix visiting my many friends. Joe Craigmyle drove us up to the Hopi and back to Flagstaff where we stayed with Platt and Barbara Cline, going to the bottom of the Grand Canyon, before coming to Salt Lake City.

403

Here we found work picking cherries, hoeing beets, etc. I irrigated one night for a Mormon and got odd jobs washing dishes in a restaurant or unloading trucks. Mary got jobs at housework. We visited the town of Layton about 20 miles north trying to get work in the fields, and also talked to the local priest but he was not a bit interested in any work among the migrants. A friend told us that a Catholic student at the University had raised $240 for us to start a House, so we looked around and found this location near the employment office and skid row. A friend in the east gave us $100 to pay the rent ahead. We got 2 months free rent and paid the 2 months ahead which brought us up to November First. Meanwhile I slept on the floor here and we looked around for furnishings, carrying bits of lumber from the alley's on our way from Mass early in the morning. Ren Mabey, a seminarian, and ex Mormon, whom I had met several years before in Mt. Angel, Oregon, mopped our floor and gave us a few furnishings. We bought a second hand small roller top desk, and a rocking chair. When we went to get the money collected for us by the student it turned out that he could not be found, but Mary worked and we were able to make it.

We had picketed that August 6th until August 21st and fasted because of the atom bomb dropped at Hiroshima 16 years before. In our leaflet headed in old English *Thou Shalt Not Kill* we quoted Joseph Smith as saying, "even the Congress of the United States has no power to make a law that would abridge the rights of my religion." Two young men were sentenced to die at Utah State Prison and their friends asked me to speak at Liberty Park at a protest meeting. The attorney general said that it was against the law to picket the prison, so I wrote to the sheriff and the warden saying that Mary and I had picketed at Sing Sing and we would picket here. The young men got a reprieve the night before the execution and we did not have to picket. The radio and television gave us good coverage and the afternoon daily, *The Deseret News* (Mormon) had a headline: " '*Anarchists' Picket In City Against Taxes, Killing.*" I had met the brother of Ernie Linford, one of the editors of the Morning paper, the Tribune, owned mostly by the Catholic Kearns family, in Santa Fe, and had looked up Mr. Linford when I came here. In his column he good naturedly headed it saying *"Hennacy's Coming,"* and continued: "You may have lived such a sheltered life that you don't know this one-man-revolution, but you likely will soon know him by reputation, if not personally." Then he tells of my radical history and intention to open the Joe Hill House. The police did not interfere with our picketing and we were seldom called "Communist." One young Catholic who had formerly read the CW in Laramie gave us $15 to get the electricity turned on. We met a sort of Rosicrucian who bought us 6 cots and mattresses, but when he saw the statues that priests from across the track had given us he didn't come around any more. One of these priests who was head of the Catholic Youth asked me to write an article for their paper against war and capital punishment and to speak to the youth at Lourdes High School, but a few hours before the meeting he told us that the Bishop did not want anything "controversial" discussed. We had written to the Bishop when we came telling him of our plans and sending him our leaflets and asking for an appointment. After six weeks we received a letter from him saying that he did not approve of our activities. We did not expect him to but we thought we might as well be friends with him. The Catholics have 8 churches here and the Mormons have 200 so they want to be overly respectable and conservative, so of course anyone half as radical as we were would be out of bounds.

Joe Hill

Joe Hill, born Hillstrom in Sweden, but as he wrote songs for the I.W.W. (The Industrial Workers of the World) the radical union of the first quarter of the century, his name came to be Joe Hill. Big Bill Haywood of Salt Lake City had been one of the organizers of this union which sought to help the transient and the poorly paid laborer. I had belonged to it from 1912 to 1922. The story goes that they were called "Wobs" because a Chinese restaurant owner who fed them for free during a strike in Seattle couldn't pronounce "I.W.W." so as they came in for free eats he would ask them "You Wobble, Wobble?" They would hold meetings on streetcorners and the Salvation Army would sing, so in order to be heard they made up parodies on the Christian hymns. The best known was Joe's *The Preacher and the Slave:*

Long-haired preachers come out every night,
Try to tell you what's wrong and what's right;
But when asked 'bout something to eat
They will answer with voices so sweet:

Chorus

You will eat, bye and bye,
In that glorious land above the sky;
Work and pray, live on hay,
You'll get pie in the sky when you die.

And the starvation army they play,
And they sing and they clap and they pray.
Till they get all your coin on the drum,
Then they tell you when you are on the bum:

If you fight hard for children and wife—
Try to get something good in this life—
You're a sinner and bad man they tell,
When you die you will sure go to hell.

Workingmen of all countries unite,
Side for side we for freedom will fight:
When the world and its wealth we have gained
To the grafters we will sing this refrain:

Last Chorus

You will eat, bye and bye.
When you've learned how to cook and to fry;
Chop some wood, 'twill do you good,
And you'll eat in the sweet bye and bye.

The chorus of *The Tramp* is especially good:

Tramp, tramp, tramp, keep on a tramping
Nothing doing here for you;
If I catch you 'round again,

You will wear the ball and chain,
Keep on tramping, that's the best thing you can do.

The I.W.W. called for all those who worked in one industry to belong to one union, as in the Brewers Union. In the 1890's when Eugene V. Debs organized the American Railway Union and everyone who worked for Jim Hill on the Great Northern struck at once they won the strike in a short time. Debs was one of the organizers of the I.W.W. It is said that Father James Hagerty wrote the famous preamble of the I.W.W. which begins with these words, *"The working class and the employing class have nothing in common . . . between these two classes a struggle must go on until the workers of the world organize as a class, take possessino of the earth and the machinery of production, abolish the wage system. Instead of the conservative motto, A fair day's wage for a fair day's work, we must inscribe on our banner the revolutionary watchword, 'Abolish the wage system.".... By organizing industrially we are forming the structure of the new society within the shell of the old."*

No wonder when in the winter of 1913 there was a strike of 5,000 miners at nearby Park City where Joe worked and his revolutionary songs were sung "to fan the flames of discontent" the wealthy Catholic and Mormon mine owners felt disturbed. Joe had been in jail in the free speech fights in San Diego and San Pedro in California. There the authorities did not allow street meetings. Thousands of the Wobs went to jail, sang Joe's songs, were beaten and killed, but they won freedom to talk. On the famous May Day in 1912 the "bindle stiffs" burned their lousy bunk houses in the lumber camps and there was a revolutionary urge in the air.

On the night of January 10, 1914 a former cop by the name of Morrison, who had been attacked twice by robbers in recent months was killed in his small grocery store at 8th Street and Southwest Temple by two armed men. The older Morrison son was also killed, the only witness being the 13 year old younger son. One of the robbers was shot. That same night Joe Hill was shot with the same kind of a bullet as that which the Morrison's shot at the robber. Joe had Dr. McHugh, former Socialist candidate for Governor, attend to his wound. Later the Dr. turned in a report of the treatment of Joe, and he was arrested and charged with the killing of the Morrison's. He claimed that he had been shot in an affair over a woman, but gentleman as he was, he refused to name any names. It is thought that the girl was Hilda Erickson in Murray, and that a former suitor of hers, a hanger on of the Wobs, by the name of Otto Applequist, was the one who shot Joe. It least Otto was not to be found the next day. It could be that Hilda tried to take the gun away from Otto, and that Joe was shot in the scuffle. There was no reason for Joe to have robbed the Morrison's. In the preliminary hearing the 13 year old Morrison boy said it was a shorter man that Joe who did the shooting, but at the trial the boy was frightened into saying "It might have been Joe." The same tactics were used in the trial of Sacco and Vanzetti. Joe fired his inefficient court appointed lawyers but was finally found guilty. While his appeal was going on under the able Judge Hilton of Denver as counsel, an ex-army man openly killed an I.W.W. leader and was quickly acquitted. Tom Mooney at the AFL convention in San Francisco introduced a motion which was passed unanimously for justice for Joe, and President

Wilson asked twice for a reprieve. The school principals of Salt Lake County publicly approved of the Mormon Governor Spry who stood fast against the radicals. The only person of importance here who said that the whole thing was a frame-up was Virginia Snow, the daughter of the President of the Mormon Church, who taught art at the University of Utah and was fired for her courage. Joe was executed at the old Sugar House state prison on Sept. 19, 1915. He had written the song Rebel Girl while in prison and dedicated it to Elizabeth Gurley Flynn. No friends were allowed to witness the execution. He gave the order to "fire" prematurely, but the guards were not ready. He refused any dope or liquor and stood up like a man. His ashes were distributed in every state but Utah and in many foreign countries. Dr. McHugh later wrote to the Governor and asked for $500 reward for turning Joe in, but he didn't get it. In the archives a friend of mine found a letter written from me in 1915 from Columbus, Ohio asking for clemency for Joe Hill.

Later the song was written *"I Dreamed Last Night I Saw Joe Hill"* and it is sung all over the world today. Mary painted a mural of the execution of Joe Hill which in size is 12 by 15 feet and is the prominent feature of our House. As you see Christ is in it as another One who was framed. The I.W.-W. wouldn't print this picture because it had Christ in it and the Catholic papers won't print it because Joe Hill is in it. Mary also painted a mural of the Holy Family, a picture of a Russian Pilgrim, something resembling a Russian Ikon, St. Joan and the Wicked Bishop, etc. We believe we are being true to the memory of Joe Hill by feeding the tramps and transients for whom he cared, and in having no Bible-banging. We do have radical meetings each Friday night.

At one window we have this quotation from Debs: *"While there is a lower class I am in it; while there is a criminal class I am of it; while there is a soul in prison I am not free."* And in the other window this wisdom from John Dewey: *"A good man is one, who, no matter how bad he has been is getting better; a bad man is one, who, no matter how good he has been is getting worse."*

HOW WE GOT STARTED

A friend gave us an electric hotplate and we cooked on that. Finally some Ute Indians who were up on trial for chasing an Indian Bureau man off the reservation, stopped in their truck and brought two stoves from a priest across the track. It took us several weeks to get the down payment and the authorization for gas, but finally we could cook on a gas stove. My friend Francis Gorgen stopped in for a visit of a day or two. It seems that again by reverse action we were to be helped, for a priest sent a young Catholic alcoholic to us and he slept here nights. He ate where he worked it seemed, and told us that he had bought us a hot water heater, which was soon delivered. Upon seeing the heater Francis said he would stay over a few days and connect it up. While looking for the connections he bought us a gas refrigerator second hand and connected it and the stoves up also. By this time the folks who had brought the heater came and got it back, for our friend had not paid a cent on it, and was already in jail for some other larceny. I looked around and went to buy a heater from a company second hand. The man, who was a Baptist, said if we were doing good work he wouldn't take any money for it, so Francis soon had it in working order. I got two laundry tubs second hand but some welding needed to be done before they could be connected. A man came with a portable welder after hours and when he had finished he said," Hell, I wouldn't charge you anything, for I used to hop freights myself." Francis finally stayed 3 weeks and the kitchen was in running order. Later I bought a shower bath for $35 and Francis installed it. Meanwhile our friend was out of jail and was collecting money and cashing checks for more liquor, all in the name of our House. I got the Mormon daily to print a notice that no one was collecting money for us. I went to one paint company and got 2½ gallons of light grey paint; then I told the next company about it and they gave me the same, and another company upped it to 4 gallons, and our walls were clean. I went to a paper company and had to ask them for new toilet paper, so they gave me a carton of it. Then to three other companies who each give a carton a year. A cracker company brings us crackers, and a few coffee companies have given us coffee. I had written to General Foods telling them that here was the opportunity to have Postum given free instead of coffee, but they had no imagination and answered no. The Hershey man brings us plenty of cocoa. Mary and I carried 120 lbs. of wheat on our backs for nearly a mile; and it is ground on the old coffee grinder I had in Milwaukee when my girls used to grind their own cereal for breakfast. Nearly all the bread companies said if they gave to one they would have to give to all. I told them to break down once and see how it felt. Finally one baker allowed me to get 2 baskets of bread three times a week, and another hearing about it allowed us 2 baskets once a week. The Spudnut folks gave us doughnuts twice a week and likewise a pie company. But milk and egg folks wouldn't budge.

Mary and I went around to the merchants saying, "We are pacifists, anarchists, subversives, and Catholics too radical for our Bishop, but we need sugar, etc." We got it. Readers of the CW over the country who know me send bits of money at times, so I make it alright. $100 a month is enough. I know that if I do the best the best will be done by me. Few Catholics in town help us but in time they will get over their fear. Mary had been in California working among the migrants in the fields around Tracy and Stockton, and painting murals for the Mexicans and the Quakers. Now in San Francisco she wrote in the January 1963 CW: "I was down in the kitchen of St. Anthony's Dining Room when the Archbishop was dishing out meals to the men, and I wrote to Ammon that someday perhaps Bishop Federal will go down to Postoffice Place and do the same thing for him. Stranger things has happened." And although one of the leading priests advised us that, "It is more meritorious to obey a stupid and mistaken priest than it is to obey your conscience, for that may be self will," and although he stands for capital punishment and war, it also it not impossible that such men may change. Cardinal Suhard, an old man in Paris, saw that the workers were not going to Church and he started the Worker Priests.

Public Relations

The Mormon radio, KSL, interviewed me here at the House, asking me what our rules were. I said "no liquor and no cops." Coy Ringo was doing life for murder and had escaped from the state prison, stabbing a guard. I was asked if I would hide an escaped murderer. I replied that "I sure as hell would. In the Middle Ages anyone whom the law was after could find sanctuary in a Church. Now the Mormons and the Catholics see which one can shoot them first." This was released twice on the radio and I had several elderly Mormons come in and ask if I was the man that would protect criminals. In asking the merchants for food, one of them wanted me to get a clearing from the Chamber of Commerce. I went there and explained our ideas and was asked what my racket was. I told them that Mary and I would not sit out on the cold curb early in the morning waiting for some padrone to pick us up if we had any racket. Nor would we spend 14 hours going to and fro to a job and working picking cherries and then get a rubber check for our trouble if we had a racket. I said that the Salvation Army only allowed transients to stay there one night a month, and if they didn't have a social security card they would turn them in to the police. That the cops had police dogs after the men in the alleys at night, so where the state left off it was the place for anarchists like us to begin.

The health department came around and said that it was unsanitary to sleep men on the floor. I said where were they going to sleep the men. They said I should have double bunks with mattresses. My reply was that the men would fall out of the bunks and crack their skulls, and besides I could only have room for a very few such bunks while I could sleep 70 on the floor. But it was still unsanitary they said. I told them that there must have been some regulation from folks like them that Christ shouldn't have been born in a stable.

The police came in and wanted to know the name of some man. I told them that I didn't ask any questions. They said that by law I ought to take the names of all who came. My reply was that inasmuch as I did not charge anything I did not have to take names. It was not long until the police brought men in late at night, or even in the daytime for us to sober up in our "cooler" under the stairway. They are friendly now as we take a lot of grief off of them.

Four times the FBI came in looking for someone. I shut my eyes and told them that I couldn't see, and if anyone whom they wanted was in here I wouldn't tell them anyway; that besides I didn't like that stinker, J. Edgar Hoover. Later they took our literature and do not bother us. A man from the Fire Department came in and said that this place was a fire hazard. I told them that I slept on the floor by the door at night and was up most of the night so that if there was any fire I would know it, and that we took matches away from any drunks we kept in the cooler. He looked around and said, "Well, I guess 60 men in 60 doorways are more of a fire hazard than 60 men all in one room here."

Several people from the Federal Building where we had picketed came over and gave us $5, refusing to give their names, but saying they liked the work we were doing. The Mormon afternoon paper generally prints a small item each week telling of the subject of our Friday night meeting. I spoke several times at the university, and at a luncheon at the Presbyterian Westminster College. Hundreds of students, mostly Mormons, have come down

409

from the university to interview me about our House and to report back to class, and as a result students often come to our Friday night meetings.

Elizabeth Gurley Flynn gave us a framed picture by Art Young from the old *Masses* of a reward wanted for Christ, the vagabond, *"wanted for sedition, Criminal Anarchy, Vagrancy. and Conspiring to Overthrow the Established Government. Dresses poorly said to be a carpenter by trade, ill-nourished, has visionary ideas, associates with common working people the unemployed and bums. Alien — believed to be a Jew. Alias 'Prince of Peace. Son of Man-Light of the World,' and Professional Agitator, Red Beard, Marks on hands and feet the result of injuries inflicted by an angry mob led by respectable citizens and legal authorities."*

Picketing for Garcia and Rivenburgh

These young men had been raised in reform school, and Garcia had at the age of 16 been put in the state prison among old tough prisoners. He was held and forcibly raped by a score of men. Later in trouble among homosexuals one man was killed. Three were charged with the murder. One got life, and Jesse Garcia and Mack Rivenburgh were sentenced to death. In March of 1962 they were again sentenced to die on the 13th. I wrote a leaflet entitled THOU SHALT NOT KILL and picketed the Governor and Board of Pardons daily for 12 days. The night before the execution they got a reprieve. Mr. McNamara, a Catholic Sociologist from New York City lectured at the University against capital punishment for a week in January, mentioning these cases and Garcia's married sister and myself and Mrs. Ethel Hale distributed these leaflets after the evening lectures at the University. One young woman, after taking a leaflet, came back up the steps and asked if I were Mr. Hennacy. I admitted it. She said she was the warden's secretary, and that they read the literature I had sent them.

It is reported that an Eastern Catholic Governor appointed 25 people on a commission to report back to him on the subject of capital punishment and that 20 of these were of other religions than Catholic, and 5 were Catholic priests. When the problem was decided by this committee, 20 were against capital punishment and of course the 5 who were for it were the 5 priests. I wrote to every minister in the City telling them that unless they took a stand against these executions that their hands would be bloody. The Catholic Chaplain at the prison spoke to me on the phone and was sorry about the pending executions but would not say anything about it openly, and of course the Catholic Bishop ran true to his conservative form in only being interested in the quiet of the bank and of the grave: nothing to disturb the collecting of money. The only one of the clergy who replied was the Unitarian minister who wrote openly in the newspaper, as I did also, against capital punishment, and who spoke against the executions in the pulpit. He said that the time had not yet come to picket, but at the time of the executions he would stand with me at the prison gate at dawn in silent protest.

A young, self centered egoist, who was writing a book about Joe Hill came and lived here from the middle of November 1961 for ten months, picketed with me for about ten days, and an employee of the Utah Historical Society picketed also until the heat got too much concerning his job. I do not blame him, but was glad to have his help. The television and radio reported my opinions fairly, and the Mormon daily took our pictures. It was quite a walk up hill to the Capitol on an empty stomach as I picketed the hour at noon, so finally I rode on the bus, and walked home downhill. Beautiful blonde Molly Fisher, whose folks had been missionaries in South America, had heard of our House and picketed with me for 2 weeks while waiting in the City for a friend. As always in my picketing after a time I got my second wind and for as much as 11 days I did not lose a pound. I continued with my regular work getting the food and sleeping on the floor by the door nights. Mrs. Mildred McAlister, a Quaker woman, head of the local chapter against capital punishment, and Professor Paul Vernier of the University who had been visiting Garcia for years, spoke at hearings before the Pardon Board. I could not get out to the prison those nights because I was needed here to keep peace among the drunks who happened to be especially troublesome just then. Finally, the night before the execution, on September 13th, Garcia got life, but Rivenburgh, discouraged at this 6th time he was facing the firing squad, took poison in his cell. These young men were both Catholics, but no priest was present at Rivenburgh's funeral in the cemetery where the young Unitarian minister officiated. I was present and was ashamed of this callousness which placed Catholic dogma and cowardice ahead of humanity.

Several times when coming back from picketing, Molly and I gave our leaflets to the young LDS missionaries assembled for an outing as we passed by. Before the scheduled execution in March, Mrs. Hale and about 20 others held a protest meeting on the Capitol steps on a snowy night. The radio gave us publicity, but some Jack Mormon rowdies tried to break the meeting up, without success. The letters in the papers during these days were mostly by Mormons who, because of their dogma of blood atonement believed in capital punishment. I found this also in my picketing. The Saturday before the scheduled execution in September, Mrs. Hale and an elderly Italian from Magna, Utah, participated in a poster walk with me on Main Street at noon. Others promised to walk with us but in this conservative environment it is difficult to get people to come out and be different. Poulson's case was carried up in the courts, and he lost his appeal. He never should have been left out of a mental institution, but he was paroled to his mother. He might as well have been paroled to a chair for he had continual record of sex offenses. He went to the police in Provo and said that he was going to get in trouble again and they had better lock him up, but the police said he hadn't done anything yet. The next day he killed a babysitter. As in the case of Garcia and Rivenburgh this young man was a product of reform schools and state institutions. Whatever guilt there is lies with the state as much as with the individual. The Supreme Court denied his appeal, so I may be picketing and fasting for him.

Who Comes to Us?

About a third are Jack Mormons, a third Irish Catholics, and a third Oakies or Arkies from the South, with a sprinkling of Negroes, Mexicans and Indians. About 25 town bums come and go. Many of them get kickbacks from their landlords from rent that the relief pays for them; and also they sell their meal tickets for half price back to the restaurant and have money for booze. In their prosperity, they pay double price to bootleggers on Sunday and holidays when the state liquor stores are closed. Only beer is sold in taverns, and no taverns are on the main street in down town Salt Lake City. You have to have a dollar permit to buy from the state liquor store. Several men know about my ideas on drinking and have given me their liquor permit cards to tear up. Drinking is not the cause of crime or of discord; it is an *effect* of a discordant and frustrated life. Overprotection by the mother in the home, the fears taught by religion, too much of the rod, and a general sense of the futility of living are causes which drive people to drink or dope to get away from their troubles. When a person desires to sober up, the AA is a great help, but the people I see here do not want to sober up: what they want is one more jug. Preaching to them does not do any good. As I have said before the only way to cure drunkards who do not want to be cured is to put them on some island or far away mountain where a saloon is too far away for them to get at. Then have work for them to do and no one making a profit from their labor. Let them have chicken for dinner every day if they want it; strawberries and cream, or whatever they can raise. Let the place be supervised by one who does not drink himself, and who will pour out any moonshine made from sugar, raisins, etc. locally. In most institutions the bosses get cream, butter, steaks, while the men get skim milk, oleo and hot dogs. Let all eat the same food. There is Antelope Island in Great Salt Lake. Men cannot be rehabilitated when there is a tavern on every corner.

"Eli Begay, sober," said a young Navajo at midnight. I let him in. Another time he came with an Indian friend, saying, "Eli Begay, drunk. Let my friend in for he is sober. I go away." Indians do not have much sense of time and while I will turn away a town bum after ten o'clock, I have more patience with Indians. If I am not sure if the man is a transient or a town bum I·will give him the benefit of the doubt. By the time I am awakened, up a dozen times a night, every night, I seek to minimize this grief. Many town bums have learned to come by nine p.m. and they can be in the cooler and sober up. I repeat that there is a difference between kindness and weakness. If I find a bottle on them at night I pour it out and put them out. I announce this policy each night before bedtime.

Cooks who come here and help me say that all cooks are drunks, and in fact I have not found a sober one. On our first Thanksgiving Day in my innocence I thought that the cook was preparing the meal: a turkey given us by a woman who worked at the Post Office, with trimmings. But he was in the back room, passed out. Alba Ryan, an old friend who had been a nurse with the Loyalists in Spain, had stopped for a day or two and took over and we had enough for all. Alba is a fine woman but sentimentally she said, "No one is boss around here; we are all one big family." I spoke up and said, "I am boss, though not a very efficient one or I wouldn't let the cook get by with his boozing. There has to be someone here to see that this place doesn't deteriorate into a dirty box car." This cook had told Mary that he wanted to be a Catholic and went to Mass once with her, and then tried to bum her for money to get drunk on. Other cooks sold whatever they could get for liquor. One fat fraud collected about $25 for my birthday, baked a cake, gave me a new typewriter ribbon, and next day went on a drunk with the remainder. I have had scores of men help out with washing the dishes, peeling potatoes, scrubbing the floor, etc. They get a job for a day and get drunk and move on. If they come back sober and they are needed I take them on again. In the beginning I used to buy them packaged cigarettes, but I quit that for I found that they always had enough money for booze, so they could buy their own cigarettes too. For the last eight months I have an aged cook whose friends buy him liquor. He is responsible, keeping the ice box and his room where sugar, canned goods, etc. are stored, locked. Often men get a day's work and buy some meat, eggs, coffee, and treat the men who work here and eat with them. Several sentimental people have thought that everyone on the line should get this extra food. There is not enough to go around. These men who do the work get a cot to sleep on. If they can get a little work on the side that is fine.

Often a Jack Mormon will give me a dollar as sort of a tithe, for he would not dare go back to his Church for they would want him to quit smoking and drinking. Men who get a steady job can sleep here and we give them sandwiches until they can get a payday. Scores have said that when they get paid they will help us, and they mean it, but between their payday and us there is the tavern and they are soon broke again. Many men have been around here for months, helping us at times, and have told tall tales about their former prosperity, and of leads they have for wonderful jobs now, but it is nearly all romancing. Men have worked for days for padrones who cheat them, mainly at cleaning bricks, at $7 a thousand. They may give them a dollar now and then for lunch and then they go bankrupt or disappear. Or they leave the employment office nearby with the promise of a job which terminates five miles from town with 50 cents an hour, or the promise of a payday tomorrow. These cheating employers think that the "bums" will work for very little because they are poor, or they will not bother to stay in town and will leave, and therefore will not have to be paid.

At Night

The sign on the door says that 9 p.m. is bedtime. This is meant to keep the town drunks away after that hour, but any transient is welcome any time. As Indians do not have much sense of time I let them in unless they are too drunk to stand up. We have a "cooler," a place under a stairway where we keep garbage and can accommodate 5 white drunks or six Indians, for the latter curl up like kittens and take little space. The cops often bring men in to sober up whom they are tired of pinching. Often two men will bring a comrade in who has passed out and have him sleep it off here. Two men kept me up all night with the shakes, but I guess it was worse on them than it was on the rest of us. Around midnight I wouldn't allow a drunken Navajo inside and in a minute he had thrown a vodka bottle through the window, and I was combing glass out of my hair for a week. All Indians stayed away for 2 weeks, thinking I might turn some of them in for the damage. At times I get up half asleep when there is a knock on the door and I am not sure if the man there is a stranger or a town drunk. I give them the benefit of the doubt. Sixty men sleeping on the floor without anyone snoring! It has happened a couple of times, but generally I have to get up and turn a man over several times on this account. And sometimes a drunk will escape our eyes and commence to babble in his sleep, and then he will have to go to the cooler. At times one of these drunks will urinate wherever he happens to stand, and one morning I got up to turn on the light and stepped in a mess that "Five by five," an enormous Mexican, had deposited on the floor. Of course he said that he was innocent but the evidence was all over him. While on the subject, one afternoon I was resting in the cook's room when the phone rang and I got up to answer it. I noticed a stream of water flowing from a corner by the bedroom door. It couldn't have come from the bathroom. Two drunks had slipped in and were sleeping on two nearby beds. I woke them up and asked which one had urinated in that especial corner. Each said that he was innocent, and one of them noticed the St. Francis and the Wolf medal that I was wearing and asked what that was. I told him not to change the subject, that the subject was piss, and not holy medals. Coming back from Mass one morning I found that the yardmaster at the freight yard had brought five men up in his car for breakfast, saying that it was better to have them here than to pinch them.

Social Work?

Both Catholic and other religions have wondered if I have been able to rehabilitate the derelicts who come here. These men have had enough preaching. They know better than anyone else what is the matter. They only feel sorry when they get out of jail or when they have a headache. Several men have given me their liquor permits to tear up, but this was only temporary, for in a few weeks they were drunk again. They have a quiet place to read, or if they are sleepy they can go in the cooler and sleep. I would not have a radio or television with all the noise. Several men have come here broke and have sobered up, got a job, and settled down to a good job and a married life. They have come back and told me about it. There may be others. I set them the example of being sober and willing to do any of the tedius or disagreeable work around here. They know I go to Mass daily and that I say prayers for all of them. Prying into their lives does not do any good. When they want any help from me, or the AA they will ask for it. I have faith enough in what I am doing to take the long view and do not have to build up my morale by having them sign on the dotted line that they have been "saved." That is up to God.

The Daily Routine

I get up at 5 a.m., turn the lights on, roll up my blankets, put jelly between two slices of bread, while the cook makes cocoa, and two others get the chairs and tables ready. Often someone offers to sweep the sidewalk but if not, I do it. Then I read the morning paper or write letters until time to go to 6:30 Mass. Back at 7:30 and have breakfast if I am not fasting. The first mail comes at 8:00, and by 8:45 I am on my way with the rubber-tired cart from the super-market for fruit and vegetables which they have saved for us, at two stores about a mile away. Often one of the men goes with me and we are back by 10:00 with potatoes, carrots, apples, onions, lettuce, and even avacados and strawberries and melons at times. One place gives us dented cans or cans with the labels off. On Mondays and Thursdays, I go to another store, coming through the Temple grounds where the guards greet me kindly. Monday morning I go for candy to a wholesale house; and for salt, sugar, spices to other places when needed. At 3:30 three times a week I walk 18 blocks (long Mormon blocks like between the Avenues in New York City) for bread, and twice a week I walk 35 blocks for spudnuts and pies. I ride home on the bus. Folks ask me why I don't get a car or have some of my help get these things. They do not understand that the tax man would get the car, and that most of my help would peddle the bread or pies and doughnuts for booze before they got home. If I have time in the afternoon, I try and sleep or rest for a few hours but often drunks are making too much noise. During the day and before 9:00 p.m. visitors or students often come in to ask questions. On Friday night I always speak on some radical subject, with a notice being generally printed in the Mormon *Deseret News*. Students come to the meetings often. Afterwards we serve cocoa and cookies. This is a 24 hour a day job. Once I went away to Colorado speaking and the drunks had nearly taken over by the time I got back. Folks have suggested that I get a bigger place, but this is enough.

A Parable

One Sunday while listening to the Buddhist sermon in Japanese, I had the following thought and wrote it out afterwards as a Parable:

A man built a house on the upper side of a road, "to be a friend to man," as he had spent many years traveling over the country and desired to rest a bit. The storms came and the winds blew and the fire poured down from above, and he saw the floods and debris going by where the road had been. He held out a lifeline secured at one end to a huge rock at the side of his house, and upon part of which the house was built. The name of the house and of the rock was called "Independence."

Most of the people went by on bits of raft or old tress, saying that they were going to the "promised land," for if they grabbed the lifeline they would get wet, and would have to struggle and might get drowned, while this way they could go half-merrily along. The man shouted that there were rapids below where they would surely get wrecked, but most of them laughed in a crazy manner, meanwhile drinking from a bottle labeled "social security," and they smoked from a pipe labeled "peace." One or two were not drinking from the bottle or smoking from the pipe and they looked up and grabbed the line and manfully struggled to this oasis.

Panhandling

Currently there is a campaign on by the police against panhandlers. They have ceased bothering me for they know I feed them here. My friend Ren Mabey had a letter in the morning paper saying that Buddha and St. Francis were beggars; that if the fact that they spend their donations for liquor was the excuse for not giving them anything, then the police should go after the liquor traffic, but this is a source of profit to the state and at times a source of graft for the cops. I don't believe in putting men in jail for panhandling. My solution is not to give them anything except to take them to a restaurant for the coffee or food they ask for, and nine cases out of ten they don't go, for what they want is a jug. Men getting over a drunk have really not eaten for five days and then I will give them half a dozen bowls

415

of soup if they want it. Then there is an elderly packrat who would carry a ton of junk from garbage cans into our place and hide it here and there if we would allow it. Stuff that is already spoiled, and old clothes with holes in them. Fellows tell me that he has shown them his bank book and that he gets a pension. He does not eat here but cooks food in the tourist park.

If I paid a man $200 a week to run this place, it is not likely that he would stay the second week, for he would not put up with the grief that is a part of a flop-house on skid-row. (My old wob friend Guy Askew says the proper term is skid-road.) Some Gypsies live two doors away and their youngsters called a colored man who was here "nigger," so he pushed a Gypsy man through our window in a fight, only it wasn't the right Gypsy. The landlord has insurance so it was fixed. One drunk slammed the door in anger because I wouldn't allow him to lie around drunk in the front room, but told him to go to the cooler and sober up. It was on Valentine Day I remember. Then we didn't have a pay phone, and the minute it happened Mary phoned from California asking how things were. I told her the nice sign she had painted on the door was lost midst the thousand pieces of glass on the floor. Another big bellowing bull of a drunk put his foot in the door and dared any or all of us to make him get away. He said that I was making a fortune out of feeding bums lousy soup; that he could beat the hell out of me, etc. After half an hour he cooled off and went away and at 10 o'clock that night asked if he could sleep on the floor. There is no use in arguing with a drunk: you only hear wine talking, not the man. I bought 8 bath towels and it wasn't long until the only one left is the one I have for myself. I bought paper towels for the men to use but instead of putting them in a box for used towels they clogged up the toilet. I couldn't talk the towel company into giving us a roller towel service free so I pay $3.09 a week: one of the few flop houses with such service I expect. Even then the men cut part of the towel off of the roller. They finally got the idea that the company would not bring me any more towels if they continued.

Men get off the freights four miles away and it is often late by the time they get here. Salt Lake City is surrounded by desert for 500 miles every way you go, so men who ride the freights are tired and hungry and need a place to rest. They are welcome here any hour of the day or night. Several times young couples came along on scooters, broke, and I allowed them to stay in the cooler a night or two, and in flush moments I have paid for a woman to stay in the cheap hotel upstairs. The Jewish Social Service, Lutherans, Unitarians, and Catholics send men here at all hours. At midnight, a woman 3 miles away phoned saying that a drunk man was sleeping in her house. He had done painting for her that day and had not sobered up yet. She was a widow and her priest said to call the cops to get him out, but she didn't like to do that, so the priest said to call me. She sent him here in a taxi. He was hardly able to walk but with my help made it to the cooler. An enormous man sat on the floor and dared us to put him out. It would have taken half a dozen men and most of the windows would have been broken, so we had to do as Peter Maurin says: *to put up with each other the way God puts up with us.* I wouldn't mind an adult pacifist to help me at times, for free.

416

Pious frauds come around and want to make our place into some racket of collecting clothing and selling it; or collecting money house to house. One such fellow had been to many monasteries he said. He wore scapulars all over his coat and offered to go right out and collect money for our place. I told him to get out and stay out. Another bewhiskered "Messiah" was flashing money in the tavern and was robbed and raised a fuss about it. He made the excuse that Christ associated with winebibbers, but I told him that Christ didn't flash any money but went "without script or purse." Then a whisky faced lout come in from Chicago wanting to know if "Big Brother" had been here yet to start a mission and make "big money selling jewelry." Maybe I could get in on it if he recommended me. I chased him too.

Catholics have told me that I am "earning merit" if I do this for Christ's sake, but that otherwise it is all wasted time. Some radicals tell me that I ought to be "making the revolution" instead of patching up the system and coddling bums. The religious want me to bookkeep my good deeds like a Boy Scout. I tell them that of course I see somewhat of Christ in every man but I joined the Catholic Church for the Sacraments and for my appreciation of Christ and many fine saints, but I didn't have time to bookkeep "indulgences" and that my prayers at Mass were direct to Christ and not to any mediaries. I tell the radicals that the Joe Hill House is a base where I can with honor picket military bases nearby, picket against the execution of prisoners, hold forth to students who are curious about radicalism, and have a meeting very Friday night where no Board of Directors can tell me "not to be so radical or you'll slow up money coming in." I am a free man in a slave-minded society.

Latest News of Joe Hill House

Since the first edition of this book was printed in January of 1965 the Joe Hill House at 1131 So. 1st West was closed because neighbors were frightened about the town bums and transients who resided there. We finally vacated in Feb. 1966. After a trip of ten weeks over 29 eastern states we returned home and rented a place out in the county. Mayor Brack Lee had told the Health Department to find us a place. I put in 44 windows and painted the place inside and out, and the Unitarian young folks helped me clean the yard of weeds. We had 17 trees, one a weeping willow, and many yellow roses. A Mormon across the street who lived next door to his Bishop told me that if I brought my ex-convicts there he would break the windows and run me off the street. He said that the work I was doing was a good work but not to do it around him. So in August of 1966 I rented a place at *3462 So. 4th West*, two blocks west of the huge Vitro smokestack, and half a block from the end of the Roper freight yard of the Rio Grande. This is a seven room house with a fireplace, and we get free wood from nearby by going after it in our grocery cart. There are two more rooms in the garage fixed up for transients. It is among junk yards of old cars and away from neighbors. I walk down the highway for two miles where I get free groceries from two super markets.

Friends of the Public Library arranged a meeting in the auditorium in November of 1965 for the 50th anniversary of the execution of Joe Hill. A Mormon youth who is now on a mission for his church sang a Joe Hill song along with Bruce Phillips and two others. I gave a short talk, as did Bruce.

417

Students have formed a Joe Hill Memorial Committee which seeks to erect a monument to him in Sugarhouse Park where he was executed when the prison was there in 1915. Gibbs Smith, a student at the U wrote a book about Joe Hill which will be published in February of 1968. I have read it and I think it is the best yet written on the subject. The Canadian Broadcasting Company sent me a half hour film on Joe Hill. I have shown it many times at our House. Foner's book on Joe Hill is fairly good. It was reviewed in *Dialogue,* a liberal Mormon quarterly edited in Stanford, Calif. I met the editor, Eugene England, and read the review which was by a Prof. Jensen of Cornell. England asked me to write 1000 word criticism of this review, which was academic and missed the significance of the I.W.W. in western and Utah history. It was printed in the Fall, 1967 issue.

While I was on a speaking tour the city passed an ordinance requiring a permit before anyone could picket. I had announced I and others would picket on a certain Saturday. The police came on a Friday night saying I could not picket in the morning. I did not know of the ordinance but as the saying goes, ignorance is no excuse. So we phoned a city commissioner and the city attorney but they would do nothing. I told them I would go down the next day at noon to picket and they could officially tell me not to picket and I would put off the date for a week and get the permit. I went down and they said to go ahead and picket. At another time I went before the City Commission and asked permission to picket and the Mayor, Brack Lee, said the ordinance was not meant for me, to go ahead and picket. On April 15, 1967 we had 150 marching. I led them with a sign asking Bishop Federal why he did not pay attention to Pope Paul's plea for peace. We rang the bell at the chancery office, and eyes peeked through the side curtain but the door was not opened. The next day a sermon was preached giving the support of the war, as the U.S. Bishop's had officially stated. At another time a group carrying the Torch for Peace, which had been lit in Hiroshima, and was now being carried by foot from San Francisco to Washington, D.C., appeared in Salt Lake City. A young returned missionary who had left the Mormon church because of its conservatism, led the march down town. The Torch was taken to different radio stations and newspaper offices and everyone was given the opportunity of holding it and leaving their fingerprints on it. I held the Torch and rang the bell six times at the chancery office in order to give the Bishop the same chance of holding it as others had, but the door was not opened. On October 21, 1967 as a part of the world wide opposition to the war, 415 of us marched 17 blocks down town and I again rang the bell at the chancery office. This time the sacristan, an old friend of mine, opened the door. I handed him a copy of the Sermon on the Mount, and a clipping from the *National Catholic Reporter* telling of 26 prominent Catholics who had just come out against the war. This was to be given to the Bishop. The paper said that we would not be allowed to have a meeting after the parade at the Federal Plaza, so I was getting ready to be arrested on the free speech issue, but the authorities allowed us to speak. I began by saying that there were three wars going on just now. One, that of 170,000 hunters who today were out shooting deer and pheasants in Utah. Two, 500,000 U.S. soldiers in Viet Nam were shooting Cong and peasants. Third, a million Negroes, Indians, migrants, and we radicals were in revolt against Johnson and his war and the system of exploitation which he headed. That we would not win but we would keep up the fight. I said that Joseph Smith's grandfather was the head of the Boston Tea Party which broke the law; that Smith was a radical, but now the bankers had charge of the Mormon Church the same as they had of the Catholic Church, and not even the right kind of a banker, for they should listen to Marriner Eccles who in January of 1966 had come out against the war. He is a millionaire Mormon who lives here in Salt Lake City. Others spoke also, and for once the morning paper gave a full report with pictures of our activities.

In the fall of 1967 some Bircher minded people spread the rumor that armed Negroes would invade Salt Lake City and seek to blow up the Mormon Temple. So one Sunday morning 150 police and soldiers were there to protect the Temple. Stories of four car loads of armed Negroes being in town were never confirmed. Governor Rampton and the morning paper made fun of this incident.

During the winter of 1966-67 I picketed for two months when Poulsen was supposed to be executed. His lawyer finally got a reprieve. And again during the summer of 1967 I picketed for about two months upon the imminance of his 7th execution date. Finally on the "cruel and unusual punishment" clause of the 8th amendment he had an indefinite stay of sentence. While I was picketing someone yelled, "Free Poulsen and shoot Hennacy." One event which complicated clemency for Poulsen was that around Christmas time in 1966 two paroled convicts killed six people. I was asked on the radio if I would be picketing for them and I said that I would when their death sentence came nearer. They also have had their cases appealed.

With all of my boasting about overcoming evil with good will I had to practice it in quite a dramatic way on the last day of my picketing the post office in August of 1967. A Korean veteran abusively cursed me and said he had killed better people than Hennacy in Korea and if I passed him twice he would beat me black and blue. He would do time for it. I told him, as I had told a man in Phoenix in 1948 that he had the right to beat me up and I had the right to picket; that made us even. After I had passed him the second time he raised his fist and moved towards me. This went on for half an hour. I thought "this was the time," but finally he left. In 1966 the tax man called me in saying he had orders from Washington to check up on me. They must still be checking, for I have heard nothing from them.

Joan and I have made several trips to the coast and to visit the Doukhobors, driving in British Columbia over a small mountain where a sign said "anarchist mountain." I spoke on CBC in Toronto and Vancouver. We were pleased to meet the Diggers in the Haight-Asbury district in San Francisco. I spoke to them in their Free Store. They are named from the followers of Gerrald Winstanley who in 1649 tried to cultivate vacant ground in England. I have met countless Hippies and wish them well in their divorce from our materialist civilization. I have also met pseudo-Hippies who descended like locusts upon Joe Hill House with their pot and acid. Two of the young men who took acid all last winter told me now they had learned their lesson and they were off of all drugs for good.

I have spoken in four Mormon churches and one polygamous, at the University here, and in high schools where my message has been taped.

Many young folks going from coast to coast have stopped to rest at Joe Hill House. A young priest spent part of his vacation painting the House, along with a young pacifist who happened to be there. Cajun did his time against the war and came to visit us with his pretty wife.

Two books have recently been published on anarchism and pacifism in which chapters have been given from my book, and favorable comments made. These are, *Patterns of Anarchy,* by Leonard I. Krimmerman and Lewis Perry, Doubleday Anchor, $1.95; and *Nonviolence in America,* edited by Staughton Lynd, American Heritage Series, $3.45.

Many priests have recently left the Church. I think the principle that applies here with *Papal Power* is the same that applies with the surfacing of *Black Power.* As long as slaves were kept in chains, either chains of fear or chains of steel, there was little revolt. But allow them a small glimpse of freedom which came with Martin Luther King and the Montgomery boycott, and there is no holding back on how far they will go against "whitey." Likewise before Pope John XXXII priests and nuns would whisper and laymen would practice some form of contraception, but it was all very quiet. But with the Second Vatican Council this lid was lifted, and now the revolt is open. Father Hafner said in his talk to the Newman Club of Monmouth College in Long Branch, N.J.: "The Church has become established, respectable, comfortable and corrupt. It no more resembles the community of brotherhood and love described in the Acts of the Apostles than an army barracks resembles a home."

Health without Medicine

Pacifists, anarchists, Catholics, and most of my friends are friendly to me, but when it comes to the subject of medicine they generally disagree more violently than they do to my other radical ideas. It seems they like their aspirins. When a person says that they do not believe in medicine they are generally called Christian Scientists. I have read all of Mrs. Eddy's books and for ten years I attended their Church and read their lessons daily, and of course took no medicine. Neither did my daughters take any medicine, nor my wife. However my opposition to medicine is not based on the denial of disease, which is the Christian Science basis. To deny a thing does not remove its cause. Only in the case where disease is based on'fear, and if Christian Science or any other idea can get rid of this fear, then can it heal the disease.

I do not know of any one who has my ideas entirely on this subject. The person from whom I have received the most understanding is Dr. Herbert M. Shelton, whom I mention previously in this book. He is editor of *The Hygienic Review,* Box 1277, San Antonio, Texas. He has written many books on the subject. His idea is that disease is remedial, and is only an effort of the body to get rid of a toxic condition caused by wrong living, wrong eating, wrong thoughts. Another man from whom I received enlightenment is a former Christian Science practioner, William Walter, of Aurora, Illinois. He was so successful that the Christian Science leaders wanted to know his method. When he told them, and didn't parrot the cliches of the Christian Science Church sufficiently or mention Mrs. Eddy's name often enough, he fell in disgrace from that church and started one of his own called *Eschatology,* with practitioners in many cities. I read their literature which said that every disease is caused by a *certain* sin, so if you cease that sin you will get well. This group, like the Christian Scientists supported war and had no sense of social responsibility. Whether they performed healings after the death of Mr. Walter I do not know.

Dr. Shelton teaches that because of our wrong way of living and eating our systems become clogged with impurities, and according to our inherited bodies we become susceptible to discomforts which medical folks call diseases. For instance in one person this toxemia results in diarrhea, in another boils, in another vomiting, in another fever, and finally when they have lived stupidly for long enough they get cancer. One of his sayings is that the stupid perish. The way to health he says is to cease eating *any* food, that is to go on a *complete* fast, drinking only preferably distilled water, to rest in bed, get plently of fresh air and sunshine, and get rid of any mental worries, and the body will heal itself. When you are well you will become ill again if you continue your evil habits, so you should become a vegetarian, cease any smoking, drinking of alcohol, tea, coffee, cocoa, soft drinks. And of course never take any medicine of any kind. He says that medicine given to a dead body has no effect. That any foreign substance in the body is ejected by nature, such as pus collecting around a splinter in your finger and thus it is driven out. So medicine taken into the body is vomited or ejected somehow. This is the body acting on the foreign substance, not the medicine acting on the body. He says that the improvement in health is due to better sanitary conditions and not to vaccinations or inoculations. The wonder drugs kill more people than they are supposed to cure. He has had many thousands of people come to his rest home who are nearly dead, having tried every other way, and less than a score have died there. Many regaining their health and living for many years. The AMA in states like New York and Ohio have caused the imprisonment of doctors who use his methods.

I admit that it is well to have doctors who know the parts of the body so that in the case of an accident when a person is unconscious, bleeding, etc., it can be attended to. Many reputable physicians will not indiscriminately give blood transfusions for they know that derelicts who sell their blood either do not know that they have had malaria or jaundice, or are in such a rush to get money to go on another spree that they lie about it, so that many deaths are caused by the injection of this impure blood into patients who are already ill. The death of many people is caused by the use of the so-called wonder drugs which have side effects upon the body not known until they have been tried upon patients. And people vary in their reaction to these poisons injected into their bodies under the guise of "helpful drugs." I am not mentioning in detail the sleeping pills which cause the birth of deformed babies.

There are four causes of diseases. *First,* the body which you have inherited which may be prone to certain weaknesses, such as heart trouble, diabetes, rheumatism, tuberculosis, etc. Or the habits of living which people in any certain occupation or in any certain geographical environment are accustomed to. Such as Navajos smothering themselves in their stuffy hogans, coal miners whose work makes them liable to rheumatism, etc. So every one has a *web of circumstance* which may help or hinder them throughout life. *Second,* the presence of fear. No matter if a person believes in God there are many who are forever fearful of everything that might happen. They are afraid of snakes, darkness, heights, cats, dogs, etc. These fears may come from frightening childhood experiences which they have never overcome. They may be afraid of certain diseases, and as the Bible says that which they fear has come upon them. *Third,* there is the matter of stupidity. Some folks are told what to do but they are too stupid to understand or too inept to do anything for themselves. They can't sleep; they don't seem to digest their food. They are always ailing. If they were a bit alive they would look around them and see the people who are healthy and they would ask questions and perhaps learn something. They suffer from too much mucous in the form of catarrah, yet they must drink milk and eat starchy foods and imbibe more mucous. They have arthritis yet they keep on eating bloody meat, sweets and starches and get worse. They go from one fake patient medicine to another and never learn. *Fourth,* there is this matter of *sin.* If any certain disease is not caused by the first three mentioned then it is caused by a certain weakness or sin. I will enumerate a few. Asthma is caused by smother love, the overprotection by the mother or other female relatives of children, especially boys, so that in order to breathe they have to get away from under the wings of the mother hen and breathe on their own. You find the grown boy whose mother must spread his bread for him, who hovers over him forever. She does not trust in God no matter how much she may go to Mass. Fears of ragweed, etc. on her part will prepare the boy for hayfever. Allergy specialists have told me that boys suffering from asthma and hayfever have been sent away to boarding schools and recovered in a few months, but as soon as their mothers visited them they commenced to breathe hard and choke. They have to get weaned sometime. In the case of anemia or tuberculosis a person may have lost their loved one, their job, or their faith, so there is no use of living. Neither is there any use of dying. They have nothing to live for so they just fade away. A study was made in Switzerland for years by doctors of tuberculiar patients and its was found that with one lung the patient could live if he had some reason for living. In some cases a love affair was patched up, in others an interest was found in life. Vain and greedy folks want to be first in everything. They rush around and overtax their heart. When they die someone else will perform the work. Diabetes is a gluttons disease. They eat and eat until they can't eat any more. The person who is forever fighting and arguing may very well be always bothered with the common cold. In more aggravated cases when food is not digested because of the anger which happens many times at meals colitis ensues. Years ago experiments were made at Harvard University where cats were fed liver and then a dog was presented to them and their stomach's were in a turmoil for hours. Continual disturbance may cause gall stones. But in the case of the stolid temperment where there is not anger in the form of action but where the supposed insult is covered up and the person sulks and hates and will not speak, tumors and cancer ofter occur. God sends love, but you only grouch and hug this hatred to yourself until it eats you up. There is no cure for real cancer, although often a benign tumor is diagnosed mistakenly as cancer. You have met the stiff-necked person who stubbornly will not listen to a new idea. He is always right, even in his parochial ignorance. Thus rheumatism, arthritis, or constipation is brought on by stubbornness. Opposition to ideas of others is always personalized. I often say that the difference between this kind of a person and myself is that I am *firm* while he is stubborn. Then there are the scare diseases: polio, the virus, and all sorts of epidemics. "Do you have the virus yet?" Every pain is called a symptom of the current fad in disease. Babies who have no sins fall ill because of the fog of fear surrounding them.

Now suppose you have a bad inheritance, are afraid, stupid, and a sinner of many varieties, what can you do about it? If you have already taken insulin for years, fasting will be of little help for you will be liable to go into a coma, but in the first stages fasting will help you. It may require several fasts of from 30 to 70 days before your body is in a condition of health. But if you go back to your evil habits you will get sick again. Do not try fasting at home where all oppose you. Go to some health home like that of Dr. Shelton's.

Time magazine of 1-15-63 reports that Dr. Frederick R. C. Johnstone of Vancouver General Hospital tells that of those who were given antibiotics that infections were three times that of those who received none. He states that "antibiotics kill off the weaker germs and leave the field wide open for the more dangerous bacilli to multiply." And in the *San Francisco Examiner* of Nov. 20, 1962 Dr. Philip Thorek of the Illinois Medical School says, "Many thousands of people are dying this year because of blood transfusions, often after the surgeon has done his work skillfully and without apparent complications." "Transfusions could be lethal," Doctor Thorek said, "because donor blood may be incompatible to the patient who receives it. Such incompatibility, the surgeon said, may occur for many reasons, including wrong composition, too much or too little of a given chemical in the donor's blood; wrong concentratin, the content that the patient needs; and, wrong rate of administration, too much blood given too fast can put a deadly burden on the heart that must pump it, while too little given too slowly may fail to correct the deficiency. Also, Doctor Thorek said, blood given may be weaker or stronger in total chemical; donor blood may carry the invisible and unfilerable germs of debilitating or mortal diseases, including hepatitis, malaria and syphilis."

The Associated Press of May 29, 1963 tells of Mrs. Elaine Johnson of Los Angeles who completed a supervised fast in Wadsworth Veterans Hospital where she fasted for 117 days and lost 136 of her 315 pounds. And during the previous winter we all read of the man and woman plane wrecked in Alaska who went 43 days on snow water and lived.

When I criticize churches and the state I do not infer that individual churchmen and politicians are knowingly wicked people, but as I have told judges when I am in court, they are in a bad business. Likewise with doctors, who many times are humane and self sacrificing, but who like the others, they have been brought up not to question the way they make a living. I have had mature doctors agree with nearly all of my ideas on medicine, but what can they do about it when people are so foolish and want to take poison to cure them instead of changing their way of life. The whole anarchist philosophy teaches the responsibility of the individual, and not dependance upon clergy, politicians, doctors, lawyers, etc.

I met a woman, now a member of The Order of Aaron, who, when much younger, had been taken to a hospital here in Salt Lake City for an operation. She was in great pain, and as the doctors assembled for the operation she asked them if there was not someone she could first call upon to pray and "lay on hands" for a successful operation. She did not belong to any church, but from reading the Bible in her youth she had this idea. They left the room and called some Mormon Elders in who prayed, and in a few minutes she was healed and did not need the operation. This was indeed faith. Then she commenced to read the Book of Mormon and joined their church. For over ten years she faithfully tried to be a good Mormon but the more she read in their books the more she saw that they did not practice the United Order and were lax in their fidelity to The Word of Wisdom. Finally she joined this new group which I describe in the chapter on Communities. Some hysterical people may be temporarily healed by such evangelists as Oral Roberts, but as he does not preach right living, but only faith, it is likely that those whom he has "cured" will again become ill, for the cause of their illness was not effected. Likewise at Lourdes a few healings occur each year. Mormon Elders are upon call to heal the sick and as I live here, I will undoubtedly learn more of this part of their religion. Their Word of Wisdom stresses a clean life. Doubtless some Christian Scientists heal those whose illness is caused basically by fear, but as their church increaingly has been commercialized, along with all others, not much can be expected from them in the matter of health.

Moral Rearmament

I have referred previously in this book as to the Moral Rearmament group being the worst fraud in modern times. I refer to it again upon reading a full page ad in the *New York Times* in which they list sixteen ideas which they are for, and opposite them ideas which they are against. For instance they are FOR Intelligent National Security and AGAINST sexual deviates in high places who protect potential spies. They are FOR peace but AGAINST Pacifism. They claim to be absolutely pure and make this as an excuse to uphold rent, interest, profit, and armaments of the capitalist system, and boast of the labor leaders and Communists whom they have turned from their wrong way of life to the MRA which bolsters up capitalism. What makes them such a fraud is that they claim to be better than those outside of their belief, meanwhile their personal salvation that they boast so much about does not prevent them from supporting every evil of capitalism except race prejudice; yet we never heard of any of them leaving their lives of luxury and joining picket lines or freedom-riders.

First Customer

When Mary and I were picking cherries and before we had started this house we worked with a man who lived upstairs in the Japanese Hotel who was seldom sober. He thought we ought to be a financial success in our new "restaurant" and kept telling us that he would be our first customer, for unless we had a first customer we would never have any more and would not succeed. So my orders to all of the help is that any time the "first customer" comes in, drunk or sober, he is to be served what he wants. After his cup of coffee or soup he ceremoniously gives us a dime "so we won't go broke," and we take it in that spirit.

Carl, the cook who has been here the longest, has drank liquor all of his life and has no intentions of stopping now at the age of 79. He never gets loud. I tell him not to bring liquor in the house, so he has friends who buy him a drink at the tavern nearby. One night he had half of a glass of liquor under his bed and went to rejuvenate himself when he found a dead mouse in it. This news was too good to keep, and we all had a good laugh over his mousetrap. I will not buy any mouse traps, telling them that if they want to take their cigarette and liquor money and buy a trap they can do so.

One goodnatured man who stayed here all one winter and help get food from the market, and who claimed to be an old time I.W.W., left and took with him anything that he could steal in order that he would not run short of liquor on the way. My gloves did not fit him but he stole them. A cook also stole my gloves, and others have stolen raincoats, shoes, cigarette lighters, and anything that they can pick up. One drunk whom I had put out a score of times for bringing in liquor was sobering up in the cooler, and hidden in his shirt was an alarm clock that we found missing, and hid under his pillow was a bottle partly full of liquor. I poured it out and made him leave, for he knew better. All of these men are bigger than I am but they seldom offer any opposition, except to blandly lie and say they are not drunk, when they can hardly stand up. One fellow was drinking from his bottle in the night and insisted that it was not *his* bottle. I told him shame for stealing someone else's liquor, and poured it out and put him out. I do not snoop around searching for bottles, but when I step on them I empty them. The men take it good naturedly. I know it is a losing battle and I do not expect to win.

Christmas Message 1962

"*Truth is forever on the scaffold; error forever on the throne*" (but you don't have to be a part of it). People are naturally good, if it doesn't cost them anything, but in this mercenary larcenized age let nearly all professedly religious people think that they may not get a promotion, or someone else may get their jobs, then the primeval beast appears to defend the status quo.

They say that they are saved and that they believe in heaven, but they really don't believe in the hereafter, for their religion teaches them that they cannot take it with them, so they hold on tight to their fortunes and consider that they are poor if they have to dig into their principal, because they do not receive enough dividends or interest.

Whether through inheritance of the example of beneficent friends or relatives many folks of any religion or of no religion are a fine example of ethical living. They may believe that St. Peter, Mohammed, Mrs. Eddy, or Joseph Smith received a special revelation superceding all others, and that their Church is the True One, and they may follow most of the rules laid down by their leaders, but, as Tolstoy says, this does not prevent them from being kind, considerate, self-sacrificing and truly noble people. An outsider meeting them would tend to be attracted to their religion because of the good example they present. But the real truth is that if they changed religions or belonged to no religion they would still be the same fine people. Thus the anonymous woman who gave us a turkey one year and two hams last year belongs to no church and her husband is a former Catholic who belongs to the Japanese Buddhist Church. The Mormon Bishop who sent us 240 pints of syrup, and the Greek Orthodox who gives us a basket of candy once a week, as well as other Mormons who help us here at our mission are good examples of their religions, while the Catholics who boycott us are a bad example.

There are others, and I expect they are the great majority, who have had a bad physical and emotional inheritance and environment and who, whether they know it or not, are motivated by the fears which their religions or their material environment presents to them. So they go through the forms and ceremonies, or go to psychiatrists, and are forever in a state of frustrated doubt, which even to admit, frightens them into going through forms and ceremonies to ward off evil. No matter what they may say, their attitude is placating the devil rather than worshipping God. The mercenary leaders of these churches grow fat on the fears of their dupes — and they may themeslves be placating the Evil One (all in the name of God). They are not to be blamed overly much for they have been conditioned that to read or think of anything "controversial" is a sin, and with these blinders their religion is clearly what Marx said, an "opiate." If they change religions they are no better for their whole pattern is based on fear of losing their souls.

Some can enter Orders, or on the outside blindly stress the virtue of obedience, and not being of an inquiring mind, but being of the "sheep mentality" they are relatively happy in thinking that they will be saved. "Why give freedom to sheep? They only bleat," says Max Stirner.

There are a number of others who, no matter what their previous environment has been, that faintly see through all this fear and fraud but feel incompetent to deal with it, so they eat, drink, take the newest dope, and like to think that they are happy. They may be fine people who spread good cheer or they may be larceny minded.

We find men elevated as leaders, or as leader of a religion who accept war, exploitation, capital punishment, and all the modern evils, and they see no contradiction between the wonderful ethics pronounced by the leaders of their religions and their denial of these ethics in their daily lives. Now at Christmas time they have a faint glimmering that comes through and they for the moment really mean what they say when they call for brotherhood, peace, kindliness, yet they are surrounded, and they consciously keep themselves surrounded by yes men and lickspittles so that nothing is really ever done that will cripple their power or decrease their revenue.

A person is tempted to agree with Charles Erskine Scott Wood who years ago wrote the book, *Heavenly Discourse*, in which God, St. Peter, Christ, etc. are discussing what is going on in this crazy world, and God is dodging the prayers that are sent up to Him. If one were to believe that the Jews were God's chosen people and they would multiply as the sands of the sea, then they could also believe that He thought He would take another chance and send Christ to bring the people around to His ways. But the Orthodox killed him. Then when His Church continually denied Him after Constantine, killed millions in religious wars and massacres, and had their Inquisition in Spain and America, it is conceivable that God would find the Prophet Mohammed. But the Mohammedans did almost as bad as the others. Then it could be that when Joseph Smith prayed and asked God which was the *real* religion that he was told that none of them lived up to their function, and that he was told to start the real one; that there was progression in spirituality in this world and in other worlds besides this one, and that he was to collect the "saints" who would lead this life in their United Order with no rich or poor and in the agricultural simplicity in which all religions have had their origin. While Catholics had generally forgotten the healing of the sick which was done in the early days before they became dominant, the Mormons practiced it, and they still do.

Mrs. Eddy came along "divinely inspired and without human hypothesis" and founded her Church, and in the same time the Seventh Day Adventists thought the world was coming to an end and at a certain date and set up their religion as a "one and only" featuring Saturday as a Holy Day instead of Sunday. At this time Alexander Campbell felt that there should be *One True Church*, so he founded the Campbellite Church or Disciples Church which was to be that Church.

Looking over the world today it can easily be seen that no church, despite their protestations, has any intention of following the Sermon on the Mount. In fact, if you talk about it you will get into trouble with politicians who have been elevated to run the churches.

It could be that God also tried to bring His program across by inspiring individuals rather than to start another church and so brought forth Gandhi among the Hindus, Tolstoy among the Russians, and Sweitzer among the Protestants, and John Woolman and Rufus Jones among the Quakers, as he earlier tried to remind Catholics through St. Francis, St. Catherine, St. Joan, and the young girl at Lourdes.

What can an honest, sincere, and wide awake person do who belongs to any of these religions or none of them? All religions are a mockery of God no matter if they were once started by inspired Prophets. Truly the Catholic Lord Acton said that "power tends to corrupt, and absolute power corrupts absolutely."

All that anyone who belongs to any church can do is to know that inspiration is not dead: that "all things work together for good to those who love God." And as Thoreau said to take one world at a time, and work within the groups where he is located, and those who are not too far corrupted will appreciate it. It would seem that organized religion is bound to be corrupted. When God plans to resurrect those of any or of no religion and start a new world is anyone's guess. The billions spent on going to Venus or the Moon, when we can't run our own world, is based on military domination of the world by the U.S. or Russia. All organized churches go along with this "my country right or wrong" and in this respect are most evil institutions (that is except the Quakers, Brethern and Mennonites) who support taxes for war and obedience to governments, national and world. It would seem that the True Church is composed of those in all churches or in no church who courageously live up to the highest teachings of their Prophets. No new Church needs to be started or it would become as bad as the others. Stay in the Church of your choice, or remain outside, and be a witness by your life for Truth against the rulers of this world and the rulers of the Church who prefer Caesar to Christ.

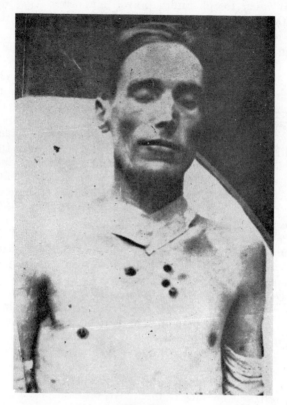

JOE HILL
EXECUTED BY THE STATE OF UTAH
NOVEMBER 19. 1915

Esther Dahl, Joe Hill's sister,
Living in Sweden in 1964.

CHAPTER 21

THE MORMONS

1961 to present

Salt Lake City, Utah

HANDCART MIGRATION

"Are you going to be a Mormon now?" asked a Catholic friend when he heard that I was going to live in Salt Lake City.

"If it is the best I will: you wouldn't want me to follow the second-best, would you?" And a Mormon asked me if I was on a mission. "Sure," I replied.

It is with a friendly feeling toward Mormons that I came here. It is in the spirit of honest inquiry that I have attended Sacrament meetings nearly every Sunday at the University Ward, and I have read a score of books pro and con about the Mormons. I have also attended the Reorganized Church and the polygamous *Church of the First Born of The Fullness of Times.* I realize that it is presumptuous to write about the Mormons with less than three years in Salt Lake City, but I have done the best I could to understand their religion, studying The Book of Mormon and The Doctrine and Covenants and Pearl of Great Price. I will learn more and more as I continue to study and to meet Mormons.

If I believed in the revelations of Joseph Smith I would be a Mormon. My great-great-grand-parents on my mother's side were Quakers and Baptists who lived not far from the uproar of the Kirtland, Ohio community. Alexander Campbell had belonged to the Achor Baptist church where I was baptized at the age of 11, and he left it and went to Brush Run, Pa. to start his Campbellite church, being inspired by God that one more *true* church was needed, he said. The Mormons and the Campbellites converted each other back and forth in and around Kirtland. If I had been a young man then it is possible that I might have followed Smith who was a radical who wanted a society without any rich or poor, all living together as brothers. He called in 1844 when he ran for President for the slaves to be bought off from their masters and freed, and for the prisons to be emptied and schools established in their place. Although as it will be shown in this chapter later, that Brigham Young and others were anti-Negro. Now in 1963 Mormon missionaries are being sent to Negroid Africa. The cynical here say it is because they do not wish to alienate the Negro vote if and when George Romney, the Mormon Governor of Michigan, chooses to run for the Presidency. The Mormons succeeded in communal life for a longer time where the radical colonists, such as Robert Owen and the followers of Fourier failed.

I am not giving the history of the Golden Plates or of the persecutions of the Mormons. In the appendix I list books as references upon which I have based opinions which I give in this book. Others can read for themselves. Tolstoy told Ambassador White that,"the Mormon people taught the American religion" and that "on the whole he preferred a religion which professed to have dug its sacred books out of the earth to one which pretended that they were let down from heaven." [14] Although these plates were supposed to be sent from heaven to the Hill Cumorah.

When Smith was accused by members of his church of not being a good prophet because he had trusted in people who defaulted, he prayed to God and God told him that *"Some revelations are of God; some revelations are of man; and some revelations are of the devil."* At another time some of his followers expected pious dignity from him and he told them that *"a prophet is only a prophet when he is acting as such . . . at 4 in the afternoon I went out with my little Frederick to exercise myself by sliding on the ice."*[2] At another time he had healed many of the sick and told his followers not to bring any more for he felt like wrestling. He would challenge any person and he usually won. It was likely that the faith folks had in him produced much of the healing. In fact he was astonished at his success. A Campbellite preacher came and wanted a sign, saying that he would believe and bring all of his congregation with him. Joseph explained his ideas but the pious fool insisted upon a miracle, so Joseph said, "What will you have done? Will you be struck dumb, blind? Will you be paralyzed, or will you have one hand withered? Take your choice, choose which you please, and in the name of the Lord Jesus Christ it shall be done." The preacher replied that this was not the kind of miracle he wanted. Joseph answered, "Then sir, I can perform none. I am not going to bring trouble upon anyone else to convince you."[3] One is reminded of Christ refusing to show off when the Devil tempted him to turn stones into bread, jump down from the Temple, or to be given charge of the whole material world. And by the way, it is just this charge that all Christian churches had succumbed to serving Caesar instead of God that provided the reason for a new religion.

A visiting English clergyman asked Joseph why he got drunk. His answer was so that his followers would not worship him too much. He said "I am not so much a Christian as many suppose I am. When a man undertakes to ride me for a horse, I feel disposed to kick up and throw him off, and ride him." And he told the Englishman, "I love that man better who swears a stream as long as my arm, yet deals justice to his neighbors and mercifully deals his substance to the poor, than the long, smooth-faced hypocrite. I do not want you to think that I am very righteous for I am not."[4] In his journal for March 13, 1843 he said, "I wrestled with William Wall, the most expert in Ramus, and threw him. In the afternoon held a church meeting." When asked to say a blessing at a meal he said, "Lord we thank Thee for this johnny-cake, and ask Thee to send us something better. Amen."[44] Those who have seen Burt Lancaster in the movie *Elmer Gantry* have met a likeable half-rogue, who, no matter what he did, was charming. I expect that Joseph Smith was an imaginative sort of Huck Finn, surrounded by religious excitement. When he said that the people on the Moon were 6 feet tall, were dressed like Quakers and lived a thousand years,[4B] no one could prove that he was wrong. Werner says that "in his youth Joseph Smith was torn between the fear of not being saved eternally and the desire to have a good time from day to day. Fortunately for his peace of mind he was able to reconcile the two by having himself appointed to have a good time."[5]

It is conceivable that he prayed to God to tell him what was the true religion and it would not take much honesty to see that all religions had long forgotten the Sermon on the Mount. Joseph must have had some rebellious feelings and he likely would have heard of his great-great-grand-father who was chairman of those who formed the Boston Tea Party.[6] If a person does not believe that Joseph found the Golden Plates, or if he found them, that the message was not the truth, or garbled truth, how can they be explained? I have read of the argument that he copied them from Spauding's book, and I have read the parallels between Ethan Smith's book printed in Putney, Vt. in 1823 and The Book of Mormon concerning the American Indians and I do not think the evidence is conclusive that Joseph ever heard of these books, for when he got his revelations there was no holding him back, and his wife and Oliver Cowdry and Martin Harris would nearly be worn out writing down what he told them while burying his face in his hat with the magic stone or stones which it is said produced The Book of Mormon. Oliver Cowdry may have helped in the grammer of The Book of Mormon and may have cut out a few hundred "verily's" and "It came to pass'es." The witnesses, most of whom apostasized later, still held to the fact that they had seen the plates, and that Heavenly Personages had spoken to Joseph Smith and to them, but Cowdry, David Whitmer and Harris said later that these Heavenly Personages had appeared to them and told them to get out of the Mormon Church for it was corrupt. As Joseph himself said revelations came from three sources so his may have been a mixture. Perhaps the credulity of his followers pushed him on. He may have deluded himself without being

431

consciously fraudalent. He did not pretend to be a man of the character of Gandhi or of St. Francis. But he did the thing they never tried to do: to establish a new religion. In Hiram, Ohio, where he was beaten and left for dead, the next morning he preached forgiveness· to those who had beaten him, some of whom were in the audience, and he made three converts. he was here at his best. When he strutted in uniform before the Nauvoo Legion and when he had Law's and Bennett's press destroyed he was at his worst. He was more realistic and much more of a likeable human being that the dour Alexander Campbell; than the Fox sisters who founded Spiritualism in the New York area where he lived; than the fanatic Miller who expected the end of the world. He would seem more honest than Mrs. Eddy, who, in 1866, got ideas from Quimby in Portland, Me. but who said that these ideas were "uncontaminated by human hypothesis and divinely authorized." She also said to follow her only inasmuch as she followed Christ and the Sermon on the Mount and that it was better to suffer death than to inflict it. Yet most minority religions make a great point also of obeying the law and of being super patriotic. This comes from a desire to be accepted, even though many of their other principles would tend to make them unacceptable. So it is that both the Christian Scientists and Joseph Smith when accused of being subversive could point to their patriotism and law obedience tenents. Mrs Eddy, like Joseph Smith and the Mormons who came after him, made changes in the "inspired" word, which if it was inspired ought not to need changes. He did not go as far as John Humphrey Noyes in the Oneida Community of free love. On the whole he was a charming man who brought happiness and hope to thousands. I do not think that he was a conscious imposter or rogue, except when his wife Emma heard about his sleeping with Fannie Alger, the young girl who lived with them, and he produced the revelations on polygamy to placate her.

Kimball Young thinks that Joseph Smith was a parapath, that is a person who cannot tell fact from fancy.[7]

Mrs. Brodie has written about Joseph Smith: "Tolerant of the foibles of his friends, since he could not easily forget his own, he provided a heaven where all men would be saved . . . Since his wife and children were dear to him, he made the marriage covenant eternal . . . Since power was sweet to him he gave to every convert the promise of dominion over a star . . . He made the frontier evangelist seem by comparison all sound and fury . . . His people believed the best of him and thereby caused him to give his best."[8] In the section on polygamy I will try to give a sympathetic account of his troubles and glories with the fair sex.

It could be that God told Joseph to start a new church for the previous ones had defaulted, but that power corrupted him as it has all other religious before and since.

Mormon Theology

M. R. Werner says, "If The Book of Mormon was inspired by God, it was his second rate work."[9] I have read it and I find more murder to the page than in the Old Testament, while some of the stories seem thinly disguised from similar incidents in the Bible. Although in Joseph Smith's ver-

432

sion of that man being called to judgment who calls his brother "a fool," he gives the spiritual translation which is also given in the Douay Version which the Catholic Church gives, as opposed to the materialistic version of the King James edition which says "without a cause," which nullifies the whole idea that Christ is trying to bring out.

Werner further states, "The Book of Mormon is the story of the wanderings of three ancient peoples. One of them, the Jaradites, came directly from the Tower of Babel, and the other two came from Jerusalem or thereabouts. These people after prolonged sufferings, dissentions, and wars, finally arrived on the American continent. The two tribes from Jerusalem were headed by one Lehi, who led his people forth about the year 600 B.C. He died in the wilderness and bequeathed the leadership of the expedition to his youngest son Nephi. But the other brothers disputed their father's will, and the family split into the Nephites, advocates of the youngest son, and the Lamanites, followers of the oldest son, Laman. There was constant war between these two peoples, and finally the wicked Lamanites wiped out their righteous brother, after both tribes had arrived in America. In 420 A.D. the whole American continent was in the possession of the Lamanites, from whom the American Indians are descended. It was the task of Joseph Smith, Jr. to redeem the continent, which, by the way, is the Promised Land, for the righteous Nephites."[10]

The Book of Mormon is uninteresting and dull. Even if all this story were true I see little reason for founding a new religion on it. For folks to live a communal life and according to the Word of Wisdom, to come out and be separate is the only way that a religion could stay pure. But the scores of revelations whereby Joseph tried to move people around and to serve his whims certainly came from anyone but divine origin. Their theology is not more far fetched than others, for all religions have picked up myths and have accommodated themselves to current fetishes and superstitions.

"In the grand council called to ratify the Father's plan, a great difference arose. The majority, led by the firstborn of the Father, our elder brother, Jesus the Christ, was ready to accept the plan with all its conditions. The minority, led by Lucifer, a 'son of the morning,' feared the isolation and the pains and ills of earth. For them Lucifer proposed that they should be sent to earth, but that provisions should be made by which they would suffer no pain and would not have to make any sacrifices. All of them would be restored with earthly bodies irrespective of their works on earth. Lucifer and his followers were thrown out of the council, and as opponents of God's plan, became the devil and his angels, who strive ever to tempt men to disobey the laws of God ... By the help of Adam, another great spirit in the council, Jesus organized the earth, and to atone for the act that brought man under the ban of death, he himself suffered death. Through Jesus the leader all men upon earth call upon for aid from the Father ... our first parents chose life on earth with its inevitable death. That was the fall of man. All men, saints and sinners will be resurrected ..."

"As the eternal intelligences were given a spirit body with which to explore the spiritual world, so this other body was needed as a tool in the exploration of the material world. Eternal progression requires contact and acquaintanceship with the whole universe ... in conformity with the free agency bestowed upon all intelligent beings God called a council of the spirits to hear the plan . . . man must battle with the conditions of earth to which his body is subjected. That would foster faith, intelligence, and courage. The evil one would be allowed to range freely upon earth; and man would have to resist temptation. This would discipline the will and turn it into righteous paths. After a short period upon earth, man would be separated from the material body, in the experience called death. However, the body would later be restored to him in a purified state."[12]

This explanation by Apostle Widstoe, more of a philosopher than most Mormon writers is included here as being the clearest that I have found. In contrast to Brigham Young who continually talked about sending people who argued with him "cross lots to hell," Widstoe says "There can be no talk of hell . . . except for the very few sons of perdition, but undoubtedly the regret for lost opportunities will be keen among those in the lower degrees of glory."[13] I have heard a Jesuit priest say that there was a hell but you couldn't prove that any one was in it except the devil, and as far as heaven went we have the word of Christ that the Good Thief would see him that day in Paradise. Whether this was a preliminary entrance into heaven we will let the theologians discuss. Widstoe continues, "A religion without a hell seemed impossible to the misled preachers of Joseph's day. The law of progress continues in full operation for every soul throughout eternity . . . all blemishes and imperfections will be corrected before the unending unity of body and spirit takes place . . . The dead retain in the spirit world the power to learn, to understand, and to choose. Did not Jesus say he was going to preach to the 'spirits in prison?' "And it is this baptism for the dead, which like the prayers of Catholics for souls in purgatory that helps those who are dead.[14]

Adam-God Theory

"While Adam and Eve in Joseph Smith's philosophy were raised to a foremost place among the children of men second only to the Savior. Their act was to be acclaimed."[15] It remained for Brigham Young to bring the Adam-God theory forth, which is not mentioned by Mormons much today. Efforts have been made to explain it away, but on April 9, 1852 he gave his famous Adam-God sermon: "

"When our father ADAM came into the Garden of Eden, he came into it with a *celestial body,* and brought Eve, one of his wives, with him. He helped to make and organize this world . . . He is our Father and our God, and only God with whom we have to do." This created quite a stir and in defending Brigham the headline in The Millenial Star of Dec. 10, 1853 had this assertion. "Adam Is Really God! And Why Not?"

This would seem bad enough but in his same April 9th, 1852 speech Brigham said: "When the Virgin Mary conceived the child Jesus, the Father had begotten him in his own likeness. He was not begotten by the Holy Ghost. And who is the Father? He is the first of the human family . . . Jesus, our elder brother, was begotten in the flesh by the same character that was in the Garden of Eden, and who is our Father in Heaven. Now let all who may hear these doctrines, pause before they make light of them, or treat them with indifference, for they will prove their salvation or damnation."

(Journal of Discourses Vol. 1, Pages 50-51) Widstoe makes a distinction between the Holy Spirit and the Holy Ghost: "The Holy Spirit or 'the light of truth' is the spirit that proceeds from 'the presence of God to fill the immensity of space'. It is manifested in all natural phenomena. It penetrates all men. By its agency, the Lord may communicate with man, and may receive help from God. The Holy Ghost, on the other hand, is a Personage, the third member of the Godhead, to whom has been committed many important phases of the plan of salvation . . . prophecy, healing and the gift of tongues."[16]

Werner says that "On Feb. 16, 1832 Smith and Rigdon saw Christ who told them that there were three orders of eternal bliss. The Celestial (Sun) order was conferred only on devout believers such as Smith, Rigdon, and their most faithful followers . . . the Terrestial (Moon) order, consisting of those who had received the testimony of Jesus after they had died . . . and the Telestial (Earth) order came one grade below and consisted of people who had never accepted the testimony of Jesus, such as the Jews, who would only be saved from eternal damnation in the resurrection."[17] (Sun, Moon, Earth) inserted by author.

By 1844 Joseph had developed the idea of many gods which was not in The Book of Mormon. Neither was the cardinal principle of baptism for the dead in The Book of Mormon. Of course God could make new revelations, which is also a part of Mormon principle that He is an evolving God; that He was once man, and that we will come to be God, which is another mixture.

Here Brodie sums up Mormon theology by saying, "What Joseph had created was essentially an evangelical socialism, which made up in moral strength what it lacked in grandeur. Nearly every man had New Testament title — deacon, teacher, priest, elder, 'seventy,' or bishop. Each title carried a certain rank, progression from lower to higher being dependent upon a man's faith, his zeal for the church, and the goodwill of his superiors in the hierarchy."[17A]

One of the most objective accounts of the Mormons was made by an Englishman, *Richard Burton*, who visited Salt Lake City in 1859 and wrote *The City of Saints*. He says: "The Mormons are like the Pythagorians in their procreation, transmigration, and exhaltation of souls; like the followers of Leucippus and Democratus in their atomic materialism; like the Epicurians in their pure atomic theories, their summum bonum, and their sensuous speculations; and like the Platonists and Gnostics in their belief of the Aeon, of ideas, and of moving principles in element. They are fetichists in their ghostly fancies, their *evestra*, which became souls and spirits. They are Jews in their theocracy, their ideas of angels, their hatred of Gentiles, and their utter segregation from their great brotherhood of mankind. They are Christians inasmuch as they base their faith upon the Bible, and hold to the divinity of Christ, the fall of man, the atonement and regeneration. They are Arians inasmuch as they hold Christ to be 'the first of God's creatures' a 'perfect creature but still a creature.' They are Moslems in their views of the inferior status of womankind. in their polygamy, and in their resurrection of the material body; like the followers of the Arabian prophet, they hardly fear death, because they have elaborated 'continuation.' They take no leap in the dark; they spring from this sublunary stage into a known, not into an unknown world."[18]

As to the mechanics of Joseph's revelations it is possible that he received word from God to start the *real* Church; but that prankster spirits gave him dimensions of buildings, advice as to whom to trust and whom to expel; that he had a gift to receive something similar to automatic writing, or even "hunches" as Edgar Cayce in our own generation received. And, as will be shown in the section on polygamy. it is plain that when Emma heard about his cohabitation with the two young girls in his household, that in defense he made up regulations to placate her, disguised as revelations from God. In contrast Brigham Young said that Joseph had had enough revelations and he did not need to give many, but when anyone contradicted him he said he was inspired and should be obeyed or, "I will unsheathe my bowie knife," "we will slay them," "cut their throats," their heads chopped off . . .,"[19] St. Paul at times said he was inspired and at other times spoke "of himself." Mohammed had epileptic fits and it has been said that this was "mine infirmity" of St. Paul. Joseph's grandfather Mack had them and it has been said that Joseph had them but outgrew them. This does not prove anything, except that it might have been that in some seizure he had visions.

I. Woodbridge Riley, in a scholarly work published by Dodd, Mead, Co. entitled *The Founder of Mormonism* in 1902 said that Joseph suffered from a form of epilepsy inherited from his grandfather but that he outgrew these "trances" by the time he was 30. He says, "Smith's method was so far the commonplace method of the trance medium. The act of fixing the eyes on one particular point (as the peepstone in his hat. A.H.), supplimented by a state of quietitude through prayer, prepared the way for the influence of self-suggestion. His external acts are one thing, the subtle and self deceiving nature of his hallucinations another. He knew no more about the subconscious self and the law of association of ideas, than he did of the fact that his 'Reformed Egyptian' resembled the irregular and spasmodic writings of hypnotic subjects." Riley also felt that in 1844 when he was at the height of his meglomania in military uniform his utterance as follows was psychotic: "I know more than all the world put together. I combat the error of ages."

I also read the Biographical Sketches of his mother Lucy Mack Smith, published in Liverpool, England in 1853, which told of his digging for treasure. This has been edited out of recent editions of the life of Joseph Smith.

The effort of the Church historian Hugh Nibley in his booklet *No Ma'am, That's Not History,* published in 1946 by Bookcraft in Salt Lake City is a pitiful attempt to answer Fawn Brodie's book *No Man Knows My History.*

Brigham Young

His family was the poorest in the frontier town where he was born in New England June 1, 1801. They did not have a horse, cow, or any land. His father made a living as a basket maker. His father had been in the revolutionary army and was very strict; " It was a word and a blow but the blow came first,"[20] Brigham said. Brigham had but 11 days of formal schooling; but he could take a clock apart and put it together again. He was very handy in many trades and made his living as a painter and glazier, but quit be-

436

cause it was a common practice to adulterate paint and cheat, and he wouldn't do it. He was very independent and didn't like to be pushed around. When his father wanted him to take the temperance pledge he said to him, "No sir, if I sign a temperance pledge I feel that I am bound, and I wish to do just right, without being bound to it; I want my liberty."[21]

His sister and brother had read the Book of Mormon and accepted it, having received it as a gift from Joseph's brother William, but it took him two years to make up his mind. He was baptized a Mormon April 14, 1832 at Mendon, N.Y. but he had not yet met Joseph Smith. When he did he commenced to speak in tongues. When he was young, two of his best friends were Henry Wells, the founder of Wells Fargo Express Company, and Isaac Singer, inventor of the sewing machine.

He had married Miriam Works with whom he had two daughters, Vilate and Elizabeth. She was baptized into the Church shortly before she died of tuberculosis. Later he married thirty year old Mary Ann Angell. When he came to Kirtland, Ohio he turned over all of his property to the Church, and when five years later he was driven out he had nothing.

He was on a mission in Boston when Joseph was murdered, and he came back to Nauvoo just in time to prevent the dour and fanatical Sydney Rigdon from taking over the Church. When he was speaking to the Mormons the story goes, that he grew in stature and his voice changed so that he resembled the martyred Joseph. He persuaded those assembled to have the Council of 12 rule the Church, but he was not elected Prophet and second President until December 1847 in Salt Lake City. Emma never recognized him, saying that Joseph had said that his son was to rule the Church, but the boy was then too young. Brigham commenced to finish the Temple where he and others would be sealed to wives, and to prepare the emigrating to the west. He took over some of Joseph's wives, but not Emma, the first being the poetess Eliza Snow. Emma later married a non-Mormon, Capt. Bideman, and they ran a tavern in Nauvoo.

Coming across the plains he was everywhere organizing families into tens and hundreds, planning singing and dances to keep up the spirit, planting seed for food at Winter Quarters, and going ahead with a smaller group to seek The Promised Land. One man grumbled a lot and Brigham announced that all who had complaints should bring them to this man and he would shout them forth as Chief Grumbler. This shut him up.

These Mormons were from the poorer classes in England, Scotland and Wales and although they were called Latter-day Saints, it is obvious that many came to escape misery, and as the saying goes, "for the loaves and fishes," except that these were scarce on the plains. Someone had to be the Moses to lead them and he had to feel that he was called by the Lord to do so. When the U.S. Government called for 500 soldiers to go to California, Brigham saw that the money they got would help the others so the 500 soon volunteered. It happened that his prophecy was fulfilled when he told them, "I promise you in the name of Israel's God that not a man of you will fall in battle,"[22] for they did not get into the Mexican War. He told the men also "If you are sick, live by faith, and let the surgeon's medicine alone if you want to live.[23] Saying he himself would rather die a natural death than be helped out by a Doctor.[24] He said, "Let the sick do without eating, take a little something to cleanse the stomach, bowels, and blood, and wait patiently, and let nature have time to gain the advantage over the disease."[25] A Doctor had written to Brigham from the East asking what the prospects were. Brigham answered him. "The Mormons thought little of one who could not build his own house, irrigate his own land, and raise up a crop of wheat, corn, beans, peas, and potatoes. If the Doctor wanted to come under these conditions he would be made welcome, but if he had any thought of accumulating wealth, he would be wasting his time."[26]

Just as he could organize the trek across the plains so could he organize the many wives and 56 children of his household. Anyone who was late missed the meal, as a warning bell rang 5 minutes before the meal. His children did not have to go to Church on Sunday but they couldn't play games, ride horses, or sew doll clothing. True to his New England tradition he was against gambling. And he organized the women to glean the fields for wheat and corn for the poor. Naturally he was pestered by folks who asked his advice. He told them "not to ask for counsel when they were sure they were not going to take it." He could hand it out but he could also take it, for when he had tongue lashed a Bishop in public he told him to keep his temper and not leave the Church. The Bishop answered, "Don't worry brother Brigham, this is just as much my Church as it is yours."[27] At that Brigham chuckled. Once a one-legged man asked him to pray for another leg for him. Brigham answered that he might do so but what was the use for when he was resurrected he would have to have three legs and be in a worse predicament. The man hobbled away satisfied.[28] The English traveler Burton describes Brigham speaking at the Tabernacle: "He sat with his high hat on when he came to the platform. When he took his hat off that old man held his cough; that old lady awoke with a start; that child ceased to squall. Brigham bent over and expectorated in a spittoon, he took a slow drink of water, and commenced to speak powerfully and extemporaniously."[29] He did not keep pigs and never ate pork. He told his wives to give the children milk and hard bread for breakfast, no meat, and plenty of fruits and vegetables.[30]

Tom Thumb visited Salt Lake City and met Brigham and said that he didn't understand "about this here polygamy." Brigham told him not to worry for when he was his size he couldn't understand it either."[31]

A woman came up to Brigham crying and said her husband told her to go to hell. He looked at her solemnly and said "Well, don't go; don't go."[32] When his 51st child was born he rushed home from a trip to be present at the birth. She, Clarissa, tells of getting two pigeons each morning from the pigeon house, and turning her back while the overseer wrung their necks. This was for her father's breakfast. He only ate two meals a day. This is the recipe for his only hot drink. It has been variously spoken of as Brigham tea, or Mormon tea: 4 oz. each of ground bayberry, poplar bark and hemlock; 2 oz. each of ground ginger, cloves, and cinnamon; and one ounce of cayenne pepper." This would surely be a *hot* drink. He would not have his hair cut, but had it singed by barber Squires.[33] This is the grandfather of a Jack Mormon friend of mine here, who is also a barber. He reads the CW and the *National Guardian*. On December 9, 1850 the Territorial Legislature passed a bill giving Brigham Young control of City Creek and Canyon on the payment of $500. This was clearly a monopoly.[34]

438

Water and wood were made public property when Salt Lake City was set up. Land was given by lot and the blocks were made large so that no one need be cramped; a bachelor got nothing, but a man with more than one wife could get land for an extra house. Brigham said: "We have no land to sell to the Saints in the Great Basin, but you are entitled to as much as you can till, or as you need for your support provided you pay the surveyor for his services, while he is laboring for you; and at a future day will receive your inheritances on the farming lands as well as in city lots; and none of you have any land to buy or sell more than ourselves; for the inheritance is of the Lord, and we are his servants, to see that everyone has his portion in due season."[35] Brigham did not tarry but went east to Winter Quarters to help the next group get along. Once when religious services were being held, word came that emigrants were arriving. He at once dismissed the meeting and told the women to get hot food for them. They could always pray and sing but now was the time to feed the hungry.

After a few years there came a Reformation and a listening to the Word of Wisdom which said that no tobacco or liquor should be used and that men should not lead immoral lives. One of the leaders was Jedediah Grant, father of Heber J. Grant, who later became President of the Church. At a meeting Brigham arose, and asked all members present who had committed adultery to stand up. To his surprise and chagrin three fourths of them got to their feet. A Bishop arose and asked if the men had not misunderstood Brother Brigham's question. He thought that the elders did not understand that the question referred only to the time since they had repented of sin and joined the Church . . . but when put to them again . . . the men all remained on their feet."[36]

Captain Van Vliet said that Brigham kept his people captive so he offered to provide free transportation and the best of supplies to anyone who desired to leave Utah territory, on the condition that the government would provide similar means to all those in the East who wished to migrate to Utah. The Captain was won over and said he would resign from the Army rather than molest the Mormons."[37] "Winter saints" were those who came with a stock of goods from the East and only stayed long enough to sell them and depart. A certain Mormon in another small town had a vacant lot that he was not using. One day he saw a man building a house on it and asked him "how come?" The man said the Bishop had told him to build there, for nothing could be held not in use or for speculation. The owner asked the Bishop by what authority he did this and he went away satisfied with the reply: "By the authority of the Priesthood of God."[38] And a fellow who charged high prices for corn was told to refund the overcharge "or his head might roll in the snow." He made the deal right.

In 1857, jealous politicians and clergy persuaded President Buchanan to send 2500 troops to put down the "rebellious Mormons." Brigham sent young Lot Smith with his guerillas to burn the fields, destroy everything in the path of the troops, scatter their cattle and horses, etc. Finally some Army Commissioners came to protest. Brigham had already moved nearly 40,000 people south to Provo, leaving only a skeleton crew to set fiire to the city if the troops entered. Before thousands in the Tabernacle he told the Commissioners: "What has the U.S. government permitted mobs to do to us in the past?

Gentlemen, you can answer that question for yourselves . . . we have been plundered and whipped, and our houses have been burned, our fathers, mothers, brothers, sisters, and children butchered and murdered by the score. We have been driven from our homes time and time again; but have troops ever been sent to stay or punish the mobs for their crimes? No. Have we ever received a dollar for the property that we have been compelled to leave behind? Not a dollar. Let the government of our country treat us as we deserve. That is all we ask of them. We have always been loyal and expect to continue so. But hands off! Do not send your armed mobs into our midst. If you do we will fight you, as the Lord lives . . . if you bring your troops here to disturb the people . . . Before the troops reach here, this city will be in ashes, every tree and shrub will be cut to the ground, and every blade of grass that will burn will be burned. Our wives and children will go into the canyons and take shelter in the mountains; while their husbands and sons will fight you to their last breath. .And as God lives, we will hunt you by night and day til our army or yours is wasted away . . . if you want war you can have it; but if you wish peace, peace it is."[39]Then the thousands of Mormons sang the rousing song "Zion." Soon the army marched through the deserted town and 40 miles away set up a camp. Brigham used magnificent strategy and won.

In the sections on Blood Atonement and on Polygamy I will deal with aspects of Brigham's character and of his beliefs which savor of Old Testament vengeance; and in the section on the United Order I will tell of his idea of the Kingdom of God on earth. Brigham held property as trustee in trust for the Church and also had business of his own. Godbe, a merchant, left the Church because Brigham crowded him in business, and the four Walker brothers would not pay tithe and were also crowded by Brigham, and they left the Church and started the Walker Bank, which even today has a huge sign seen for miles. It was this attainment of power which made enemies for the Church and led to the oppressive laws from Washington, D.C. As in Nauvoo, the destruction of the press of the opponents of Joseph Smith brought the mob down on him, so here this monoply stirred up envy among the politicians and clergy. Brigham was not a theologian, yet he came forth with some wild ideas that were not in the Book of Mormon. He was primarily an organizer and statesman; an honest and upright man in most of his dealings. The Church has produced no one since his death with a modicum of his fearlessness, or with a tenth of his ability. Despite his greatness he ordered that no monument be placed over his grave; just a flat stone. So north of where East Second Street South begins, off First Avenue there is an enclosed graveyard with Brigham's grave and the graves of several of his wives. However, when thousands of tourists come to see the Temple and the Square, the huge statue of Brigham Young stands with hand and arm stretched out to the Bank, and with his back to the Temple. This is joked about by Gentiles to suggest the worship of wealth by the Mormon Church today, but the members of other churches do not come with clean hands, and they, as the Indians say, speak with forked tongues, for all churches worship Mammon, and do so not in the name of latter day prophets and martyrs, but in the name of that Christ who drove the money changers from the Temple.

From the 4th Chapter of First Nephi where Zoram slays Laban, through the whole Book of Mormon to the next to last chapter of Moroni there is more bloodshed, treachery, cannibalism and ungodliness to the page than you can find in our Old Testament, notwithstanding that many of the words of Christ are paraphrased and His parables given in different settings, and He says that He comes to supercede the law of Moses and brings the Sermon on the Mount, and the people do live in peace and brotherhood for generations until they again become corrupted. Despite all these warnings of what comes to those of evil heart who seek vengeance, Brigham Young emphasized the necessity of the shedding of blood to atone for sins. It would seem that the death of Christ on the Cross was of no avail.

In 1893, William Smith, Joseph Smith's brother, testified in court as follows: "I left Nauvoo in 1845 because my life was in danger if I remained there, because of my objections and protests against the doctrine of Blood Atonement."[40] In a debate with George A. Smith, who advocated imprisonment rather than hanging, Joseph Smith says: "I was opposed to hanging, even if a man kill another. I will shoot him, or cut off his head, spill his blood on the ground, and let the smoke thereof ascend up to God; and if I ever have the privilege of making a law on that subject, I will have it so."[41]

And Brigham said, "Suppose you found your brother in bed with your wife, and put a javelin through both of them, you would be justified, and they would atone for their sins, and be received into the kingdom of God. I would at once do so in such a case; and under such circumstances. I have no wife whom I love so well that I would not put a javelin through her heart, and I would do it with clean hands." And "if you want to know what to do with a thief that you may find stealing, I say kill them on the spot, and never suffer him to commit another iniquity . . . I know this appears hard . . . if you will cause all those whom you know to be thieves, to be placed in a line before the mouth of one of our largest cannon, well loaded with chain shot, I will prove by my works whether I can mete out justice to such persons, or not. *I would consider it just as much my duty to do that, as to baptize a man for the remission of his sins.* That is a short discourse on thieves, I acknowledge, but I tell you the truth as it is in my heart." (Journal of Discourses, Vol 1, pages 108-109)

And in the Temple February 8, 1857, Brigham said: "This is loving our neighbor as ourselves; if he needs help, help him; and if he wants salvation and it is necessary to spill his blood on the earth in order that he may be saved, spill it . . . that it the way to love mankind." And again Brigham said: "I could refer you to plenty of instances where men have been righteously slain, in order to atone for their sins." (Journal of Discourses, Vol 1, pages 108-109)

In 1857 troops of the U.S. Army were headed toward Utah. A migrant train of 150 well armed and well loaded folks from Arkansas came toward California. They were told to hurry westward and not to go the southern route. Attached to them were a few boisterous "Missouri Wildcats," one of whom boasted that he had the very gun that killed "Old Joe Smith." They would pass through towns and seeing chickens along the road would snap their heads off with their long snake-like whips. George A. Smith went ahead of them telling the Mormons not to sell any produce to this group. Finally they camped near Cedar City at a place called *Mountain Meadows*. Bishop Haight and Col. Dame met and as the ecclesiastical, and Army or Militia leaders, decided that the blood of the Prophet should be avenged. The Francher train was too well armed and could not be overcome without much loss of Mormon men, so it was decided to inflame the Indians to surprise them. This was done, but a few white men helped and the Mormon leaders did not want word to get out that they had had anything to do with it, so to cover up it was decided to bring a white flag and call for a truce, and then murder them all at a certain signal. John D. Lee, as farmer to the Indians went along and he saw men, women, and children killed, but 17 children of tender age were saved and later sent back to Arkansas. The murderers took a solemn oath not to divulge their bloody deed. Brigham sent word not to harm the Francher party, but it was his bloodthirsty talk all these years that built up this episode. The Gentiles over the country made a great fuss about it. Warrants were made out for the leaders for years, but they hid away. John D. Lee had been at Nauvoo and was an adopted son of Brigham. He colonized southern Utah and Lee's Ferry at the Colorado River was named after him. He had 19 wives and 64 children. Without a word and in the midst of his work for the Church he was excommunicated and most of his wives left him. Haight and Dame were out of the country and it is supposed that Brigham knew Lee would be caught in time and if he was to be the scapegoat then it were better that he not be a member of the Church when arrested. He was tried and offered immunity if he would implicate the Church but he would not do so, being true to his oath taken after the massacre. I read his two volume diary and the book about him by Juanita Brooks of the Utah Historical Society. When Lee was excommunicated, Brigham said that "under no circumstances should he ever be admitted as a member again."[42]

To placate the Gentiles an all Mormon jury found Lee guilty and sentenced him to be shot. He had been out on bail and a messenger from the Church telling him to skip bail and it would be paid, did not reach him in time. Lee felt that he had spilled innocent blood and that the only way he could atone for it was by shedding his own blood, so I doubt if he would have fled if he had received the message in time. He was shot near his coffin and grave at Mountain Meadows on March 13, 1877. Before being executed he said, in part: "It seems that I have to be made a victim — a victm must be had, and I am the victim. I am a true believer in the gospel of Jesus Christ. I do not believe everything that is now being taught and practiced by Brigham Young. I do not care who hears it. I studied to make this man's will my pleasure for thirty years. See, now, what I have come to this day! I have been sacrificed in a cowardly, dastardly manner. What confidence can I have in such a man (Brigham)! I have none, and I don't think my father in heaven has any!"[42]

And 5 months and 6 days later Brigham was dead. The lawsuit of his last wife, Ann Eliza, coupled with the guilt he must have felt because the reputation of a Church must be secure even by the betrayal of a friend, must have lessened his will to live. It is a black mark upon his character.

But somehow truth comes out, so despite Brigham's command, on Thursday, April 20, 1961, the First Presidency and the Quorum of Twelve met in a joint session and 'It was the action of the Council after considering all the facts available that authorization be given for the re-instatement to membership and former blessings to John D. Lee.' *"On May 8 and 9 following the necessary ordinances were performed in the Salt Lake Temple."*[43]

It only took the Mormons 85 years to admit their error; it took the Catholics 400 years to make Joan of Arc a saint. And no penitance has yet been shown for the St. Bartholomew Day massacre of thousands of Protestants by the Catholics, although the advent of the Worker Priests of unhappy memory was perhaps a gesture in the cosmic plan to be interpreted as always by mercenary clerics.

Brigham said "If a white man steals shoot him. If an Indian steals teach him better." Brigham said of laws: "Strip a justice of all the legal mists and fog which surround him in this day and age; leave him no nook or corner of precedent, or common law ambiguous enactments, the accumulation of the ages, wherein to shelter, and it is my opinion that unrighteous decisions would seldom be given."

The first murder trial in Utah was that of Howard Egan in 1851 for killing a man whom he caught in bed with his wife. His lawyer argued that if he had not done this he would have shared his wife's guilt and by killing the man he wiped the slate clean. He was acquitted with honor, for had he not been an instrument in "blood atonement."

The laws in early Utah were also bloody, the first four ordinances of the High Council providing 39 lashes for stealing, or being "disorderly or dangerous" and for adultry or fornication. The General Assembly on December 2, 1850, in Section 10 declared that in the case of murder, "he, she, or they shall suffer death, by being shot, hung, or beheaded." None was ever beheaded, as each one sentenced could choose the method by which they were to be executed. A thief had to pay back four fold, according to Section 28.[44]

Polygamy

"Wherefore, my brethern, hear me, and hearken to the word of the Lord; for there shall not any man among you have save it be one wife; and concubines he shall have none." Jacob 2:27 Book of Mormon

"Inasmuch as this church of Christ has been reproached with the crime of fornication, and polygamy: we declare that we believe, that one man should have one wife; and one woman, one husband, except in the case of death, when either is at liberty to marry again." First edition of Doctrine and Covenants section 101:4, printed in 1835, but taken out in 1876 and Sec. 132 on plurality of wives put in its place.

Revelation of Plural Marriage July 12, 1843 in Nauvoo. Joseph's secretary, Wm. Clayton states: "Joseph and Hyrum Smith came into the office . . . they were talking on the subject of plural marriage. Hyrum said to Joseph, 'If you will write the revelation on celestial marriage, I will take it and read it to Emma, and I believe that I can convince her of its truth, and you will hereafter have peace.' Joseph smiled and remarked. 'You do not know Emma as well as I do.' Joseph then said, 'Well, I will write the revelation and we will see.'" . . . Hyrum then took the revelation to read to Emma. Joseph remained with me in the office until Hyrum returned. When he came back, Joseph asked him how he had succeeded. Hyrum replied that he had never received a more severe talking to in his life.' (History of the Church, by Joseph Smith, Introduction to Vol. 5)

On August 29, 1852 Orson Pratt first publicly announced that the Mormon Church believed in plural marriage. This was in Salt Lake City.

Brigham Young said: "Now if any of you will deny the plurality of wives and continue to do so, I promise that you will be damned."[45]

Wilford Woodruff said in June of 1879, "I will not desert my wives and children and disobey the commandments of God for the sake of accommodating the public clamor of a nation seeped in sin and ripened for the damnation of hell. I would rather go to prison and to death."[46]

Lorenzo Snow, Fifth President of the Church said, "The severest prosecutions have never been followed by revelations changing a divine law, obedience to which brought imprisonment or martrydom. Though I go to prison, God will not change his law of celestial marriage." [47]

Polygamy renounced by President Woodruff, September 24, 1890 and ratified by the Church by the General Conference October 6th. "I Charles Penrose, wrote the Manifesto, with the assistance of Frank J. Cannon and John White, and it is no revelation from God, for I wrote it, and Wilford Woodruff signed it to beat the devil at his own game. Brethren God has not withdrawn this everlasting principle, or revoked it, for how can he revoke or withdraw an everlasting principle?" (This statement made at an Elders Conference,in London in 1908, and reprinted in the January 1929 issue of TRUTH.

This is Woodruff's revelation: "The Lord showed me by vision and revelation exactly what would happen if we did not stop this practice . . . all ordinances would be stopped . . . many men would be made prisoners . . . I went before the Lord, and I wrote what the Lord told me to write." In part "Inasmuch as laws have been enacted by Congress forbidding plural marriages, which laws have been pronounced constitutional by the court of last resort, I hereby declare my intention to submit to those laws, and to use my influence with the members of the Church over which I preside to have them do likewise. There is nothing in my teachings to the Church or in those of my associates, during the time specified, which can be reasonably construed to inculcate or encourage polygamy; and when any Eider of the Church has used language which appeared to convey any such teaching he has been promptly reproved. *And I now publicly declare that my advice to the Latter-day Saints is to refrain from contracting any marriage forbidden by the law of the land.*"

On October 6, President Lorenzo Snow offered the following: "I move that, recognizing Wilford Woodruff as the President of the Church of Jesus Christ of Latter-day Saints, and the only man on the earth at the present time who holds the keys of the sealing ordinances, we consider him fully authorized by virtue of his position to issue the Manifesto which has been read in our hearing, and which is dated September 24th, 1890, and that as a Church in General Conference assembled, we accept his declaration concerning plural marriages as authoritative and binding." The vote to sustain the foregoing was unanimous. 10-6-1890. Page 257 Docterine and Covenants.

The Second anti-polygamy Manifesto-April 3, 1904, by President Joseph F. Smith prohibiting all plural marriages.

Verse 26 of the 132nd section of the Doctrine and Covenants teaches that only by the shedding of one's blood may he atone for murder. It is no wonder that in the Mormon dominated Legislature of 1962-63 a bill to abolish capital punishment did not get to first base. Seeking to be respectable the Mormon Church does not openly preach "blood atonement" these days any more than it advocates the old "Adam-God" theory, but these ancient bloodthirsty beliefs keep them from being true Christians.

The reader will now have a background to follow in detail — this story of deceit, bravery, and cowardice on the subject of polygamy. When the average person thinks of the Mormons he thinks of polygamy, and unless this subject is dealt with clearly and fully there is no understanding of the Mormons.

To begin with I should state that I have read the Booklet issued by the Reorganized Church of Jesus Christ of Latter-day Saints, Independence, Mo. entitled *"Joseph Smith Was Not a Polygamist.* Because Emma would not admit anything about his wives or the revelation on polygamy shown to her by Hyrum Smith, and because there is not a court record of any marriages this Church denies that Joseph Smith ever thought of polygamy. A person either has to believe this flimsy evidence or that of scores of people who knew Joseph and his wives. I believe the latter.

Here is the evidence to prove that Joseph had many wives before he dared to tell Emma about it. In the testimony in the Temple, Lot Case page 320-321, Lorenzo Snow, Fifth President of the Mormon Church said that Joseph Smith sealed or married his sister Eliza in April of 1843 and the revelation on polygamy was July, 1843. Benjamin F. Johnson stated, "As I could not long be absent from my home and business, we soon returned to Ramus. On the 15th day of May some three weeks later the Prophet again came and at my home occupied the same room and bed, with my sister, that the month previous he had occupied with the daughter of the late Bishop Partridge as his wife."[48] *Emily Partridge* relates as follows (from Historical Record, page 240) "The Prophet Joseph and his wife Emma offered us a home in their family, and they treated us with great kindness. We had been there about a year when the principle of plural marriage was made known to us, and *I was married to Joseph Smith on the 4th of March 1843,* Elder Heber C. Kimball performing the ceremony. My sister Eliza was also married to Joseph a few days later. This was done without the knowledge of Emma Smith. Two months afterwards she consented to give her husband two wives, providing he would give her the privilege of choosing them. She accordingly chose my sister Eliza and myself, and to save family trouble Brother Joseph thought it best to have another ceremony performed. Accordingly on the 11th of May, 1843 we were sealed to Joseph Smith a second time, in Emma's presence . . . From that very hour, however, Emma was our bitter enemy. We remained in the family several months after this, but things went from bad to worse until we were obligated to leave the house and find another home."

John D. Lee was many times a bodyguard of Smith when he went to sleep for a few hours with his young wives.[49] Records of the Nauvoo Temple show those women sealed to Joseph Smith. Lucinda Morgan Harris was the wife of William Morgan who was murdered for revealing Masonic secrets.

Then she married George Harris but Joseph slept with her off and on for four years and Harris was present when she was sealed to Joseph in January 1846. Prescinda Buell visited Joseph twice at Far West jail. Her husband left the Church and she said she was not sure whether Buell or Joseph was the father of her son Oliver. Erastus Snow said that "my wife's sister, Louisa Beman, was his (Joseph's) first plural wife, she being sealed to him by my brother-in-law, Joseph B. Noble, April 5, 1841." Zina Jacobs lived with Joseph while her husband was on a mission. After Joseph's death she left Jacobs and married Brigham Young. Mary Lightner married a non-Mormon but gives a sworn statement that she was sealed to Joseph "in the Masonic Hall, over the old brick store by Brigham Young in February 1842 and then again in the Nauvoo Temple by Heber C. Kimball." She bore Lightner ten children, although one of them might have been Joseph's, and lived to be 95. Eliza Snow married Joseph at the age of 38, June 29, 1842, Brigham Young performing the ceremony. Later he married many single girls, but he seems to have picked on the wives of his friends. In Utah when polygamy was above board there does not seem to be any marrying to others than virgins. The above data is from Fawn Brodie's *No Man Knows My History*, and from *Tanner's Mormonism*.

I am not going into detail about Brigham's wives other than to mention that he was a very busy man and romance did not seem to be a part of his nature, procreating being a part of his duty. Werner writes that Brigham Young, Jr. and his father both courted Lizzie Fenton but the boy got her.[50] But at the age of 61 he became passionately in love with Amelia Folsom, cousin to Grover Cleveland's wife. She was 25 and when he married her she insisted on a house of her own, and until that was built she ate at a table alone with Brigham, and he escorted her all over town. She never had any children. He sent a rival on a mission. There were no lame, deformed or blind children among his 56 children. There were three sets of twins.[51]

One excuse for polygamy often given is that there were more females than males in Utah, but this is not true. For in those days one census showed 5,055 more males than females. George Bernard Shaw gives a better explanation: "Polygamy when tried under modern democratic conditions, as by the Mormons, is wrecked by the revolt of the mass of inferior men who are condemned to celibacy by it; for the maternal instinct leads a woman to prefer a tenth share in a first rate man to the exclusive possession of a third rate." In fact it was only the more prosperous and more responsible men who attempted polygamy. At any time not more than 10% of the Mormons practiced it.

The one best book on the subject is *Isn't One Wife Enough?* by Kimball Young, the grandson of Brigham Young. The only defect in it is that he told nothing of his own childhood in a polygamous family. He was head of the Department of Sociology at Northwestern University, and made a case history of 175 polygamous families and gives numerous illustrations of how it all worked out. He had doubts about the truth of Joseph's revelations. He found 53% were successful, a fourth moderately successful, 23% had considerable conflict. Nearly half were in a high economic level; one third medium, and one-sixth were poor.

He tells of the first wife, who, if her husband was sleeping next door with his second wife, and did not get up early enough to suit her, would awaken him by throwing stones on the roof. In another family where they all lived in one house, as the children grew older all the boys would sleep in one big room and all the girls in another, no matter who the mother was. He tells of one family where the father and mother were much in love, and the two wives he married were a matter of duty to "live the principle." These wives were engaged to young men but they liked the old man whom they wanted enough to live in polygamy. All these wives had the same ideas of desire for an education, a beautiful and peaceful home. The new wives were aggressive but the first wife didn't mind it for she knew despite all that she was "first" in her husband's affections. Another man's wife had died and he wanted to marry two sisters but their mother wouldn't allow it unless he married her too. This might be the perfect solution to the mother-in-law problem, for he married her first, and then the sisters. One sister didn't have any children and she took care of the other sister's children when needed, and it was a real happy family. Polygamy, if accepted by the wives made for unselfishness. With such a large family there had to be some system so each child had certain work to do. Today if sisters marry different husbands and live nearby they will help each other in child-birth, nurse the other's baby if one has more milk than another, so in the days of polygamy, if sisters were married to one man they helped each other in the same way. If it happened that one was better at some function such as sewing, washing clothes, buying at the store, etc., then naturally that function devolved upon that certain wife. One could take care of the children while the rest went to Sacrament Meeting and there wouldn't be the babble of children at the meeting, while in mono- gamy someone had to miss the sermons while the other partner took the squalling child outside. And if a woman was ill, some of the other wives could do her work and take care of her children and she need not worry. While Brigham Young had his favorite wife Amelia Folsom and other men might have had any especial wife with whom he was deeply in love, with many it would seem that the women didn't get much fun out of it, as the men procreated as a "duty" rather than with amorous intent.

Jonreed Lauritzen's family pioneered the town of Short Creek, Arizona, in the "strip" north of the Grand Canyon, and he lived there for many years in this settlement of polygamists, although he, himself was not one of them. In his most recent novel, *Everlasting Fire*, deals of life in Nauvoo.

The description of the cooperation between the wives who all love the same husband given by the Indian wife Coziah is the best that I have read on this subject. Where life does not get dull for there was a chance of a new sister-wife coming along almost any day. The publisher would not permit any quotations from the book. Those interested can read for themselves: Doubleday Co., New York City, 1962. Price $5.95.

Kimball Young says that President John Taylor and Apostle Erastus Snow each had a segregated establishment for a wife, and the families had relatively little to do with each other except at reunions and special events. This limited both conflict and cooperation. Then there were some families that couldn't take it. Another man had a freighting business and no one knew when he was coming or going. Once he came at night and his oldest girl wouldn't allow him in her mother's bedroom, saying there were too many children already.

The following is from The Journal of Discourses, Vol. 4, pages 55-57, by Brigham Young: To the women who were whining, "I am going to give you from this time (Sept. 21, 1856) to the 6th of October next, for reflection, that you may determine whether you wish to stay with your husbands or not, and then I am going to set every woman at liberty and say to them, now go your way, my women with the rest, go your way. And my wives have got to do one of two things; either round up their shoulders to endure the afflictions of this world, and live their religion, or they may leave, for I will not have them about me. I will go into heaven alone, rather than have scratching and fighting around me. I will set all at liberty. 'What, first wife too?' Yes, I will liberate you all." None of them left.

Werner reports that someone asked, "How many wives have you Mr. Young? 'Having wives is a secondary consideration; it is within the pale of duty, and consequently, it is alright. But to preach the Gospel, save the children of men, build up the kingdom of God, produce righteousness in the midst of the people; govern and control ourselves and our families and all we have influence over; make us of one heart and one mind; to clear the world from wickedness—this fighting and slaying, this mischievious spirit now (1871) so general, and subdue it and drive it from the face of the earth, and to usher in and establish the reign of universal peace, is our business, no matter how many wives a man has got, that makes no difference here or there.' "52

After the manifesto there were plural marriages, even in the Temple by Elder Lorine Woolley, but nothing could be proven. And during the preceding ten years when over a thousand men had gone to prison there was still many who felt that *really* no matter what was said in public that the Lord would not allow this law to be changed. One man had been in jail three times and said that he would live openly with his wives. He did so and was not bothered again. The two best books on this subject are *The Family Kingdom*, and *I Have Six Wives*, both by Samuel Woolley Taylor, grandson of President Taylor who died in exile. The first book is about his father John W. Taylor, an Apostle who married three more wives after the Manifesto and was finally excommunicated for it. He is quoted by his son as saying that the *persecutions came "because we insist on competing for wealth and political advantage with the Gentiles. If we kept to ourselves and minded our own affairs strictly, nobody would care how many wives we had."53* It is said that President Taylor had a revelation that the plural marriages should continue secretly and that he told Lorin Woolley definite instructions on this matter. This was given to President Taylor when he was in hiding at the Woolley home in Centerville on Sunday evening, September 26, 1886. Members of the Council had been pressing Taylor to issue a Manifesto rescinding polygamy. He told them to come back the next day and he would ask the Lord about it that night. He did so and the next day showed them the revelation given to him saying that the principle was everlasting and was not to be rescinded, but the Committee would not allow it to be promulgated for it would mean jail for all of them. So Taylor chose 5 of them and gave them orders to continue the priesthood secretly until the time would come when polygamy could be open again. Later when Taylor was dead and his son John had been excommunicated for taking on his 4 wives since Woodruff's Manifesto rescinding polygamy and Joseph F. Smith's second Manifesto in 1904, one of these 5 asked John W. Taylor to be head of a new Church. He refused to do so saying, "The Church has disowned me but I will never disown my Church. I will never join with any bitter group working for its downfall. I will never repudiate the Principle, but I here and now repudiate all men who try to use it in an attack on the Church."[54]

Taylor says of his father: "When he was in town it was a gala occasion with a holiday aspect. It always meant a gathering of the clan with Mother, Aunt Nellie, Aunt Roxie and Aunt Rhoda beamingly preparing the feast, a couple of dozen brothers and sisters on deck together with several dozen kids from the neighborhood.[55] Perhaps because he was away so much he was a heroic and legendary figure, not only to all his children but to all his wives . . . the stars never left the eyes of his wives, and its glow was reflected in the eyes of the children. If John W. Taylor sacrificed career, position, and opportunities for his families, he had the satisfaction of having his love for them returned in full. He never tasted the bitterness of having paid a great price for a bad bargain. His families were the all important thing to him in this world and the next, and to his family he was the all important man."[56] On August 25, 1917, shortly after his death, the Mormon Church issued a statement that he had been "excommunicated from the Church . . . the excommunication has never been revoked, rescinded, nor in any way modified . . . Joseph F. Smith, Anthon H. Lund, Charles W. Penrose, Heber J. Grant,"[57] signed the statement. This story of a happy polygamous family is charming and ought to be read by all who want a fair picture of the subject. It is not many men who could have six wives and make each one feel that she was really the most special.

An equally charming book, but more critical of polygamy, for the author does not believe in it, is *I Have Six Wives*. It is a case history, the author having read the diaries of these wives, of a man now living in Salt Lake City with six wives, and having done time for it twice, but now he seems not be bothered by the authorities. I met him five years ago when I first visited and spoke in Salt Lake City, and I have since met him and some of his wives and children. Naturally the correct names are not given in this book, as the purpose was to explain how one polygamist of the thousands living in Utah, Idaho and Arizona function in these modern ways. He says, "What were the stresses and strains of this type of life in the modern age? Golda was physically the largest wife and the most aggressive. She obviously was queen of this establishment, as befitted the senior wife. This was as it had been. There was outspoken Amy, small and dark; Faith, slender and gentle; Becky, with auburn hair and the spirit to go with it, serene with classic beauty; the sisters Pepita and Sybil, Pepita thin and intense, Sybil fair, calm and placid . . . Why? What led them there?"[58]

.When the author was visiting the family one night the husband asked if it was not about bedtime. They all went to bed without a word, 26 of them. The author had only one child and it was a battle to get her to bed, he said. The polygamous father smiled and said, "With a family like mine there *has* to be order." None of this family had ever been on relief, even when he was in prison.[59]

Mr. Taylor visited Short Creek, Arizona, in the strip north of the Grand Canyon several times. Over a million dollars has been poured into this desert community by polygamists from Salt Lake City and Los Angeles. The young men work in neighboring towns and turn their wages over to the leaders, but the older leaders seem to have a monopoly of young wives. This is called the United Effort rather than the United Order, for they are only "trying." The first big raid was March 7, 1944, when polygamists were arrested in three states. In Salt Lake City, 15 men were sentenced up to 5 years on the charge of "unlawful cohabitation." Their attorney presented a list of 886 caught-in-the-act sexual offenders on record in the city the previous year. All of them had been fined from $5 to $50 and released without publicity. The Mormon Church activated this persecution. The second raid was July 26, 1953 at Short Creek where Governor Pyle sought to build his political fences by sending 100 troops on a Sunday morning to arrest these terrible polygamists. (The whole thing backfired and he was defeated in the next election mainly because of this foolish self-righteous attack.) Byers, the hero of *I Have Six Wives,* had left a day and a half ahead of the raid. As in previous Mormon history, the reason for the raid was not polygamy, this was the excuse; the real reason being that the ranchers were being school taxed to support all these kids, and the Mormons could outvote the ranchers if they took the idea.

When Governor Pyle's troops arrived the children were lined up in their best clothes singing *God Bless America.* 385 in all were arrested, mostly children, and taken to Phoenix where Judge Lorna Lockwood promised that the children would not be taken from their mothers, but this was done anyway. I left Phoenix for New York City about that time and the last $5 I made I gave to the Catholic lawyer who was defending them in court. Two years later Taylor visited Short Creek and they had the schoolhouse over on the Utah side, and the families were living together again. I know of one woman of this group whose husband was a drunkard, who drove a truck to Mexico taking her children with her. Under the name of LeGrande King Taylor, writes about one of the worst frauds among Mormons, polygamous or regular. This man's real name is Leroy Wilson and he wrote to me for years when I was in Phoenix trying to get me to persuade the Hopi to allow him to build some enormous earth covered area for the Hopis to hide in. He had got hold of a CW in Chicago and thought I might be added to his sucker list. He lived on a mountain west toward St. George, with all kinds of junk machinery and cars and trailers, the latter for his wives. He was a big bag of wind who made everyone else live on cracked wheat while he ate steaks on his trips over the country getting suckers to bite on his many inventions. *TIME* magazine told a few years later of someone murdering him, and the sheriff figuring that a good deed had been done. Taylor says of him: "But to ask a question of LeGrande King was like fighting a pile of feathers, as I can certify. Brother LeGrande didn't evade — he simply engulfed you in a torrent of words."[60]

Jonreed Laurtizen, the writer, had left when one of his teen age daughters stood a good chance of getting engaged to a polygamous boy. This is likely the first time in America where hostages have been taken legally. Taylor asked these polygamous men why they didn't go to Los Angeles where they wouldn't be bothered by the law. They answered, "But that wouldn't advance the cause. We will never win the fight with secret practice. Somebody has to keep the issue alive." Frank E. Moss was the Federal D.A. in 1956 (he is now U. S. Senator) and his position was not to have big raids but only to take them to court upon complaint. He says, "The problem that confronts us is that these men have established families and have a great many minor children. They are supporting their children to the full extent of their ability. In that respect they are acting in accordance with the standards we apply to good citizenship. They don't seem to bother their neighbors. They are not offensive and are not committing other crimes or carousing. They are quiet and sober citizens. We shouldn't disturb them."[61] This would seem to be a sane attitude, and much better than those puritans who bought a home for wives who wanted to escape polygamy in Brigham's time, and all whom they got to live there was one non-Mormon prostitute. Uranium has been found at Short Creek. If they become prosperous that will be a greater test than persecution. The Short Creek case came to the Supreme Court and was decided against them, and queer as it may seem, the liberal Justice Douglas was against them while the Catholic Frank Murphy, and Justices Jackson and Black were for the Mormons. It is conceivable that if a case came up again the Supreme Court could declare polygamy legal. Then the Mormon Church, if it had nerve enough, could allow it to come up from the underground. It is difficult to get any statement on a controversial issue from the heads of the Mormon Church. John J. Stewart of Logan, Utah, in his small book, *Brigham Young and His Wives, 1961,* a Mormon writer, says, "Seven of ·our nine Church Presidents have lived plural marriage,[62] and that this principle still is and always will be a doctrine of the Church." Taylor says that "No Mormon can denounce discarded practices without renouncing his heritage. Where can the line be drawn between the belief in and the practice of?" [63]

". . . the restoration of the Church and Gospel of Jesus Christ, is to prepare for the second coming of the Savior, which is nigh at hand; to help usher in His great millenial reign, when the Gospel in its fulness, including plural marriage, will be lived by worthy members of the Church,"[64] said Prof. Stewart. And he further states, ". . . plural marriage is the patriarchal order of marriage lived by God and others who reign in the Celestial Kingdom. As well might the Church relinquish its claim to the Priesthood as the doctrine of plural marriage."[65]

I have attended church meetings of the *Church of the First Born of the Fulness of Times* with a mailing address in El Paso, Texas, and a colony 200 miles south in Mexico. About a thousand polygamous live there, while Short Creek has about 300. The congregation are mostly young folks in the lower economic bracket, earnest and likeable. They talk about the consecration of worldly goods to the Church but feel that it can't be asked of people much these days who seldom own anything clear, but have it in hock. I will continue to visit their meetings. Old timers with whom I have talked say that there are 18 groups of polygamous living, mostly in Utah. Nothing is done about it unless there is a complaint, and as with moonshiners in Kentucky, no one likes to be a "stoolie," and it is difficult to get a conviction.

My friend John Marshall Day has completed a thesis on the Fundamentalists, and especially the Short Creek group whom he visited for two days, but by that time they refused to give him any more information. He states that the older men in the village who come from the most prominent polygamist heritage have the most wives and seem to have the pick of the young girls. For some strange reason more girls than boys are born there. When young men went to war and came back on furlough they were encouraged to marry; the reason being it is thought that the group wanted the allotment checks. This economic basis is also shown in that in the depression in 1935 and Short Creek wives listed the same husband to get their relief checks. This awakened the authorities to the polygamous situation, and as more got on relief and as more children came of school age the Arizona ranchers were worried about the expense and put the heat on Governor Pyle to do something. There is a story of an Arizona official who came by chauffeur driven limousine the 400 dusty desert miles, and in a few minutes he said, "If I had to live here, I'd want more than one wife myself," and he hurried back to civilization without another word.

The leaders assigned by President John Taylor to work in secret and keep the polygamous faith were in order, John W. Woolley, Lorin C. Woolley, J. Leslie Broadbent, John Y. Barlow, Joseph Musser. The current Apostle is Roy Johnson. The polygamists criticize the Mormon Church for sending missionaries in style instead of "without purse or script" as in the old days, and they say that no revelation has been given the heads of the church since they apostisized on polygamy. Mr. Day thinks that the fact that Short Creek is not sustaining and that the young men and girls go out in the world and work to bring money back to the colony will evenutally bring outside ideas there and the young folks will not so readily do as they are told.

Mr. Day points out that the Mormons, like the early Christians, started as a sect and developed into a church and gave up enough of their ideas to accommodate themselves to the outside world. They all started out dreaming of a utopia; the dimensions of which were determined what they lacked here. The religions founded in a desert country dreamed of a heaven or utopia like unto a Garden of Eden. The Eskimos thought of heaven as a nice warm place and their hell was a cold sky.

The fact that these fundamentalists accepted state aid is as much of a defeat of their ideal, as that of the Mormon Church in doing away with polygamy. If they despised the Gentile government why did they try to live off of it?

Negroes

Generally speaking the Mormon Church has denied Negroes membership of first class in their Church. There is not as much pressure for them to change as there was in the case of polygamy. As stated before the appearance of George Romney on the political scene may encourage the Church to ease up on the record of the Church on this subject. Joseph Smith has been quoted for and against slavery and while the latest he said on the subject was when he was running for President in 1844 to the effect that slaves should be bought from their masters by money received from the sale of public lands, and freed. It is possible that this might have been a political plank, rather than a sincere expression of his thought.

However, it is a matter of church history that Elijah Able, a negro, was ordained an Elder March 3, 1836, and a Seventy, April 4, 1841. In 1883, as a member of the Third Quorum of Seventy, he left Salt Lake City on a mission to Canada. It was said that because he had labored in the construction of the Temple he was elevated to the Seventies.[66]

William E. Barrett, Vice President of Brigham Young University says in *The Church and the Negro People:* "It appears that one person of Negro blood had been ordained an Elder by William Smith while he was on his mission in New York State as evidenced by a letter appearing in *Journal History,* June 2, 1847, 'At this place (Batavia, N.Y.) I found a colored brother by the name of Lewis, I am informed, has a son who is married to a white girl and both are members of the Church.' "[67]

Joseph F. Smith in a funeral service for a colored Mormon by the name of 'Aunt Jane' said, "She would in the resurrection attain the longings of her soul and become a white and beautiful person."[68] And in a letter from the First Presidency, July 17, 1947, to Dr. Lowry Nelson: "We are not unmindful of the fact that there is a growing tendency, particularly among some educators, as it manifests itself in this area, toward the breaking down of race barriers in the matter of intermarriage between whites and blacks, but it does not have the sanction of the Church and is contrary to Church doctrine."[69] What egotism for Joseph F. Smith? How does he know that a fine looking colored person *must of necessity* prefer to be white?

In the *History of the Church* (Vol. 3, page 29) the question is asked of Joseph Smith, "Are the Mormons abolitionists?" The answer is "No, unless delivering the people from priestcraft, and the priests from the power of Satan, should be considered abolition. But we do not believe in setting the Negroes free." Also, while an abolitionist spoke in the early 1830's in Kirtland, Ohio, Joseph in the Messenger and Advocate, and as quoted in his *History of the Churhch* (Vol. 2, pages 436-438) said that the attendance was very few, "the gentleman to hold forth his arguments to nearly naked walls . . . I do not believe that the people of the North have any more right to say that the South shall not hold slaves, than the South have to say the North shall . . . but I can say, the curse is not yet taken off from the sons of Canaan, neither will be until it is affected by as great a power as cause it to come; and the people who interfere the least with the purposes of God in this matter, will come under the least condemnation before Him."

Brigham Young said, in *Journal of Discourses* (Vol. 7, p. 290), "The Lord put a mark upon him, which is the flat nose and black skin. Trace mankind down to after the flood, and then another curse is pronounced upon the same race — that they should be 'the servant of servants'; and they will be, until the curse is removed, and the abolitionists cannot help it, nor in the least alter that decree." And again in Vol. 10, page 110, he says, "Shall I tell you the law of God in regard to the African race? If the white man who belongs to the chosen seed mixes his blood with the seed of Cain, the penalty, under the law of God, is death on the spot. This will always be so."

Joseph Fielding Smith, next in line to the Presidency of the Mormon Church, and who is Church Historian, was asked about Negroes being allowed in the early Mormon Church as Elders. The reply dated June 10, 1960 said, "Negroes were not ordained in the early Church." This is in contrast to the statement of David O. McKay, who is more liberal, and who is now President of the Mormon Church, who said in a letter of Nov. 3, 1947, "I know of no scriptural basis for denying the priesthood to Negroes other than one verse in the Book of Abraham (1:26) . . . The real reason dates back to our pre-existent life." Note that he says nothing about the Old Testament Cain and Ham, etc.

Orson Pratt gives the theory (*Journal of Discourses,* Vol. 1, page 63) "Among the Saints is the most likely place for the spirits to take their tabernacles, through a just and righteous parentage. They are to be sent to that people that are the most righteous of any other people on earth; . . . This is the reason why the Lord is sending them here, brethern and sisters; . . . The Lord has not kept them in store for five or six thousand years past, and kept them waiting for their bodies all this time to send them among the Hottentots, the African negroes, the idolatrous Hindoos, or any other of the fallen nations that dwell upon the face of the earth."

Joseph Fielding Smith further explains the idea (*Doctrines of Salvation,* Vol. 1, P. 61): "There is a reason why one man is born black and with other disadvantages, while another is born white with great advantages. The reason is that we once had an estate before we came here, and were obedient, more or less, to the laws that were given us there."

James Boyd Christensen in his Masters Thesis, University of Utah, says, "In 1850 Utah was the only western territory that had Negro slaves. It was one of the few places in the United States where Negro and Indian slavery occurred in the same locale in the same period. It is interesting to draw a parallel between the attitudes of the Mormon colonizers toward Negro slavery and the Indian slave trade. In short, they countenanced slavery of Negroes among them while they abhorred the slave traffic among the Indians and legislated against it."[70]

"The U.S. census for 1860 gives the number of colored persons in the Territory of Utah as 59. 30 free colored and 29 slaves." And this from the Salt Lake Tribune of May 31, 1939, "Patrick J. Sullivan, employee of a Salt Lake Abstract firm, while searching the record for real estate information, came across the copy of a bill of sale for a Negro boy named 'Dan' in a book containing transactions for the year 1859. The slave was sold by Thomas S. Williams of 'Great Salt Lake City' to William H. Hooper, same address, for $800."

Just as polygamy and the Adam God theory were contrary to the Book of Mormon so is this degradation of the Negro, for in *2 Nephi* 26:33 we read, "he inviteth them all to come unto Him and partake of his goodness; and he denieth none that come to him, black and white, bond and free, male and female; and he remembereth the heathen; and all are alike unto God, both Jew and Gentile." Of course churches that accept capital punishment and war all in the name of God deny Christ and His New Testament, for Philip baptized an Ethiopian, and Jeremiah asks, "Can an Ethiopian change his skin?" Peter is told that God is no respector of persons for "God hath shewed me that I should not call any man common or unclean . . . But in every nation he that feareth him, and worketh righteousness, is accepted with him."

In the 1963 session of the Utah legislature several hundred members of the NAACP and others demonstrated for civil rights legislation, and as a result one of the several bills were brought out of committee and passed and signed by the Governor, repealing laws which did not allow mixed marriages of different races. But Utah still remains the only state outside of the deep south that does not have laws of fair employment, fair housing, and of access to public accommodations for those of all races. This is no doubt because of the prejudice in Mormon theology against the Negro. However, the speakers at the Civil Rights meeting at the Unitarian Church were nearly all liberal Mormons from the University who were not afraid to thus go counter to the teaching of their Church and Lowell Bennion spoke against capital punishment at the Senate Hearing. He is a prominent Mormon educator. Catholics do not seem to be interested in this subject in Utah, although some priests belong to the NAACP. The Catholic idea of refusing to mix with other denominations, even for a good cause, seems to have prevented them from attending Civil Rights meetings with the Unitarians. In May 1963, upon motion of non-Mormon Mayor "Brack" Lee, the City Commissioners passed a resolution unanimously favoring the serving of Negroes in all restaurants and public places. This was taken because a Negro reported that he had been refused service in a restaurant, but this is a recommendation, not a law.

Mormons Weigh Stand on Negro — May End Ban on Complete Membership in Church, by Wallace Turner. Special to the *New York Times*. Salt Lake City, June 3 (1963). The top leadership of the Mormon Church is seriously considering the abandonment of its historic policy of discrimination against Negroes. Because the Church of Jesus Christ of Latter-day Saints has a lay priesthood to which almost every adult male member belongs, the effect has been to limit Negroes to second-class membership. "We are in the midst of a survey looking toward the possibility of admitting Negroes," said Hugh B. Brown, one of the two counselors serving President David O. McKay in the First Presidency of the Mormon Church. "Believing as we do in divine revelation through the President of the church, we all await his decision," Mr. Brown said.

Mr. Brown, a 79-year-old former attorney, said he believed that if the change were made, it would be a doctrinal revision for Mormonism of a magnitude matching the abandonment of polygamy in 1890. The whole problem of the Negro is being considered by the leaders of the church in the light of racial relationships everywhere," Mr. Brown said. "We don't want to go too fast in this matter. We want to be fair." Under Mormon doctrine, the President is the chairman of the prophets. He is always the senior member of the Council of Twelve Apostles, each of whom is considered to be a prophet, a seer and a revelator. A major doctrinal change would be discussed with high church councils before its enunciation by President McKay.

There are now about 2,000,000 Mormons, and only a few hundred of these are Negroes. Members of all races, except the Negro, are in the priesthood. The church also has forbidden Negroes the right of marriage in a

Mormon temple. In addition, the marriage of Negroes to members of other races is forbidden by the church.

Throughout Mormon writings is the hint that the ban might someday be removed. Brigham Young once asked himself how long Negroes were to endure the curse of Cain. He thought it would be "until all the other descendants of Adam have received the promises and enjoyed the blessings of priesthood and keys thereof." More positive hope was held out by President Wilford Woodruff, who led the church when polygamy was abandoned. He said: "The day will come when all of that (Negro) race will be redeemed and possess all the blessings which we now have." The Mormon church, Mr. Brown emphasized today, has never closed the door to Negroes, nor to the possibility of removing the limitation on their participation in church affairs.

In a telephone conversation June 8th, Hugh B. Brown told Jerald Tanner that he was misquoted in the part concerning the change of policy, however, he expressed his approval of the article by saying that it was "on the whole very fair."

Within a few hours after the *New York Times* containing this article had been on the stands or public containers downtown, all copies were gone. Mr. Tanner reprinted the article in a one page leaflet.

The Word of Wisdom

The Word of Wisdom was given by Joseph Smith February 27, 1833 and it forbids the use of tea, coffee, strong drinks and tobacco. The Church authorities today have changed the records trying to prove that Joseph and Brigham were strict on this matter. Joseph himself admitted that he often became drunk, and in Nauvoo he installed a bar in the Nauvoo House only to have Emma tell him their either she would move across the street or the bar had to go. Emma stayed. Elder Clark preached against drinking and Joseph publicly reproved him saying that Noah got drunk and yet he was counted by God to be a righteous man. Joseph had a pious sober clerk by the name of Robert Thompson. To wake him up Joseph told him one day, 'Robert, I want you to go out and get on a bus, go and get drunk and have a good spree. If you don't you will die.'[71] In less than two weeks he was still sober but by that time he was dead and buried. In Carthage jail soon before they were killed, all, including Joseph drank wine that the guard brought. John D. Lee tells of many times when working on the Nauvoo Temple they got a barrel of wine and drank all they wanted. Brigham Young on October 8, 1859, spoke against drinking "until you really need it." When his Discourses were printed this sentence was left out. At first the Utah Hotel which is owned by the Church did not sell tobacco or liquor. Now it sells tobacco and all who bring their own liquor can get accommodation of the extras that go with it. And KSL, which is owned by the Church, advertises tobacco, coffee and beer.

I have heard Mormon leaders at their Sacrament Meeting at the University declare that while they obeyed the Word of Wisdom that a person could do all this and be selfish and greedy and miss the real meaning of the Gospel. As stated elsewhere when I came to Utah I ceased drinking tea and coffee as a courtesy to the true Mormon way of life and Mary ceased smoking cigarettes. There are jokes told of Mormons who put their beer cans in their neighbor's garbage.

Tithing as practiced in the Mormon Church is something that Mormons pride themselves on, and Gentiles are generally envious of the ease with which they get money. As given by Joseph Smith, "The celestial law requires one-tenth part of all a man's substance which he possesses at the time he comes into the Church, and one-tenth part of his annual increase ever after. If it requires all that a man can earn to support himself and family, he is not tithed at all." (*Millenial Star,* Vol. 9, page 12)

The Mormon Welfare Plan in its present state was inaugurated during the 1930 depression. At 7th South and 7th West they have a huge elevator full of wheat, a milk processing plant where milk from a dozen stake farms is brought and made into evaporated milk, powdered milk, butter, cottage cheese and cheese, and a cannery that any can use, paying only for the tin cans. Those Mormon families that would ordinarily be on county aid can come here and get canned food, milk, meat, clothing, or whatever they need. No money is exchanged. Those who are not able to come to the warehouse have it delivered daily or weekly in plain trucks. There is a weaving department, furniture repair, shoe repair, and a barber shop. Many men from our Joe Hill House go there and work a day or two and get what they need. The Mormons pay taxes to the county and state for the aid given to Gentiles but they tithe themselves to help their poorer brethern. On the first Sunday of each month all good Mormons fast for two meals and turn this money over to their Bishop to pay for rent, utilities, etc. for the poor. When this fast is broken they have their monthly testimony meeting where any member can get up and tell of the blessings of his or her religion. I have attended many of these fast meetings, even when on my 45 day fast, and the Bishop generally had some of the congregation drive me home. It was all down hill going home but I appreciated their thoughtfulness. As at Quaker meetings, Christian Science Wednesday evening meetings, and service club, and sales meetings there is a lot of mutual backslapping, and some very monotuous conversation, but at times a sincere and eloquent note does come through.

Perhaps half a dozen wards will get together and have a stake farm to produce milk, or produce, or have a chicken ranch, cattle ranch, or as near Mesa, Arizona, a cotton ranch. In Houston, Texas, they produce peanut butter. They have a 240,000 acre cattle ranch in Florida, and citrus juice is canned in Florida, Arizona and California and sent in exchange for applesauce, etc. from Utah. Some years ago when there was a big flood in upper California the Mormon Relief was days ahead of the Red Cross or any other help. Many elderly folks work at the warehouse to pass the time away or because they want to help. All this is in the old Mormon pioneer tradition and is something that those who depend upon the Welfare State could also do if they were not spoiled by the handout system of public relief. Mormons who got help when they are handicapped are encouraged to work to pay back if they are able to do so later.

The United Order

Reference has been made in this chapter to the United Order. This was tried out in Kirtland, Far West, Nauvoo, Salt Lake City, Brigham City, Orderville and other Utah towns. The idea was that upon joining the Mormon Church each one should consecrate all that he had and turn it over to the

457

Bishop. He in turn would judge how much was needed to keep the family going and if the man did not have enough he was given back enough to keep him in necessities. All surplus wealth was meant to be given over for the Church to administrate to those in need. The panic of 1837 toppled over the Kirtland economy, and persecution in Far West and Nauvoo prevented this plan from working. Brigham Young saw "winter saints" coming to Utah with a stock of goods and after selling them go away, or he saw Gentiles getting a lot of business. He then started the ZCMI (Zions Cooperative Mercantile Institution) which nearly bankrupted the Gentiles. Now a $17,000,000 business is done in their two stores in Salt Lake City. The idea was a good one for the Mormon economy, for scores of industries were started and people were helped. But eventually in Brigham City the cooperatives got into the hands of a clique, and in Orderville the big wages to be made in the nearby mines weaned away the members. The increasing secularization of life in this century has made nearly all other cooperative effort into being that in name only, or as in the case of the Amana Community, they went directly into the capitalistic way of life. The inertia of most people tends to allow the direction of community life to get into the hands of the few, and while the leaders may be unselfish, it is seldom that their children inherit ideals. In 1880, the 50th anniversary of the founding of their church, a jubilee was declared, and tithes owed were cancelled, and all debts were supposed to be forgiven." In 1980 such clemency would break up the banker clique that controls the church.

Mormons Evaluated

> Joseph Smith when he was young,
> Saw a golden censer swung . . .
>
> A Moses or an Abraham
> Felt that nations in him swam . . .
>
> He spun the world four thousand years
> Back to Jacob and his steers . . .
>
> And the new age caught them up,
> Stilled the psaltery, drained the cup . . .[72]

Robert P. Tristram Coffin

V. F. Calverton, who wrote, *Where Angels Fear To Tread*, concerning many communities, gave this report on the Mormons: "The Book of Mormon was founded upon theories no more fantastic than those of the Bible; it was interspersed with the doctrine of the day, rife with paradoxes and contradictions, and shot full of irrational and incredible supposition and conceptions."[37]

William Mulder and A. Russell Mortensen, in their *Among the Mormons,* a sympathetic anthology of their beliefs, say in the introduction, "Joseph Smith's unfolding theology seemed tuned to all the reform fiddles of the times. He filled the breathless years with experiments in theocracy and communitarianism and temperance and polygamy, with expectations of millennium and the Second Coming, with world evangelism and practical programs of emigration and colonization, with aspirations and nonconformities which the frontier, despite its vaunted individualism could not abide."[74]

Kimball Young, grandson of Brigham Young, feels that a score of prominent families control the Mormon Church and that they have lost that purity and desire to be different according to their faith, and have succumbed to the secular way of life.

Prof. Richard T. Ely of the University of Wisconsin, wrote, "The organization of the Mormons is the most nearly perfect piece of social mechanism with which I have ever, in any way, come in contact, excepting the German Army alone."[75]

The Mormon Prof. Leonard J. Arrington in his *Great Basin Kingdom*, said, "Church policy broke with the past by actively soliciting financial assistance from outsiders. And the concessions made to those outside financial interests paved the way for absentee ownership and control. Eventually, the levithan of American finance capitalism finally ruled Utah as it had long ruled Montana and other western states and territories.[76] "The self sufficient kingdom may be said to have been brought to an end. A more acceptable adjustment between spiritual and seculiar interests was attained. And with this adjustment, the church no longer offered a geographic and institutional alternative to Babylon. Faith became increasingly separated from community policy, and religion from society. Individualism, speculation, and inequality — once thought to be characteristics of Babylon — were woven into the fabric of Mormon life."[76A]

Dr. Robert J. Dwyer, wrote as his doctrinal thesis at Catholic University of America, *A Gentile Comes to Utah*. He is now the Catholic Bishop in Nevada, and formerly lived in Salt Lake City. He says, "There seems to be less profanity, rowdyism, rampant and noisy wickedness among the young Mormons than among the youth of any other town or city where I have been."[77]

Roy B. West, Jr., a former Mormon missionary in Germany, but now out of the Church, writes a sympathetic book: *Kingdom of the Saints*. He concludes, "Heber J. Grant was President from 1918 to 1945. He was a member of or chairman of so many boards of directors that skeptical members of the church often asked themselves how much time President Grant had for spiritual affairs. His administration gave rise to fears that the Church had become an organization destined to be administered by aged patriarchs of an ultra conservative cast-men whose judgments were too likely to be affected by the least lively minds among their subordinates. David O. McKay President from 1951 to the present. His first actions showed him to be a more vigorous and strongminded administrator than most of his followers had anticipated. He curbed the authority of some of Grant's most conservative leaders, whose business interests and political bias had much to do with determining church policy . . . the member who once had a voice in advising his superiors through the priesthood quorums finds his way barred by men in the lower ranks of authority who are too afraid of the men above them to risk carrying criticism up the ladder of leadership."[79]

M. R. Werner wrote a critical life of *Brigham Young*. He says of Joseph Smith, "It is impossible to determine exactly whether the golden plates of the Book of Mormon were an imaginative delusion of Joseph Smith's, or whether they were a piece of conscious fakery instituted at first for fun and later developed for their financial possibilities. His later acts seem to favor the opinion that he had succeeded in deluding himself, however much he may have been interested at first in deceiving other people.[80] It is my conviction that Joseph Smith wrote the Book of Mormon without the aid of God, and that the book itself shows evidence of being a product of Smith's environment.[81] The important question is not whether Joseph Smith was divinely inspired, but whether he thought he was divinely inspired."[82]

Prof. Thomas F. O'Dea, a Catholic teaching sociology at the University of Utah writes on *The Mormons,* and concludes, "The conservative, literalist, fundamentalist group seems now to control the church, and these principles of church organization — lay leadership, seniority as the basis of promotion, selection on other bases than theological learning, and control of appointments by conservative elements — make the advancement of liberals into church leadership very unlikely in the next several years. Yet it is these very liberals, shut out from leadership, who in the church's educational system are saving many of the youth from apostasy. President McKay, while a man generally respected by all groups within the church, is not unfriendly to the liberals.[83] Moreover, it would seem a grave mistake for a religious movement to concentrate its attention on this — worldly activities, since it is precisely this—worldliness and activism that modern man appears to find inadequate. For organized religion to offer competition in spheres of life in which non-religious organizations do better — spheres themselves inadequate to the facing of deeper human problems — is to be found wanting. The basic need of Mormonism may well become a search for more contemplative understanding of the problem of God and man. And it is precisely here that the intellectuals — the products of Mormonism's great vale of education — may make important contributions. It is a tremendous presumption to attempt to judge the future of a movement like Mormonism, yet it is my suspicion that those who emphasize the obsolescence of Mormonism, those who see the end of them in a stereotyped lack of creativity and a routine running down, who believe that this Mormon world will end not with a bang but a whimper, are wrong. There is still too much vitality — the characteristic Mormon vitality — remaining for such a prognosis to be likely."[84]

Now after reading these books and studying their conclusions, and after asking questions of my many Mormon friends I will venture the following opinions. Bear in mind that the preceding pages of quotations from authors who evaluate are thoughts that I can in part agree with, or I would not have selected them.

But first let me describe for non-Mormons what the Sacrament Meetings of the Mormons are like. In cities where there are few Mormons, the meetings begin at 7 or 8 o'clock p.m. and last for about an hour. The Bishop announces who will take part and then calls upon, say a young man to open the meeting with prayer. Then about half a dozen young men distribute the bread after some such prayer as, "Oh God, Eternal Father, bless this bread taken in remembrance of the body of thy son Jesus Christ that we may partake of it in remembrance of Him." And likewise when the water is distributed in small cups. Then a song is sung before and after, and perhaps a young girl reads from a piece of paper or recites from memory a 4 minute talk on some Biblical hero. Then maybe a young couple play a duet or sing

460

a song. Then perhaps two returned missionaries tell of their experiences, after which there is a song and a prayer. If there is any business it is conducted first, such as voting by hands to "sustain" an appointee to some church function. No one ever votes not to "sustain" any person. Here in Salt Lake City at the University Ward where I attend there are at times musical selections, but as the membership is composed mostly of students there are no young folks taking part. At times there will be but one speaker as when a Dr. burned a cigarette and put nicotine on a mouse causing its instant death, in a talk against smoking. Or when the Chaplain at the state prison spoke of affairs there. He did not tell of the tear gassing of inmates and afterward I chided him about it. Speakers have read from Tolstoy's *Kingdom of God Is Within You,* quoted from Thoreau and Gandhi, and one of them said that if Christ was speaking today across the tracks none of them would hear Him for they were respectable folks and wouldn't go across the tracks, shame them! Also about a Mormon who kept the Word of Wisdom and paid his full tithe, but needed humanizing as he was unsociable and greedy. Then on the first Sunday of the month is a Fast Meeting where those present have missed two meals and turn the money over to the Bishop to pay rent, utilities, etc. for the poor. The Bishop said some members must live very frugally for the price of their meals were only 8 cents each. These meetings, after the sacraments and songs, are testimony meetings where anyone can get up and speak, being similar to the Wednesday evening meetings of the Christian Scientists. At times these testimonies are tiresome and one gets the feeling of being at a Rotary Club or Fuller Brush salesmen pep meeting, but at other times very sincere thoughts are given. Each talk in all of the meetings is ended with the expression "I bear testimony in the name of Jesus Christ that the Gospel is true." And most of the congregation concurs by saying "amen." A scribe sits on the platform and takes an account of what goes on and the number of those present, both Mormons and Gentiles. Unless the usher who passes by me knows me I am offered communion and I whisper to him "I am Gentile." In towns where the Mormons are few, or I am told in Mormon towns out in the state, there is a spontaneous welcome of a stranger, but here in Salt Lake City the Bishop may welcome you but most others pay little attention. Of course now that I have been attending for two years, many of the folks know me and speak to me. On a rainy day some of them have driven me downtown.

On days when I attend the Greek Orthodox I seldom see a blonde there, but here at LDS (the Mormons seldom call themselves "Mormons," but use the abbreviation "LDS") most people are blondes, as the converts have come from the north of Europe. The Bishop announced one day that during the past year there had been 26 marriages in the ward, and 20 of them had been in the Temple "for time and eternity." At another time he called for three volunteers on a Saturday to work on the Stake Farm. There is Sunday School in the morning and MIA (Mutual Improvement Association) on Tuesday nights at the Mormon Institute. The latter is attended by hundreds and consists of talks given by noted Mormons. At all of these meetings, parents bring their small children, but if there is too much noise they are taken outside for a time. The whole atmosphere at the Sacrament Meetings is informal, announcements being made of births and deaths. A speaker generally prefaces his remarks by saying "Dear Brothers and Sisters."

In Catholic Churches you very seldom hear a good sermon. It is usually a call for money or a denunciation of Communism or birth control, or at the best a dreary lot of hell-fire theology. At the Greek Orthodox Church the sermon is short and tends to be ethical instead of commercial. At the Japanese Buddhist Church the sermons are in Japanese, but are translated into English. They are primarily directed to the children, but adults can get the idea. Both the Buddhists and the Mormons are happy people, as contrasted to the dreary fear of hell or of the Communists that one generally hears in Catholic and Protestant churches. As I have said before the Unitarian Church tends to be a good, or a bad, book review, although you are sure to get a social message there, instead of theology. The attendance at the Mormon Church is interesting and not dull, and I always look forward to going there. I attend the Catholic Church to receive the Sacraments, and only occasionally in the poor churches across the tracks do I hear a sermon worth listening to.

Around the time of Joseph Smith, an Indian chief asked a missionary why, if God had caused a Bible to be written had He not written it so it could be understood; that he would wait a year and see if the new brand of Christian just arrived was as tricky and bloodthirsty as the previous one.

It is possible that the boy Joseph sensing the bankruptcy of all existing religions, had prayed to God and did receive a vision from on high. It is obvious that there is little that is heavenly in the Book of Mormon, filled as it is with tales of murder and deceit, and paraphrased from Biblical stories. Even if it were true as history it is not important enough for a guide in these tempestuous days. Something more is needed than the old "eye for an eye" philosophy. It is obvious that midst his digging for buried treasure and his playing around with peep-stones young Joseph found that he could put across as bonafide whatever he fancied. It is also obvious that his revelation on polygamy, however it resulted in building up Utah, came to cover up his affairs with young girls and with the wives of those sent away on a mission. Whether prankster spirits or imps or his own bubbling imagination was the cause of his continued revelations is something that can only be guessed at. Certainly power corrupted him and led to his death, for there was nothing holy or inspired in his strutting around in uniform and driving out of the Church and out of Nauvoo any who questioned his secret wives or his open delusions of grandeur.

Out of equalitarian dreams of Robert Owen and Fourier and the ferment of new religious thought of the times he did evolve his Word of Wisdom, which even today is worthwhile and which is something where the Mormons excel other religions. Their attempt at the United Order is also praiseworthy and could be even approximated today if it were believed enough. Perhaps because they chickened out on polygamy, they unconsciously emphasize the Word of Wisdom to cancel their guilt.

Brigham Young did not pretend to be holy. He was a great organizer and without him the Mormons would likely have been no more than a tiny sect split into warring factions. He gathered from afar, not Saints, but varied kinds of people, and welded them into communities of cooperative effort. His threat to burn Salt Lake City was a masterly strategy, keeping the U. S. Army at bay. He dealt with kindness toward the Indians which was something new in those days. But, like Joseph, his assumption of dictatorial power brought on the crisis whereby the Mormons had to cease their open polygamy, and control of the economics was limited. The expulsion of those who dared not "sustain" his policies, or who opposed his monopoly of sugar and salt and other business ventures, and the handing over to Porter Rockwell or Bill Hickman and their Danites for punishment those who opposed him, is no more to be approved than the modern tyranny of a Hitler, a Stalin, or a Franco. If polygamy was directed by God then to chicken out on it under persecution was cowardly. The assertion of the Church that the Constitution was divinely inspired, in lieu of the studies of Beard, the historian, is silly, and it's adherence to man made law rather than that of God, as nearly all other churches teach, is part of their worship of Mammon.

"The Constitution had been drafted by men representing special economic interest. Four-fifths of them were public creditors, one-third were land speculators, and one-fifth represented interests in shipping, manufacturing and merchandising. Most of them were lawyers. The old Articles of Confederation, to which the States had subscribed in good faith as a working agreement, made all the provision for their own amendment; and now these men had ignored these provisions, simply putting the Articles of Confederation in the waste-basket and bringing forth an entirely new document of their own devising. Jefferson had criticized it because it had no Bill of Rights and did not provide against indefinite tenure of office." From pages 176, 177 of Jefferson, by Albert Jay Nock, Harcourt, Brace Co., N.Y. 1926.

The Mormons often say that the Constitution was divinely inspired and opened by prayer. The truth is that Franklin, no especially religious or moral man himself, suggested this prayer daily, but the motion was not passed, Alexander Hamilton saying they were not in need of "foreign aid." And the fact is that those who called the Convention lied about its purpose, for they intended to form an entirely new centralized government to keep the farmers and the poor from ever over riding the rich and powerful. The Articles of Confederation were only to be changed by unanimous vote, but they changed it to a two-thirds vote and had to use many tricks to get that accord. Rhode Island and North Carolina let the new Constitution become a law without ratifying it. Beard says it was as much by accident as intent that we did not have a parliamentry form of government like England. The proceedings were secret and it was only by the fact that Madison kept notes that 50 years later we really knew what went on.

The mechanics of church government whereby conservative old men elect each other to rule is something which the Catholic Church has been doing for nearly two thousand years, resulting in their stagnation spiritually. The Mormons have had less time to become corrupt but they have done very well at it.

Since the time of Brigham Young, Mormon leaders have tended to be business men, as Catholic Bishops and Cardinals are also chosen, without much pretension of being holy men, and with little vision beyond the collecting of tithes and the expansion of their political and industrial power.

On the positive side there is a Mormon tradition of self-help, rather than looking to the government, which is as counter to the this welfare-state age as was the original Mormon teaching to orthodoxy. They pay taxes for the relief of the poor Gentiles, but do not moan about it, and feed their own people by their fasting and self denial. This is in contrast to most Catholics who cry because they pay taxes for public schools and have to support their own parochial schools, so now that a Catholic President is in power they ask for federal aid. If Catholics disciplined themselves as the Mormons do in not using liquor and tobacco, and not depend upon gambling for an income, they could support their own schools. This emphasis upon a clean life on the part of the Mormons is their greatest asset. There is also an occasional healing by the "laying on of hands," perhaps practiced with the old sincerity of the Christian Scientists, or of the early days at Lourdes. There is also the emphasis upon inquiry and there is no index of the books which Mormons must not read. When I have attended Buddhist services twice a month I have often met young Mormons there.

Individual polygamists whom I have met, and those called "fundamentalists" whose literature I have read or whose clandestine meetings I have attended, predict the destruction of "Anti-Christ" who is in control of the official Mormon Church, somewhat like the Jehovah's Witnesses and some Protestants call the Catholic Church "the whore of Babylon" and predict the destruction of all but the select few — the 144,000 who have kept the faith. These folks accept the debasement of the Negro, support of war, obedience to the government, except in the case of polygamy. They seem as bad as regular Mormons in their denial of civil rights to minority races. But, as stated previously, I have met a few radical pacifistic and anarchistic polygamous who do not belong to any group. As Prof. O'Dea states, there is still much of the old time Mormon vitality and integrity, which calls for those who are not afraid to make their church something like it was supposed to be. Here they are predominant. All they have to do is to be rebels. I am interested in the polygamous because they are a minority group, not because I favor polygamy, but they have their rights to practice their religion, if they take the punishment, that comes with it.

It has been said that if a person is a good Mormon he doesn't have time to do much else. Their praying for the dead in the Temple is as sensible and authentic as the Masses for those in purgatory by which Catholics keep their priests busy. Their theory of a pre-existent life coincides with the Hindu, Rosicrucian, and Hopi Indian teachings, and would seem to be more reasonable and just as Biblical as the "hell and damnation" of the orthodox Christians. But their emphasis upon "blood atonement," the degradation of the Negro, and their emphasis upon worldly success as a proof of the favor of God leaves the Mormns no better than other religions which worship the Golden Calf in the Name of Christ.

Because of the pressure of Communism, and the in-roads which the Jehovah's Witnesses are making upon orthodox religions; and also the storefront churches which "Bible-bang" the old time religion, that the fashionable churches have replaced with their social worker attitude to life, there is room for those millions who have not heard of Mormonism to be converted to this strange theology. They could have 20 million members instead of 2 million and their influence would not be as great politically and economically, outside of Utah, as the Catholic Church, the Mohammedans, the Buddhists, or Hindu religions in those countries where they are dominant, or even the Baptists in the "deep south."

The future lies, not with any of the organized religions, all of which have gone to seed, but with that spirit abroad in the world which typifies Gandhi, Martin Luther King, and Albert Sweitzer, men who escaped from the restrictive bands of their religions, and who present a positive message of hope, self-sacrifice and joy, rather than the piling up of money and the building of new religious edifices. Who will be the Gandhi of America? This is the challenge!

A speaker at one of the Sacrament Meetings of the Mormons which I attended told of the Christian who asked God to guide his footsteps, but the fellow, like most church members, never moved. He was content to mumble prayers.

Let young Catholics listen to the theologian Father Hans Kung, who, at the Vatican Council, calls for the abolition of the Index, the freedom of worship for Protestants in Spain and Portugal, and the right of the individual priest to obey his conscience rather than the medieval closed mind of his superior and who quotes the "Grand Inquisitor." Let them listen to the criticism of the Jesuit Father George Dunne who has told off stuffed shirt superiors all of his life and has insisted in speaking "controversially." Let them listen to Dorothy Day who visited Pope John XXIII asking him to allow a Catholic to be a conscientious objector, instead of, like most Popes, asking for peace, but always supporting war. And let them listen to Pope John who tried to "get out of the bag" into which the conservative Curia bureaucrats had placed him. Let them listen to Pope Paul VI who it is hoped will continue Pope John's ideas.

Let young Mormons have the courage to refuse to sustain ancient bureaucrats among their leaders. (The Danites won't get you now); let them believe what they like about "the Gospel of Joseph Smith being true," but, as Tolstoy says, let not this belief keep them from pioneering spiritually as their forefathers did materially. Let them know that Negroes are also their brothers; let them know that there is something higher than "obeying the law of the land." Let them be courageous in helping to remove their state of Utah from the ideology of the deep south on the subject of civil rights. Let them stay in their Church, for a new one would in time become just as corrupt; let them have the courage of Joseph Smith and Brigham Young in searching for truth and in living it against many odds. They have the heritage of good bodies from their Word of Wisdom; let them be a leaven instead of an indigestible lump in the body politic.

ACKNOWLEDGMENTS

1A. From page 87 of *Autobiography of Andrew White*, N. Y. 1907.

1. From page 39 of *Brigham Young*, by M. P. Werner, Marcourt, Brace Co., N. Y. 1925.

2. From page 94 of *Brigham Young*, by M. P. Werner, Marcourt, Brace Co., N. Y. 1925.

3. From page 12 of *Kingdom of the Saints*, by Roy B. West, Jr., Viking Press, N. Y. 1957.

4. From page 153, Werner.

4A. From page 353 of *Joseph Smith*, by John A. Widtsoe, Deseret News Press, Salt Lake City 1951.

5. From page 63, Werner.

6. From page 100, Widtsoe.

7. From *Isn't One Wife Enough*, by Kimball Young, Henry Holt Co., N. Y. 1954. Direct quotations not allowed.

8. From page 404 of *No Man Knows My History*, by Fawn M. Brodie, Knopf, N. Y. 1946.

9. 10. From page 47, Werner.

11, 12, 13, 14, 15, 16. From pages 155, 156, 157, 159, 165, 169, 171, Widtsoe.

17. From page 84 Werner.

17A. From page 100 Brodie.

18. From page xx, West.

19. From pages 83, Vol. I, *Journal of Discourses* and Vol. 2, pages 186, 311, 322.

20. From page 2 of *Life Story of Brigham Young*, by Susa Young Gates and Leah D. Widstoe, Macmillan Co., N. Y. 1930.

21. From page 8, Werner.

22. From page 73, Gates and Widtsoe.

23. From page 23, Werner.

24. From page 279, Werner.

25. From page 220, 227, Vol. 15, *Journal of Discourses.*

26. From page 213, West.

27. From pages 261, 329, 318, 338, Young and Gates.

28. From page 462, Werner.

29. From page 278, West.

30. From pages 307, 323, Gates and Widtsoe.

31. From page 390 of *Desert Saints*, by Nels Anderson, U. of Chicago 1942. Special permission of the author.

32. From page 265, Werner.

33. From pages 16, 19, 48, 72 of *One Who Was Valiant*, by Clarissa Spencer and Mabel Hamer. Published by the Caxton Printers, Ltd., Caldwell, Idaho. Used by special permission of the copyright owners.

34. From page 578 of *The Story of the Mormons*, by Wm. A. Linn, Macmillan Co., N. Y. 1902.

35. From page 195, West.

36. From page 220, West.

37. From page 257, West.

38. From page 91 of *The Great Basin Kingdom*, by Leonard J. Arrington. This and following qoutations used by special permission of Harvard University Press. Book printed in 1958.
39. From page 190, Gates and Widtsoe.
40. From page 98, Temple Lot Case court record in Missouri.
41. From page 296 of Vol. 5, *History of the Church*, by Joseph Smith.
42. From pages 208, 209 of *Mountain Meadows Massacre*, by Juanita Brooks. This and following quotation quoted by special permission of The U. of Oklahoma Press, Norman, Oklahoma. Book printed in 1962.
43. From page 223, Brooks.
44. From pages 94, 146, 147, Anderson.
45. From Deseret News, November 1, 1855.
46. From page 504, Arrimgton.
47. From page 114, Historical Record.
48. From letter of Benjamin F. Johnson to George S. Gibbs, noted from page 153 of a mimeographed book entitled *Mormonism*, by Jerald Tanner, 566 Center St., Salt Lake City 16, Utah, 1963. Price $3.00.
49. From page 149, Werner.
50. From page 355, Werner.
51. From page 56, Werner.
52. From page ix, Werner.
53. From page 33 of *The Family Kingdom*, by Samuel Woolley Taylor, Mc Graw Hill, N. Y. 1951.
54. From pages 274, 279, Taylor.
55. From page 251, Taylor.
56. From page 262, Taylor.
57. From page after page 262, Taylor.
58. From page 19 of *I Have Six Wives*, by Samuel Woolley Taylor, G reenberg, N. Y. 1956.
59. From page 20, Taylor in above book.
60. From page 150, Taylor in above book.
61. From page 271, Taylor in above book.
62. From page 22 of *Brigham Young and His Wives*. Quotations reprinted by special permission of the author, Prof. John J. Stewart, and Mercury Publishing Co., Salt Lake City. Book printed in 1962.
63. From page 167, Taylor in above book.
64. From page 73, Stewart.
65. From page 47, Stewart.
66. Rrom page 577 of *L.D.S. Biographical Encyclopedia*, edited by Andrew Jensen, Assistant Church Historian.
67. From page 7, 2nd section of *Mormonism and the Negro*, Wm. E. Barrett, Vice President of Brigham Young University.
68. From page 15, 2nd section, by Barrett.
69. From page 47, Stewart in 1st section above book.
70. From page 171, Tanner.
71. From page 166 of Vol. 2, *Journal of Oliver B. Huntington*, typed copy at the Utah Historical Society, quoted on page 188, Tanner.
72. Reprinted from a poem by Robert P. Tristam Coffin, by special permission of Macmillan Co., N. Y. City.

73. From page 133 by V. F. Calverton from *Where Angels Fear To Tread.* Bobbs Merrill, N. Y. 1941.
74. From page 9 by William Mulder and A. Russell Mortensen in *Among the Mormons*, Knopf, N. Y. 1958.
75. From page 185 of *The Mormons*, by Prof. Thomas F. O'Dea, U. of Chicago Press, 1957.
76. From page 386, Arrington.
76A. From page 409, Arrington.
77. From page 40 of *The Gentile Comes to Utah*, by Fr. Robert J. Dwyer. Special permission for quotation by Catholic University of America, Washington, D.C. The book was printed in 1941.
78. From pages 345, 346, West.
79. From page 361, West.
80. From page 31, Werner.
81. From page 60, Werner.
82. From page 64, Werner.
83. From pages 230, 231, O'Dea.
84. From page 262, O'Dea.

The Church of Christ, Temple Lot, also called the Hendrickites, composed of 12 churches and 3,000 members in the vicinity of Independence, Mo. contrived to buy the two and three-fourths acres which Joseph Smith dedicated as the place for a temple in Zion. All Mormons would like to have this lot. The poor who own it won't sell it to the prosperous Utah Mormons, yet they can't build anything themselves on it. The *Bickertonites* have 45 churches and 2,000 members and have published the *Book of Mormon* in Italian. They edit a paper called *Gospel News*. Bickerton was baptized by Sydney Rigdon in 1845. The followers of James J. Strang, who was once King of Beaver Island in Wisconsin, number about 250 with 6 churches. Their high priest lives in Artesia, N. M. There are also 100 followers in Burlington, Wis. of original Strang group.

BIBLIOGRAPHY

Brigham Young, by M. R. Werner, Harcourt, Brace Co., N. Y. City 1925.

Diaries of John D. Lee - 1846-1876, Edited and annotated by Robert G. Cleland and Juanita Brooks, Huntington Library, San Marino, Calif. 1955.

John D. Lee, Pioneer Builder, Scapegoat, by Juanita Broks, Arthur H. Clark Co., Glendale, Calif. 1962.

The Mountain Meadows Massacre, by Juanita Brooks, U. of Oklahoma Press, Norman Oklahoma 1962.

No Man Knows My History, by Fawn Brodie, Knopf, N. Y. City 1946.

The Mormons, by Prof. Thomas F. O'Dea, U. of Chicago Press, 1957.

Joseph Smith, by John A. Widtsoe, Deseret News Press, Salt Lake City 1951.

Arizona Pioneer Mormon, David King Udall, by Pearl Udall Nelson, Arizona Silhouettes, Tucson, Arizona 1959.

One Who Was Valiant, by Clarissa Young Spencer and Mabel Harmer, Caxton Printers, Caldwell, Idaho 1940.

Kingdom of the Saints, by Roy B. West, Jr., Viking Press, N. Y. City 1957.

Under the Prophet in Utah, by Frank J. Cannon and Harvey J. O'Higgins, C. M. Clark Pub. Co., Boston, Mass. 1911.

The Everlasting Fire, by Jonreed Lauritzen, Doubleday Co., N. Y. 1962.

The Gentile Comes to Utah, by Fr. Robert J. Dwyer, Catholic University of America, Washington, D.C. 1941.

Joseph Smith, by John Henry Evans, Deseret News Press, Salt Lake City 1946.

The Great Basin Kingdom, by Leonard J. Arrington, Harvard University Press 1958.

Isn't One Wife Enough? by Kimball Young, Henry Holt Co., N. Y. 1954

The Family Kingdom, by Samuel Woolley Taylor, McGraw Hill Co., N. Y. 1951.

I Have Six Wives, by Samuel Woolley Taylor, Greenberg, N. Y. 1956.

Where Angels Fear To Tread, by V. F. Calverton, Bobbs Merrill Co., N. Y. 1941.

Among the Mormons, by Wm. Mulder and A. Russell Mortensen, Knopf, N. Y. 1958.

Deseret Saints, by Nels Anderson, U. of Chicago Press, 1942.

The Story of the Mormons, by Wm. Alexander Linn, Macmillan Co., N.Y. 1902.

Joseph Smith and His Mormon Empire, by Harry M. Beardsley, Houghton Mifflin Co., Boston 1931.

Life Story of Brigham Young, by Susa Young Gates and Leah D. Widtsoe, Macmillan, 1930.

Grave of Five Haymarket anarchist martyrs,
hung Nov. 11, 1887. Waldheim cemetary, Chicago

EPILOGUE

The following excerpts from Dostoevsky's *Grand Inquisitor* seem to me timely today as when they were written many years ago. The underscored sentences are in part my emphasis. I am a Catholic who remains in the Church but criticizes it.

He came down to the hot pavements of the southern town in which on the day before almost a hundred heretics had, ad majorem Dei gloriam, been burned by the cardinal, the Grand Inquisitor, in a magnificent *auto de fe,* in the presence of the king, the court, the knights, the cardinals, the most charming ladies of the court, and the whole population of Seville.

He came softly, unobserved, and yet, strange to say, every one recognized Him . . . The crowd weeps and kisses the ground under His feet. He stops at the steps of the Seville cathedral at the moment when the weeping mourners are bringing in a little open white coffin. In it lies a child of seven, the only daughter of a prominent citizen. The dead child lies hidden in flowers. 'He will raise your child,' the crowd shouts to the weeping mother. The Priest, coming to meet the coffin, looks perplexed and frowns, but the mother of the dead child throws herself at His feet with a wail, If it is Thou, raise my child! she cries, holding out her hands to Him. The procession halts, the coffin is laid on the steps at his feet. He looks with compassion, and His lips once more softly pronounce, 'Maiden, arise! 'And the maiden arises...

There are cries, sobs, confusion among the people, and at that moment the cardinal himself, the *Grand Inquisitor,* passes by the cathedral. He is an old man, almost 90, tall and erect, with a withered face and sunken eyes, in which there is still a gleam of light. He is not dressed in his gorgeous cardinal's robes, as he was the day before, when he was burning the enemies of the Roman Church—at the moment he was wearing his coarse, old, monk's cassock. At a distance behind him come his gloomy assistants and slaves and the 'holy guard.' He stops at the sight of the crowd and watches it from a distance. He sees everything; he sees them set the coffin down at His feet, sees the child rise up, and his face darkens. He knits his thick gray brows and his eyes gleam with sinister fire. He holds out his finger and bids the guards take him. And such is his power, so completely are the people cowed into submission and trembling obedience to him, that the crowd immediately makes way for the guards, and in the midst of death like silence they lay hands on Him and lead Him away. The crowd instantly bows down to earth, like one man, before the old inquisitor. He blesses the people in silence and passes on.

The guards lead their prisoner to the close, gloomy vaulted prison in the ancient palace of the Holy Inquisition and shut Him in it . . . The Grand Inquisitor himself comes in with a light in his hand . . . 'Is it Thou? Thou? . . . I know too well what Thou woulds't say . . . Why then are Thou come to hinder us? For Thou hast come to hinder us, and Thou knowest that. *Tomorrow I shall condemn Thee and burn Thee at the stake as the worst of heretics. And the very people who today have kissed Thy feet, tomorrow at the faintest sign from me will rush to heap up the embers of Thy fire . . .*

The old man has told Him he hasn't any right to add anything to what He has said of old. One may say it is the most fundamental feature of Roman Catholicism . . . "All has been given by Thee to the Pope,' they say, 'and all, therefore, is still in the Pope's hands, and there is no need for Thee to come now at all. Thou must not meddle for the time, at least.' . . . Thou hast given us the right to bind and unbind, and now, of course, Thou canst not think of taking it away.

Christ's temptations after fasting 40 days— . . . But seest Thou these stones in this parched and barren wilderness? Turn them into bread, and mankind will run after Thee like a flock of sheep, grateful and obedient, though forever trembling lest Thou withdraw Thy hand and deny them Thy bread. But Thou wouldst not deprive men of freedom and didst reject the offer, thinking, what is that freedom worth, if obedience is bought by bread? . . .

And we alone shall feed them in Thy name, declaring falsely that it is in Thy name. Oh, never, never can they feed themselves without us . . . Thou didst promise them the bread of Heaven, but, I repeat again, can it compare with earthly bread in the eyes of the weak, ever sinful and ignoble race of man? And for the sake of the bread of Heaven thousands and tens of thousands shall follow Thee, what is to become of the millions and tens of thousands of millions of creatures who will not have the strength to forego the earthly bread for the sake of heavenly . . . But we shall tell them that we are

Thy servants and rule them in Thy name. We shall deceive them again, for we will not let Thee come to us again. That deception will be our suffering, for we shall be forced to lie . . . .

If Thou wouldst have given them bread they would have worshipped Thou. . .Thou wouldst have satisfied the universal and everlasting craving of humanity — to find some one to worship . . . these pitiful creatures . . . what is essential is that all may be *together* in it. This craving for *community* of worship is the chief misery of every man individually and of all humanity from the beginning of time. For the sake of common worship they've slain each other with the sword. They have set up gods and challenged one another, 'Put away your gods and come and worship ours, or we shall kill you and your gods.''

There are three powers, three powers alone, able to conquer and hold captive the conscience of these impotent rebels for their happiness — *those forces are miracle, mystery and authority.* Thou hast rejected all three and hast set the example for doing so.

Second Temptation of Christ — Cast Thyself down from the pinnacle of the Temple. And couldst Thou believe for one moment that men, too, could face such a temptation? Is the nature of men such, that they can reject miracle, and at the great moments of their lives, the moments of their deepest, most agonizing spiritual difficulties, cling only to the free verdict of the heart? . . . Thou dids't not come down from the cross . . . for again, Thou woulds't not enslave man by a miracle. Thou didst crave for free love and not the base raptures of the slave before the might that has overawed him forever. But Thou didst think too highly of men therein, for they are slaves, of course, though rebellious by nature. . . .

Canst Thou have simply come to the elect and for the elect? . . . *We have corrected Thy work and have founded it upon miracle, mystery and authority.* And men rejoiced that they were again led like sheep . . . .

Be angry. I don't want Thy love, for I love Thee not . . . Listen, then. We are not working with Thee, but with *him* — that is our mystery. It's long — eight centuries — since we have been on *his* side and not Thine . . . We took from him Rome and the sword of Caesar, and proclaimed ourselves sole rulers of the earth . . . we shall triumph and shall be Caesars, and then we shall plan the universal happiness of man. But Thou mightest have taken even then the sword of Caesar. Why didst Thou reject that last gift? Hadst Thou accepted that last counsel of the mighty spirit, Thou wouldst have accomplished all that man seeks on earth — that is, some one to worship, some one to keep his conscience, and some means of uniting all in one unanimous and harmonius ant-heap . . . Had Thou taken the world and Caesar's purple, Thou wouldst have founded the universal state and have given universal peace . . . *We have taken the sword of Caesar, and in taking it, of course, have rejected Thee and followed him* . . . Thou art proud of Thine elect, but hast only the elect, while we give rest to all . . . how many of those elect . . . have grown weary waiting for Thee . . . some of them, the fierce and rebellious, will destroy themselves, others, rebellious but weak, will destroy one another, while the rest, weak and unhappy, will crawl fawning to our feet and whine to us, "Yes, you were right, you alone possess His mystery, and we come back to you, save us from ourselves."

Oh, we shall allow them even sin, they are weak and helpless, and they will love us like children because we allow them to sin. We shall tell them that every sin shall be expiated, if it is done with our permission, that we allow them to sin because we love them, and the punishment for these sins we take upon ourselves . . . and all will be happy, all the millions of creatures except the 100,000 who rule over them. For only we, we who guard the mystery, shall be unhappy . . . the curse of the knowledge of good and evil. Peacefully they will die, peacefully they will expire in Thy name, and beyond the grave they will find nothing but death. But we shall keep the secret, and for their happiness we shall allure them with the reward of heaven and eternity . . . And we who have taken their sins upon us for their happiness will stand up before The and say: 'Judge us if Thou canst and darest.' Know that I fear Thee not. Know that I too have been in the wilderness. I too have lived on roots and locusts, I too prized the freedom with which Thou hast blessed men, and I too was striving to stand among Thy elect, among the strong and powerful, thirsting "to make up the number." But I awakened and would not serve madness. I turned back and *joined the ranks of those who have corrected Thy work.* I left the proud and went back to the humble, for the happiness of the humble. Tomorrow *Thou shalt see that obedient flock who at a sign from me will hasten to heap up the hot cinders about the pile on which I shall burn Thee for coming to hinder us. For if anyone has ever deserved our fires, it is Thou. Tomorrow I shall burn Thee. Dixit.*

The Grand Inquisitor does not believe in God but as he says has long worshiped the devil, so he suffers as must those who "accept lying and deception, and lead men consciously to death and destruction, and yet deceive them all the way so that they may not notice where they are being led, that the poor blind creatures may at least on the way think themselves happy."

He saw that the Prisoner had listened intently all the time, looking gently in his face and evidently not wishing to reply. The old man longed for Him to say something, however bitter and terrible. *But He suddenly approached the old man in silence and softly kissed him on the bloodless aged lips.* That was all his answer. The old man shuddered. His lips moved. He went to the door, opened it, and said to Him: "Go, and come no more . . . come not at all, never, never!" And he let Him out into the dark alleys of the town. The Prisoner went away. "And the old man?" "The kiss glows in his heart, but the old man adheres to his idea."

All Christian churches deny Christ, and the worst is the Catholic. Most church leaders have been so brainwashed that they do not know this, so they are not to be blamed when they kill or silence what they call heresy, for they do not know any better. They are not to be feared or obeyed though by *real* Christians when they follow the Grand Inquisitor and his master the devil to found the "universal state and universal peace" based on executions, excommunications, exploitation and war, we Christian anarchists who know better will not follow them. We shall continue to insist upon the primacy of the individual conscience; upon a reliance on the Sermon on the Mount rather than ecclesiastical pomp and power. We know that we are following Him, rather than denying Him in His name. Neither should we who know all this punish folks like the Grand Inquisitor, for Christ did not punish him, even when he was going to burn Him, as they did St. Joan of Arc later, but returned good for evil and kissed him.

CHAPTER 22

I LEAVE THE CATHOLIC CHURCH

SALT LAKE CITY, UTAH

1965 to 1968

My second wife: Artist and Painter, Joan Thomas

Some friends say I never was a Catholic. Whether I left the Church or the Church left me depends upon how you look at the question. Now after 15 years in the Catholic Church I find that any increase in spiritual emphasis that I have gained has been in spite of and not because of attendance at Mass and taking Communion. So I do not think it worthwhile to call myself a Catholic. *In solitary in 1918-19 I made my real conversion. This was the important event of my life.* All since then, as may be said, is only on the surface.

This book being the story of my life it would not be worthwhile writing it if I remained in the same groove into which I was born. Great changes have been made in the world, and to meet those changes I have had to revalue what is important to me. These changes have not been to accommodate myself to the current, but as always to fight upstream against the current.

In Chapter Twelve of this book entitled, *I Become A Catholic,* I discuss in detail how this came about. I have often said that a person living in India would naturally be attracted by Gandhi. In this country the person with the most integrity as a pacifist and anarchist, as well as a Christian, is Dorothy Day. If she had been a Quaker or a Mormon and edited a *Quaker Worker* or a *Mormon Worker* I would have been attracted to those religions. On page 263 I quote Dorothy as saying that I should not become a Catholic because I loved her and the CW. The reasons why I became a Catholic and was quickly baptized in 1952 (too quickly I think all concerned would now agree), are still legitimate, taking my development at that time. I got along for 33 years as a Christian Anarchist without belonging to any church.

God. I believe in everything I said on this subject in 1953, but I would add on the subject of the Devil that I do not think he is a person but is only the name for that which is the opposite of good. *Hell* might be called what the Christians have made of this earth, in Christ's name. If there is such a place, as some priests say, you can't prove there is anyone in it but the Devil. So I am not afraid of going to a place which I do not believe exists. *Purgatory* is logical, but just how it works I will find out when I die. I am not worrying about it.

474

The Bible. I believe on this subject the same as I did in 1953. There may be some words from God in it, but most of it is folklore. Outside of what Christ said on divorce, and the usual interpretation of "give to him that asked of thee," I believe in all that Christ said. I think that He meant that we should not be selfish. I would not give a bum money to spend on booze but I do give the bum a place to sleep and something to eat in my Joe Hill House. I do not agree with the old Jewish idea of a divorced person not allowed to be remarried. (The Greek Orthodox Church allows two re-marriages, but not three.) I think that a person can make a mistake on every other decision in life, so why cannot they make a mistake in being married? Former Mayor O'Dwyer of New York City, Jackie's sister, Henry Luce, and the President of Peru were allowed to be married after being divorced. The 16 rules of annulment of marriage by the Catholic Church seem to me not to be based upon the saying of Christ, but upon pull and expediency. I asked the Chancery office to annul my common-law marriage, and they wouldn't think of it.

The Early Christians. I agree with what I wrote on this subject in 1953, although I see little hope of the Catholic or any other church in trying to live like the early Christians.

Paul and the Churches. I believe on this subject what I said in 1955, that Paul spoiled the message of Christ.

Prayer. There can be spiritual power when spiritual people recite the Rosary, as I wrote in 1953, but today, for me there is no meaning in praying to Mary or the saints, but only to Christ and God. I revere St. Francis, Joan de Arc and Bernadette of Lourdes and get lessons and inspiration from them, but I do not believe in the legend of Fatima or of Guadalupe. Each person can choose their own saints.

The Catholic Church. A Christian Anarchist has no business belonging to such a reactionary organization. I do not believe in original sin, indulgences, the infallibility of the Pope, or obedience to any church official if it is against my conscience. I am not interested in earning "merit" or in being saved by priestly incantation. Of course I do not believe in confessing to a priest. Many Catholics never can forgive themselves because of the sense of fear and guilt taught them, and they go to priests again and again in a useless round. I believe in the virgin birth of Christ and in personal immortality; in all of Christ's miracles and in the resurrection. That we can be "saved" from sin by following Him, whether we belong to any church or not. I believe in God the Father and that the *real* members of any church are those who follow Christ, and also those outside of any church. I consider myself a member of this *real* church along with St. Joan de Arc, who was burned as a heretic by the Catholic Church. I made a will some years ago in which I desired to be cremated and my ashes put on the graves of the Haymarket anarchists in Waldheim cemetary in Chicago. Later the Catholic Church allowed cremation.

Communion. The supposed effect of this sacrament has seldom changed Catholics into desiring to follow Christ, or there would not be this wholesale denying of Christ daily.

Freedom, exists as a theory in the Catholic Church. Let priests and nuns picket for strikers and Negroes and supposedly liberal Bishops like Bishop Lucey of San Antonio are just as quick to punish them as Cardinal McIntyre is in Los Angeles. Here in Salt Lake City I know priests who read the *Catholic Worker* and the liberal *National Catholic Reporter* and who really know better than to support war and the conservative system of society around them, but the fear they have makes them subservient to their conservative Bishop.

Love is a word used without meaning by the clergy. From the Pope down to the layman the emphasis upon pomp and wealth and prosperity while the world starves and wars go on is a denial of Christ.

Heresy is a word that has no meaning to me now, for I renounce the whole system of Catholic or other theology which is based upon the fear of hell and the hope of getting into heaven by all sorts of dubious bargains.

Reincarnation. I still think that this idea is the most logical, but really there is no answer to the problem of evil. If I don't believe in reincarnation and it is true I'll be reincarnated whether I believe in it or not. If it isn't true, believing in it will not make it true. It is how you live that counts.

There are others "not of the fold" who remain followers of Christ. I choose to be among them. There is no reason for joining any other church for they all support exploitation, and mostly they support war. And I sure don't want any Ammonites following me around.

On page 334 I mention that I was asked if I was an anarchist or a Catholic first. I said that I was first a Catholic, and being an anarchist came sixth. Now I would rephrase my emphasis as follows:

1. To be an anarchist-pacifist and oppose as much as I can all war and violence, and the state which lives by these methods.
2. This also means to be a Christian, a follower of Christ. Outside any church.
3. To seek to understand and to love your enemy.
4. Not to expect to make the world see this now, but to continue my one-man-revolution, no matter what the result is to me personally.
5. To help the poor, especially the transients, for this is where the state leaves off and the anarchist begins.
6. Not to smoke, drink, eat meat, or take medicine, and to approximate the life of the poor among whom I live.
7. As stated in the following paragraph I recently married out of the Church, so in addition my personal emphasis is:
   a. To make my wife, Joan, happy, and help her and myself to grow in every way.
   b. To continue to be awake enough to oppose war and exploitation in this crazy world; not to chicken out.
   c. To search for more truth as to what is best for myself and the world.

* * *

Two and a half years ago, soon after this book was published, I married a young lady, Joan Thomas, to whom I especially dedicated this book. The priests in Salt Lake City who knew about it forbad us to ever take communion. Although other priests over the country who knew the circumstances, said that the Church would change its mind some day on divorced persons remarrying, and offered to give us communion. As an anarchist I know it was not logical to get a divorce and be married by a justice of the peace in Nevada. As I was running the Joe Hill House I did not find it possible to go to Idaho, the only state in the west where Common-law is legal. If I was a polygamous I would not mind doing time for it, but I had no desire to interrupt the Joe Hill House by doing time for bigamy or cohabitation. The latter is a law made here to catch the polygamous. I have found Joan to be a very courageous woman, and the best, as far as character is concerned, of anyone I have met. Also, in all fairness to her I should add that she does not agree with me in all things, although she is a pacifist and an anarchist. She uses both these terms non-politically and on the spiritual plane which commences with St. John of the Cross's, "the just man is above the law." We both consider it a mark of genuine love that two persons with such divergent views are able to get along so well. She promised in so far as our marriage is concerned not to be wife as such, but to be my best friend as she holds friendship to be far more important than marriage. She is a believing Catholic and has not left the Church. She does not believe that our marriage is valid, but believes our friendship is.

* * *

I value the friendship of many priests, nuns and laymen in the CW movement, and others whom I have met in my travels, and I list Dorothy Day among the fifteen great people in American history. Although her statement in the CW that she would obey Cardinal Spellman if he told her to keep quiet on the war is not a part of her *real* philosophy, but just a pious exclamation, uttered, I think, because most liberal Catholics were then condemning him because Fr. Berrigan had been sent to South America for his opposition to the war. Dorothy always is for the underdog. I doubt if she would obey Spellman if it came to a show down.

We have all helped each other. And of course I regret to have to cause them pain in leaving the Church. I have attended Mass here in Salt Lake City daily for years. With very few exceptions I have never met a Catholic here who had any conception of the social message of Christ. They are not to be blamed for their Bishop never speaks on these problems, and is only in print to praise something military or commercial, always in pious terms. If I had lived in a community like Milwaukee where Bishop Cousins allows Fr. Groppi and priests and nuns to picket against closed housing, or if I lived in Oklahoma City where Bishop Reed allows the open parish which meets informally in homes I might possibly have tried a little longer to remain in the Church. But here all that is mentioned is The Legion of Mary, Boy Scouts, Fatima, bingo parties, and attacks on Communism and birth control, and of course always praise of the military.

While my becoming a Christian, a pacifist and an anarchist in prison in 1918-19 was gradual and without any outside influence, except the Bible and Tolstoy, my becoming a Catholic took fifteen years of association with the Catholic Worker and was a sort of osmosis, although the direct cause as given on pages 264, 265, 266 was a culmination of this CW atmosphere. The fifteen years from 1952 to 1967 allowed me to speak in scores of seminaries and hundreds of Catholic churches and schools and to meet the most liberal Catholics. I met French Worker priests and looked forward with hope to the efforts of Pope John XXIII and Pope Paul VI. I finally had to realize that only surface changes would ever come to the Vatican or the Pentagon, for they are built upon the basis of unlimited power and they are afraid of truth, not realizing as someone has said that, "truth has nothing to fear from truth." They both will move only so far as they are pushed. When an especially obnoxious prelate dies there is always one trained by him to take his place.

In the past 49 years I have changed my mind regarding religion three times and each time many of my friends decried these changes. I have tried life in the largest church and found it wanting. I can still sign myself, "In Christ the Rebel" without belonging to any church. I am still a rebel in my 75th year, against war, exploitation, capital punishment, and race hatred. I still look forward to the day when there will be more Christian Anarchists. I am not discouraged to be nearly alone in my one-man-revolution. Young folks will come along, perhaps some whom I have helped awaken, and they may do much better than I have done.

Readers of my book in this country and in other countries of course are familiar with the conservatism of the Catholic Church and it is no news to them that in the Mormon state of Utah that church should run true to form. During the six years that I have been here I have written to the Bishop mildly at first, and then with more spirit, thinking that at least when the two Catholics, Garcia and Rivenburg, were to be executed he might say something. He wrote a short note saying he was opposed to my activities. I have twice been asked to speak to Catholic audiences here and the meetings have been cancelled. As a matter of record and as a challenge to those Catholics who continue to obey a Bishop who continually refuses to accept the social teachings of Christ, I include the last letter that I sent to him dated August 29, 1967.

Dear Bishop Federal:

I am puzzled about how to reach your conscience. In the past I have first asked you gently to take a stand against the death penalty involving two Catholics. When you paid no attention I got a little rough in order to wake you up, but you still hide away from expressing yourself on social problems. The Boy Scouts and the Salt Lake Palace receive your attention, but the war in Viet Nam against which half a dozen Bishops have expressed themselves does not stir you. When I led 150 people on April 15 asking why you did not follow the lead for peace given by Pope Paul, the only answer was a sermon the next day giving the Bishops' approval of the war. You do not have a warmonger over you like Bishop Sheen has in Cardinal Spellman, yet he was not afraid.

President McKay and Joseph Fielding Smith are in their 90's and they may not change in their very conservative views of their time. It seems that for the Catholics in Utah you have determined to stand 100 years behind the times and allow no change in your remaining term, which should be longer than that of McKay and Smith. Why should any liberal Mormon convert to such a Catholic Church as you present in this state? As I have asked before, what does it take to wake you up? I doubt if Joseph Smith or Moroni came back they would be able to change the Mormon Apostles, I also doubt if Christ came you would know it, for He would likely be on the other side of the tracks and be dressed poorly, and if He came to the Cathedral He would be ejected as a bum. He has said to forgive and to love. He would likely overturn the bingo tables in your churches. By your silence you emphasize gambling, the worship of money, and the execution of Poulsen, and the war in Viet Nam.

I respect the testimony of Msgr. Moreton, who was formerly chaplain of the state prison. He always opposed capital punishment. But when I attended hearings of the Board of Pardons in Poulsen's case the Catholic Chaplain sat there cowardly and said not a word. Surely he knew better. Why are priests under your jurisdiction afraid to speak up? The Protestant Chaplain and the head of the Council of Churches, a Mormon professor, and a Jew, and the Episcopal Dean spoke for clemency. I repeat, why are Catholic priests afraid or not interested?

A Professor at the U sent out a questionnaire on capital punishment to 500 people. He was surprised to find many Catholics against it. He asked if any member of the legislature would pull the trigger to execute a prisoner. None of them would. You and they elect others to do it for you. Peter and all of the Apostles said to obey God rather than man. Why do you deny God and obey man?

Whenever we are picketing downtown against capital punishment and war we will come up to the Cathedral for a minute in protest against your docility.

Many people have come from out of town and phoned your office asking where the Joe Hill House of Hospitality for Transients is located, and have not been told. We are at 3462 S. 4. W. (2 blocks south of the Vitro smokestack.) Poulsen's 7th execution date is set for Tuesday, September 5.

Sincerely in Christ
Ammon Hennacy

A couple of years ago a young man interviewed me. He was writing a book about people of the right and of the left. This week I received his book, *The Farther Shores of Politics,* by George Thayer, Simon and Schuster. In his chapter on The Peace Movement he discusses my anarchist and vegetarian ideas especially and says that I have "actually renounced his Catholicism."

CHAPTER 23

THE PRICE
OF COURAGE

January, 1970

i

I begin this final chapter with an apology. First although I love psychology, I am not a psychologist, and fascinated as I am by theology, I am no theologian. There are going to be countless errors in what follows, although I am going to try to be as objective and honest as I can. Next, although I am a writer, I consider myself a novelist, not a biographer—my mind does not work in the form of the biography, although in this instance, it's going to have to attempt this. Readers may wonder why I don't seek help with the writing of this final chapter, but it is because this is something I feel, for all my inadequacies, I must do alone.

Now I must state—quite blatantly—that according to the law of the Church, Ammon's and my friendship was a mortally sinful relationship, and that every time we took Communion together we were guilty of the Flesh and Blood of Christ. But I didn't believe we were guilty (or obviously I wouldn't have had us go up to the Communion rail). At this moment I don't believe we were guilty. Confession would not comfort me in the least, anymore than I feel Am needed the Sacrament of the Sick to get to Heaven (I belive God possibly wanted him signed with this Sacrament to mark him as a Catholic, however, which may be why Am didn't die immediately on the picket line). Here is where the supreme wisdom of the Church comes in: A man is bound in duty to follow (subjectively) his conscience, even if (objectively) that conscience is wrong and he not know it. For myself, I guess—if my conscience is wrong—I still don't know it.

Also, I *believe* that belief (or Faith) is *not* knowledge. I've believed that all my life (belief may very well be knowledge) and this is theologically incorrect. "Correct" theology would say Faith is knowledge based on reason, or else Faith is a higher form of knowledge. And yet for an example—half the world does believe in reincarnation which is incompatable with Christian dogma (I don't believe in reincarnation, but Ammon definitely did; if reincarnation is the truth, I believe Am is done reincarnating), but I'm not so sure we can throw the burden of proof on those who do believe in reincarnation. Why does half the world believe in it? Why couldn't it be true? I'm not going into this in the interests of reincarnation, but simply to show I don't feel reincarnation can so easily be thrown out the window by faith based on reason, and calling itself knowledge. If belief were knowledge, would we need to distinguish so between the two words? We would not need to always say 'I believe in God the Father Almighty.' We could say sometimes 'I know God the Father Almighty,' a presumption no one on this earth would dare. I remain steadfast to my 'Belief is not Knowledge' position, in spite of how, according to Catholic theology (and possibly reason) this is not correct, and also how I may be seemingly throwing out the operation of Grace. But it seems to me that with the latter it could be argued that Mormons are given Grace to see the Mormon religion, Buddhists the Buddhist, etc.

Finally, about my use of the statement, 'The just man is above the law.' That, too, is pretty tricky water theologically. We not only have to have the law, we have the law (natural laws, for example). Or as Am would say, if we don't obey traffic lights, we might easily have a bad accident. There are some laws one is better off obeying. But if it is the law that we go to war and kill our brothers, and we feel we must not, then the supremacy of the individual conscience reigns, which brings me full circle back to my second paragraph except for one further idea: If God can break his natural laws via miracles, it seems reasonable to me that He can rise above the laws of the Church when He so chooses (via what I believe is Mercy).

In all clear conscience then (which I admit may objectively be a 'wrong' conscience), I believe that Ammon's and my friendship was a thing destined by God, and yet I must continue to ask the readers' forgiveness for what is doubtless not much better than the mishmash I've always felt Am's 'theology' was. And forgive, too, the twistings, repetitions, all my many parentheses, and I suppose what in places are going to be paradoxical contradictions. Life is a Mystery. In truth, I *believe* I *know* nothing. I am almost as puzzled by everything this day, as I am when this friendship first began. Am used to say that he had never met anyone like me. Believe me, I had never met anyone like him.

ii

After a friendship of about ten years, seven of which we were very close, and five of the seven legally married, I am now put in what for me is the paradoxical position of having to write a concluding chapter to Ammon's autobiography. It is unbelievable to me that he is not here with me tonight in this house. Naively, I expected him to live as long as his mother, who died at ninety-three; he, himself, thought he would live as long as Tolstoy, who died at eighty-three. And yet uncannily, I feel his presence is near me as I write this. "Don't worry, Willow, things will work out for the best," is what he seems to be saying to me like he said so many times to me during our life together.

481

I first met him in June of 1960 in New York. I was twenty-five at the time, he was sixty-six. Like many Catholics who visit New York, I had gone to spend a day at the Catholic Worker establishment. Although I liked Ammon, he first struck me as a complete egomaniac, and after talking to him about five minutes, I wondered what in the world he was doing in the Catholic Church. He was so hostile, while his mentality, outlook, feeling, what you will, was just not Catholic. And yet from rereading the chapters in this autobiography where he deals with his joining the Church, I find that he did seem to have a Catholic sense of things—a Catholic 'sense' which possibly he lost or had to lose because of me, or else this 'Catholicism' of his, this Catholic faith, was just not very deep that it could so easily be lost, and he so easily revert back to his earlier position of the nonchurch Christian. Certainly when one is as close to a person as I was to him, it is more than ever difficult to write objectively.

But it seems to me that Ammon absolutely could not think or reason. Apart from the great truth of the Pacificism of Christ, he had gotten the other great truth in his head—the supremacy of the individual conscience. But Am's 'theology' was a mishmash. I early gave up trying to straighten it out. I couldn't. I don't think anyone could. Paradoxically, I don't think God wanted him to think or reason, in order that Am might see with such blinding clarity the Truth that is above reason. And how he saw this higher Truth was so refreshing and so much fun. Even rereading his last chapter (22) in preparation for the writing of this, I had to burst out laughing. What he said—his wonderful letter to the bishop—is 'true,' unreasonably true. If Ammon could have reasoned, he could not have so beautifully and unreasonably seen and told the truth. And with such—yes—hilarity. (He and I have had so many hilarious fun-times, that now I think our brief years together were some kind of comic journey with God, in spite of how God told Blessed Angela of Foligno, "It was not to make you laugh that I have loved you.")

To me, Ammon was a cheerful thorn in the Crown of Christ. In spite of how we are put upon this earth to do God's will via suffering (a belief—it may not be the truth), I believe that comedy is the rock-bottom level of our existence. Not tragedy. We live forever, we do not die forever. And yes, Ammon was comedy (I think he had the joy of the saints). My favorite novel, since I read it for the first time in college where I majored in Spanish, has been *Don Quijote*. Ammon was Don Quijote, who is perhaps, for all the laughter, the most serious figure in literature. And the greatest. If we did not have laughter upon this earth, we would die from grief. Don Quijote keeps us from dying. Without Don Quijote, we could not bear to live upon this earth. Even now I can hear Am saying what he said so often, "Willow, you're lots of fun. I love you." Well, Am was lots of fun, too. And if he was Don Quijote, maybe I was some kind of Sancho Panza pricking the balloon of all the praise and glory heaped upon him which made men see him as a myth, a legend, and not as a man. (Honor belongs to God, not men.)

One of our biggest jokes was how I was losing all his friends. I had a relatively 'poor' childhood, and am, I suppose, a master at outsnubbing the rich before the rich can outsnub me (like being invited to dinner and refusing to eat anything at the table and going into the kitchen and looking in the refrigerator for something to eat). Yes, I know, it isn't necessarily wealth that makes a person rich or poor, but the quality of the heart; certainly I should have acted with the charity with which Am acted; except I simply can't understand how people who own a lot of stuff can be poor in spirit. And these childish deviltries were perhaps done on a less comic level by a person who very early had to learn to survive in a harsh and bleak world. But Am laughed afterward as much about the stunts I pulled as I did (and I doubt if I really lost any friends for him, except the alms were getting less and less the longer we were together, until they had dwindled to almost nothing). But I can recall effortlessly his magnificent charity at houses of very rich people where I wouldn't take a bite and he cheerfully ate tortillas and beans that the rich people served him to prove that they were of the people. (When I was growing up, the best food was always served to guests.) But these are minor things and in truth, I think it was just that people considered Am so much family, took him so much for granted. He was never a guest, he was one of the family sitting down with them. And yet not really, or when I met him, he would not have been so lonely.

Regardless, I think everyone, including myself, took Am too much for granted, and that none of us realized that even his gallant heart could wear out. He should not have been doing all the tramping around he was doing this winter. And yet who can say? He and I always agreed that a person should be allowed complete freedom to follow his or her destiny, even if that destiny was death. He said a woman always made a man chicken out. That's what he liked about me, that I didn't try to make him chicken out. One of the first things I asked of him when we started becoming well-acquainted (he told me after this was when he really fell in love with me), was that if anyone ever attacked me physically, he was in no way to use violence to protect me—even if it meant my death. He said no one had ever said that to him before (I was testing the sincerity of his convictions, but I meant what I said), and he promised he wouldn't. If he hadn't promised, I would have dismissed him as a milksop and a coward like I've found every man I've ever met (except for my father and my grandfather). Even a small thing like dependency on cigarettes or coffee seems to me cowardly. And so perhaps this—my death in front of his eyes—could have happened. Also, we talked thus: If on a certain day we both knew that if he went out picketing that day, he would be shot down, he still must go. Either my death or his—either would have to be rather than that he should—yes—chicken out on God. What I am talking about here is the price of courage. The price of courage is death. Since I was about five, I have said no matter what the cost, even if I ended up dead from starvation, I would never cease to write. My writing is not important like the things Am lived and died for, but because of my attitude to my work (I believe to write is

God's will for me), I can understand his attitude—to his own life. Thus besides Courage, I am also talking here about how a person must do what he believes is God's will for him to do (pacifism would probably be considered God's will for Ammon), regardless of the cost to him or to those he loves.

Dorothy always said, Pay attention to what Ammon does, not what he says. This is true for anyone. One can have the greatest faith or reasoning ability in the world, and have not charity. Likewise, if one has charity, which I believe Am had to the degree of sainthood, it doesn't much matter what one believes or how one reasons. I think if one in clear conscience worshipped the Devil, and went around doing good, that good would pass muster with God. We are judged in the end only by our Charity.

Ammon and I corresponded with one another for about two years after that initial New York meeting. In June of 1962 my first husband left me (I consider that one of the greatest blessings in my life that my first husband, whom yes, I did care for, walked out on me,—otherwise, I would never have become close to Am). In August, I went to Salt Lake to picket and fast with Ammon, but I couldn't stand the picketing and the public world in which he lived, so I went home again, back to Minneapolis, but he and I continued to correspond. The following August (1963), I went back out again to Salt Lake, and this was when I began to realize that maybe he and I would not have to live such a public life and we began to talk (or he did—I was still doubtful) about making our friendship a more or less permanent one. I went back to Minneapolis for my car (I had come these first two times by bus) and returned in October. Very shortly, he started asking me to marry him. For some time, I said no, but finally on April 12, 1965, we got married in Elko, Nevada. Prior to that, on February 9th of that same year, we drove through Las Vegas on a speaking tour and said private vows in the church of St. Joan of Arc there.

Now is where the complications come in. By all Catholic laws, this was a mortally sinful relationship, especially for me, since I did not leave the Church as Ammon did—my dearest Ammon, who really never seemed to me to have any conception of what sin was all about, beginning from the first day I met him in 1960 in New York. I don't think he knew what it was to turn from God, and oddly enough, I could not feel that in my friendship with Ammon that I was turning from God either. Certainly in all these years, I never went to Mass without feeling I must also go up and take Communion (which I did); likewise, regardless of what Ammon said about his having 'left' the Church, I saw nothing wrong in his coming with me to Mass and Communion whenever he wanted to. I never dragged him or forced him to come (I couldn't have—no one could make Ammon budge one inch on anything he didn't want to do); if he didn't feel like coming with me, that was okay, too. But nearly always when I asked him if he'd like to come with me, he would come—willingly, happily, even if the priest did give a sermon which Am railed against afterward (usually we aimed for daily Masses to avoid the sermons). Personally, I didn't care whether or not he came. I wanted him to do as he wanted to do. I was happy when he came like I am happy he had the Sacrament of the Sick and a funeral Mass, but if he didn't come with me, or hadn't had the Sacrament of the Sick and the funeral Mass, I was not—or would not have been —unhappy or concerned in the least about his soul—so much *faith* do I have in his charity—and in God's mercy.

This is Ammon's autobiography, not mine. So I'm not going into the complicated subject of my own self, except to say that God made use of what I define as a manifestation of neurosis, to have me do all my life, it seems, but particularily from the time I was about seventeen (not just during my friendship with Ammon), what otherwise I would not have done. From the age of seventeen for sure, I feel I have been pushed, manipulated, by God, so that in no way could I lead an ordinary, conventional life. If I tried to keep to the ordinary, or the conventional (this is something apart from my devilish trickery such as outsnubbing the rich), it was as if God took over to put me through a hell in which I finally learned that if I didn't do what I believed God wanted me to do, even if what God wanted seemed objectively 'wrong,' the hell would take over and the hell was worse than all rights and all wrongs.

As I say, this is too complicated for a few paragraphs (I may not be correct either, but at this moment I believe I am), and I intend possibly in his biography to go into the subject more. What I'm actually driving at in this instance is something perhaps either very stupid or very shocking or presumptuous (and again, I may not be correct in this) —that though Ammon 'left' the Catholic Church, the Catholic Church, through me, did not leave him. Even I am somewhat shocked by what I do hope is not proud presumption or else just plain stupid female rationalization of possibly unconscious guilt, for most or all people would say that if he hadn't met me, he wouldn't have left the Church. But I don't think this is true. As he told me so many times, regardless of our marriage—and the longer we were together, the more hostile and vicious he became towards the established Church—in fact all established religion—sooner or later he would have left. I probably got him out sooner and here is where my own ability to reason comes in (at least I hope I am being *reasonable*). Even back in New York that first meeting in 1960 (as I have already stated), I wondered how a person who believed as he did, could call himself a Catholic. For even then, his thoughts were revolving towards the nonchurch Christian attitude of Chapter 22. To me, Ammon couldn't be a Catholic, if by being a Catholic meant believing in a certain dogma, creed, or religion. So far as truth went, I thought he should not call himself a Catholic, and yet now I am struck by the uncanny realization that God probably continued to call him a Catholic. And again—perhaps to call him through me. (This has absolutely nothing to do with me as a person. God will do with us as He will and use us as He will. God could have used any number of persons or methods to 'call Am' a Catholic. The ways of God are infinite.)

For myself, I have never considered leaving the Church. Part of my sticking with it, is my love of St. John of the Cross, although St. John of the Cross is not the Church and one cannot be a Catholic because of one saint. Obviously not. My rock-bottom faith rests on the Eucharist. I don't care what changes they make in the Church—about birth control, the celibacy of the priesthood, divorce laws, etc.—as long as the Eucharist remains, through God's grace, I remain. And yet once more on this subject—I would not swear that the Eucharist is the Flesh and Blood of Christ. I believe it is, but I can't feel that my belief or the belief based on the reasoning of wise men make it the truth (nor can I deny the obvious Grace poured out on all religions, not just the Catholic). All people can agree on what a hand or a leg is used for. But all the people who profess that their individual faiths are The Truth don't agree. I believe that the Church is the Truth, but I don't know that it is and I may be wrong.

As has been inferred already, Ammon and I did have a very happy life together. I think God—here again, acting as Mercy above His laws as He acted throughout all of Ammon's life; without question, for me Am is St. John of the Cross's just man who is above the law—finally took pity on Ammon's loneliness—so much the public man without one private friend—to finally give him a private friend. When I met him, Ammon, for all his host of friends, was incredibly lonely. That was one of the things he told me, that second summer before I went back by bus to Minneapolis to supposedly get my car, that he would consider it heaven if I stayed with him, because then he'd have someone to talk to. He got lonely sometimes. (Lonely—and someone to talk to! He who talked to so many!) In truth, I didn't plan to come back. But hell began and I came. I was to run back and forth a fair number of times, each time persuaded by him to return (he was the most persistent man I have ever met) and yes, pushed to him by God, so it seems to me, before I finally gave up and married him.

We had our bad times together, of course. But the best times were worth all the bad times. I would go so far as to say now that for myself, all these hells I have known in this life, hells stretching back into my earliest childhood long before the age of seventeen when the worst hells began, were all worth it, if they were the price I had to pay for this friendship with Ammon. And I think maybe there were the price. One cannot have Heaven without Hell. God does know what He is doing, even if we think He doesn't. No matter how much He is cutting away at one's already scarred heart, tearing away at the scars, as I feel is being done to me how through Ammon's death, I still believe that God knows what He is doing. "Though He slay me, yet will I trust Him."

January fifth, 1970, Ammon began picketing for Lance and Kelback, two convicted murderers. He always said he wanted to die on the picket line, but thought maybe someone would shoot him down (I was to carry on the next day if this happened). January eighth, on the way up the hill to picket the Capitol, he had a heart attack. Friends, not realizing what had happened (Am thought he was sick to his stomach), brought him home. I immediately called the doctor and drove Am to the hospital. Only the doctor and I knew about the heart attack then, for if Ammon could make it through three days, he would probably pull through, and I thought it best if I had to tell people the worst, to wait and see if the worst occurred. But actually, I was too heartsick to talk about him to anyone and wished only to pray to God to ask that Ammon might live. While he was in the intensive care ward, I asked Ammon if he would like to see Father K—. He said No. I said no more about it, for that was one of the things we never did to one another, try to enforce our private beliefs on the other person. As I have said, Ammon came happily with me to Mass, but he didn't have to. I would never have nagged at him to make him come with me. God has prior ownership over every one of us. Each of us belongs first to God. Am and I agreed on these big basic things. (I don't think we ever quarreled over anything that wasn't very trivial and unimportant—and yes, humorous—and usually, we always made up in above five minutes.)

The eighth was Thursday. Friday I picketed for him, and Monday and Tuesday. Sunday the doctor had him taken from intensive care and I told people about his heart attack, and at the same time assured them he would live, for I thought God had answered my prayers and Ammon would not die (he didn't, but I meant to life on this earth). Wednesday morning the doctor phoned and told me to hurry down to the hospital. I asked was Ammon going to die? The doctor said just to come down. I did. Ammon had died.

He had been eating breakfast when he suddenly slumped over. Later, the autopsy showed that part of the heart wall had caved in. Weakened heart walls would not show up in a physical, for I had had him have a physical last September and the doctor had said he was in excellent condition. But hard work during excessively long fasts is extremely hard on the heart. And disregarding the fasts, all his life Ammon worked tremendously hard. The chaplain had been called after what is termed 'clinical death'. A person can be revived from this— which Ammon was. He then lay there unconscious and with a definite heartbeat when the priest arrived. Hearing is the last sense to go, but whether or not Ammon heard the priest when he administered the Sacrament of the Sick, neither the priest (I got all these facts from him), nor any of us know. As the priest shouted in Am's ear who he (the priest) was, what he was going to do, and then did it (administered the Sacrament of the Sick), there was no outward response from Ammon, which does not mean that the soul was not making some inward response. But the latter, again, we do not know. Am died about twenty minutes later. When I arrived, I was told that he could have a funeral Mass, which I then went ahead and arranged, choosing Our Lady of Lourdes church as Am was fond of Bernadette (one of the three saints in whom he believed).

At no time did Am make any final confession. For instance, the night before, Am and the priest had a visit, but the priest didn't want to upset him (we still thought he was going to get well), and left it to Am whether or not religion would be discussed. Am didn't mention religion.

Now I have stated things as honestly and objectively as I can. Many or most (simply because of the Sacrament of the Sick having been administered) will in clear conscience be able to call Ammon a Catholic. But I cannot. In clear conscience and in all honor, I must call him what, so far as I *know* from our life together, he wanted to be called—a nonchurch Christian. In general, I would say that what he wrote in what up till now has been the final chapter of this book, was what he believed in up to the moment he died, (except what do we know about the moment of death?) plus he definitely told me he believed in reincarnation; also he held all his beliefs with more hostility towards the Church.

As I would not inflict my beliefs on him while he was living (or try to), so I will not inflict them upon him now that he is dead. In the same way he never tried to encroach on my own destiny or beliefs. No matter how poor we were, I never heard from him anything else but, "You keep on with your writing, Willow, we'll make it somehow." Nor did he ever in the usual arrogant, masculine fashion think he would be conferring some honor upon me to bring me the use of his name. If a woman wants to take a man's name, okay, but if she doesn't, okay, too. All men and women are of equal worth in the eyes of God.

If he had violently opposed going to Mass and had never gone with me, I would not have had him have a funeral Mass. For all his talk of not believing in Transubstantiation, he did not for instance, take the offered bread and water at a Mormon service we attended (neither did I). If he genuinely hated Catholics (or yes, the Church—I don't think Am was capable of genuine hatred for anything, for all his hostile talk), I would not have allowed him to be (or he would not have agreed to being) brought to Holy Cross hospital, although again, in all fairness he was taken there merely because our doctor (who is not Catholic) has his patients taken there. Here again, I feel I can see the working of the Hand of God, for if Dr. E— had his patients taken to University or some other hospital, Am would have gone there, and undoubtedly would not have had the Sacrament of the Sick, which again, I don't think he needed to get into Heaven.

As I say, I am trying to be as honest as I can—and it is up to every reader to decide however he or she sees fit. I am stating how I have decided, but certainly no one else has to decide this way (although naturally I would like it if everyone called Am a nonchurch Christian—so long as the person wasn't going against his conscience to do so). Much as I believe God wanted him to be marked as a Catholic upon his death, I must go by what I know. I find our whole life together, his and mine, so very strange, and also, although I may be wrong, I feel that the same kind of paradoxical destiny which drew us together is not yet over. Even my mother used to say that the good Lord (her term for God) must have brought Ammon and me together for some reason. (My family, too, love Am dearly.) Well, everything happens for the reasons of God.

I should be ending this book with a grand paean of praise to a great man, but I will let the world do that, and make what it will of how in his last chapter he said he had left the Catholic Church, and how in this chapter I say It did not leave him, while at the same time I cannot call him a Catholic. In the hospital he was so happy that I went out picketing for him. (Friends are carrying on at present as I have so much work connected with his affairs; also, I must add that Al, one of the former Joe Hill men who had been picketing with Am since the fifth, was there the days I picketed, also, so I didn't have to picket alone, although I expected when I went that first day that I might have to—I was thankful I didn't have to.) That to Am was one of the great tests of whether or not a person was a radical—whether or not he picketed. Am had always said I was a natural-born anarchist. Thus we became even closer during his illness. He said that this (the heart attack) was probably the best think that had ever happened, because it brought us more close together (got me out picketing, he meant). He said as he always did that he loved me best of all, and of course I told him the same. All my life I've been a fanatic for courage. Courage is the most important thing to me. Except for my father and my grandfather, Am's the only man I've ever met whom I could call A Man of Courage. He used to say so many times when he came home from tramping around town, how wouldn't it be terrible if he had to come home to some lonely room and cook some sloppy meal for himself. During his lifetime he knew so many lonely rooms.

So let the world praise and love him as it will, and think perhaps how very stupid it is for a neurotic woman to puzzle over whether or not the man she loves, the man who is at this moment with God (he may not be, but I believe he is), the living God who stands above all religions, creeds, dogmas (the God Who is Mercy), this man who was her best friend for he eased the hell of her hells so that she might learn how to deal with them, even as he said that she was his best friend— perhaps because she eased the loneliness of a public figure whose inner figure people did not realize existed, so powerful was the public one— anyway, how silly for this woman to conjecture as to whether or not such a man died a Catholic. After all, what difference does it make? So far as the charity and vision of his life goes, it makes no difference, but because I can reason to a degree, I must reason, and especially in this instance because I do not want to do anything concerning Am that he would not have wanted me to do. He trusted me. I think possibly Am was an early Church Christian sent at a time when the Church has become too monolithic, and when another world war could destroy the earth. His beliefs seem to me in the main early Church and primitive, but that complicated subject, too, I must try to work with in the biography.

The pardons board was to hold a hearing on the Lance and Kelback case January 14th. Ammon dictated to me this message January 11th, from the intensive care ward of the hospital. Friends then planned to read this message to the pardons board. For reasons, the scheduled hearing was not held, and this message remains Ammon's last words to the world. Ironically, if the hearing had been held, this would have been read the 14th—the day Ammon died.

"The latter day Christians today have given the Jews a bad name by quoting to justify capital punishment, 'an eye for an eye, a tooth for a tooth.' But it wasn't really as bad as that. For in the earlier Bible times, if a man knocked out an eye of another man, according to tradition, he'd be lucky to get off with being lynched at once. The Jews were trying to lessen the severity of this so that if a man knocked out the tooth or eye of another man, he wouldn't be lynched, rather just forfeit his own eye or tooth. He wasn't asked to overly compensate for that injury. All that I'm trying to do is to go a bit farther like Christ did—that he without sin should first cast the stone. Some day Christians of this state and other states will not take upon them the vegeance of the Old Testament God, but will do as Christ and Ghandi said to do—return good for evil. I have been picketing and saying this for the last nine years in Salt Lake City and will continue to do so as long as I live."

* * *

May Am's ashes be scattered over the graves of the saints and the martyrs, of whom he was one.

Ammon and his mother

Ammon in front of last Joe Hill House

Church of St. Joan of Arc in Las Vegas, Nevada
(The real Church in which Ammon believed)

Index